I once intended a dedication to Pleasant Porter, Ira Hayes, Leonard Peltier, and other icons who shaped my early awareness, but that's too complicated. This book is for Susan, JohannaKate, and Katie, the best partners a mountaineer could ever have.

Contents

PART 3
Rock

PART 1

Mountaineering

Mountaineering means more than climbing mountains. The meaning of mountaineering covers a wide range of activities, from casual day hikes to extended technical expeditions in extreme and remote environments. Mountains, wilderness, and the alpine experience touch everyone differently, and everyone comes away having been uniquely changed by the mountains they climb. For most of us, our particular understanding of mountaineering is intensely personal, yet every citizen of Earth is captivated by the grandeur of high mountains.

1
Introduction

Backpackers travel into the backcountry to get a closer look at the scenery—to see a little farther. Mountaineers usually describe their journeys as a means of looking more closely into their own selves—to see a little deeper. Climbing mountains compels that. Every detail, from the smallest to the most obvious, must be constantly attended to, a process both exhausting and exhilarating. Exhilarating, because the criteria for success are absolute and absolutely objective; they are chosen by the mountain, not by the mountaineer. Every person is equal when judged by mountains. Success requires mountaineers to appraise their own physical and mental capacities and to know, or discover, the extent of their reserves of competence, commitment, and courage. Mountaineering does not build character so much as it reveals it, and mountaineering is among the few activities outside of combat in which you knowingly trust your life to the capability and judgment of your companions, and they to yours. On the other hand, as Edmund Hillary put it, "you climb for the hell of it."

Such juxtapositions are part of the appeal—and the cruel irony—of mountaineering, but the definition of mountaineering is neither entirely subjective nor objective. Mountaineering is a component of alpinism, the broad appreciation of mountain regions that includes issues of sport, recreation, tourism, protection of biodiversity and natural resources, appreciation of indigenous peoples and cultures, access, and even sustainable development. I'll touch on these areas in *The Mountaineering Handbook*, but my principal scope ranges from wilderness-backpacking specific to mountaineering (because hiking is necessary to reach the climb) to basic alpine climbing, though most summits can be reached by easier means. Alpine climbing is traditional ("trad") climbing in the realm above tree line, where mountaineering skills are required. Trad climbing uses ropes, removable anchors, and other climbing hardware, mostly for safety. In a mountaineering context, such climbing can take place on rock, snow, ice, or a combination—even to the extent of climbing rock using crampons and axes.

The Mountaineering Handbook is about decision making. It's not a compendium of legacy techniques or a museum guide to climbing equipment; it's certainly not a gear review. There are plenty of other books devoted to these areas. To make good decisions, you need solid facts. In many cases I'll provide actual numerical data. Don't let this be daunting; you'll never need to memorize these numbers, just use them to separate good information from poorly informed hearsay and old wives' tales. You'll learn exactly how "light" is light, how "strong" is strong, and how "good" is GORP. There's no question this book reflects my own experiences and viewpoints, but for the most part you'll find it technical rather than philosophical. In fact, you may at first find it *too* technical. That's the nature of technical climbing; it's part of what distinguishes mountaineering from backpacking. Don't worry; you won't need to absorb every detail at first—which is a good thing, because there are plenty of them.

I'm aware that technical climbers tend not to be technical—above all they're practical. I'll be practical, too, and I'll make the technical matters easy to understand and easy to refer to as your experience grows. More than that, I'll give you step-by-step coaching, with text and illustrations, on the best practices of the world's leading alpinists and on the thought processes they go through when confronting technical problems. I'll show you how even the most advanced techniques are basically simple—simple is good for alpinists, because it equates to fast and safe. For example, we'll use a very small number of knots, but I'll show you how the pros tie them quickly with one hand; you won't find this approach in any other text.

When writing this book and getting into the research and fact checking, I was astonished to find that many books and magazines, even the most respected, advise methods that are out-of-date and inefficient, and sometimes downright dangerous—at least that's my opinion. The reason this is possible is that climbing and mountaineering seldom stress systems to their limits. In most cases, just about any reasonable technique will let you muddle through; you just won't be efficient, and

you'll sacrifice your safety margin, whether you know it or not. You'll gain experience, but the problem with experience is that it becomes self-validating. In the absence of catastrophic evidence to the contrary, experience takes on the appearance of wisdom, even when it only means making the same mistakes over and over. *Mountaineering: The Freedom of the Hills* is a classic if there ever was one—I own three editions—and it's helped get a lot of people into the mountains. Nevertheless, part of my motivation in writing this book is to present a more modern and efficient approach to mountaineering, one that's focused on the latest tools and the safest, most practical techniques, while filtering out the remainder. By drawing on a wide variety of sources as well as my own experience, even conducting original research when necessary, I've taken a fresh, new—some might say iconoclastic—approach to general mountaineering that I think you'll enjoy.

WHO'S IT FOR?

Perhaps you're an avid backpacker who's eager for the next level of growth in your exploration of alpinism. You may never have tied into a rope, but your passion to explore higher and more challenging peaks is growing. You're ready for more difficulty and more commitment, ready to extend your wilderness seasons into late autumn and early spring, ready to peer a little more deeply into what you're made of. Perhaps you've looked through the many books on rock or ice climbing and found the content overwhelming. You know that only a fraction is useful to you—but which fraction? What's accurate? What's up-to-date, and what's hopelessly obsolete?

Or you might already be an active rock climber, but you've never hiked farther than from the parking lot to the first bolt. You're nagged by the feeling that there's more to climbing than clipping draws. You are starting to feel the call of the high, the cold, the remote. You're up to the challenge of routes without chalk, but you know there are many skills you'll have to add—climbing snow with confidence and crossing glaciers safely among them. You're impatient with old-school teaching because you know much of it is wrong, but what's right? There's so much contradictory information out there—where to start?

Perhaps you're already an experienced mountaineer with dozens of peaks under your belt, but it's been a while since you sharpened your systems. You have the feeling that your methods may be getting rusty and that you could benefit from the latest advances in lightweight mountaineering, training, nutrition, and new-school methods. You don't want a gear catalog; you want solid information to help organize and update your repertoire of skills.

If you fit any of these descriptions and if you're eager to get more out of your alpine adventures, you'll find this book was written especially for you.

The Mountaineering Handbook will extend the backpacking you already know to new skills that will take you higher into more difficult terrain— the world of third- and fourth-class climbing. I start out with the basics, assuming only that you have backpacking experience (if you need to brush up basic skills, I've put some great references in the Resources section of the Appendix). If you're already a climber, you'll find this book's material on fifth-class climbing to be an eye-opener; its new

concepts will answer critical questions on moving fast, building anchors, and self-rescue. If you're looking to update your mountaineering skill set, I'll show you ways to safely increase your speed, efficiency, and enjoyment of the alpine world. Along the way, from beginner to experienced climber, I won't simply give you a long list of optional techniques, as if all were equivalent—that's the approach others take. Instead, I'll show you specifically the best ways to use the most modern, but basic, equipment to deal with the real challenges mountaineers confront—not all of which involve climbing. The equipment and methods I cover will take you safely to the top of nearly any peak in the Sierras, Cascades, Rockies, or Winds—and just about anywhere else. *The Mountaineering Handbook* is your most direct route from basic material on moving fast and light on the trail (Chapter 3) to advanced topics such as self-rescue (Chapter 25) and glacier travel (Chapter 26), and you'll find a wealth of new information that's unavailable in any other single source. I'll help you build an informed base of knowledge that will open up the great majority of mountaineering possibilities and, should your ambitions take you that way, give you a solid foundation for an even more adventuresome exploration of rock and ice.

2

Let's Go Climbing Together

Throughout this book I write in the same way I chat with my mountaineering friends, not the way I'd lecture to a class. If you're new to mountaineering and especially to climbing, you may feel inundated by the unique argot climbers use; be sure to check the Glossary in Appendix C and the Index whenever you encounter an unfamiliar term. Mountaineering will also immerse you in unfamiliar circumstances—some of which are potentially life threatening. To help you get a handle on the patois of climbing and to put the subjects I cover in context, how about we enjoy a mountaineering outing together? Along the way I'll describe our prototypical climb and point out the chapters of this book where you can find more detail to inform the decisions you'll have to make when you set out on your own.

GET YOUR HEAD READY

Mountaineering is hard to define, for me at least, because it encompasses so many activities and environments, as well as being highly personal. If you want to explore the best of what others have written, and get thoroughly stoked in the process, check out the great books by and about mountaineers that I sketch in Chapter 28; they're about the experiences of mountaineering, not the techniques.

To get an overview of the kinds of climbing (from scrambling to the serious stuff) that we might encounter on our outing, Chapter 8 explains ratings and grade systems and puts them in the context of mountaineering. We'll start out hiking, but to reach the summit, we'll face some snow or ice climbing (check out Chapter 16) and a final section of roped and belayed climbing on rock (see Chapter 14).

GET YOUR SKILLS READY

There are a few basic skills that are of fundamental utility to mountaineers. These include wilderness navigation, mainly the use of map and compass but including electronic tools such as altimeters and GPS receivers. You'll find a fresh approach to basic and intermediate navigation in Chapter 4. Having a handle on mountain weather forecasting will save you considerable grief, too, and that's covered in Chapter 6. Wilderness first aid is too complex to be covered in a single chapter or even by a book. Sign up for a hands-on course in first aid for wilderness environments after you read the introduction and overview in Chapter 21; there's an excellent text listed in Appendix B, Resources.

FAST AND LIGHT

Fast and light has lately become an in-crowd phrase among mountaineers, or at least among marketing departments that want to sell to would-be mountaineers. You'll find it's more about skills and attitude than about equipment purchasing. I start out in Chapter 3 discussing specific techniques for moving fast on the trail. Then I devote Chapter 17 to methods mountaineers use to go light, trading skill for weight without jeopardizing safety. Throughout the book I emphasize making lightweight a priority when selecting and using equipment. In every chapter you'll find constant emphasis on moving fast in the mountains, with special detailed sections on speeding up rock climbing in Chapter 14 and snow climbing in Chapter 16. If you follow my advice, you'll be carrying significantly less weight and moving faster than others who haven't gotten the message.

GET YOUR BODY READY

Of course, you could do as many others do and simply head for the mountains on fair-weather weekends. If you want to get the most out of your outings, as well as be able to make the most of light and fast techniques you'll learn from this book, you'll want to invest in endurance and strength training specific for mountaineering. New-school training is the subject of Chapter 20. To keep your body optimally hydrated and fueled so you can sustain a successful pace on our outing, you'll want to devour the contents of Chapter 19, Performance Nutrition for Mountaineers.

GET YOUR GEAR READY

From whatever direction you approach it, mountaineering—especially lightweight mountaineering—places unique demands on equipment. Selecting the best equipment for your personal objectives is important, and having good guidance is important for avoiding the vast quantities of seldom-used gear that most of us have accumulated through years of ill-considered acquisitions. Finding specific guidance focused on mountaineering is difficult. Most equipment that you'll find in outdoor shops is intended for recreational backpackers with no interest in lightweight mountaineering. Don't expect the annual reviews of popular magazines to be focused and impartial, much less critical. The basics are covered in Chapter 18. I avoid mentioning specific products and emphasize the reasons for demanding or rejecting salient features of footwear, backpacks, clothing, sleeping systems, shelter systems, mountaineering stoves, and water purification; and of course, I offer my own "ten essentials" list. Be prepared for a number of surprises in this chapter. Since our outing will involve technical climbing on snow and rock, you'll want to inform your climbing gear selections by reading Chapter 10, Equipment for Rock Climbing, and Chapter 15, Equipment for Snow and Ice Climbing. You'll find much more than just gear lists; these chapters are about the practical use of mountaineering hardware. A fundamental choice for all mountaineers is the selection of a climbing rope; the options are actually somewhat complex and involve choices of climbing style, as you'll learn in Chapter 9, which serves as an introduction to a climber's decision-making processes.

Even after you've acquired the equipment you'll need, you'll want to give it a thorough going over in the days before our climb. This not only helps to sublimate your cabin fever, but it ensures that everything is in working order, that stresses from the last outing have been repaired, and that consumables have been replenished.

GET STARTED

We meet Friday after work, drive to a restaurant near the mountain, and revel in gluttony, knowing that we'll face high-calorie-burn days on our climb (that's the excuse anyway). Then we drive to the trailhead, throw out our bags next to the truck, and crash in the darkness. Saturday involves a tough hike to our base camp, so we get up at first light and go through the ritual of equipment sorting, ensuring we'll have what we need but don't carry duplicates. We've checked the weather report according to Chapter 6, and the sky above doesn't suggest trouble, so we'll be able to use lightweight bivy sacks instead of tents; no need for water purification, as you'll learn about alpine water sources in Chapter 18; we've got home-dried meals—those and other factors will keep the weight of our packs very manageable. After a light breakfast of body-builder powder in cold water, we hit the trail in lightweight boots. We begin our on-the-go hydration-nutrition plan, consuming an ounce of maltodextrin gel and 7 ounces of water every 20 minutes, as Chapter 19 recommends. And we hammer. Our light packs allow us to maintain about 3 miles per hour up the trail until we come to a decision point, where we head cross-country. You've plotted this point on your map because you've read Chapter 4, so when we think we've reached it, you confirm by taking a compass bearing on a nearby gully. Fortunately there's a use trail, so we can keep moving fast, as we've agreed. The use trail soon becomes indistinct; we've moved from the sub-alpine ecosystem into the alpine—the world above tree line.

BASE CAMP

We decide to push our base camp right up to the small glacier on which the real climbing begins. Fortunately, someone has built a rock ring for a tent site. Unfortunately, someone hasn't read Chapter 22 and failed to pack out their poop—the site reeks. We find another flat, sandy spot that's plenty big enough for both of us since we're using bivy sacks. Camping right below a glacier or snowfield is often inadvisable, but the weather is mild, and we're on the windward side of the mountain, so we won't freeze. We still have daylight while we get our clothes and equipment ready for the next day. We find water running from under the glacier and collect enough for tomorrow, since the little stream may be gone in the morning, as cautioned in Chapter 5. We fire up the micro stove and bring our home-dried meals to life. As the sky darkens and stars appear, we finish our meals watching the lights of distant towns and highways. Life is sweet.

THE ALPINE START

Sweet, that is, until your watch starts chirping at 3:30 A.M. Out come the headlamps. Now it's all business—no one wants to dillydally when it's cold and dark. The alpine start is such an important part of mountaineering, I'm surprised that few texts mention it; here you'll find all of Chapter 7 devoted to the subject. Pull on the heavy boots (should have kept mine in the sleeping bag) and wolf down a breakfast of powder in cold water (which I did keep in the bag, so it hasn't frozen). Everything gets zipped into the bivy sacks, and they get held down with big rocks. The insulating jackets go into the sacks last, and we're wearing lightweight wool underwear and wind shells (you've studied Chapter 18). We're chilled as we get started, but we're out of camp just before 4:00 a.m. The eastern sky is starting to glow.

THE APPROACH

Exactly where the approach ends and the climb starts is seldom marked by signposts. We decide that since we expect to use a rope, the approach ends when the rope comes out. We stumble across talus to the glacier's snout by headlamp. Glaciers and travel on them are discussed in Chapter 26. The small glacier is mostly dry (bare ice), so we put on our crampons but we don't rope up. We don't expect serious crevasses, and any that are extant should be visible. I elect to climb with ski poles that have self-arrest grips; you opt for a mountaineering ax. The details of this decision and the associated techniques are covered in Chapter 16, Climbing Snow and Ice.

The glacier is small, so the only real trouble we expect is crossing the *bergschrund*—where the moving glacier separates from the permanent alpine ice above. We see that any stones that fall from the rock higher up could make it all the way down to where we are. That's just one reason for our early start—and for the helmets we're wearing. Objective hazards and how to manage them are examined in detail in Chapter 5. The glacier steepens, and the ice seems to get firmer; I'm beginning to wish for an ax about the time we reach an easy stance at the 'schrund.

THE CLIMB

Throughout the book there's the constant question of whether first to describe how to use a piece of equipment or to begin instead by describing its attributes. In the climbing chapters, I begin with lots of functional details on the equipment, so you'll understand the reasoning when I explain later how it's put to use in various scenarios.

Getting over the bergschrund will involve a little bit of moderate ice climbing. I don't know how it might be later in the day, after the sun warms it, but now the ice is aerated, brittle, but firm. That will make for easy climbing but poor protection. I reach up and sink an ice screw after trying to chop away the worst of the ice. The screw goes in a bit too easily; I wish for a Screamer, a force-limiting runner described in Chapter 11, Climbing Forces, and Chapter 12, Anchors; my technique is covered in Chapter 16, Climbing Snow and Ice. You're able to pound a picket (snow stake) into the ice at the 'schrund for your belayer's anchor. None of this is ideal, but it'll probably work. In anticipation of moderate climbing and no falls, we've chosen a 115-foot half rope to use as if it were a single; this choice and associated cautions are explained in Chapter 9, Your Climbing Rope. We tie in to the rope according to the wisdom of Chapter 16 and check each other's safety connections, as always. You've got a daisy-chain runner cinched to your climbing harness for easily adjustable connections, so you clip it to your picket and set up a loose belay. Belaying the leader is discussed in Chapter 14, with more detail on belaying for snow and ice in Chapter 16. I stow my poles and take out my axes, carry the two remaining screws and pickets, and head out. The climbing isn't too bad; in fact, it feels good to be getting warmed up and actually climbing.

I place another screw before the top of the 'schrund and then haul myself over. The climbing is easier above, so I run it out a bit before I place my last screw and drive in a picket as far as I can. I equalize these placements with a long runner made with a loop of nylon webbing. Building complex anchors is discussed in detail in Chapter 12. I set up a Münter hitch to belay you up, and I'm happy to feel the first sunshine as I take a breather and suck down some water and gel while you curse the picket you're trying to remove.

Soon you've clipped yourself to my anchor, and we congratulate ourselves on passing the first major difficulty. We can now see other peaks in the distance and, fortunately, few clouds in the sky. We conclude that the climbing above is moderate, and we're feeling strong, so instead of belaying, we'll be faster to continue up by simul-climbing. That means we'll both be moving at the same time, without establishing belays except for the first and last, while always keeping two anchors on the rope between us. Simul-climbing and other techniques for moving a party expeditiously are discussed in Chapter 24.

ONTO THE ROCK

The ice continues to steepen, but we reach the top of the alpine ice in good style. We take advantage of the security in the moat, where the snow pulls away from the rock above, to take a breather. We both have a light lunch, as taught in Chapter 19, and we're pleased with our progress and to be getting off the ice before noon. We can remove our crampons and heavy boots, stow our axes, and get ready to climb the rock above. I expected the rock to be dry, so I brought along rock shoes; you've chosen to climb in your hiking boots. In poor conditions we might have continued in heavy boots or even kept our crampons on for the entire climb. If we found ourselves forced to climb rock and ice with axes and crampons (dry tooling), we'd probably conclude that the climb was more than we were up for.

The rock above is easy but exposed. We elect

to stow the rope for a while and do some third-class climbing. Eventually we conclude that the safety of the rope is worth the extra time belaying will require, and we decide to continue in fourth-class style, using the rope and infrequent anchors for safety. Climb rating systems are discussed in Chapter 8. We establish Anchor #1, as detailed in Chapter 12, and set up a belayer's anchor for you. There are plenty of rock features where we can use long runners for anchors, so we spare the "small rack" of protection hardware ("pro") that Chapter 10 discusses. I lead out, placing a few pieces, and set up an anchor to bring you up, using my Gi-Gi belay device in autoblock mode, as explained in Chapter 14. That allows me to drink and eat gel easily while you climb. We're moving fast.

After two rope lengths of fourth-class climbing we reach the base of the summit plateau, where easy fifth-class climbing confronts us. Happily, the pitch looks short, and we're still on schedule. We continue to apply the skills of Chapter 14, and I again lead out, carrying the small rack, less one piece used for your belayer's anchor, but confident that the doubled runner making up Anchor #1 is solid.

The climbing is a little harder than I expected, so I place more protection, which takes additional time. The pitch is also longer than it looked, taking more time. I'm distracted from an unpleasantry that confronts me when I finally pull over the last difficulty: I didn't notice that the wind direction has been shifting, and there's now a full-on gale coming from the other side of the mountain—the summit plateau is sand and gravel blowing horizontally, with an occasional chunk of ice flying up from an unseen snowfield. My position is secure, but I struggle in the wind to find placements where I can build an anchor to bring you up. Plus, I'm chilling fast as my sweat is evaporated by the wind, so I'm also trying to pull on my hood and tighten down every opening in my clothing. I finally get in two chock anchors and a questionable runner that I sit on to keep from being blown away. I yell for you to hurry up, but you can't hear me, of course. Our plan to move fast has just run out of gas. It's realities like this that I discuss in detail, that you won't find mentioned in other texts. Am I the only one who finds themselves climbing in poor conditions?

You and I have climbed together before, so you know that if the rope stops and then starts moving up again because I'm taking up slack, our understanding is that it's time for you to get climbing. Which you do, but it seems to take forever. I fervently wish I hadn't placed some of those chocks so firmly (although it seemed like a good idea at the time), especially my favorite 0.5 TriCam.

When you finally arrive at the belay, the wind seems even stronger. You're freezing, too. I ask why it took so long, to which you reply, "That damn TriCam!" We assess our options, screaming at each other in the wind. "Do you want to go for the summit register?" "We'd have to crawl to make it." "I say we bail." "But we're almost there." "I'll go if you will." "Naw, let's get out of here." The wise decision, for any number of reasons. Today there won't be a lazy respite on the summit, no guessing at the identities of distant peaks, no browsing the register for the names of friends and heroes. We're miserable, sandblasted, and we know there are more challenges facing us. Chapter 27 is devoted to risk management, decision making, and keeping fear under control.

RETREAT

At this point we can't make it to the easy descent route we'd planned, and we'll have to rappel the pitch we've just climbed. There are two problems: no place to easily set up a secure rappel anchor, and the rope isn't twice as long as the pitch we've just come up. We're able to slot a really secure chock, which we conclude is better to leave behind than to go with only a questionable runner. We extend the anchor with a long runner, and you even volunteer a carabiner to make the rope a little easier to pull down. Thanks, because getting the rappel rope stuck now would be a major problem, addressed with detailed dread in Chapter 13. We add another runner anyhow, as a temporary backup, and you sit on it to keep it in place. To deal with the length of the rope, you take out a 6 mm retrieval cord, and we connect it to the rope, just as described in Chapters 9 and 13.

I've set the anchor, so I go down first. Even though the wind is howling and we're both freezing, we systematically go over our mutual safety system checks—spelled out in detail in Chapter 13. I get ready and unclip my tether, get a thumbs-up from you (no point in trying to shout), and scoot over the edge. I don't throw down the rope or retrieval cord, not in this wind; I just play them out of my pack—after all, I wrote Chapter 13. This takes longer than usual, and the retrieval cord barely makes it to the bottom (I make a mental note). When you feel the rope go slack, you get set up and start down while I keep the rope and cord from being blown to perdition.

BE RESOURCEFUL

We're both down the hardest section, but descending fourth-class rock is much scarier than climbing up it. We're forced to set up several more rappels. Now we're hours behind schedule. We've collected a lot of beta (climbers' data) on this mountain, and we think we can move along the moat and eventually find an easier way down, without having to descend the glacier ice. We stow the rope and climbing gear in our packs, change shoes, and get moving. Our extemporaneous route takes yet more time and isn't completely successful. We're forced to descend a few hundred feet of ice. The ice isn't difficult, but we're tired. We remind each other to take it slow and avoid a careless stumble, because we're not roped up—there'd be no point without anchors, and that would take way too long. My poles turn out to be really handy for maintaining balance as I descend. Even though we've kept a sense of where we are on the mountain, we still have to endure a miserable traverse across talus to make it back to camp. Good thing we brought headlamps, though we originally expected to finish in daylight. There's now a big lenticular cloud flying off the top of the mountain; we exchange looks that say we're glad we're not still up there.

BE TOUGH

As we stumble back to our camp we can barely see the bit of surveyor's tape we set out to make our rocks easier to find. The recovery meal recommendations in Chapter 19 go out the window. We're knackered. We cram whatever we can into our mouths while we hurriedly cram everything else into our packs. We pick up some water and remind each other to make a last check of our campsite (good thing, I'd have left my camera).

Then we hit the trail in darkness. There's no trail at first, so we consult each other, check our compass by headlamp, and follow the few remaining stars. When we come across the trail we shift into autopilot speed hiking. Hours later we finally make it back to the trailhead and briefly consider crashing. Instead, we conclude it's better to drive home carefully in the wee small hours and then recover at our desks on Monday. I always keep some lattes stowed for just such exigencies.

We managed to finish without any dire emergencies, such as those that Chapter 25, Self-Rescue, prepares for. We didn't call for help, even though things could have gone very badly. We didn't get the summit, but it'll be there another day, and so will we; we met the test.

HAVE FUN

We shake hands, slap each other on the back, and then pile into the truck to head for home. Each of us smiles in the darkness as we pull out of the trailhead parking lot, with that old mountaineering maxim running through our thoughts: "You don't have to be having fun to have fun."

This climb has touched the surface of many topics that will be explored in much greater depth throughout *The Mountaineering Handbook*. I hope you've enjoyed our climb together, and if you have, I'm certain you'll enjoy the book you're about to read.

PART 2

The Approach

Mountaineers know that much of an outing can be consumed merely by getting to the climb, so much so that this part has its own name: the approach. Each approach has its own characteristics, but in every case you'll want to move quickly, efficiently, safely, and comfortably.

3
Moving Fast on the Trail

Mountains are dangerous, and the faster and more dynamic you are under dangerous conditions, the safer you will be.

So wrote Yvon Chouinard in his essay on fast and light more than two decades ago; it's an emphasis you'll find throughout this book, too. The concept of *fast and light* is central to modern mountaineering and has been since the writings of Lionel Terray and Chouinard. Moving fast is key to mountaineering safety, success, and fun. It starts with the approach hike and continues on the climb and descent.

ON THE APPROACH

Every successful mountaineer I've known hikes god-awful fast. Not that they run—heck, I'm the one who's running, trying to keep up. Long strides, high cadence, I dunno. And they're fast on easy trails, rough trails, steep trails, and no trails. Big packs or small. Up or down. I've spent many sea-sons watching fast mountaineers from behind as they cover ground; that's given me plenty of opportunity to analyze how they do it. Fitness doesn't seem to be the main issue. Certainly fast mountaineers are fit—you'd have to be. But fitness alone is no guarantee of speed—or success—as a mountaineer. Here's a list of what I have concluded is important to moving fast on the trail, in order of significance.

Get the Rabbit Habit

The main attribute of fast mountaineers is simply their habit of moving fast. That's good news, because it means that you, too, can develop the habit. When you're hiking, think about your pace every once in a while. You'll realize that you could be moving faster, but probably you're just ambling along comfortably. So increase your speed. Not to the point of maximum heart rate, certainly; you need to learn to pace yourself, too. Pace is the dominant attribute of a mountaineering outing. But chances are that you can move along just a bit faster with minimal additional effort if you remind yourself to do so. Your pace is mostly a matter of habit. A while later, after you've been distracted from awareness of your pace, you'll realize that you've let your speed drop back to your old rate. So pick it up again. Eventually, after many hikes, your habitual pace will be reset faster and faster. You'll be moving along significantly faster than you once did, but without feeling like you're killing yourself as you hike. You may have to find new hiking companions unless they, too, reset their habitual pace.

Hike

In other words, reduce the proportion of time you spend not hiking. Don't stop to take off your pack for a drink, drag out a camera, stash your jacket, find a snack, check your e-mail, or whatever. Keep the items you'll need attached to yourself such that you can access them while on the move. Study your route in advance and keep it in your head, so you won't have to stop and reconnoiter at every decision point. If you find that you absolutely must stop, think about how to eliminate that reason for stopping the next time you're out.

Go Light

I return to this theme often. Learning and practicing the techniques of lightweight backpacking—as applied to mountaineering—is fundamental to enabling and enjoying fast travel on the trail. Chapter 17 is devoted to the specific skills involved in lightweight mountaineering. You'll never keep up with that guy with the 30-pound pack if yours weighs 60.

Take Five-Minute Breaks

But only five minutes, and not too many. Taking the load off your feet, checking your map, or swapping your gel flasks every hour or so may be what allows you to move fast all day, but don't let your five-minute breaks end up taking 15 minutes, or your hope for speed is doomed. This is especially difficult to enforce in a group, so the leader may have to become Ming the Merciless in order to keep breaks few and short. Definitely stop and remove insulation if you find yourself overheating (resolve to start out chilled the next time); if you're too cold, hike faster. Be sure the group knows in advance that there will be an emphasis on moving fast; then leave for dead those who won't comply.

Hike in Small Groups

And well-selected groups. Estimated travel times should be increased by about 1 percent for each additional member of the group, maybe more if there's significant disparity in the fitness, preparation, or motivation of group members. Larger groups also take longer to get going in the morning; draconian measures may be needed to get a group out of camp anywhere near the appointed hour. Saying that a group can be only as fast as its slowest member doesn't capture the truth—invariably a group is even slower than its slowest member. Little time is saved by letting groups spread out, because slow hikers get even slower, and there's always the danger of serious time loss if a party member goes missing. On the other hand, a motivated foursome of climbers with harmonious attitudes and abilities can be faster than a solo hiker. Call it competitiveness or just the constant presence of three other reminders not to slow down. Larger groups somehow never achieve this synergy, so fast hikers avoid them.

Maintain On-the-Go Hydration and Nutrition

In this book's chapter on performance nutrition (Chapter 19) you'll read prescriptions for consuming water and for nutrition during high-output activity. Following such guidelines is absolutely critical for maintaining a fast pace for many hours or days.

Use Trekking Poles

At first, trekking poles may seem like distractions, just something else to worry about when working your way over irregular terrain. Maybe they're a put-off because they strike you as yuppie fashion accessories. After an outing or two you'll begin to appreciate their value. I don't buy the shock absorption claims, but they certainly do add a little extra boost on uphills and stability on downhills; both effects make for faster travel. Even on flat trails where they have less benefit, just holding the shafts seems to eliminate puffiness in my fingers. I recommend the cheapest models having two key features: three-section shafts with sturdy locks (so they can be collapsed when climbing or scrambling) and tips that stick to rock. The best tips I've found are those that employ a tungsten carbide cylinder with a raised star pattern on the business end. Be sure the tips can be serviced and that replacements are readily available, because they go fast. Some manufacturers claim that their plastic ends are deliberately intended to break in the event of an accident . . . hmmm. Locking mechanisms are the weak link; the twist types seem eventually to fail in one way or another. Some mechanisms don't allow the shafts to be locked when fully collapsed. Keep experimenting with length when terrain varies, and learn to use the wrist straps effectively. Once you've used trekking poles to climb snow or assist in a dicey stream crossing, you'll be sold, but use them as an aid to (not a replacement for) good hiking technique. Evolved trekking poles are also becoming a new-school tool for serious alpinism, as I discuss in Chapter 16.

ON THE CLIMB

Learning to move fast while actually climbing is as important as moving fast on the approach, but far more difficult. Once you've started a climb, time is one of your biggest enemies. It conspires with other threats—weather, objective dangers, and darkness—to thwart your success. Moving fast on the mountain increases your odds because it retains options you'd otherwise lose to the clock. Since most mountaineering takes place on moderate terrain, it's especially important to learn to move fast when things are interesting but not especially challenging; that will give you more time to handle technical difficulties. The principles for climbing fast are very similar to those for hiking fast, but to them you must add refined judgment and routefinding ability, proficiency with technical climbing skills, and the efficient organization of members of a group who are roped together, literally or figuratively, in pursuit of their objective.

4

Wilderness Navigation

All who wander are not lost.

Whether you think this well-worn phrase comes from Shakespeare or Tolkien, you can be certain it didn't come from a mountaineer. Mountaineers know that the truth is that many wanderers are indeed lost. I'll cover basic and intermediate navigation skills that will ensure that if you happen to wander, being lost won't be the reason.

Wilderness navigation has many facets:

Navigation refers broadly to the process of finding your way to your objective. Sometimes you'll be able to do this using nothing more than signposts along the trail, referring to your map from time to time for reassurance and confirmation that you aren't committing a giant blunder. On rare occasions, perhaps after you recognize that giant blunder, you'll have to use your compass, topo map, and well-honed skills to bring your navigation actions and your navigation intentions into agreement.

Routefinding is more an art than science. It refers to evaluating the terrain ("reading the mountain") in order to judge the best course to follow and then making lesser decisions along the way in order to follow your intended course safely and efficiently—sometimes right down to finding places to put your hands and feet. Routefinding may mean choosing from among several options for attaining your objective—a snowfield, a scree slope, or a pitch of technical rock; whether to climb a gully or a ridge; whether to follow a trail or go cross-country. The best route may depend on the season and weather, the condition of your party, the amount of daylight available, the equipment you're carrying, and the consequences of misjudgment.

Orientation is the whole business of locating your position on a map. Many times you don't particularly care precisely where you are, so long as you're in the correct drainage or on the expected ridge and are headed in the right direction. Other situations may demand considerable precision; a capable wilderness navigator can, under hospitable conditions, confidently establish location well within a few hundred feet using no electronics beyond the synapses in her brain.

Orienteering means finding a specific, arbitrary location. The skills required to do this quickly have been turned into sports (orienteering, geocaching), but those skills are also valuable to the mountaineer who needs to find a particular campsite, locate a cache, or return expeditiously to a hidden trailhead.

NAVIGATION WITH MAPS

The way wilderness navigation is usually taught is excessively academic. It's based on military map and compass use; artillery shells may travel long distances on a single bearing, but backcountry travelers seldom do. I hardly ever use a compass, because it's usually too much trouble and because I keep track of where I am by staying aware of the terrain around me and exploiting more fundamental skills.

Neophytes often approach map and compass skills as if the compass were the more important of the pair, perhaps because it has moving parts and appears more complex. The opposite is true; a rare glance at the compass to reaffirm your sense of direction is often all that's required, but maintaining constant correlation between your location in your surroundings and your position on your map is crucial to avoiding the wanderer's pitfall in unfamiliar terrain. Key to doing that is getting your head around the basic concepts of topographic maps. This is easy for some people, while others struggle, but one day it will click for everyone who persists.

The real world is complex and three-dimensional. It's made up not just of land features but of vegetation, rivers and streams, snowfields and glaciers, roads and trails, and man-made structures. In addition, maps feature intangible devices that help interpret and locate features; these include political boundaries, section survey lines, and UTM grids, which are covered later. Selecting and representing all the important features is a significant challenge. The amount of information on USGS quad maps is far more than wilderness nav-

TOPOGRAPHIC MAPS

The fundamental navigational reference for mountaineers in the United States is a system of topographical maps produced by the United States Geological Survey (USGS); Canada and Mexico have similar systems. I'll stick to the most common for wilderness navigation in the United States (except for Alaska): the 7½-minute USGS quadrangle, commonly called a "quad." These maps divide up the surface of the globe using latitude (the angle from the center of the earth north or south of the equator, reaching maxima of 90° at the poles) and longitude (the angle heading east or west from the Greenwich meridian, reaching maxima of 180° near the international date line in the Pacific). At the equator, a degree of longitude spans 60 nautical miles (a nautical mile is 6,076 feet, 1,852 meters, or 1.151 miles). USGS 7½-minute quads divide the earth's surface into curvilinear rectangles that are ⅛ of a degree of latitude and longitude on each side, typically (in the middle latitudes) covering an area roughly 6 miles east to west by 9 miles north to south; they'd be almost squares at the equator. Away from the equator, their curved sides and narrower tops become more evident but are significant only in higher latitudes such as Alaska. The standard scale is 1:24,000, or roughly 2½ inches on the map for a mile on the ground (42 mm per km); some quads are metric, displaying elevations in meters. There are also 15-minute maps at 1:62,500, no longer printed, or 1:63,360 (inch = mile) for Alaska. Canada and Mexico maps use metric dimensions and a scale of 1:50,000. Topo maps report the date on which their underlying data were collected; mountains seldom change, so maps of wild areas may be updated less frequently than those showing urban areas. This could mean your map's depictions of man-made objects, such as trails, roads, bridges, and buildings, are 30 years out of date.

igators require, but they're the only widely available option. Part of the challenge in using these maps is mentally simplifying the information presented and focusing on just the basic terrain information you need.

To follow along, get your hands on any old USGS 7½-minute quad, because the colors are important.

Brown is used to represent contour lines, except on snowfields or glaciers, where blue is used. The usual elevation difference between adjacent contour lines is 40 feet or 20 meters, sometimes less in flat regions, and rarely is more than one value used on a single map; the interval used is shown in the map's margin. Every fifth contour line is made heavier, and the elevations of heavy contour lines may be printed along them in brown text.

Blue is used to represent water-related features, such as streams, lakes, and glaciers. Contour lines and elevation data on glaciers and permanent snowfields will also be printed in blue.

Green is used to represent vegetation, from heavy forest to scattered scrub. Grass, low brush, or widely scattered scrub won't be indicated. The actual margins of vegetation may be indistinct and may vary considerably from when the map was created.

Black shows trails and lesser roads, using dashed lines, and other man-made objects. Think of black as a tip-off that the physical thing represented may be absent when you look for it or that another similar object may have appeared in the terrain but isn't yet shown on the map.

Red shows larger roads and highways, and survey boundaries and data.

Purple is used to show updates of previous versions of the map that have not yet been confirmed by physical survey and fully incorporated.

Contour Lines and Terrain

Fundamental to topographic (topo) maps is the representation of terrain by lines of constant elevation, called contour lines. The key to using topo maps effectively is learning to associate contour lines with the terrain they depict. There are many analogies intended to help grasp the concept. To some, contour lines are like rings in a bathtub that show where the waterline was. (You're a mountaineer, right? I'm assuming you have rings in your bathtub—if you have a bathtub.) If you had a nice little mountain sitting in the middle of your bathtub, as some mountaineers do, each water ring formed on it would trace a single elevation level all around the mountain, no matter how complex its shape. For more fastidious mountaineers, I've shown four views of a bit of terrain.

The first of these figures is a section of the Convict Lake 7½-minute quad around and to the southwest of Convict Lake, California. I've highlighted terrain features, so you can compare their representations from figurative to literal. The next

illustration is computer generated from microwave radar data overlaid with the digitized quad, showing the same region. Then I show a view of Mini Morrison from across Convict Lake using the same digital data. Finally, I show a photograph I took of Mini Morrison from the same location as the previous computer-generated perspective.

If these figures don't make the concept come together for you, keep working at it. There's a real benefit, some would say a necessity, to being able to look at a topo map and readily visualize the terrain it represents. Here are some hints that might help:

Contour lines closer together depict steeper terrain. To get a sense of this, consider the map's scale. At 1:24,000, five contour lines spaced at 40-foot intervals amount to 200 feet or 2,400 inches of elevation difference in the terrain. Two hundred feet on the ground is a tenth of an inch on the map. When you see five contour intervals, identified by heavier lines, about 0.1 inch apart, you know that the vertical distance and the horizontal distance are the same, meaning that the slope grade is about 100 percent or the slope angle is 45°. A rock slope that steep would likely present a climbing challenge requiring a rope. If the separation of five contour lines is twice that, 400 feet or 0.2 map inches, the slope would be 50 percent, or about 27°; that's steep, but not intimidating. Use the scales in the map's margin to measure such distances, using the scale that matches the units in which elevation is shown (feet or meters). Measuring the percent grade of a slope (rise divided by run) is easy on a topo map, but you'll need trigonometry to convert grade to slope angle. It's common to switch back and forth between these two ways to say the same thing. Following is a chart of common grades and slopes. I've included an overlay navigation tool in the Resources appendix that will allow you to read slope angles directly from maps; it was designed for ski mountaineers because slope angle is so important to them, but anyone can use its features.

In very flat places there will be no contour lines, and at cliffs the contour lines will come together, or nearly so. Forty-foot intervals may conceal many unpleasantries. A 79-foot cliff might not be shown at all; a field of 50-foot boulders might

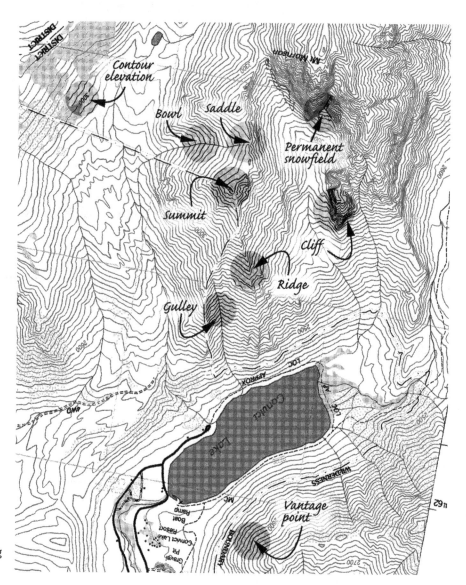

Section of USGS 7½-minute quad "Convict Lake" showing terrain features.

appear smooth and seduce the unwary into considering cross-country travel; an innocent looking creek might turn out to have steep, high banks; and what appears to be pleasantly open terrain may prove to be impassible brush. Learning to anticipate such unwelcome possibilities comes from experience, nearly all of which will be bad.

Getting Acquainted

Now zoom your brain out and get a lay of the land. If you see a blue line on the map running through the apexes of V-shaped contour lines, that's a stream, and the contour lines are showing a valley, not a ridge. Closed contour lines that don't enclose others indicate summits, not depressions (which are much more rare and are indicated with closed contour lines having little downward pointing ticks). Many summits have a black X printed on them, an elevation indication, a benchmark indication (BM), or a triangle symbol. Ponds and lakes are always at the bottom of depressions, never on summits. The V's of valleys and chutes point uphill, whereas V's or U's representing ridges point to lower elevations. Gullies invariably result

Computer-generated "aerial" view of the same region.

Computer-generated view of "Mini Morrison" with Mt. Morrison behind.

A photograph of "Mini Morrison."

in creeks, but ridges never do. Gullies tend to come together (converge) to end up as river valleys. Ridges come together at summits. Saddles are easy to distinguish from crests. A dashed blue line, indicating an intermittent stream, is a gully giveaway, but don't expect to find water when you reach the symbol—it seems that intermittent stream indications are a cartographer's inside joke. Sometimes you'll have to follow a contour line until it becomes part of a feature that you can confidently associate with terrain; rarely you may have to follow two heavy contour lines until you can find elevation numbers that will tell you which lies above the other.

HANDY NAVIGATION FEATURES

Features with special utility for wilderness navigators include *handrails*. A handrail is a feature that's easy to identify, easy to notice if you've crossed it

GRADES, ANGLES, AND GRADIENTS OF SLOPES, AND THEIR MAP REPRESENTATIONS

Grade (%)	Angle (°)	Gradient (ft/mile)	Five lines (map inch)	Comment
1.75	1	92	5.71	
6	3	320	1.67	Steep highway
10	6	530	1.00	Typical trail; incredibly steep highway
14	8	740	0.71	Average of the road to l'Alpe d'Huez
20	11	1,060	0.50	Steep trail; maximum of l'Alpe d'Huez
40	22	2,100	0.25	
50	27	2,640	0.20	Slope is 1:2, (elevation)/(distance)
67	34	3,540	0.15	Slope is 2:3, (elevation)/(distance)
70	35	3,700	0.14	Angle of repose; steep black ski run
75	37	3,960	0.13	Terrain is 25% longer than map distance
100	45	5,280	0.10	1:1; Scary climb for some unless roped
200	63	10,560	0.05	
236	67	12,460	0.04	Contour lines touch: cliff

or lost it, and easy to follow. Examples include ridges, streambeds, large bodies of water, cliff bands, and trails. Wilderness navigators seldom have the luxury of man-made handrails, but sometimes a railroad track or power line will serve if it can be identified with confidence; beware: man-made objects are highly generic. Even a contour line might serve, if it leads where you want to go and you can travel at a fixed elevation, though traversing in the mountains is usually inadvisable. You don't have to be on the handrail, just keeping track of it at a distance may give enough guidance as you travel.

An *attack point* is a feature that you expect will be visible throughout an entire leg of your route, so that you can head for it without hesitation even if your travel is forced to become circuitous. When you approach your attack point, verify your position; then use your map to select the next attack point and assure yourself that it will lead where you intend to go. A distant summit may work; you don't have to actually reach an attack point for it to be useful, you just have to know where your actual objective is with respect to the attack point.

A *collecting feature* is a feature, usually near your route, that's easy to identify and will help you establish where you are on your route. Examples are bridges, trail junctions, stream crossings, and passes. A collecting feature that prompts an action, such as taking a side trail, turning left or right, or heading cross-country, is what I call a *decision point*.

A *catching feature* is something that lets you know that you've overshot your intended decision point. This can be as simple as a change in direction of the trail or slope of the terrain, or as obvious as a road or river. Catch features don't have to be relegated to cross-country travel; especially where new trails are numerous or in winter when there are no visible trails, establishing a catch feature, and keeping an eye out for it, can help you avoid becoming an accidental wanderer.

What navigators call *pace counting* is a last resort; counting inches is especially difficult off trail. Mountaineers do better with a good judgment of distance and hiking speed. Estimate where you *should* be and see if you can identify confirming terrain features. Your accurate sense that you've traveled a particular distance will help reduce the number of possible locations that you must evaluate.

Bearing off or *aiming off* refers to the sensible decision not to head directly, or what you think is directly, toward an objective. Rather than take the chance of missing the target in featureless terrain, or terrain where features are obscured by trees or by a whiteout, you may conclude that you'll save time by heading for a catching feature of which you can be confident. If you're heading for your car parked along a road in forest, for example, you may want to be confident that when you reach the road you'll turn left to find your car. If you head directly to where you think your car is parked, but you arrive at the road and don't see it, you have a 50 percent chance of wandering. Could be worse if you've parked at the end of a road and you realize, as darkness falls, that you should have come upon your car hours ago.

Micro-Navigation

Zoom in and take a look at the contour lines that lie near or across your route; especially those within a hundred feet or so. Every terrain feature may not be represented on the map, but you can be certain that any little wiggle in a contour line has some corresponding feature in the terrain. If you're doing critical navigation, it's important to look for these wiggles on your map as you move along your route and to associate them with the features they depict; you may even want to trace your progress with a pencil. If the features you expect aren't visible, it's likely you've wandered. If you do a good job with this, you'll always know your location within a few dozen feet, terrain permitting, and you may seldom find a compass necessary. If you want to become a capable wilderness navigator, this is a skill you'll need to practice.

Moving Fast

A constant theme in this book. Identifying terrain features as I've just discussed will allow you to move at maximum speed when that's feasible, such as on a good trail where coarse navigation by keeping track of collecting features is sufficient. As you approach a decision point, you may slow your pace and look for more details to confirm your location. Finally, you may revert to micro-navigation to locate the cache you left before the snowstorm. Don't use slow micro-navigation on the trail if there's a catching feature that will give warning should you overshoot your decision point.

Being There

When you actually stand in the terrain with your map in hand, you'll want to orient the map to match the terrain. Open your compass, set its declination-corrected bezel to 0°, and lay the edge of its baseplate along the edge of the map. Now rotate the pair together until the compass and the map point north. Even if you end up looking to the south, making the map's text upside down, associating the map and terrain is difficult if they aren't aligned; confusion lurks nearby. If you'll be doing a lot of comparisons between your map and the terrain, scratch a north-south line in the ground to give yourself a constant reference. In all of this, keep your head screwed on: note the sun's position, think about the direction you're facing, and ask yourself if things really make sense.

How Steep Is It?

You may be surprised that this question has an answer—three answers really: The angle of the slope is either steeper than 35°, equal to 35°, or not as steep as 35°. What's with 35°? It's so special that it has a name: the *angle of repose*. It turns out that should you attempt to pile up similar irregular objects, the steepness of the pile reaches a limit depending mostly on the size of the objects. Try to pile them steeper, and they just roll down. That steepest angle possible is called the angle of repose. You can see it in the pile of highway maintenance gravel under the end of the conveyor belt. For smaller dry talus, scree, and coarse sand, the angle of repose is between 30 and 40°; 35° is close enough, or you could use 34°—a slope with a ratio of rise to run of 2:3 and a 67 percent grade. Bigger talus and boulders can be piled more steeply than scree or sand, but often only temporarily.

If you're standing on a scree slope pitched at the angle of repose, you'll feel reasonably secure even if the slope extends far below. That's because if you slip, you'll only slide down a bit, just like the other objects around you. On the other hand, if you attempt to hike up, you'll also slide down—

along with a lot of the material you're standing on. Secure, but a miserable way to gain altitude, as mountaineers come to know. Descending a slope at the angle of repose can be very quick and safe; a boot glissade on scree or sand is almost as facile as glissading on snow.

The sense of security you feel when standing on a 35° talus slope vanishes when the slope is covered with snow or ice. A 35° slope makes for an easy snow climb, but looking down that frozen slope wearing skis, boots, or crampons definitely increases the fear factor—you have the acute sense that a slip could lead uncontrollably to a nasty fall, and you're right. The steepest black runs at ski areas are 35° because they're basically snow-covered talus slopes. For a snow slope to be steeper, the underlying terrain must be rocky, or the snow must have been piled up by wind deposition. Permanent snowfields, storm-plastered rock, icy couloirs or gullies, and glaciers are not bound by this rule; these can be quite steep.

What's the utility of this factoid? If you see a distant peak and notice a scree-filled gully running up it, you can be sure that the steepest part of the gully, usually right at the top, cannot possibly be steeper than the angle of repose. Steeper slopes can only get that way if they contain material that's more solid than talus or sand. This will help you evaluate the grade, even when foreshortening distance makes things appear more vertiginous. Knowing that a snow-covered scree slope is about 35° is also handy because this angle is prime terrain for deadly slab avalanches. Reviewing your topo and knowing that a climbing route is steeper than the angle of repose tell you that it must at a minimum have some rocky sections; that could be good or bad.

RESORTING TO YOUR COMPASS

So far we've done a lot of navigation, but we've barely touched a compass; that's good. There will come a time, however, when there are no handrails, no good attack points, no catching features, and micro-navigation draws a blank. Time to take out that compass and know how to use it.

The compass is very simple, as befits a wilderness tool, but its uses can be very sophisticated. It has two primary functions: taking a bearing in the field and plotting a bearing on a map. *Taking a bearing* means measuring the angle from your nose to a terrain feature with respect to north; this bearing can be corrected to geographic north, or true north, by applying the local declination. *Plotting a bearing* uses the compass solely as drawing tools (protractor and straightedge), and the needle is totally ignored; bearings are expressed as the angle with respect to true north and may be drawn between any two points on the map.

Magnetic Declination

Conveniently, the earth has magnetic poles near its geographic poles, which allow simple instruments to be used for basic navigation. Inconveniently, the magnetic poles are not exactly at the north and south poles, so error (declination) corrections must be made that depend on your location on the planet. The declination that applies in a topo map's area is printed in its margin and indicated by a little diagram. Magnetic north is in arctic northern Canada, about 800 miles south of the geographic north pole at approximately 83°N by 114°W; it's drifting toward Siberia, decreasing declination in California by about a degree every

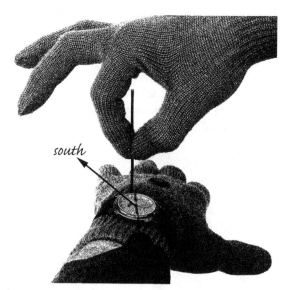

Point the hour hand at the sun using the shadow of a twig; south is halfway to 12.

When it comes to selecting a compass, consider your needs. If you expect to be practicing the level of navigation skills taught in this section, you'll want a baseplate compass with a mirrored cover and a means of adjusting the declination. It will have a bezel with 2-degree calibration marks and a clinometer to measure slope angles. Slightly down market would be a similar compass with no declination adjustment feature. This is the type that I always carry in my "ten essentials," though I also carry a more sophisticated compass when I expect to need it. Don't expect much satisfaction using a lesser instrument, such as a compass without a mirror or one having 15° calibrations. Still, any compass is better than none when you need to remind yourself of the general direction of north.

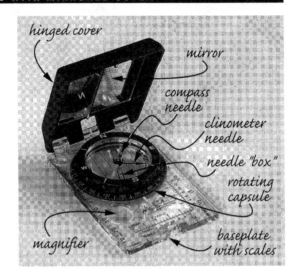

25 years. It even wanders around a bit during the day. The location of the magnetic pole means that mountaineers in the Mississippi valley (about 114°W) will see their compass needle point directly to the north pole. Mountaineers elsewhere are not so lucky (except for having mountains). On the West Coast, compass needles will point to northern Canada, but true north lies at an angle to the left; in Seattle, the difference is about 19°. This angle is referred to as an easterly declination. The situation will be reversed on the East Coast, where the Canadian pole will result in an error to the west. In Alaska the declination is over 20° east.

When taking bearings, deal with declination by using a compass that compensates by offsetting its needle box from true north. If you must opt for a simpler compass, don't try to compensate for declination arithmetically (arithmetic in the backcountry is a recipe for trouble). Instead, apply a strip of tape to the underside of the needle capsule, angled for the declination where you will use the compass, to serve as a "box" for the needle. If you can't manage even this, get into the habit of applying the declination correction to the bearing once it has been taken by rotating the capsule while counting degrees of correction. This is easier than doing mental arithmetic, especially if the declination adjustment crosses 0 = 360°.

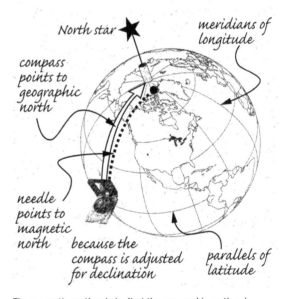

The magnetic north pole isn't at the geographic north pole.

But wait, there's more. Since compass needles actually follow the flux lines of the earth's magnetic field, as a compass approaches a magnetic pole its needle will point increasingly downward; right at the magnetic pole (it's actually a small region) the needle would attempt to point vertically into the earth. This effect might cause needles to hang up in their capsules, so compasses are man-

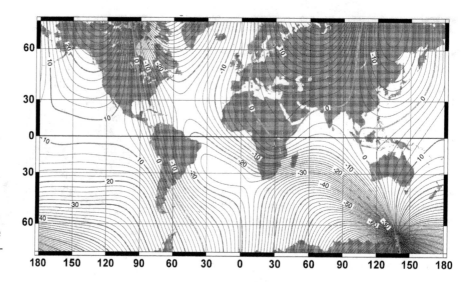

World magnetic declination chart, 2000. (Data from the National Oceanic and Atmospheric Administration.)

ufactured with imbalanced needles to compensate. Six cryptically labeled regions around the world have been defined, and compasses intended for a particular region may not work well elsewhere; some compasses have needles mounted with tiny gimbals in fat capsules and claim to be universal.

Resection

The main use for a compass, apart from establishing the direction of north, is determining your location on your map. Unfortunately, navigation geeks leap to this use before exhausting the simpler means I've just discussed. Using a compass this way is called *resection* (or commonly, *triangulation*); it's based on bearings you take of terrain features and then plot on your map. If you already know that you are somewhere on a particular feature, such as a trail, stream, or ridge, a single bearing to a known point tells you where you are along the feature. That simplicity is seductive, but there are a number of problems with triangulation, even apart from the errors in taking a bearing. In a forest, your restricted line of sight will leave you hardpressed to get a good sighting on a distinguishable feature; same story in unfamiliar alpine terrain where summits may be unrecognizable, obscured, or indistinct. In open areas, features may be so distant that they are useless. And inclement weather

may hide even nearby terrain. Think of triangulation as a last resort.

TAKING A BEARING

Taking a bearing is straightforward, but a bit of technique will allow you to approach an accuracy of about 2°. Start by identifying a target that you can locate on your map. Face the target and hold the compass in front of you at arm's length with the mirror cover opened about 60° so that you can look over the cover at your target and simultaneously use the mirror to look down on the needle capsule. Hold the compass with both hands, and use your fingertips to rotate the bezel easily without changing your grip. If your new compass bezel is balky, a *tiny* drop of silicone oil on the capsule bearing surfaces makes the movement smoother. Align the various marks on the compass with your target; these alignment marks include the line down the center of the mirror and the pivot point of the needle. Rotate the capsule to align the north, or red end of the needle to approximately match the box marks in the needle capsule; then carefully rotate the bezel to make those marks exactly parallel to the needle (a process called *boxing the needle*). Be sure the compass is horizontal and that no iron objects are nearby (especially no magnetized objects, such as another compass or your iPod headphones). Fine-tune the bezel rotation as you bring everything into exact alignment. The bezel now reads the bearing from you to your target. If you need better precision, take a few more readings and average them.

The first time you deploy your compass, you may be confused about which mark to use as the pointer to the bearing angle; compasses with hinged covers resolve this confusion (it's the mark at the hinge), but take care not to use the opposite mark when plotting bearings—a blunder easily made.

The targets you select can be any readily identifiable feature. The ideal feature is a sharp summit that's closer than a mile. Be cautious about man-made features, as water tanks and antenna towers come and go, and they all look alike. Features more than a mile distant will introduce more error. A 2° error taking a bearing on a distinct feature a mile distant represents 180 feet (about 35 m on a feature 1 km distant). More distant features increase the error, so check your map for possible candidates within a mile radius (2½ inches on the quad) of where you think you are. Summits aren't essential; a cliff band or a narrow chute that you can confidently associate with a representation on your map will do as well. Always give your conclusions a reality check: check your topo map for squiggles in contour lines indicating terrain features near where your plotting puts you, and then look

Taking a bearing on Mini Morrison.

around to see if you can identify those features in the expected locations nearby.

BEARING OF THE SLOPE

One useful bearing that may not be obvious is the bearing of the slope on which you're standing. It's the most direct way down the slope, a line that perpendicularly intersects the slope's contour lines. A skier might refer to it as the slope's *fall line*. You can use this targetless bearing to distinguish the slope you're on from others on your map. This can help you eliminate candidate locations. For example, when you know you're on a trail, the bearing of the slope can help decide where on the trail you are— or aren't. Slope bearing is a clue that could be useful when few clues are available.

A *back bearing* is the exact opposite direction of a conventional bearing, useful to confirm your travel direction by checking your starting point. Rather than adding or subtracting 180°, simply use the alignment mark on your compass that's opposite the direction-of-travel mark (the one you *always* use otherwise), or use the white end of the compass needle instead of the red end.

With a bit of practice you can visually estimate bearings within about 15°, so you may not even need a compass once you've established a true north reference; this also helps with a reality check of your plotting. Take a guess at the bearing and see if your compass comes close. For me, 15° is the width of my outstretched first and little finger; 15° is also the angle the sun and moon move in an hour—handy for estimating remaining daylight.

PLOTTING A BEARING

Transfer the bearing you've just taken to your map. You don't even have to read the bezel to do it. What you do need are north-south lines on your map to serve as references. If you have a map printed after 1989, and it indicates a small UTM grid declination (see the section on GPS and UTM later in the chapter for an explanation), you're in luck, because you can use the UTM grid. Otherwise you might be lucky if the target is near the edge of your map, and you can use the margin. If you're intent on precision navigation, you should have ruled your map with lines parallel to the sides and spaced about an inch apart. Don't be easily seduced by red section lines; these are not guaranteed to be orthogonal to meridians and parallels, though many are. Certainly don't invite chaos by attempting to deal with declination by ruling reference lines along magnetic north instead of true north; use a quality compass and deal with declination in your compass.

When plotting bearings you've taken, completely ignore the compass needle. The map doesn't even need to be horizontal. Lay your compass on the map with the cover opened fully. Locate your target on the map and position the compass edge on it. Now fiddle with the alignment of the compass baseplate until the meridian lines of the needle capsule align with true north-south lines on your map (you don't need to refer to or even know the actual bearing angle, just don't rotate the capsule). You now know that your position is somewhere on the bearing line that lies along the side of your compass (the dotted line in the illustration). If you're on a handrail or known trail,

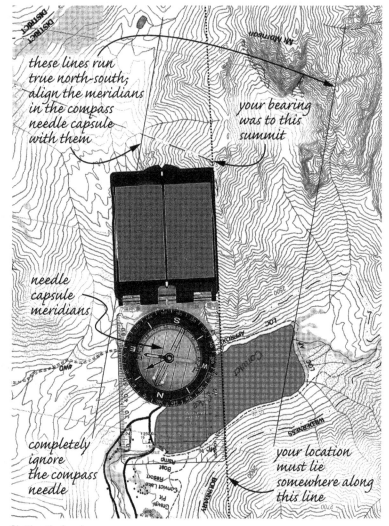

these lines run true north-south; align the meridians in the compass needle capsule with them

your bearing was to this summit

needle capsule meridians

completely ignore the compass needle

your location must lie somewhere along this line

Plotting the bearing on your map.

the intersection of that feature and the bearing line shows you your location. If you need to take another bearing, hopefully about 90° to the first, do so and plot both bearings. Your location is near where the two lines intersect, with an error proportional to the quality of your targets and skill of your bearing taking and plotting—hopefully within a few degrees or a few hundred feet. The more bearings you can take and plot, the more confident you can become of your exact location.

MEASURING A BEARING ON THE MAP

If you've drawn a line on your map connecting two features, you can use your compass to measure the

bearing of the line (just be sure to keep your direction-of-travel arrow pointing from the "from" point to the "to" point as you measure the angle from the first point to the second). Lay the edge of your compass along the line and rotate the needle capsule until the meridian lines on the capsule align exactly with true north-south lines on the map. When everything lines up, the compass bezel will indicate the line's bearing. Declination doesn't figure in, because adjusting your compass's declination only rotates the capsule's needle box (which you're ignoring) with respect to the bezel; it doesn't rotate the capsule's meridian lines.

When you take a bearing in the field, you must

be physically at the "from" point; the "to" point is your target. But when you plot bearings on your map, this isn't necessary. For example, you may plot in advance a bearing *to* a target you're sure will be recognizable *from* a decision point on your map. As you travel the route, you keep taking bearings to the target until you match the one you plotted; you are then at the decision point.

The most common error in both taking and plotting bearings is to flip the compass by 180°. Everyone does it once in a while. Be sure to keep straight what is the "from" point and what is the "to" point as you plot or take bearings. Good advice for every navigator is to take a deep breath, check the sun, and give your plotting an idiot test to confirm that it actually makes sense.

FOLLOWING A BEARING

Following a bearing means—after determining your location and intended direction of travel—setting that bearing on your compass and using it to guide your travel. The most effective way of doing this is to select a suitable attack point. If that isn't feasible, select a general direction that provides a handrail and catching feature; a drainage without complexity would be an example. If none of these sensible methods are feasible, you could be forced to simply hike while holding your compass with the needle boxed and hope to move consistently in the direction it indicates. This is lame. An example might be finding yourself in a forest where you're unable to see suitable terrain features for guidance or taking bearings, or when caught in a whiteout on featureless terrain. In such circumstances you can easily become a lost wanderer despite your map and compass, so be sure to establish catching features if at all possible. In extreme cases, you may find it necessary to spread out your party ahead of you along a line in the direction of your bearing, yelling or whistling at the lead person to tell them to move right or left as you consult your compass. By leapfrogging party members while you navigate from the rear, it's possible to maintain a reasonably straight course of travel, terrain permitting, but this is a painfully slow exercise, as anyone who has been fogged out on a glacier can tell you.

As you travel in the field there are many subtle techniques that you may need to invoke when you leave the trail—like navigating around obstacles, following intermittent handrails, and aiming off unseen objectives. These more advanced skills use the techniques I've already discussed in combination with plenty of practice and common sense—all critical to becoming an accomplished wilderness navigator. The most valuable skills are learning to use terrain features to guide your travel so you never have to resort to using a compass.

handy manual protractor

1.5 to 2.0°
- 140' to 180' at 1 mile
- 25 to 35 meters at 1 km

(use trig to calibrate yourself)

about 15°
- about 1,400 feet at 1 mile
- distance the sun moves in 1 hour

=========

about 140' long
about 38 per mile

trail dash marks for trails and dirt roads on USGS quad maps

if you are hiking briskly at 3 miles per hour, on a 1:24,000 (7½') map you can estimate . . .

3 MPH means 8 map inches per hour
3 MPH is not quite 2 trail dashes per minute
1 mile is 2.6 map inches . . . takes 20 minutes
1 map inch = 2,000' . . . takes 8 minutes
1.64 map inches = 1 km . . . takes 13 minutes

1 km is about .62 (5/8) mile
1 mile is about 1.61 (8/5) km

over a distance of 1 mile, a bearing error of 1° amounts to a distance of about 92 feet

over a distance of 5 miles, a bearing error of 5° amounts to almost half a mile

Handy rules of thumb (and finger).

ALTIMETERS

The availability of inexpensive electronic pressure (and temperature) gauges has resulted in the appearance of altimeters in more and more gadgets, including wrist watches, radios, bicycle computers, and GPS receivers. The quality of such instruments varies considerably and unpredictably. To use one proficiently you need to understand why it might go wrong.

A barometric altimeter is an air-pressure gauge calibrated in elevation. This calibration is possible because atmospheric air pressure (essentially the weight of the column of air above the instrument) decreases in a regular, roughly exponential manner as altitude increases. It does so according to a complex model of the atmosphere called the International Standard Atmosphere. There are many factors in addition to altitude that affect air pressure; the grace with which a particular instrument deals with these sources of error strongly impacts the accuracy of its readings. Price is not a good predictor of grace.

Errors Due to Weather

The accuracy of an altimeter can be stated in terms of the number of contour lines of uncertainty in its reading. Topo maps themselves have 90 percent of their tested elevations accurate to within a single contour line interval (±20 feet). The factor that most affects altimeter accuracy is weather; this makes the instrument a great aid in weather forecasting, but it plays havoc with its use as an altimeter. Sea-level air pressure ranges from about 950 to 1,050 millibars (normal is 1,013.25 mbar, 101.325 kPa, 760 mm-Hg, or 29.93 in-Hg); even on a stable day, variations of ±1 mb are common. This corresponds to an apparent altitude change of ±30 feet—more than a contour line. It's not uncommon for mountaineers' altimeters to show an apparent change of altitude of 100 feet (two or three contour lines) in the course of a day of camping in stable weather. If the weather is changing, a common 1 percent barometric change amounts to over 300 feet of apparent altitude change. In major storms an anomalous change of 1,000 feet is possible. Chapter 6, Mountain Weather, has more detail on using an altimeter as a weather forecasting tool, but suffice it to say that your altimeter has no way to distinguish whether you have carried it up the mountain or whether a low-pressure system has arrived; only you can make that interpretation.

Errors Due to Temperature

Temperature also has a significant, if recondite, impact on altimeter accuracy. The manufacturers of most instruments claim to have compensated for the temperature of the instrument itself (actually, of its sensor chip). You can test this by putting your altimeter in the freezer compartment and seeing if your refrigerator relocates to your roof or basement. If an altimeter is truly temperature compensated, you can keep it on your wrist or inside your jacket without concern about affecting its readings. Compensation for air temperature, however, is another matter altogether.

Part of the International Standard Atmosphere is a profile of the temperature of the atmosphere at various elevations; there are many complexities, but the profile comes down to the *average environmental lapse rate*, about 3.6 F° per 1,000 feet (6.5 C° per 1,000 meters). This is a handy number to remember, for many reasons. The ISA profile calls for a temperature of 59 °F at sea level and 30 °F at 8,000 feet. That might be true over the ocean at night (the most common condition throughout the world), but it won't apply to mountains on a summer day. Specifying a temperature profile is necessary, because temperature affects air density, and that affects the weight of the column of air above the altimeter. If air in that column is warmer than what the ISA calls for, it will be less dense; that means that movement up or down within the column of air will result in less pressure difference—the altimeter will be less sensitive than it expects to be, based on the ISA. Here's an example: Let's say you're leaving Mammoth Lakes for a climb of Bloody Mountain on a summer day when the temperature is 70 °F. You set your altimeter to read Mammoth's 8,000-foot elevation (an offset adjustment of about 600 feet lower than what it would read if the temperature were 30 °F). The air temperature is 40 F° higher than the ISA expects, so your altimeter will be significantly less sensitive than it's calibrated for. If you climb only 1,000 feet, your altimeter will read about 88 feet—more than two contour lines—too low, with proportionally more error as you climb higher. If on such a day you were to leave a summit after resetting your altimeter to the known elevation of 14,000 feet, and then descend toward 10,000 feet, your altimeter will tell you that you reached 10,000 feet about 350 feet (eight contour lines) after you actually pass it. Establishing the correct air temperature requires keeping the altimeter in free air, not on your wrist or inside your clothing. Temperature inversions are common in mountains and can be 25 F° in winter. There's no easy way for a mountaineer to correct for nonstandard air temperature and inversions, and there's no way the altimeter can know if the temperature above it is higher or lower than the ISA profile expects; manufacturers are little help sorting this out. You can guess at the effect by thinking that if the air seems warm, your altimeter will be less sensitive, maybe by 5 to 10 percent; if you think it's unusually cold, your altimeter may be more sensitive than it should be. Air temperature effects could be a serious problem if you rely on your altimeter to make critical routefinding decisions.

Errors Due to Wind

Another factor that influences air pressure, and therefore the readings of barometric altimeters, is wind. Higher air speed over mountains causes a decrease in air pressure (due to the Bernoulli effect—the same thing that gives airplanes lift). As air masses move across mountain ranges, the air velocity increases at saddles and summits and along crests; this produces orographic pressure waves. High winds can cause an increase in altitude readout of as much as two contour lines, depending on terrain. Keep this in mind if you reset your altimeter on an especially windy saddle or summit.

Reality Check

There are other factors that affect altimeter accu-

racy in lesser ways. The standard approach to dealing with all these sources of error is to reset your altimeter any time you're at a known altitude by reference to your topo map, such as at a lake, summit, or trail juncture. For example, to maintain a one-contour-line accuracy during your Bloody Mountain climb, you'd have to reset your altimeter at every dozen contour lines of gain or loss. This should make you wonder: if you can accurately ascertain your exact elevation that frequently, why do you need an altimeter for navigation?

Your Compass as Altimeter

As a navigational tool, altimeters should be viewed only as an adjunct to skilled use of map and compass. It's possible to estimate altitude using the clinometer feature of your compass, by checking whether you are higher or lower than features around you whose distance and elevation you can determine from your map. Tip the compass on its side and use the mirror to view the clinometer as you sight along the baseplate. Commit to memory the factoid that a 1° angle spans 92 feet at a mile distance. For example, if your clinometer tells you that a known summit two miles away (according to your map) is 2° higher than you (according to your compass clinometer), you have determined that you are about 370 feet lower. This is probably as accurate as using an altimeter, and the clinometer's error sources are consistent and free of unknown influences.

Because of the variety of factors that affect altimeters and the variability of success of different models in dealing with them, a group of mountaineers carrying altimeters will be provided with hours of harmless fun discussing why their readings differ. If you want an instrument primarily for weather forecasting, a special-purpose model that measures and records wind speed, humidity, dew point, and air temperature, as well as altitude and barometric pressure (and of course date and time), would be a better choice at a price and weight that compares favorably to fancy but less accurate wristwatch altimeters. I admit that I often carry a gadget that has an electronic compass, thermometer, altimeter/barometer, and alarm clock. My reasons are that the quality of such instruments has gotten very good, the readout is easy to see even at night, I need the alarm function anyhow, and the cost and weight are no more than for a watch. Plus it even stores data snapshots, plots data, and uses trends to forecast weather; what's not to like?

NEW-SCHOOL MAPPING

Old-school navigators learned to fold their quads to leave the names visible and to carry all those needed to cover their routes, sometimes carefully cutting them up and taping them together. New-schoolers use mapping software to print only the areas they need. With that capability, however, comes peril. First, there's a lot of potentially useful information printed in the margins of USGS topos—I strongly recommend against cutting them off. Most of this information is lost by software. You'll likely find that the elevations your software reports as you move the mouse over a displayed map do not coincide exactly with elevations in the map image; this happens because the elevation data comes from a separate database, not directly from the digitized map, and the data often align imperfectly. Computerized map printing also opens the door to software mischief, most notably the "fit to page" printing feature, which results in non-standard scaling. Not only will this negate

your developing sense of scale and terrain, but it will render useless most navigation tools, such as the scales on your compass, your UTM romer, and the tools I've included in the Resources appendix. Always use 1:24,000 scale and check from time to time to ensure that your software hasn't found a clandestine means of being helpful.

I've described ruling north-south lines on USGS quads, but software may allow such grids to be printed automatically. You must decide whether you want lat/long lines or UTM grid lines; they are seldom orthogonal, or perpendicular (see the section on Grid North).

Mapping software can do more than just print maps and draw grids. You can draw your proposed route over the screen image and then analyze its length and grades. Old-school navigators twiddled little wheeled gadgets along routes to estimate length, or attempted to trace routes with their compass lanyards and then transfer the lengths to the scales printed on map margins, followed by application of squiggle factors based on experience. New-schoolers can zoom in to add enough detail to route tracing that, on a $7\frac{1}{2}$-minute quad, errors become insignificant. Not only is this easier, but most software can report both distance on the flat map and the greater distance along the ground. Determining altitude at any point is simple. Software makes it easy to determine the grade of route sections and to assess whether selected terrain features will be visible or obscured at particular vantage points (they'll be visible if the grade of their sight line to the observer is greater than that of intervening features). It's possible to establish waypoints on the electronic map that can be transferred into GPS receivers; such data will transfer in the other direction, too, making it possible to draw routes on software maps from GPS waypoints collected in the field or from other mountaineers.

By the way, you'll discover that the maps you print at home (or at work when the boss isn't looking) are vulnerable to the slightest amount of water, due to the inks in most color inkjet printers. Keep yours safe in a waterproof map pouch from Watchful Eye Designs (and I mean *really* waterproof, not a flimsy zip seal bag).

GPS AND UTM

The Global Positioning System can be made extremely complicated, but let's not, because the simple basics are all you need. GPS has three components: the constellation of military-run satellites orbiting the earth each day, a few ground stations that talk to the satellites and keep them honest, and millions of receivers like yours that use signals from the satellites to establish their locations on the surface of the earth, their altitudes a little less accurately, and high-precision time. The Europeans operate a supplemental system called EGNOS, to be followed by an independent GPS-like system called Galileo starting operation in 2008. Modern handheld receivers are capable of receiving up to 12 GPS satellites at once (for better reception in dense forests and narrow canyons); positional error is usually "less than ±15 meters (±49 feet) RMS, 95% of the time." Many receivers are chock full of fascinating features and readouts, such as crude electronic compasses and basic barometric altimeters that compliment their GPS altimeters. GPS receivers run on batteries that last up to a dozen hours when all features are being used.

Datum

To set your GPS receiver to provide helpful information you must first select the datum that corresponds to that of your map (yes, you must be adept at using topo maps, even if you supplement with GPS). A datum is a mathematical model of the earth, which isn't precisely spherical. Select from a built-in list of hundreds. Most handheld GPS receivers default to datums called NAD83 (North American Datum of 1983) or WGS84 (World Geodetic System of 1984), which are essentially equivalent. USGS maps use the older NAD27 (some use NGV29 for vertical coordinates—ignore this); Canadian maps may use either NAD83 or NAD27. The USGS has flirted with NAD83, 1:25,000 scale, and metric measure, so be sure to refer to the marginal notes of the map you use. Set your receiver correctly, because the difference can be hundreds of meters—yes, GPS and UTM use metric measurement. Topo maps usually show the offset between NAD27 and NAD83 by little crosses near their corners. If you're a new-school navigator using mapping software (no little crosses for you), you'll have to set your software to your datum of choice and ensure that it prints at 1:24,000, even if the contour lines on the maps you print are metric.

Coordinate System

Next, you'll want to set your GPS receiver to display location in your favorite coordinate system. Latitude-longitude (lat-long) could be used. Then you'll have to select degrees, minutes, seconds as used on many maps; degrees and decimal minutes as used in aircraft navigation; or decimal degrees, which are seldom used but which make calculations easiest and might be the default. Using lat-long can be a real head scratcher in the field, so for short distances, spanning less than a few quads for example, mountaineers should select UTM.

UTM

Universal Transverse Mercator is a mapping projection. Projections are schemes for representing the surface of the three-dimensional earth on a flat, two-dimensional map—there are many varieties, each a compromise in some ways. A *mercator* projection, named after the 16th-century dude who conceived it, depicts the earth on the surface of a cylinder that's parallel to the earth's polar axis. It makes Greenland look bigger than South America though it's actually a fourth the size, but sailors like it because it makes lat-long lines perpendicular everywhere; you can see an example in the previous map of declination. A *transverse* mercator depicts the earth on a cylinder that's *perpendicular* to the earth's polar axis. This is useless information, but it's fun to try to get your head around the concept and imagine how lat-long lines would be drawn. That bizarre distortion is avoided by the UTM scheme of depicting only narrow slices of the spherical earth.

Knowledge of UTM is important even if you don't own a GPS receiver, because it's becoming increasingly common for mountaineering trip reports or guide books to locate key points using unambiguous GPS coordinates as a supplement to highly ambiguous descriptions of surrounding

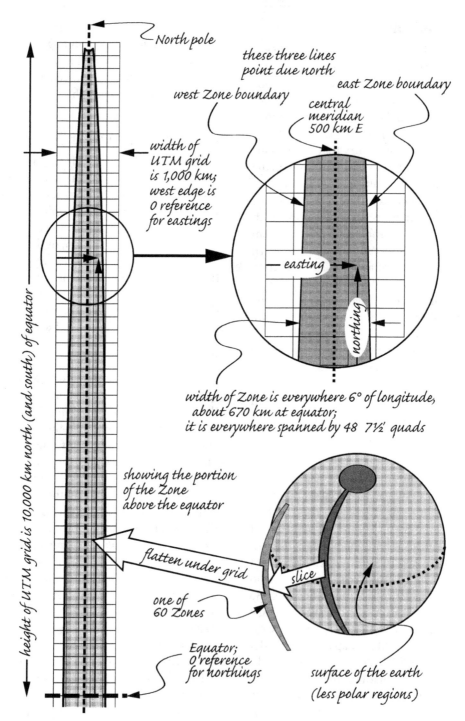

North pole

these three lines
point due north

west Zone boundary

east Zone boundary

central
meridian
500 km E

width of
UTM grid
is 1,000 km;
west edge is
0 reference
for eastings

easting

northing

width of Zone is everywhere 6° of longitude,
about 670 km at equator;
it is everywhere spanned by 48 7½' quads

height of UTM grid is 10,000 km north (and south) of equator

showing the portion
of the Zone
above the equator

flatten under grid

slice

one of
60 Zones

Equator;
0'reference
for northings

surface of the earth
(less polar regions)

The UTM grid.

terrain. Hopefully, the person writing the trip report will be familiar with UTM, uses it in preference to whatever default comes up on their GPS receiver, and reports the datum. If you have the UTM coordinates, you can readily plot the points on your map. You can also make a simple calculation of the flat distance between two points using the Pythagorean theorem, even without plotting anything. Things are not so simple if coordinates are reported in lat-long, even if the reporting scheme matches the degrees-minutes-seconds scheme used on USGS quads. (You do remember the Pythagorean Theorem, don't you?)

Zones

To get a sense of how UTM is designed, imagine the surface of the earth as being like an orange. Now slice the orange from pole to pole, making 60 tall, narrow slices. These 6° slices are numbered 1 to 60, beginning at the international dateline in the Pacific and heading east all the way around the globe, er, orange. Whack off the ends, which represent polar regions—they use another type of projection. Now peel and flatten each slice to make it two-dimensional; some distortion of latitude lines (called *parallels*) will result—no biggie. Each slice will be about 674 km wide at the equator and 100 km wide at the truncated ends; each slice is called a *zone*. Now center the slice under a grid of 1 km squares that is 1,000 km wide and 20,000 km tall; the grid will completely overlap the slice. Points on the slice are described by their *x* location, measured to the east from the western edge of the grid (not from the edge of the slice). This dimension is called an *easting*. The slice of terrain and the overlaying grid are centered, so the middle of the zone will be at an easting of 500 km (500,000 meters); there will be no eastings less than about 160 km or greater than about 840 km, reflecting the grid's overlap. The *y* (vertical) coordinate is measured from the equator (at 0 meters) and increases toward the north pole; it's called a *northing*. In the southern hemisphere, *southings* start from the equator at 10,000 km and decrease toward the south pole. Coordinates everywhere will always be positive and are based on easy, consistent metric measurements (because the system was designed for soldiers).

Bands

If the zone number and hemisphere are specified, it's possible to unambiguously describe the location of any point on the globe. To remove the need for a hemisphere label, each zone is further divided into 20 horizontal bands, all but the northmost band spanning 8° of latitude. Bands are labeled alphabetically from C at the south end of the zone to X at the north end, skipping I and O (to avoid confusion with numbers 1 and 0). Global locations are completely specified by their zone, band, easting, and northing (or southing). UTM is used with many applications and mapping systems, not just USGS topo map quads. I've thrown a whole lot of info at you; fortunately you don't have to memorize any of it once the basic concepts soak in. Besides, you'll know if you're in the southern hemisphere because the sun will arc strangely to the north, and familiar constellations will be upside down—and there's the Southern Cross.

Shorthand Notation Used with UTM Coordinates

First, let's look at the longhand specification of a point using UTM, taking the location of Mt. Whitney as an example. In geographic degrees-minutes-seconds coordinates it's located at 36° 34' 45" N latitude and -118° 17' 33" W longitude. In UTM coordinates it's in zone 11, band S. With the NAD83 datum, the easting of Mt. Whitney is 384,356 meters, and its northing is 4,048,961 meters; using the NAD27 datum its easting is 384,436 meters, and its northing is 4,048,764 meters. The summit would appear to be displaced 180 meters (590 feet) if the wrong datum is used, dropping that little stone house right down the Mountaineer's Route; more significantly, this amount of error is certainly enough to cause you to go off route in tricky terrain.

A complete representation of the location of Mt. Whitney, according to the NAD83 datum, would be

11S 384356 mE 4048961 mN

The easting, reading to the right, is always given before the northing, reading up. Some GPS receivers omit the band, let you specify the hemisphere in your receiver setup, and then display Mt. Whitney's location as

11 3 84 356
40 48 961

In some representations, the final digits, representing single meters, will be dropped to indicate that the precision is being given only to 10 meters. Two digits would be dropped if the requisite precision is 100 meters.

USGS topo maps simplify the coordinate expressions when no confusion would result (for example, when referring to a single, specific 7½-minute quad map). Two numbers in the easting and northing specify a particular UTM 1,000-meter (1 km) grid line; these are the "principal digits":

11S 384436 mE and
4048764 mN

The Mt. Whitney quad would show a fine black grid line or blue ticks along the edge of the map area at the 384th 1,000-meter easting grid line and at the 4,048th 1,000-meter northing grid line in the zone, among others. (Most USGS maps also show ticks, usually labeled in feet, associated with State Plane Coordinate Systems; the details are too complex and useless to mention, just ignore them.) Principal digit UTM ticks on this map would be marked

^{3}84 and ^{40}48

The superscripted initial numerals deemphasize resolution that is too coarse to be of importance on this particular map. If these ticks happen to be cardinal on a particular topo map, in the SE and NW corners, they would be marked more completely as

^{3}84000 m$_E$ and
^{40}48000 m$_N$

SECRET CODE

Even more information can be removed from UTM coordinates by conjoining eastings and northings, omitting the superscripted prefixes that are unneeded if you stick to a specific single quad, and dropping digits representing unwanted precision. In this manner the summit of Mt. Whitney at 384436 mE and 4048764 mN would be described as being at UTM 844488, to a precision of 100 meters (about 328 feet). This representation is diabolically cryptic, but now you know how to decode it when you find it in a route description or guide book. Without the name of the USGS quad to which you are referring, such representations are ambiguous and indecipherable. My personal opinion is that ink is cheap and confusion is not, so complete longhand UTM coordinate representations are to be preferred.

Locating a Point on a Topo Map Using UTM Coordinates

Here's where the UTM system shows its convenience compared to lat-long. On the Mt. Whitney quad, the summit of Mt. Whitney, with an easting of 384436 meters, will be located to the east (right) of the ^{3}84 grid line, a little more than one-third of the way to the ^{3}85 grid line further right. That establishes its east-west location. With a northing of 4048764, its north-south position will be above the ^{40}48 grid line, about three-quarters of the way to the ^{40}49 grid line next up. Transparent overlay scales or grids, called *romers* or *roamers*, in 1:24,000 or 1:25,000 (metric) scale, are available to help plot UTM coordinates on maps, and I've included a pattern for one in the Resources appendix that you can print yourself. The meter scale in map margins may be all you need. If the 1,000-meter grid lines are printed or drawn on the map, you might get close enough just by visual estimation.

GRID NORTH

Gird your grid: there's another subtlety in the relationship of UTM grid lines and lat-long meridians and parallels on quad maps; it arises because they are based on different projections. On the flattened slice of terrain (orange peel) with which we started, the longitude lines (meridians) converge at the poles. On our UTM projection and grid overlay, meridians above the equator on the west side of the zone (slice) appear to curve toward the east, and on the east side of the zone they appear to curve westerly. UTM grid lines, on the other hand, are everywhere parallel and perpendicular, which is a big appeal for using UTM. However, this also means the UTM grid only aligns with longitude meridians (*all* of which lead true north) near the center of zones, at an easting of 500,000 meters— a grid line that would be marked $^5 00^{000}$ ^{m}E on a USGS map. If you zoom in on the six-degree wide zone away from its center and examine one of the forty-eight 7½-minute quads that span the zone, you find that the conic projection used for USGS quads results in maps—bounded as they are by lat-long parallels and meridians—that are more or less (but not exactly) rectangular and square to the page. This implies that UTM grid lines will *not* be square to the page, especially for quads near the east and west edges of the zone. The UTM grid that covers the quad will appear tilted but not distorted. Getting your head around this concept admittedly takes effort, which may be unjustifiable in practice. The offset angle of the UTM grid with respect to meridians depicted on a particular quad is called Grid North, and newer USGS maps add a GN declination arrow to the marginal diagram that shows the declination angle of magnetic north (MN) with respect to true north (TN or ★). The greatest east or west GN declination on any 7½-minute quad will be a couple of degrees.

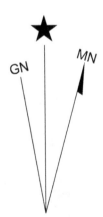

UTM GRID AND 1983 MAGNETIC NORTH DECLINATION AT CENTER OF SHEET

A quad map's depiction of geographic north, magnetic north, and grid north.

So?

Now that you're convinced that a GPS receiver is a world of wondrous complexity, you might ask, "But what good is it?" The answer depends on whom you ask. If you ask me, I'd say that for most mountaineering, you can better spend your money and weight budget elsewhere. Sure, a GPS receiver is barrels of fun to play with, but it mainly tells you where it is (or was); it's a *position* instrument whereas a compass is mainly a *direction* instrument. You wouldn't use a GPS receiver to follow a route instruction such as "From the summit, the only descending ridge that doesn't cliff out is the one at 58°." A GPS receiver determines its position with amazing precision, but in most cases precision is not required beyond that obtainable with thoughtful observation of your surroundings and maybe a compass—you still need a real map and map skills to take advantage of your GPS. Knowing the coordinates of a location tells you little about how to get there or even how far away it is. There are exceptions, of course, where a GPS receiver could be handy. Finding a cache or retracing your route in a whiteout or finding your location in a deep forest (or at night) where compass navigation is problematic would be examples, as would be the person who chronically becomes lost—just be sure that if you depend on your GPS receiver you don't let its batteries go dead. Pick a receiver that uses rechargeable AA batteries or allows easy battery swapping and get at least one spare (most units won't lose data when you replace batteries); be sure the unit has a backlight display and is water resistant. Worry more about weight than about a big, flashy display. Software and hardware can add fun features, of course, but for most outings I'd suggest that you simply learn to use your map and compass, and pay more attention to the world around you. That's what draws you to the mountains in the first place.

ESTIMATING TRAVEL TIME

The best means of estimating the time required to travel a particular route is based on experience, yours or others', including trip reports of previous parties. Still, wouldn't it be handy if there were a simple way to calculate an estimate? Turns out that for simple routes, there is such a calculation. The basic idea behind this family of calculations, called Naismith Rules, is to figure hiking speed on trails, hiking speed cross-country, and time to add to account for altitude gain.

When hiking on easy, flat trails, reasonably fit and moderately loaded backpackers move along at about 2.5 miles (that's about an inch on a quad map) per hour, or about 25 minutes per mile, 3 to 5 km per hour. This corresponds to an energy consumption around 600 calories per hour. Determined, athletic backpackers do better; figure 3 mph or more. Speed drops significantly if the trail is rough and more significantly if the terrain is so rough that the trail disappears altogether. You might figure 1 mph through boulders and half that if things are really awkward, but Naismith formulas are intended mainly for trails. To your trail travel estimate you add additional time if the easy trail ascends—an additional hour for every 1,000 feet or so, maybe more if you don't follow my guidance and you're carrying a heavy pack. To such an estimate you would add more time for rest stops, large group inefficiency of about 1 percent for each additional person, and other delays. Above 10,000 feet your performance will drop more, depending on your degree of acclimation.

Expressing these rules of thumb mathematically results in the approximation

$$T = R/3 + C + H$$

where the time, T, in hours, will be given by adding the road or trail travel distance, R, in miles (figuring 3 mph) to the cross-country distance, C, in miles figured at 1 mph, to the altitude gain in thousands of feet, H. This is a very crude estimate, so H is omitted (not subtracted) for segments involving downhill travel, even though the difference over rough terrain may be nil. You can easily modify this formula based on your own hiking speeds; I find it gives times that are too long by at least 50 percent for a small group of conditioned and motivated mountaineers.

Burn, Baby, Burn

Another approach to estimating travel time is based on the energy consumption required and available. In Performance Nutrition for Mountaineers, Chapter 19, I point out that, depending on level of fitness, mountaineers may burn 600 to 800 or more calories per hour when working hard. If the caloric requirements of a route could be estimated, the travel time could be calculated based on nominal calorie burn rate. As a gross estimate, figure on burning 100 calories per trail mile, 200 calories per cross-country mile, and 400 calories for every 1,000 feet of elevation gain. To that sum, add about 65 calories per hour of estimated travel time for basal metabolism. The sum will estimate the energy required for the route; divide that by the rate you can, or would want to, put out, and the result will estimate the travel time for you that the route requires.

For the Obsessive-Compulsive Mountaineer

If you're planning a trip well in advance or for a remote location, you can find calculators on the Internet that will give you sunrise and sunset data for any place at any time of year, and by digging further you can find the corresponding angle of the sun above the horizon (architects use this all the time). If you really want to get fancy, you can use your topo map to see at what time your camp might receive sunshine or when your snow slope descent might see the sun recede behind the local crest, with attendant temperature drop. The sun appears to move 360° per day or 15° per hour, so you can use the grade of the occluding terrain to determine how many hours after sunrise the sun might strike your frosty little tent.

LOST

Getting lost means that you or your party comes to the realization that the certainty of your location has somehow wandered away. It can happen gradually, as your hiking trail turns progressively into a rabbit track, or suddenly, as you encounter an unexpected feature. The usual reaction to this conclusion consists of stopping immediately and taking out map and compass to reorient. Occasionally this works. In the worst case, becoming lost could mean retracing your path back to the last place where you knew your location with certainty, even if that's the trailhead. It never means stumbling ahead in hopes of rejoining your intended route. Travelers who proceed ahead hoping to come across the route invariably become wanderers who are most certainly lost. For mountaineers, becoming lost can be more serious because it could imply that you're in terrain that all looks the same; for example, you're ascending a gully and develop the deep suspicion that it isn't the gully you had intended. Or you're descending a ridge, and that little voice in the back of your head that's been nagging you for half an hour finally gets your attention. Or you're skiing down a most excellent run and realize near the bottom that you're no longer heading homeward. You consult your map and can't determine for sure if you're on the correct route or the one that ends at an impassable cliff. Reversing your path is exquisitely unattractive and could result in an unplanned bivouac. You're lost.

The cure for all cases of being lost is the same: stay found. Maintain constant association between your location in the terrain and your intended route on your map. Start with reviewing your route by spreading out the topo maps on the kitchen table and uploading the terrain into your brain, along with potential handrails, attack points, catching features, and, yes, bailout options. Be sure all members of your party are acquainted with the intended route, even if that comes only at the trailhead as you point it out on the map before heading off. And always let someone who won't be coming along know your intentions. If you're the leader of a more serious outing, you may decide to prepare a formal route card, with enough detail and identified decision points to make you confident of successful navigation. Leave a copy with your significant other unless he's in the party.

Then, as you travel, maintain confidence that you're proceeding according to plan, in terms of both route and timetable. Encourage everyone in your group to chat up the route and voice any suspicions that something could be wrong. Turn around often, especially at decision points, to get an idea of what the return route will look like. If you really anticipate problems returning along your route, because of the possibility of bad weather perhaps, mark your route with wands or strips of surveyors' tape from your ten essentials (see Chapter 18); toilet paper also works until it rains—just be sure to remove any of these forms of trash as you return. An alert party is unlikely to become lost unless beset by unexpected events. A weather change is such an event, or the realization that travel in a green area on your topo map means that you're unable to see terrain features you hoped to use for navigation. The implication is that some objective hazard threatens the group; dealing with that hazard and ensuring the safety of the group is more important than adherence to a route plan or timetable. Rockfall or avalanche avoidance, for example, can result in the necessity to travel on unplanned routes. Running out of daylight in combination with positional uncertainty is a very good reason to resign yourself to a comfortable camp (or uncomfortable bivouac) and cease compounding your troubles until the next morning.

If you're traveling solo, you must assess whether you're truly lost, or whether you're just uncertain of your specific location and a bit of reconnaissance will resolve doubt. Factor in whether you believe that a search for you will be initiated. The worst possible things to do are travel in darkness, wander out of the sensible search area, cross barriers such as rivers or passes where searchers will expect you to stop, fail to leave clues in obvious spots, or find yourself trapped by a terrain feature, such as a dry waterfall in a gully, that maroons you in an unlikely place of hiding. Searchers look for clues, not persons, so leave plenty, such as deliberate foot prints showing your direction of travel, bits of surveyor's tape, arrows and your initials scratched into the dirt or made by lining up pebbles on larger rocks, bundles of grass bent over in your direction of travel and wrapped with more grass, or even written notes. Most of the material written about what to do after realizing you're lost relates to hikers lost in the woods; travelers in high mountains may enjoy more visible landmarks, but should they become lost their predicaments require unique solutions. For example, building a smoky fire may be impossible above tree line, on snow, or in strong winds; there may be no one close enough to see it or to reach you in a reasonable amount of time if they do see it. As I write, thousands of firefighters are battling a nearby 250,000-acre fire that has destroyed thousands of homes and cost a dozen lives; it was started as a signal by a lost hunter. Instead of pyromania, avoid becoming lost in the first place.

Separation Anxiety

If you're new to mountaineering, you might wonder how it's possible for a small party of mountaineers to become separated in broad daylight. Actually, it's ever so easy and happens all the time. If everyone knows the route, there's usually no problem, but should a member of the party become truly lost, there must be a clearly understood assessment and response plan. Absent that, don't allow the party to become widely separated for fear of a tremendous waste of time reuniting a lost member. At a minimum, reunite at every decision point. For the lost member, who's most often trailing the others, the first thing to do is to stop, even though you're behind. If that lost person is you, and you can figure out where you are, then continue ahead to rejoin the group, but frequently consult a map to test your hypothesis. If you're mapless and clueless, stay put or move only a short distance to a location where you'll be more visible. It's remarkable how invisible a person becomes in the scale of mountainous terrain, even back in the unmissed days when Day-Glo clothing was in fashion.

If you're among the searchers, you should rely on the plan your party has formed for the route, or even route segment, in question. You did make an if-lost plan, didn't you? The first attempt at reunion involves group shouting and group listening. I've never known shouting to work (for anything), but three blasts on one of those deafeningly loud whistles will reach out better than you might expect. Most parties have an understanding that if darkness intervenes, safety of the searchers requires that efforts will be discontinued at nightfall. The next morning, searching won't resume until some understood time, such as two or three hours after first light. This gives lost members enough time to find their way back to the group or at least to make themselves more findable, and prevents them from being overcome by guilt and desperation at being unfound, as they know that no one will maintain a night search or set out first thing next morning.

ANOTHER WAY OF NAVIGATING

When I was just a tyke my grandfather would take me into the forest and try to teach me about wild things. He'd point out animal tracks that I could barely see, yet he was able to tell the sex of the animal, how fast it was moving, and what it was doing when it made the tracks. I was amazed, so I'd beg him to show me these things every chance I got. I once asked my granddad how he could walk so much in dense forests and never become lost, seemingly without any effort at all and certainly without map or compass. He responded with a story told in a very matter-of-fact way. He said that for thousands of years our ancestors (my family is Native American) had been walking over the land, over all of America, to the top of every mountain and down every river. (My father joked that they "turned over every rock and looked under every bush.") My grandfather said that our ancestors left their spirits in special places to guide future generations, so that we wouldn't become lost. He said that if I found one of those special places and listened for the spirit voices, they would guide me. Wow, was I impressed! I nagged him with queries about how to find such places and what the spirit voices might say and every other silly question. He answered that these were things that could be learned, but not taught. That was his answer for a lot of my questions. Ever since then, throughout my life, I've looked for special places, and I've tried to hear the spirit voices of my ancestors. Never in my life have I ever been lost.

Well, of course, you might say. That's just a story to teach common sense to impressionable kids: pay attention to things around you; maintain a sense of where you are and where you're going; be comforted by your environment, not fearful; calm down and make sensible decisions; come up with a plan and follow it. Certainly good advice, and I'm passing it on to my daughter. My grandfather became one with his ancestors long ago; I give you his story for what you care to make of it. Trust his counsel, and the spirits may speak to you, too.

5 Mountain Hazards

Every mountain accident has its human ingredient.

That's what Reinhold Messner thought; in fact, he may have thought that humans can overcome objective hazards by force of will. In my view, objective hazards are those that arise from the mountain environment, whereas subjective hazards are those arising from human behavior and can therefore be influenced. Rockfall is an objective hazard; failure to climb so as to avoid rockfall is a subjective hazard. Objective hazards are unaffected by human intent, but the risk of objective hazards can be managed by competent decision making. When climbers are affected or afflicted by objective hazard, the common conclusions are either that they were the victims of unlucky accidents, or that they exercised poor judgment. Luck and judgment have little didactic utility, but decision making can be systematically improved. Good decision making is informed by facts, so let's have a look at some facts about objective hazards.

ROCKFALL AND ICEFALL

Mountains are constantly in the processes of formation and destruction; the steeper the grade and the more extreme the weather, the faster the mountains are converted to talus and talus to sand. Different rock types vary in their susceptibility to weathering, but generally more northerly ranges and faces are broken down more actively. Seasonal weather cycles cause the fracturing of mountain faces, so the two safest seasons are summer and winter. In winter, loose rock is frozen in place, and ice remains solid; when spring arrives, receding snow and ice allow many stones to fall and leave others delicately balanced. In summer, melting is complete, and less rock is fractured and released until fall weather resumes the attack on the mountains. Daily melt-freeze cycles cause a higher incidence of rockfall as the day progresses and sunlight warms the rock. Global warming appears to be reducing the year-round snow and ice that glue loose rock in place on many mountains, with the result that the choss, or loose rock, is coming down at record rates. Unusual drought has the same effect.

The key to enjoying the mountains while avoiding involvement in the erosion process is minimizing your exposure to falling rock and ice. That means selecting routes appropriate to the season and avoiding those prone to rockfall when conditions are unfavorable. Avoiding the daily cycle of rockfall and icefall usually means getting an early start on the day; the classic alpine start begins early enough in the predawn to pass route sections with stonefall hazard while rocks are still frozen in place and before meltwater begins releasing missiles. Rockfall can be avoided by sticking to ridge routes and avoiding gullies and couloirs, particularly those that funnel rockfall from cirques above.

When you're unavoidably exposed to rockfall, a few tactics may improve your lot. Most basic is wearing a hard-shell helmet. When you're in a mountain shooting gallery, be constantly alert for falling rock and try to have sheltered spots at hand. You may have to decide whether it's better to quickly ascend a gully or to take more time while traversing back and forth to minimize your exposure in the fall line. In a party of climbers, you may have to cross an area exposed to rockfall one at a time while others remain sheltered; this consumes a lot of time and is another reason to keep groups small. When rock does fall, it often comes as a shower of rocks that have dislodged others. As soon as you hear, see, or cause falling objects shout the customary warning, "Rock!" and hunker down under your helmet, pressing against the rock in whatever shelter you can quickly reach, using your pack to shield your back. If you're belaying, lock off the belay and hide under your helmet. Don't look up in hopes of dodging the rock unless you're certain it comes from very nearby, perhaps from your clumsy partner. Looking up seems to attract falling rocks. Don't follow the old-school advice to bend your head forward and cover the back of your neck with your hands. When climbing with others, in your party or below another party, either climb very close together, so that dislodged rocks can be sidestepped, or avoid climbing directly below others. Be aware that rocks that have fallen

some distance can bounce and ricochet in amazingly unpredictable ways. On more technical terrain, test every hold for looseness by pounding it with the palm of your hand, and pull down rather than out as you move up. Warn your following partner of any loose rocks you discover, and replace them gingerly. A rope is a great device to use for creating your personal rockfall; particular care is required to avoid doing so when rappelling and as you pull down the rappel rope. Protect your rope from rockfall by minimizing the amount that's exposed; keeping all but what's needed in a rope bag is a great way to do this.

Rockfall is not to be taken lightly; after falls, it's the second most common cause of mountaineering mishap. Just about every mountaineer has been whacked by rocks; usually that results in a bruise and a sigh of relief, but it's not uncommon for bones to be broken. I've seen climbers killed by rockfall, and it ain't pretty.

RAIN

Rain is much more serious than just a cause of discomfort and slippery footing, made worse if the rain freezes to verglas, a thin coating of ice. Rain causes a significant increase in rockfall and icefall—bad if you're being rained on, but possibly beneficial if you climb soon after the rock dries. While you're being rained on, rain not only attacks frost that may be retaining rocks, but it also increases and contributes to meltwater, which will cause substantially more rockfall. Even a light rain increases rockfall by simply decreasing the angle of repose. That's the steepest slope at which loose rock can be piled, so if it decreases, rocks that would otherwise be stable if they were dry will slide down. Wet talus and scree slopes become especially treacherous.

Rain also increases the danger of avalanche; the details depend on the locale of the snowpack (maritime or continental), history of the snowpack, and other factors. But the consequence of rain on snow is invariably a bad thing for avalanche hazard, and the ill effect, even if not immediately expressed, may persist as a dangerous potential for many months. Things will be particularly bad on steep snow, where rain may cause water to run on rock beneath the snow and significantly reduce adhesion. Rain on a glacier will weaken snow bridges, even if it doesn't make crevasses more visible. When rain wets rocks and ropes, the force required to pull down a rappel rope essentially doubles; this may also double the chance that the rope will become stuck—not what you want to deal with in the rain. Rain that wets an unprepared climber's clothing substantially increases heat loss; this can result in hypothermia even though the air temperature is well above freezing. Finally, as stony mountains are inefficient at retaining water, rain, snow, or hail can result in gulley routes becoming a series of waterfalls and rivulets—no fun to climb or descend. Even brief and remote thundershowers can result in rapid flooding that sends debris crashing down creeks and can quickly raise stream flow to dangerous levels, possibly cutting off retreat routes. If you've only thought of rain as an excuse to blow off climbing and drink beer, your sloth is vindicated. Spend the time learning to interpret weather reports, or for the full benefit, practice aid climbing or dry tooling at the local crag, which will be empty.

RIVER CROSSINGS

You may think that I'm single-mindedly accumulating reasons to start climbing days at a painfully early hour, but hazardous stream crossings are yet another justification. It's often said that the most dangerous components of many climbs are the stream crossings necessary to reach them. Streams that originate in glaciers and snowfields flow most freely after the warmth of afternoon sunshine; in early morning, small flows may disappear completely (a good reason to collect plenty of water in the evening, if that's your source). Early morning is the best time to cross such creeks and their larger confluences. If you arrive at a crossing late in the day to see boot prints on the trail disappearing into a robust creek and reappearing on the other side, you know the likely cause. The safest option may be to camp nearby and cross the following morning; that will give you ample time to remind yourself to plan better in the future.

Any crossing of cold, swift water deserves respect and time allowed for crossing safely. Such crossings are made all the more dangerous if visibility through the water is obscured by cloudiness caused by glacial flour (finely ground rock dust) or sediment brought in by a recent storm. Rapidly moving water causes stones and gravel to move readily when disturbed, providing treacherous footing that compounds the current's force on your body. Modest streams can be crossed using common sense: scout up and down for helpful features, hope to find logs in a forest or gravel bars near a glacial terminus, check your map to see if upstream tributaries offer the possibility of crossing the water in increments, or search your map for nearby stretches where the grade is lower and the stream may be wider and therefore less deep. Your map may even remind you that a hike to a bridge or pack trail ford is preferable to dealing with the stream as it immediately confronts you.

Crossing swift water requires skill and practice, like any other mountaineering challenge. With skill, crossing crotch-deep water is possible, but water that roils over knee height will thwart many. Pick a crossing with a take-out point that allows moving diagonally downstream. Give thought to the consequences of falling in, so avoid crossing immediately above more treacherous stretches, undercut banks, brush-choked banks, strainers (piles of tree limbs or logs through which water flows), and submerged logs. The usual strategy is to remove your socks and insoles but wear your boots; you could also wear just your spare socks if the water is clear and shallow enough that you can see that the bottom is reasonably smooth. Release your pack waist belt and sternum strap and be sure that everything on your pack is well secured. Cross facing upstream, shuffling your feet and planting your trekking poles upstream for balance. (Be sure to pop off the snow baskets.) If several people are crossing, the decision must be made whether to cross one at a time, with others standing downstream as spotters prepared to extend assistance to anyone who falls in, or whether crossing as a group will be more effective. There are several tactics for crossing as a group. The most accomplished person will cross upstream, and the others will form a line in the eddy below, holding hands or clinging to the pack of the person upstream. This method works best if only one person moves at a time, so someone needs to give direction and organization. Using a long tree limb on the upstream side of the group makes this technique even more effective unless obstacles in the stream require the group to weave around. A rope can be strung across the stream as a handline if anchors are available that will allow it to be stretched tightly from the put-in point to the take-out point well downstream. Move across the rope on its downstream side and never attach directly to the rope because of the danger of becoming trapped underwater if your feet are swept away; clipping your pack to the rope makes sense if you're confident you can escape your pack should you slip. Using a rope in this way can be very effective if it permits some serious hauling back to keep your feet planted solidly as water roils up your legs.

If you do fall in, shuck your pack, face downstream with your feet up to cushion the brunt of anything you hit, and attempt to bob your way to the nearest bank. Use every possible effort to avoid becoming trapped in a strainer or streamside hazard, but don't attempt to stand until you have reached a bank or calm water. Look for spotters who may be extending poles or swinging a cordelette your way. If you've managed to extricate yourself, you'll be cold and exhausted; you deserve the good fortune of having your pack end up on the same side of the stream so you can put on dry clothing and prepare a warm meal.

Cold-water immersion causes loss of muscular coordination due to rapid shell cooling, rendering even strong swimmers dysfunctional after only 5 minutes in ice-cold water. A person who suddenly inhales water may lose consciousness within seconds, and about one such victim in eight suffers from larynx spasms that cut off their airway. Respiratory failure should be treated immediately with positive pressure ventilation (a component of CPR), without first removing water from the lungs. Rescued victims of cold-water immersion should be given basic life support and treated for hypothermia even though they appear to be dead. Victims who are pulled from the water may recover spontaneously within a couple of minutes, but cold water is an irritant to the lungs that may cause life-threatening pulmonary edema to develop later. Anyone who has inhaled a significant amount of water or who has lost consciousness during an immersion incident should be monitored and evacuated.

LIGHTNING

The one statement about lightning that can be made with conviction is that lightning is replete with murky science and fascinating, frightening stories. I'll stick to a small dose of the latest murky science, to give a perspective on those stories.

Cumulous clouds form by convective lifting, which can be strong over mountains. As clouds form, they accumulate static charges (technically, they separate static charges). This happens high in the sky over flat land, such as Florida's Lightning Alley, but cloud bases may be close to the earth over mountains. Lightning may be visible when a storm is about 15 miles distant. If you can hear thunder, the storm is probably no more than 6 to 10 miles away; count the seconds from the flash to the boom and divide by 5 to estimate miles (sound travels about 1,130 feet per second). Storms in mountains are commonly not evident until they are closer than the striking range of lightning.

As a cloud gets bigger, perhaps becoming cumulonimbus, its static charges increase. The charge begins leaking into the atmosphere from the bottom of the cloud in connected arcs called step leaders. Step leaders are each many tens of yards (meters) long and aren't aimed at any specific feature of the terrain below, they just hop to the next most favorable point in the atmosphere below the cloud, generally heading downward toward the earth; the process is somewhat erratic and happens very fast, in a few milliseconds.

Meanwhile, on the ground below the cloud, a charge of opposite polarity accumulates and begins bleeding off into the air in what are called streamers. The earth below the cloud is a ground plane, meaning it has an essentially infinite supply of both positive and negative charges. Sharply pointed objects form corona and streamers more readily, but they'll form on just about anything as the charge builds in reaction to the charged cloud above. Pine trees have lots of sharply pointed needles, making the tall ones effective single-use lightning rods. When charge intensifies and streams off of climbers, they report things like their hair and pack straps standing on end and their climbing hardware "buzzing like bees" due to the electrical discharge into the atmosphere nearby. These are very bad things to experience, because the next thing to happen is that a step leader jumps to a streamer, making an ionized path that connects the earth to the cloud. Bam! Lightning strikes. Intense streamers form in many places as step leaders get nearer; unsubstantiated reports suggest that these streamers can be powerful enough to cause injury even if a step leader selects another streamer for the final jump. The high-current, high-frequency lightning bolt is only an inch or so in diameter, but it's so intense that ordinary concepts of electricity are inapplicable.

Combine that with the fact that stone and snow, even wet, are not particularly good conductors of electricity, and the truths about ordinary lightning come to light. The first truth is that the lightning bolt isn't aiming for anything specific when its step leaders start out from a cloud that may be miles away—not a pine tree, nor a summit, and not a hapless climber who has misjudged the weather. Lightning doesn't always strike summits or ridges, or even the highest point around; lightning may ignore rocky summits and strike lower, where the ground is more conductive—or it may not. Sitting on your rope or pack or sleeping pad will offer no protection from a strike that has already passed through thousands of feet of air, a much better insulator.

As lightning strikes an object, it heads down it to the earth and then spreads out. The lightning current heading for ground is so powerful that it can create damaging induction currents in other objects, even if it doesn't hit them—fences, cables, and phone lines, for example, or maybe you. As it's heading down whatever it hits first, lightning may jump to another, more attractive object or may jump over the ground surface for 20 yards or

more. These jumps are called side strikes and surface arcs. As the bolt enters the earth, it may not spread out evenly (as the sheet-resistance-of-earth theory claims) and may continue, especially if the ground is rocky, along zigzag ionization paths much like it did in the air. The upshot of this is not to be near any object that may be hit because side strikes can reach out farther than the height of the object struck. Although ground currents do generally decrease farther from the strike point, this is not a uniform phenomenon: you may be bypassed by ground currents from a nearby strike, or you may be unfortunate enough to be affected by an intense ground current path at some distance from a strike. Engineers drilling tunnels under the Alps discovered that blasting caps could be set off by lightning strikes miles above.

So where do we stand, so to speak, as mountaineers? First, prevention is the best approach, maybe the only one that's effective. This means watching the weather and not being in high places when thunderstorms are forming and especially not when they arrive. Start early; get off the upper mountain before the afternoon cumulous clouds develop. If unexpectedly caught by a lightning storm, abandon the route and head down the mountain quickly. The mountain will surely survive; if you do, too, you can climb it another day.

It's true that a tall, perfectly grounded conductor will provide a "cone of protection" from strikes that's about twice as wide at its base as the object is tall. The problem with this notion is that lightning is difficult to model because of its intensity and high-frequency energy. If lightning decides that a nearby object is more seductive (because it offers lower impedance to ground than a taller object that the lightning struck first), a side flash to that object can occur with any fraction of the strike's energy. Rock is a poor conductor, so side flashes from tall rocks should be expected. I've personally been hit and burned by a side flash. They're the reason that taking shelter in shallow caves or overhangs is always discouraged—the lightning will side-flash over the cave opening and through you (you're mostly salt water) rather than follow stone around the cave. This would imply that the best location with respect to a tall, isolated tree would be at a distance of about twice its height; this may also give relief from flying shards of wood when the struck tree explodes from steam pressure. Another reason not to be near an object that you would hope provides a cone of protection is that unpredictable ground currents are sure to be stronger close by. Cones of protection exist for radio towers, which have excellent ground systems, but maybe not for power lines, which typically don't; certainly trees are not protective. For natural objects and mountaineers, the cone of protection idea is invalid; it's best not to be near any tall objects during or near electrical storms.

I've mentioned the common fallacy that sitting on your pack or sleeping pad provides protection from being struck. Sitting on a rope or pad isn't enough to discourage ground current (which actually means side flashes from the ground) from jumping up to you. There's plenty of voltage available to jump up to a climber, sleeping pad or not. Remember also that rock is a pretty good insulator (granite is made of quartz and feldspar, or silicon and aluminum oxides, both insulators); crouching on a low boulder is at least as effective as crouching on your wet pack, rope, or pad. Don't stop for such actions; continue heading down as fast as possible, rappelling and leaving hardware if you need to. If things get really nasty, and you feel a tingling sensation, your hair stands on end, you see a blue glow on objects around you, or your equipment starts buzzing, these corona effects indicate a nearby strike may be forthcoming. Continue to hurry down in a crouching position if you can, but if you're caught in the open and are certain that a strike is imminent, crouch on a low boulder and cover your ears with your hands. It seems sensible to keep your feet close together; definitely don't lie down. Remain in this position until the storm cell has passed. These actions won't prevent you from being struck, but there's a chance they may help you escape side flashes from the ground, and covering your ears may help prevent tympanic damage from thunderclaps. Lightning heats the air so hot and so fast that an explosive shock wave is created that can extend out several hundred yards before it dissipates into ordinary thunder. Victims have been blown out of their

clothing and off mountains by such blasts. There's no scientific evidence that advice in this paragraph or any similar advice is effective; on the other hand, I'm unaware of any report that a person crouching on a large rock has been toasted.

What is effective in reducing lightning hazard is getting off exposed features such as peaks and ridges, avoiding large open areas such as mountain meadows, staying as low as possible and avoiding being the highest object nearby, avoiding large bodies of water, and avoiding large metal objects, such as bicycles, machinery, and especially fences and other long metal conductors. There's no evidence that proximity to small metal objects, such as axes, tent poles, ski edges, or climbing hardware, increases the likelihood of being struck, so don't waste time jettisoning them. I've never seen a solid report that a struck climber's rope caused a problem, even for climbers whose nylon jackets were melted to their arms. Whether a wet rope is a more attractive conductor than nearby wet rock appears to be academic. Being inside an auto seems to protect, but not always. The best cover may be in a forest away from summits or ridgelines; don't lean on the trees. It's stupid to camp on a ridge when cumulous clouds are forming, whether or not a storm cell is visible. If your group is threatened, spread out by about 50 yards and hope that a survivor knows CPR. Anyone struck needs thorough medical evaluation even though injuries appear superficial. New research shows that mountaineers struck by lightning suffer free radical damage that can be mitigated by dietary supplementation with antioxidants.

What are your chances of getting nailed? Impossible to say. There are several hundred casualties and 60 to 90 lightning fatalities in the United States each year, most in south Florida and about half affecting young males out in the open. Colorado, among the top ten states, has about a dozen casualties annually; Alaska, none. The high survival rate is probably because the high-frequency aspect of lightning means that it doesn't overcome the body's skin resistance and penetrate very far, and because many victims are probably hit by weaker side flashes.

AVALANCHE

Avalanche accidents are not accidents of slope angles, snowfall, winds, and weak layers in the snowpack. Human factors are the primary cause of avalanche accidents.

Words to the wise from Dale Atkins, avalanche researcher and forecaster at the Colorado Avalanche Information Center. Ski mountaineers are far more likely to be affected by avalanches than are climbers. The reason is simple: backcountry skiers seek out steep, freshly fallen snow—the very terrain that climbers want to avoid. Nevertheless, there are two or three dozen backcountry travelers killed by avalanches each year in the Lower 48; most are highmarking snowmobilers roaring up steep slopes, but a small number of climbers are included. To put that number in perspective, it's about the same as the number of people killed by trees at ski areas or by elevators, but they're just as dead.

Skiers are well aware that they venture into avalanche terrain; many carry transceiver beacons to help locate buried victims (actually, these should be called "corpse locators"), avalanche probes to fine-tune searches, and shovels to dig out victims and make pits for evaluating the snow pack. Climbers may carry shovels at best. This means that climbers are forced to focus on avoiding avalanches rather than worrying about what to do after being caught in one. Pity that skiers often lose this perspective, as 50 percent of avalanche fatalities occur from trauma during the slide (in one gruesome example, the victim was disemboweled by his own broken femur). Still, snow can be the easiest way up steep slopes—far more enjoyable than the same slope without snow, when it would be endless scree. So what should climbers do when confronted by steep snow? The same thing skiers should do: don't believe that your equipment will allow you to survive an avalanche—avoid them altogether. Avoiding avalanches means understanding why they occur.

It isn't enough to say that avalanches are snow sliding down a mountain. Why snow slides is of great interest to mountain travelers. Snow releases only when the forces holding the snow in place are overcome by gravity. Usually this implies changes in the snow pack, a process called metamorphism that's mainly driven by changes in the weather. Usually avalanches require some trigger event to cause the snow to release and slide rather than continue its natural processes of transformation that will lead to stability and eventually to névé (frozen granular snow) or runoff.

Maritime, Intermountain, and Continental Ranges

Avalanche danger and the character of avalanche-prone snow depend considerably on the general locale of the mountains involved. In *maritime* ranges, such as coastal British Columbia, the lower Cascades, the Sierra Nevada, and Patagonia, the snow tends to be deeper and more dense; the air tends to be relatively warm. Greater snow depth and warmer air mean that the temperature gradient within the snow pack will be lower. Temperature gradients contribute to the metamorphism that sets up conditions for instability and avalanches. Maritime ranges undergo melt-freeze activity all winter, which tends to stabilize the snow pack, as does their heavier, higher moisture content snow. Such ranges tend to have *wet snow avalanches*, which travel on the surface and are less likely to be deadly than slab avalanches; that doesn't mean they're benign, as they can carry huge amounts of heavy snow and can be especially dangerous in chutes and other terrain traps. As a consequence of climate, maritime ranges see relatively few avalanche fatalities. In general, backcountry travelers are safe if they stay out of maritime mountains for at least a day after storms and follow the basic rules of avalanche avoidance.

Interior ranges, such as the Colorado Rockies, the Alaska Range, the interior of British Columbia, and the Himalayas, have what's called *continental* snowpack. The snowpack is thinner and the air is colder, leading to higher temperature gradients within the snow. This contributes to more pronounced metamorphism, which creates new crystal types within the snow. These faceted crystals, called *depth hoar* among other names, adhere poorly to each other, resulting in *sugar snow*—the kind that you can't pack into cohesive snowballs. When sugar snow warms and the corners of its crystals melt, the result is extremely unstable; mountaineers call this *rotten snow*, and it is rotten to travel on as well as making rotten conditions for the avalanche of overlying snow dumped by a spring storm. Especially when new snow is deposited atop such an unstable layer, by storms or by wind (which can move much more snow than what falls during storms), the conditions are primed for *hard slab avalanches*. These types of avalanches suddenly release all the snow accumulated above the instability layer—sometimes all the way to the ground if the weak layer had formed early in the season, called *climax avalanches*. Because of the profound influence of wind deposition, most hard slab avalanches occur on lee slopes. The snow may be held in place only by the cohesive strength of the upper snow, and only a small disturbance may be required for the upper snow to fracture and begin sliding on a layer of faceted crystals, which act like ball bearings. That initial disturbance can be the weight of a person, a falling cornice, or a rapid warming of 6 to 10 F° (4 to 5 C°) which makes the sugar snow just a bit more slippery. The observance of naturally triggered slab avalanches is an indication of extremely bad conditions (but not necessarily so wet snow surface releases). Often the stronger surface snow layer acts to propagate a disturbance, so the width of the avalanche immediately grows, some times many hundreds of yards. Hard slab avalanches are the killers because they contain lots of snow, involve a significant fraction of the snowpack, and move very quickly for a considerable distance from where they originate.

In continental ranges, avalanche danger typically builds during the winter and involves changes going on invisibly in old snow, deep within the snowpack. Hard slab avalanches are common there, and any hope of forecasting depends on skilled snowpack analysis over a long period of time; avalanche cycles are not tied to storm cycles. In maritime ranges the snow typically stabilizes during the winter, except immediately after storms, and incidents tend to involve snow at the surface. Wet snow avalanches are more common there, and forecasting can effectively use meteorological data. In intermountain ranges—between the maritime and continental (such as Utah's Wasatch)—snow can start out weak but build strength as spring approaches. Based on Canadian figures, about 15 percent of avalanche deaths occur in coastal ranges, and the remainder occur in the interior or Rockies; 90 percent occur in the alpine region at and above tree line. Intermountain ranges can have maritime conditions on their western slopes and continental conditions on slopes that face east.

If you're already out there and it starts to snow, you can base some of your decision making on the storm itself. Depending on your locale, snow falling at 1 inch per hour can be marginally safe, but farther inland and at higher elevations, a steady rate of $\frac{1}{2}$ inch per hour may foretell grave avalanche danger. Snow that falls warm (in the mid to upper 20s °F or above -5 °C) will likely bond to the surface it covers, even if the storm progressively cools. Cold snow will bond and stabilize more slowly and remain subject to wind deposition longer; if the storm then warms, the heavier new snow falls on more poorly bonded colder snow and creates extra instability. Wind moves snow around very effectively and doubling the wind speed can move 8 times as much snow; winds of 15 to 20 miles per hour can turn a modest snowfall of less than a foot into dangerous conditions in just an hour or two. Such moderate winds deposit snow on the lee side of ridges, while stronger winds dump snow into gullies and scour other terrain; both set up avalanche potential. Wind also pulverizes the snowflakes, giving wind-deposited snow twice the density, if not more. Keep in mind that wind also blows at night and can create conditions that threaten your campsite even though snow isn't falling where you are. Big mountain faces aren't a prerequisite for killer avalanches. Most fatalities occur in slides running 200 feet or less, and most slab avalanches are less than a few feet deep. This means that danger can lurk in bowls and gullies along the route to the climb, where a small slide can deposit many tons of snow into a terrain trap and on top of you.

Grade Is Key

Slab avalanches tend to run on slopes of 30 to 45°. On lower grades the down slope pull on the surface snow is less, giving the snow more opportunity to build strength, while on steeper slopes snow tends to slough off during storms and so doesn't build up the weight that contributes to deadly releases. Wind deposition of snow on lee slopes confounds that rule. Wet loose surface avalanches can start on lower angle surfaces, sometimes lower than 20° when the snow is soaking wet, but these slides don't produce deadly statistics the way slab avalanches do.

On a 7½-minute topo map a 35° slope will be indicated by bold contour lines that are 0.143 inches apart; that's not an especially useful fact, so either refer to my Telemarker's Rule in the Resources appendix, or use the map's scale to estimate 290 feet (on a metric map that slope will have bold contour lines that are 0.235 inches apart, or use the map's scale to estimate 143 meters). Remember from the navigation chapter (Chapter 4) that the *angle of repose* of talus and scree is about 35°, giving you a clue if you have seen the terrain without snow cover or if you have developed a sense of how steep the angle of repose feels; 35° is about the steepest continuous slope of black diamond ski runs.

When things start warming up as winter ends, the air temperature approaches ground temperature, and the temperature gradient decreases to the point that the snowpack is said to go *equitemperature*. Around this time, metamorphism rounds the snow crystals and bonds them together, which, along with the weight of the snow, causes the snowpack to compact and become increasingly more stable against slab avalanche formation. The snow can eventually become slush during the warmth of the day, and wet slides on the surface may occur that release spontaneously at a single point and fan out as they flow down hill. The snow may freeze into a solid crust overnight even when the air temperature doesn't fall below freezing, making for good climbing in early morning, though conditions can become scary if the soft surface turns back into ice before you descend late in the day; wind increases heat exchange at the snow surface by hundreds of times. Eventually, if it hangs around long enough, the snow compacts and turns into tiny balls of wet ice, called corn snow, which is great for skiing and glissading—and it is relatively safe even on steeper slopes so long as the water-soaked snow isn't more than ankle-deep over firmer snow beneath. Diurnal melt-freeze cycles help strengthen spring snowpacks, but in continental ranges a protracted period of thaw, caused by continuously cloudy weather for example, may set up avalanche conditions if the lower layers of the snowpack haven't yet stabilized. Rain on snow with weak or icy layers is a particular concern, as the water may run down to and then along such layers and result in considerable enduring weakness hidden within the snowpack. The rain may have fallen long before you arrive, so it pays to monitor weather conditions for some time, look for rain runnel patterns on the snow, and dig a pit to examine the snowpack structure.

The Pits

If you were to dig a pit to check the snow, what would you find? You'd want to dig a pit with a smooth, vertical, uphill side, all the way to the ground in a continental snowpack, and then brush the vertical side with a glove. What you don't want to find is layers of sugar snow and layers of crusty ice. These indicate potential instability layers on which upper snow can slide. What you'd hope for is fairly consistent, firm snow that can be formed into snowballs, all the way down to the ground.

Do-It-Yourself Avalanches

Ninety-five percent of slides that catch backcountry travelers are triggered by someone in the party, as opposed to occurring naturally. Talking loudly isn't enough to start an avalanche, you must actually physically disturb the slope. The unavoidable implication is that faulty decision making is responsible for people getting caught in avalanches. At the head of the list of faulty reasoning is the assumption that being in a group makes one safer, that another party's tracks confirm safety, or that your lack of accidents in the past confirms the acuity of your instincts. Mother Nature, however, doesn't care about any of that.

Avalanche Avoidance

I'm constantly amazed that there are mountaineers who are intensely conservative in their rock climbing, who always wear helmets, who filter every drop of water, yet who will glance at a steep snow slope and charge right across. Avalanche professionals carefully analyze what's going on within the snowpack, but for most climbers a few rules will serve much better than complex snow science. Here are basic tenets of avalanche safety:

▲ Check the avalanche conditions report for the area where you intend to travel; call an appropriate agency or use the Internet. The best sources vary and will depend on where you climb (see the Resources appendix). Most incidents occur when conditions are Considerable, because travelers think they can evaluate the danger and escape trouble.

▲ Use a topo map to plan your route. Avoid being on or beneath slopes steeper than 30° when the danger is Considerable or High (stay home if it's Extreme).

▲ Avoid being on or below obvious avalanche paths, cornices, and steep slopes where wind has recently deposited heavy loads of snow.

▲ Avoid convex surfaces, especially on lee ridges; this is where slab avalanches most frequently start.

▲ If you observe settling or whumpfing of snow as you travel on it, or if the surface cracks and the cracks spread, you're in the middle of bad conditions and need to retreat pronto.

▲ Avoid traveling in terrain traps, such as gullies and constricting chutes that are beneath steeper slopes or wind deposition areas (where the wind slows down and drops its load).

▲ Travel on the windward side of ridges; alternatively, climb steep slopes where snow doesn't accumulate so long as they aren't beneath accumulation areas higher up. Southerly slopes stabilize faster and may be safer.

▲ Spread out climbers by at least 30 feet when traveling in questionable terrain, thereby endangering only a single person at a time; don't rope up. Don't climb in a vertical pattern, with some climbers in the fall line below others. If the terrain or conditions appear hazardous, cross one at a time while others watch from safe locations.

▲ If a member of your party is caught, try to see where he is carried and note the last place he was visible. If conditions are safe, start searching downward from the last-seen point. Listen and look for clues on the surface, such as clothing and equipment; probe to the full depth of your extended trekking poles with the baskets removed (that will be about 3 feet; almost no rescues are made from greater depth), start in likely spots and then revert to a 2-foot grid pattern; keep searching for at least an hour even though after 15 minutes a buried victim's chances aren't very good.

▲ Don't assume that snow-covered summer hiking routes are safe, even below tree line.

▲ Don't get fooled into thinking that you're safer in a group—the reverse is true.

Also, don't put much stock in those recommendations for "swimming motions" if caught; worth a try perhaps, but slab avalanches move about 80 miles per hour. About the only thing that will help you is for some part of your body or gear to end up above the snow so that your companions can find you and dig you out immediately; that's why waving a trekking pole in the air may be helpful. Keep your pack on, because it's less dense than you and may help you float in the moving snow. After avalanched snow stops moving, it sets up very solidly, very quickly, like snow that's been plowed. As you are sliding, keep your mouth shut in hopes of avoiding getting it plugged, and keep your fingers crossed.

What if you've avoided avalanche terrain but find you need to camp in a valley with obvious slide paths all around? Where will you be safe? The answer is complex, but a rule of thumb can be applied. Camp on a slope that is pitched 10° or less, which won't encourage avalanches to keep moving. Use the clinometer on your compass to select a relatively safe distance from likely start zones for naturally occurring avalanches by ensuring that the angle from your campsite up to the natural avalanche start zone is about 23° above horizontal for intermountain ranges. Avalanche professionals call this the *alpha angle*. Move away from the steep slope where avalanches might start until the angle drops to 23° or less. In maritime ranges the angle might be a few degrees more (you could be safe closer to the start zone), and in continental rages it will be a few degrees less.

ALTITUDE

The human body is amazingly adaptable, and nowhere is that more evident than in the process of altitude acclimation (acclimatization). The classic example is that a climber who was dropped on the top of Everest would lose consciousness in a few minutes and die within an hour, yet over a hundred climbers have struggled to the summit without supplemental oxygen after several weeks of adaptation.

The earth's atmosphere contains about 20 percent oxygen (and 80 percent nitrogen, 0.03 percent carbon dioxide), but as altitude increases, the total atmospheric pressure drops approximately logarithmically from 760 mm-Hg (101.3 kPa or 29.93 inches of mercury) at sea level. At 12,000 feet (3,660 meters) the barometric pressure is only 480 mm-Hg, so there are roughly 40 percent fewer oxygen molecules in each breath. As an interesting factoid, the earth's rotation causes the atmosphere to be thicker at the equator, so there's about 15 percent lower pressure at the summit of Denali than at the same elevation in the more equatorial Himalayas or Andes. With less oxygen available, humans must adapt. Most people can quickly go to the 8,000-foot altitude at Vail or Mammoth Lakes with little ill effect, but the way specific individuals respond to higher altitudes, with acclimation or without, is unpredictable, and the processes of acclimation is still incompletely understood. Everyone's brain swells somewhat, but people handle it differently. A few responses to reduced oxygen are certain: respiration rate increases (the hypoxic ventilatory response), resting heart rate increases, and the number of red blood cells (which carry oxygen) increases after several weeks of adaptation (apparently the rate of red blood cell increase in women is independent of menstrual cycle phase). At first your respiration increase is suppressed because hyperventilating also results in more carbonate—dissolved carbon dioxide—being removed from your blood, which tells your body to slow respiration. After a day or so the kidneys respond by increasing throughput (altitude diuresis); this dumps carbonate and allows your hyperventilation response to develop fully. Your increased respiration attempts to maintain the same amount of available oxygen as at lower elevations, but it's never enough. There are other subtle adaptations at the hormonal and cellular level. The vast majority of these metabolic changes are complete by 3 to 4 weeks at altitude, but structural changes such as capillary density and growth of mitochondria take many weeks to months. If ascent is sufficiently slow, these adaptations are usually successful, but when ascent is too rapid and adaptation is incomplete, the symptoms that result are called altitude illness. This has implications for the many mountaineers who live near sea level and head for peaks on weekends.

Normal Adaptation and AMS

Most persons adapted to sea level can quickly ascend to some certain altitude with few problems; typically, that altitude is around 9,000 feet, but it's specific for each individual and his or her history. Going just a bit higher, even a few hundred feet, may result in symptoms of Acute Mountain Sickness. Typically symptoms include headache, dizziness, nausea, and lassitude; simply being fatigued and out of breath does not mean AMS. After a night at 9,000 feet, a person has begun adapting, and the level above which symptoms appear rises, perhaps by 1,500 to 2,000 feet (450 to 600 meters), but again the adaptation is individualistic (genetic). If ascent exceeds this amount, AMS symptoms may appear, and acclimation will be impaired; this is particularly true if the climber sleeps at the higher altitude. If you ignore significant symptoms and push beyond whatever your adaptation differential is to sleep higher for yet another night, your symptoms will become more severe, and acclimation will be impaired. Things won't get better until you return to the altitude where you were symptom free. After full acclimation, a mountaineer can spend at least a week at low altitude yet retain enough adaptation to avoid AMS when going high again.

At intermediate altitudes of 3,000 to 10,000 feet (900 to 3,000 meters), up to 25 percent of unacclimated travelers may experience AMS symptoms and sleep disturbed enough that REM (rapid eye movement) rest is impaired. Those who go to, and especially who sleep at or above, 10,000 feet (3,050 meters) experience an adaptation process, and at least 75 percent of unacclimated persons suffer mild symptoms until acclimation is successful. Those who are exercising appear to be more vulnerable. Women and people over 50 tend to be affected less; children are affected to the same degree as adults. Some people acclimate quickly and can ascend rapidly; others acclimate slowly and have trouble avoiding symptoms even on a slow ascent. There's no easy method *ab initio* to predict who's likely to get sick at altitude. For poorly understood reasons, the same person may get AMS on one trip and not on another, despite identical ascent rates. People with serious lung, heart, and blood diseases are more likely to develop AMS. Complete acclimation requires at least several weeks, depending on whom your parents were, but that just means relief from symptoms of high-altitude illness—it doesn't mean your performance will be the same as at sea level.

Adaptation includes increased resting heart rate; if yours was about 60 at sea level, it may become 70 or higher at 10,000 feet, but your exercising heart rate will drop from, say, 170 to 155. After a week you start producing more red blood cells, and that lets your blood carry more oxygen though it can also make you more prone to clot formation. It can require up to 12 weeks over 10,000 feet (3,050 meters) for this process to be complete. As you acclimate, your respiration rate will increase, breaths will become deeper, and lactate accumulation during submaximal exercise will decrease, compared to unacclimated levels. You'll likely pee up to an extra half liter (16 ounces) per day, so you'll need to compensate with additional water intake. Your brain will swell slightly, causing

GETTING YOUR HEAD AROUND ALTITUDE

Whatever their physiological responses may be, people deal with the debilitating effects of altitude in different ways. Some decompensate, emphasize their discomfort, and are miserable, making their companions miserable, too. Others keep their fecal matter coalesced by using various strategies that include disassociation, involvement in teamwork, deliberate focusing, self-esteem reinforcement, and short-term goal setting. Climbers who are successful in summiting high mountains invariably use mental training as one of the tools that help them deal with oxygen deficiency.

---

headache and nausea to various degrees. Some individuals experience swelling in their hands and feet; avoid accentuating that tendency by abstaining from a high salt intake. You'll suffer loss of appetite, with or without AMS, so consider a liquid carbohydrate diet that you can control. When you're sleeping, your breathing may become irregular (called periodic breathing or Cheyne-Stokes respirations), with breathing becoming increasingly deep until punctuated by a brief period of no breathing at all (apnea). That can be scary if you wake up not breathing or hyperventilating, even though it is more or less normal and isn't altitude illness; taking 125 mg of acetazolamide (Diamox) before sleep may take care of it.

Of course, we all ignore the recommendation to ascend for sleep less than 1,500 feet per day above 9,000 feet, and most mountaineers get away with accepting mild symptoms during outings of a few days or until adaptation catches up after four or five days. We can squeak by because edema does not appear instantly but builds over 12 to 24 hours, so AMS symptoms usually start appearing about 8 hours after ascent. The symptoms may appear some time after you've stopped climbing, or may never appear if your presence at altitude is a day climb. Not infrequently climbers develop AMS during the first night after they go high. Be prepared to descend any time if significant symptoms persist. Mild symptoms may be only a nuisance but cannot be completely ignored; it is dangerous to continue ascending in the face of significant altitude illness symptoms. As they say, it's OK to have altitude illness symptoms (that's just nature's way of telling you), but it's stupid to die from altitude illness.

Mild Becomes Moderate If You Ignore It

What I've described is *mild* AMS. A prevalent symptom of the more serious *moderate* AMS is headache that cannot be relieved by simple medication, such as ibuprofen (600 mg is usually effective). If symptoms also include nausea and vomiting, and especially decreased coordination (ataxia), it's time to take stock and be prepared to take action. Other stresses, such as hypoglycemia, dehydration, and exhaustion can produce similar symptoms, but don't assume that AMS can be ignored. Don't expect things to improve by just taking it easy. If you've been at your altitude for three days or more, another problem is more likely to be the cause of the symptoms. A good test for moderate AMS is for the climber to stand with feet in a straight line, heel to toe, crossing arms with hands on opposite shoulders and eyes shut—like a sobriety test (hopefully that's an unfamiliar reference). If the climber can't stand for a full minute, there's trouble. Ataxia will prevent success with this test—a clear indication that immediate descent is required. It's important to get the victim down before the ataxia reaches the point that he cannot walk on his own, making an evacuation by litter necessary. Sometimes descending only a few hundred feet is all that's required to relieve symptoms, and 1,000 feet is almost always effective. The climber needs to remain low for at least 24 hours and allow symptoms to subside before cautiously resuming the climb.

HACE

AMS is a continuum of symptoms, from annoying to life threatening. At the severe end of the range is *high altitude cerebral edema* (HACE). HACE occurs when the leakage of fluids into the brain increases intracranial pressure to the point that health of the brain becomes at risk. Coma and death can result. *Severe* AMS is indicated by more pronounced symptoms as well as shortness of breath even when at rest, inability to walk, decreasing mental status and worsening judgment,

and fluid building up in the lungs (called HAPE, which sometimes accompanies HACE). AMS headaches tend to be painful and persistent. Severe AMS requires immediate descent of 2,000 to 4,000 feet, even if that requires an immediate litter carry. A climber with severe AMS is at risk of death and will not be able to recover without aid from companions. Even after symptoms subside, as they generally do following descent, lack of coordination while walking may persist for days; some fine motor skills are lost for months.

Although HACE is sometimes described as coming on suddenly, edema takes so many hours to develop that the apparent suddenness may be because symptoms were attributed to other causes or were simply ignored. The vast majority of cases of HACE occur above 14,000 feet (4,300 meters) and affect climbers who continue to ascend despite having symptoms of AMS. The propensity to ignore symptoms and continue on is especially strong in a larger group. By the time things should be obvious, a climber's mental state may be too impaired to recognize his own symptoms. This means that recognizing AMS and preventing it from progressing to HACE is a group responsibility as much as an individual responsibility. Learn the early symptoms of altitude illness and be willing to admit when you or your companions have them. Remove any stigma from descending. Never ascend to sleep at a higher altitude with significant symptoms of altitude illness. Descend if your symptoms get worse while resting at the same altitude.

HAPE

Another form of altitude illness due to lack of acclimation is fluid leaking from capillaries of the lungs into the alveoli, shutting down air exchange—a climber literally drowns in his own secretions. This condition is called high-altitude pulmonary edema (HAPE); it's responsible for most deaths due to high-altitude illness. Because edema comes on slowly, HAPE may not appear unmistakably until the second night at altitude (it rarely appears as low as 9,000 feet, or 2,700 meters). HAPE occurs more frequently in the cold and among young, fit climbers and much more frequently among those who have experienced it previously. New research suggests the root cause of HAPE is inadequate sodium-driven clearance of alveolar fluid, likely arising from a gene defect; that's what increases blood pressure and leads to edema in the lungs. Inhaling the drug salmeterol (a beta agonist in Severent and Advair, used to treat asthma and pulmonary disease) may prevent HACE because it stimulates sodium transport in the lungs.

The initial symptoms of HAPE are shortness of breath and an occasional dry cough, but these are easily ignored amid the respiratory stress of exercise at altitude. Other symptoms of the progressing condition include extreme fatigue, difficulty catching a breath at rest, fast and shallow breathing, a nasty cough that may produce frothy or pink sputum in late stages of the illness, rales (gurgling or rattling inhalations that sound like a paper bag being crushed), and ultimately cyanosis that makes the lips or fingertips, especially nail beds, turn pale or bluish. HAPE may be accompanied by HACE symptoms, and it may lead to them; cerebral symptoms predominate in some people, and pulmonary symptoms predominate in others. HAPE rarely appears after 4 days at the high altitude. When symptoms appear, immediate evacuation to lower altitude is necessary and invariably effective; delay may be fatal. HAPE worsens with exertion, so severely afflicted victims may need to be carried down.

HAPE usually resolves quickly after descent to the altitude at which the climber last slept without symptoms; after one or two days, recovery may be complete, and climbing may be cautiously resumed. Usually, returning to the altitude where problems occurred previously will be uneventful.

HAPE can be mistaken for other illnesses, some serious for mountaineers if not recognized and treated. These include high-altitude cough and bronchitis; with these there is no shortness of breath at rest and no severe fatigue. Pneumonia symptoms may resemble HAPE, and both may result in a fever, so fever is not proof of pneumonia instead of HAPE. The differential test for all these is descent: HAPE will improve rapidly, but the others won't. As HAPE is the more imminently life threatening, descend first, and if that doesn't work, then treat with antibiotics, not the other way around. Asthma may also be confused with HAPE, but if conventional treatment for asthma doesn't bring immediate relief, assume HAPE and descend; interestingly, asthmatics often do better at altitude than at sea level.

Drugs to Treat Altitude Illness

The previous discussion has focused on things that every party can do to diagnose and treat high-altitude illness. In addition, there are several drugs used to treat altitude illness that could be administered by a skilled practitioner. Most are prescription medications with potentially serious side effects that are not easily foreseen and that are difficult to treat in the field. They're not in the category of "Here, try one of these." Nevertheless, you'll hear about all of these, so here are the facts.

OXYGEN

Administering oxygen starting at 2 to 4 liters per minute and continuing at 1 to 2 liters per minute works on all varieties of high-altitude illness and works quickly; best of all, it has no side effects. It does not aid in acclimation.

DIAMOX (ACETAZOLAMIDE)

Acetazolamide speeds up the process that causes your kidneys to dump carbonate and lower blood pH (making the blood more normally acidic). This allows your breathing to improve, particularly at night. The net effect is to speed up acclimation, approximately by a factor of two. Beware: acetazolamide *does not eliminate* AMS, HACE, or HAPE; if you have symptoms, don't continue ascending until they abate, even though you are taking Diamox. The old-school dose recommendation in the *Physicians Desk Reference* is three 250 mg tablets daily, but the modern prescription for mountaineering at altitude is 250 mg daily in two 125 mg doses, beginning a day or so before ascending and continuing until you have been at your high point for 2 days. This dose is equally effective and results in fewer side effects; it is recommended as a prophylactic measure for those with a history of AMS. There's no rebound effect, so discontinuing acetazolamide merely returns your acclimation rate to normal. For most mountaineers, acetazolamide is unnecessary, but for rescuers who must ascend more than 1,600 feet in a day, or for climbers and trekkers who fly in to high altitudes and want to begin ascending immediately, it has proven beneficial in reducing the incidence and severity of AMS symptoms.

Downsides include increased diuresis (acetazolamide is a diuretic), so be sure to actively maintain hydration. Acetazolamide may cause rare allergic reactions, so a test of a few days well prior to use is a good idea. It also has minor side effects that go away upon discontinuing the drug: a metallic taste in your mouth, bad-tasting carbonated drinks, and tingly fingers or face. Acetazolamide appears to slightly reduce exercise capacity—another reason it should not be used unless it's actually needed.

DECADRON (DEXAMETHASONE)
This potent steroid drug decreases brain swelling and reduces intracranial (inside the skull) pressure; it can be lifesaving in people with HACE. The dosage is 4 mg every 6 hours (injection will be necessary if the victim is vomiting); obvious improvement usually occurs within about 6 hours. While acetazolamide treats a cause of altitude illness, dexamethasone treats only the symptoms; it doesn't aid in acclimation, but merely buys time, particularly in situations where administering oxygen or descending is infeasible. It is of no benefit for HAPE. This points out a serious problem: dexamethasone masks AMS symptoms and may lead climbers to take actions that result in serious HACE. A climber whose symptoms have been relieved by dexamethasone should not resume ascending until 12 hours after discontinuing the drug, to let the effects of the drug wear off and reveal any symptoms that show high-altitude illness is still present.

Side effects include euphoria in some people, or upset stomach, trouble sleeping, and an increased blood sugar level in diabetics. It has a rebound effect upon discontinuation—meaning that you may be worse off when you stop taking the drug than when you started.

NIFEDIPINE
This calcium channel-blocker (beta-agonist) drug normally prescribed for high blood pressure seems able to decrease the narrowing of the pulmonary artery caused by low oxygen levels, thereby improving oxygen transfer. The dosage is 20 to 30 mg of slow-release nifedipine, every 12 hours. It can be used to treat HAPE (not AMS or HACE) both after onset and prophylactically, but its effectiveness is not nearly as dramatic as the treatment of HACE with dexamethasone. Nifedipine can cause sudden lowering of blood pressure, so the patient must be warned to get up slowly from a sitting or reclining position. Nifedipine is OK for trekkers maybe, but not what climbers want to experience unless they really must.

ASPIRIN
The prophylactic use of a gram of aspirin daily (three 320 mg tablets) beginning the day before ascending and continuing during acclimation reduces the incidence of headache at altitude (whereas exercise tends to increase it).

GINKGO
Reputable studies have shown that Ginkgo biloba prophylactically reduces AMS symptoms, but conditions and dosages have been highly variable in the various studies, as they are in the sources of the herb (check ConsumerLab.com). A typical regimen is 120 mg of Ginko extract twice a day orally, starting 5 days prior to ascent and continuing while at altitude; this seems to cut the incidence and severity of AMS symptoms by more than half. Other studies have shown good results with half that dose starting the day prior to rapid ascent, but one study compared Ginko to acetazolamide and found Ginko biloba to be ineffective against AMS. Be cautious about using Ginko in combination with high doses of aspirin or other anticoagulants.

OTHERS
Many other substances have been studied for their ability to treat or prevent altitude illness, but in most cases the research is sparse. Antioxidant vitamins (4 capsules daily after meals containing 250 mg of vitamin C, 100 IU of vitamin E, and 150 mg

of alpha-lipoic acid) have been shown to improve AMS symptoms and to increase appetite in Everest climbers; there are no side effects. A number of other prescription drugs have been used or investigated as treatments for altitude illness. These include furosemide, normally used to treat congestive heart failure, but a possible candidate for treating severe HAPE that is currently out of favor. Theophylline, found in tea and commonly prescribed for asthma, has been successful in treating AMS in some studies but it has dangerous side effects and is not recommended. Prednisolone at 20 mg daily, appears to significantly curtail Acute Mountain Sickness without impairing normal adaptive responses to hypoxia. Even morphine has been tested as an adjunct to treatment of HAPE, especially with oxygen. Of potential interest to some climbers, Viagra (sildenafil) has been proffered as a prophylactic treatment for HACE, because it increases the effect of nitric oxide, the deficit of which is part of the mysterious, possibly hereditary, physiology of altitude illness. A recent study (summer 2004) at Everest base camp using the dose typical for its better-known purpose showed benefits in hypoxic adaptation and an increase in exercise capacity; it's the first drug ever to claim this benefit. Social side effects have yet to be explored in the scientific literature.

You may hear about hyperbaric (pressure) chambers, such as the Gamoff or Gamow bag, made of fabric. The weight and bulk of these bags make them feasible only for larger groups of climbers. Two hours minimum inside a bag that's pumped up to the pressure of a lower altitude (about 2 psi) has the same, but more immediate, effect as descent, comparable to low-flow oxygen. Be wary of a potential rebound effect when the cat gets out of the bag.

General Strategies for Avoiding Altitude Illness

To avoid altitude illness, first learn your own body's typical response to climbing at altitude and avoid overreaching; stay hydrated; avoid alcohol, most sleeping pills, and depressant drugs; don't continue ascending if symptoms appear, and do descend promptly if symptoms worsen. Hydration cannot be overemphasized; there are many effects of altitude that conspire to cause dehydration, but blood plasma volume is a principal component of aerobic capacity, so allowing your plasma volume to drop due to dehydration will devastate your cardiovascular fitness. Overhydration, however, is of no benefit. When mild symptoms of AMS appear, the usual therapy is rest, fluids, and mild analgesics (acetaminophen, aspirin, or ibuprofen—medications that will not cover up worsening symptoms). Avoid foods that contain nitrites and sulfites, which can cause migraine: cheese, chocolate, citrus fruits, processed meats, and apparently monosodium glutamate. AMS tends to get better as your body acclimates, and simply resting at the altitude at which you became mildly ill is often adequate. Improvement usually occurs in 1 or 2 days but may take as long as 3 or 4. Taking Diamox as a treatment for AMS can speed up recovery at rest. Descent also increases the recovery rate. There are other causes of headache for mountaineers, particularly dehydration; if you drink a liter of water and take one of the analgesics listed above, and the headache goes away quickly and totally (and you have no other symptoms of AMS) your headache wasn't caused by AMS. Never ascend, especially to sleep, when you're experiencing the symptoms of AMS, and descend promptly if symptoms worsen.

HEAT AND COLD

Hot and cold environments challenge the body peripherally and at its core. The terms *hyperthermia* (exceptionally high body temperature) and *hypothermia* (subnormal body temperature) describe core effects; each is a continuum of responses usually described in three stages of severity indicating the degree to which the body's normal chemical processes are altered. Although there are any number of medically defined symptoms of the various conditions, the one most apparent (I'm figuring you aren't going to be frequently checking your companions with a rectal thermometer) is a diminished mental condition. Unfortunately, the deteriorating mental status that accompanies hyper- and hypothermia may result in victims failing to assess their own condition and take appropriate action. In other words, mountaineers need to watch out for each other and intervene before things deteriorate inexorably.

Heat Response

The body's initial response to heat challenge is to compensate by dilating blood vessels in the skin (shell/core effect) and increasing sweat production. This can occur even in cold weather if there is solar heating or a person is overdressed. Sweating cools very effectively because of the large amount of heat energy removed by evaporation. As long as there's enough blood volume and sweat production to keep up with the heat challenge, the body's core temperature will remain normal (below about 102 °F, 39 °C, for a vigorously exercising athlete). This stage is called *heat response*. The individual can keep it going by maintaining hydration and electrolyte replacement, as discussed in Chapter 19 on performance nutrition, and he can help his body compensate by the usual means of increasing comfort, including reducing his activity level.

Heat Exhaustion

If a person continues to be exposed to heat challenge while her body's efforts to keep its core temperature normal aren't supported by copious hydration and electrolyte repletion, she becomes dehydrated, and early-stage volume shock sets in, even though her core temperature doesn't rise appreciably. This stage is called *heat exhaustion*. The victim will be thirsty, weak, nauseous, and may have heat cramps. Her mental state deteriorates, and she may become irritable and less rational. Heat exhaustion is serious and demands immediate treatment, but the treatment is simple: remove the heat challenge and rehydrate. Reduce the patient's activity, get her into the shade, remove her clothing, fan her. If the patient is vomiting, give small amounts of fluid. Replenishing electrolytes isn't critical to emergency treatment, but do so if it's easy. Don't give large amounts of salt as a treatment for heat cramps; a quarter teaspoon in a quart of water is enough, or use diluted sports drinks. Look for restored urine output and mental state as indications of recovery, which could take up to 12 hours. Suspect heat exhaustion any

time a person becomes ill while exercising in the heat, especially if their mental state seems altered.

Heat Stroke

If hyperthermia progresses, the condition is called *heat stroke*. The body's heat response becomes completely overwhelmed, and the core temperature will rise above 104 °F (40 °C). Pulse rate and respiration increase, and mental status declines to the point of severe agitation, seizures, and even coma. Skin characteristics can be inconclusive. This is a life-threatening medical condition that requires immediate intervention; the patient is dying and could do so within minutes absent effective treatment. Treatment involves radical efforts to cool the patient, such as removing his clothing, spraying him with water, and vigorously fanning him. Don't dunk patients in cold water, which will cause immediate constriction of peripheral blood vessels and could wildly swing the patient, already in a bad state, into hypothermia, but you could pour cold water on the patient's head and neck. Giving fluids orally to an unresponsive heat stroke patient may be unsuccessful and too slow anyhow, so IV fluids are a priority as soon as advanced life support is available. Monitor the patient and beware of a return to elevated core temperature. A heat stroke victim must be evacuated and could suffer long-term physiological damage.

In Chapter 19, Performance Nutrition for Mountaineers, where I spend considerable time on hydration and electrolyte repletion strategies, I mention acclimation to heat challenge. This effect applies to a number of body responses, but it can take weeks or months to develop, depending on which response you're talking about. Don't rely on it to benefit you; just be aware of it when you compare your heat response to those of other mountaineers.

Cold Response

When challenged by cold, the body responds by reducing blood flow to the skin (shell/core effect again) and slight shivering. The affected person is not uncomfortably cold, and his mental state is normal, but his skin is pale and cold. A cold-challenged climber's speech may be slightly slurred, and he may stumble a bit. If this goes on for long, the body may be unable to produce enough heat to prevent a drop in core temperature, so the prudent mountaineer will increase insulation, reduce the cold challenge (usually by getting out of the wind), and throw more fuel on the fire by eating and drinking. It doesn't hurt to empty the bladder, either, as it'll become filled due to cold diuresis. Failing to maintain hydration impairs the body's ability to respond to cold challenge.

Mild Hypothermia

If the individual doesn't respond effectively to a cold challenge, her body's core temperature will drop. This can happen quickly, by falling into a creek, for example, but usually it happens slowly. In persons exposed to rain, snow, wind, and cold, the onset of hypothermia may be insidious. The first warning may come with violent shivering, serious fatigue, or withdrawal, stubbornness, and hallucinations as the body temperature drops below 91 to 95 °F (33 to 35 °C). Hypothermia can result from other problems that reduce the body's ability to respond to cold challenge, and it may contribute to other injuries by impairing judgment and dexterity. Climbers must be especially attentive to the condition of their partners any time slow-onset hypothermia is a possibility; absence of complaint is not always a good sign. Mild hypothermia is a serious condition; it indicates that the body is near its limit of ability to maintain core temperature. Unconsciousness and cardio-respiratory arrest may follow rapidly unless resuscitative efforts are begun immediately. Rewarming is the first priority, and any technique is good as long as the patient is cooperating. Remove wet clothing. Put the patient in a sleeping bag with bottles of hot water or another mountaineer. Shivering is good. Feed the cooperative patient high-glycemic-index carbohydrates like the maltodextrin gel I tout, or anything with simple sugars, preferably in a warm solution; the complete meal can come later.

Severe Hypothermia

If the body's core temperature continues to decline, a hibernation-like condition sets in. Shiver-ing stops, pulse and respiration decline substantially, blood circulation is cut off to much of the body's shell regions, and the patient becomes unresponsive or comatose. Patients may be given up for dead, particularly if they're found in this state, as they might be if they are storm or avalanche victims. The treatment for severe hypothermia is significantly different from that for moderate hypothermia, but it may not be possible to obtain a definitive rectal temperature reading, which would be below 90 °F (32 °C). The main indicator is, again, decreased mental capacity—the patient will be unable to cooperate. Severely hypothermic patients should be wrapped in insulation, protected from wind, and transported to a hospital; field rewarming is a last resort. The patient should be handled very gently because the cold heart muscle is susceptible to irritation and may go into fibrillation. Keep the patient horizontal because shell blood vessels will no longer contract, and blood will escape the core. If evacuation is not feasible and rewarming must be attempted, the patient should be put in two sleeping bags zipped together with two other mountaineers and rewarmed non-aggressively. The concern is that cold blood from the shell will enter the heart and cause fatal cardiac arrest.

Frostbite

As the body shunts blood circulation to the core in response to cold, extremities become vulnerable to freezing. Frostbite begins with *frostnip*, the freezing of superficial layers of skin at temperatures below 20 °F (-6 °C). The affected area will be white or grey, or pink in dark-skinned climbers, and will feel firm and insensitive. To prevent the development of frostbite, the affected areas should be rewarmed immediately, which will be painful. Long-term care isn't required, but the area will likely be more susceptible to cold injury in the future. Frostbite is another matter.

Frostbite is the condition in which not only skin on the surface is frozen, but also the underlying tissue. Ice crystals may be visible on the surface, and the affected extremity feels as if it were wooden. In cases of frostbite that can be evacuated, it's best to prevent additional freezing but to

Wind is the thief of warmth. In 2001, the ancient windchill chart was revised to reflect more realistic conditions; it raised the windchill temperature at high wind speeds by as much as 20 F° (11 C°).

Wind Chill chart - US units
Temperature in °F

Calm	45	40	35	30	25	20	15	10	5	0	-5	-10	-15	-20	-25	-30	-35	-40	-45
5	42	36	31	25	19	13	7	1	-5	-11	-16	-22	-28	-34	-40	-46	-52	-57	-63
10	40	34	27	21	15	9	3	-4	-10	-16	-22	-28	-35	-41	-47	-53	-59	-66	-72
15	38	32	25	19	13	6	0	-7	-13	-19	-26	-32	-39	-45	-51	-58	-64	-71	-77
20	37	30	24	17	11	4	-2	-9	-15	-22	-29	-35	-42	-48	-55	-61	-68	-74	-81
25	36	29	23	16	9	3	-4	-11	-17	-24	-31	-37	-44	-51	-58	-64	-71	-78	-84
30	35	28	22	15	8	1	-5	-12	-19	-26	-33	-39	-46	-53	-60	-67	-73	-80	-87
35	35	28	21	14	7	0	-7	-14	-21	-27	-34	-41	-48	-55	-62	-69	-76	-82	-89
40	34	27	20	13	6	-1	-8	-15	-22	-29	-36	-43	-50	-57	-64	-71	-78	-84	-91
45	33	26	19	12	5	-2	-9	-16	-23	-30	-37	-44	-51	-58	-65	-72	-79	-86	-93
50	33	26	19	12	4	-3	-10	-17	-24	-31	-38	-45	-52	-60	-67	-74	-81	-88	-95
55	32	25	18	11	4	-3	-11	-18	-25	-32	-39	-46	-54	-61	-68	-75	-82	-89	-97
60	32	25	17	10	3	-4	-11	-19	-26	-33	-40	-48	-55	-62	-69	-76	-84	-91	-98

Wind speed in miles per hour

frostbite in 30 minutes
frostbite in 10 minutes
frostbite in 5 minutes

Wind Chill chart - metric units
Temperature in °C

Calm	10	8	6	4	2	0	-2	-4	-6	-8	-10	-12	-14	-16	-18	-20	-22	-24	-26	-28
2	7	5	2	0	-2	-4	-6	-9	-11	-13	-15	-17	-20	-22	-24	-26	-28	-31	-33	-35
4	3	0	-2	-4	-7	-9	-11	-14	-16	-18	-20	-23	-25	-27	-30	-32	-34	-37	-39	-41
6	0	-2	-5	-7	-9	-12	-14	-17	-19	-21	-24	-26	-29	-31	-33	-36	-38	-40	-43	-45
8	-2	-4	-7	-9	-12	-14	-17	-19	-21	-24	-26	-29	-31	-34	-36	-38	-41	-43	-46	-48
10	-4	-6	-8	-11	-13	-16	-18	-21	-23	-26	-28	-31	-33	-36	-38	-41	-43	-46	-48	-51
12	-5	-7	-10	-12	-15	-17	-20	-22	-25	-28	-30	-33	-35	-38	-40	-43	-45	-48	-50	-53
14	-6	-9	-11	-14	-16	-19	-21	-24	-26	-29	-32	-34	-37	-39	-42	-44	-47	-49	-52	-54
16	-7	-10	-12	-15	-17	-20	-23	-25	-28	-30	-33	-35	-38	-41	-43	-46	-48	-51	-53	-56
18	-8	-11	-13	-16	-18	-21	-24	-26	-29	-31	-34	-37	-39	-42	-44	-47	-50	-52	-55	-57
20	-9	-12	-14	-17	-19	-22	-25	-27	-30	-32	-35	-38	-40	-43	-46	-48	-51	-53	-56	-59
22	-10	-12	-15	-18	-20	-23	-26	-28	-31	-33	-36	-39	-41	-44	-47	-49	-52	-55	-57	-60
24	-10	-13	-16	-18	-21	-24	-26	-29	-32	-34	-37	-40	-42	-45	-48	-50	-53	-56	-58	-61
26	-11	-14	-16	-19	-22	-24	-27	-30	-33	-35	-38	-41	-43	-46	-49	-51	-54	-57	-59	-62

Wind speed in meters per second

frostbite in 15 minutes
frostbite in 10 minutes
frostbite in 5 minutes

postpone rewarming until it can be done in a controlled environment. If that's not possible, establish a warm environment and ensure that the patient is warm, fed, and hydrated. Give 1,000 mg of ibuprofen to reduce pain and blood clotting and allow at least 15 minutes for it to begin taking effect (as long as the patient is protected from additional freezing, there's no urgency). Immerse the affected extremities in hot water (about 105 °F, 41 °C), which to you will feel hot but not intolerable. Add hot water to keep the immersion bath warmed during the process, which will be excruciating for the patient. Once the affected tissue is rewarmed, it will be very delicate; treat it tenderly and never allow it to refreeze. The frostbitten tissues will become inflamed, and blisters will develop; necrosis may be evidenced by the tissue turning dark blue or black. The affected extremity should be bandaged and splinted, and in no event should the patient use them (which might mean a helicopter or litter evacuation). If a frostbitten extremity begins rewarming as its owner rewarms, treat the condition immediately, and don't attempt to stop the rewarming process. Frostbitten tissue is very susceptible to infection and must be treated as a high-risk wound.

Trench Foot

Trench foot, or immersion foot, is a condition caused by prolonged exposure to wetness and cold (but not freezing). It can affect hands as well as feet and is especially indicated in climbers who wisely use vapor-barrier boot liners but unwisely fail to dry their feet every night. The indications are those typical for inflammatory reactions: swelling, tenderness, red or pale blotchiness, and occasionally blisters. Affected areas are more prone to infection and injury, not to mention pain. Treatment is basic: start giving the feet (or hands) the opportunity to dry out and warm up for several hours each day. Be especially wary of minor injuries, which can easily become infected.

SUN AND UV

The ultraviolet component of sunlight causes skin damage and aging and can promote the formation of squamous tumors and melanoma, not to mention sunburn. About 10,000 people die each year from sun-caused cancer. Mountaineers are especially vulnerable to injury by sunlight because the amount of ultraviolet radiation increases about 4 percent for every 1,000 feet (300 meters) of elevation gain. The general solution is to avoid exposure by wearing a wide-brimmed hat or a sun curtain around your helmet, wearing gloves and long-sleeved shirts, and using a waterproof sunscreen with SPF of 35 or more. The albedo of snow is nearly 1, so the reflected sunlight can even burn the inside of your nose and roof of your mouth. If exposure at altitude will be lengthy, wear glacier glasses with a nose shield and use sunblock with zinc or titanium oxide pigment (clown makeup). Certain antibiotics, such as tetracycline and doxycycline, increase sensitivity to light. Thin, light clothing may be more comfortable on sunny days, but unless the fabric is specially treated it provides less protection from ultraviolet rays than darker fabrics. Carefully choose eyewear that blocks 100 percent of UV light. Quality sunglasses will have an anti-reflective coating on the inside of the lenses, to prevent light from being reflected back into your eyes; that's the purpose of the side shields on glacier glasses (which pass 4 to 10 percent of visible light, compared to the usual 15 percent).

Snow blindness is a condition in which corneas become roughened and even clouded by exposure to UV radiation, resulting in pain, redness, and swelling. The injury doesn't manifest itself until many hours after exposure, by which time the damage is done. Treatment for snow blindness is straightforward because of the cornea's rapid healing. Remove contact lenses and resist the urge to rub itchy, burning eyes. Protect your eyes from light with soft bandages; I find that contact lens saline drops temporarily reduce discomfort. Comfort and light sensitivity will return to normal in a day or so, but be extra vigilant about wearing sunglasses thereafter.

6
Mountain Weather

Once more the ruby-coloured portal open,
Which to his speech did honey passage yield;
Like a red morn, that ever yet betokened
Wrack to the seaman, tempest to the field,
Sorrow to shepherds, woe unto the birds,
Gusts and foul flaws to herdmen and to herds.

And to mountaineers. When Shakespeare wrote the raunchy *Venus and Adonis* in 1592, he wove into it the common wisdom that a red sky in the morning portends bad weather, though in the evening it suggests the opposite. The disciple Matthew offered the same wisdom centuries earlier. Basic weather forecasting skills are handy for mountaineers as well as poets and prophets, even though meteorological terms and concepts may seem arcane at first. Weather profoundly affects the pleasure and safety of mountaineering in a number of ways throughout the year, and weather also strongly affects avalanche conditions in winter.

WHAT YOU ALREADY KNOW

If you know anything at all about weather, it's probably that weather systems track from west to east. You may also know that in the northern hemisphere winds circulate in a clockwise direction around high-pressure centers and counter-clockwise around lows. And you may even know that local weather forecasts are more problematic near the West Coast, because much depends on exactly where storms originating in the Pacific or Gulf of Alaska actually make landfall; in the East, there are fewer mountains and more data history for accurate forecasts. You might already be in the habit of checking the weather forecast for the area where you expect to be climbing and change your objective or cancel plans altogether if things look bad. Hospitable weather is key to fast, bold climbing, and to comfort and success on every ascent. I have a partner who's learned to read the National Weather Service forecast discussions, with their arcane terminology and computer models (*discus-*

sions are where the NWS meat is found). He carefully picks days to climb and never gets stormed on the way the rest of us seem to.

Even with the official forecast (or official guess) under your belt, you may also know that high mountains and ranges are capable of making their own weather, because of the environment and the relief of the mountains themselves, and that conditions at various parts of a mountain system can be very different and change rapidly—whatever the forecast may say for lower elevations. To arrive at an accurate forecast, you need to factor in the effect of local conditions, based on your own observations. If you have an altimeter, you can note trends in atmospheric pressure, but your main data will come from observing clouds.

CLOUDING THE PICTURE

Gross weather forecasting is based on estimating the consequences of moving air masses, fronts, and pressure systems. Air masses are large volumes of air with horizontally uniform temperature and moisture; they assume the character of the ground below so they're called polar, tropical, continental, marine, etc. Fronts are the margins where air masses meet and do battle. Pressure systems are regions of the atmosphere where the barometric pressure is definitively higher or lower than normal (normal is 29.93 inches or 760 mm of mercury; or 1,013.25 millibars, mb; or 1,013.25 hectopascals, hPa, or more correctly but less commonly, 101.325 kilopascals, kPa).

Clouds are the most evident indicator of weather. You probably already know that clouds on a summit, no matter how fluffy and innocent in appearance, usually indicate blustery conditions there. Lenticular clouds, so-called because of their lens-like shape, indicate high winds aloft. When near a summit they may not rule out pleasant conditions elsewhere, but when lenticulars, and especially multiple stacked lenticulars, form far downwind of summits, windy conditions are likely to be widespread, and gusts on summits and ridges throughout the mountain range may be insufferably strong. Time to consider Plan B.

When Weather Gets a Lift

The fundamental concept behind an understanding of bad weather, or at least precipitation, is lifting. For significant precipitation to develop, air must be lifted (and there must be humidity and instability, too). Clouds form when warmer, moist air is lifted higher into the atmosphere; moist air is less dense than dry air, so it will rise even if it's at the same temperature. Rising air expands, and expanding air cools; when the air cools to the temperature of the dew point (technically, to the lifting condensation level) invisible water vapor condenses on microscopic particles to form visible water droplets or ice crystals—clouds. If cloudy air continues to rise, it cools further, and water may fall out of the clouds as precipitation of many kinds. The reverse is true of descending air, which usually leads to pleasant conditions.

There are several ways that lifting significant enough to produce mountain storms can occur. *Frontal lifting* describes air forced upward by the displacement of one air mass by another. Convection or *convective lifting* occurs when solar heating at the earth's surface causes warmed air to ascend into cooler air above, like hot-air balloons. The speed of the rising air may be 10 miles per hour. Convective lifting produces big cumulonimbus clouds that are associated with thunderstorms, such as those that seem to occur over the Rockies and Tetons almost every summer afternoon. In such clouds, convective lifting can exceed 50 miles per hour. *Upslope lift* is produced when air rises as it moves over gently rising land. The eastern sides of the Rockies are famous for big snowfalls during upslope conditions when a powerful winter low to the south brings Gulf moisture; upslope lifting is intensified by orographic lifting. The same effects may cause wet or snowy weather on the western slopes of any North American range. *Orographic lifting* describes air forced upward as it moves over a mountain range. It's the most powerful lifting mechanism, ten times more powerful than frontal lifting, and accounts for the majority of precipitation in the western United States and Canada. Orographic lifting is the primary reason that mountain weather differs from flat-land or ocean weather and the forecasting thereof. Moun-

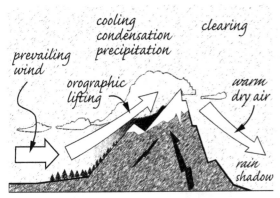

Orographic lifting.

tains and ranges affect local weather, and it's the local weather that affects mountaineers.

Meteorologists use a plethora of Latin words to classify clouds according to their altitude and appearance. We can start more simply. *High clouds* are composed of ice crystals. These clouds, variously called cirrus, indicate moisture high aloft and warn of an approaching weather system in 24 to 36 hours. *Middle clouds* (6,500 to 20,000 feet), often forms of stratus clouds, may be composed

of water droplets, resulting in well-defined edges, or ice crystals, resulting in wispy edges. Certain midlevel clouds indicate arriving weather systems that may be some hours away; other types, such as "fair weather cumulus" scattered in a blue sky, indicate high pressure and fair weather. *Low clouds* (having bases from ground to 6,500 feet) are the source of rain or snow because precipitation falling from higher clouds usually evaporates before it hits the ground. In mountains you may be well above 6,500 feet and in the thick of things as storms develop.

Some cloud types are of specific interest to mountaineers. *Cumulus* clouds look like clumps of white cotton, usually with grey, horizontal bases. They're formed by convective lifting of moist air above solar heated ground; they almost never form when the ground is below freezing. Cumulus clouds may be formed or enhanced by orographic lifting in mountainous regions. *Cumulonimbus* clouds are heavy, dense cumulus clouds with massive vertical development produced by powerful convective lifting; their tops reach 20,000 feet or higher, where ice crystals and cirrus-like cloud

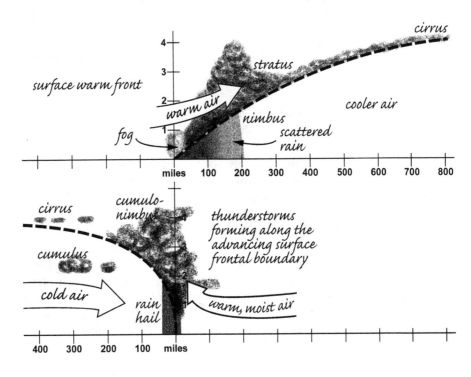

Warm front and cold front over flat land.

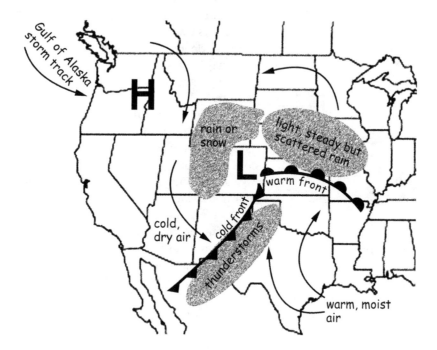

Basic weather map.

components form. Their bases are usually dark and accompanied by virga (wisps of precipitation that don't reach the ground), hail, or heavy showers that can dump a million pounds of water or more, showing just how powerful lifting effects can be and why, given the impermeable nature of mountainous terrain, climbers should avoid narrow drainages when even distant thunderstorms could produce flash flooding. *Orographic* clouds seldom form when the atmosphere is stable, but with a little instability orographic lifting leads to stratus clouds or to cumulus clouds if the air is even more unstable. Instability along with high moisture may lead to cumulonimbus clouds. Solar heating of mountain ridges causes nearby air to be warmer than air at the same elevation over valleys, increasing convective lifting that adds to orographic lifting and results in more cloud formation during the day that will abate in the evening when solar heating abates. Orographic *lenticular* and *cap clouds* indicate high winds (more than 40 miles per hour) even though they don't appear to move; this is because they form as the wind moves up windward sides of mountains and dissipate as

the air moves down lee sides—the air moves, but the cloud remains stationary. *Banner clouds* form off the lee side of sharp peaks when strong winds create a wake vortex there that pulls condensing air into it, making for great photos.

CLIMATOLOGY

I might as well mention climate, the big picture of weather. There are four main factors that influence climate:

Latitude mainly influences the amount of solar radiation and relative proportions of day and night. This effect changes during the year because the earth's rotational axis is tilted 23.5° degrees relative to the sun—the latitudes of the Tropics of Cancer and Capricorn.

Altitude affects air density, precipitation, wind, solar radiation, temperature (by about 3.6 F° per 1,000 feet), and atmospheric moisture. Every 1,000 feet (300 m) of rise in elevation is approximately equivalent, in terms of climate, to traveling 350 miles (560 km) farther north, at sea level.

Continentality means distance from the coast.

The principal mountain ranges of the Americas run north-south, roughly perpendicular to the usual progress of weather systems. This isolates the climates of maritime, intermountain, and continental ranges and creates major differences in local weather and snowfall. Continentality has a significant effect on avalanche conditions. Usually, western slopes of North American mountain ranges are wetter because moisture is lost as eastward-moving air ascends as it passes over them.

Regional patterns of wind and ocean currents affect our weather. In summer the Bermuda-Azores High brings warm, moist air from the Gulf of Mexico into the United States and contributes to the development of thunderstorms in the Midwest. The Pacific High over the Gulf of Alaska causes weak northerly winds along the West Coast, bringing clear skies, low humidity, and warmer temperatures, save for local effects such as the spring marine layer fog along the California coast. The persistent California Low forms over Arizona, between these two highs, and the summer jet stream moves high over Canada. In winter, the Bermuda-Azores High continues to dominate weather in the eastern United States, but the Pacific High weakens and drifts south, exposing the West Coast to strong winds from the Aleutian Low that forms over the Bering Strait. These westerly winds bring extensive precipitation, as frontal systems drive maritime air into western mountain ranges. The storm track is typically north of California, through Washington and Oregon, and across Utah. The weak Great Basin High forms in the intermountain region, pouring colder winter air into the Great Basin as the mountains cool, especially at night. The jet stream in winter drops down from Canada to pass over the West Coast and California.

These descriptions are typical, but very general. Weather systems that are exceptions to these patterns are often given special names, like the "Pineapple Express" that comes out of the Pacific from the southwest to bring warm rain to northwest coastal mountains. Each mountain range has its own typical weather pattern. The Pacific High tends to block storms from the Gulf of Alaska during the California Sierra summer climbing season, but rare tropical storms from the west coast of Mexico can bring monsoon moisture into the Great Basin and Eastern Sierra. The precipitation that results is often widespread and copious, so Sierra climbers should watch for clouds moving in from the south, thickening clouds, and rising humidity. If rain occurs at night, a rarity in the summer Sierra, the arrival of a tropical storm system is confirmed; in combination with convective lifting, cumulous clouds can form that develop into powerful thunderstorms during the day. Learn from experienced mountaineers about the seasonal weather patterns typical for the areas where you intend to climb. You'll find they are amazingly consistent (the weather patterns, that is, not the mountaineers).

PREDICTING MOUNTAIN WEATHER USING LOCAL OBSERVATIONS

Using local observations to forecast short-term weather changes means observing *trends*, and that means checking weather maps and forecasts, or discussions, for a few days before your climb and keeping an eye on local weather indications and your ear on your NOAA weather radio even as you hitchhike to the trailhead. A smattering of meteorological knowledge and your personal observations and experience make it possible to forecast short-term local weather with surprising accuracy. Just what a mountaineer needs. Mountain terrain affects wind, temperature, precipitation, and, to some degree, clouds, but not barometric pressure, so I'll start there.

Barometric Pressure

Barometric pressure is always corrected to sea level even though station pressure (actual pressure at the instrument) is measured, because altitude effects on air pressure would confound analysis. Falling barometric pressure (an altimeter indicating ascent even when you don't move) indicates the arrival of a trough aloft or a cold front at the surface and therefore the possibility of an approaching storm. In far western mountains especially, the storm may be diverted elsewhere, or its frontal lifting may be increased by orographic lifting that would augment precipitation; in other words: things could go either way. If you're referring to an altimeter, 40 to 60 feet of altitude gain over 3 hours means a mountaineer should keep an eye out for lowering clouds or a swing of the wind to the east or southeast; if 60 to 80 feet of gain is observed, consider bailing on your summit bid and selecting a more conservative alternative; if you see more than 80 feet of anomalous elevation gain in 3 hours, it's time to head for the cars. Two hundred feet of change while you were sleeping in your tent indicates the possibility of a storm within several hours, and 1,000 feet of overnight gain—not uncommon in big mountain ranges—means you're right in the middle of a serious storm. A few days of steady or rising pressure suggests that a period of fair weather has arrived.

Temperature

Temperature is a poor prognosticator of weather, because so many things affect it locally. Air temperature decreases at about 3.6 F° per 1,000 feet of altitude gain (2 C° per 300 m), called the average environmental lapse rate. To be a little more precise, figure 3 F° if skies are very cloudy, and 5 F° for every 1,000 feet if skies are clear (1.6 and 2.7 C° per 300 m). If you use these relationships to estimate the freezing altitude, be aware that snow can accumulate a thousand feet lower. On clear, cold nights, air that has cooled as the result of radiative heat loss drains down into valleys from higher up (katabatic winds). The effect should influence the decision of where to set up camp, favoring locations several hundred feet above valley floors. Temperature inversion is an increase, rather than decrease, in air temperature with altitude. In mountain valleys in winter this common effect can be as much as 25 F° in 3,000 feet (14 C° in 1,000 m); the good news is that temperature inversion accompanies stable mountain weather. Nights with gentle breezes will be warmer because wind stirs things up and brings some of the warmer, inverted air down to ground level. Things will be warmer overall on cloudy nights, because the

cloud cover reflects heat back to the earth. The second night of a mountain storm is likely to be the coldest because the coldest air lags behind the leading edge of a cold front, and also because the skies will have cleared, leading to more radiative heat loss from the earth. If the temperature is lower than 5 °F (-15 °C), snowfall is unlikely because air that cold cannot hold enough moisture for significant precipitation.

Wind

Surface wind gives few clues about mountain weather because it's so profoundly affected by the mountains themselves, even to the extent of apparently reversing the direction of the prevailing wind. Wind in valleys tends to follow the sides of canyon walls rather than the direction of the wind aloft, and wind through gaps or passes can be twice the speed of surface winds elsewhere. Snow plumes trailing off peaks are another indication, like lenticular and cap clouds, of strong winds. In summer, mountain thermals originating on southerly slopes can create strong up-valley winds, 10 to 15 miles per hour or more, that are unrelated to prevailing winds; in the evening, these winds reverse, and colder air coming down results in down-valley breezes that may be even stronger below snowfields or cliffs (so don't camp in such spots). As air moves up slopes (orographic lifting), it cools, it may lose moisture, and its speed increases dramatically, sometimes doubling or tripling. This effect is augmented by clear skies, lots of rock exposed to the sun to encourage convective lifting, and light prevailing winds. When orographic winds cross ridges and descend, their speed drops and the air warms, an effect greater than the cooling effect. These descending air currents are the warm, dry Chinook or "snow eater" winds, called Föhn or Foehn in Europe, Canterbury in New Zealand, and Zonda in the Andes. Such warm winds can cause unpleasant gusts for campers, and their rapid temperature rise of 20 to 40 F° (10 to 20 C°) can also lead to weakening of snow bridges, rising creeks, and an increase in avalanche hazard. Speaking of avalanche danger, wind is the main factor influencing localized snow deposition in winter, more important than snowfall itself. Lee slopes of some peaks may be areas of relatively calm winds, but on abrupt lee slopes strong descending winds can lead to turbulence, erratic wind patterns, and downdrafts of from 10 to over 30 miles per hour, which will impair helicopter rescue and give erratic altimeter readings. These wind effects can be very pronounced on glaciers, even in the absence of storms—be prepared, even if the wind is mild when you begin setting up camp.

Clouds

Clouds of any type indicate that moist air has been lifted, a requirement for precipitation and a common indicator of a weather change to come. Clouds alone, however, do not mean that bad weather is inevitable. For example, it's common in summer mountains for a clear morning to be followed by cirrus clouds growing during the day, for midlevel clouds to gather, and for scattered cumulous and lenticular clouds to develop later—day after day with no inclement weather appearing, or if there is any it may be confined to an increase in wind or to afternoon storminess on scattered high summits while fair weather continues everywhere else. If there is moisture in the air and the potential for convective lifting, thunderstorms may develop; forecast discussions report the amount of precipitable moisture (an inch is a lot) and indicate the potential for convective lifting, "pops." To make accurate predictions it's important to become familiar with the seasonal cloud patterns common to the ranges where you intend to climb and to check the most detailed local forecasts you can digest, even though you know that the range and your summit objective may have very different weather than that forecast for lower elevations. On the Net you can find all manner of static and animated forecast information, starting with national weather maps, visible satellite imagery showing clouds, radar imagery showing precipitation, infrared imagery showing intense weather systems, and new 3-D imagery to help your visualization. You can drill down and find maps of lightning strikes, surface winds, and forecast model predictions. When you've reviewed these, incorporate your own knowledge of clouds that you observe

to create a forecast advising your personal climbing plan. It's not as difficult as I make it sound.

INTERPRETING CLOUDS

Fronts and troughs cause lifting and cloud formation, so thickening and lowering clouds, especially in the western sky, likely indicate the approach of a weather system and potential storm. The clouds appear to lower because the arrival of colder or more humid air with a front lowers the altitude where clouds form. Cirrus clouds indicate high winds aloft that can carry moisture many hundreds of miles. This means that the appearance of cirrus clouds, especially a solid layer of cirrus clouds on the western horizon, may indicate a storm approaching in 24 to 36 hours. Cirrostratus clouds can result in a halo around the sun or moon; generally, the closer the halo is to the sun or moon, the denser the clouds and the closer the storm—maybe within 24 hours. As cirrus clouds thicken and lower, they may become altostratus, a sure sign of an arriving weather system. Cirrus clouds dim the stars at night, but altostratus clouds hide them completely, so if the stars disappear, beware.

Cumulus clouds form for many reasons; if they're few and scattered, they may exist merely to enhance photos. If they rapidly grow larger, taller, and darker, stronger lifting is indicated, and a serious, if localized, storm may soon appear even though no frontal system is passing. Cumulous clouds may develop into widely scattered thunderstorms; take care that hail and lightning isn't scattered on you. When multiple layers of clouds appear, and especially if scattered clouds that were hanging lower down in mountainous areas begin to rise, it's a certain sign of bad weather approaching within 12 hours. If a solid layer of higher clouds is visible through breaks in lower clouds, storms are likely to persist.

Cap or lenticular clouds indicate strong winds over mountains. If lenticulars grow, descend, and are joined by additional clouds, it's an indication that more moisture has arrived and is being lifted by high winds, indicating an imminent storm or at least weather change. Snow plumes also indicate high winds over summits and ridges, because the wind force is exceeding the shear strength of the snow. Freshly fallen snow can be lifted into the air by winds of only 5 miles per hour, but older, consolidated snow or wind slab being blown about reveals much higher wind speeds.

Clearing weather follows thinning and rising clouds, indicating a diminishing supply of moisture. Low-lying fog or layers of valley haze in the morning also suggest that lifting isn't taking place, and air is stable. It's a common experience for mountaineers to climb above clouds and to look down on cloud tops that obscure the landscape below; this indicates stable weather, but if those clouds begin rising, conditions will soon change for the worse. The appearance of small cumulus clouds that diminish or disappear during the day is another indication of stable weather, as will be just about any form of scattered mid- or lower-level clouds that don't become taller or thicken during the day—ruling out processes that indicate lifting of additional moisture and a weather change for the worse. Even light cirrus clouds from the north or northwest don't indicate an interruption of fair weather. Morning dew or frost also suggests improving weather. The end of a snowstorm and thinning cloud cover is indicated by smaller snowflakes falling, and the passing of a winter cold front is suggested by a change to rimed (granular) snowflakes (graupel) created by turbulence in the front that's about to pass.

Thunderstorms cannot only drench you with cold rain and marble-sized hail; if you're on an exposed ridge or summit they can subject you to lightning strikes—one of mountaineering's most unwelcome experiences. Climbers must take the hail seriously, too, wherever they are. During the writing of this book, a thunderstorm dumped over a foot of hail on a bewildered Los Angeles. Thunderstorms are indicated by an increase in size and rapid thickening of scattered cumulus clouds, or by the approach of a line of large cumulus or cumulonimbus clouds accompanied by an advance guard of altocumulus clouds. At night, increasing lightning in the direction of the prevailing wind gives the same warning. If there is mid- and high-level moisture in the atmosphere above hot and dry air at lower levels, conditions are ripe for an approaching trough to join with convective lifting to trigger thunderstorms in the heat of the afternoon; weather forecasts may refer to these as "scattered" but they seem always to pick on mountaineers. The dry air lower down may evaporate much of the actual precipitation, but that will cool the air and accelerate it downward, possibly resulting in very strong surface winds as the down-rushing cold air hits the ground. Massive and growing cumulus clouds hanging over a ridge or summit, day or night, are another harbinger of thunderstorm activity and a reason to consider abandoning your summit bid.

FOG

Fog is mostly an inconvenience, or photo opportunity, for mountaineers because it occurs only when winds are relatively calm. There are three common causes for mountain fog. Radiative heat loss may cause fog to form over ground made very damp by recent rain, an effect seen most commonly in fall when nights are long and skies are clear, augmenting heat loss. Advective fog forms in spring or summer when moist air from bodies of water moves over land and cools—call it marine fog. Advancing warm fronts may produce fog when precipitation falls out of warmer upper air into colder air below, causing the cool air to become saturated with moisture. If the colder air cools more during the night, fog may form that doesn't burn off but dissipates only as the warm front arrives. In fact, fog in general doesn't "burn off" because it scatters more heat than it absorbs; fog dissipates when the sun warms the ground below and incoming drier air starts dispersing the inversion that caused the fog.

LIFTING THE FOG

Will reading this section make you an expert meteorologist? Probably not, especially if it's all new to you. Hopefully it'll allow you to make better use of official weather forecasts and to begin to associate your personal observations with the weather that follows. Try it, it's a fun way to add depth to your romance with Mother Nature. Having an expert point things out, especially cloud types, is very helpful to get you going. The important things to remember are that clouds indicate that air has been lifted high enough to cause condensation, so something is going on—clouds are necessary but not sufficient to produce precipitation. When clouds seem to lower, it's because the altitude where the temperature becomes cold enough to cause condensation is descending, indicating that more cold air is arriving and that things are becoming increasingly unstable. The appearance of clouds often follows patterns that give clues as to what kinds of weather will follow. Having no visible clouds indicates no moisture and, except over deserts, no lifting or instability. Understand that even armed with an accurate, wide-area weather forecast, you should expect that peaks and ranges can affect localized wind and precipitation. That's where your new skills and observations will help you make critical decisions affecting the comfort and safety of your outing.

The Alpine Start

Back in the Midwest when I first started climbing, my friends and I would start the day in the cavernous confines of The Alpine, a restaurant that ladled out great heaps of the artery-clogging fare for which Wisconsin is famous. After we were completely bloated we'd stagger out into the sunlight, fall into cars, and head for the local crag, satisfied that we were beginning our day with an alpine start.

Not even close. But the alpine start is a part of mountaineering tradition that well deserves its place, whether it means getting going at the crack of midnight, in the wee small hours, at oh-dark-thirty, or by first light. The reasons for an alpine start are many, and maximizing the number of hours available to complete the climb is only the most obvious. It's about safety, not comfort. Many unanticipated events can conspire to use up your available daylight and your margin of safety. By getting an early start you give yourself the best chance to avoid the consequences of a set of options that's ever diminishing, like sand in an hour glass. Descending is inevitably more dangerous than climbing, and retreating in darkness is the most dangerous descent of all.

WHY START EARLY

Climbing in the early morning is usually easier and safer. Snowfields are firm, making step kicking or cramponing easier. Later, as the snow warms, it may turn into bottomless slush that makes for a miserable, wet ascent. If you complete the climb early enough, you have the option of waiting until that slope is in good shape to descend by glissading. If sloth robs you of time, the once-inviting snowfield may have turned icy as shadows fall late in the day and temperatures along with them. That could make the descent much more dangerous, even if you're prepared with crampons or a rope. If you're unprepared, the temptation will still be strong to shave your safety margin to nil in order to continue down rather than become benighted. A decision to be avoided by starting early.

Rockfall may abate during the night but resume with fury as soon as the sun warms the stone. One of the scariest mornings I can remember saw our party shortcutting beneath an icefall as fast as we could possibly move—not because of the ice, but because the upper surfaces of the seracs (blocks of ice) were covered with all manner of rocks lightly frozen in place. We knew that as soon as the sun came over a ridge and warmed those rocks, many would be on their way down in search of lazy climbers. Getting an early start up a couloir gives you the best chance of encountering the least amount of rockfall and icefall.

In the pleasant months of summer climbing, many mountain ranges see thunderstorms appearing in early afternoon. That's the time by which you want to have already left the summit, for several reasons. The most obvious reason is to avoid being drenched with rain and assaulted by lightning. Rock is more slippery when wet—this not only makes it more difficult to climb on, but wetness encourages rockfall. The worst example of rockfall I've witnessed was a huge afternoon release of wet rock; two climbers perished.

Approaches as well as climbs should be started early, especially if they involve stream crossings, glacier travel, or bergschrunds. Snow bridges over crevasses weaken in the warmth of the day, and melting snow can substantially increase afternoon stream flow, making crossings more difficult and dangerous.

MORNING BEGINS AT SUNDOWN

Getting an early start begins the night before or even the day before, with an ample dinner, casual but complete preparation, and a good night's sleep. Lest you think you're alone in your wakefulness, let me assure you that just about every mountaineer has trouble getting a restful night's sleep before a climb. Anxiety is compounded by altitude and unfamiliar, often uncomfortable, surroundings. Minimize the worry by taking care of everything necessary to get you off promptly the next morning. That means having all your climbing gear accounted for and packed; your food and water packed; breakfast planned; a water bottle for

the night; and your climbing clothes ready. There's nothing like keeping mental track of a growing to-do list to keep you awake.

TURNING OFF THE LIGHTS

Most climbers have personal recipes for getting to sleep; here are a few popular menu items:

▲ Overeating, especially pasta and cheese
▲ Alcohol, carbonated and otherwise
▲ 5-hydroxy l-tryptophane
▲ Antihistamines, like Benadryl or Benahist, containing diphenhydramine HCl
▲ Diamox (acetazolamide), 125 mg if the problem is nighttime respiration disturbance (periodic breathing) when new to altitude
▲ Drugstore sleepers, such as Unisom, containing doxylamine succinate
▲ Prescription sleepers like Ambien (Zolpidem, zolpidem tartrate) that act quickly, don't disturb breathing at altitude, and avoid the morning hangover
▲ Prescription benzodiazepine sedatives (Valium, Halcyon, Xanax, Versed, etc.)
▲ Valerian root or other herbs
▲ Melatonin

If you choose any of these, don't experiment on your first big outing. You want to wake up alert and motivated, not hung over. If you're sleeping at 8,000 feet or higher, be especially cautious with any substance that depresses respiration or acts as a diuretic (as do many of these and their kin); such side effects contribute to Acute Mountain Sickness. The best high-power option by far is Ambien; avoid the depressants.

I usually don't have problems falling asleep. I take care of the anxiety-minimizing preparations, set the alarm, pop in my earplugs, and drift into the arms of Morpheus; melatonin plus B-12 make for pleasantly vivid dreams. My problem is staying asleep. Winter makes this worse, when there are 14 hours of darkness and nothing to do but stare at the insides of your eyelids. A pee bottle is handy, even in summer, to minimize interruptions of torpor. The coldest time of night is the hour before dawn; that's usually good for enough contributory discomfort to pry one's eyes open—might as well get up and out.

Mountaineers learn to get out of the bag and get in motion promptly. That helps with attitude as well as with staying warm. Some who weren't successful getting to sleep may want to start the day with modafinil (Provigil, Alertec), and so might even some who were. Some need coffee to get them going; some find coffee gets them going uncontrollably. Hot cocoa has smaller fangs and helps more with hydration. Few mountaineers seem to relish a big breakfast of any kind as part of a genuine alpine start; I'll discuss eating options in Chapter 19 on performance nutrition.

THE DREAD BIVOUAC

When all else fails, and your alpine start or lack thereof fails to save you from the likelihood of a bivouac, don't despair. There are hardly any mountaineers who haven't found themselves high on a mountain, shivering in the darkness while watching the lights of warmer places twinkling in the distance below. They've survived, and you will, too. Maybe they learned a little more about suffering, but the mountaineers who faced the greatest danger were the ones who thought that a few hours of discomfort should be avoided by descending in darkness or deteriorating conditions. Resist the temptation to forsake your safety margin by rappelling into unknown terrain, descending an iced slope when you prepared only for snow, or exposing yourself to other objective hazards, simply to avoid a night out. Better to accept a few hours of discomfort waiting for first light. An unplanned bivouac in winter or in a storm can be more threatening and last longer, but if that's a possibility, you should carry the minimum equipment that will get you through. There are plenty of stories about backcountry travelers who thrashed around off route in the darkness, getting themselves lost, fatigued, and hypothermic, but there are far more numerous, though less interesting, instances of climbers who did the sensible thing and hunkered down. For these sensible climbers, their greatest danger may have been dehydration and boredom. All this, by the way, applies to the typi-

cal summer bivouacs facing North American climbers. At high altitude and in extreme cold, bivouacs can become fatal.

Yvon Chouinard is often quoted as admonishing that if you take along bivy gear, you *will* bivouac. He was warning not only about the consequences of the additional weight carried but the consequences of accepting the attitude (or possibility) of defeat even before your climb sets off— not to mention the powerful disincentive of an option that will entail even more than the customary amount of suffering, should it become inevitable. So don't plan on an unplanned bivy, but there are things you can prudently take along to avoid truly dire consequences if unforeseen circumstances cause delays and you become benighted. These items won't contribute much weight or consume much space in your pack; together they're lighter but more effective than an old-school shell parka:

Wind jacket. I'm expecting that you'll carry a hooded wind jacket as part of your normal clothing in the mountains. If that isn't the case, you'll want to prudently pack one in case your estimate of time or weather proves inaccurate. For greater protection but less versatility, elect a waterproof, nonbreathable hooded rain jacket of lightweight fabric. Either option can be carried for less than 4 ounces.

Balaclava. A balaclava provides the greatest warmth for least weight because it covers your head and neck, your areas of greatest heat loss. A light version should be in your ten essentials.

Gloves. If you aren't carrying climbing gloves, consider liner gloves for emergency use only.

Socks. Heavy socks would be a good idea if there's any chance of an extended climbing day when you're otherwise wearing only light socks.

VBL. A vapor barrier sleeping bag liner offers serious protection from the elements should you get caught out. A VBL made from silnylon weighs only a few ounces and is a better choice than "space blankets." A similar alternative would be a bivy sack, which in modern fabrics will weigh as little as 8 ounces and could fit two compatible climbers in an emergency.

When you have to concede that you're facing several hours of discomfort, invest the last daylight finding a spot that's sheltered from wind and stonefall, preferably east facing. Put on all available clothing. Sit on your rope with your feet in your pack. Pull your arms inside your jacket and cinch up all openings. Cuddle up with your companions. And suffer. Be comforted by the words of Gaston Rébuffat:

The man who climbs only in good weather,
starting from huts and never bivouacking,
appreciates the splendour of the mountains
but not their mystery, the dark of their night,
the depth of their sky above . . . How
much he has missed!

PART 3

Rock

In this section I'll cover the basics of roped climbing in a mountaineering context, though most general mountaineering in North America targets summits that can be reached without a rope. Many people find mountaineering immensely satisfying without ever roping up; they happily use nontechnical skills for 99 percent of their climbing. But there's no definitive separation of the skills underlying third-class climbing—where a rope is carried "just in case"—and fifth-class climbing. The fundamentals are the same; they relate mainly to safety, so if you carry a rope, you need to master the skills. Fourth-class climbing is essentially easy fifth-class climbing with long runouts, whether the medium is rock, snow, or ice. The climbing moves on lower fifth class may be a little more difficult or continuous, and the medium a little more vertical, but the equipment and techniques required are substantially the same. Fourth-class climbing doesn't mean fifth class done ineptly, and when a third-class climb requires a rope, because of exposure or objective hazards or if a rappel is required, you'd better be in command of proper equipment and sound technique. Good technique isn't complicated; in fact, a skilled climber will reduce complexity to the minimum—she wouldn't carry extra equipment or waste time fiddling with inefficient methods. The material in this part may strike you as highly technical as you read it, but work out the techniques using your own equipment, and you'll see that I've actually kept things pretty simple, even though the material is more up-to-date than you'll find elsewhere.

8
Climb Rating Systems

*Climbing difficulty ratings is one of those
subjects that every climber understands,
but on which no two agree.*

CLIMB WITH CLASS

Since the early days of mountaineering, climbers
have invented systems to tell other mountaineers
how difficult their routes were. Some systems are
based on the most difficult section of a route, some
on the length or overall difficulty, some on the
techniques required. The Sierra Club established a
system of grading their outings based on six classes
of hiking or climbing first proposed by Willo
Welzenbach in the late 1930s; this system forms
the basis of route grading in the United States.

Class 1 refers to hiking on a trail.

Class 2 means rough hiking that requires using
hands for balance, such as crossing a field of large
boulders.

Class 3 routes require using hands in addition
to feet for actually moving up the rock. It's climbing, even though a rope isn't used.

Class 4 means that a rope will be used for
safety.

Class 5 climbs mean the leader will be belayed
and will place intermediate anchors—sometimes
called "running belays," anchors, protection, or
simply "pro"—through which the rope moves upward along with the leader.

Class 6 (a term no longer used) referred to
climbing where anchors and man-made devices
bore the climbers' weight and were used to aid ascending, whereas fifth-class climbing meant that
only features of the rock are used for climbing, and
the rope and other hardware are solely for safety.
The modern term is *aid climbing*.

Fifth-class climbing that uses no aid is called
free climbing, and climbing, including aid climbing, that uses removable anchors instead of pitons
or bolts is called *clean climbing*. *Free solo* climbing
doesn't mean climbing alone; it refers to climbing

a route without a safety rope where one would normally be expected.

You'll notice that fourth- and fifth-class climbing—free or aid climbing—involve the use of ropes, anchors, and belays. There are many ways to go about this; Chapter 9 discusses selecting ropes in the context of the various ways ropes can be used. Chapter 12 discusses anchors, and Chapter 14 discusses belaying—securing a climber with a rope. Anchors for belaying the first climber—the leader—are established at the start of each pitch, and anchors for belaying subsequent climbers—the seconds—are established at the finish of each pitch of climbing.

The class rating system is a combination of grading the difficulty of the most difficult section of a climb and the techniques used to ascend it. Typically, the person who first climbed the route gives it a rating that future guidebook writers are loathe to alter—however preposterous it may come to be seen. If the route description were generous it might say, for example, "mostly Class 2, with a few Class 3 moves at the summit." Without this detail the route would simply be rated Class 3, and you wouldn't know if it involved 1,000 feet of Class 3 or just a single move. Approach hikes are generally not rated unless they're more involved than Class 1 or 2.

Climbers understand that what's one class of climbing for most parties might be handled another way by others, for any number of reasons. "It was late, so we decided to Class 3 the whole thing" means that they didn't use a rope. "The ledges were covered with snow, so we roped up," means that the party decided that using a rope would be prudent irrespective of the route's rating. Generally, ratings are assigned based on optimum conditions. Objective hazards, and even subjective considerations, may influence the actual techniques and equipment that you'll want to use.

The rating of a climb is certainly not the whole story. If you think about it, the south col of Everest is just a fourth-class route, maybe third, and it's been climbed in 8 hours. The summit of Mt. Whitney, the highest point in the lower 48 states, is accessible by a Class 1 trail that's 11 miles long and gains over 6,100 feet, beginning at over 8,000 and ending up at 14,495 feet (4,418 meters). Weather, trail conditions, and the effects of altitude turn back many. In late summer when there's no snow or ice on the trail, a reasonably fit hiker can complete the round trip in about 11 hours. Many parties take 2 days for the round trip even under these optimal conditions. A super-fit runner wearing flimsy shorts and a singlet has done it in less than 4 hours. Don't assume that the class rating someone assigned to a route effectively describes its difficulty for your party or for all conditions you may encounter.

THE YDS

As more and more new fifth-class routes were climbed in the early days, it became apparent that one grade was not sufficient to express the range of difficulties that rock climbers continued to conquer. Easy/moderate/hard didn't suffice, either. In 1956, the "decimal system" first appeared in a guidebook to Taquitz, a Southern California crag. Fifth class was divided into ratings of 5.0 to 5.9 ("five oh" to "five nine"; the decimal point is not pronounced). At the time 5.9 seemed to be the greatest difficulty that would ever be possible to climb. Itinerant climbers took the system to the Valley, and despite its origin, it came to be called the Yosemite Decimal System. Climbers continued to push their limits, however, and harder climbs began to bunch up at the 5.9 level—no one wanted to be the first to rate their climb 5.10. Finally in 1967, an existing aid route (again at Taquitz) was climbed free that was so difficult (it's now rated 5.11a) that it blew the limit off the system, which became open-ended. Today the first rock climbers are reaching 5.15.

Low levels of fifth-class climbing are virtually indistinguishable—certainly less so than the higher levels, which are often subdivided into a, b, c, and d, or + and −. Haggling over whether a climb is 5.1 or 5.2 would be an attempt at humor. Appreciable difficulty begins at about 5.6. I've found that a reasonably agile teenager, wearing skateboard shoes, can climb (but not lead) easy 5.6 sport routes without falls on the first attempt, without much instruction. This leads to the ob-

Along with difficulty ratings, climbing has become specialized in other dimensions. *Gym climbing* on a wall to which plastic holds are attached is an indoor version of *bouldering*—climbing short but difficult routes using only hands and feet (and gymnastic chalk). *Sport climbing* refers to fifth-class routes that are typically one pitch long and where bolts (machine screws drilled into the rock that hold hangers to which carabiners can be clipped) provide closely spaced anchors; sometimes carabiners on runners are pre-placed. *Trad* (traditional) *climbing* refers to fifth-class climbing that uses removable hardware (chocks, cams, etc.) to establish anchors in natural features of the stone, though popular routes may have bolts or fixed pitons at belay stances. *Ice climbing* typically refers to climbing frozen waterfalls, but becomes *mixed climbing* if rock is thrown in. *Aid climbing* refers to fifth-class rock climbing where climbers' weight is more or less continuously on anchors, which are moved up for ascending. *Big wall climbing* refers to multipitch routes on large, vertical faces usually involving several days and the techniques of trad, aid, and bolted climbing. *Mountaineering* may add snow and ice climbing to any of these techniques on routes in mountainous terrain.

---

servation that it isn't the climbing difficulty that makes mountaineering routes challenging so much as it's the technical difficulties (tying knots, placing protection, establishing anchors), objective dangers (routefinding, loose rock, snow on ledges), and psychological challenges (remoteness and being 1,000 feet over nothing but crisp, clean air). The recommendation is often made to take your gym- or sport-climbing ability and drop it at least two levels to get the rating you would find manageable in the mountains—the challenge of sport bolted 5.10 climbing at the local crag compares to 5.8 in a mountaineering context.

The rating of a route's free climbing is separated from that of any aid climbing involved. For example, you may see routes rated "5.9 A2." Aid climbing has evolved into a highly specialized form of climbing with six grades that are based on the security of anchor placements and the consequences of falling. A0 refers to rappelling or hanging on a securely anchored rope without moving up; A1 means that placing secure anchors is easy, and you might "French free" the climbing (just

pull on your anchors to surmount a difficulty). A2 means that placements are mostly sound, but some are tricky to place. Beyond that, mountaineers seldom use aid and don't carry the specialized equipment, if only because serious aid climbing is incredibly slow; most mountaineers would look for easier ways to the summit.

ICE WITH THAT?

If you've gotten the idea that the climb rating schemes can be somewhat nebulous, the ratings for ice climbing will solidify your convictions. To be fair, the big pleasure of snow and ice climbing is that it constantly changes. To attempt to rate difficulty with the same precision that might be possible for rock is untenable; consequently, the range of ice climbing difficulties from uninteresting to impossible are compressed into only eight grades, 1–8. To distinguish between climbing frozen waterfalls or flows and climbing frozen, consolidated snow (névé), ratings are prefaced by WI (water ice) or AI (alpine ice). The ratings for alpine climbing don't include whatever difficulty may be encountered in crossing the bergschrund—that can change from day to day and could be WI5 or AI1 depending on weather and snowfall (or you may resort to rock climbing to avoid the 'schrund altogether).

WI1 and AI1 Virtually a flat walk that requires crampons but not tools (axes).

WI2 and AI2 The steepness is up to 60 or 70°, and one ax is required.

WI3 and AI3 The steepness increases to 70 to 80°, but the ice is easy, and resting places and belay stances are readily available. Two axes will be needed. Steeper and more difficult ice in the mountain environment usually results from melting and refreezing, so water ice ratings tend to be more appropriate above AI3.

WI4 Feels like vertical. Steepness may be 85°, but the ice is of good quality, accepts confidence-inspiring protection, and belay stances are available.

WI5 There are extended sections of vertical ice, and the remainder is strenuous and nearly vertical.

WI6 Already about as steep as you can get; the ice quality deteriorates, and protection becomes more difficult to place; serious strength and skill are required.

WI7 Pitches are steep, possibly overhanging, and devoid of secure placements for tools or crampons. Diminished protection options results in significant danger to climbers.

WI8 The ice is terrible and poorly bonded, protection is nearly non-existent, and the pitch is highly strenuous and may involve mixed climbing.

If the climb involves both rock and ice, the rock difficulties can be rated separately, using the YDS for the rock if it's fifth class. If the climbing is really mixed and involves dry tooling (climbing rock using the same ice axes and crampons used to climb the ice), M ratings will be used, in principle extending from M1 to M11 or M12. The relationship of M ratings to comparable YDS or other rock difficulty ratings is still being debated, here and abroad.

You may also encounter water ice ratings given with roman numerals in seven levels. These aren't the same as the alpine route grades discussed next. They indicate the commitment required by the route, remoteness, difficulty of approach and descent, and objective danger as well as climbing difficulty. Not our subject matter.

MAKING THE GRADE

After you know how hard the hardest part of the route is, you'll also want to know something about the overall challenge of the climb. To do that the National Climbing Classification System established grades that apply to alpine climbs—climbs in the mountain environment. Grades take into account the maximum and average difficulty of the climbing as well as its length and other factors. As grades increase, so does the requirement for mental as well as physical stamina. Here's roughly how it works:

Grade I Any degree of technical difficulty; the route will require several hours to complete and will offer no difficulties of access or descent.

Grade II Any technical difficulty, but requiring half a day for the climbing; usually two or three pitches.

Grade III Any level of technical difficulty on the route; the climbing uses up most of the available daylight, perhaps because of a lengthy approach.

Grade IV A long, multipitch route in an alpine environment with an approach that may be subject to mountain hazards. Requires an entire day for the climb, hopefully not more.

Grade V A long, sustained multipitch route with significant exposure to mountain hazards on the approach and a difficult descent. The climbing requires more than a day—thus a bivouac.

Grade VI Hard climbing in an alpine environment that may include aid climbing and more than 2 days to complete, sometimes weeks.

Grade VII Such routes are rumored to exist, but none in the Lower 48. Baffin Island and a few in Alaska. For more insight read Reinhold Messner's *The Seventh Grade*; it's not about middle school.

By including the grade, a more or less complete idea of the climb's difficulty can be conveyed; for example, a route might be labeled "III, 5.9, A1." Interestingly, it often happens that the actual grades of popular routes are now easier than when they were first established. That's because good information on climbing details simplifies routefinding, belay points now have fixed protection or bolts, and skills and equipment have improved—plus the boldness and athleticism of rock and ice climbers continues to advance.

Other Systems

So far we've seen that any single rating system doesn't cover all the aspects of a route that could affect its difficulty. In some regions, local systems have been developed to address the problem. For example, the Mountaineers, who operate in the Pacific Northwest, have lists of climbs rated according to the number of days usually required, technical difficulty and exposure, and physical effort needed. They even indicate appropriate months of the year for climbing. In most areas, you'll have to dig this level of detail out of guidebooks and trip reports. Most guidebooks have tables converting any specialized rating systems that may have become the convention in the areas they cover to the YDS or even to European or Australian systems.

Outside the United States

These descriptions of climbing ratings apply to the United States. Elsewhere, they may be familiar or unknown; local systems prevail. Britain, for example, has perhaps the most bewildering ratings, with two overlapping systems for rock climbing alone. In the Alps a French system is used with seven mountaineering grades ranging from *facile*, to *très difficile*, to *abominable*. Would that the Sierra Club had been so eloquent.

WHAT DOES ALL THIS MEAN TO MOUNTAINEERS?

First, rating systems and their historical evolution need a little more discussion. The entire business, from the assignment of third, fourth, or fifth class to the YDS and grades is highly subjective; more generously, one might say the ratings are adaptable. The beauty is not precision, but rather flexibility—new routes are given grades by a consensus comparison to accepted grades of established routes, and the end result is pretty much understandable. Attitudes have changed over the years, though. Some noted first ascentionists are legendary for giving their routes lower ratings than most folks think they deserve, apart from any additional difficulty contributed by the mountain environment. Especially before 1970, alpine ratings tended to be lower, and guidebook writers have been reluctant to change the ratings from those assigned by the persons who first established the routes ("put them up"). Some geographic areas tend to rate climbs harder, others easier.

If you look at fifth-class alpine routes, you may notice that the hard classic lines tend to concentrate at 5.9. This is due to the historical effect mentioned before, and it's also because that's about as hard as even a skilled mountaineer would want to tackle, especially in heavy boots. The mountain environment makes harder climbing particularly difficult and time consuming—it can push the nature of the route into Grade VI territory where several days may be needed on the climb, requiring bivouacs, hauling supplies, and so on. If a difficult line must be followed, mountaineers will often resort to aid. That accounts for the many routes rated 5.9 A-something. Mountaineers intent on a summit are not shy about resorting to the occasional sling (or partner's shoulder) to create a foothold that makes a move or two much more manageable in mountain boots.

Exposure

There are many elements that influence the difficulty of a climb, not all of which may be reflected in its rating, however complex and complete it may be. These elements include the actual difficulty of the climbing, the length of the climb and descent, objective hazards, remoteness, altitude, and other aspects of the mountain environment. One of the elements most difficult to quantify is *exposure*.

Exposure is the property of a route, or section of one, that makes climbers (sometimes even hikers) acutely aware of the imminent possibility of falling. It typically involves the visualization of a plummet down rock, snow, or air (a "screamer") that leads without recourse to an unpleasant terminus far below (a "crater"). Milan Kundera expressed an alternative view in *The Incredible Lightness of Being*, saying "Vertigo is not the fear of falling, it is the fear that you will be unable to overcome the urge to hurl yourself into the void." For Milan, maybe.

The reactions to exposure are those typical of fear: dry mouth, sweaty palms, and altered mental function. Every person experiences these reactions to one degree or another, and they aren't altogether bad. If your altered mental function means becoming more focused and more deliberate, your response would be helpful in dealing with a critical situation. If, on the other hand, you lose effective control of your motor skills or become so fearful that you cannot move up or down (you're "gripped"), you and your party may be in big trouble until you regain control and focus your extra adrenaline on dealing with the situation before you, bit by bit.

For some, exposure keeps them off tall ladders and out of mountains. Most climbers mitigate their reaction to exposure as their experience builds. Some climbers become exposure junkies, turning fear into exhilaration and exalting in standing precariously atop airy summits with their arms outstretched, while their climbing partners avert their eyes. It's sometimes said that those with a powerful fear of falling have the most to gain from mountaineering while those with no fear of falling have the most to learn.

What, Then, Is Third-Class Climbing?

Let's suppose your partner calls and says, "How about we do Widow Maker Peak? I hear it's third class." Do you have any idea if it's within your range of ability (or available time)? About all you know is that someone, probably the first person to take the particular summit route your partner has in mind, said that somewhere it involved actual climbing, but they didn't need a rope.

The first thing you'd want to do is turn to trip reports, guidebooks, and more experienced friends to find out what others have said about the route. You could learn what kinds of terrain might be encountered and get a sense of whether the third-class climbing was only a few moves or a long, exposed, knife-edge ridge. Will you be crossing a snowfield that might be your best friend or worst enemy, depending on the season or time of day? What about objective dangers such as rockfall or even hazardous stream crossings on the approach? You'd see who put up the route (Fred Becky, Norman Clyde?) and when. You'd try to find reports of trips undertaken at the same time of year as when you intend to climb, and you'd read closely for routefinding tips and for clues as to why the parties took the time they report. You might find topo drawings showing crude illustrations of the route and its approach and, with luck, maybe some photos that will help you get a feel for the climbing and spot route-finding difficulties. Unless you already know the area, you'd hope to find guidance about campsites, the availability of water, and other amenities. You'd drag out your own USGS topo maps (or fire up your mapping software) and look for additional guidance and a sense of the terrain in the area.

Compiling and analyzing all this information ("beta" as climbers call it) will give you a basis to decide if Widow Maker Peak will be interesting and appropriate to your team's skills—and who should be on the team. It'll also help you decide what equipment, clothing, and food you'll require. Perhaps your partner would be uncomfortable with the "exhilarating exposure" one trip report describes, so you'd want to bring a rope just in case. A trip report may suggest a rope would be useful for rappelling parts of the descent even if not required for the climb up. A rope could be the heaviest thing in your pack, so you wouldn't want to bring it if adequate beta could help you rule it out; simply knowing that someone rated the route Class three isn't enough. And any time you carry a rope, every member of the party must carry a few extra items that make for safe rope use. Same story for crampons, ice axe, helmet, and other items that may or may not be required for a Class three climb or its approach.

The class ratings, although expressed in terms of techniques and whether hands or ropes were used, also suggest the degree of difficulty presented by the climb. Climbing on the route could involve low fifth-class moves, but in context the climb could still be rated third class because the exposure is minimal, and the hard sections are short. Realize that many characteristics of the route can each have dimensions from trivial to terrifying, but the route could still fit a Class three appellation. In sum, the route could be anything from a boring trudge that doesn't justify wasting a weekend to an epic that leaves you benighted far from the trailhead late on a cold Sunday night. It's up to you to know what decisions must be made and to gather the information necessary to make them wisely—and carry extra weight if your beta is incomplete.

What about Fourth Class?

Historically, fourth class meant that a rope was used but not intermediate anchors; the leader climbed without meaningful protection, and the second climbed while belayed from above (on a "top rope"). This style of climbing originated in the days when ropes were short and weak and had no energy-absorbing capability; pitons had not yet been invented, and carabiners were unknown. That was long before modern, easily placed and removed anchors, strong webbing, and longer ropes—it was an era that spawned the maxim "the leader must not fall," because doing so would also

---

pull down every climber tied to the rope. There's no reason to use this anachronistic and unsafe technique today, even on snow. Intermediate anchors, in addition to providing safety, also direct the rope around obstacles and allow longer pitches; they protect the belayer as well as the leader.

The implication is that there's a gradation in degree of difficulty, exposure, and use of protection as the class rating changes from third to fourth to fifth, but there are no definitive demarcations. At least, that's my opinion. In third-class climbing, the rope would be used rarely, seldom for belaying the leader, and usually only for a short distance—an exposed move or two, a chossy or iced-up section, or if a member of the party didn't feel up to the challenge. Fourth-class climbing would mean using a rope by most parties somewhere on the route, but intermediate anchors would be few and would be placed when convenient or mainly to protect a difficult or exposed move. Fifth-class climbing would mean that the climbing moves, while not necessarily more difficult than in fourth-class climbing, would be more continuous, as would be the exposure; intermediate anchors would be placed more regularly, with the expectation that they might be called upon to protect a leader's fall. Any of these situations would require competence in belaying and constructing anchors. Much of mountaineering lies in a gray area between technical and nontechnical, but third- and fourth-class climbing is not merely incompetent fifth class.

Any time you tie into a rope, the decision-making challenges go up by an order of magnitude compared to third class, even if the difficulty of individual climbing moves doesn't. Fourth-class climbing can entail all the technical complexity of fifth-class climbing. In particular, any time a leader is being belayed, anchors must be built with skill, no matter what the climb's rating might be. Leaders must be competent climbers, comfortable with exposure—the main incentive for a rope on fourth-class pitches. To climb fourth class you'll need to know how to belay, how to set up secure anchors, how to place appropriate protection for you and your partner as you climb, how to move expeditiously on rock, ice, or snow, and how to conduct safe rappels.

When you plan for a fourth-class climb, unless you're absolutely convinced otherwise by very solid beta, you know you'll have to carry a rope and you'll likely use it. From that you know that you'll also carry a harness to tie in to the rope, slings to establish belay anchors at least, carabiners to clip in, and shoes suitable for more serious climbing—and more. You might also expect increased routefinding challenges and the possibility of increased objective hazards, compared to third-class climbing. You also know that whenever you tie in to a rope, you'll eat up time. Maybe you conservatively figure an hour total per roped pitch. More weight, more stuff, more time.

On the other hand, a competent climber may elect to ascend some fourth-class pitches with the simplest rope system of all: no rope. Indeed, many skilled climbers will choose to solo selected fifth-class pitches and stretches of alpine ice for which others would set up belays. Most climbing crags have a low fifth-class route that better climbers refer to as the access gully, and they just scramble up and down it. Every mountaineer constantly balances risk against reward; if you climb with others, their decisions as well as your own will impact your safety and likelihood of success.

For third-, fourth-, and easy fifth-class alpine climbing, it isn't the difficulty of the movement on rock or ice that presents the main adversity. The challenges come from all the complex judgments, mountain hazard management, technical skills, and interpersonal skills that are necessary to complete a safe and enjoyable climb. They're what I'll focus on throughout this book.

9

Your Climbing Rope

There is no more familiar icon of mountaineering than a coil of rope. Carrying a rope, and using it proficiently, marks your transition from hiker to climber.

THE BASICS

Exploring the considerations involved in choosing a rope for mountaineering is a good introduction to the technical aspects of climbing. Making the choice isn't especially easy. Most ropes are made for rock climbing—they're called "general purpose." A few rope models are designed for gym climbing or guiding or ice climbing. Your best choice for mountaineering will take a little thought, an understanding of what's implied by the various rope specifications, and an appraisal of your own objectives.

Kernmantle

All modern climbing ropes, and cordage, too, have what's called "kernmantle" construction, meaning that they're made of a twisted core covered by a braided sheath, both made of generic nylon fibers. The core fibers are steamed to make them shrink up then twisted into inter-twisted strands, giving the core the effect of a damped spring, which is what gives kernmantle ropes their energy-absorbing capability. The sheath, accounting for about a third of the rope's weight, mostly protects the core and makes the rope run more smoothly, but without the sheath the rope would barely hold a single test fall. The sheath can be made looser or tighter, thinner or thicker, and woven in different ways to achieve desired trade-offs between abrasion resistance and suppleness.

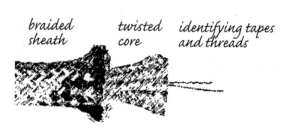

braided sheath   twisted core   identifying tapes and threads

Kernmantle construction.

Dynamic/Static

The first distinction you'll encounter is between dynamic and static ropes. Many years ago climbing ropes had no ability to absorb energy, with the result that a serious fall could result in the breaking of anchors, climbers' bodies, and very likely the rope. The UIAA (that's Union Internationale des Associations d'Alpinisme, of which the American Alpine Club is a member) long ago set an upper limit of 12 kN (kilonewtons, or about 2,700 lb.) for the force a rope could convey, because they figured this is the maximum that a climber could survive. Dynamic ropes must have enough energy-absorbing capability so that they deliver no more than 12 kN in a worst-case fall; this means they can be used for lead climbing, the only time a fall of such severity might occur. Static ropes, better called semi-static or low-stretch ropes, are designed for caving, rescue, rappelling, canyoneering, hauling, expeditionary fixed lines, top roping, gym climbing, and, if you believe me, glacier travel and a few other applications where falls won't be serious. They have about a third the stretch of dynamic ropes and deliver up to twice the fall force, making them unsuitable for lead climbing but OK for many other purposes. Climbers have been taught to look at static ropes the way chickens look at snakes—as if merely touching them might cause a fatality. In actuality, semi-static ropes should be acceptable for falls having a fall factor of about 1 or less, which is nearly all falls (much more on fall factors in Chapter 11). Static ropes are not only less stretchy than dynamic ropes but, partly as a consequence, they're also less prone to abrasion damage. Static ropes were once easy to spot: they were mostly white. Standards now require static ropes to be monochromatic with simple color stripes; dynamic ropes can be as gaudy as you like.

Cord and Webbing

Accessory cordage also has kernmantle construction but isn't necessarily designed for stretch; in fact, the makers brag about low stretch. Cordage certainly has some stretch, but it isn't specified—only ultimate breaking strength. Climbing webbing doesn't have the kernmantle spring effect built into in its construction, but 100 percent nylon webbing still has significant stretch and energy-absorbing capability, comparable to static rope. Though you know it's there, don't bet your life on energy-absorbing stretch from the cordage in chock slings or cordelettes, or from your webbing runners. There is virtually no stretch or energy absorption in webbing made with the fancy new high-strength fibers, such as Spectra/Dyneema.

SINGLE, HALF, TWIN

The next distinction you'll encounter for dynamic ropes (I'll skip over the two distinctions of static ropes) involves their mode of use. The most common mode in American climbing would be as a *single* rope, meaning that climbing, belaying, and other applications use only a single strand of rope. Ropes intended and tested for use as a single rope are marked on their end bands with ①.

Halves for Double

Ropes for the next most common mode are called half ropes; they're used for double-rope technique so were once also called double ropes or doubles. They're used in pairs and are clipped into alternate anchors, after the first. The claimed benefit of double-rope technique is that wandering climbs can be made to have less rope drag, and that both ropes are unlikely to be cut simultaneously by rock edges or rockfall (or the wayward ice axe). Falls on half ropes tend to be softer than on single ropes, but somewhat longer. The soft fall is not so much because of the more stretchy ropes, but because it's harder for the belayer to grip the rope that's holding the fall while also gripping the other rope that isn't—resulting in a more dynamic belay (more slip at the belayer, therefore a less forceful stop). Half ropes are marked at their ends with ① — a circled ½—and they are tested a bit differently than single ropes.

Twins

The most uncommon mode in the United States, thought to be a good solution by committed mountaineers even though unavailable at Return

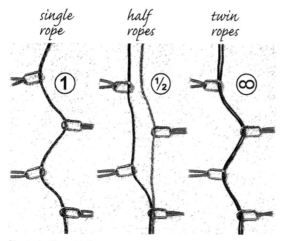

single rope

half ropes

twin ropes

Single, half, and twin ropes.

Every Item, is using two specially designed skinny ropes in exactly the same way you would one single rope: clipping both ropes through every anchor. The benefits include the ability to make full-length rappels without bringing another rope and less likelihood that both ropes would be accidentally cut at the same time (an event that has never been reported in the history of climbing). Ropes made for this mode are called twin ropes and, curiously, are marked at their ends not ②, but ⑧. Twins provide the highest safety margin. A pair weighs about as much as the heaviest single rope but less than a pair of half ropes. Falls on older twin ropes tended to be somewhat harsh unless the belayer let out a bit more length on one of the ropes; newer models have brought forces down to the level of singles. Twin ropes, like half ropes, are designed to be used as a matched pair. Best not to mix brands or types.

On the subject of end marks on ropes, you may encounter others. A ⓒ designates ropes intended for canyoneering (rappelling down a watercourse). Unless you need a low-stretch rope that floats, don't bother. You may also encounter ⓞ on ropes meant for touring/mountain walking (whatever that is); these tend to be very light, short, and not intended to take significant falls. End bands may also show the length of the rope in meters, the technical standards that it meets, the manufacturer, and other details.

You may see standards abbreviations on ropes and other hardware. The mark C€ (Communauté Européenne or Conformité Européenne or just an abstract logo, depending on whom you believe) isn't intended as a mark of quality; instead it indicates that the product's manufacturer claims compliance with applicable directives (eurospeak for standards). These can include certain requirements for quality and performance and, in the case of "personal protective equipment to protect against falls from a height," safety. Climbing hardware products must have the mark to be sold in Europe. The number following the mark indicates the test facility, not the directives or standards that the product claims to meet, so you may find different products with the same number, or similar products with different numbers. The CEN (Comité Européen de Normalisation or European Committee for Standards) issues EN (European Norm) standards specific to the type of product and which may have any number of safety, performance, and testing requirements. The EN standard for dynamic climbing ropes, for example, is EN 892. The UIAA standard 101 is comparable. The UIAA mark is sometimes printed inside a little mountain-shaped logo. You may also encounter reference to ISO 9000. This is a paperwork standard that doesn't indicate quality or performance but signifies that the manufacturer's processes, including quality testing, are well documented. It suggests that the manufacturer has its act together overall. You'll increasingly see ISO 14000 certificates, indicating the manufacturer implements and documents an acceptable environmental management policy.

WHAT SPECS ARE UNIMPORTANT?

What rope specifications are important to mountaineers? We can start with those that aren't important: claimed diameter, falls held, elongation, and breaking strength top the list. Total weight certainly is important to a mountaineer, as you'll probably carry the rope on your back a lot farther than you carry it while actually tied in. This favors a thinner, shorter rope; modern manufacturing can produce thinner ropes with adequate strength by reducing sheath thickness, but that results in more abrasion damage and shorter life. Climbing ropes that see a lot of falls (those used in sport climbing, for example) tend to age (get stiff and lose strength, which happens first near the ends), but general mountaineering ropes seldom take hard falls. If you're taking hard falls in the mountains, you've either made an inappropriate choice of hobby, or you're engaged in advanced alpine rock climbing and should be reading another book. Mountaineering ropes tend to suffer most as the result of abrasion damage to the sheath; this doesn't harm the core until it becomes obviously severe. Reducing abrasion damage suggests a fatter (and heavier) rope might be best. Fat ropes generally have thicker sheaths; they stretch less and therefore rub back and forth less against the stone, while rappelling, for example.

How Phat Is It?

Diameter is the most commonly quoted, though least reliable, rope specification. The number is basically a marketing tool, and the actual diameter varies widely from the one quoted, even for ropes from a single manufacturer. You can't even easily measure diameter yourself, because ropes aren't perfectly round, certainly not after they've been through a rappel brake. Anyhow, a tenth of a millimeter is only about 0.004 inches—a hair's width. Since all ropes are made of nylon fibers, a better way to see which one is fatter is to compare their weights per length. This is given in grams per meter (g/m) and tends to be accurate, though I suspect the ropes are weighed when bone dry to avoid the several percentage points of water weight that "dry" nylon absorbs from air. A heavy single rope will weigh about 80 g/m, while a light (i.e., thin) rope will come in closer to 55 g/m; some half ropes approach 40 g/m and twins 35 g/m (climbers refer to such ropes as "dental floss"). Unfortunately, you can't simply multiply by the length and end up with the rope's total weight, because manufacturers generally cut their ropes from several percent up to 25 percent longer to account for shrinkage after the rope gets wet; naturally, the amount of extra length is unspecified and unpredictable.

Falls Held Rating

Falls held is another unimportant specification. For single ropes, it refers to the number of factor 1.78 falls holding an 80 kg iron weight with 2.6 m of rope that can be sustained by the same spot in the rope over a 10 mm edge in a special testing machine under certain conditions. Half ropes are tested individually with a 55 kg weight. Twins are tested together. Got that? If not, don't worry. The exact test specifications have been tweaked over the years to try to make results more consistent between test facilities. Don't expect precision with this very severe test, and don't fret about the reported numbers. Climbing ropes must sustain at least five such falls (12 for twins) to be UIAA 101 or EN 892 rated, which all are. If your rope has seen hard, high fall factor impacts, and you see stiff sections, thin sections in the core, flat spots, or strange kinks then retire it immediately. Otherwise, in typical fourth- or fifth-class mountaineering your rope will never come near this kind of abuse. Five UIAA falls is plenty; more is just icing on the cake and isn't a reliable indicator of strength or durability in actual use—even the manufacturers say so.

Tests have shown that simply lowering a top-roped climber with a belay device substantially reduces the number of test falls that a rope will hold. It only takes the equivalent of a few days of sport climbing to reduce the falls held number by half—and that's without taking any falls whatsoever. The lessons would be 1) use old ropes for top roping and reserve your new rope for leading, and 2) rappel off the top anchor of sport climbs instead of being lowered. Few climbers actually follow these suggestions.

In a more reassuring test, the UIAA simulated sport climbing leader falls so that exactly the same point on the rope was stressed over and over (that's unrealistically severe, despite what you might conclude from watching sport climbers). The rope held well over 200 falls. Halfway through it was severely flattened and blackened by the top carabiner, and eventually it broke its sheath before failing altogether. The main stress that mountaineering ropes undergo comes from rappelling, and even though rappelling will cause the rope to lose falls held strength, nobody agonizes about this effect, and you probably shouldn't either.

Rope Stretch

How about elongation? There's dynamic elongation, which is the maximum percentage stretch in a factor 2 test fall. Static elongation is the percentage stretch with the 80 kg weight at rest. Elongation is measured only on the first drop with a new rope; after that the rope gets progressively less stretchy with successive hard drops, and its energy-absorbing ability (the very reason we use dynamic ropes) decreases. Dynamic stretch is a roundabout way of getting at the impact force. The greater the dynamic elongation, the gentler the fall will be (as felt by the climber and also by the belayer and rope anchors), but more stretch will make the fall longer. Single ropes stretch to about a third longer under test conditions that simulate a serious fall; 40 percent is the maximum dynamic stretch allowed by the UIAA, so some ropes probably come close to that figure. That's 40 feet of stretch in a 100-foot section of rope. You've noticed this effect if you've seen a top-roped climber take a fall on the first moves—a gentle fall on a long rope can let the climber hit the deck even with a tight belay—a reason for using static ropes for top roping or gym climbing. The main danger to a falling mountaineer isn't being jerked to a halt in midair by the rope; it's smacking into something beforehand. Dynamic ropes have static stretch, sometimes called working elongation, of less than 10 percent with an 80 kg weight. Diameter, elongation, and falls held are all a balance of compromises (or optimizations, if you prefer) in rope construction.

Breaking Strength

What about the ultimate tensile strength—the force it would take to actually break a rope? This isn't often given for dynamic ropes, although it is for static ropes, webbing, and accessory cord. Breaking a dynamic rope would be like trying to break a screen door spring by pulling on it. You'd have to do a lot of pulling—essentially destroying the spring—before you got close to actually breaking it. If you must know, a climbing rope will hold around 30 kN (the range is about 5,500 to 7,500 pounds of force); that's certainly the strongest link in the safety chain and nothing to worry about. The UIAA says no modern climbing rope has ever been broken by fall forces alone—the complicity of a sharp object is required.

WHAT SPECS MATTER?

OK, then, what rope parameters *are* important to mountaineers?

Impact Force

Take a close look at impact force. That's roughly the maximum force a new rope will transmit to a climber in a factor 2 test fall—the worst case. Modern single ropes and twins show less than 10 kN; half ropes less yet. Now you can see why ultimate breaking strength is unimportant: if the maximum force you could apply through the rope in a worst-case fall is less than half the rope's ultimate tensile strength, the rope won't be broken by fall forces.

Ropes that show lower impact forces in the test machine tend to produce more gentle falls in actual use—where fall factors average less than 0.3. This means lower peak forces on climbers and, just as importantly, lower peak forces on climbing anchors. A rope that starts out with a low force rating is especially important to mountaineers and trad climbers because in many circumstances friction on the rope through intermediate anchors and against rock will reduce the effective length of rope that's absorbing fall energy and reducing fall forces.

Cut Resistance

Another standard reports a rope's ability to resist being cut when stressed over a sharper edge than the 10 mm edge that simulates a carabiner in a fall test machine. The argument could be made that by specifying a 12 kN maximum impact force, the UIAA has shifted the main rope safety issue from impact force to the ability of the rope to resist being cut by a sharp edge—that's the rationale for this new test (UIAA 108). Tellingly, single ropes for which this specification is reported show only one or two falls held. One fall is the minimum that will pass, but the test is optional, hard to reproduce, and therefore controversial; as I write, the UIAA has suspended its use. At the moment the designs that allow passing the test make ropes either unusually stiff (because of added internal fibers) or unusually soft (to absorb lots of energy).

Feel of the Rope

Another important characteristic is the "hand" or suppleness of the rope. You'll spend a lot of time handling your rope, tying and untying knots in it, and belaying with it; a stiff rope is simply less fun to deal with. Manufacturers sometimes report knot diameter (the hole inside an overhand knot with a 10 kg weight on the rope). Smaller numbers suggest the rope is easier to bend, but the truth is that you have to actually handle ropes to make a judgment on feel, even when comparing different models from one manufacturer. You may also encounter a specification for sheath slippage on the core; nearly all modern ropes quote 0 percent.

By adjusting all the variables of rope construction—sheath percentage, sheath tightness, braid patterns, core twists, core heat shrinking, and secret sauce—manufacturers produce ropes that are optimized in various ways, including weight, durability, impact force, falls held, suppleness, and so forth. Except for the secret sauce, the final results come from trade-offs that affect all manufacturers in much the same way, so knowledgeable mountaineers can select ropes with the best balance of characteristics for particular applications, though no one rope will be truly universal.

Dry Treatment

In addition to the structural characteristics just mentioned there is also the matter of "dry" treatment. Think of it as a silicone (or Teflon) treatment to inhibit water take-up—or think of it as marketing hype. The UIAA found no differences when they soaked ropes at length, and only a few treated ropes actually repelled water in the first place. Some manufacturers treat the core fibers as well as the sheath and call such ropes "extra dry." The treatment eventually loses whatever effectiveness it might have as the rope is used or gets wet (or washed). At least one manufacturer claims that a reaction process makes their treatment permanent, but all treatments are trade secrets without standard tests for durability or effectiveness, so it's hard to say. Wash-in products are available for retreatment, but they cost about $25 per application.

If your rope gets soaked, perhaps as it's dragged across a sunny snowfield, and then freezes solid when it gets into the shade, you'll certainly wish it had a brand new dry treatment that actually worked.

The main benefit of keeping a rope dry is avoiding an increase in weight and an attendant loss of strength. The weight gain can be more than 50 percent, so you could easily end up carrying more water in your rope than in your water bottle. UIAA tests show that a soaked wet rope (but surprisingly not a frozen rope) loses about 60 percent of its falls held strength, and a considerable amount even if the rope is only slightly wet—even for ropes claiming a dry treatment. Thankfully, the strength returns when the rope dries. Dry treatments are also claimed to make ropes last longer due to reduced grit uptake and they may make ropes more supple and a bit stronger because the fibers slip around each other more easily. Such claims are in the category of secret sauce. There's an urban legend that the wax-based carrier commonly used in the United States to apply dry treatments retains more dirt in the rope than the solvent used in Europe, so new American-made ropes may tend to turn your hands black more than imported ropes. Weird.

RECOMMENDATIONS FOR MOUNTAINEERING ROPES

Your climbing rope is the key component of the safety chain—the whole system that includes slings, anchors, belays, and even your climbing partner—that protects you from disaster. Having absorbed the technical stuff presented so far, you can knowledgeably balance the trade-offs and select the rope that will work best for you, but here are my recommendations:

Stay Single

If you already have a 10.5 mm, 50 m (160 foot) general purpose climbing rope and don't want to invest in another just yet—fine, go with what you've got. It'll do everything you need it to; it'll just be on the heavy side (about 8 or 9 pounds). If you have a 60 m long, 11 mm rope (about 10 or 11 pounds) you could even use that; just expect a little difficulty getting it in and out of some belay devices, and be sure your partner carries it. Sixty-meter ropes are becoming common, maybe even necessary, for new sport routes, but sport climbers hate fat ropes. Guides, for whom durability in constant use is critical, may favor fatter 11 mm ropes.

Thin Is In

If you're going to be using your rope only for third- and fourth-class mountaineering, consider a 50 m dry-treated half rope used as if it were a single. Using a rope for a purpose for which it isn't intended requires some explanation and cautionary warning. The bases for this choice are lightness (about 5 or 6 pounds) and your determination not to take falls on it, certainly not big falls, or it'll be relegated to early retirement. For easy slips on rock or long slides on snow, a half rope meets the requirements and is a common choice among mountaineers. When tested as a single, half ropes hold several test falls; that's certainly adequate for basic mountaineering, where the main use will be rappelling, hopefully not catching big falls. A similar option would be one of the new lightweight single ropes that approach 9 mm and are intended for expert sport climbing. Though heavier than a half rope and far more expensive, you'll have the comfort of knowing that they're intended for use as a single rope, even though they barely pass the five falls held test. They're lighter because the sheath is made thinner, so they're less durable. Ropes with decent durability and feel along with a light weight will be developed, and at least one, the spendy Mammut Revelation (9.2 mm, 55 g/m), seems to be there now. Skinny ropes require extra care and technique when belaying or rappelling, as they won't produce as much friction through mechanical belay/rappel devices as do fatter ropes (Mammut ships a Matrix belay/rappel device with each Revelation); there's more on this in Part 6, Advanced Techniques. No one deliberately climbs in the rain, but opt for the slightly higher cost of a dry-treated rope if you anticipate using it on snow or ice or if you want some hope that being caught in a mountain storm won't soak your rope.

When selecting ropes for lightweight climbers (120 pounds or less) or belaying kids, focus on half ropes used as singles. This will better match rope parameters to the weight of the climber. Fatter ropes mean harder catches for light climbers.

Short Is In, Too

If you're feeling bold, another choice would be one 70 m half rope (you may have to shop around to find one) cut in half. After carefully melting down the cut ends, you'll have two 35 m (115 foot) ropes—each a low-cost, sub-4-pound solution that's plenty long enough for most mountaineering. A few manufacturers even offer lightweight 30 m (100 foot) ropes. Mountaineering routes, except for those on snow and alpine ice, are seldom vertical, invariably wander, make for poor communication, and often include traverses. Long pitches can become almost impossible because of rope drag through broken terrain. And long pitches are rarely necessary for general mountaineering. Neither are long rappels, which become an invitation to causing rockfall and ropes getting stuck when pulled down. So why carry a long rope? The claim is that a longer rope might allow more options to reach or set up a belay, but many experienced mountaineers carry a 30 m rope quite happily for fourth-class and low fifth-class routes; even a 25 m (80 foot) rope isn't uncommon. That's because these mountaineers have found that the additional weight of a longer rope isn't worth it for the climbs they encounter. If your partner carries one of the halves and you the other, you can use one 35 m rope for almost everything; use two together in half-rope mode on a tricky fifth-class section or for crossing the bergschrund; and join the two for rappels that will be longer than you could make using a single 50 m (160 foot) rope. Some climbing shops carry discounted short ends left over from making standard length ropes.

One exception to the shorter-is-better thinking might be if you anticipate long routes on alpine ice or snow where you'll actually belay (as opposed to simul-climb, where shorter ropes are adequate if not preferable). In such a case, having a longer rope and being able to use the entire length (having enough protection hardware, for starters) could reduce the number of pitches and therefore speed up the climbing, going up and going down. Longer rappels can save time and increase your options in certain situations, particularly over snow and ice. This scenario might also apply to steep glacier climbing, but not to unbelayed glacier hiking, where even short ropes are often shortened further in the course of roping up. Some climbers might prefer at least a 50 m rope for glacier travel if they anticipate using one rope for crevasse rescue—the only requirement for long rope length on most American glaciers; others might prefer a shorter rope and carry a 7 or 8 mm cord separately to result in lighter weight and greater flexibility.

Increasing Your Options

As your technique, experience, and ambitions develop, you may want to consider carrying a second rope, a skinny one, to increase your options. We're talking very skinny: 6 or 7 mm accessory cord. Experienced climbers frequently use this technique; there's no reason not to consider it, as long as you know what you're getting in to. The motivation is to gain nearly all the additional flexibility of having a second rope, but paying very little weight penalty—100 feet of 7 mm cord will weigh just over 2 pounds. Part 6, Advanced Techniques, explores the benefits and the cautions when using a light cord as part of your safety system.

It Takes Two to Tangle

And that's just part of the problem. The previous recommendations pertain to single ropes. Some mountaineers might wonder about double-rope technique. For most mountaineering and even most alpine rock climbing, double-rope technique wouldn't, in my opinion, be the first choice, or even the second. That statement's bound to raise eyebrows, so I'll offer my reasoning to anyone willing to wade through. If you list the benefits of doubles, most can also be met by twin ropes; many can be met by a single plus a light retrieval line. In other words, the benefits mostly come from carrying the second rope, not from climbing with it. The main problem doubles claim to address, rope drag, is a bit of a straw man. Double-rope technique was developed in an era when

only carabiners were used to clip pro, before long runners became widely accepted. Nowadays, long slings can and should be used to keep a single or twins draped to reduce rope drag, which can then be less than using half ropes. On irregular mountaineering climbs using double-rope technique, you often find yourself climbing some distance on just one of the half ropes, in which case you're essentially relying on a half to perform like a single while you drag the other like a haul line. A route that seriously wanders will be a drag any way you lace it, and few routes actually involve moving far left, placing pro, moving far to the right to place pro, moving back left, and so on. Longer slings are more generally effective at reducing rope drag on wandering routes, and they also help control pull on placements from undesirable directions. Sport routes should have their bolts located to minimize rope drag, and with it any benefit of using half ropes.

More importantly for most mountaineers, double-rope technique is complex and thus unwelcome, and the mountain environment makes it even more so. Consider a typical pitch: the belayer must sort out two piles of rope and keep them separate and untangled; you can use a single pile, but that invites tangles and exposes both ropes to the same rockfall. Good rope management at belays is essential to climbing expeditiously; doubles make that harder, even if you're smart and use two rope bags. The leader begins climbing and soon clips to the first, solid anchor with both ropes (to prevent a factor 2 fall on the belay). The second should now offer about 10 percent more slack on one of the ropes, to avoid high forces on the leader and first anchor, should he take a fall on both ropes simultaneously. When the leader reaches the next clip, he'll call out "Red!" or whatever color rope he intends to clip (a good reason to avoid black half ropes—rhymes with "Slack!"); the second will feed out on this rope to give enough slack for the leader to make the clip, while locking off the other rope in the belay device. After the clip, the leader resumes climbing, and the second will take in the rope that was clipped, while feeding out the other until the leader passes the clip, whereupon the second must feed both ropes simultaneously, but not necessarily equally. This prestidigitation is made extra difficult if Münter hitches are used for belaying, whether on a single carabiner or two, and whether belaying the leader or the second. Try it, you won't like it.

Throughout the pitch, the leader must constantly think about how the ropes have been clipped, or the rope drape may become more zigzagged, rather than less, and drag will increase. For example, if the red rope is clipped first on the right side, then to the left, then to the right, it will incur more drag than if always clipped to the right, but this isn't always easy to sort out when climbing mountaineering routes, especially along with looking for pro placement opportunities, taking care to keep both ropes outside both your legs, and minding the other chores of leading, such as hyperventilating and cursing. Good communication between leader and second must be maintained throughout the pitch; if it's somehow impaired, by rock obstruction or wind noise, for example, this whole process devolves into exchanges of profanity and insult, as in "Slack on the *other* rope, you moron!" When the leader belays the second up, she must also diligently take care to keep the ropes untangled while taking them in at different rates.

One other specious benefit often proffered for doubles is that the leader can give the second better protection on a traverse. For this to be the case, the leader must belay the second from high above the traverse, but while crossing the traverse and climbing to that higher stance, the leader will be effectively leading on only one half rope. This special case really doesn't deserve notice; besides, good anchor placement using singles and twins also solves the problem.

It's true that practiced climbers can learn to deal with the complexity of double-rope technique. The question would be, why bother? The insurance provided by doubles is only against an agent serious enough to cut one rope but not both (a crampon might fit that description, though it turns out that stabbing a rope with a crampon doesn't weaken it much at all). Half ropes stretch substantially more than singles and are thinner, making them slightly more likely to be individually cut during a fall and less resistant to abrasion. Twin ropes provide comparable protection against

two simultaneous rope failures, and modern twins have moderate fall forces but much higher falls held ratings than halfs. Twins are much lighter than doubles and compare favorably to a light single plus additional haul line or rappel retrieval cord. My opinion is that double rope technique persists mainly because climbers are creatures of habit; it will eventually disappear, to be replaced by single-rope technique for most forms of climbing except for serious alpine and mixed routes, where twin ropes will increasingly become the experts' choice. End of rant.

HANDLING AND CARING FOR YOUR ROPE

Your first chore will be uncoiling your new rope. It comes to you without twists, so if you simply start using it, you'll create one twist for every loop in the original coil. Instead, put your hands through opposite sides of the coil and unreel it onto the floor by cranking your forearms around, same way you'd uncoil a skein of yarn.

Flaking It Out

I have no idea where the term "flaking it out" came from—mariners, you can be sure. It simply means putting the rope into a neat pile bit by bit and, in the course of doing that, taking out all the knots, tangles, and twists. This ritual is essential each time you use the rope, lest you find yourself distracted by tangles in the middle of a tense situation. If you're flaking out the rope to set up a rappel, try starting with both ends at once and flake the rope into two piles simultaneously so you finish holding the middle point.

MOUNTAINEER'S COIL

There are three methods of coiling your rope. The first is, unfortunately, called the *mountaineer's coil*. Picture a burly guy in lederhosen with a big coil of hemp line across his shoulder and you've got the idea. There are any number of ways to make this coil, including coiling the rope in one hand, wrapping it around widespread bent knees, and wrapping it around a knee and a foot. Usually, the rope is coiled doubled, starting at the free ends and working toward the middle. When you've got the rope almost all coiled, fold back the finish end (the middle of the rope) to create a pair of loops, and follow the illustration below to finish the dress that ends up tightening the loops to secure the ends. Most people also tie the middle loop and free ends together with a square knot.

The benefit of a mountaineer's coil is that you can throw it over your head and one shoulder, even with a pack on, and Bob's your uncle, as the Brits might say. There is, however, one serious downside: the mountaineer's coil twists the rope. This isn't a matter of technique, it's just a fact that every turn around the coil unavoidably creates a 360° twist. Twists will turn the coil into a stack of figure eights, or if you managed to carefully remove the twists as you made your nice, neat coil, the rope will become twisted when it's uncoiled, same as a brand new rope. Because of the twists it causes, thoughtful climbers never use this method; flaking out the twists and kinks is simply too troublesome and time consuming.

With one possible exception: when new-school climbers tie into a rope for hiking on snow, alpine ice, or glaciers, they typically attach with only part of the rope length between them, then one or both of the end climbers coils the remainder. That coil wants to be readily accessible, so the mountaineer's coil is a reasonable option among several, and the length of rope that must be untwisted is relatively short. Some would argue that getting a mountaineer's coil over their helmeted heads is awkward, and having a coil of rope hanging over all the other paraphernalia glacier hikers need

to tie onto themselves is just too annoying when there are better options; include me in that list.

BUTTERFLY COIL

The *butterfly coil* avoids twists because it lays the rope back and forth rather than wrapping it around and around. One popular method is to lay the doubled loops around the back of your neck; this makes it quick and easy to get a neat coil, even in wind, rain, or darkness. There are various ways to secure the loops using the ends of the rope, depending on the way you'll carry it. One method uses the ends to create shoulder straps and a waist belt, allowing the rope to be carried like a miniature backpack.

That's the issue with the butterfly coil: how to carry it. If you're already wearing a pack, the "mini-backpack" method can be awkward; it may even come undone after you clamber around. You could also just tie the rope to your pack. Some packs have straps at the top specifically for this purpose; the coils lay sideways across the top of your pack, under the top pocket if you're using one. Some climbers attach the coils to their packs with the straps intended for securing a sleeping pad; they look bedraggled after the rope shifts around from an hour of hiking. Because it doesn't twist the rope, the butterfly coil is preferable to the mountaineers' coil—just sort out the carrying style that suits you best and finish the coil accordingly.

BAG IT

Then there's the third method, the new-school method. Though it's uncommon among moun-

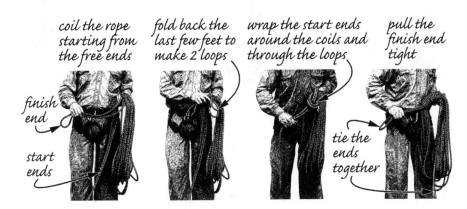

coil the rope starting from the free ends

fold back the last few feet to make 2 loops

wrap the start ends around the coils and through the loops

pull the finish end tight

finish end

start ends

tie the ends together

Finishing a mountaineer's coil.

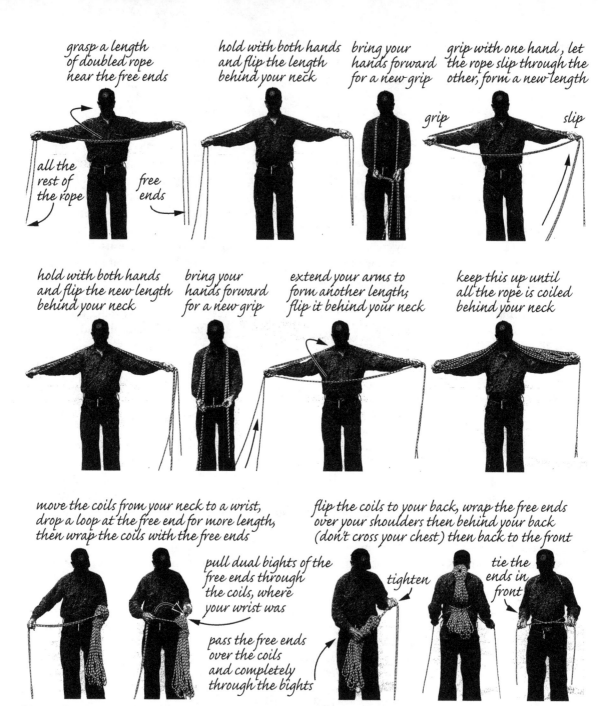

grasp a length of doubled rope near the free ends

hold with both hands and flip the length behind your neck

bring your hands forward for a new grip

grip with one hand, let the rope slip through the other, form a new length

grip

slip

all the rest of the rope

free ends

hold with both hands and flip the new length behind your neck

bring your hands forward for a new grip

extend your arms to form another length; flip it behind your neck

keep this up until all the rope is coiled behind your neck

move the coils from your neck to a wrist, drop a loop at the free end for more length, then wrap the coils with the free ends

pull dual bights of the free ends through the coils, where your wrist was

pass the free ends over the coils and completely through the bights

flip the coils to your back, wrap the free ends over your shoulders then behind your back (don't cross your chest) then back to the front

tighten

tie the ends in front

Tying and finishing a butterfly coil.

taineers, it is, of course, the one I recommend: bag it. That's right, just put your rope in a sack. You can use a basic store-bought rope bag, which will have the optimum longish shape, waterproof fab-

ric, a drawcord end closure, maybe a full-length zipper, and some attachment points. Sport climbers use bags that open up to make a sheet that keeps the rope off the ground, but these have too many heavy features for mountaineering. You can also just use a plain old stuff sack. Get one with a longish shape in the smallest size that fits, like one for a small tent. The benefits of sacking are many: you don't have to coil the rope at all, just stuff it in. Well, stuff it in carefully and let the working end peek out; that way the rope won't get knotted, and you won't have to flake it out—just pull the rope out of the bag as you need it—belay out of the bag! That saves the time needed for coiling the rope and flaking it out. Better yet, your rope will be protected from dirt, rain, snow, solar UV radiation, and the errant boots of your clumsy partner. It'll be easy to attach to your pack (lower, like a sleeping pad, or higher, across the top), and your rope can't get knotted and twisted. Use the bag as a means of keeping the rope tidy at belay stations. The only down side is the few additional ounces of weight, but I sometimes use the rope bag as a pillow or a butt pad for sitting on snow, so it can do multiple duties—always a plus for mountaineers.

For any of these options there's an underlying requirement: carry the rope in such a way that you can access it quickly and easily. Make sure that you can get it out if you end up face down in an arrest position or hanging in a crevasse—even upside down. You don't want the rope stuffed deep inside your pack just when you, or someone in your party, decides they really need a rope now!

Keep It Clean

When your rope comes into contact with rock, sand, or dirty snow, it picks up grit. When you use your rope, that grit works its way into the rope's fibers and will eventually weaken it. That's one reason ropes are so sacrosanct with climbers. Just step on someone's rope if you want to be given a thorough dressing down; even my dog understands this and takes extraordinary measures to avoid stepping on a rope.

Keeping your rope clean means washing it. Some climbers think of washing their rope as an biannual, cosmetic ritual, but that doesn't cut it. Cavers, whose whole world is cold mud, rinse out their ropes at every opportunity, even while down a cave. Mountaineers should do the same. If your rope gets dirty, and there will be an opportunity to dry it, rinse out the rope in a creek. You can squeeze the dirty water out by running the rope through a belay device under a little tension; that also works for getting water out of a rope that was accidentally soaked. Otherwise, resist the temptation to preserve its dry treatment, and wash your rope any time it looks dingy or you know it was dragged through dirt. Washing will also remove the aluminum that carabiners leave on your rope, and that will help keep black marks off your hands and clothing. Some rope manufacturers even wash ropes to condition them before they're performance tested. Here's how: forget advice about needing a front-loading washing machine or a mesh bag to prevent tangles. Finding a big mesh bag is a problem, and it'll mean a large weight swinging around on one side during the spin cycle. Simply bunch up your rope with a *lineman's coil* and throw it into any old washer. Pull the ends through the last loop to keep the coil from unraveling in the wash. Tying a lineman's coil takes less than a minute and results in an easily washed mess that won't tangle in a washing machine and that can be untied instantly by pulling out the ends in the terminal loop.

Wash your rope in cold water with a small amount of ordinary laundry detergent; there's no need to use special soap, although Sport-Wash would be ideal, but definitely don't use bleach. Run it through two rinse cycles or more if you see lots of foam in the rinse water. Don't leave soap or detergent in the rope fibers because that will encourage water adsorption. Use liquid fabric softener in the final rinse. Fabric softener? Sure—it may be a very bad idea for your pile and waterproof clothing, but it makes your rope more supple; tests show it also increases a rope's life.

Finally, dry the rope by laying it in loose loops where it's out of the sun and gets good air circulation. I wouldn't recommend extraordinary means of drying a rope or storing it in a location where it'll be dried by heat. Manufacturers warn against using a hot clothes dryer. Be sure the rope is thoroughly dry before you put it away; that could take several days in New Orleans. Dampness won't damage the nylon, but it could support mildew

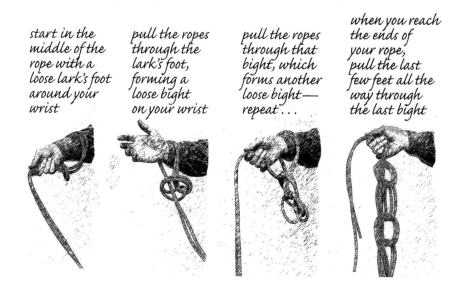

start in the middle of the rope with a loose lark's foot around your wrist

pull the ropes through the lark's foot, forming a loose bight on your wrist

pull the ropes through that bight, which forms another loose bight— repeat . . .

when you reach the ends of your rope, pull the last few feet all the way through the last bight

Tying a lineman's coil.

growth. Even if you use fabric softener, your freshly washed rope will be a bit stiffer than usual at first, and it'll be about 5 percent shorter, too (a loss of about 7 feet for a 50 m rope). This shortening increases the strength and reduces the impact force, so it's not a disaster—and the length returns as the rope is worked. Your rope's "dry" treatment may become less effective, but your rope will have no loss of strength.

Avoid Damage

Speaking of damaging the rope, what else might cause that? Other than physical damage (your partner stepping on the rope with crampons would be a good example), nylon is attacked by acids, but it's fairly resistant to salt, gasoline, grease, and oil. It's also unaffected by chemicals common around a campsite, like stove fuel, Gatorade, mosquito repellent, and alcohol. If you get some gas or sunscreen on your rope, just wash it thoroughly. If you get auto battery acid on your rope, even diluted, it's best to retire the rope; acid damage can be invisible and has accounted for more fatalities than have healthy ropes broken by climber falls. Vinegar is also an acid that will attack nylon. Ultraviolet light from sunlight will degrade nylon and make it brittle, but the sheath keeps UV off the rope's core; nevertheless, keep your rope

out of high mountain sunlight (in a rope bag) whenever possible.

The Telltale Mark

Another potential cause of damage is using a felt marker pen to mark the middle of your rope. The mark could save time when setting up a rappel or let you signal the leader at the halfway point. There's some controversy about this. One manufacturer sells a pen specifically for the purpose. Tests by other manufacturers find that any brand of pen they tested, including those sold for rope marking, caused around 50 percent lower falls held when the mark was put right on the loading edge of the test machine. That's enough evidence for me: no middle mark pens. No word on whether ordinary fabric dye, which works well on nylon, could be used to mark the middle, but you'd think it would be OK since the sheath fibers are already dyed. If you really want a middle mark, an option would be a rope having a pattern change in the sheath to indicate the middle; some ropes even have pattern changes to indicate the last 5 meters at the ends. Rumor has it that some of these ropes soon develop bulges in the sheath where the pattern changes. Pen marks can be hard to find in fading light so at least one manufacturer marks the middle with whips of brightly colored thread that can be felt as well as seen; a few climbers use that method, too, even though they must replace the thread from time to time. You'll feel a hesitation when such a mark goes through a belay or rappel device. Don't use tape; you might not notice if it slips, and you could rappel to the end of one side prematurely. The middle mark serves mainly as a reassurance that you haven't screwed up and made one side appreciably shorter than the other; don't hang the rope from rappel slings or rings at exactly the same spot on the rope every time to avoid accumulating stress at one small point.

When to Let Go

Finally, there will come a time to put your old rope out to pasture. Mark it or cut it to be sure it won't accidentally get put back into service (or braid it into a cool doormat). To wear a $C\epsilon$ mark, products must have a stated lifetime. Rope manufacturers puzzle over this, but usually say 3 to 5 years. Some tests suggest ropes lose about 2 percent of their tensile strength per year, even if not used. In actual practice, it's not the age of a rope but the amount of use that determines its life (and death). Indeed, the most likely cause of rope failure is high-tension abrasion over an edge; that will cut a rope surprisingly quickly. Unused and properly stored, a rope could last decades. Tests on 25 year-old ropes show that they will hold at least one test machine fall; in other words, they would not likely be broken by actual use. This isn't a recommendation to use ancient ropes. Not only might they be unsafe, but rope technology has come a long way in 20 years; an early 11 mm kernmantle rope may have done well to hold three test falls.

Mountaineering ropes are unlikely to experience hard falls, but if yours does, carefully examine it for irregularities in the core and retire it if you find any flat spots, skinny spots, or lumps. Dump it if the sheath is cut or worn enough for the core to become visible, even slightly. The most likely wear a mountaineering rope will experience is fuzzing up the sheath due to abrasion on rock or multiple Münter hitch rappels; that alone doesn't mean the rope has been seriously weakened. Ultimately, you may just want to replace your rope because it looks ratty enough to scare your climbing partner, and you're longing for a colorful, new, confidence-inspiring rope.

10
Equipment for Rock Climbing

*I once believed that man is unique
among animals because he alone is a maker
of tools. Then I discovered that other
animals also make tools; man is merely
unique in his dependence on tools.*

You've probably already noticed that your local outdoor shop, mail-order catalogs, and Internet sites are bulging with all manner of climbing paraphernalia. It's a natural human tendency to acquire as much of this stuff as possible, even absent any conceivable use. Fortunately, for mountaineers (and their spouses), their necessary and useful equipment list is relatively sparse. Some of the items I'm going to mention are out of the ordinary and may be hard to find; American shops may not carry them, and some magazines have a policy of not reviewing equipment that isn't handled by mainline distributors. You have only to step into a climbing shop in a large European city, or check their Web sites, to discover there's a much bigger world out there.

I'll begin by repeating my worry about discussing the features of a piece of equipment before describing its use or, equally unsavory, discussing its use before most of its features have been laid out. As a compromise, I'll discuss equipment first but focus on uses rather than features. While I struggle, don't get bogged down. Feel free to keep moving ahead, even if some points aren't perfectly clear, and refer back to this section when you read the subsequent chapters on forces, anchors, rappelling, and climbing, where the equipment gets put to use. The equipment described here pertains to basic technical rock climbing as it arises in general mountaineering; equipment for wilderness backpacking is covered later, in Chapter 18.

CLIMBING HARNESS

Gone are the days when it makes sense for mountaineers to carry only a rope and expect to attach themselves to it using a "bowline on a coil." You can check Appendix A, Additional Skills, to see how that's done, but it's another of the old-school "skills" that should never come into play if modern climbers are playing heads-up ball. Any time a rope is carried, even on a third-class climb, every member of the party should at a minimum carry a 48-inch open runner and an HMS carabiner. Smarter yet would be to also carry an alpine harness.

Diaper Seat

If your only uses of a rope are certain to be limited to short, nonvertical rappels or for security on easy ground, a diaper seat harness is certainly adequate and can readily be made from a long sling. You wouldn't want to take a leader fall with one or hang for very long, but strength and security are not issues. Form your perfectly sized diaper seat from a custom-tied runner made of 1-inch webbing; the closest commercially sewn sling length will be 48 inches (120 cm), or maybe 44 (110 cm) if you can find one. The following illustration shows how to arrange such a sling to make a diaper seat.

As with all other harnesses, test your diaper seat construction skills and runner length by hanging in it to confirm that your center of mass is properly supported and there's no tendency for you to get turned upside down, even while wearing your climbing pack. Note in the illustration that a short runner has been used both to extend the rappel brake and to avoid triaxially loading the carabiner (loading from more directions than the

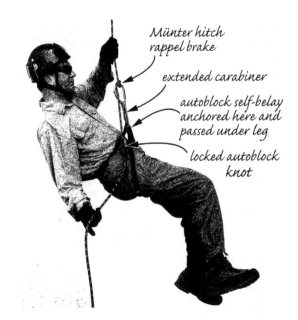

Hanging in a diaper seat.

end-to-end orientation for which carabiners are designed).

Alpine Harness

If you're going to go near a rope very often, you should invest in a commercial mountaineering or alpine harness. It isn't expensive or heavy, and you can use it as a rock harness while you're learning to climb. Pick a model that doesn't require stepping through leg loops to put on, as rock climbing harnesses do. This will eliminate most models, but a

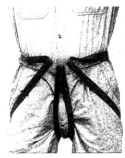

diaper seat harness improvised with a 56-inch runner

back view

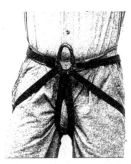

simply clipping loops cross loads the carabiner

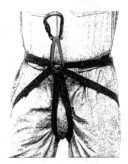

use a 12-inch runner to hold the loops and extend the carabiner

Diaper seat improvised climbing harness.

few good choices remain, all intended specifically for mountaineering. The reason for this requirement will become apparent if you try to put on a conventional climbing harness wearing heavy boots, crampons, or snowshoes. Good for humorous hopping exercises and a face plant; unsafe in the mountains, where you may find yourself deciding a harness is needed only after you encounter precarious conditions. A climbing harness's waist belt (sometimes called the "swami") invariably closes with a buckle that requires being doubled back. Different harnesses do this differently, so be sure to follow the manufacturer's instructions; also learn how other models work so you can check your companions every time you rope up. Alpine harnesses are specifically designed to facilitate dropping the leg loops; work out how you will execute a biobreak or add pant layers while remaining tied in to the rope, one way or another.

You may at first be dismayed by the absence of a belay loop on alpine harnesses. If one were used, it could make it impossible to remove the leg loops without unbuckling the harness. Strangely, some people are paranoid about using the belay loop if their harness has one, yet it's the strongest component of the harness. Its purpose is not just convenience; it prevents untoward loading of the large locking carabiner that is part of the typical belay system. A belay loop isn't really a requirement, but it's a good idea to use it for belaying and rappelling because it extends the HMS carabiner away from possible tangles in clothing around your waist and allows the carabiner to move around to line up with applied forces while being prevented from being pulled far to the side of the swami. A alternative is to create your own belay loop by cinching a 1-foot runner through the leg and waist belt loops where you'd normally tie in to the rope; this will give you a strong loop that's a bit longer than a conventional belay loop—exactly what you'd want for rappelling and belaying while wearing bulky clothing.

An alpine harness will have no padding, the assumption being that your clothing will provide all you need, which won't be much because you'll avoid falls, hanging, and protracted hanging belays. Padding just adds to the bulk of layers of clothing and backpack waist belt around your middle; it will make you more likely to sweat there and may freeze when you stop sweating or encounter cold precipitation. Use shoulder slings to supplement your harness's gear loops if you're carrying more than a few items or if your pack's waist belt interferes. Never use gear loops to attach yourself to anything, and never use the haul loop in back, if there is one, as a tie-in or belay point, even if the one on your harness is rated at runner strength, as it should be.

BELAY/RAPPEL BRAKES

There are three types of belay devices worthy of consideration: none, a simple plate or tube device, and one of the new devices having an autoblock mode.

No Device

I'm not talking about old-school hip belays and the Dülfersitz rappel; I'm referring to uses of the Münter hitch—a skill set that belongs in the repertoire of every mountaineer. You'll find considerable detail on the Münter hitch when it gets put

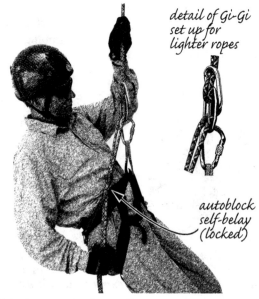

detail of Gi-Gi set up for lighter ropes

autoblock self-belay (locked)

Alpine harness set up for rappelling.

one of many ways to cross-load or triaxially load a carabiner–bad

better; the big end carries the most loops

best; the carabiner is extended and resists being wrong-loaded

The wrong way and better ways to load a carabiner; note the handy 12-inch runner.

to use in Chapter 13. With a Münter hitch, you can rappel or belay using only the rope and the HMS carabiner you always carry—or most any other carabiner in a pinch—whether you're using single ropes, halfs, or twins. Some mountaineers, especially in Europe, use a Münter hitch as their principal means of rappelling and belaying, but it isn't as familiar in the United States. Climbers have almost come unglued when I've used a Münter hitch belay at sport climbing crags. The essential skills of using a Münter hitch also serve as backups when you drop your hardware or encounter challenging circumstances, and there are many instances where it's the tool of first choice.

Plates and Tubes

This category is the most common among the many commercially available devices. All plates and tubes work the same way, creating friction (i.e., amplifying the force of your grip) by forcing the rope to snake through them and around the big locking carabiner with which they work. The most popular today, certainly the best marketed, is probably the Black Diamond ATC. BD has introduced a new model with an incredibly original name, doubtless suggested by Bill Gates: ATC-XP. It provides a second mode with additional friction for use with smaller ropes or for rappelling with light single ropes or heavy packs. The ATC-XP

joins several competitors making similar claims, all of which are asymmetric, meaning that if you get them turned around you'll have more or less friction and stopping power than you expect. At least one model has been miniaturized specifically to be used with skinny twin ropes, when normal belay/rappel devices provide insufficient resistance; it tends to overheat when rappelling. If your belaying and rappelling requirements are modest and infrequent, you can shave weight and complexity by using one of the simple fat plate devices (alpine plates)—or just use a Münter hitch.

Autoblock Devices

Autoblock means that these devices can be rigged to automatically lock off a belayed seconding climber; they also allow two seconds to be belayed up independently at the same time if you have two

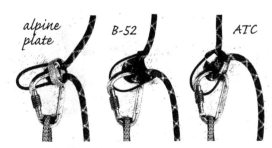

alpine plate   *B-52*   *ATC*

Common belay/rappel brakes.

strands of rope—a great time-saver when there are three in a party. Use these devices normally for belaying the leader; that's not what the autoblock mode is for, and autoblock doesn't mean a hands-off belay—these devices aren't like the heavy Gri-Gri belay contraption, or the Trango Cinch for skinnier ropes, popular with sport and gym climbers, that's supposed to automatically lock the rope in the event of a leader fall. Confusingly, the oldest of autoblock devices is called a Gi-Gi; it's just a small plate with two slots and carabiner holes at either end. In autoblock mode the rope from the second goes in at the top of a slot near the hole where the anchoring carabiner is attached; it then goes around a second carabiner behind the plate, out through the same slot below its entry point, and into the belayer's hand. Should the second fall, the rope will pinch into the slot, trapping the holding side of the rope and locking off the second; the belayer can then tie a safety knot in his end of the rope and take photos, deal with tangles, or in general be less attentive. Both hands are needed to take in rope, and you absolutely must always hang on to the belay rope, just as with other belay devices, until the autoblock function locks the rope. Bringing up a second using the autoblock can be handy, a bit like using a Münter hitch belay (which tightens firmly but doesn't lock); however, releasing the autoblock is challenging, unlike the Münter hitch. A Gi-Gi has lots of clever uses, including rappelling, belaying the leader, ascending, hauling, and adaptation to thinner ropes; you just need to work them out and commit them to memory. Plenty more to come on using the autoblock function.

There are other belay/rappel devices that can be used in autoblock mode, including the Petzl Reverso and Reversino, the Cassin Più or GTC, the New Alp Mini or Magic, the Mammut Matrix, and the Trango B-52. These can be anchored by a single carabiner, like the Gi-Gi, but Trango says the B-52 should be used with two identical anchor carabiners (three total) when belaying two seconds at once; you can use two opposed nonlockers. I'll confess that I've used my B-52 with only a single anchor biner, and even with two 8 mm ropes, it seems to work just fine for both seconds. If you intend to frequently belay two seconds in this manner, you may want to search out a Kong Gi-Gi; it has a ridge on one side that helps a bit to separate activities on the two ropes, and it's easier to release from autoblock. The Matrix is specifically designed with thin rope features as well as the autoblock option and the helpful little ridge on the back. In all cases, use an autoblock carabiner with a simple oval cross-section; the ropes will run smoother with less unwanted friction.

All these devices, autoblock or not, can be used as a tube or plate device. The Petzls and B-52 are nicely smooth when rappelling or lowering another climber—superior to conventional tube or plate designs, where the typical pattern is for too much friction at the start of a rappel and too little at the end. Using them in autoblock mode makes it easier to winch up the second under tension, a technique that can speed up climbing when aesthetics is secondary (i.e., mountaineering). Neither are symmetrical, but the force required for the B-52 to hold a fall remains manageable if you happen

Autoblock belay/rappel devices that work with thin ropes.

Matrix

Gi-Gi

Reversino

B-52

The term *autoblock* has two uses in climbing. It refers to the property of a belay brake device that allows it to be configured so that tension on the rope to a seconding climber (or climbers) will jam the belay rope and hold it. This will hold the fall of a seconding climber but isn't intended to hold leader falls or to be used hands-off. *Autoblock* also describes a knot and setup used to automatically hold the rope below a rappel brake, locking it in the event the rappeler's grip fails (a self-belay); the force multiplication effect of the rappel brake means that a weak knot suffices, one that can be released by pushing on it without taking tension off the rope. *Autolock* is the property of specialized mechanical belay brakes, such as the GriGri and Cinch, which strongly grip the rope automatically in the event of a fall, including leader falls; some climbers, particularly lazy sport climbers and aid climbers, use these devices hands-off.

---

to flip it around. Claims that the B-52 has lots more holding power than an ATC in normal mode aren't supported by my own measurements; the difference is small when simulating a leader fall catch. When flipped, the B-52 does offer a more dynamic catch, and it's far easier to get a frozen rope into it than into an ATC. Compared to the Reverso, the B-52 offers both smoother rappels and significantly more holding power on small ropes, when the Reverso requires about twice the grip force on the part of the rappeller (so use a Reversino instead). Like the B-52, the Reverso can be flipped to result in two degrees of braking or used with two carabiners to add more resistance (about 40 percent more, same as most other rappel

brakes). Petzl's instructions discourage using the Reverso with ropes smaller than 8.5 mm in adverse conditions or when belaying two seconds in autoblock mode; that's what the newer Reversino is for. The Reverso can get scary at the end of a skinny rope rappel, very scary on a single skinny rope, so I prefer a B-52 or Gi-Gi, but the Petzls have ardent fans, too, and I suspect the Matrix will pick up adherents as it becomes better known. If you're planning to use ropes that are 9 mm or smaller, be sure to thoroughly test your belay and rappel techniques under full loads, and use an autoblock self-belay setup when rappelling, as detailed in Chapter 13.

Finally, read the manufacturer's instructions carefully (you may have to work out the details of complex little cartoons). It requires special skill and more than a little strength and agility to release an autoblock to lower a second who's fallen and who's putting tension on the belay. On easy ground or when the second can ascend the rope, this may be only a small problem, but it's not something you'd want to try to work out for the first time in the middle of a serious climb. There are detailed instructions later.

Devices to Avoid

Many common belay/rappel brakes were designed before the advent of thinner ropes, modern techniques, and emphasis on lightweight equipment. Don't even consider a figure-eight belay/rappel device, even if you were given one as a stocking stuffer as a kid; they're too heavy, twist the rope big time, don't provide sufficient stopping power on light or single ropes, can convert accidentally to a

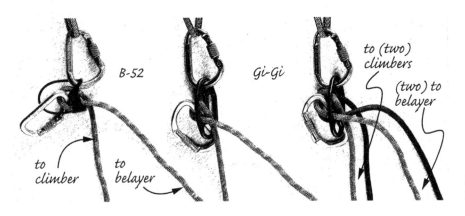

to climber   *to belayer*   B-52

Gi-Gi

to (two) climbers   *(two) to belayer*

B-52 and Gi-Gi belay brakes in autoblock mode.

lark's foot lock up, and can twist around so that they wank their carabiner's gate. Also, forget the classic Sticht plate, with spring or without. These products were advances in their day, but that day has passed. Definitely don't consider carabiner brake contraptions, but not because they put excessive force on carabiner gates (an uninformed myth); it's just far better to use a single carabiner and a Münter hitch. You'll certainly encounter old-school mountaineers who treasure these legacy devices and defend them mightily; just smile with sympathy.

HELMET

You may have come across the spine-tingling photos showing Alex Buber soloing a 2,000-foot overhanging face on the Tre Cime in Italy's Dolomites—38 continuous pitches of climbing up to 5.12. Wow! In the photos you can see that he's climbing without a rope, and you can also see that he's wearing a helmet. When asked about this apparent incongruity, he replied that it would be far too dangerous to climb there without a helmet, because of rockfall potential on the upper pitches. Lesson well learned, from someone who's intimately acquainted with danger.

Every active sport has its specialized helmets, and the smarter practitioners wear them. Climbing has two general types. One type is designed to protect your head if it smashes into the rock. The other protects your head if rocks smash into it.

The first variety is light, generally made of rigid foam with a thin plastic shell, and offers side as well as top impact protection. These helmets tend to be "single incident" devices, however; an incident can be a climbing fall or a thoughtless toss of your pack. These helmets are favored by rock climbers on routes where rockfall is not a problem because they're light and have streamlined shapes that look trendy in photos. As far as I know, none can withstand more than a single test impact measuring protection from rockfall, and many won't even do that after a few years of normal use. If you wear one, be sure the rockfall that nails you contains only one rock.

The other helmet variety is basically a thick plastic or fiberglass bucket that fits on your head with a strap suspension system designed to spread out the force of impacts and to continue to do so after years of hard use. These helmets are heavier than the "bicycle helmet" variety, 16 ounces compared to 12, but they're much more durable. They have the potential to be cooler in warm weather, depending on their ventilation design. This type of helmet is favored by mountaineers, despite the possibility of lessened protection from side impacts, because they're more durable and offer superior protection from rockfall. There's one model that's not only lightweight but survives many more of the top-impact tests than other helmets because it's made of carbon fiber and Dyneema fabric. As you might imagine, it costs about twice as much as other models. I've put patches of special shock-absorbing foam on the lateral insides of mine.

As a sensible mountaineer, you'll probably pick a helmet of the latter type, or maybe one of the models that's sorta in between. Thereafter, the most important consideration, once you've addressed weight and stylish color, is fit. Select the appropriate helmet size and be sure you adjust the retention straps correctly; when that's done well, a self-inflicted whack from any direction won't cause the helmet to move around on your noggin. It's amazing that you can see in climbing magazines, among the small fraction of climbers who are photographed actually wearing a helmet, many who don't have theirs adjusted correctly. Don't be one of them; it looks really stupid for serious climbers to wear their helmet far back on their head. Do be among those who apply a bit of reflective tape to the front and back of your brain bucket, to make yourself easier to spot by headlamp during those alpine starts (or post-sunset stumbles back to camp).

CARABINERS

Your first carabiner selection will be the big pear-shaped HMS locking carabiner that you use with or as your belay/rappel device. Pick a model that has personal appeal for you; you'll be fondling this one a lot, and your life will hang on its performance. You'll sometimes have several slings and knots tied to this biner, so get one of the larger sizes. Large pear-shaped models are the only aluminum climbing carabiners designed specifically to have multiple things connected to them. A big circular arc at the top makes for smooth double-rope rappels by loading both ropes evenly; avoid models with more asymmetric big ends, which don't. That should also buy you a larger diameter on the rope-bearing surface, another contribution to smoother rappels; just make sure you can fit it through your autoblock belay/rappel brake; not every model will fit through the slots in a B-52, for example. Seek out a nicely swinging gate with a smooth screwlock that you think you'll like when wearing gloves on cold fingers.

This is a good time to introduce the difference between *strong* and *secure*; it comes up often. It may be counterintuitive, but screwing down the gate of a locking carabiner does not make it stronger, it just prevents the gate from opening accidentally, thus making the carabiner more secure. Locking carabiners have a little play in their gates when screwed fully shut, to allow the gate to be opened deliberately when body weight is loading the carabiner. Carabiners bend a little even from just body weight; without a little play, the gate screw might bind so tightly while you were hanging on the biner that you couldn't open the gate to add another sling or clear a rope. That wouldn't be good, so standards require gates to open with 0.8 kN (180 lbf, or pound-force, which I'll explain later) applied. If additional weight is applied or the carabiner is subjected to the force of a fall, the body of the biner will bend several millimeters

match 'em   flip either one

Back-to-back biners.

more until the free end of the gate locks into its catch; this prevents additional bending and accounts for the much higher closed-gate strength compared to open-gate (when the test is performed with the gate deliberately held open to simulate an accident). Nonlocking carabiners also allow their gates to be opened with a body weight load, thus the reason for using lockers at critical points. Don't be paranoid about having locking biners everywhere. Certainly at your waist or at busy belay stations where there is lots of rope, slings, and traffic, but otherwise nonlockers, especially wire gates, are adequately secure. You can always use two non-locking carabiners back-to-back to get more security for twice the weight.

An option if you want a locker in an emergency but don't have one is simply to use tape from your first-aid kit to tape the gate shut and prevent it from opening accidentally. If you wisely abandon a carabiner at a rappel anchor to make the ropes easier to retrieve, just put a Band-Aid on the old biner you found in the parking lot to turn it into a locker.

For the general-purpose carabiners you select, pick ovals or near ovals. Their larger size and symmetrical shape makes them functional in every application, and throughout this book you'll see examples where oval carabiners, straight gate or wire gate, work effectively where more radically shaped, asymmetrical carabiners would function poorly or not at all—another illustration of the importance of equipment versatility to mountaineers. Avoid tiny carabiners with narrow cross sections and asymmetric shapes, however seductively light they may be. Wire gate ovals are comparably light, but mountaineers carry so few carabiners that weight

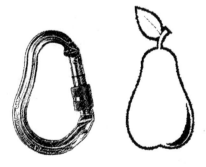

Pear-shaped HMS carabiner and inspiration.

isn't a critical issue—versatility is. Carabiners with lighter wire gates are reputed to be less prone to unintended gate opening when the biner is jerked around or vibrated by a fast-moving rope, and they're also less prone to being surreptitiously held open by packed snow or ice. The wire gate design has a long history of reliability in marine hardware. Although it doesn't seem so, wire gate biners with straight spines can even be used to make carabiner brake rappel devices, but don't use them in a way that puts a rope or sling in contact with the gate—the gates are plenty strong, but the narrow wires could damage the nylon. Start out with at least as many carabiners as you have runners; a dozen, say. In your starting collection, include a couple of small, lightweight locking carabiners of any shape.

Carabiners, even wire gates, have moving parts that require maintenance. They pick up grit in their hinges, gate screwlocks, the spring-loaded pusher pins inside solid gates, and even the pivots of wire gates. In your maintenance routine, first examine your carabiners for burrs that may come from minor gouges or hinge pin imperfections; remove these with fine sandpaper or a file lest they snag your rope and runners. Soak your dirty biners in hot soapy water and brush their moving parts with your partner's toothbrush. Rinse them in hot water and allow them to dry. (Personal confession: I just run mine through my dishwasher with hand soap.) Squirt the hinges, gate screws, and pusher pins with Kroil (the best choice, and the best kerosene-type, light oil lubricant), WD-40 (that's WD for Water Displacing), or a very light silicone lubricant, and then towel off as much as possible as you exercise the gates. If you haven't done this in a while, give it a try; you'll be impressed at the improvement it makes in the crisp action of your gear. Do not use a heavy oil, wax, paraffin, or dry lubricant such as those recommended for bicycle chains; this is definitely the wrong application for such products, and they'll gum up your carabiners (and cams)—that could result in sticking parts and dangerous performance.

RUNNERS AND SLINGS

The options are runners sewn or tied from nylon webbing in full or narrow widths and open runners sewn from narrow webbing that combines nylon with high-strength fibers (Spectra or Dyneema, same difference). Old-school mountaineers are very familiar with 1-inch tubular webbing, either Mil-spec or the stronger "climb spec" material. This webbing is sometimes made into commercially sewn slings, but more commonly mountaineers tie their own, usually using a knot that I believe the climbing world can and should do without. I might as well digress to discuss the water knot, beer knot, and double fisherman's knot.

The *double fisherman's knot* is technically a bend because it joins two cords. A double overhand knot on another cord is very secure, but even when tightened firmly it'll still slip along the other cord until it hits a stopper knot; it is, in fact, a slip knot. It also makes a great stopper knot. If two double overhands are tied back-to-back on each other's cord, each forms the stopper for the other, and the resultant knot (OK, bend) is very secure. The double fisherman's knot is actually two double overhand knots tied back-to-back. Don't think that the *single* fisherman's knot is weak—it's the knot that manufacturers use to test chocks with user-tied slings, and these are plenty strong, often rated stronger than the wire cable versions of the same chocks. The double fisherman is one of the most useful knots for a climber. It's not only strong, in that it causes a minimal reduction of strength compared to the cord without a knot (all knots cause a reduction in strength to some degree, the double fisherman loses an unusually small 20 percent), but it's also very secure. So secure, in fact, that it becomes difficult to untie once it has been loaded, especially if wet.

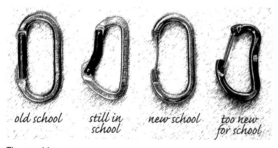

old school   still in school   new school   too new for school

The carabiner crew.

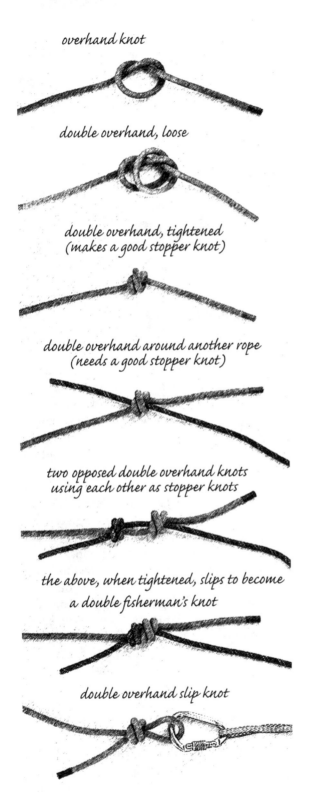

overhand knot

double overhand, loose

double overhand, tightened
(makes a good stopper knot)

double overhand around another rope
(needs a good stopper knot)

two opposed double overhand knots
using each other as stopper knots

the above, when tightened, slips to become
a double fisherman's knot

double overhand slip knot

The overhand knot and the double fisherman.

The double fisherman's knot is exceptionally secure, but always leave extra cord hanging out. How long tails should be is endlessly debated; technically, a length of only three times the diameter of the cord is necessary for complete strength (of any knot), but this seems too short to allow for possible shortening due to tightening and mishap. Better to leave six to ten diameters; ten is what chock manufacturers suggest. Old-school climbers insist that the knot must be tied so that the two overhand knots snug together, and the turns appear to form a continuous spiral, as illustrated, but the actual strength is unaffected if one of the double overhand knots doesn't match the other, so long as each is tied correctly. Learn to tie the knot neatly if there's time, but if time is of the essence and you get it backward, don't bother fumbling around for cosmetic perfection.

The double fisherman's knot, er, bend, is used just about anywhere climbing cords, even webbing, need to be joined—of the same or widely different diameters (which may now make sense to you, given its progenation). It works especially well on the narrow nylon webbing I favor. It's used to make cord slings for protection hardware, to make cordelettes, and in some cases to join ropes prior to making a double-rope rappel. It works as well in webbing as cord, and it's the best knot to use for on-the-climb joining of a webbing sling to make a rappel anchor. (Don't use flat webbing for climbing; only the more common tubular webbing will result in high-strength knots.)

The *water knot* (aka tape knot, ring bend, and rethreaded or retraced overhand knot) is also familiar to climbers, most commonly for joining webbing. It has none of the virtues of the double fisherman's knot. It's not particularly strong, losing 50 percent or more of the webbing strength and resulting in a loop that's less strong than a single strand. Neither is it secure; every expert recommends checking water knots frequently for two reasons. First, the knot doesn't self-tighten, so it can loosen just by rough handling. (Try this demonstration: tie a water knot in 1-inch webbing. Now roll the knot around between the palms of your hands, maybe wearing gloves to get some friction. The knot will disintegrate before your eyes.) Somehow this tendency to loosen is bizarrely perceived as a virtue—in case you ever want to untie it, the knot is way ahead of you! Second, if lightly loaded and subjected to repeated tugs, the water knot will creep and eventually untie itself—such loads are exactly what occur to a rappel anchor. I think it's crazy to use a knot with such credentials, especially when better options are available. Old-school climbers don't dispute the negatives, but somehow they really cling to this knot—better the devil you know, I suppose, than learn something new. If you must use it, leave very long tails and be aware that taping them down doesn't make the knot stronger or more secure. Better yet, learn a better knot (bend).

The *beer knot* will be the bend of choice when new-school climbers tie runners from 1-inch (25 mm) webbing. The beer knot is strong, keeping about 80 percent of the webbing's strength, same as the double fisherman. It's also secure; it self-tightens so it doesn't fall apart like a water knot, and it doesn't creep. A beer knot that's been soaked in water and tightened under body weight will be difficult to untie, but certainly not impossible; untie it to open a runner and then close the runner with a double fisherman's knot if you need to secure a webbing loop around a terrain feature to create an anchor.

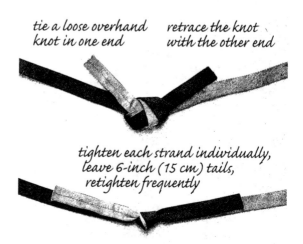

tie a loose overhand knot in one end

retrace the knot with the other end

tighten each strand individually, leave 6-inch (15 cm) tails, retighten frequently

Tying a water knot, if you must.

Recommended Runners

Mountaineers starting out with a new-school attitude should first look at commercially sewn 100 percent nylon runners; these are readily available if you search, and they're more reliable than tied runners, even using a double fisherman's knot (the only choice for tying runners in skinny webbing). In nylon, sewn runners aren't too expensive: less than $5 for a 48-inch (120 cm) runner, half the price of Spectra/Dyneema webbing. Choose 48-inch length (8-foot circumference) runners of narrow, heavy-gauge tubular nylon webbing ($^{11}/_{16}$ inch, 18 mm; or better, $^9/_{16}$ inch, 15 mm, if you can find them). Start with ten (yes, ten . . . well, OK, six and four of 24-inch, 60 cm length). Also include one 12-inch (30 cm) runner—lots more on this handy guy later. This is the maximum number you would carry; never carry slings you know you won't use. Modern nylon webbing is plenty strong and plenty durable (a $^9/_{16}$ sewn runner can test over 20 kN, but maybe not one tied with a double fisherman's knot, and certainly not one tied with a water knot). Sewing works because the stitches and webbing distort under load just enough so that all fibers share the stress; making the sewn area stronger than the webbing itself is just a matter of applying enough stitches of sufficiently strong thread.

Narrow nylon runners save weight and facilitate a number of applications better than 1-inch webbing—and save money, too, compared to

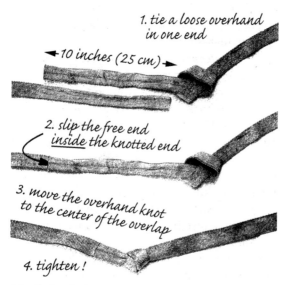

1. tie a loose overhand in one end

10 inches (25 cm)

2. slip the free end inside the knotted end

3. move the overhand knot to the center of the overlap

4. tighten!

Tying the beer knot.

Sooner or later it creeps into the awareness of my climbing partners that I sew some of my own runners—long after they've noticed the beer knots on my 1-inch runners. Sewing your own runners makes them cheap and readily available in whatever sizes are needed. You can also make extra-long or extra-short runners for protection hardware. (Scary as it might seem, protection hardware runners require lower strength ratings than general-purpose runners, and the stitches need hold only about half of that.) There's nothing sacrosanct about sewing runners; what's required is calculating the necessary number of stitches and sewing them uniformly—a burly household sewing machine will do. To calculate the number of stitches, just divide the strength of the webbing by twice the strength of the thread (because there are two threads per stitch), then include a safety factor. Use heavy-duty, DB92 bonded polyester thread, which comes on a spool of about 2,500 feet. If you can find this stuff, know what needle to use, and can adjust your needle and bobbin tensions to sew webbing, you probably qualify to sew runners. I use a buttonhole foot and sew bar tacks, but long patterns of straight stitches along the length of the overlap area have historically tested better, they're just more difficult to sew neatly. Testing is the real challenge. You'll want a loop strength of about 20 kN, that's 4,500 lbf—about the weight of a car, and the limit for narrow nylon webbing. That suggests one way to test your runner design: use a big vehicle to slowly tow a small vehicle with a runner as you lock the small vehicle's brakes. If a runner bursts at the stitches, add more to your design; stitches count more than neatness. Having large-diameter anchors ("bollards" in testing parlance) moves the load to the stitching and reveals weaknesses. Never test any equipment that you'll actually use near its strength limits; that's just for testing your design. Manufacturers proof equipment to half strength; any equipment, commercial or homemade, that has seen loads near rated strength should be retired, with gratitude. All things considered, you'll be impressed by the strength of your homemade runners; hopefully, your partners will be, too.

Spectra/Dyneema. Narrow webbing loads carabiners more optimally; wide runners cause a reduction in the strength of carabiners by causing more force to be spread to the gate side instead of the spine side. This might seem like a plug for the new 8 mm Spectra/Dyneema runners, but I suspect these threads are too specialized for most mountaineers, and too spooky, too (they look like shoe laces). Nylon webbing can be cut and retied, but Spectra/Dyneema webbing doesn't hold knots, so only with pure nylon can you safely open a runner and retie it around an object. Same story with the master point knot of a cordelette-type anchor; don't expect Spectra/Dyneema runners to hold such knots without slipping. Nylon webbing can be used to make friction knots on rope; narrow webbing works best. Spectra/Dyneema webbing is slippery and therefore not recommended for this application; plus, should it slip, its low melting point will likely lead to melted fibers and who knows what else. Spectra/Dyneema webbing will not hold friction knots on snowy or icy ropes; nylon may. A 48-inch runner is long enough to use doubled when you might otherwise have to open a 24-inch runner. Long runners can easily be doubled, tripled, or knotted to shorten them when they're carried. A 48-inch runner is long enough to make a cordelette-style, non-extending connection to two anchors. When setting up snow anchors, such as deadmen, a long runner reduces the tendency for the load to pull the anchor up and out. Although it may require a shortening knot, a 48-inch runner is the shortest standard length that can be used to make a chest harness for glacier travel safety, and it will make a passable ice axe leash in a pinch. A 48-inch runner can be used to tie a Klemheist friction knot and still have enough length remaining to tie a serviceable foot prusik. Finally, it requires at least a 48-inch runner to make an emergency diaper seat harness. All these applications will be covered in detail later. The classic adage is that a mountaineer can never have too many runners, nor can they ever be too long.

Even though I mostly preach the accepted gospel that webbing and accessory cord don't provide energy-absorbing capability the way climbing ropes do, I must confess: they do. At least the nylon versions do; the high-tech fiber versions don't. This is important for the thoughtful mountaineer to realize, but unfortunately, it can't be counted upon. If you actually measure samples of tubular webbing, you find a surprising amount of energy-absorbing stretch, sometimes more than static (low-stretch) climbing rope. Ditto 6, 7, and 8 mm accessory cord. A bit of stretch in webbing or cord might reduce peak fall forces and might help balance forces among static equalized anchor placements that you'll learn about in Chapter 11. The problem is that this property isn't specified or controlled by the manufacturer like the impact force of climbing ropes is. Even though I don't rely on it, I factor it into my decision to prefer nylon

MODERN FIBERS IN CLIMBING GEAR

Ever since nylon 6,6 revolutionized textiles, the search has been on for something better. Strong fibers in the aramid family include Twaron, Kevlar, and Technora. These are two or three times stronger than nylon and are very temperature resistant, but they exhibit autoimmune failure: when repeatedly flexed or knotted, the fibers cut each other, and the cord weakens. Technora holds up three times better than Kevlar, which is disappearing from the climbing market. A newer high-strength fiber is Spectra or Dyneema; these are trade names for the same fiber, produced mainly for nautical cordage. The stuff is technically gel-spun ultra-high molecular weight polyethylene; it has high strength (3.5 times that of nylon), good fatigue resistance, and very little stretch. It has other of polyethylene's characteristics, including a low melting point, resistance to dyes (so it's usually white), resistance to UV radiation, a light weight (it floats), and exceptional slipperiness. Because it's so slippery and won't hold knots, runners made of Spectra/Dyneema fibers blended with nylon are invariably sewn (never tied), usually with Spectra/Dyneema thread. An exception to this is Ultratape, which uses a lower percentage of Spectra with its nylon and polyester fibers and is woven to put the Spectra on the interior; it'll hold most conventional knots. Kernmantle cordage with Spectra/Dyneema in the core must be tied with triple fisherman's knots to avoid the failure mode in which the core slips out of the knot and the sheath then breaks. It's important to note the poor temperature performance of Spectra/Dyneema; it shouldn't be allowed to reach 125 °F (50 °C), or it'll begin to weaken. This could easily be reached in the trunk of a sun-baked black VW or in a dishwasher being used by a lazy climber to wash factory-slung SLCDs (spring-loaded camming devices). Vectran fiber is as strong as Kevlar, melts at a higher temperature than nylon, and will hold knots, but it has poor UV resistance, so it must be incorporated inside sheaths of another material. Its flex fatigue is better than Kevlar, but not as good as Technora. A new fiber in industrial and nautical use is Zylon (PBO). It has the same fatigue and UV resistance problems of most other high-tenacity fibers, but speaking of tenacity, this stuff is second only to carbon fiber. A $\frac{1}{8}$ inch (3 mm) cord tests at 5,000 pounds. Manufacturers are constantly working to maximize the benefits and minimize the down sides of all fibers, using a wide array of techniques including combining them. In the end, for all-around performance, nylon is proving pretty hard to beat.

runners and cordelettes to high-tech versions for most mountaineering purposes.

Carry your runners over your neck and one shoulder, or clipped to your gear rack—be it a shoulder sling or gear loops on a harness waist belt. The method you select depends on whether you want bulky stuff dangling at your waist or whether you want to be waving your arm over your head as you access a sling. On a typical mountaineering climb I often use both methods simultaneously. A 24-inch runner makes a nice length for an over-the-shoulder sling and readily loops between two carabiners to rack and deploy neatly. A 48-inch runner can be doubled and joined with a carabiner to make an over-the-shoulder loop; the carabiner prevents tangles with other runners, and unclipping it allows removal of the runner without swinging it over your head, which can tangle on your helmet or pack or cause unwelcome commotion when leading on steep ice or delicate rock. Crampons strapped to your pack, especially, are magnets for runners that have to be removed over your head and pack; this tangling is amusing only when it happens to your partner.

Even if you prefer to invest in Spectra/Dyneema runners, you should have a few nylon runners, too, for those applications where Spectra/Dyneema runners perform poorly. Some old-school mountaineers carry one very long length of webbing, 20 feet or longer; new-schoolers carry cordelettes instead.

Wearing a 48-inch runner over your shoulder.

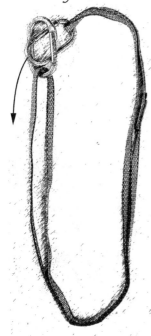

pass one carabiner through the other

with 48-inch runners, make a second pass

to deploy, unclip all strands except one (it doesn't matter which ones you pick) from either carabiner

(it's magic)

clip all four strands

Shortening a sling to rack it.

CORDELETTE

A cordelette is a long loop of cord or skinny nylon webbing. The cord is traditionally 7 mm nylon utility cord, but 6 mm would be fine, too. If someone suggests 6 mm isn't strong enough, ask them how strong it needs to be (two strands of 6 mm cord will hold 16 kN, or 3,600 lbf). An alternative would be 5.5 mm Tech Cord or Gemini2, which have Technora interiors and polyester sheaths. A loop made from 20 feet (6 m) is about right; join Tech Cord or nylon utility cord with a double fisherman's knot. The nylon cord will resist flex fatigue far longer than Technora and is more limber as well as being a third the cost. Six mm cord is especially tactile and can be pressed into use as a serviceable prusik. Like nylon webbing runners, nylon cordelettes have a small amount of energy-absorbing capability that will lower peak forces; Technora cord doesn't. Cordelettes are standard tools for trad climbers, and they're becoming more common among mountaineers. Fifth-class climbers will likely carry at least two because of their utility. Cordelettes are typically used for setting up an anchor with three joined placements, but they can be used any time you need a really long runner. The ones made from nylon cord are so affordable you can leave them behind at rappel stations without regret, and they test almost as strong as those tied with pricey Technora cordage. Make yourself two or three. Or purchase a sewn alternative, such as Web-o-lette, which is just a long piece of Ultratape webbing having short loops sewn into the ends. Carry an additional large locking carabiner that will become the master point of the anchors you build with cordelettes.

It's possible to use a long runner as a two-anchor "cordelette" or an especially long runner as a

A cordelette ready for racking.

conventional cordelette. Using Spectra/Dyneema webbing in these applications is questionable. The slippery webbing won't hold knots, so the knot at the master point of the cordelette's anchor system could slip in the event a component placement is pulled out by a fall, allowing significant extension—or worse.

Daisy Chain

A daisy chain is a specialized runner popular with trad climbers and new-school mountaineers, known to Brits as a cow's tail—curious animistic naming analogies again. A daisy chain is a long runner with secondary stitching that leaves it with little bulged out openings every few inches. Select the short, 45-inch (115 cm) version. A daisy chain cinched to your harness's tie-in points and accompanied by a dedicated, locking carabiner is standard equipment on trad climbs; it should be for roped mountaineers, too, and not only because it holds your alpine harness together. Adjust the length by clipping from one (and only one) of the pockets; they're rated at 3.5 kN (787 lbf; more in Chapter 11 on kilonewtons and pound-force). You'll see constant admonitions not to clip adjacent pockets lest a fall rip out the stitching between them and leave your anchoring carabiner as a free agent. Mountaineers will find a daisy chain and its dedicated biner handy for many uses: for security when arriving at a belay, putting a backpack on belay or connecting it to a glacier travel setup so it can be retained if exited, and as an excellent temporary tie-in until you've checked your rappel setup and are ready to descend. A daisy chain can also be used as a conventional runner, but only full length.

PROTECTION HARDWARE

If you look forward to more challenging roped climbs, prepare yourself with the other necessary accoutrements for building anchors. At some point you'll see a route description with the recommendation to bring a rope and a "small rack." What the heck is that? The meaning is different for mountaineers or rock climbers contemplating a fifth-class route. After the early 1970s and Doug Robin-

don't clip two pockets!

Daisy chain.

son's clean climbing essay in the Chouinard catalog, it no longer meant "a handful of pitons." Today it means at least half a dozen mid-sized pieces of removable aluminum protection hardware: "pro."

Most moderate, roped mountaineering climbs can be protected mostly using long runners. If hand- and footholds are ample, it's likely that opportunities to place pro will be, too. That means that you won't need extremely large pieces, which are heavy, or very small pieces, whose placements are far more difficult to evaluate for security and more difficult for the second to remove. Start out with wired chocks (aka nuts, rocks, stoppers) in the range of finger to two-finger width. My personal preference is to use wired versions in the smaller sizes, but to use chocks with longer, homemade Tech Cord runners in the middle and larger sizes. Tech Cord runners are lighter, can be made longer than usual, and work well enough for maneuvering hardware into place; tie them dog-bone style (with the overhand knots of the double fisherman's knot around both strands) for neater dress. When you make your own Tech Cord runners, you'll confront the remarkable strength and temperature resistance of Technora; I use sharp wire cutters to cut the cord and then cut an additional $\frac{1}{16}$ inch off the inner fibers before pushing the sheath back over the end and melting it with a flame. When you select chocks, start with proven, conventional shapes.

Hexes Are Passive Cams

Next consider hexes (Hexcentrics, Exentrics, Rockcentrics, Quadratics). These are stoppers having irregular hexagonal profiles that can impart a slight camming action if placed properly—pulling on their runners tends to make them rotate and wedge themselves more tightly in place. Some models have curved sides, some straight. Placed endwise, they behave like chocks. Hexes once fell out of favor but are being used more frequently these days as trad climbers rediscover their benefits, and they give confidence to mountaineers, compared to the alternatives, when whacked into icy cracks. Hexes offer the width options of active cams at far lower cost and weight, but it does take skill to place them effectively, utilizing their camming action to best effect. Choose wired hexes (those with factory-swedged wire cable runners) or slung hexes (hexes with attached runners made of cord or webbing). The wired versions can be reached more easily into and out of placement locations, like wired nuts. Problem is they don't readily remain in proper camming position and tend to be dislodged by the rope more easily than the slung versions. Hexes having webbing slings instead of wires are lighter and cam better, but they're more fiddly and fingertippy to place, especially in smaller sizes that fit into placements where your gloved fingers won't. The "slings" can be commercially sewn Spectra/Dyneema webbing furnished with the hexes or user-tied from 5.5 mm Technora cord—a good compromise compared to stiff wire cables. Some users tie or (wink, wink) sew slings that are essentially double length, making an additional runner unnecessary in many cases. Some users tie slings in slightly different lengths to make size identification easier and so that pieces don't bang into each other as much when hanging on the rack.

A good combination is to use wired nuts for placements that are so narrow that you can't readily get your fingers around the pro, and use slung hexes when the placement location is wider and in horizontal cracks. In traditional hex sizes, the most useful would be numbers 5 to maybe 8 (but the bigger ones do make those nice cowbell sounds so familiar to trad climbers).

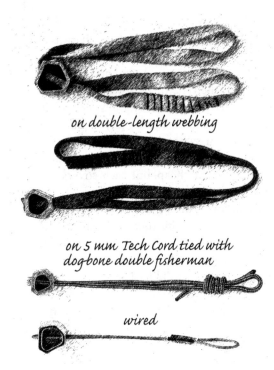

on double-length webbing

on 5 mm Tech Cord tied with dogbone double fisherman

wired

A selection of hexes.

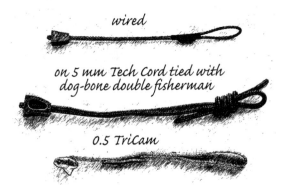

wired

on 5 mm Tech Cord tied with dog-bone double fisherman

0.5 TriCam

A basic selection of chocks.

Active Cams

I know you're just dying to go out and spend your lunch money on some *real* cams: spring-loaded camming devices. Indeed, these contraptions have revolutionized trad climbing by making pro placements quick and easy where they were hitherto impossible. On the other hand, they're heavy, expensive, and unnecessary for most moderate mountaineering climbs. Hexes and TriCams can offer the width options of an active cam at far lower cost and weight. Active cams are not foolproof, or even idiot-resistant; it's just that they work in many places where conventional pro won't. Avoid the extremes of their size ranges and learn to place them to mitigate their profound propensity to perambulate when perturbed. You'll pay as much for a couple of these guys as you will for all the rest of your rack, in both money and heft. If you can't resist, definitely avoid the smaller sizes—those that fit cracks an inch wide or narrower. The reason is the same as for small passive pro: it's very difficult to evaluate whether smaller pieces are placed effectively, and they're much more susceptible to being rendered ineffective by a small crystal on which they were wedged breaking away under the force of a fall. Small cams can also be diabolically difficult to remove. The perfect selection of a particular brand and model will depend on the type of rock where you climb (in limestone, maybe *none* is the answer), but if you're torn, here's my biased view. If you plan to acquire only one or two, consider Black Diamond Camalots. Sure, they're heavier than the competition, and they ain't cheap, but each covers a slightly wider range of placement widths and, more important for beginning climbers, they're a bit easier to remove when inexpertly crammed, fully retracted, into a crack. Moral: you'll burn less daylight trying, or failing, to recover your expensive gadget. If you're building a set of cams for mountaineering, most other modern designs weigh about the same; the Forged Friends, which have rigid stems, are the most affordable, with flexible-stem DMM 4Cams right behind. Start in mid sizes and work your way up, but not too far down. It's even more important than with carabiners to keep these mechanical wonders properly cleaned and lubricated.

Or Alternative Cams

There's another useful pro option for adventuresome trad and alpine climbers: TriCams. These things often work when nothing else will. Where other passive pro works, they work as passive chocks, too. In camming mode they tend to require practice and to be a little fiddly to place and remove, but when you set them, they feel solid, even in a slightly flaring crack or when they're close to the edge of a horizontal crack. If you want to begin experimenting with unconventional pro without the weight and expense of SLCDs, consider TriCams. Start with the #1 and maybe #2. A #2 TriCam has about the same size range as a comparable Camalot active cam, has comparable strength of placement, but is a third the weight and cost. There are climbers, me included, who don't leave the belay without the #0.5, the fabled "pinkie," so called because of the color of its sling, and dear to the hearts of many trad leaders, but maybe not their seconds.

PERSONAL SMALL RACK RECOMMENDATION

Here's what I carry for a small rack. Chocks: Wired #6 Rock (15 x 22 mm); #7 (18 x 31 mm), #8 (21 x 35 mm), and #9 (24 x 38 mm) with Tech Cord slings that I tie extra long. Hexes: #6 Hexcentric (27 x 39 mm) with Tech Cord sling, #7 (33 x 46 mm) and #8 (39 x 54 mm) Hexcentrics with double-length home-sewn webbing slings. Rock sizes are for the classic Wild Country version, and the hex sizes are for Black Diamond Hexcentrics; for some reason manufacturers use non-equivalent numbering systems. That's a total of seven pieces, with the #6 Hex and #9 nut fitting about the same size placements. If you want to add more pieces, first double up on the nuts except for the #9 and add a larger hex; this heads you in the direction of building a "light alpine rack," acknowledging the realities of roped mountaineering while keeping a watchful eye on flexibility and weight. Mid-sized SLCDs can come later. Slung nuts and hexes, especially those with unusually long slings, may not need additional runners in order to prevent their placements being dislodged by the action of a wavering rope, the way pro with wire cables would be. And don't forget that #0.5 Tri-Cam. These eight pieces together weigh just over a pound (0.5 kg).

TriCam in a vertical crack.

As you contemplate that small rack, consider its possible applications. Building anchors comes first to mind, then protecting the lead, then maybe backing up rappel anchors; don't forget that the second may also need to set anchors in the event that a self-rescue situation evolves. When you've become competent placing pro and are graduating to routes where more than a small rack will be required, you can grow your gear toward smaller sizes of wired nuts and to larger sizes of whatever works for the rock you climb—if it's dry rock, that may inevitably include SLCDs, or if your stone of choice is icy, you'll carry TriCams and maybe even pitons if the icy rock is remote. As a mountaineer

with growing ambition, you'll start to select pro on the basis of how it might work for aiding on the routes you look forward to, not because you're specifically looking to do aid, but because Mother Nature might demand it. For alpine climbing, versatility is paramount, even when it conflicts with the other principal criterion, light weight.

But What about Pins?

Ever notice that pins don't have strength ratings like other pro? I wasn't going to go there, but pitons (pins) can be a valuable adjunct to an alpinist's rack, the main pain being the need to carry something (heavy) to bash the suckers in. The objection to pitons is that they dig progressively bigger openings in the rock as successive climbers place and remove them in the same spot. They're considered more acceptable on remote and less-traveled routes, and some ethicists say that once placed they should be left fixed; those ethicists tend to be seconding the climb. If you're going down that road despite protests, here are my recommendations for a small collection that a skilled mountaineer might use in uncertain circumstances: one to four Knifeblades (KBs), one or two short Bugaboos, one or two Lost Arrows (LAs) in whatever size appeals to you while avoiding the largest, and two to four of the smaller Angles. Several manufacturers make equivalents, some in titanium. Pitons require skill and practice to place, just like other pro. Drive them in until the sound they make shows obvious solidity; if the head touches the rock before your confidence level reaches 99 percent, remove the pin and start over. If the head is far from the rock even though the pin rings with strength, consider tying it off with a slip-knotted runner. Stacking pins is beyond the skill set of mountaineers, who should be able to find better and more confidence-inspiring placement opportunities. I'm assuming that you'd carry pins only to set an anchor when desperately facing icy or chossy conditions, maybe on a loose desert peak, maybe to rap off and retreat. This is not a circumstance that your average mountaineer would want to face, but for desperate conditions you might also consider carrying a DMM Ice Hook or one of its kin to drive into frozen turf in hopes it remains long enough to resolve your desperation. Europeans fond of climbing grass might carry Warthogs for that purpose. If you're into extremism, you could always hammer in your ice tool's spare pick.

NUT TOOL

Don't forget a nut tool. Although many mountaineers forego these devices, if you're serious about placing pro, you should also be serious about removing it, quickly and easily. A nut tool is especially useful when you're using cams and pro having soft (not wire cable) runners, plus it's a great device to use to clean grunge out of a crack where you'd like to have a chock actually hold.

RAP RING

No, we're not talking ostentatious urban bling. It's a good idea to use this form of mountaineering jewelry any time a rappel station is likely to be used repeatedly, or when there's any chance you might have to lower a climber using the rappel anchor. Rappel rings, aluminum or titanium, aren't beefy enough to inspire universal confidence, so some climbers are excessively wary of them, even though they're rated over 10 kN. You'll learn in Chapter 11 that rappel forces will be only 10 percent of that, but you can add a short tied or sewn runner as a backup, as shown in Chapter 13.

KNIFE

Knife? All trad climbers and, I'd argue, all mountaineers should carry a knife while climbing and keep it handy for emergencies. Some climbers duck-tape a Ka-Bar or standard issue Marine Corps bayonet to their legs, but that approach creeps up on overkill. I hang a tiny Swiss Army knife around my neck on an OSHA-approved releasable lanyard. (*Never* put anything around your neck that could inadvertently turn into a garrote.)

Knifeblade, Bugaboo   Lost Arrows   Angles

A selection of pins.

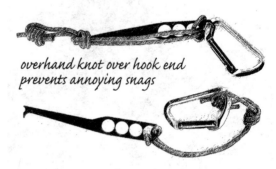

overhand knot over hook end prevents annoying snags

Nut tool with keeper cord.

The blade is adequate for cutting old slings, the scissors for cutting tape, and the tweezers for removing cactus spines from your partner's derriere. Nothing beefier is necessary. Old-school mountaineers romanticize about slashing a prusik loop to free it, but only because they haven't learned the Münter-mule (which you will, later). There are many tales of climbers who became imprisoned in runners or halted by clothing sucked into rappel devices (best use the scissors to deal with this; a blade near a loaded rope has also led to many tales) or mountaineers who needed to cut off the end of their rope to make emergency rappel slings. Or maybe they needed to hack off an entrapped part of their body: an arm, a foot, a ring finger imprisoned by a jammed ring—the list of actual acts is endless. Read Joe Simpson's chilling *Touching the Void* to see how Simon Yates used a little Swiss Army knife on Joe. Carry a small knife where you can readily access it, but where it won't readily access you.

11
Climbing Forces

Be forewarned that you may find this section excessively technical, even if you haven't already made that objection to other parts of the book. Unfortunately, that's the nature of the beast—technical climbing is technical. If your eyes tend to glaze over as you wade in, feel free to skip ahead, but realize that the discussion lays the groundwork for many of the points I make that run counter to old-school "wisdom." The forces encountered while climbing and the best ways of dealing with them are indeed difficult to grasp. Most climbers are hazy about the magnitude of climbing forces and the strength of hardware; they often believe that forces are much higher than they actually are, and they don't appreciate where in the safety system the highest peak forces appear or, for that matter, from which direction. Uneducated climbers tend to attribute anchor failures to lack of strength or simply bad luck. Worse, climbers may develop untenable confidence born only of the absence of disaster in their recent past. Erroneous and misleading information on climbing forces

and anchors appears even in texts by respected authors, contributing to the Scylla and Charybdis of overconfidence or paranoia. Don't be surprised if you read contradictory material elsewhere.

PHYSICS 001

Might as well dive in by discussing ways of describing mass, force, and weight; getting these tangled up confounds discussions of climbing forces. For scientific work nearly the entire world uses a version of the metric system called the International System of Units, abbreviated SI (from the French *Le Système International d'Unités*). In the SI scheme, mass (an intrinsic property of matter) is expressed in *kilograms*. Force, a consequence of mass being accelerated or decelerated, is expressed in units called *newtons*, named after Sir Isaac himself. In the avoirdupois system used in the United States, things are not so simple, or maybe they're too simple, especially for those who were dozing in freshman physics class. The avoirdupois system has several schemes with units scaled to particular applications. In the version I'll use, both mass and force are expressed in *pounds*. There are other schemes in which mass is expressed in slugs or force in poundals. NASA uses an even screwier system in which force is expressed in pounds and mass in slinches; it was trouble managing conversions of units from this scheme that led to the demise of the Mars Climate Orbiter space mission and tens of millions of dollars, so don't feel like you're alone if you find this stuff daunting.

Although Americans express both mass and force in pounds, these are very different things. Confusion centers on the notion of weight. Colloquially "weight" usually means mass. When your doctor puts you on a scale to measure your weight, she does so by balancing your mass with calibrated masses built into the scale. But . . . when you step on your bathroom scale at home you're actually measuring force—the force, resulting from your mass being acted upon by the acceleration due to gravity, that's pressing down on the spring inside your scale. Both scales read the same (unless, like me, you lean to the side of your bathroom scale to shave off a few pounds). In fact, they both read the same even if your weight is read out in kilograms. Confused? Maybe you could be a NASA engineer.

To help keep things straight, I'll use "pound-force" (lbf) to refer to force. One pound (lb) of mass is approximately 0.4536 kilograms (kg). One pound-force is about 4.448 newtons; one thousand newtons (1 *kilonewton*, kN) is approximately 224.81 lbf. An apparently stationary object requires a force, expressed in lbf, approximately equal to its mass, expressed in lb, to prevent it from falling into the earth. For example, a 1 lb object hanging on a rope would put a force of approximately 1 lbf on that rope. I say "approximately" because gravity varies by about half a percent depending on where in the world it's measured. If that object had the good sense to be stationary in Canada, every kilogram of its mass would require a force of approximately 9.807 newtons to restrain its descent. That proportion gives rise to another unit of force, the *decanewton*, sometimes abbreviated DaN but correctly daN or, to be excruciatingly correct, dekanewton and still daN. It's equal to

10 newtons. The dekanewton is commonly used because it's conveniently close to a kilogram-force (the force on its rope caused by 1 kilogram), which makes it equal to about 2.248 pounds-force (lbf). I won't grind you with the distinctions of energy and momentum; hopefully, you remember that from high school. If all this seems arcane, you're right. All you need to remember is that 1 kN is about 225 lbf.

STATIC FORCES

In a simple system like climbing (simple compared to that errant Mars mission), there are few sources of forces, mainly the weights and movements of climbers' bodies. I'll distinguish two types of forces: static and dynamic. Static forces are those occurring when all the objects in a system are at rest with respect to each other; typically static forces come from the weights of the objects. Dynamic forces arise when objects are being speeded up or slowed down. Dynamic forces don't just turn off and on; they build up to a peak and then taper down to static forces when things stop moving. It's peak forces that break anchors, hardware, and climbers. Peak forces are often hard to determine empirically, but they are what's most important in a safety system.

Hanging and Rappelling

The simplest example of significant climbing force is the weight of a climber hanging on a rope. Obviously, the force on the rope is equal to the weight of the climber, unless she's metric, in which case we'll need to multiply her weight by 9.8 N/kg (from a few paragraphs back); so a 75 kg (165 lb) climber just hanging puts a force on the rope's anchor of about 0.74 kN, or 165 lbf. This is a static force.

We now have the first glimmer of utility in these numerical calisthenics. Remember in the discussion of climbing gear in Chapter 10 I said that carabiner gates were required to open when holding a load of 0.8 kN or less? If our climber were hanging from a biner, she knows she'll be able to open its gate—deliberately or accidentally. She's plenty safe hanging there, however, since the open-gate strength of carabiners is required to be at least 7 kN, ten times the force her weight is putting on it.

What if our hanging or rappelling climber were to put as much force as possible on that climbing rope, by wildly jumping around and jerking the rope (but not climbing up and falling on slack rope)? In climbers' parlance this is referred to as "bounce testing" and might be employed to check an anchor's security. The magnitude of this peak force would be a good thing to know, so such forces have been measured. It turns out that you can just about double the force of your weight if you really work at it, making the highest peak force on the anchor about 1.5 kN from our example climber.

This discussion reinforces another concept introduced in Chapter 10: the difference between *secure* and *strong*. Certainly a rappel anchor must be secure, because it is the sole connection between the descending climber and his religious views on the hereafter. It does not, however, need to be particularly strong, because the possible peak forces are somewhere south of 1.5 kN (337 lbf), something a loop of burly shoelace might hold. The lesson is to be very attentive to the security of the rappel anchors you build, making sure that knots are tied properly, that anchors won't somehow release themselves, that carabiners are clipped as they should be, that the directions of applied forces are taken into account, and that locking carabiners are used where appropriate; the strength issue will probably take care of itself. In other words, rappel anchors don't have to be bomb proof, they have to be goof proof.

Lowering or Belaying a Climber

In this example of belaying, the rope from the climber runs up to a carabiner and back down to someone holding it with a belay device; this setup is sometimes called top roping with a slingshot belay. The belayer sensibly keeps the rope slack free, so the climber can't fall any distance before the rope goes tight. Forces are basically static. The force on the climber's strand is simply the climber's weight, which is 0.74 kN in this example. Because of friction on the rope through the top carabiner, the force felt by the belayer will be reduced to 60 to 70 percent of the force from the hanging climber, or about 0.50 kN. The actual ratio is highly variable in practice, depending on characteristics and history of the rope, diameter of the carabiner, angle of rope wrap, and so on—typically there will be a one-third reduction of force when the rope passes through a carabiner used as a pulley, as in this example. The anchor holding the carabiner must sustain both forces simultaneously, for a total of about 1.2 kN (275 lbf). If the climber jumps around and deliberately

static = climber weight
+ dynamic = jumping around
────────────────────────
= force on anchor = 2x climber weight

Forces from a hanging climber.

force on anchor = force on climber's strand
+ force on belayer's strand (about 1/3 less)

force on climber's strand = *static = climber weight*
    due to
+ dynamic = jumping around

force on belayer's strand = *static = 2/3 climber weight*
(lower due to friction) *+ dynamic = 2/3 jumping around*

total peak force on the top anchor due to
a slingshot belay or lower = 3 1/3 x climber weight,
or 1 2/3 if the climber doesn't jump around
and attempt to maximize his applied force

Forces from a climber hanging on belay.

applies the maximum force of 1.5 kN, the peak force at the belay would be about 1 kN, and the peak force at the top anchor would be the sum, 2.5 kN (560 lbf).

There are some interesting points here. Our force analysis always focuses on the critical top-most anchor—if it fails, the entire safety system fails. The top anchor must hold a force that's *more* than the weight of the hanging climber, but not twice that weight. If a frictionless pulley were used instead of a carabiner, the force on both strands would be equal, so friction actually reduces the force on the top carabiner as well as at the belay. Friction makes it possible for a lighter person to hold a heavier climber on a rope passed through at least one carabiner.

Hauling with Pulley Systems

The purpose of constructing a pulley system is to decrease the force that a person pulling on a load must exert to move the load. Typically, the load is either a climber who has fallen and is hanging on the rope or is a bag of supplies known affectionately as "the pig." I'll get into pulley systems in detail when I cover self-rescue in Chapter 25, but it's common to read cautions that the anchors for pulley systems must be exceptionally strong because of the higher forces possible. In fact, the opposite is true. The pulley system actually reduces the forces

on pulley anchors and distributes the total force of pulling up the climber, or pig, over all the anchors and the puller. For example, in a pulley system having a 3:1 mechanical advantage, the puller feels one third and the anchors feel only two thirds of the load.

DYNAMIC FORCES AND LEADER FALLS

The forces I've been describing are basically static, but the main purpose of the roped safety system is to prevent injury to climbers in the event of a fall, when forces will be dynamic, and peak forces will be much higher than static forces. There are two approaches to examining exactly how much higher peak forces could be: start at the climber end of the rope, or start at the belayer end. The usual approach is to start at the climber end, but that leads to paranoia and is a poor guide to reality. I'll start at the belayer end.

A falling climber could generate some pretty high forces; the purpose of the roped safety system and the belay is to bring the falling climber to a stop slowly enough that the peak forces don't rise to the point that they break the safety system or injure the climber. In the bad old days, when ropes had little energy-absorbing capability, it was incumbent upon the belayer to execute a dynamic (slipping) belay as the principal energy-

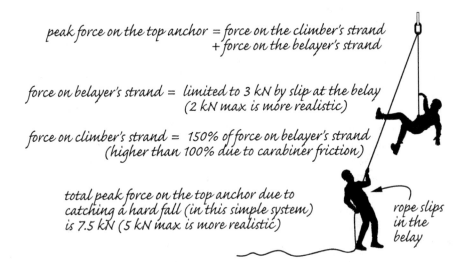

peak force on the top anchor = force on the climber's strand + force on the belayer's strand

force on belayer's strand = limited to 3 kN by slip at the belay (2 kN max is more realistic)

force on climber's strand = 150% of force on belayer's strand (higher than 100% due to carabiner friction)

total peak force on the top anchor due to catching a hard fall (in this simple system) is 7.5 kN (5 kN max is more realistic)

rope slips in the belay

Forces from a climber falling on belay.

absorbing component of the safety system. The hip belay was developed for this, but it works only if the belayer wears gloves to reduce friction burns to his hands and to avoid complete loss of control of the rope as it slips around him, converting motional energy to heat. Belay brakes and energy-absorbing ropes came along that made for big improvements.

The belay brake (belay/rappel device) acts as a force multiplier, increasing the belayer's holding power, static and dynamic. Static holding power depends on grip strength, posture, fatigue, rope diameter, and other things; it varies widely. Figure 0.18 kN (40 lbf) for one strong hand for about 1 second or 0.1 kN (25 lbf) for half a minute. This force is important when lowering another climber or yourself, but not in catching a fall. The force on the rope caused by a falling climber comes on suddenly, so you might expect that it would be difficult to establish a strong grip quickly enough; you'd be correct. It turns out, however, that you don't have to.

The highest force that a falling climber generates occurs only for a fraction of a second, when the peak force at the belay also occurs. The belay peak force arises as the rope accelerates the belayer's hand, arm, and part of his upper body, jerking them toward the belay brake. This force ranges from 0.15 to 0.3 kN (about 33 to 67 lbf); it can be

reduced by about 15 percent if the belay setup allows the belayer's entire body to be pulled or lifted, but that benefit is limited to around 3 feet (1 m) of motion even in the hardest fall—something you'd want to build into the belay setup whenever possible. Forces throughout the safety system subside to static levels in about a second. If the peak force would rise higher than the belayer and force multiplication designed into the belay brake can hold, rope will slip through the belay brake until energy is dissipated and the force on the rope diminishes. The belay basically acts to spread the fall energy over time and limit the maximum, peak force on the rope at the belay.

Static or Dynamic Belay

A static belay is one without any rope slip, as if the rope were tied off; a dynamic belay allows rope to slip while absorbing energy and limiting forces. All actual belays are dynamic to some degree, even with a GriGri. But is that a good thing or bad? In fact, what's the basic purpose of a belay? This is an important point that climbers need to get their heads around, but it isn't one that's brought out in other texts, including The Classic.

As in the previous example of top roping forces, the force on the topmost anchor is the sum of the forces on the climber's strand of rope and the belayer's strand. In other words, the safety system component that receives (and must withstand) the highest force during a fall is the topmost anchor. *The purpose of the belay is to keep the force on the topmost anchor as low as possible.*

Static belays maximize forces throughout the safety system while dynamic belays reduce them, but if the belay is too dynamic, the climber will fall farther than necessary. The goal, then, is to produce a belay that's sufficiently dynamic to keep the force on the topmost anchor comfortably below failure; there are many ways to do that. If the topmost anchor can't possibly fail, the goal becomes making the belay sufficiently dynamic that the force on the climber isn't too severe as she's brought to a halt. Accomplishing these goals is highly contextual; the strength of anchors depends on many factors, including the medium in which they are placed (rock, ice, or snow). The distance a climber could fall safely depends on the terrain. The force conveyed to the climber (and anchors) as she's brought to a stop depends on the energy-absorbing characteristics of the rope and other energy-absorbing components of the safety system. The ideal belay will always be a guess and a compromise; knowing the principles is the place to start. The guiding focus in trad climbing and mountaineering is reducing the peak force on the topmost anchor.

Maximum Force from the Belay

The hip belay, when used with a modern climbing rope, can hold a maximum force on the rope of about 1 kN without considerable slipping; that's not enough for belaying a leader, so we'll leave it out of the discussion. Belay brakes (belay/rappel devices) have been designed for compromise between rope slip and rope hold when used by a typical belayer on one strand of rope, and also when used by a typical rappeller on two strands of rope. Older designs were intended for fatter ropes; newer models accommodate modern, thinner ropes, sometimes by offering asymmetrical braking features that give a choice of holding power. Adding an additional carabiner to tube and plate brakes increases their force multiplication by about 40 percent. Still, all brakes hold the rope only up to some force limit without slipping. For old-fashioned brakes used with modern ropes,

that maximum force on the rope and belayer is about 2 kN (450 lbf). Modern devices increase that to as much as 2.5 kN. The least intrinsically dynamic brake in common use is the Münter hitch, which slips around 3.5 kN in its stronger orientation and around 2.5 kN in its weaker orientation. Figures are for single ropes and depend somewhat on rope diameter and other factors.

If we take these figures and consider friction through the topmost carabiner, the strand of rope holding the climber will be limited to a maximum force 1.5 times greater, or about 3 to 5.25 kN. That's the peak force on the climber irrespective of any force reduction by rope stretch. The top anchor will be subject to at most 5.5 to 8.5 kN peak force during *any* possible fall in this simple system. Those figures are probably less than you expected.

Is this good or bad? Is it the whole story? If it were the whole story, it would be good, and you'd

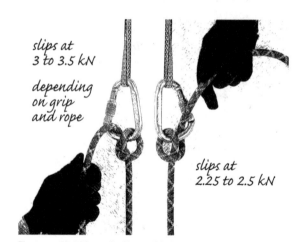

slips at 3 to 3.5 kN

depending on grip and rope

slips at 2.25 to 2.5 kN

The two orientations of a Münter hitch.

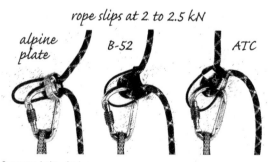

rope slips at 2 to 2.5 kN

alpine plate   B-52   ATC

Common belay devices.

already know more about safety system forces than the majority of climbers, but there are other factors that could substantially increase or decrease these forces.

Force on the Climber

The UIAA long ago established an upper limit of 12 kN (2,700 lbf) for the force an energy-absorbing rope could transmit to a fallen climber; they figure that's the maximum force a climber's body could endure without fatality. This number comes from old studies of Scandinavian military parachutists, but when a parachutist pulls the rip cord he's had time to get into a favorable position that, along with his specialized harness, lessens the consequences of impact caused by the chute opening. Falling climbers don't have these luxuries and wouldn't know what to do if they did. Nevertheless, for want of a better number, 12 kN is it. That's more than twice the number we just figured, so what's up? A couple of things. The 12 kN is a test number, whereas our figure is more practical. More importantly, the 12 kN would occur only in the worst-case fall, one in which the topmost anchor fell out or never was placed, the falling climber went past the belay before hitting the end of the rope, and the rope was tied off, not belayed.

The highest possible fall factor is usually said to be 2, but it could be higher if a substantial part of the climber's tether is made of materials that don't absorb energy, such as a long Dyneema sling or daisy chain. A factor 2 fall results when the climber falls from directly above a solid anchor to which the rope is tied. In such a fall, the climber (and anchor) would feel a peak force equal to the impact force rating of the rope (typically 8 to 10 kN), plus or minus some details.

Let's take a look at the force on an example climber using a typical climbing rope. If the climber falls from 4 m (13 feet) above the anchor where the rope is tied for a total fall distance of 8 m (26 feet) on a 4 m length of rope—a factor 2 fall—the peak force felt will be around 10 kN. The rope would stretch about 35 percent (1.4 m or 4.5 feet) while delivering that force. Rope stretch is not figured into fall factor calculations. If the same climber took a 16 m fall on 8 m of rope (same fall

The length of a fall doesn't determine the peak force on the fallen climber. To some mountaineers this is counterintuitive, but to others it makes perfect sense. The reason is that while a longer fall results in higher energy, there's a longer length of rope available to absorb that energy. A longer fall on a longer rope results in the same peak force as a shorter fall on a shorter length of the same rope. The details require knowing properties of the rope that aren't among those usually quoted by manufacturers. For a given rope and climber weight, the peak force on the falling climber caused by catching the fall with a *tied-off* climbing rope is proportional to the square root of a simple ratio: length of fall divided by length of energy-absorbing rope. This ratio is called the *fall factor*, and it is central to the analysis of fall forces.

$$\text{fall factor} = \frac{\text{length of fall}}{\text{length of rope absorbing fall energy}}$$

tied off (no belay, no slip)

Fall factor.

factor of 2), the peak force and rope stretch percentage would be the same.

Real-World Falls—Shocking!

A force of 10 kN would reflect a shattering fall, probably enough to injure the climber or end the day, but in a realistic factor 2 fall the fallen climber wouldn't experience anywhere near that force. Why not? Because the rope wouldn't be tied off, it would be belayed, and the belay would slip. The belayer might get rope burns and might release the rope, but even a Münter hitch could only apply 2.5 kN to the belayer's rope and to the climber. Rope will slip at the belay until enough energy was absorbed to drop the force on the rope below the 2 kN applied by a typical belay brake. This is the basis of the energy absorbers designed for via ferrata, climbing routes on fixed iron rungs that, for protection, use a nearby cable with periodic anchors. Rope slippage is proportional to the fall distance: a whopping 10 feet would be added to our example 26-foot fall. Providing the climber didn't hit anything on the way down, this factor 2 fall would result in only mild forces on the climber and belayer's anchor (2 kN); not much more than a hanging climber could create by jumping around on the rope. This example should convince you, however, to wear gloves when belaying.

So a real-world, belayed factor 2 fall puts only 2 kN on the fallen climber and the belay. I'll bet you find that surprising; it's certainly not what you'll read elsewhere. What will surprise you even more (unless you're a physicist) is that the amount of force and rope slip at the belay is independent of the rope characteristics; they'll be the same for a stretchy half rope used as a single, a typical 10.5 mm single rope, or a static rope.

Let's take another example, this time a factor 1 fall, where the distance of the fall is equal to the length of energy-absorbing rope. If the climber ascends 4 m, places an anchor, climbs up another 4 m, and then falls (8 m, 26 feet), the maximum force on the example climber would be about 3 kN (675 lbf), and the force on the top anchor would be 5 kN (1,125 lbf), because, again, the belay would allow the rope to slip (about 6.5 feet, 2 m) at a force at the belay of 2 kN. Using a static rope would result in about the same forces, but more slip (10 feet, 3 m).

If you've been schooled by tradition, you're wondering, "What the heck is going on here? This isn't what I've been led to believe! How come a factor 1 fall hits the climber harder than a factor 2 fall? How come a static rope results in the same forces as a wimpy half rope? How come the forces are so low?" The simple answer is that the rope

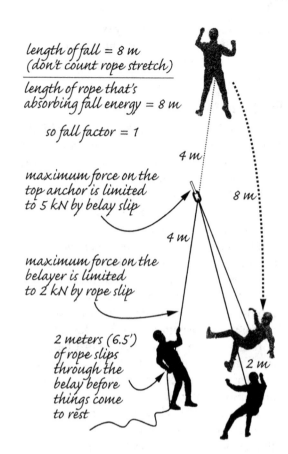

length of fall = 8 m (don't count rope stretch)

length of rope that's absorbing fall energy = 8 m

so fall factor = 1

4 m

maximum force on the top anchor is limited to 5 kN by belay slip

8 m

4 m

maximum force on the belayer is limited to 2 kN by rope slip

2 meters (6.5') of rope slips through the belay before things come to rest

2 m

Fall factor example: a factor 1, tied-off fall.

isn't the only component of the safety system that lowers peak forces. The belay plays a big part, and that's by design.

In typical climbing situations the fall factor is often 0.3 or less, lower yet on sport climbs. During an 8 m fall of factor 0.3, the force on the falling climber will hit a peak of 3 kN (675 lbf), the belay would feel 2 kN, and the top anchor 5 kN, same as before, but the belay would slip only 3 feet. That's with a typical 10.5 mm single rope; a half rope used as a single would result in slightly lower forces and no rope slip. An 8 m factor 0.2 fall on a 10.5 mm rope will result in the same forces, but no rope slip at the belay. A static rope would result in the same forces, but twice as much rope slip.

To summarize, during high-factor falls, energy absorption at the belay (due mostly to rope slip, which can be considerable) soaks up most of the fall energy and keeps forces low; at fall factors around 0.2 (depending on the rope), the belay doesn't slip, and the rope's energy absorption keeps forces even lower. This is probably surprising to you, but there's more to the story.

REAL-WORLD INFLUENCES ON FALL FORCES

Factors That Reduce Fall Forces

The previous computations assumed that the climber is an iron weight tied directly to the rope. A real climber is a flexible object attached to the rope by a conforming harness; distortion of the falling climber's body will reduce forces about 5 percent, and harness distortion will absorb another 5 percent in typical falls. Even the tightening of knots under load will absorb some of the fall energy, maybe 3 percent. Lifting of the belayer's body may also reduce peak forces by a significant amount, maybe 10 to as much as 20 percent, if design of the belay system permits (this is the only influence that can be controlled by climbers). The overall consequence is that fall forces for short falls are less than those calculated, because of all these various factors that absorb energy and reduce peak forces. How much less depends on many things, even the climbers' positions and postures, but the falling climber would more likely be shaken, not disturbed, in a fairly short though high-factor fall.

The belayer, too, would be shaken, but hopefully wouldn't release the rope or be pulled into an unsafe position. A fall that occurs after several anchors have been placed may see peak forces at the belay reduced further as anchor carabiners and runners are jerked into alignment by the tightening rope. On the other hand, carabiners and runners have no energy-absorbing stretch, even though they may contribute to the lengths of falls.

FORCE-LIMITING RUNNERS

It may seem curious to name a product for what it prevents instead of what it promises to deliver, but that's what Yates did with Screamers. These are conventionally sewn runners that are folded and sewn again in such a way that the secondary stitching rips when the applied force exceeds a certain level, typically 2 to 2.5 kN (450 to 560 lbf). In ripping, the Screamer absorbs energy and limits the peak force until all the secondary stitches are gone. Screamers and their several competitors are intended to be used at questionable intermediate anchors, not at the waist of the leader or at the belay; they limit the force on the placement, not the climber. The ripping point is just above the sum of the peak force from a thrashing climber, 1.5 kN, plus that from the belayer, 0.5 kN, so they rip only in some kind of actual fall, not from hanging or thrashing on the rope.

There are comparable gadgets that have been developed for safety on via ferrata, where climbers are typically attached to an anchored vertical cable, and fall factors much higher than 2 are possible. These devices, which can replace Screamers, are typically based on a short length of rope that slips under control of friction; they can be reused if the rope in them is rethreaded, whereas ripping runners can't be rejuvenated. In the process of ripping or slipping, force limiters absorb energy and reduce peak forces, typically by about 15 to 20 percent.

Factors That Increase Fall Forces

The previously discussed influences help explain why sport climbing falls are not as severe as you'd expect (and why the sport is popular). Sport climbing anchors are placed close together and in optimal locations; this means that fall factors are low after only a couple of anchor clips, and the rope usually runs reasonably straight. Things are very different for trad climbers and mountaineers, who may choose or be forced to place widely spaced intermediate anchors on wandering routes.

MR. FRICTION IS NOT YOUR FRIEND

Not if you're the leader, he isn't. It's not uncommon for the trad leader to be out of sight of the belayer almost as soon as she leaves the belay stance; wandering and increasing friction on the rope continues from there. The friction of the rope around intermediate anchor carabiners, plus any friction against rock over which the rope runs, reduces the effective length of rope that's absorbing fall energy, increasing the effective fall factor. When there are several anchors along the lead rope, even in a reasonably straight alignment, the effective fall factor can be double that calculated simply by the length of rope from the belay to the falling leader. If the rope also runs, even slightly, against rock in between those intermediate anchors, the effective fall factor can reach three times the one calculated, increasing the force felt by the climber and top anchor by 75 percent. Sharp bending of the rope at intermediate anchors or over rock makes things much worse. It can readily happen that only the rope from the climber to the next-to-last intermediate anchor is absorbing energy and reducing peak forces. A consequence of so much friction on the climbing rope is that the alpine leader can sometimes take a fall without the belayer even realizing it. Friction can mean there's little energy-absorbing slip at the belay, which essentially becomes static. That is not a good thing.

Every such situation is different, but the general rules for avoiding increased forces are to use long runners to keep the rope as straight as possible, avoid having the rope running against rock and around corners, and place pro more frequently at the beginning of a pitch and farther apart at the end. These principles can restrict the feasible length of wandering mountaineering pitches.

Few climbers fully appreciate the factor-increasing phenomena; they just hate leading when there's significant rope drag. It underscores the recommendation that choosing a rope having a low impact force rating is important for mountaineers—they may often find themselves relying on short sections of rope to absorb energy and reduce peak forces on themselves and their anchors.

The highlights of the preceding discussion include the following:

▲ Forces caused by a fall are likely to be lower than expected, especially at the belay.
▲ Forces are likely to be highest at unexpected points, particularly at the topmost anchor.
▲ Slip at the belay is what limits forces during harder falls; the rope has little effect.
▲ Rope characteristics limit forces (by stretching) during easy falls.
▲ Forces on critical elements of the safety system (the fallen climber and the topmost anchor) are significantly increased by rope friction at anchors and against rock.

STRENGTH OF SAFETY SYSTEM COMPONENTS

Let's take a look at the strength of individual components of rock, snow, and ice climbing safety systems.

Personal Equipment

International strength standards for climbing harnesses require them to sustain a force of 15 kN (3,380 lbf). The details of this specification are a bit nebulous, but suffice it to say that the harness is stronger than the climber. There are plenty of knots sufficiently strong to connect the rope to the climbers' harnesses; none will fail to hold 15 kN. The belay loop, if your harness has one, is at least as strong. Your main HMS carabiner will probably be 25 percent stronger than the standard's minima, or about 25 kN along the main axis and 9 kN cross-loaded or with the gate open.

Carabiners

All carabiners sold today will be adequately strong. Notice the pictograms on the spine. There's a double-headed arrow pointing lengthwise and an adjacent number indicating the rated strength along the major axis when the gate is closed as normal. The UIAA/EN 362/EN 12275 minimum standard is 20 kN (4,500 lbf). Oval carabiners are allowed to pass with 18 kN, but few weasel. A double-headed arrow pointing across the carabiner indicates the strength when the biner is cross-loaded between its spine and gate; the minimum for this test is 7 kN (about 1,500 lbf). The remaining symbol is supposed to suggest a carabiner with the gate open; the minimum strength is also 7 kN, tested along the major axis. Ovals can skate by with lower numbers on this test, too. These strength numbers are based on single tests of new carabiners; manufacturers usually proof test each carabiner to half the closed gate strength, leaving telltale divots when they do. Contrary to old-school wisdom, carabiners do not lose strength when they are dropped (even off Yosemite's El Cap) or abused, unless they are visibly severely damaged. Mangled carabiners or any that have been loaded near their limits, which happens very rarely in climbing, should be destroyed.

Anchors in Rock

The strongest rock protection is undoubtedly a sling around a tree or permanent rock feature. Many fourth-class and parts of fifth-class climbs can be protected using runners, without hardware other than carabiners, and mountaineers endeavor to do so whenever possible (which is whenever they have enough long slings). Natural anchors should be good for the strength of the runner, ranging from over 20 kN for sewn slings to around 9 kN for a tied loop of 5 mm accessory cord.

Manufacturers of climbing hardware protection are required to quote strength ratings; these ratings include the strength of the main device, any associated runners or cable crimps, and the device's holding power in rock—which depends on the quality of both the stone and the placement. Hmmm. Anyhow, strength ratings given for medium to large chocks, passive cams, and active cams are usually in the range of 10 to as high as 20 kN (2,250 to 4,500 lbf). Pro that fits cracks smaller than around 10 mm (½ inch) has lower strength ratings, and the really tiny ones may be

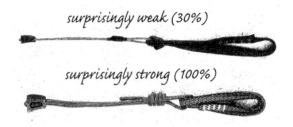

surprisingly weak (30%)

surprisingly strong (100%)

Connecting a runner to a chock without using a carabiner.

rated at only 2 kN and are only for holding body weight when aid climbing, not holding falls. All such strength ratings are somewhat hypothetical in that they assume a solid placement, good rock, and the testing force applied in the most favorable direction.

If you're running out of carabiners, the question is sometimes raised as to whether a runner could be connected directly to the runner that's permanently connected to the chock (commonly a wire cable), without using a carabiner. Definitely don't use a lark's foot (aka girth hitch) to connect a sling directly to a wire cable, but it turns out that passing a webbing runner through a cable loop and clipping the ends (so there are four strands supporting the load) results in surprisingly little loss of strength. If you tie your own chock runners with Tech Cord, as I recommend for the middle sizes, the loss of strength of another runner connected without a carabiner is insignificant.

Anchors in Ice

Just as rock has natural protection, so does ice. If you throw a sling around a substantial icicle, be sure that its base is well formed into a big, solid ice flow. Absent the good fortune to find a handy icicle, the other natural pro options are ice bollards and the Abalakov V-thread. *Ice bollards* should be as strong as the equivalent diameter of icicle in the same quality of ice, but bollards are intended only as rappel anchors, so a kilonewton or so is all the strength required. Making them secure lies in the craft of the ice sculptor, and security is the real issue. Security comes mainly from undercutting the rear edges of the bollard and ensuring that the rope will not pull from an untoward direction. Be diligent and expect to invest some time chipping away; in fact, unless you have no other option or unless a natural feature of the ice contributes, crafting ice bollards takes an inordinate amount of time.

The *Abalakov V-thread* is one of those elements of climbing that, like the European Death Knot, leaves you incredulous when you first encounter it, yet it's potentially stronger than a more reassuring ice screw. This natural ice anchor is made by drilling two intersecting holes in solid ice using a long ice screw, after clearing away any rotten ice on the surface. You want the angle between the holes to be 60°. If you have two screws, leave the first one partly sticking out as a visual reference for targeting the second hole; after the second hole is started you can remove the first screw and peer down its hole in hopes of seeing the second screw appear. Five, six, or seven millimeter cord or $\frac{9}{16}$-inch webbing is threaded through the V-shaped channel by teasing it down one side and snagging it with a wire hook poked in from the other; use wire in your ten essentials or a coat hanger you brought for the purpose. Cord is easier to work than webbing. Tie the ends of the cord or webbing

into a loop with a double fisherman's knot. The holes don't need to be angled down or up, and they might better be drilled in a vertical pattern, one above the other, depending on how the ice looks (in a little gully, for example; remember that the weight of ice causes it to favor horizontal fractures). As with ice screws, place v-threads in recesses rather than on bulges. V-threads are more secure than ice bollards and take less time to establish, but they require a long (17 or 22 cm) ice screw; long ice screws are not the most useful. V-threads are less prone to melting out than screws. Popular ice climbing areas become festooned with V-threads by mid-season, and by summer the rock is strewn with abandoned cord loops—a chance for gear scavengers to clean up the environment. V-threads are used as rappel anchors or for belaying the second, meaning a worst-case force around 1.5 kN (340 lbf). There's no way to determine the actual strength of a given V-thread placement, but figure 5 kN if the quality of the ice and your handicraft inspire confidence and the distance between the holes is at least 4 inches (10 cm). You'll get double that strength if you can drill intersecting holes twice as far apart. V-threads in good ice have been tested to nearly 20 kN, so their use as a leader belay anchor (Anchor #1) is certainly conceivable and potentially better than a screw; I've never seen this actually done. I'm unaware of any tests of V-threads in hard alpine ice (in contrast to water ice), but I suspect they would work as well as comparably sized bollards, which means well enough for rappel anchors on the slopes involved.

Ice screws and ice hooks are the only popular hardware alternatives from among many that have been experimented with since curved-pick ice axes made climbing near vertical water ice feasible. Ice hooks are somewhat specialized, highly variable in their placements (which tend to be in rock or frozen dirt as much as ice), must be hammered in and chopped out, and are only infrequently relied upon by mountaineers, so I'll stick to ice screws. Modern tubular ice screws have polished, well-spaced, high-relief threads. Tests have shown that these threads, when the screw is placed in "good" ice, are more effective at anchoring the screw than the picket effect of the screw body. In good ice, the

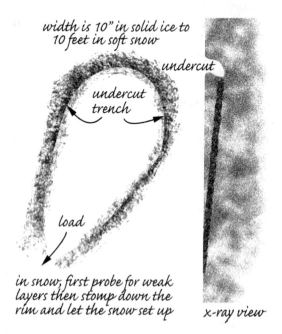

width is 10" in solid ice to 10 feet in soft snow

undercut

undercut trench

load

in snow, first probe for weak layers then stomp down the rim and let the snow set up

x-ray view

A snow or ice bollard.

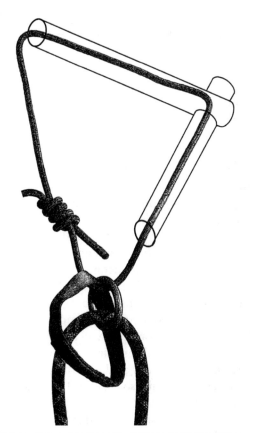

An Abalakov V-thread anchor with rap ring and backup runner ready to rappel.

cause the screw will bend and fail in the weak surface ice; weak surface choss must be removed to put the screw head in solid ice. This is particularly important on a glacier or at the base of a waterfall, where even the best ice may be aerated, and reaching anchor-grade ice may require considerable excavation. The screw alone is stronger, even if it can't be placed fully into the ice, than if it's tied off at the surface of the ice with a slip knot runner or the wire of a wired nut, unless the extended length exceeds 5 cm (2 inches)—which would be a scary-looking placement. In "not so good" ice, placing the screw perpendicular to the surface or angled 5 to 15° away from the direction of pull may be the strongest option, but not good ice is even more variable than good ice.

What is "good" ice? Pretty much what you'd expect: ice that has formed slowly into solid flows from meltwater, not from frozen water spray or metamorphosed snow. Usually such ice will be on lower-angled surfaces and may even be transparent. Warm ice tends to be more plastic and to resist fracturing better than very cold ice, so screw placements are stronger. Bad ice, which all ice is to some degree, looks like white foam plastic and may have obvious air pockets. If cold, it's brittle; if warm, the ice may turn to slush as you climb. If the screw is warmed by sunlight on its exposed features or by water running behind the ice, it will melt loose surprisingly quickly, making its threads useless. I can assure you that having water come running out of an ice screw as you place it is unwelcome for a number of reasons, not the least of which is your sudden awareness that it may fall out even before you can clip it, yet you have limited options and limited time to explore them. Think of a good ice screw placement as having a strength of about 10 kN, a mediocre placement as having a strength of 5 kN, and an exceptionally good placement as having a strength of 15 kN in the real world. Learn to clip ice screws with your fingers crossed.

When placing multiple, equalized screws in ice flows, my dictum of placing anchors more or less vertically in line with the applied force (as opposed to side by side as most texts illustrate) becomes even more important than on rock. This is because ice tends to fracture horizontally due to

screw should be angled about 15° *toward* the direction of the expected pull, for maximum holding power. This is contrary to old-school advice to angle the screw away from the direction of pull. When properly placed in really good ice, an ice screw can hold over 20 kN. That's the good news. The bad news is that ice is a highly variable medium, and the variation from placement to placement even in good ice is quite wide and difficult to predict. If subjected to the same statistically based specification as other pro, an ice screw nominally rated at 10 kN might need to be rated at only 5 kN to account for the variability of the ice in which it's placed. Longer screws are slightly stronger than shorter screws, but most strength comes from ice near the surface; if that ice is "bad" or fractured, a longer screw helps only a little, even though it reaches down into solid ice. That's be-

internal stress caused by its weight; you don't want to enhance this effect with your anchor sites. Place your ice screws as far apart as feasible, 2 feet at least, to prevent one screw from weakening the ice of its neighbor or the failure of one screw fracturing the ice where the other is placed. If you're considering purchasing a couple of screws in hopes of coming across ice of good enough quality to place them, have a look at the Petzl/Charlet Laser Sonic. These have the expected integral crank for placement ease, but the handle end is a rotating bolt hanger; this allows you to remove and even place them with the runner or a keeper cord attached— no more dropped screws bounding down the gully below you, making chimes that sound like a cash register. Place them at your waist like any other screw, but you can be clipped in before you start cranking.

Anchors in Snow

If you think ice protection is screwy, you'll find that snow protection is a real crapshoot. In favorable snow, anchors can be amazingly strong, but in snow like you'd want to ski on or kick steps in, considerable skill and time will be required to construct worthy anchors. Same story if the snow is firm, but highly sun cupped. The exact nature of

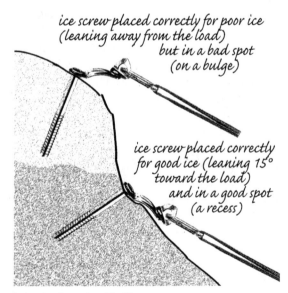

ice screw placed correctly for poor ice (leaning away from the load) but in a bad spot (on a bulge)

ice screw placed correctly for good ice (leaning 15° toward the load) and in a good spot (a recess)

Ice screws in good and bad ice.

the snow may not be apparent, so you can seldom be certain of the results of your efforts. To make things worse—or better, if you're lucky—snow is constantly changing, even minute by minute. Here are some guidelines to help you understand the potential strength of snow anchors and how to make the most of them.

SANS HARDWARE

In soft snow, a strong snow bollard must be huge, maybe 10 feet across—requiring at least 40 feet of rope and excavating a lot of snow. If the snow is that soft, there's little reason for an anchor because climbing is secure enough without a belay, especially on a slope of low enough angle that stumbling around and constructing a big bollard is feasible. A large bollard in heavy, well-consolidated snow can be very strong, maybe up to 10 kN, but success is hard to predict; a sound snow bollard looks exactly like one that will allow the rope to slice through a weak layer in the snow. Snow bollards are used mostly as descending anchors on lower-angled terrain, so they need withstand only about 0.5 kN.

The aim of a snow bollard is to contact a sufficiently large surface area (length) of rope against a sufficiently large amount of sufficiently firm snow. Snow that has been worked (stomped) tends to harden after several minutes; damp snow can turn very solid, as you see with the snow left by plows. Usually, building a snow bollard in old snow in a shaded area beats building one on nearby sunny snow. You'll want to stomp down the snow around the bollard periphery, on the inside of the bollard's rope channel; the snow outside the rope or the depth of the bollard's ditch doesn't affect strength. Start the stomping process as you define the bollard's teardrop shape, and evaluate the snow's hardening as you refine the undercut. If the snow is too firm to work with your feet, you're in luck—a smaller bollard, maybe only a few feet across, is justified; just make sure that it isn't only the surface that's firm.

If you imagine yourself constructing a bollard on steep snow in order to descend a steeper section immediately below, consider this: one of the most common starting points for avalanches is a "pillow" of snow—a convex bulge. In other words, the very spot where you're about to dig a big trench through the surface layer of snow that may be under tension and ready to release. If a ski cut could cause a release, cutting a big slot and tromping around while doing so seems foolhardy. If you do manage to slice off the bollard with the rope, you're in double trouble because it'll join you for the ride down.

What about a *hip belay*? After all, we're not talking about a super steep slope or hard falls on snow. Wouldn't the inherent weakness of a hip belay be turned from a liability into an asset when belaying on snow? The answer is yes. If you want a weak, dynamic belay, a body belay on snow might be just the ticket. A hip belay can be expected to hold a kilonewton at most, and the rope will slip even then; it will slip more if the rope is snow covered, and the belayer is wearing insulated gloves. Holding the rope will be the limiting element if the belayer digs a deep U-shaped channel to sit in and is well braced, basically becoming a cogent deadman anchor with a frozen butt. Adding additional backup protection is probably pointless, for if it were actually secure, hardware protection would be a better choice for the belay anchor than a belayer's body. Running the rope through a carabiner at your waist will increase your holding power and decrease the tendency for the taut rope to twist you around, though it isn't likely that a hip belay will be called upon for power.

MINIMAL HARDWARE, MINIMAL STRENGTH

There are many situations in which a mountaineering party might need a weak belay when climbing or descending steep or icy snow. Hard core types might do without, but a typical party will be far safer to expend the additional time to establish anchored belays. That means knowing how to set them up efficiently and what results to expect. Old-school texts often don't get it right.

Boot-Ax Belay. In every mountaineering text you'll see an illustration of the classic boot-ax belay. Invariably the illustration incorrectly shows the hands reversed from the strongest position, even in The Classic; either leg can be uphill but

Sitting hip belay on snow with both strands of rope through a single carabiner at the waist.

the hand position is critical to getting the maximum wrap of rope around the boot. Strength is not the boot-ax belay's forte, but you might as well get all that's available. In strong snow, when it'll be difficult to force the ax shaft all the way down (but do it anyway), a proper boot-ax belay without crampons can hold 2 kN (450 lbf), maybe a bit more if the belayer has a high tolerance for pain. In softer snow, holding power will be significantly less, even when wearing crampons and even after stomping down the area around the placement and giving the snow time to set up. Hopefully, soft snow will also result in gentle falls, or none, because any belay using an ax is likely to whack the belayer when it pulls out. One problem with this belay is the difficulty of safely taking in rope; fancy flailing in an awkward position is needed. Nevertheless, the weakness of the belay (keep in mind it's the topmost anchor) makes it imperative to take up rope quickly and minimize slack to the climber. The boot-ax belay is more efficient handling descenders than climbers and is best used to guard against short slips turning into long slides.

The Stomper. Another classic, weak belay that's frequently illustrated in a suboptimal orientation

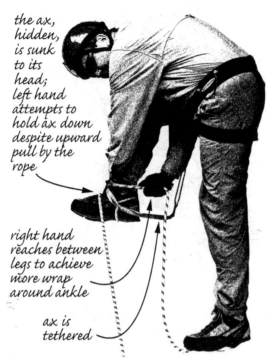

the ax, hidden, is sunk to its head; left hand attempts to hold ax down despite upward pull by the rope

right hand reaches between legs to achieve more wrap around ankle

ax is tethered

The boot-ax belay.

is the boot-carabiner-ax belay. Note that the belaying carabiner's runner should go through the hole in the ax head or, unless it's otherwise tethered, the ax may be lost if the belay fails. Like any other hip belay, even when correctly executed, the stomper belay is limited to holding little more than a kilonewton, depending on the belayer's grip strength and pain threshold; it's for slips on slopes, not falls on ropes. The boot-carabiner-ax business doesn't add significant brake action; it merely redirects the rope. The force on the carabiner will be approximately equal to the sum of the force on the rope from the fallen climber plus the force being held by the belayer, or roughly 150 percent of the force the falling climber applies. A Münter hitch belay would make better use of any strength a snow placement provides—that would be the new-school approach. Using a Münter hitch on a boot-carabiner-ax belay for ascenders is a pain in the back, because you'll have to bend over and use both hands to take in rope. It works great, however, for descending mountaineers and is easier on backs than the boot-ax belay, ascending or descending.

Torn between the boot-ax belay and the stomper? Go with the latter. Rope management is easier, it's less directional, it allows the belayer a better view of what's being belayed, it's less likely to cause injury by the flying ax should the belay fail, it causes less pain on the belayer, and it's slightly more robust. Both belays are best used for the second or descenders, not for belaying leaders who could take significant falls.

Laying It on the Line. What about a self-arrest on snow—how strong could that be? This is of certain interest because a self-arrest might be the anchor that stops another climber who's fallen, particularly into a crevasse—a potentially serious fall, even though the fall factor cannot exceed 1. A well-

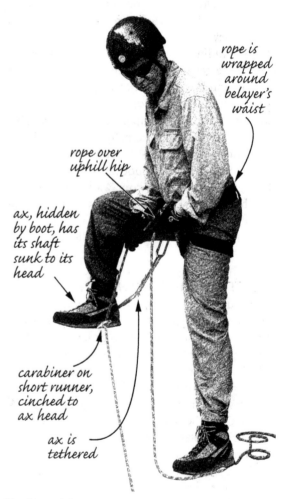

rope is wrapped around belayer's waist

rope over uphill hip

ax, hidden by boot, has its shaft sunk to its head

carabiner on short runner, cinched to ax head

ax is tethered

The stomper belay.

executed self-arrest in good, horizontal snow can momentarily withstand 2 or 3 kN once solidly established; the limiting factor is the ability of the arrester to briefly endure the pain of holding the force on his harness, reminiscent of medieval torture methods. If you consider the length of rope between glacier hikers, the likely fall distance, and the force reduction by snow (especially if knots are tied in the rope), you arrive at a maximum force on the falling climber of around 2 kN—pretty close to the strength of a single self-arrest. The key to traveling safely on crevassed glaciers and keeping fall forces manageable is to keep the rope linking travelers as tight as practical and for the belayer(s) to attentively go into self-arrest as quickly as possible upon a fall. If the party is inattentive, delays arrests, and allows excessive slack in the rope (or carries coils!), fall forces could exceed the ability of self-arrests to hold, allowing what might have been only an individual's slip to turn into a party's desperate tumble toward the abyss.

THE PICKET LINE

Hardware anchors for snow are of two kinds: pickets and deadmen. A picket is an aluminum stake with a T-shaped cross section intended to be driven into harder snow or softer ice. They are available in 2-foot and 3-foot lengths, but the 3-foot versions are just evidence of desperation (understandable, if you're seeking strong anchors in soft snow) and take longer to place; there's little strength to be gained from the 3-foot versions. The strength of a picket depends on the quality of the snow or alpine ice into which it's driven, mainly the surface strength. Whack them in as far as you can, angled about 15° away from the likely direction of pull, and attach the connecting carabiner or runner at or only slightly below the surface; attaching the load higher substantially weakens the placement, and attaching it lower creates an upward force unless the runner is entrenched. You'll have a reasonably capable anchor, one that could even be used for a leader belay anchor or intermediate climbing protection. When the snow is soft, stomp it thoroughly in front of the picket; it's the strength of the snow or ice at the surface that limits the strength of driven pickets. A picket that's had an

end exposed to the sun for a time may only be resting, not anchoring; you may be able to slide it up and out with your fingertips. Place pickets with their heads below the snow surface whenever possible and cover exposed metal with snow to prevent solar melt out; just be sure that a pull on the runner will not bring them up and out. Whacked well into glacier ice, pickets make appropriate rescue anchors, given the way rescue systems distribute loads. Some pickets have a stainless metal end covering to hold up against repeated pounding into firm snow or névé; if you're planning a lot of this, bring along a hammer tool and spare your ax. In the end, the strength and security of a driven picket is more about the snow or ice than about the aluminum; you might figure on a placement strength of from 1 to 6 kN, depending. Hopefully that will be all you need, or hope you'll be able to place two and combine their strengths.

A mountaineering ax can be used as a driven or buried picket. You can even purchase pickets that appear to be headless axes. Axes are B- or T-rated according to several tests (see Chapter 15 for details on ax features). You'll be using a B-rated ax having a shaft rated to hold 2.5 kN. That rating applies to the head resisting being ripped off. You can do better using the ax as a picket if the snow is firm and well stomped in front of the placement, and if you attach a runner through the hole in the ax head and stomp the shaft down until the ax head is at or just below the snow surface. Angle the shaft of the ax about 15° away from the direction of pull and hope for 3 to 4 kN, best case, because that's all the ax itself can handle. With ideal alpine or glacier ice you could even use the pick of your ax as a driven picket and attach the load-connecting runner to the hole in the spike. If you're holding a companion who's fallen into a crevasse, this may be your only option; place your pick with conviction. If you've climbed vertical ice, you know that a remarkably short length of pick or crampon point can support body weight, so it shouldn't be surprising that the entire pick sunk to the shaft would support substantially more if conditions are favorable, which would be unfavorable for attempts to deeply embed the shaft of the ax. Figure a couple of kilonewtons, maybe more unless the head pulls

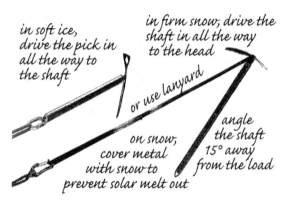

in soft ice, drive the pick in all the way to the shaft

in firm snow, drive the shaft in all the way to the head

or use lanyard

on snow, cover metal with snow to prevent solar melt out

angle the shaft 15° away from the load

Mountaineering ax used as a picket.

off, and figure on some effort digging out the pick if it doesn't.

DEADMEN TALES

A deadman is any object buried in snow for use as an anchor. The trick is to cut a narrow slot for a straight and direct connection to the deadman, and then to drive or bury the deadman perpendicular to the slot and the direction of pull. A picket makes a great deadman, better than a horizontally buried ice ax shaft, but nowhere near as good as a buried ski. Nontraditional objects might serve in desperation, including a snowshoe, a lassoed backpack stuffed with snow, or even your partner's sacked tent with poles; use slip knots to attach runners around the objects. After digging out the hole for the deadman, stomp snow around the buried object and allow a few minutes for the snow to set up before loading the anchor; soft snow will harden considerably after it's been worked this way, and heavy wet snow may become ice hard. The resultant placement can be remarkably secure. In heavy summer snow I've called off the pulling test out of fear of damaging the shaft of my ax; an entire party of mountaineers was unable to pull out a ski buried under only a few inches of snow (attach the runner with a slip knot and be sure it won't be cut by the ski edges). In the same conditions, an 8-foot wide snow bollard could be sliced out by the determined pulling of three people.

In good (heavy, damp, not too cold) snow, a picket deadman might hold 8 kN, close to metal failure. In cold, fluffy snow you might be lucky if your deadman holds 1 kN. This means a picket is stronger as a deadman that is connected at its center than as a driven picket that is connected at its end; theoretically it should be twice as strong. Using a carabiner to attach the runner to a picket isn't the best way to achieve this strength; a webbing runner passed through two holes and over the ends better spreads out the load. Even cinching a runner directly through a single hole will be sufficient (not "girth hitched" around the picket, which tends to crush the picket as it tightens). Use one of those 4-foot runners I recommend; the longer the better. Always stomp down the snow well ahead of a deadman in hopes it will set up with improved strength, but your results will vary unpredictably. The snow-stomping business is critical to the strength of any deadman placement, and you always want to construct a burial pit that's large enough for plenty of backfill with stomped-on snow; dig the pit from the load side, so your feet will be stomping snow as you dig. If you must attempt a deadman anchor in soft snow as part of a rescue, you'll want to equalize together as many snow anchors as you can set up; I'll cover complex anchors later, in Chapter 12.

Vertical Burial. A picket used as a deadman can be placed vertically, attached by a runner in the middle and entrenching the runner ahead of the picket. Horizontal placements are vulnerable to weak layers in the snowpack, so always probe the snow before you plan your burial. A vertical picket deadman is 20 percent or more stronger than a horizontally placed picket deadman. It's certainly faster to place in firm snow, but be sure you don't lose the opportunity to stomp the snow around the hardware to gain strength, as you'd always do when establishing a horizontal placement. In optimal conditions you might hit 9 kN before failure of the picket itself occurs, especially if you use my method of attaching the runner to distribute the force over the picket.

In order of increasing strength in the same snow we have: a picket driven completely into the

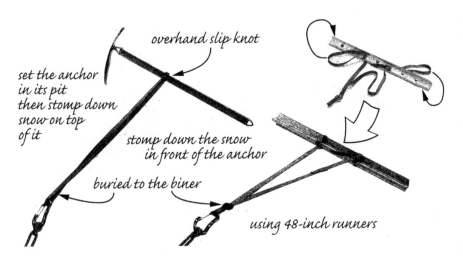

set the anchor in its pit then stomp down snow on top of it

overhand slip knot

Horizontally buried pickets as deadmen.

stomp down the snow in front of the anchor

buried to the biner

using 48-inch runners

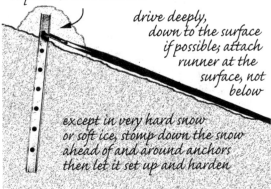

cover with snow to prevent solar meltout

drive deeply, down to the surface if possible; attach runner at the surface, not below

except in very hard snow or soft ice, stomp down the snow ahead of and around anchors then let it set up and harden

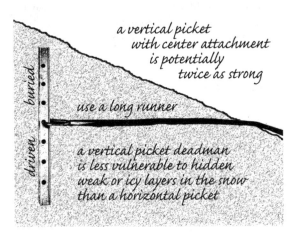

a vertical picket with center attachment is potentially twice as strong

buried

use a long runner

driven

a vertical picket deadman is less vulnerable to hidden weak or icy layers in the snow than a horizontal picket

Picket as a vertical deadman.

snow, the same picket buried horizontally as a deadman, and for the greatest strength the same picket placed vertically as a center-connected deadman.

An ice ax can also be buried as a deadman. Attach a runner to its middle using a slip knot. Failure of the shaft sets a strength limit around 4 kN, and you might get close to this in heavy, well-stomped and set-up snow. You get slightly more strength using the lanyard to hold both ends. In general, any deadman held by its ends is stronger than if held by its middle.

NOT CALLED FLUKES FOR NOTHING

Snow flukes are deadmen made of bent sheet aluminum with cables that attempt to hold the plates at favorable angles, causing flukes to increase their burial depth when pulled on. I assume that a fair number of these things get sold, but in my personal experience they aren't worth their weight on the pack. Standards call for a mechanical strength of 6 kN (1,350 lbf), which suggests that strength in snow will be less. I've had better luck with the flat versions with bent edges than those with a single bend in the middle, but neither inspired confidence. They either pulled out outright, or moved off to the side and pulled out, or dived down to a frozen layer and pulled out along it (be sure to probe for a hidden ice or weak layer before placing a snow fluke—especially important

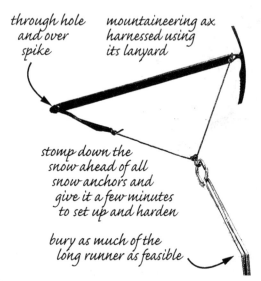

through hole and over spike

mountaineering ax harnessed using its lanyard

stomp down the snow ahead of all snow anchors and give it a few minutes to set up and harden

bury as much of the long runner as feasible

Mountaineering ax used as a horizontal deadman.

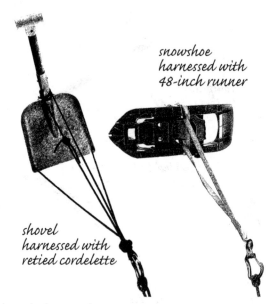

snowshoe harnessed with 48-inch runner

shovel harnessed with retied cordelette

Improvised snow anchors.

on a snow-covered glacier). There may be snow conditions where good security is possible, but pickets are more secure and much more versatile in my opinion. In a pinch, you could use your shovel blade or a snowshoe as a snow deadman by constructing a harness from that length of 6 mm cord you wisely carry; their large area makes for impressive holding power, especially if the snow in front is firm or well stomped.

Flukes' weakness might be inevitable given their size. All things being equal, the holding power of any deadman is proportional to the area resisting the pull against the snow, so a picket deadman and a fluke with similar areas should be comparably strong. For example, a 2-foot-long by 2-inch-wide picket will have approximately the same area as a 6-inch by 8-inch fluke. All things are not equal, however, as the fluke's cable holds it at an angle that reduces its effective area and strength. If the fluke works its way down to an ice layer, that angle can increase, and the fluke will hold even more poorly. Flukes should be buried as deeply as feasible, behind stomped-on and set-up snow. In good, well-stomped snow their tested strength can be impressive, but just stuffing them down into snow is ineffectual. Never place multi-

ple flukes in a line, as any movement of the first fluke through the snow will create a weakness that will make the following flukes much less effective. Don't use a fluke as part of a joined ("equalized") anchor system if their typical movement could compromise other placements.

THE MORE, THE MURKIER

Multiple snow anchors involve some subtleties that don't arise on rock. Multiple, connected anchors are an effective approach to compensating for the variable and unpredictable nature of snow. The strength of a snow anchor placement depends

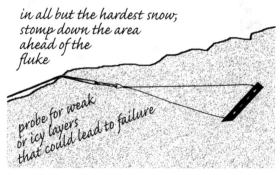

in all but the hardest snow, stomp down the area ahead of the fluke

probe for weak or icy layers that could lead to failure

A correctly placed fluke.

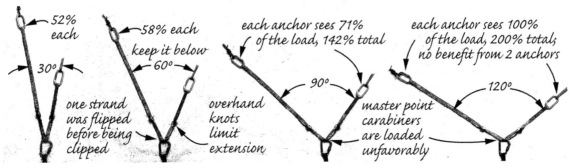

Force multiplication; anchors above, loads below.

not just on the snow in immediate contact with the hardware, but also on the snow that lies broadly in front of the anchor in the direction of the load. In old-school texts you see illustrations of anchors made with, for example, two perpendicular ice axes in contact. Such a placement is far weaker than placing the axes widely apart and connecting them with an equalizing runner—obvious once you realize that it's the snow around the axes and not the axes themselves that limit strength. When snow at one ax fails, any ax close by will also fail. When setting up equalized anchors, it's reasonable to assume that snow placements are equally strong if placed far enough apart so they act independently—that's the new-school approach, where cordelettes come into play.

If worse comes to worst and your snow placement fails, expect that failure under load will be sudden. Not only will you no longer have an anchor, but you may be threatened by flying hardware with pointy ends. Flukes in poor snow fail progressively and may even travel some distance under the surface without losing what strength they have; the snow acts like a force limiter. If you notice that a vertical picket is being pulled toward its load, back off immediately because that's an indication that the supporting snow has been compromised, and catastrophic failure is imminent.

Summary Observations

The UIAA has taken care to specify the key hardware components of the safety system by requiring minimum strengths that will prevent any single element from being an obviously weak link. The *security* of anchor placements, not the *strength* of their hardware, is what determines their overall benefit to the roped safety system. The upshot is that the safety of climbers depends on their personal knowledge and skill in using and placing secure anchors—climbers' fate rests in their own hands.

FORCE MULTIPLICATION

The safety goal of the skillful roped climber is to place secure anchors and minimize the forces on anchor placements, especially the topmost anchor. Unfortunately, there are a number of subtle ways that forces can be increased beyond what might be expected. These scenarios are referred to as *force multiplication*. Force multiplication can be categorized as lever effects or pulley effects.

Lever-Effect Force Multiplication

Force multiplication can arise when two anchors are thoughtlessly connected. If the angle formed by the runners connecting the anchors rises above 30°, the forces on the anchors increase above their expected share of the load. When the included angle reaches 120°, each anchor will experience a load equal to 100 percent of the applied force. In other words, at that angle and higher there's no strength benefit in having two anchors—*both* anchors bear the full force, defeating "equalization." Furthermore, the direction of the force is sideways instead of in the direction of the rope's pull.

It's unfortunate that many illustrations in climbing texts show anchors side by side, often with connecting runners at high angles. To avoid sneaky force multiplication, a proficient new-school climber is always searching for anchor placements that are essentially *in line* with the applied force, whether in rock, ice, or snow.

Another example is the construction of an anchor by looping a short runner around a rock feature.

The forces on the rope used in a Tyrolean traverse or on the webbing used in a slack line can be incredibly high. In order to avoid an initially wild ride down the first half of the rope and a major grunt hauling yourself up the remainder, the rope of a Tyrolean traverse needs to be as flat as possible. That means the rope must be tight, and that means a very high included angle at the point where the traversing climber is hanging, almost 180°. Tyrolean traverses should be avoided, and when set up just for fun, they should be made with beefy static line and *really* beefy anchors and backups.

Another example is a hand line set up to protect members of a mountaineering party as they traverse an exposed section of rock or steep snow during a climb—a technique often illustrated in mountaineering texts, including The Classic. The anchors at the ends of such a line must be exceptionally strong and secure, because lever-type force multiplication increases the tension on the line to greater than the force of a falling climber.

Lever-type force multiplication can also develop on protection that's placed in opposition. Sometimes the exact angle is difficult to determine, but you can be sure that high forces can arise.

In addition to force multiplication caused by

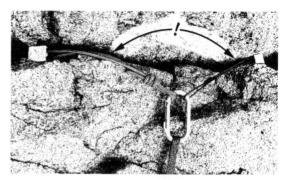

Sneaky force multiplication.

the high included angle of the chocks' runners, the carabiner in this placement illustration is triaxially loaded, which significantly reduces its strength.

Pulley-Effect Force Multiplication

We've already encountered the most common example of pulley-type force multiplication, the upper carabiner in a belay system acting as a force-doubling pulley.

Another example arises when placing protection pieces in opposition. You might at first think this setup is clever: the lower chock protects against an upward pull and the upper placement resists a downward pull, and the two hold each other in place. Don't be seduced. The force on the

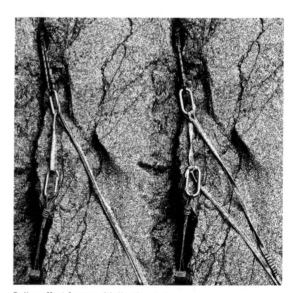

Pulley-effect force multiplication and a cure.

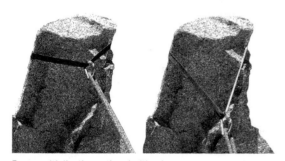

Force multiplication, reduced with a longer runner.

upper anchor will be twice that on the rope, twice what it would be if the upper anchor were used alone—force multiplication at work.

The problem is fixed by tying a clove hitch at the upper carabiner with both strands or at each carabiner with a single strand, as shown; your choice will depend on the consequences to the security of the placements when the anchor is loaded.

There are numerous other examples of where force multiplication arises in climbing and mountaineering. Some instances may be benign, others not. If you're a physics geek you might be able to perform a vector analysis of what's going on, but if you're like most of us, you should just develop an informed intuition and rely on it. If a setup looks squirrely, it probably is.

12
Anchors

Now that you have a solid grounding in hardware, climbing forces, and force multiplication, let's take a look at anchors with an eye on force management throughout the roped climbing safety system. Later in the chapter we'll work through actual climbing scenarios using these techniques.

The whole idea of the roped safety system is to prevent calamity in the event of a slip or fall. The downside is that belayed climbing is slow. That means the climbing party will require more time on the route and will be exposed to objective hazards for a longer period. A party that lacks confidence and elects to use a rope may actually be less safe than a more expeditious party moving unroped; it all depends. There's no point in using a rope for climbing protection if you don't know how to set up anchors proficiently. Unfortunately, most of what's taught about building anchors is misguided. I'll cover anchors and how to place them, but first let's tie in.

TYING IN

You've followed your harness manufacturer's instructions and have buckled it correctly, and you've checked that your partner has as well. Now it's time to tie into the rope. I'm about to confront another sacred cow of old-school climbing—hang on. There are probably at least a dozen common ways for a climber to tie a rope to her harness. I'll discuss two; you can forget about the other ten. The most common knot, taught to beginners by every text and every guide and every climbing school, is the retraced or rethreaded figure eight, also called the figure-eight follow-through. It's basically a figure eight on a bight (a bight is a section of rope that curves back on itself) with the bight passing around the harness tie-in points. There are a number of useless embellishments to this knot that have themselves become cows almost as sacred. You'll see climbers using this knot and swearing that it's the best and safest option. They are wrong.

The knot I recommend is superior in every technical way. It began decades ago without a name but has come to be called the Yosemite bowline.

Be forewarned: arcane arguments about knots are favorite ways for climbers to harmlessly waste time. An Internet search will find endless discussions in which people assert one view or another about knots with absolute conviction but without any actual data. When respectable data are produced, preconceived assumptions about knot strength and security are invariably demolished.

Old-School

The most popular knot for tying in is the rethreaded figure eight. I hope you won't use it yourself, but your partner might, so you should be able to see that it's tied correctly when going through the ritual of mutual safety inspections that precedes every roped climb. I've included instructions for efficiently tying a rethreaded figure-eight tie-in in Appendix A, Additional Skills.

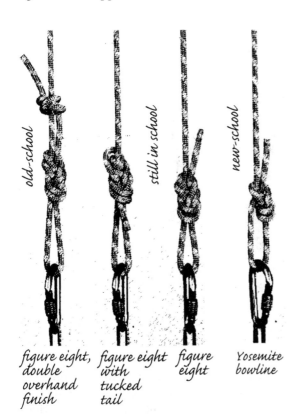

figure eight, double overhand finish

figure eight with tucked tail

figure eight

Yosemite bowline

Common ways to tie in.

One common old-school myth is that a rethreaded figure eight requires an additional knot as a backup, finish, or lockoff. A single or double overhand around the main rope is the usual recommendation. Strangely, you see this prescription all the time, yet experts who've done actual testing have long complained that any additional knot provides no increase in strength or security, it just adds complexity, time, and bulk—if you have enough rope tail to tie a lockoff knot, you don't need a lockoff knot. Somehow this wisdom is ignored. There's never been an example of a rethreaded figure eight failing as a tie-in. You may hear about "failures," but they turn out to be cases where rethreading wasn't completed properly. The most famous example of this is the 70-footer into a tree that Lynn Hill took lowering off Buffet Froid; she failed to complete her knot, and her partner failed to check her. Failing to complete a figure eight can easily happen if you're distracted while tying it; that's one of the knot's shortcomings.

To address the objection to having the tail of rope just hanging there, sport climbers increasingly forgo the lockoff knot and just wrap the end back into the lower turns of the figure eight. This makes for a neater knot but isn't expected to add strength or security; it does make the knot easier to untie. If you're seriously paranoid about the security of your rethreaded figure eight, you should have a look at the figure nine; it's a figure eight with an extra half twist that tests slightly stronger than a figure eight; it's undoubtedly more secure.

New-School

The knot I've used for decades, nowadays called the Yosemite bowline or bowline with Yosemite finish, is superior to the figure eight as a tie-in. The illustration shows an efficient way to tie it. The motions may seem a bit tricky to learn, but they soon become something you can manage, in extremis, in the dark with one hand, while being rained on. It's much faster to tie than a rethreaded figure eight. The trick to this efficient method is the flip in the third step.

There's none of that old-school "rabbit goes out of the hole and around the tree" business. After the flip, it's pretty easy to finish the knot correctly.

hold the rope
near the
sharp end,
palm up;
you'll learn
what length
to allow

standing
line

sharp
end

lay the sharp end over the standing line, palm down;
with a scooping motion, turn your hand palm up to
create a loop while simultaneously flipping the
sharp end down then up and through the loop—
this should be one smooth, continuous gesture

(this is the key maneuver for making the knot)

swing the sharp end
behind the standing
line and into
your fingers; pull the
sharp end through
the loop—this is
now a bowline

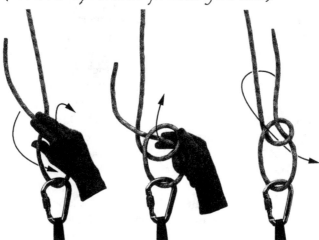
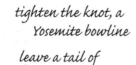

continue with the
loose bowline;
follow the
standing line
with the sharp end

tighten the knot, a
Yosemite bowline

leave a tail of
about 6 inches

back side

Tying a Yosemite bowline.

You want to end up with 5 or 6 inches of tail remaining; no finish knot is needed because it wouldn't add strength or security. It doesn't matter which side of the standing line the tail end finishes on, but I recommend always finishing on the right, as shown, so that you end up with a shape that be-

comes familiar. Also note that after the fifth step you have a complete bowline, which would be an adequate tie-in if you happened to fall before completing the knot. A bowline is a strong tie-in knot, but it can loosen if it's subject to wiggling, which explains why there are so many different embel-

Attribute	Rethreaded figure eight	Yosemite bowline
Most familiar	✔	
Strongest		✔
Simplest, so easiest to inspect by skilled practitioners		✔
Fastest to tie by skilled climbers		✔
Easiest to untie, especially when wet and frozen		✔
Easiest to tie with one hand		✔
Uses least amount of rope and is least bulky		✔
Secure against "ring loading"		✔

lishments, all seemingly called the "double bow-line." In a photo of Edmund Hillary and Tenzing Norgay Sherpa on Everest, you can clearly see the knot at Hillary's waist that binds him to his partner—it's a bowline.

Old-School versus New-School

There will be plenty of groaning by those who've accepted as a matter of faith that the rethreaded figure eight is the best knot for tying in to a rope, probably also with a finishing knot. There's no science behind that belief. The most tenable argument is that, since the rethreaded figure eight is so common, it's more likely that one tied incorrectly will be spotted. The counter argument is the experience of climbing instructors who admit that beginners frequently don't get it right. Even world-class experts like Lynn Hill mess it up, so it seems like a simpler knot would be better. The table has a rundown of some of the rational arguments, but not all arguments are rational.

A final few comments, then you'll have to decide for yourself. I've strength-tested rethreaded figure eights against Yosemite bowlines many times; it's an easy test, dry, wet, or frozen. Advantage: bowline, but many knots are adequately strong for tie-in—that's not what determines the best choice. More important for mountaineers are the ease of tying the knot quickly and correctly and the ease of untying it. If you've ever tried to untie a figure eight that's been wet, weighted, and frozen, you know how difficult that can be, especially with fingers that are themselves becoming frozen. Even

a nice, dry figure eight that's taken a fall or borne weight will be recalcitrant.

"Ring loading" or "wrong loading" refers to applying a perpendicular load to the strands as they enter the knot. This can arise if someone else,

ROOM FOR ONE MORE FOOT

As long as I've trashed the rethreaded figure eight, I might as well continue appearing extraterrestrial by trashing the figure eight on a bight. Somehow this knot has become ubiquitous in climbing; I'd argue that it could be dispensed with almost entirely. Here's why: Its purported advantage over the easier-to-tie and equally effective overhand on a bight is that it's easier to untie after it's been loaded; if it isn't loaded, that advantage is nil, so you might as well use a simple overhand when you need only a backup knot. When the knot *will* be loaded, at the master point of a cordelette anchor system used for top roping, for example, then go ahead and use the figure eight on a bight (or bights), but clip a carabiner through it to make it easier to untie (after removing the biner). Otherwise, don't waste time struggling with a shortage of cordage—just tie a simple overhand. If ease of being untied is truly important, there are other knots that are superior. If you need a stopper knot, the mule knot is much easier to untie. The Yosemite bowline is more universally useful, and it's a better choice than the figure eight on a bight for making a loop near the end of a rope. If you need to make a loop in the middle of the rope, the butterfly knot has advantages, including using less rope and being easier to untie; it doesn't suffer the wrong loading problem of the figure eight on a bight that causes the loop to shrink if the rope is tightened. Just because you see other authorities using the figure eight on a bight without giving it much thought, don't assume that you, too, must stay in this rut. New-school mountaineers know better.

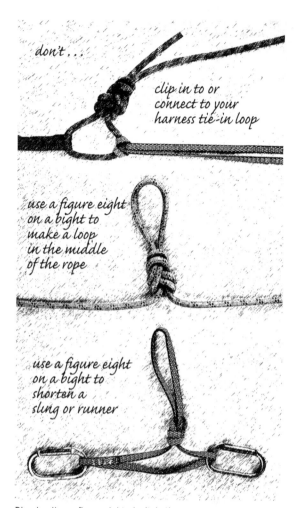

don't...

clip in to or connect to your harness tie-in loop

use a figure eight on a bight to make a loop in the middle of the rope

use a figure eight on a bight to shorten a sling or runner

Ring loading a figure eight; don't do these.

a rescuer perhaps, clips to you; if you unthinkingly clip to a convenient loop in a complex rescue rig; or if you follow bad advice to belay or rappel off that loop instead of your harness's belay loop or an attached runner. Avoid loading a figure eight this way because it'll fail by rolling over itself at surprisingly low loads; a loose figure eight fails at even lower loads rather than tightening up. The Yosemite bowline does not have the problem, but clipping to its loop is a bad habit anyhow.

SIMPLE ANCHORS

Now you're finally tied in to the rope with the overall intention of using the rope to safely catch

a falling climber—on an anchor. I'll use the term *anchor* to refer to one or more connected placements, and *placement* to mean a single attachment to rock, snow, ice, or a tree. So let's talk about anchors.

Natural Protection

Many fourth- and even lower fifth-class mountaineering routes can be protected mainly using natural anchors and long slings, a blessing and a curse. The blessing is that these anchors can be almost ideal: they're strong, don't require hardware, are usually multidirectional, and are usually self-evident in their application and in their discovery. The curse is that mountaineers who've learned to rely on natural anchors don't develop good hardware-placing skills, a craft that requires diligent practice. On the other hand, climbers with a trad background tend to spend effort placing hardware anchors immediately adjacent to terrain features that would make superlative natural anchors. Sport climbers can't find the route without chalk marks; don't place pro without a Bosch, and don't own any long slings.

Common advice when encountering a sturdy rock horn is to throw a girth hitch around it. That

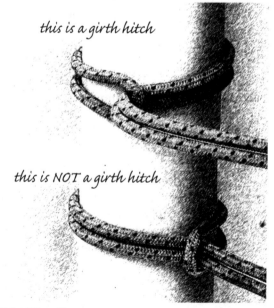

this is a girth hitch

this is NOT a girth hitch

Girth hitch and ?

engenders a rant about another of my pet peeves: the *girth hitch*. Maybe because the name is catchy it gets used frequently in climbing, but the actual knot is hardly ever used; it should never be.

If the other hitch isn't a girth hitch, what is it? That's my quandary. Girth hitch is a handy though incorrect name, but the correct common names for the other knot, *cow hitch*, *lark's head*, and *lark's foot*, are undeniably clumsy; they don't even agree on which end of a lark the knot is supposed to resemble, or what animal. I'm snake bit, as my granddad might have said.

The girth hitch is an example of sneaky force multiplication—its very purpose is to use force multiplication to increase the constriction force around the hitched object, but that reduces strength, usually testing about 50 percent less. Use a girth hitch to cinch a pack to an obdurate mule or to compress a stuff sack, but don't use a girth hitch as part of a roped safety system.

The lark's foot has this problem to a lesser degree, depending on what professional riggers call the "choker angle," so climbers should avoid habitually using a lark's foot (which they call a girth hitch) when better options are available. Loading a girth hitch or lark's whatever on only one of the two strands will result in failure, and connecting two runners with a lark's foot will reduce strength by about 30 percent; a carabiner juncture retains full runner strength.

If you need a hitch that will apply a little constriction to keep it in place, use an overhand *slip knot* (not a clove hitch—pointless and more diffi-

Stronger than a lark's foot, but not multidirectional.

cult to tighten). A girth hitch holds only while it is tensioned. Substitute a slip knot for a lark's foot any time you can get the runner over the end of whatever you're hitching to. The slip knot uses half the length of runner compared to the lark's thing, which could be important when the hitched object is large.

If you can't get the loop over the object you're hitching to (a tall tree or a hueco—a pocket passage in a rock face), use a longer runner and just wrap it around the object.

This configuration is exceptionally strong because the load's being held by four strands of

form a bight and loosely grasp a strand nearby

flip your hand over to make a loop around your fingers

pull the bight through the loop and tighten

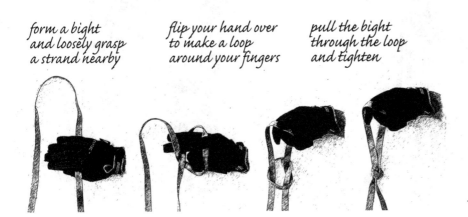

Tying a slip knot.

webbing, but its holding power isn't multidirectional. Note that the wide end of a pear-shaped carabiner should be used for holding the most strands, as shown, while the narrow end holds the rope. To get the absolute maximum strength out of a runner slung around an object, wrap it twice or more around so that the knot is isolated by friction.

This will result in a loop that has double the strength of the webbing and is multidirectional. You can do this with a retied runner, a looped runner, and even a doubled cordelette clipped and wrapped to get four times the cord strength for winching your Hummer—just don't put a high bending load on the carabiner's spine.

There's nothing quite so comforting as throwing a runner around a well-rooted tree. A live tree only an inch or so in diameter is incredibly robust, as anyone who has ever skied into one can tell you. If Mother Nature is kind enough to provide you with an anchor tree, be kind to it, and leave no trace of your use.

Hardware Placements

Placing hardware protection is among the skills that can't be learned from a book, yet artfully and expeditiously placing protection is fundamental to roped climbing; that's why we're discussing it first. Mountaineers on a technical climb typically make few placements far apart, so you'll want to be con-

fident that the anchors you place are solid. Text and photos can offer hints, but learning to place pro well demands hands-on practice and, preferably, mentoring from someone who's put in the years to get good at it. Even if you can place pro reasonably well, evaluating placements for strength and security also requires time in grade. It's not uncommon for someone with considerable climbing skill developed at top roped or sport crags to buy a new rack and head to the alpine world thinking, "How hard can it be?" They might even climb for a few years under this delusion. I did. But then you take a fall, zipper your pro, and come to the realization that there's more to it. Better get serious about learning the skills.

LEARNING TO PLACE ANCHORS

Start learning to place rock pro standing on level ground and placing pieces on whatever rock features you come across. Most pro is asymmetric; try placing pieces in multiple orientations in the same crack, sideways and slipped around. When you place a piece, yank on it from different directions; put some force on your yanks, use a big hammer or barbell weight if you dare (wear a helmet and eye protection). Try placing pieces in opposition to resist pullout and see if you can actually make it work. Move up to multiplacement anchors and yank on them; you'll be surprised how long it first

Joining knot isolated by friction; two wraps are even better.

Hummer goes here

Joining carabiner is isolated by friction; anchor is multidirectional.

takes you to set up a multipiece anchor. Place gear on top rope and practice criticism/self-criticism with your companions. Lead on a loose top rope and repeat the pitch several times trying new placements or eliminating the pro that was easiest to place on the first lead. Climb an easy pitch on aid, maybe top roped; then try aiding a 5.10 crack for real. Aiding will make you place a lot of pieces and hang on every placement; that will focus your attention on their quality. You'll really learn how your placements behave with body weight applied. If you can convince an experienced trad leader to coach you or let you second their leads, it'll cut months, and maybe a fall or two, off your education. Carefully examine their placements as you remove them, and ask them when you see something new—or amiss. If you're lucky, they may second your easy leads and offer comments. Graduation comes when you have the composure to capably place protection after you've climbed far above your last piece—that's mountaineering.

PLACING NUTS

I'm assuming you won't be placing bolts or pitons for a while. You may come across old pitons on classic climbs; they're a good opportunity to practice redundant placements. If you encounter rusty quarter-inch bolts with spinning homemade hangers, they're a good opportunity to practice avoidance. The protection you're most likely to place will be nuts, chocks, rocks, stoppers, tapers, or wires—all names for the same thing, and the easiest type of hardware to place. The principle is obvious: these chunks of aluminum want to be placed in openings in rock that constrict in the direction of applied force. Normally that direction is down, but it could also be out if outward force is possible, as it often is. Chocks want to be placed with as much aluminum in contact with the stone as possible. Brush off surface grit, and beware of any small crystals that could prevent pro from seating completely but break off under stress. Give the piece a smart tug to seat it. The strength of the tug depends on your confidence level, appraisal of dislodging forces, and the trouble you want to leave for your second's cleaning chores. Don't be satisfied with a hardware placement that has any

Stopper with runner tied dog-bone style.

movement or rattle whatsoever. If the crack has ice or snow in it, don't hesitate to hammer the piece into place.

PLACING HEXES

Hexes by whatever name are a bit more trouble to place than stoppers, but they inspire confidence when well placed because it's easy to visually confirm a good placement and to feel that the placement doesn't rattle. Don't just use your hexes like chocks—learn to take advantage of their cam action. Placing a hex in camming mode requires it to be twisted and rotated a bit as it's placed; you may need to get your fingers down into the crack and hold the hex as you seat it. Getting the placement right can require two hands, and the hex may be poorly seated until you give it a tug to initiate its cam action.

PLACING TRICAMS

A TriCam can be placed like a conventional stopper, with its sides in contact with the rock. Its real power is its camming mode, which is what makes TriCams shine when placed in horizontal and slightly flaring cracks; they also work in shallow pockets and even manky or icy cracks. The general idea is to place the TriCam so that the "stinger" point is in a small depression or behind a nubbin, and the webbing on the opposite side isn't touching the rock, but both of its guide rails are; the result is three-point contact. Make sure the piece is positioned well before you release it to grab its sling and give it a tug to solidly set the placement. Pull a placed TriCam from side to side to test for good contact or the possibility that rope movement might dislodge it.

Removing smaller TriCams can be tricky; these tend to be useful for the leader but intractable for the second, especially if they have borne weight.

Hexes with double-length runners placed as a chock and in camming mode.

A TriCam placed in a horizontal crack.

The SLCD promise of instant anchors in tough spots is seductive, but it can be just as tricky to place active cams correctly as passive hardware, and they're not always as reliable. They work well in parallel or slightly flared cracks in smooth, solid rock, but they don't work at all in icy or snowy cracks. A climber's first reaction to SLCDs might be concern that they are insecure, because unlike passive pro, you can't really "set" them with a tug; they can be wiggled around even when soundly placed. Put a long sling on them if they could be wiggled by movement of the rope, which might cause them to walk to a less favorable location, powered by their springs. Many cam placements will auto-align to a new direction of pull without unwelcome consequences—but don't bet your life on it. An active cam placed in a constricting crack and wiggled by the rope may walk backward until it opens fully and loses its wedging action, whereas a nut or hex might be perfect for such a placement. Avoid the extremes of fully expanded or contracted placements by choosing another cam size or crack size. On typical mountaineering climbs, where there are plenty of placement options and plenty of time to place hardware compared to desperate trad climbs, SLCDs may bring more weight and distraction than satisfaction.

COMPLEX ANCHORS

There are many instances when a single placement is inadequate; usually not because of strength, but because the likely direction of applied force doesn't align with the most favorable direction for the placement or it can't be determined with confidence. Even if you encounter a pair of sound bolt hangers, there are many different ways to set up an anchor and connect yourself. You'll also take a different approach to building anchors for belaying the leader versus belaying a second. Mountaineers usually find more placement options, including natural anchors, than trad climbers and are often spared the construction of elaborate, multiplacement anchors—which is a good thing for someone carrying a "small rack." Nevertheless, building multiple placement anchors is a fundamental skill for all roped climbers.

A Word from the Opposition

Simple anchors are sometimes made with the placements *in opposition*—one or more pieces are placed as directionals to secure another placement against pull from an unfavorable direction. The anchor is constructed as a single system, without the expectation that one placement will survive if another fails. Watch out for sneaky force multiplication and *triaxially loaded* carabiners. The opposition anchor illustrated has significant flaws, yet experts have written that it's a "standard and relatively effective setup." Readers of this book will understand that it isn't, even though it may sometimes be your only option.

Misplaced Serenity

There are well-established acronyms intended to teach the necessary characteristics of anchors. You usually see SRENE or SERENE, sometimes ERNEST and once upon a time RENE; often the explanations are screwy. Here's my take, not necessarily conventional, on what these letters mean.

S should mean *strong* and *secure*. These are not the same: a shoestring around a tree is secure but not strong; a runner draped over a rock bulge may be quite strong but easily displaced and therefore not secure.

R means *redundant*. Redundancy is constantly going through climbers' minds. Every component of the safety system should be redundant, so that if one element fails, another will back it up and prevent disaster. The concern applies to holds,

A bad, but common, example of chocks placed in opposition.

anchors, hardware, knots—everything. For example, avoid having your entire climbing team secured by a single carabiner; strong as carabiners are, a single biner is not redundant. Redundancy is not always possible in the real world, but it's always desirable.

E means *equalized*. This means that the load is shared equally by more than one of the anchor system's component placements. Weak placements such as anchors in snow, aerated ice, and choss benefit greatly from equalization (nevertheless, I recommend you don't take hard falls on such anchors).

NE means *non-extending*. This means that should one component of the anchor system fail, the load will not be allowed to move significantly before other components gracefully take over.

On first blush the SRENE concepts seem self-evident, but they actually obfuscate fundamental principles of smart anchor building. Those principles must be somewhat subtle, because so many people, including claimed experts, seem to have an imperfect grasp of them. I'll spend a little extra time so that you won't be among those people.

Invariably, the person offering these acronyms fails to understand which anchor is most important; that's why I began by discussing climbing forces. That discussion pointed out that the most important anchor is the topmost; it's the one that always takes the highest force. If it holds, the safety system remains intact, but if it fails—deep doodoo. The anchor that supports the belayer holds less than a kilonewton, less than 3 kN peak force even if it takes a factor 2 fall, but unfortunately that's the anchor where most climbers are taught to focus SRENE concepts. The topmost anchor constantly changes as the leader advances and places additional intermediate anchors; it wouldn't make sense to build every intermediate anchor using multiple placements—so where am I going with this? The anchor that critically deserves the focus of your attention is the *first anchor after the belay*; I'll call it Anchor #1.

The Importance of Being #1

In Chapter 11, Climbing Forces, you learned that the highest fall factor, 2, occurs only in a fall di-

rectly on the belay anchor. That's the end of most climbers' education, but you also learned that this fall would result in peak forces on the climber and belayer of only 2 or 3 kN, because of rope slip in the belay. You also learned that a factor 1 fall would result in higher forces on the climber and the topmost anchor than would a factor 2 fall—more evidence that the topmost anchor needs to be stronger than the belayer's anchor. The most crucial topmost anchor is the first one placed, that's Anchor #1.

The real danger of a fall onto an anchor is that force might come from a direction that wasn't properly factored into the construction of the anchor, causing the anchor to fail—not because of lack of strength but because of lack of security. Multiple placement anchors can be equalized for a force in one direction only, unless extension is allowed—that's not the situation for the most common use of a cordelette. In other words, more than likely only one placement of the multiplacement anchor is actually taking nearly all the force, but the anchor builder doesn't really know which one (otherwise, why place several?). With three placements each rated at 10 kN, there's no imaginable force that could overcome the anchor if it were truly equalized—more reason to focus on security rather than strength.

Don't be the climber who thinks, "Hmmm. This placement will be weak because it will get pulled sideways, and this placement is lame because the rope could dislodge it, and this placement is dubious because one of the cam lobes isn't touching, but if I tie them all together with a cordelette, the result will be strong!" Lashing placements together hoping to achieve strength from multiple weaknesses or wishing that one of the placements will somehow be oriented well enough to hold the fall is an ineffective shotgun approach—the "infinite number of monkeys" school of anchor building.

This naive strategy can be mitigated by focusing on the first anchor after the belay, Anchor #1; in general, it's the most important anchor in the safety system and, fortunately, it's amenable to thoughtful construction. The direction of forces on it will be known. The largest force will be downward, if the leader falls before clipping another placement or if the subsequent placement fails during a fall. The direction of force from the belayer will be fixed, too, so it can be factored into the anchor's design. A far smaller force from a predictable direction might occur if the rope tightens on subsequent anchors and pulls it outward or upward. If the belayer is pulled off his stance by the force of a fall, the leader and the belayer could both end up hanging from Anchor #1, but even in a worst-case scenario, the total force on Anchor #1 will be less than the strength rating for a single piece of pro (because of energy absorption by the rope and slip in the belay). This suggests that the focus when constructing Anchor #1 is making it secure, rather than making it strong.

Extended Equalization

This discussion doesn't mean that SRENE concepts are wrong, just that they are usually poorly understood and applied. There's no better example than calling for both equalization and non-extension (E together with NE). Despite the implications of acronyms, you can't actually achieve non-extension and equalization simultaneously. Equalization is an appropriate goal when the strength of an individual placement might be inadequate to hold anticipated forces; that could arise on snow or ice, but it's seldom a problem on decent rock. Placements in rock are typically quite strong, but only when pulled from a particular direction—a direction that may not coincide with the force anticipated when the anchor was built. To deal with that, other placements can be included in the anchor system as *directionals*. This is not the same as equalization, at least not in the mental process that goes into designing the anchor. For example, you may use a hardware directional to keep a sling around a rock horn from being pulled off it, converting a strong anchor into one that's also secure by controlling the direction of applied force.

STATIC EQUALIZATION

Static equalization describes multiple placements joined by cords of fixed lengths; it's how you typically use a cordelette. Static equalization usually

A sling around a rock horn, held in place by a directional.

results in the minimum extension of the anchor's master point should one of the component placements fail, but it balances forces on its placements only if the applied force is precisely from the anticipated direction in three-dimensional space. Locating placements far apart creates undesirable force multiplication, but locating them close together results in more force imbalance (loss of equalization) if the actual direction of the load doesn't align as you intended. How big is that problem? If two runners join at 30°, moving the load from the perfectly equalized direction by only 10° will result in three times as much force on one of the anchors as the other; equalization is clearly lost, and things could be worse depending on the runner angle. In practice it's often difficult to estimate the ultimate direction of the applied force and it's especially difficult to tie the master point knot to tension things just right. In other words, static equalization rigs are almost always examples of redundancy and use of directionals, not genuine equalization—despite what the anchor builder was thinking or hoping to achieve. High-strength, no-stretch runners and cordelettes make this problem worse. This is an important understanding that few climbers appreciate.

REDUNDANCY

The redundancy or *backup* approach to rigging an anchor puts the load on one placement, while another placement is established to take the applied force only if the first placement fails and extension occurs. Backups are usually a poor use of placements, but somehow this approach has psychological appeal, and you often see it illustrated in texts, including The Classic.

DYNAMIC EQUALIZATION

Dynamic equalization refers to multiple placements joined so that force balancing is maintained even if the anchor isn't perfectly aligned with the applied force, or if the direction of the applied force changes. In order to achieve dynamic equalization, some amount of extension must be tolerated. The amount of extension that's possible is proportional to the amount of adaptation to change in the direction of applied force. You can't achieve E and NE at the same time.

Quite Frankly, I'm Shocked

I hate the word *shock*. It is commonly misused, suggesting lack of technical understanding in first aid and in discussions of climbing forces, where the term *shock loading* gets thrown around. If shock loading is to have any meaning beyond ordinary climbing forces, it must refer to forces that are unusually high and brief; such forces are very rare, thanks to modern safety equipment. Let's examine an example. A climber is hanging from a single 10-foot-long rope tied to a carabiner that's held by two anchors. One anchor pops out, and the carabiner drops 1 foot before the other anchor stops it cold. Most would agree that this is an example of shock loading the remaining anchor. But is it? The force from a fall is proportional to (the square root of) the fall factor. In this example, the fall factor is

1 foot of fall divided by 10 feet of energy-absorbing rope, or 0.1. Only 0.1? That would cause a peak force on the remaining anchor of at most 2.5 kN, even without considering any energy absorbed by the first anchor's failure, and that's not a dramatically hard fall at all—and that's my point. Actually, my point is that any time a significant amount of dynamic rope is in the system, "shock loading" doesn't occur. This statement will have old-schoolers sucking in their beards, but intuition about abruptly applied force is invariably poorly informed and excessively paranoid. Anchors do fail when jerked on, of course, but the failure is inevitably due to lack of security, not lack of strength.

If shock loading means extraordinarily abrupt and high force, does it *ever* occur? If a climber clips to an anchor with a Spectra daisy chain and climbs higher, then falls several feet, there's *no* energy-absorbing rope in the system at all, and forces rise incalculably high. In real-life situations where this has happened, hardware has broken, and climbers have fallen to their deaths. Shock loading was once a serious problem with via ferrata until special energy absorbers were developed. There are many components of climbing systems in addition to the rope that can absorb a little energy, so it takes brainless effort to produce damaging shock loads and, fortunately, that's rare—but it's something to watch out for in unusual circumstances.

The implication is that a moderate amount of extension doesn't result in high peak forces if there's rope in the system. Sure, you'd avoid build-

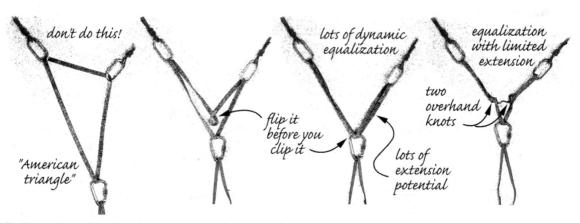

The "magic X" or "sliding X" and a balance of extension and equalization.

ing anchors that could result in really long extension, but there's little cause for paranoia in ordinary setups.

Building Anchors with the Rope

Mountaineers who fail to follow my advice of carrying an ample number of long slings may find themselves needing to set up an anchor using the rope instead of runners. If your mind goes blank despite reading the forthcoming paragraphs, you could simply use clove hitches at the anchors and at the HMS biner at your waist. With enough clove hitches, you'll be fine; this is how ice climbers sometimes establish anchors. There's nothing significantly wrong with this approach, and there's a lot to be said for it, starting with simplicity. Of course, your HMS biner and your waist will be

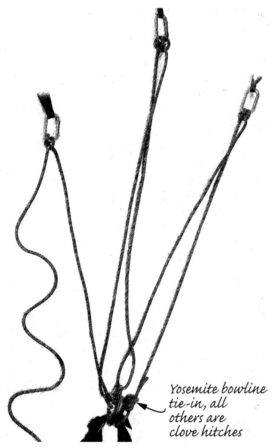

Yosemite bowline
tie-in, all
others are
clove hitches

Building a multiplacement anchor using clove hitches on the climbing rope.

crowded, and you'll have used miles of rope. You can't escape the web you've woven without completely taking it apart—and there are better ways.

Tricky knots are bad news. The Internet and climbing texts, too, are full of fancy ways to make double loop and triple loop knots for creating multiple placement anchors using the rope. Don't be led down the primrose path. Most of these knots have been created by mad geniuses who have too much spare time and who've never encountered the challenges of mountaineering: stiff or frozen ropes, snow-covered ropes, gloved yet frozen fingers, the likelihood that knots will be hurriedly dressed and tightened, the possibility that placements will fail, and the likelihood that the knot tier will be distracted by exposure, rockfall, darkness, and doubt. Multiple loop knots are especially susceptible to lame inventiveness, which is why cordelettes are such great accessories for modern mountaineers—they avoid all that malarkey. Despite the evident requirements, you see many knots that are excessively complex when simpler solutions are available. Simple is good for mountaineers; complexity is dangerous.

Madame Butterfly

A simple way top create anchor loops when your cordelettes are unavailable is to tie familiar butterfly knots—well, it should be a familiar knot. The butterfly is strong and doesn't slip when pulled from either strand or from the loop. It has many applications, but somehow climbers think of it as a specialized knot used only for creating a tie-in point in the middle of a rope, such as for a roped party on a glacier. Use the butterfly as your first choice to put a loop anywhere on your rope, except near the end, where you'd tie a Yosemite bowline loop. No fancy knots necessary.

There are many possible variations and combinations. Exactly what approach you take will depend on circumstances, such as how confident you are of your anchors, how much rope and hardware is available, equalization/extension goals, and so on. In the Additional Skills appendix I've included instructions for tying a simple knot to create two or three loops in the rope; it's the only such specialized knot in which I have confidence, from

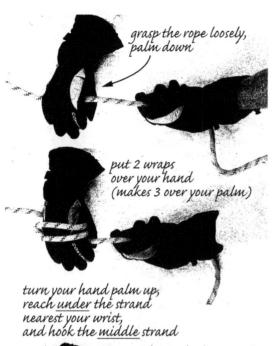

grasp the rope loosely, palm down

put 2 wraps over your hand (makes 3 over your palm)

turn your hand palm up, reach <u>under</u> the strand nearest your wrist, and hook the <u>middle</u> strand

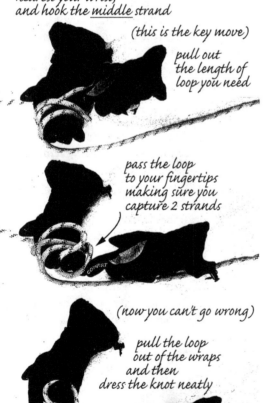

(this is the key move)

pull out the length of loop you need

pass the loop to your fingertips making sure you capture 2 strands

(now you can't go wrong)

pull the loop out of the wraps and then dress the knot neatly

Tying a butterfly knot.

Finished butterfly knot.

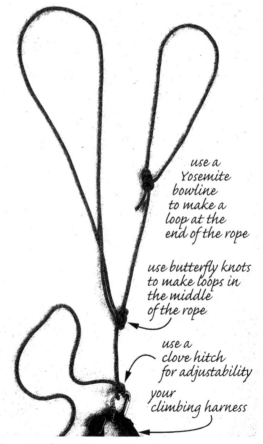

use a Yosemite bowline to make a loop at the end of the rope

use butterfly knots to make loops in the middle of the rope

use a clove hitch for adjustability

your climbing harness

Using a butterfly to build a complex anchor.

among the many that somehow find their way into print.

WHAT'S A MOUNTAINEER TO DO?

If static equalization invariably boils down to redundancy rather than true equalization, and dynamic equalization doesn't typically lead to shock loading, the old acronyms leave us adrift. What then is a reasonable, realistic approach to anchor building? Actually, this is a nontrivial quandary that few mountaineers (or trad climbers, for that matter) understand. Fortunately there are pretty good simple answers.

Focus on Anchor #1. Locate it where the leader can clip it without fear of falling beforehand; that could mean making it part of the belay anchor or making the belay anchor part of it—giving up the best anchor spot to Anchor #1 and using a less desirable placement for the belayer (a sling around a horn for Anchor #1 and a nut for the belayer, not the other way around). Analyze the direction of forces that Anchor #1 must hold and locate placements accordingly. If a good placement location doesn't align well with the expected force direction, use another placement as a directional. Strength of 100 percent for any good-sized piece of pro is all you'll ever need, so it's better to focus on guaranteeing you'll have it than on the macramé of tying together several less secure placements—unless you confront a rare circumstance when that's all that Mother Nature allows. Your primary focus should be to connect the component placements of Anchor #1, not so much in hopes they all share the load (*mutual strength*), but so that they work together to ensure *mutual security*.

If several secure placements are available, by all means use more than one; if not, start over where there are better options. When good placements are available, as mountaineers usually enjoy, as a practical matter you'll be working mostly with redundancy, not true equalization; give the rig your best shot at static equalization, but don't agonize. Adding a third placement using a cordelette increases the strength of the anchor by 50 percent, but only if the applied force is shared exactly equally by all three pieces; in practice that's hard to

achieve, so usually only two anchors actually bear the load and then seldom equally. Be sure that rope or belayer movement won't dislodge components of Anchor #1 and place additional pieces if necessary to prevent it.

If strength of placements making up Anchor #1 is a genuine concern (in weak ice or snow, usually, or a chossy rock anchor where the "rock" is kitty litter, dried mud, or frozen turf), join them with a truly equalizing arrangement. Don't apportion much time figuring how to limit extension,

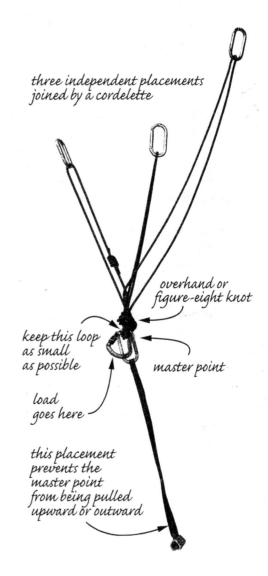

three independent placements joined by a cordelette

overhand or figure-eight knot

keep this loop as small as possible

master point

load goes here

this placement prevents the master point from being pulled upward or outward

An example of building Anchor #1.

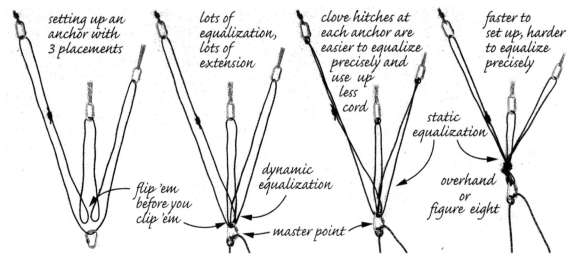

setting up an anchor with 3 placements

flip 'em before you clip 'em

lots of equalization, lots of extension

dynamic equalization

master point

clove hitches at each anchor are easier to equalize precisely and use up less cord

static equalization

overhand or figure eight

faster to set up, harder to equalize precisely

Complex anchors made with a cordelette.

unless it could be truly long (several feet), because if one placement blows, they may all go, no matter what you've done. Use a force-limiting runner (Screamer) if you have one. The relative strength among equalized placements doesn't figure in to load balancing, because you'd be foolish to include an obviously weaker placement whose failure could compromise the entire anchor system; assume every placement is equally strong when you design your anchor. Only if you have plenty of time, tie knots to allow some equalization while limiting extension.

If you really must have near-perfect, if static, equalization with your cordelette, using clove hitches at the anchors rather than a knot at the master point makes fine-tuning easier; you'll still have minimal extension.

Locate the belayer at least several feet from the master point of Anchor #1. That will allow the belayer's body to be jerked in the direction of Anchor #1 by a hard fall, and that will reduce peak forces throughout the safety system. Tether the belayer to safely limit the distance he can be pulled—up to 3 feet (1 m) is optimum, but that will occur only in the hardest falls. There's an illustration of this setup in the following section on belaying the leader.

When in doubt, use a longer runner.

13
Rappelling

Mountaineers on moderate routes may carry a rope as a precaution but use it mainly to rappel sections of the descent. Downclimbing is faster and often safer, but rappelling is faster than belayed downclimbing; sometimes it's the only option. Rappelling under even the best conditions can be tricky and dangerous; on moderate routes it can cause much more rockfall than climbing or downclimbing. I, and the climbers I know, are apprehensive about rappelling because it inevitably means that your fate depends entirely on a few pieces of equipment and the beneficence of the mountain. Mountains are not beneficent; every climber has an "almost bought the farm" story of rappelling. Whether it's true or not, there's a prevalent belief that more injuries occur while rappelling than on any other part of the climb, and rappelling injuries tend to be fatal. Tom Patey is just one of the accomplished climbers whose careers were terminated by rappelling; guides are not immune. Getting down a rappel route may not even require rappelling; it may be more expedient

for the strongest climber to *lower* tired or inexperienced climbers rather than go through the business of getting them on rappel and ensuring they will be able to complete the descent safely under their own control. The following discussion covers in detail techniques that make rappelling as safe as possible, even if you've adopted unusual rope choices, yet climbers often don't take all these precautions. I suspect that's both because they're unaware of them and because many climbers, especially beginners, don't view rappelling with the dread that experienced climbers develop. If you cut corners, you shrink your margin of safety.

GET CONNECTED

Select a rappel brake that's designed for the ropes you'll be using, particularly if they're lighter than usual. I recommend one of the newer devices that give more holding power on narrower ropes and single-rope rappels, and I like devices with an autoblock option for belaying. Connect your rappel brake's HMS carabiner to your harness using a 1-foot sewn runner, especially when you're wearing a minimalist alpine harness that may not have a belay loop anyhow. This runner extends the brake away from your clothing, which a mountaineer may have a lot of, and it facilitates using an autoblock self-belay. Your setup will include a daisy chain cinched to your harness tie-in points with a small locking carabiner on it. You could use one of the pockets in your daisy chain to extend your HMS biner and rappel brake instead of the short sewn runner and still use the remainder of the daisy to clip in for security (it's OK to use a daisy chain to extend your brake for rappelling but not for belaying; the pocket strength is 3.5 kN). Definitely learn to use the Münter hitch to rappel; it will get you through a variety of situations.

The Münter Hitch

The Münter hitch is also called the Italian hitch and Italian half hitch (but not by Italians), Mezzo Barcaiolo (MB), and the half clove hitch—which in German is Halb-Mastwurf-Sicherung or HMS, hence the name for the large locking carabiner that pairs well with the Münter hitch. Münter was the Swiss guide who brought the Italian hitch to America, and three Italians brought it from ancient mariners to climbing. The rumor that it twists the rope is overblown; the actual amount of twisting is, as for hardware brakes including tubes, dependent on the exact dress of the rope as well as the rope's design and construction. The force a

this orientation has 2/3 of the holding power

The Münter hitch in action.

Münter hitch can apply depends on the exact way the rope enters and exits the brake (coplanar works best) as well as on the rope's design and construction. The Münter hitch applies maximum holding power when the holding and held ropes run alongside each other and roughly 70 percent of the maximum when they enter and exit the hitch on opposite sides.

Figure on 3 kN or a bit more for the maximum holding force of the strong orientation of the Münter hitch, and 2.25 kN for the weaker orientation, before the knot lets rope slip no matter how firmly you hold it with your thoughtfully gloved hand.

Making a Münter

To tie a Münter hitch, forget all those goofy, fumbly ways you've seen in old-school texts, and learn the method pictured here. Using just one hand and never releasing the rope you'll amaze your friends by tying it faster than they can follow. The method is based on a backhand clip.

When you master the backhand clip, you can quickly tie a clove hitch by using two backhand clips, instead of just one to make a Münter.

If the clove hitch is new to you, be assured that it doesn't let rope slip, despite its apparent simplicity. One of its virtues is that it's easily adjusted without untying.

You can also tie a clove hitch using one hand if you've already clipped the rope through the carabiner; and yes, this does cause a twist.

From there, it's easy to convert an already-clipped rope to a Münter hitch.

To complete the discussion, I'll illustrate a Münter hitch having an additional turn, sometimes called a Super Münter (or, as you might want to call it, the ÜberMünter). This substantially increases the holding power of the Münter hitch; use it to rappel on a single skinny rope or to lower a heavy load, such as two climbers simultaneously in an emergency. Start out with a Super Münter any time you have doubts about your ability to maintain control as you let out rope. It may turn out frustratingly slow, but that's better than eye-poppingly fast.

When the Münter hitch changes from taking

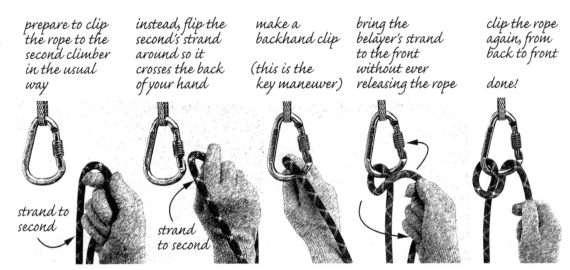

prepare to clip the rope to the second climber in the usual way

instead, flip the second's strand around so it crosses the back of your hand

make a backhand clip

(this is the key maneuver)

bring the belayer's strand to the front without ever releasing the rope

clip the rope again, from back to front

done!

strand to second

strand to second

Tying a Münter hitch.

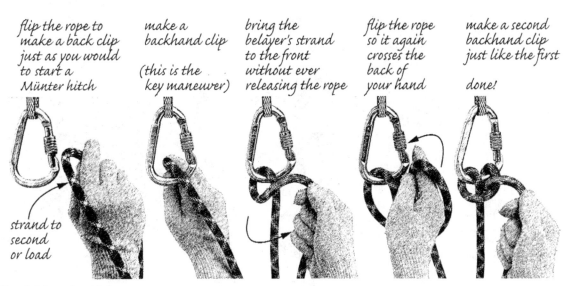

flip the rope to make a back clip just as you would to start a Münter hitch

make a backhand clip

(this is the key maneuver)

bring the belayer's strand to the front without ever releasing the rope

flip the rope so it again crosses the back of your hand

make a second backhand clip just like the first

done!

strand to second or load

Steps in tying a clove hitch.

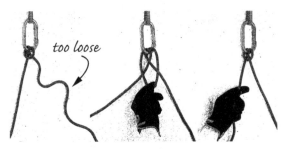

too loose

A benefit of the clove hitch is ease of adjustment.

in rope to feeding it out, as it would if a second were to fall while being belayed upward, the hitch flips through the carabiner and rearranges itself; using a big HMS biner makes this smoother. Don't agonize about getting your Münter hitch tied with the holding rope or the loaded rope against the carabiner spine; just be sure to screw down the gate. In a pinch, a Münter hitch will work on just about any kind of carabiner. Practice tying both

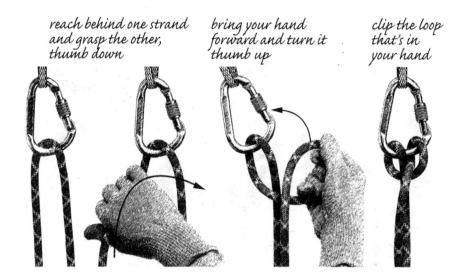

reach behind one strand and grasp the other, thumb down

bring your hand forward and turn it thumb up

clip the loop that's in your hand

Tying a clove hitch when the rope is already clipped.

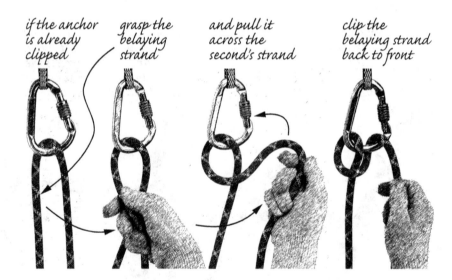

if the anchor is already clipped

grasp the belaying strand

and pull it across the second's strand

clip the belaying strand back to front

Tying a Münter hitch when the rope is already clipped.

the clove hitch and Münter hitch at your waist and at shoulder height.

RAPPEL ANCHORS

Rappel anchors may not require great strength, but they do require great security; that's what should be foremost in your mind when you start building your anchor. The emphasis on security over strength means you should be completely com-

fortable rappelling off a single, secure nut or a 5 mm cord anchor. That nut will hold fall forces, and that 5 mm cord is what you make your prusik loops out of, so their strength is acceptable; it's up to you to learn the skills to place them securely. There may be instances where attempting to create a rappel anchor from several placements could end up with a less secure anchor than if made from one—complex rigs or combining a solid anchor with another that's questionable, for example. If

adding an extra turn to a Münter hitch substantially increases holding power

The Super Münter.

I have to chuckle (or groan) every time I see texts instructing the Dülfersitz rappel. After going through the many reasons it's unsafe, they end up saying, "but you should learn it anyway, just in case." But when mountaineers who never practice this rappel reach the point of "just in case," they inevitably don't know how to pull it off. That makes it extra dangerous, because it's easy to flip out of a Dülfersitz if you don't know what you're doing. By the time you're at the point of "just in case," you've already made a huge number of avoidable dumb decisions. Amusing examples of the Dülfersitz show a climber in a harness using a prusik self-belay (a genuine recipe-for-disaster combination) or the rappeller being belayed from above (you can't use a fireman's belay from below with a Dülfersitz rappel). The climber in the first example should just use his carabiner to make a Münter hitch rappel, and the second climber should simply be lowered. The Dülfersitz is a dangerous relic from before the First World War; it's no recourse for climbers who are so inexperienced as to get themselves into a situation where it might be considered a recourse. It's especially problematic for a rappeller wearing a backpack or carrying climbing hardware. Here are some alternatives: if your party carries a rope, each climber should have, at a minimum, a 48-inch runner and an HMS carabiner—make this a hard and fast rule. Then set up a diaper seat harness and do a Münter hitch rappel—no Dülfersitz needed. If only a single carabiner is available, even a nonlocker, share it among the party for Münter rappels and tape the gate shut with a Band-Aid if you must; make a diaper seat with a loop at the end of the rope if necessary. If no carabiner is available, lower climbers rather than use a Dülfersitz. Experts agree that the Dülfersitz rappel should only be used on low-angled slopes and only as a last resort; they also agree it messes up your shoulder and your jacket. Forget about the Dülfersitz and spend the time learning to avoid such "last resorts." If you absolutely must see it properly applied, check Appendix A, Additional Skills.

you expect to set up several rappel stations as you descend a mountaineering route, be prepared with a long length of narrow nylon webbing or, better, 6 mm accessory cord that you can cut to length—which will always be longer than you anticipate. A couple of sacrificial cordelettes work, too. With plenty of cord you'll be able to take advantage of sturdy natural features such as horns and chockstones rather than using hardware to set up secure anchors; you can use that iron wire in your ten essentials to help lace cord behind rock features. The anchors you can build depend on circumstances, certainly, but let's take a look at the best way to deal with the anchor, no matter how it's constructed.

Redundancy

Redundancy is especially important when rappelling, where failures can be fatal. A comforting rappel anchor, maybe the most common on mountaineering routes, is a runner around a sturdy rock feature. Assuming the feature is indeed permanent and that you're using a sewn runner or one tied with a double fisherman's knot, this anchor should be totally acceptable. But why take

chances? There are numerous possibilities that might compromise even this ideal setup—rockfall, for example, or the rock horn that comes adrift because it turns out to be held in place by mud (true stories). The safe thing to do is create another unloaded backup placement that does not depend on the same rock feature that supports the main runner. Place a nut or runner elsewhere and rig it so that should the main anchor fail, the backup will take over with minimal extension. The last descender can remove the backup after it proves unnecessary.

V-THREADS

If you're rappelling off a V-thread, use the ice screw that you drilled the holes with as a backup. Don't put it close to the V-thread lest it weaken the ice and because failure of the V-thread ice might cause the backup to fail, too—the same thinking that says if your V-thread drilling is off target, start another attempt several feet away. Remember that a rappel will subject ice or snow anchors to continuous pressure for several minutes; hopefully they won't melt out, but always cover the anchor and its backup with snow to help keep them cool and shady. And skedaddle.

RAPPEL RINGS

Retrieving the rope is a major concern when rappelling; retrieval should always be made as easy as possible. That's one reason never to use a rock feature or tree as an anchor without also using a sling (pulling down your rope could also scar the tree and get sap in your rope); desperate alpinists even cut off the end of their ropes to make emergency rap anchors. Rappel rings also make the rope easier to retrieve, but mountaineers often don't use them, I suppose because they're reluctant to part with a couple of dollars, but it's always a good idea, especially if the anchor is likely to be used often. Rappel rings do make it a little easier to pull the rope, they prevent wear on the anchor sling as the rope is pulled down, and they make it possible to lower body weight through the rappel anchor in the event of an emergency. Never let a weighted rope slip through a runner; lowering body weight on a rope directly through a nylon sling or cord could cut through the sling after only 10 feet of travel. Leave an old carabiner behind, with its gate taped shut, if you anticipate a difficult rope retrieval or if there's any chance the rope could run through the rappel anchor under load. Pulling the rappel rope, even unweighted, causes slight melting that weakens rappel slings, a good reason that if you decide to use an existing sling without a ring or carabiner, you should rotate it so that the rope runs over a different spot. People have unwisely top roped off rap rings without consequences; their strength is over 10 kN (2,250 lbf), but be aware that loading a cord (rope or runner) across a small radius reduces its ultimate strength by maybe 25 percent, and while it's running over a small radius it's weaker by as much as 50 percent.

Rappel rings also raise concerns about redundancy; for sure, those little aluminum rings are thought provoking when staking your life, no matter how strong they test. Back up rap rings, not by using two, but by adding a small runner. The illustration shows a backup runner tied with a beer knot, but a home-sewn runner would work as well (see Chapter 10). The anchor sling must hold both the ring and its mini-runner, and the rope must run through both, too. If you use the lark's foot attachment illustrated below (perhaps because you're adding a ring to an existing sling) the anchor won't be multidirectional and self-equalizing; locate the ring thoughtfully and be sure there's no chance the ring could come unhitched.

The best place to locate the rap ring when you set up the anchor is free hanging above the rappel route; this makes the start more difficult for the rapeller, but it offers the best chance of avoiding problems when the rope is pulled down. Next best location would be well above any lip, placed so that the rope lies gently over the lip, and any rope-joining knot is below the lip. The rope will stretch a little when weighted, and the lip will create abrasion.

rappel anchor

Rappel ring with a backup runner.

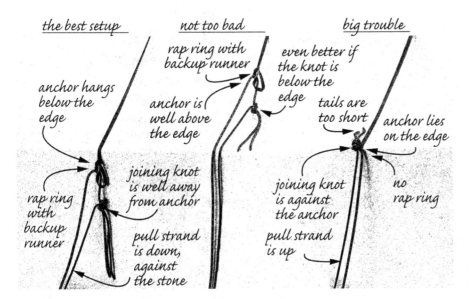

the best setup

not too bad

big trouble

anchor hangs below the edge

rap ring with backup runner

even better if the knot is below the edge

anchor is well above the edge

tails are too short

anchor lies on the edge

joining knot is well away from anchor

rap ring with backup runner

joining knot is against the anchor

no rap ring

pull strand is down, against the stone

pull strand is up

Setting up the rappel anchor.

If the rap ring must lie on rock, be sure that the pull-down strand is on the bottom, against the stone. Clear away choss near the rappel site that could be dislodged by the rope or by waiting abseilistas.

GETTING STARTED

So far, everything's been under control, but you're now about to hand your rope over to Mother Nature. If she's acting temperamental, that may be unwise. If she's benign, assume fate isn't, and be sure you're tethered to a reliable anchor with your daisy chain while preparing the rappel.

Throwing Down the Rope

If you're rappelling on two strands of one rope, flake it out into two piles simultaneously so that you can find the middle, but keep track of the ends. Lace one side through the rap ring and its little backup runner; if this is too much of a chore, borrow a carabiner from your partner's rack instead of using a descending ring. Tape the biner gate shut with tape from your first-aid kit to get the benefits of a locking carabiner without the economic consequences of abandoning one. Tie double overhand stopper knots into each of the rope ends separately. If you're concerned that the rope

might escape by sliding through the rap ring, tie a mule knot near the midpoint. Gather up half of the rope so that you end up holding the stopper knot and a few coils in one hand and most of the first half looped in your throwing hand. Throw out the middle of the strand, trying to cause the rope to uncoil substantially before it drapes perfectly down the intended route. As you release the coils, habitually yell "Roooope!" even if no one's below to benefit from the warning. If you get tangles or the rope doesn't lie where you want it, pull it up and try again. If you're satisfied with the lay of the rope, throw down the stopper knot and the few terminal coils so that all of one half is down; you don't have to give this end a big toss unless you're trying to influence its ultimate location. Throw down the other half of the rope the same way; then release the mule.

If Mother Nature would insist on blowing your ropes to the netherworld, it's best not to throw them down at all. Doing so could force the first descender to wander far off route and dislodge stones on herself with the rope while attempting to coalesce the cords, which could become trapped by the terrain. Rappelling below a stuck rope end can elicit an especially time-consuming recovery if the rappeller must prusik back up the rope to free it; deal with this by having the

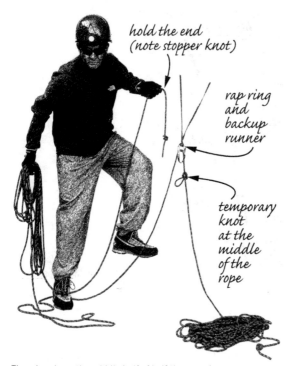

hold the end
(note stopper knot)

rap ring
and
backup
runner

temporary
knot
at the
middle
of the
rope

Throwing down the middle half of half the rappel rope.

first descender continue down on the strand that isn't stuck after the ropes have been locked off at the anchor with a prusik loop. The next climber will remove the prusik and rap down both strands, taking care not to pass the sticking point, free the rope, and continue down amazed at having survived the complexity. Instead of throwing down the ropes, the first descender can dress the rope as she heads down, while another climber feeds rope and prevents tangles; this gets you down at least halfway. If you keep your rope in a bag as I recommend, you could rap all the way down while feeding rope out of the bag (or your backpack or a stack of coils in a sling clipped to your harness). Also consider rapping on one strand of the rope while being belayed from above on the other; just be sure you are prepared to deal with the need to apply twice the holding power with your brake hand, compared to a typical twin-strand rappel. Yet another option would be simply to lower the first descender on both ropes, but communication needed for delicate lowering will be impaired by that howling wind.

JOINING TWO ROPES FOR RAPPELLING

Double Fisherman's Knot

Use the same basic procedure if you're rappelling on two joined ropes to make a full-length rappel, except that you'd pass the end of one through the rap ring before tying the ropes together. There are only two sensible knots for joining rappel ropes. The most reassuring is the double fisherman's knot. It neither requires nor benefits from any kind of backup knot; just leave tails at least 5 inches (12 cm) long. The double fisherman's knot can be used to join ropes of substantially unequal diameter. If you confront this mismatch of rappel ropes, anticipate problems in the rappel itself; you'll be rappelling on the fatter rope while the skinny one is just along for the ride. Any time you have dissimilar ropes, make sure the fatter one goes through the anchor, and pull down the thinner one first.

The double fisherman's knot should be used to join rappel ropes only when there's no chance that the rope could get hung up. This is rare. It might happen if the rappel is free hanging or over a smooth surface or when abseiling over snow or ice. Otherwise, ropes seem diabolically determined to get stuck, and a stuck rappel rope is the most time-consuming and dangerous diversion of a climb. Ropes, even a single rope, can get stuck behind a flake without any help from a knot. They also get stuck as the knot tries to pass over a clean horizontal edge. This might be surprising, but remember that there's substantial force resisting your downward pull; this force comes from the weight of the remainder of the rope and from the friction of the rope over rock and through the rappel anchor (a reason to use a rap ring or leaver carabiner to reduce that friction). A rope stuck this way seems from below to be so solidly jammed that you'd guess the knot was caught in a crack even though it's just hung at an edge; just one reason why climbing up to free a rope can be so scary.

EDK

The UIAA, AMGA (American Mountain Guides Association), and all other climbing groups that have looked into the issue have concluded that the double fisherman's knot and all other knots, save one, should be avoided unless there's certainty that the ropes cannot become stuck. The knot recommended in the alternative is the simple overhand, also called the flat overhand and, by sardonic American climbers, the EDK—European Death Knot, reflecting its Eastern European origin.

If you've been around climbing for a while, you've encountered heated debates about the EDK/flat overhand. It just looks too simple to be depended upon for the sole knot that holds a rappeller dangling over destiny. Tests have consistently shown that the unimproved flat overhand has wholly adequate strength (10 kN minimum; and keep in mind that the load on the knot is half the load on both ropes), has well-established security, has numerous minor benefits such as ease of tying and untying, and most importantly is the knot least likely to contribute to rappel ropes becoming stuck. It works fine with ropes of different diameters, with many of the performance tests having been done with joined 8 mm and 11 mm ropes. You can even securely join a 5 mm retrieval line to an 11 mm lead rope with a simple overhand; there's plenty of room to tie a backup double overhand with the 5 mm onto the 11's tail, but I've never seen the backup become loaded. Whatever the diameters are, leave long tails, typically 10 inches (25 cm) or more, and firmly tighten the knot one strand at a time. Tie the knot so that the tails tip in the direction of the pull-down force to

make for slightly easier travel of the knot over edges, and keep the knot away from the rappel ring because contact makes the pull-down start balky.

FINAL PREPARATIONS

Consider whether the first descender should take all of the rack, or just most of it; in the event of an emergency, climbers remaining may find themselves needing what just left with the first rappeller, perhaps including materials to extend the length of the rappel just a bit or to relocate the anchor if the rope proves to be unretrievable. The first climber to descend will set up her rappel device, clip in to the rappel anchor system with her handy daisy chain and locker, and release any other connection. She'll then run the rappel ropes through the rappel device, lock her HMS biner, and move

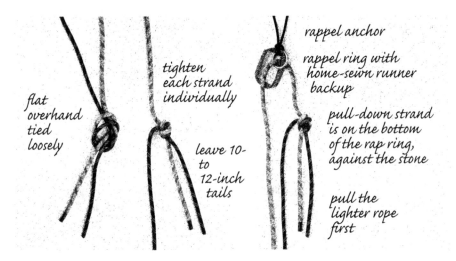

flat overhand tied loosely

tighten each strand individually

leave 10- to 12-inch tails

rappel anchor

rappel ring with home-sewn runner backup

pull-down strand is on the bottom of the rap ring, against the stone

pull the lighter rope first

The flat overhand knot (European Death Knot).

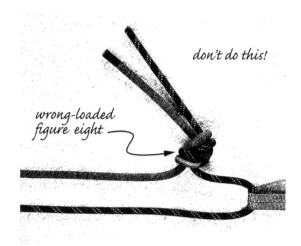

don't do this!

wrong-loaded figure eight —

Side-loaded figure eight; don't do this.

toward the starting position. Next, she'll set up her self-belay.

SELF-BELAY WHILE RAPPELLING

A self-belay is good practice for rappelling mountaineers, who may be burned out at the end of a long day or days, carrying a backpack, wearing gloves, and subjected to objective hazards or the threat thereof. The first descender is especially vulnerable to rappelling misfortune, because she'll have to reconnoiter the route, avoid causing rockfall, dress the ropes, and locate a stopping point that will accept the remaining climbers and perhaps another rappel anchor. Things are worse yet if she has to deal with skinny ropes or ropes that are wet, snow covered, or icy. There are several ways to set up a rappel self-belay; you should work out one that works for you and that you can readily put into action. Make it so easy to use that you use it without hesitation, because a self-belay adds considerably to the safety of rappels.

Old-school climbers advocate a self-belay that uses a prusik knot on the rope above the rappel device, but this virtually guarantees problems; the prusik takes full body weight and will require gymnastics to release if it inadvertently locks—which it invariably does. The knot requires being held continuously to prevent locking, but requires an unnatural release of grip if locking is needed

to avert disaster. New-school climbers use a self-belay friction knot *below* the brake device, where it holds only a fraction of body weight. A weak friction knot can be used, one that can be released by hand while it's loaded. The hand that isn't braking the descent is freed to brace the descender, flip the ropes around, or whatever. The autoblock knot is just four turns of "prusik loop" cord wrapped around the rope. The two ends of the loop can be clipped to a harness leg loop with a biner (technically making it a *French prusik*), or one end can be cinched and the other clipped. In order for this setup to work well and give the brake hand some space, the rappel brake and its carabiner need to be extended. Cinching a 1-foot runner to the harness's tie-in point is just the ticket; it also makes the rappel device more visible and keeps it away from clothing and other objects near your crowded waist. Clothing caught in your rappel device results in a thought-provoking delay. Extend the rappel carabiner with a doubled prusik loop, if you haven't a short runner.

I prefer holding my brake hand near my thigh when I abseil, so I connect my autoblock to the haul loop in back of my harness instead of to the leg loop; that gives me plenty of clearance. You need to work out what works best for you, paying

PRUSIK LOOPS

Every alpine climber should carry two or three prusik loops where they can easily be reached, in a pocket or clipped to a harness. These are just loops of 5 mm accessory cord tied with a double fisherman's knot. A 60-inch (24 cm) total length cord is a place to start; pick very limp cord so friction knots lock reliably, even on wet or icy ropes (I prefer Mammut cord). Going up to 6 mm cord is unnecessary, and it doesn't lock well on skinny ropes. Even 4 mm cord is strong enough and locks well, sometimes too well; just replace it often. There are any number of uses for these loops, including prusiking up a rope, described in Chapter 25, Self-Rescue. Prusiks, friction knots in general, and mechanical ascenders are intended only for gripping rope and holding body weight; they're not suitable for catching falls. A prusik loop is plenty strong enough to use as an emergency rappel anchor. Don't leave home without your prusik loops, and don't let them hide in the bottom of your pack.

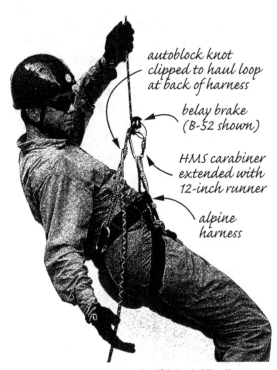

autoblock knot
clipped to haul loop
at back of harness

belay brake
(B-52 shown)

HMS carabiner
extended with
12-inch runner

alpine
harness

Rappeller hanging with autoblock self-belay holding the rope.

clip to harness haul loop
or leg loop

The autoblock knot.

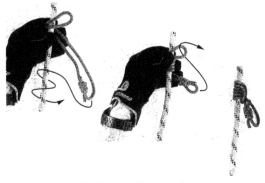

Tying a Klemheist friction knot with a prusik loop.

particular attention to making the prusik loop used for your autoblock the right length for your particular harness. If your rappel brake isn't extended far enough, or if the prusik loop is too long and the autoblock knot touches the brake when everything's tensioned, the autoblock knot won't lock—and you're history. Keep your brake hand on the ropes between the autoblock knot and the rappel brake, not on the knot itself. Don't use friction of the autoblock as the means of controlling your descent; it's there for emergency use only, should your brake hand lose control. If you intend to set the autoblock deliberately (to stop and take photos, for example), resist the temptation to hold it and let it slowly grab the ropes; it may just rub, not lock. Instead, let your brake hand get pulled up to the brake, away from the autoblock, and all should be well.

Test your autoblock setup before you head for the mountains, or even the local crag. This is particularly important if you intend to use skinny ropes (halves or twins), and especially if you intend to carry a long skinny cord to pull down a

main rope that's slim to start with. If you don't get enough grip with the autoblock knot, or if you worry about the effect of snow on your rappel ropes, a Klemheist friction knot made with cord or nylon webbing provides a bit more bite though it's more difficult to release.

CAST OFF

At this point you're clipped in for safety with your daisy chain and locker, the ropes are in your belay device, and your autoblock self-belay is in place. You may even have a mule knot tied in the ropes a short way below the rappel stance as a safety stop. Tie the release side of the mule knot downward; releasing a mule, especially one jammed on your autoblock, is manageable, but a figure eight on a bight jammed against your rappel device may require prusik climbing to free. Some climbers clip that knot to their harness, where it contributes clutter but is easier to deal with if you forget about it until it stops your progress; don't clip it to a gear loop. You'll be carrying the rack, or most of it, in case you need it on the way down or at the bottom. If you're carrying a heavy pack on a near vertical drop and are justifiably concerned that its weight could flip you over, don't wear it but clip it to your harness so it hangs between your legs. Your partner gives you a visual going over, checking the usual items: harness buckle doubled back, ropes properly through belay device or Münter correctly tied, locker locked, autoblock in place, anchor still looks good—then: thumbs up! Move to the start of the rappel and give yourself and the anchor a final inspection, being watchful that no clothing, gear, hair, or beard (it's happened) is positioned to be pulled into the rappel device or to interfere with your rope handling. Next, you'd like to haul back on the rappel ropes and give the setup a yank test for peace of mind. You'd like to retest your autoblock to be sure it will lock, even though you've thoroughly worked it out at home. When all systems are checked, yell to your partner, "Unclipping!" and then unclip your safety tether and stuff the end of the daisy chain and locker in your pocket. Tell your partner, "I'm outa here!" or "On rappel!" Shift to the final position if the start is tricky, and begin lowering yourself. Your ever vigilant partner will shout, "Hey, hoser, don't forget about that safety knot!"

AS YOU ALIGHT

The first descender's most obvious task is locating a stopping point where another rappel anchor can be built and where other members of the party can congregate, safely for themselves and safely for a person who will be descending below in the next rappel. On terrain where rockfall is a concern a series of angled rappels may be better than going straight down. If you descend to a section that seems designed to trap your rope when you try to pull it down, a big flake or flakes, for example, or a section that guarantees that significant rockfall will be kicked off by the rope or subsequent rappellers, don't continue if you're able to stop nearby. It will be faster to make two raps than to try to recover a stuck rope, and it will be safer than dodging dislodged rock. When you come to a stop, move out of the direct line of fire of rocks dislodged by the rope or feet of other rappellers; protect yourself and protect the rope from stones. Give the ropes a test pull to be sure that they're free enough to retrieve and to confirm the correct rope strand to pull. If you have plenty of rope at the new stance, pull down as much rope as possible to reduce the chances for a hang-up when the rope is finally pulled from the anchor. Anchor the ends to prevent them being blown around and to guide the next rappeller, but don't remove stopper knots. If rockfall isn't an issue, or if you can hide from any that may come down, get ready to perform a fireman's belay, even if it might not appear to be essential; just be sure those who follow you know what you're intending.

LAST IS BEST

Traditionally, the person who builds the rappel anchor goes down first. The last climber confronts the decision to remove the backup anchor before descending; this decision is entirely his own and should never be influenced by what equipment might be left behind. I had a climbing partner once who, before big climbs, would set fire to a $20 bill in the parking lot; he said it freed his mind of concern about leaving gear. This raises another issue, that of clipping in to the rappel anchors with your daisy chain while other climbers descend. There's a story about Mugs Stump being clipped to a single nut behind a lose flake as Jim Bridwell was rapping off it during the vertical blind descent from their outrageous climb of the Moose's Tooth. Mugs realized that if Bridwell popped the nut he, too, would perish, so he unclipped. Then he thought about

DISASTER RECOVERY

If one of your ropes has become damaged, you can use the damaged rope to pull down the good rope, and rappel on the good rope (or good half). A standard way to isolate a severely damaged section of rope is to put it in the loop of a butterfly knot; this knot is very strong and doesn't slip. A figure eight won't work. You could, I suppose, contrive a way to pass this knot as you descend both strands, but it's easier just to rap on the good rope and use the damaged strand as a retriever.

You may have noticed that it's often necessary to pull up on the ropes to get them to slide through your rappel brake enough to begin a descent. If the downward pull of the ropes were increased, you'll be stopped cold. It doesn't take much pull at all; one hand down below can do it. Any time climbers are rappelling it's a good idea for the first one down to hold the ropes and be prepared to pull them tight, just in case the descender somehow loses control. It's even easy for the belayer below to take complete control of the descent, if for any reason the rappeller is unable to do so.

being left alone on the vertical face without a rope, so he clipped back in. I'd say always clip in, to either the main anchor or the backup. I've never rappelled off anchors that appeared to have any possibility of failing, with snow bollards coming the closest; at least bollards don't force the decision to clip or not.

FREEING A STUCK ROPE

Everybody's down, and you begin to haul on the ropes to bring them down, too; you remember to pull the correct color and even untie the stopper knots before you start pulling, an oversight you'll make only once. You give the rope a big outward whip when you think you feel it about to leave the anchor. You keep pulling, but then the rope grinds to a halt—every climber's worst nightmare. Famous alpinists have died trying to free stuck ropes. What to do? Certainly, you'll immediately apply a lot of profanity and whipping of the rope.

When tugging and verbal abuse don't work, the next step is to vigorously apply body weight to the rope; attach a prusik or ascender to the end you have in hand. Hopefully that will start the rope creeping down. If not, have your partner join you and apply the two body weights. If the rope still doesn't move, at least you have a glimmer of hope that one person could possibly prusik up the rope and survive. If you're the technical type, you might consider setting up a Z-pulley system; that would allow you to apply about twice your weight to the hanging rope end. If you and your partner both apply body weight to the Z-pulley, that'll be about 3 kN (700 lbf)—not outrageously damaging to the rope, and only a minor challenge to your anchor-setting skills, but it establishes a modicum of comfort that prusiking up the rope will be uneventful, for a few feet at least.

If you've thought pure thoughts, there will come a time at some point during this low- and high-tech pulling exercise that the rope will come free. This isn't an altogether wonderful event, as the free rope may also be accompanied by free stones that were just recently its close companions. The likelihood of stonefall when freeing a rope demands constant attention to what's going on above; your perusal of the descent route during your rappel will give you clues and warnings. And you always wear a helmet, right?

If none of this pulling procedure produces positive results, ascent is the remaining option. First construct a serious belay anchor unless you'll be starting from the ground. If you've managed to pull down enough rope, you may be able to lead up the rock using the rope end you've got. You can use the stuck rope for aid (no style points are awarded when freeing a rope). You already know that the stuck rope will sustain your body weight should you attempt to prusik up it or yard on it when you need to; you just don't know how long it will stay stuck.

Another possibility is that you still have both ends but can't climb the rock. You'll have to ascend the ropes, but at least you can hope they're still through the rap anchor. Use prusik loops on both ropes together, or use mechanical ascenders on the pull-down strand and anchor both ropes against an upward pull, should your retention problem resolve itself precipitously.

The worst possibility is that you have only one strand and can't climb the rock. Your only option is to prusik back up the free hanging stuck rope. Using mechanical ascenders, even Tiblocs, makes this smoother than actually using prusik loops with Klemheist knots; smooth is good. Unless you're starting from flat ground, tie the rope to the anchor you've just built and connect yourself to the rope with a clove hitch below your prusiks; loosen the clove hitch and move it with you as you ascend. This time-consuming but necessary hitch will hold you in the event the rope comes unstuck and you fall past the anchor; your prusik loops are unlikely to hold a fall, and ascenders would just slide along the rope in their nonholding direction. It's also a good idea to tie a mule knot below yourself every dozen feet or so as a safety stop, if enough rope is available to do so. Advise your partner not to stand too close, as you'll be peeing in your pants as you start up the rope. (On a rare occasion when I resorted to this method, after I got up a ways I noticed that the rope began very slowly slipping downward.) Place protection, even crummy protection, on the rope below yourself at the first opportunity; until you get that first piece in, you're facing a tied-off factor 2 fall—the absolute worst possible climbing fall. You could attach the rope end to your starting anchor with a force-limiting runner, but likely it would be completely ripped if you fall before that first piece goes in. Fortunately, this scenario suggests that the free end of the up rope (the strand that wasn't pulled) isn't too far above, and the rope is still through the anchor. When you reach the free end, you'll be able to attach to both sides, and you'll be reprieved from the big drop if you're correct that the rappel anchor is still in the system. You can set yourself up as

if you were rappelling and figure out how you'll continue up the ropes with a self-belay; you may have considerable prusiking, or yarding at least, ahead.

The payoff in all these scenarios is freeing the rope. Your efforts to whip the rope and otherwise encourage its freedom should come at times when you're well anchored and watchful of rockfall. When you're able to free the rope, you must construct another rappel anchor and descend, removing any protection you were able to place as you went up. This rappel won't likely be made from a location you'd have chosen under better circumstances, and you may be distressed by all the time your retrieval has consumed. Don't cut corners as you make this rappel; it'll likely be more dangerous than the first.

Now you can see the reason for all the emphasis on taking precautions to avoid getting rappel ropes stuck and why the EDK has become popular. Not only is a stuck rope dangerous, but it can take hours to climb up to it, essentially adding another pitch of climbing and a rappel to your day, plus all the messing around and cursing. The techniques that could be required to free a thoroughly stuck rope are somewhat advanced but, if you lead a charmed life, seldom practiced.

14
Climbing on Rock

PRELIMINARIES

Before we jump into specific climbing techniques, let's review some basic protocols that mountaineers habitually apply before every climb.

Don't Leave Home without It

Your gear check, that is. It's time to get up close and personal with your paraphernalia. I know this seems like just a guy thing, but it's an important ritual before every outing. Inspect every carabiner to ensure its gate is functioning smoothly. Check the holes in your ATC or edges of your Reverso to be sure they haven't yet developed sharp edges. Check the slings on your protection hardware. Check the knots on your tied runners and prusik loops—in fact, where *is* that prusik loop? Not only does this procedure check your equipment, it also reloads your brain as to what you're bringing along. In order to bear the C€ mark for sale in Europe, climbing hardware must state a rated life; Petzl now quotes ten years, even for textile products, but recommends an inspection every 3 months. The more climbing equipment you carry, the more important this exam becomes. Nor does gear sorting require much inventiveness to turn it into an excuse to head for the climbing shop.

Tie In Your Head

At the base of the route as you're getting ready to start your climb, many things are going through your mind. Anxiety, uncertainty, self-doubt, doubt about your partner, doubts about the weather and your late start. Lots of things to think about as you look up at the route, things that tend to scatter your thoughts at the very time they most need to be focused. This is the time when you should be zeroing in on a mental routine that's as fundamental to you as the hardware manipulations you're soon to commence. Before you tie the rope to your harness, get yourself mentally tied in. All safe and successful climbers observe a few fundamentals.

What If?

The most fundamental mental exercise climbers must constantly perform is going through what-if scenarios. This means projecting your present circumstances ahead by a few decisions and actions and evaluating the possible consequences; it's what Edward Whymper meant when he wrote, "Do nothing in haste, look well to each step, and from the beginning think what may be the end." It means having your head screwed on and thinking through the consequences, not just of what you're about to do, but where that will lead, and how that will constrain or expand your remaining options. Your decisions should create more alternatives, rather than result in an ever-diminishing range of choices. What if I slip, and this anchor gets pulled from another direction? What if I lose the route, and the climbing becomes too difficult? What if I rappel down and can't find a place to stop? The reason for having started with a discussion of climbing forces is to help you make these what-if analyses more concrete and tailored to the specific climbs you confront.

Check Your Partner and Double-Check Yourself

At the beginning of every roped climb, smart climbers overtly check each other by asking, "Doubled back?" as they inspect their partner's harness buckle and "Rethreaded? Hey, what the heck is that?" as they take a close look at each other's tie-in knots. Each gives his partner a general looking over to make sure nothing is left dangling, unzipped, or unclipped. This may seem silly, unnecessary, or unmanly, but a huge percentage of the accidents of mountaineering, including those that have killed experienced climbers and guides, would have been prevented by this sort of basic, methodical, safety-checking habit. The more intense the climbing or descending becomes, the more objective dangers threaten, the more important is the ritual. It's not a statement about your lack of confidence in yourself or your partner; it's just one way to confirm that you seriously care about safety and about the person you're with. If you don't care, climb with someone else; if you do care, show it. If it seems unmanly, get over it.

Communicate

Another excellent habit that may at first seem stilted is simply stating aloud to your partner (and maybe to yourself) what you're about to do. Certainly you'd say, "I'm going to take you off belay for a second," if that were the case, but it doesn't hurt to habitually announce and ask for confirmation of even routine actions: "I'm going to unclip my daisy and start climbing, OK?" When you set up a rappel anchor, ask, "Look OK to you?" When you tie the ropes together, ask, "I'm tying a death knot, do you agree?" When you're taking down the belay anchor, state, "I'm going to take out all the pieces except that one." This sort of verbal communication is mandatory if you're about to unclip your partner or remove any safety connection.

If checking your partner and verbalizing your intentions seems awkward at first, just announce it in advance. I've never received an objection to this in all the years I've been climbing, and the first time someone taught it to me my reaction was "Hey, that's a great idea." It helps you take the measure of a new partner much faster, and much more safely. The more you're cold, tired, rained on, working by headlamp, or otherwise stressed and distracted, the more important these habits become. When the situation becomes most intense, you must become robotic about your safety checks and feedback with your partner; internationally famous climbers have perished because they didn't, and I wouldn't want that to happen to you.

BELAYING THE LEADER

After the preparation and approach trudge and route analysis and all the rest, you're finally ready to start climbing. The leader begins organizing the rack while you flake out the rope and begin to build the belay anchor. Begin, as always, with the what-if analyses: What if the leader falls, where will she go? What are the likely directions of forces? What if there's rockfall, where should the second stand? If the leader falls, where could the second be jerked? Where can the second hang out and be comfortable for the next half hour? After you've sized up the scene, it's time to use your anchor-building knowledge to deal with the possibilities. Remember the new-school rule: *all belays must be anchored.* Simply wrapping the rope around your waist and telling your partner to go for it isn't among the options for smart mountaineers.

Setting Up to Belay the Leader

By now you know to focus on Anchor #1, even if you're belaying off the deck. If that's the case, a high-factor fall is ruled out, because lithobraking will intervene. The force on the first anchor may be entirely upward and outward if the leader avoids a ground fall and places protection higher up. The first anchor will then serve only as a directional to keep higher anchors from being pulled outward by the rope, forces on it will be low, and it won't see fall forces—but don't omit it.

You also know that a primary goal in constructing the safety system is to reduce the peak force on the top anchor in the event of a fall. That means you'll want to locate yourself, the belayer, so that a hard fall can safely jerk you a few feet in the direction of Anchor #1. Only in highly unusual circumstances would you attach your belay brake directly to an anchor, because that would eliminate any force-reducing benefits of your body's movement when the rope goes tight and would result in the highest forces throughout the safety system. Strangely, most texts show the belayer doing just that: using a brake connected to the carabiner at his waist, then connecting that carabiner tightly to the belayer's anchor. This is equivalent to belaying directly off an anchor (except for making it more difficult to escape the belay should something go wrong). Instead, tether yourself, if necessary, so that you can be jerked without danger of falling or being pulled completely into Anchor #1 or smacking nearby rock including rock overhead. Rather than standing next to the leader to get a good view as the leader begins climbing, locate your stance some distance from Anchor #1 to put more energy-absorbing rope into the system and reduce forces on protection the leader places early in the pitch.

If you've gained some elevation before setting

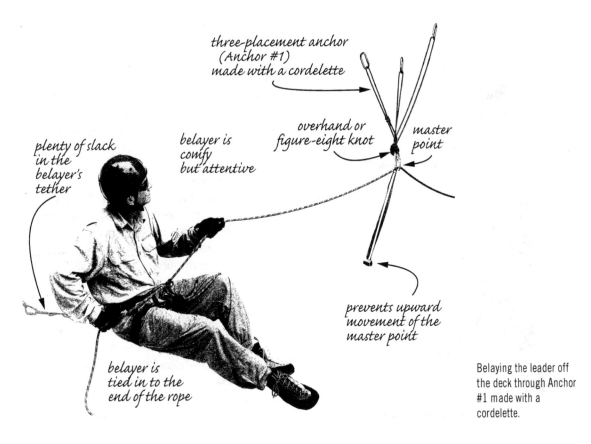

three-placement anchor (Anchor #1) made with a cordelette

plenty of slack in the belayer's tether

belayer is comfy but attentive

overhand or figure-eight knot

master point

prevents upward movement of the master point

belayer is tied in to the end of the rope

Belaying the leader off the deck through Anchor #1 made with a cordelette.

up the belay, and the leader faces a higher-factor fall, you could construct Anchor #1 as the master point of a complex anchor. Strangely (again) most texts show the fanciest anchor being used instead to hold the belayer. You know that Anchor #1 is what will take the highest force, not the belayer's anchor. Locate yourself several feet from Anchor #1, even if your belayer's anchor is of necessity a component of Anchor #1.

The belayer's hanging anchor is far less crucial than the first intermediate anchor, Anchor #1. If there's any doubt that the leader can safely place a solid first intermediate anchor immediately after leaving the belay, the belay anchor should be built as part of the first anchor system itself; this could be the case on many technical climbs except those beginning at the ground. The belayer's personal anchors or tether don't have to be strong, because they're subject to only moderate forces, but the first intermediate anchor must be burly indeed and unquestionably secure if there's any possibility it might see a high-factor fall. Working out ac-

tual numbers shows the peak force on the highest anchor can be as high as 6 to 8 kN in a simple system; the minimum for most hardware protection devices is at least 10 kN, but only when loaded from the optimal direction.

Unconventional New-School

You'll notice, I hope, that this thought process is somewhat different from what's usually taught for setting up a belay anchor. Usually, most instruction centers on building strong anchors, but often the emphasis on strength overshadows concern for security and a thoughtful analysis of the likely direction of forces. This old-school approach can result in a single directional that was placed almost as an afterthought ending up actually holding the force of the fall. The approach I've presented suggests that your major focus should not be on strength but on security, especially for Anchor #1. Don't focus on building a super anchor for the belayer; spend that effort on building Anchor #1 for the leader.

How to Scream

Now you've built the perfect anchor system for your stance and the route ahead. You've flaked out the rope, tied in, clipped your tether, and put the rope through your belay brake. Time for the climbers to get verbal for the customary mutual safety-checking ritual: harness doubled back?—yup, yup; tied in through both leg loop and belt loop?—yup, yup; that's a Yosemite bowline, right?—yup, yup; helmet buckled?—yup, yup; radios communicating? . . . and so on. Climbers usually tie into their respective ends of the rope, but if for some reason the belayer doesn't, he'll tie a stopper knot in the end of the rope so that it can't possibly escape through the belay brake. With all safety measures addressed, the leader will tell the second her initial intentions whereupon the classic climber dialog begins.

In casual conditions the lead climber will say something about being ready to climb and ask if the belayer is ready, and the belayer will respond that the belay is on and that the leader should go for it. In the teeth of the wind the climber will shout "Ready to climb!" or "On belay?" whereupon

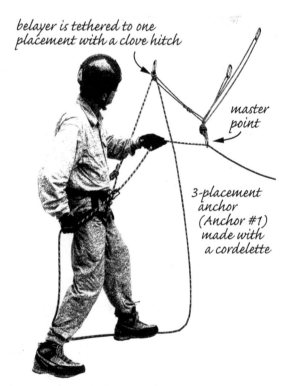

belayer is tethered to one placement with a clove hitch

master point

3-placement anchor (Anchor #1) made with a cordelette

Belaying the leader from a semi-hanging stance near Anchor #1.

It's probably worth making some of these points again, because in every climbing text I've checked, including The Classic and those I've listed in the Resources, belay anchor systems are invariably shown constructed inefficiently and sometimes dangerously. When you see a belay setup depicted, give yourself a little mental exercise and ask: Is this intended for belaying the leader or belaying the second? If for the leader, what component will take the most fall force if the leader is able to place a solid anchor before falling? What will take the most force if the leader falls *before* placing a solid piece? How much force are we talking about? Keep in mind that the absolute maximum force a belay device can put on the rope without slipping is 2 or 3 kN; if your Internet fall force simulator spits out 8 kN at the belay, plan on plenty of rope slippage in reality. Above all, think about how the belay configuration will affect the force on the topmost anchor—that's the force that must be minimized in order to maximize safety. If the setup depicted is for belaying the second, ask yourself if it would really be as efficient as simply belaying off an anchor using a Münter hitch.

---

the belayer will shout "Belay on!" and the leader will respond, "Climbing!" If the belayer is inattentive at some point, the leader may ask for more rope with "Slack!" or if the leader foresees difficulty, she may suggest "Watch me!" If difficulty prevails, she may so inform the belayer with "Falling!" but mountaineers assiduously avoid falls. Should the leader merely want to rest on the rope at an intermediate anchor, she can request "Take!" though if the belayer is old-school he won't have a clue what that means. If he understands, he'll quickly take in rope until he feels tension and be prepared to hold or lower the leader. If the leader wants to be lowered back to the stance, she might say, "Dirt me!" The belayer can inform the leader when the rope used is "Half way!" and continue to report the length of rope remaining as the end approaches. When the leader reaches the next belay station and puts in enough protection to anchor herself comfortably, she'll announce "Off belay!" whereupon the belayer can take the rope out of the belay device and respond "Belay off!"

The belayer attentively feeds rope so that no tension and a minimum of slack is on the rope; he's mindful that no tangles appear out of the flake-out pile or rope bag that might cause an inopportune hiatus in his chores. As the belayer lets out rope he'll hold the rope beyond the brake with his free hand and feed rope into the belay device with his brake hand held so that the rope in that hand is at a minimum 90° angle to the main rope; he shouldn't get sloppy and sit with both hands adjacent and hanging limply between his knees. When the rope runs through the belay brake in this orientation the brake has little holding power and that could cause rope burns for the belayer and let the falling leader drop farther than necessary—or farther. When the leader needs slack to make a clip, the attentive belayer feeds rope quickly. At serious moves, and when there's little rope drag, the belayer may take in a few feet after the leader clips a placement and moves up, then the belayer reverts to letting rope out as the leader climbs past the clipped anchor. Whatever happens, the belayer always observes the ancient admonition to *never take your brake hand off the rope!*

LEADING

From the leader's point of view, she's now organized the rack, tied in, and gone through the mutual safety check ritual. She looks up at the route and tells the second, "I'm going to head for that big flake up there and see if I can find a good stance; if not I'll keep going. You may have to take down the belay and simul-climb. OK, am I on?" Meaning, "On belay?"

Then for a tiny fraction of a second she fights the fleeting feeling of "What the heck am I doing here?" but she's seen a copy of The Mountaineering Handbook in her second's car. Assuming he's actually read it, she puts hands and feet to stone and moves up with confidence. Confidence is what leading is all about. Not overconfidence, but I suspect that's gotten lots of climbers up the learning curve until their skills and wisdom caught up, or until they took a leader fall and dumped their gear on eBay. Alpine climbing is the most committed and dangerous form of climbing, and leading through long runouts is a big part of that. Roped climbing in the mountains means keeping your fecal matter coalesced in the face of cold, exposure, remoteness, and uncertain rock. It means not falling. That doesn't mean every climb is an epic. There are many wonderful climbs that take place on sunny days on quality rock with great views, and with someone else doing the leading.

What, No Pics? A Sermon Instead

I'm going to depart from tradition and not show pictures of climbers in awkward positions or of hands and feet stuck into rocks. Books are not the place to learn to move on stone. Go climbing with someone better than you are, or go top roping at the crag, and you'll learn more in one day than you will from any book. Plus, if you're at all athletic you already know enough to climb low fifth class without instruction. What will make you a mountaineer is learning to *lead* low fifth class in the mountains, and that requires thoughtful practice more than it does consummate technique.

Learning to Lead

Strange that most climbing texts talk very little about learning to lead, yet leading is the biggest challenge of trad climbing and roped mountaineering. Leading is a head game more than athleticism or technical virtuosity. Learning to lead accompanies learning to place pro, but it's not the same thing; you can start out learning to place pro standing on the ground. It's best to separate building pro-placing skills from pushing your climbing limit; while you're learning, avoid attempting climbs that are physically difficult for you that also have challenging pro placement. My personal view is that you should begin leading easy routes early in your introduction to roped climbing, so that you don't get stuck being a rock gymnast who is freaked by exposure and runout. A principle feature of trad and mountaineering climbing, in distinction to sport and gym climbing, is that falling is mostly unthinkable; that's because it usually leads to injury since there's so much opportunity to hit something as you fall. Usually the injury isn't life threatening, but a sprained ankle on an alpine climb can be more than inconvenient, and dealing with an unpleasant fall can consume an immense amount of time. Being able to confidently climb fourth and low fifth class requires experience to

know the limits of your equipment, your personal physical and mental abilities, your ability to evaluate holds and anchors, and even your sense of when your shoes are going to stick or slip. The best way to start building this experience is to second climbs lead by better trad climbers. Next best would be leading on a loose top rope; then aiding trad routes to learn to place pro and rely on it. As I said in Chapter 12, your education is nearing completion when you have the composure to capably place protection after you have climbed far above your last piece.

A fundamental skill set of trad and mountaineering climbing is knowing how to establish and maintain the integrity of the roped safety system, and habitually doing so. This is why I've spent an inordinate amount of time discussing forces, anchors, and placing protection: to help you move your safety skills up as fast as your climbing ability develops. You'd be surprised how often climbers let safety skills lag, probably because they haven't learned to recognize risk and manage it. It's possible to go for years with dubious technique and marginal equipment, simply because most climbing doesn't stress the safety system anywhere near its limits—so any technique appears to be good technique and worthy of teaching to others. Inevitably, the distinction between ignorance of risk and competent risk management makes itself clear.

CLIMBING

No details here on where our leader puts her hands and feet, but she can be seen using good trad climbing techniques. She keeps her body close to the stone and climbs in balance. She's careful to keep the rope hanging to the sides of her legs, not between them, to avoid being flipped upside down should she fall. She checks every hold before she puts weight on it. On innocuous jugs she may merely brush off loose grit, but she's not shy about cleaning turf with her nut tool. When she approaches a flake, she'll pound it with the heel of her hand and evaluate the sound produced in hopes of spotting loose rock. Not to say she won't move up on rock that's loose, but she carefully pulls down and not out, and she avoids putting all

Rock climbing for mountaineers isn't quite the same as trad climbing at the local crag. You'll be in clunkier boots, maybe gloves, and maybe even wearing crampons. Your hands may be cold and you may be freighting a backpack in bulky clothing. The principles, however, are the same as for all low fifth class climbing: it's all about your feet; don't plan on dragging yourself up on your arms with gorilla moves (women, of necessity, learn this much faster than men). Keep your weight balanced on your feet and off your arms as much as possible and climb harder moves or hang to rest with your arms straight rather than bent. Twisting your torso while hanging from a straight arm often helps extend the other to a higher hold.

The most basic form of rock climbing is face climbing. The rules for your hands are simple: grab the rock feature that's easiest to hang on to and hang on. The big holds are called jugs, the little ones crimpers. Wearing gloves helps turn the former into the latter—that's the reason I recommend wearing thin gloves or none while actually climbing and slipping on mittens as soon as you stop in the cold.

There are two approaches for your feet, edging and smearing; they have contradictory requirements of your boots. You want stiff soles for edging (standing on a tiny ledge) and soft soles for smearing (relying more on friction). If a substantial portion of a pitch is pure smearing it's called slab climbing. Friends don't let friends climb slab, because the protection is widely spaced (run out) and if possibilities did exist, you'd use them for handholds and footholds and therefore it would cease to be slab. This means that falls will be long and abrasive. It's worth top roping steep slab until you get a sense of when your mountaineering boots can be trusted to stick. Keep your weight over your feet and use your hands mainly for balance—trust your boots. Lieback is a technique that uses an outward or sideways pull with your hands to increase friction pressure on your feet; an undercling is an upward horizontal lieback.

The other common style of rock climbing is called crack climbing. It implies ascending long, continuous cracks in the stone, not climbing fractured rock. Crack climbing is an important skill set for alpine rock climbers, but it's problematic for mountaineers. Any crack that lends itself to bulky mountaineering boots will be too wide (offwidth) for hands and protection—you are allowed either hands or boots in the crack, seldom both. Mountaineers tend to seek features on the nearby face or down inside the crack, so feasible crack climbing often becomes mixed with face climbing. Removing a mountaineering boot that you've securely wedged (jammed) into a crack can be a real struggle.

When crack climbing, as with face climbing, focus on your feet and use them to support your weight while using your hands for balance as much as possible. Apply a basic foot jam by leaning a knee to the side and slipping the toe or forefoot of your boot into the crack; bring your knee back to vertical to twist the boot and make it secure in the crack. Hand jams (and finger and fist jams) are made by slipping your hand into the crack and then tightening your fist, bunching your fingers, or in some other way creating pressure against the sides of the crack; wearing appropriate gloves or wraps of athletic tape reduces the pain. You can apply a basic hand jam either thumb up or thumb down. Try for thumbs up hand jams as much as possible, because they're easier to move up on. A good crack climber will ideally climb with her hands jammed around waist or chest high, thumbs up and not reaching up too far, and will seem to walk up the crack on her feet.

---

her weight on a single loose stone; this avoids killing her belayer just when she needs him most. She practices the "always three points of contact" principal, but she's not a slave to it. When she places protection she gives it a smart tug and then inspects it again; if the piece has extra importance, she may bounce test it, knowing that if it won't hold body weight it certainly wouldn't hold a fall. She uses plenty of long slings to keep the rope running as free of drag and hangup as possible, to keep carabiners from being stressed over edges, and to guard against pro being pulled in unfavorable directions or dislodged by the rope. She's careful about routefinding and avoids moves over questionable ground that she might be unable to reverse. Should she get off route, she's practiced downclimbing and down aiding as well as removing pro below her, so she won't get stuck. She knows this is mountaineering, after all, and doesn't hesitate to pull on a well-placed piece if the alternative is thrashing and delay; she'll even clip a sling to a placement and create a foothold. If things do get out of hand, she's prepared to leave pro and lower back to terra firma; no false economy here. She avoids falling even while knowing that anyone who leads will inevitably take falls. This leader makes cowardice her friend and will back off a climb when it doesn't feel right. Her confidence in all these skills helps her keep her wits about her in the face of uncertainty, exposure, objective hazards, and limited daylight.

Best of all, if you're the belayer new to trad climbing, you're watching this competent leader and soaking up pointers like cat whiz on a down jacket. Watching someone do it right is a great way to start learning to lead.

PLACING PRO

Apart from confidence, the first issue our leader will confront is placing pro, or at least setting anchors. I've already gone on at length about the importance of that first intermediate anchor, Anchor #1. It must be strong, and it must also be able to resist being displaced by motion of the rope or by an upward or outward pull on the rope. It might actually be the anchor that prevents successive placements from being pulled outward. Nevertheless, outward pulls will be relatively weak, so a tiny stopper is all that's necessary to deal with this issue. To repeat, that first placement needs to be made at the earliest opportunity for setting a really solid anchor, immediately after the leader leaves the belay or if necessary even making the belay's tether part of Anchor #1.

What about the next placement after Anchor #1? Well, the leader could just move onward and upward, placing pro or throwing a sling around a rock horn whenever an opportunity presents itself, but there's a more thoughtful approach, particularly if the leader has only a "small rack" and would like to make best use of the limited number of slings and pro she's hauling. First, let's assume that all placements are equivalently solid; if not, the thoughtful leader might skip questionable or time-consuming opportunities because she's aware of what's actually required to achieve maximum safety with the minimum number of placements.

And what's that? The most basic goal of placing pro when leading is to avoid a factor 1 fall or a grounder, often the same thing. Simplistically then, as you climb past that beefy Anchor #1, you'll want to make your next placement at the same distance from Anchor #1 as Anchor #1 is from the deck or the belay device, whichever is shorter.

Then Anchor #3 should be placed a distance from Anchor #2 that's just a bit closer to Anchor #2 than it is from the ground or the belay brake, and so on. If a ground fall or hitting a ledge is possible, take into account up to 25 percent rope stretch. Avoiding a ground fall or factor 1 fall with the minimum number of placements comes down to placing successive anchors exponentially farther and farther apart; for example, at 10 feet, 20 feet, 40 feet, then 80 feet. This should factor into your personal sense of "runout," as being 10 feet from your last anchor when you're 20 feet off the deck is far more dangerous than when you're 100 feet up, even though the emotional impact may not match the potential physical impact. I didn't say that pro should be placed based on how hard the climbing is; a leader certainly wants to have a good anchor before tackling a challenging move, but don't neglect placing pro on confidence-inspiring easy ground if the consequences of a mishap could be severe.

Traversing

Specific terrain features will modify this simple schema, and placing pro is ultimately more opportunistic than mathematical even if there's an engineer on the sharp end of the rope. One chore of the leader is to make placements that protect the second, who will have to follow the pitch and clean the pro. Traverses require extra thoughtfulness, because the second could face a more dangerous fall than the leader. One guide is that the leader should place pro as if she were leading the traverse in the opposite direction. The worst example for the second might be a crux at the beginning of a traverse. It's the leader's natural, and correct, tendency to place a piece immediately before making the hard move, then to move ahead quickly, relieved by easier climbing over the remainder of the traverse. When the second arrives at the crux, he must remove the pro but will then face a long pendulum fall if the now unprotected crux goes badly. Traverses also expose placements to sideways drag by the rope, so the leader may decide to place two pieces in opposition to prevent either from being dislodged. Leaders need to be mindful of such scenarios and place protection all along traverses so that the second isn't exposed to pro that's missing in action or to a pendulum fall, which can be nasty both in terms of impact at the end of the swing and in terms of creating opportunities for helmet testing durng it.

BELAYING THE SECOND

The leader has now reached an opportune location to set up an anchor system and bring up the second. Maybe she's run out of rope or into rope drag, maybe she's run out of terrain where a rope is needed, maybe she's concluded that the climbing from here on demands a full rope length, or maybe she just likes the opportunities available for setting up an anchor. Remember: *all belays must be anchored*, even on easy terrain.

This anchor is significantly easier to build than Anchor #1 for the leader. Two factors contribute to this: the peak forces will be small, not even twice body weight, and the direction of pull is likely to be known and unchanging. There may be other demands made on this anchor, such as providing a means of securing the leader and perhaps securing the second during lead changeover, but the forces associated with those chores will also be relatively small. The emphasis should be on making this anchor *secure*, knowing that *strong* will likely take care of itself. And again, this contradicts conventional wisdom.

So what would be an ideal anchor? A sling around a sturdy terrain feature or tree would be reassuring. Even in such a case it wouldn't be a bad idea to place an independent backup anchor just in case, even if the backup can't be perfectly located—but that's enough. If opportunities make it possible to construct a simple but exceptionally secure anchor, don't waste time getting fancy simply because you saw a picture of someone lacing four pieces together. In fact, if four pieces are necessary to achieve adequate security, something is probably being overlooked. Four equalized marginally placed pieces are no substitute for a single secure placement.

Now, how about the belay method? Most texts, including The Classic, show the leader belaying the second off a brake on the HMS carabiner at her waist, with a tight connection from the same biner to an anchor. This approach is as suboptimal for belaying the second as it is for belaying the leader, but for different reasons. It's still better than belaying the second through a redirect (a carabiner anchored above the belayer), which nearly doubles the force on the main anchor (the redirect biner).

The new-school method is to belay the second directly off an anchor using a Münter hitch or autoblock belay device. To make it much easier to take up rope quickly, locate the anchor's HMS biner a couple of feet higher than the belayer (was leader); now she can use both hands and pull rope through the Münter or brake several feet at a time.

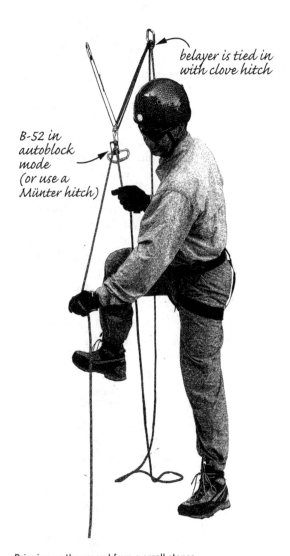

belayer is tied in with clove hitch

B-52 in autoblock mode (or use a Münter hitch)

Bringing up the second from a small stance.

If she were close to the main carabiner, she could only bring up a few inches at a time—très tedious. If she needs more distance from the anchors, perhaps to lean over and watch the second, the leader will extend both the belay biner and her tether. Don't use the autoblock biner if there's a likelihood you'll have to lower the second, unless you're prepared and practiced in this fine art (see Part 6, Advanced Techniques); the Münter hitch works just fine and is usually the best option.

This setup is quick to establish, taking in rope is efficient, the belay is more secure than belaying off your harness with a brake, and should anything go wrong, the belayer (was leader) has already escaped the belay and can immediately begin dealing with the problem, even if it's just leaning over and shouting advice. Maybe that comment about the security of the belay should be emphasized: in the most commonly taught (and, probably, performed) belay—off the waist of an anchored climber—the belayer's hands spend most of the time directly in front of the belayer and close together, particularly if the second is moving up quickly. When the rope is dressed that way, the belay brake has little holding power (see the illustration in Appendix A). Probably an attentive belayer could gain control fairly quickly, and probably he could avoid rope burns, but the real reason he chose this setup in the first place is that he probably didn't know better. Unless the terrain at the belay stance somehow precludes it, belaying directly off an anchor using a Münter hitch is the best way to bring up a second. Belaying with a Münter hitch off your waist carabiner is still safer than using a belay brake, because it maintains security continuously, unlike using a tube or plate.

The belayer (was leader) has a few other chores. She will think about the pitch below and know when the second is probably moving through the traverse; she won't keep yanking on the rope if she knows the second has reached that 0.5 TriCam she placed with vigor. She needs to keep slack out of the rope, and she needs to prevent the rope that she's taken up from becoming tangled or, worse, from dangling into terrain where it could get stuck or dislodge rocks. If she's leaning on a tight tether, the rope can be draped

I find it bizarre that respected texts illustrate climbers hanging from elaborate anchors belaying a second from their waist through a redirect higher up; usually the redirect is attached to one of the component placements of the belayer's anchor. A redirect is a carabiner that changes the direction of rope travel—the belayer is facing up, toward the redirect, while the belayed climber is below. Those climbers don't understand forces, but hopefully you do, and you know to reduce the force on the topmost anchor; in this case it's the redirect. In a fall, the redirect must hold the force of the falling climber *plus* the force from the belayer, whereas the belayer's anchor must hold only the weight of the belayer—even less during a fall while the belayer is pulled upward. In other words, the anchor is being used backward: the redirect should be on the strongest point. Heck, why not attach both the redirect and the belayer at the strongest point? Better yet, why not use a Münter hitch on that redirect carabiner? This would reduce the force on the carabiner by nearly half compared to using a redirect belay. In addition, the Münter hitch belay is safer because it doesn't cycle through an orientation in which its strength approaches nil, as does a tube/plate belay, and it's far easier to escape should something go wrong. An experienced belayer can use a Münter hitch belay to safely drink and suck down gel while bringing up the second over innocuous terrain, all the while keeping her brake hand on the rope.

back and forth across it; she could also pass the taken-up rope back and forth through a conveniently located sling. She could even use her pack as a rope bag if she hasn't followed my advice and used a rope bag in the first place. This being mountaineering, there's no reason for her not to give the second a bit of tension, maybe even a lot of tension if everyone is agreeable. Not during that traverse, of course.

SECONDING

Having heard "Off belay!" and answered "Belay off!" the second immediately begins taking down the remainder of the anchor and getting ready to climb. After an interminable period of anxiety, the rope moves up and goes tight at the second's tie-in. "That's me!" he shouts. There's no answer. He was hoping to hear "Belay on!" but the wind probably

Münter
hitch
belay
brake

handy
12-inch
runner

Minding the rope while bringing up the second.

even more anxious, "Tension!" When the second arrives at placed pro, he won't let tension on the rope seduce him into climbing too high to remove the placement. He'll leave everything clipped to the rope until he frees the hardware and then simply throw the runner over his head and shoulder with the hardware still on it and keep moving; no need to be neat and orderly for now, because there's not that much pro to collect on most mountaineering routes. He's moving up fast until—damn! it's that 0.5 TriCam!

CHANGEOVER

When the second arrives at the belay stance, the leader might say, "Why don't you come up on this side, since you're going to lead the next pitch. How'd you like that pink TriCam?" The second will clip into the master point with his daisy and locker, telling the other, "Great lead! I'm going to clip myself in here, OK?" Clipped, he says, "Off belay!" and receives the response "Belay off!" This team actively verbalizes to eliminate time-wasting uncertainty. If everyone's comfy, it's time to get on with the changeover. If the original leader intends to lead the next pitch (called *leading in blocks*) the rope needs to be dealt with neatly but quickly, and the leader must transfer pro that the second retrieved back to her rack according to her wont. A new locker (locking carabiner) will be added to the master point so the leader can recover her big HMS; the rope from her waist will be clipped through the locker and the gate locked. The second will reposition his anchor and tether and then connect the rope through his belay device. If the climbing is difficult, having the same person lead several successive pitches makes sense even if the climbers are equally skilled because the leader will have had the opportunity to rest and hydrate while belaying the second, whereas the second will arrive at the belay stance having just climbed a tough pitch. The rested leader can quickly start leading again.

If the second is to lead the next pitch (called *swinging leads*), probably easier to organize, the second can sort gear onto the leader's rack (helping to remind the second what's available) and

carried it away. The rule might be that if the rope goes tight, climb. The rule is enforced by a mighty tug from above, so after a last glance to be sure nothing has been left behind, he yells "Climbing!" and up he goes. Now, if the mountaineering leader can be unconcerned with style points, the second can fairly revel in bad style. Pulling on slings—no problem. Pulling on the rope or hanging on the rope—whatever works. The leader has set a nice Münter belay, not a hip belay, so she won't even object if the second throws a Klemheist on the rope and aids up it a bit—this isn't particularly fast, but it might be necessary to pass a difficult move or to remove an anchor in the middle of one; just figure how you're going to unwind it (the loop of rope below the second, not the knot). If the second finds he's climbing faster than the rope is moving up, and a great loop of slack has developed, he can scream to the leader "Up rope!" or, if

then transfer the entire rack to his own shoulder, assuming this team is efficiently using a shoulder sling to carry most of the gear. A new locker will be added to the master point and the original leader will grasp the rope near the second's tie-in point, clip it through the new locker, and then transfer her HMS biner to her harness and rig a belay.

These basic scenarios assume that the master point resulting from the anchor that the original leader set up to belay the second is suitable to become all or most of Anchor #1 for the next pitch. Probably it will be, unless the directions of anticipated forces suggest otherwise. Maybe a placement needs to be added to prevent upward motion, or maybe a completely new Anchor #1 system needs to be constructed to deal with the new pitch. If the anchor for bringing up the second can be used, things move quickly, because the new belayer is already near an optimum location.

Now the climbers go through an abbreviated safety-check ritual, the new belayer gets ready and says, "OK, you're on," the new leader says, "I'm outta here, wish me luck," and receives the reply, "Good luck then, you're gonna need it."

MOVING FAST ON ROCK

Throughout this book I revisit the themes of mountaineers increasing speed and reducing weight. The first time I read the phrase "fast and light" was in *Climbing Ice*, a seminal book of the mid 1970s by that seminal alpinist Yvon Chouinard. He laid out the principles and equated fast and light with safety. Increased safety is indeed the main reason for speed; a greater likelihood of success would be second, and having more fun would be on the list, too. Climbing faster means climbing more efficiently, and that's always more fun than being inefficient. Read the sections on objective danger; each hazard inevitably involves danger that's a function of when you're exposed and for how long. Climbing fast allows you to have more choices about the when and to reduce the how long. I'm not talking Hans Florine fast, just avoiding delay and moving competently. Moving fast on rock involves the same basic concepts as moving fast on the trail, starting with making it a

priority and then getting into the habit. It doesn't really require extraordinary climbing ability to move expeditiously on fourth- and low fifth-class routes; in fact, I'm not suggesting that you speed up the actual climbing movements, just optimize all the other things that consume time during a climb. The difference compared to hiking on a trail is that being fast on rock requires competence with the technical hardware of the roped safety system, and it requires being and staying highly organized with your climbing partners. These skills require practice. Let's start with an overview of the same points I mentioned for hiking fast in Chapter 3, Moving Fast on the Trail; then I'll have a look at specific techniques that will help you climb more efficiently.

THE RABBIT HABIT
Just as with fast hiking, climbing fast—or at least faster than the norm—involves making it a priority and deliberately attempting to speed your climbing overall. Speed on rock often means eliminating unconscious stalling in the face of uncertainty or self-doubt. Developing a fast habit doesn't mean rushing or cutting corners, but it does mean confronting the sloth that may have become a habit—mountaineers must change that habit if it's been developed in other forms of climbing, and you can develop the fast habit if you constantly pay attention to your rate of progress and eliminate activities that impede it.

CLIMB
This means spending less time doing things other than actually climbing up the rock. You may have noticed that the fraction of your climbs that is actually spent making movement on stone is a small percentage of the total. The easiest way to speed up overall is to spend less time doing things other than climbing. Things like puttering around, sorting out gear issues, having a snack, untangling the rope, and discussing plans with your partner.

GO LIGHT
This has more implications for climbing than hiking. Hikers who carry heavy packs often do so, when they actually think about it, to increase their

comfort. Climbers with heavy packs think their extra stuff will increase their safety—despite innumerable examples that being lighter and able to move more quickly increases the margin of safety more than carrying weight in hopes of being prepared for every conceivable contingency. All the techniques I lay out in this book for going lighter apply to climbing lighter, whether we're talking a day climb or a three-week adventure. These techniques require specialized knowledge and experience with the limitations of lightweight gear. Going light also means being more attuned to the need to bail if you realize that you have shaved your safety margin too thin for the way things are turning out.

Going light also refers to each pitch. If you're the leader you can move up much faster if you're not carrying a lot of stuff (including climbing hardware) that you won't use on the pitch. Let the second carry it.

TAKE SHORT BREAKS

This one is pretty easy when actually climbing: don't take any breaks. Don't even come close. There are many opportunities when climbing with a rope for each member of the team to suck down energy gel and water or even have a snack and take a whiz. Let your group breaks come on the summit and back in camp, whether you ever break out the rope or not.

CLIMB IN SMALL GROUPS

A competent party of three using two ropes can be almost as fast as a climbing pair, but basically two on a rope is the fastest way to climb. Larger climbing parties, even unroped, inevitably slow things down. This is not to say they should be avoided altogether; just count on taking longer in return for the additional camaraderie. In Chapter 24, Roped Parties, I address special techniques for efficiently moving larger parties on rock and snow.

MAINTAIN ON-THE-GO HYDRATION AND NUTRITION

Moderate climbing is generally not aerobic, at least not for long, but climbers still need to pay attention to nutrition and hydration. The more nearly aerobic the actual climbing becomes, the more closely your nutrition and hydration protocols must resemble those of endurance athletes and adventure racers. A lot of mountaineering occurs on relatively easy ground where it's possible to get your heart rate up for extended periods of time as you motor along. Often such terrain will be simul-climbed or third classed, so the whole party will be working hard; a glacier or alpine snow/ice climb is an example of this. If you've gotten out of the habit of moving at a rate that merely keeps your heart rate moderate, and you're fit enough to push it higher for hours on end, you'll certainly move much faster. And you'll certainly have to pay close attention to on-the-go nutrition and hydration. Even rock climbers on third- and fourth-class routes—heck, even on fifth-class routes—must avoid the debilitating effects of dehydration and glycogen depletion, which can easily occur if you don't deliberately plan to do it right.

CARRY TREKKING POLES?

Sure. Trekking poles are great for climbing and descending steep snow, often better than an ax. The parallel for rock climbing is to carry appropriate gear and use it skillfully. Just as trekking poles have become new-school tools for mountaineers, so, too, have autoblock belay devices, cordelettes, daisy chains, TriCams, Tiblocs, and even the venerable Münter hitch, so it seems.

Speedy Tips

Here are some techniques for moving fast when climbing rock; the relative importance of each will change, depending on the nature of the climb and the party attempting it, so the tips are not listed in any special order:

Don't Rope Up. Once you tie into a rope, all activities conspire to consume time. A large party sharing one rope is incredibly slow. There's no doubt that simo-soloing is the fastest way to cover ground. It's also the most risky. Somehow, free soloing while a nearby companion is also free soloing seems safer, but of course, it's not. Whether it's safer to move fast or to rope up is a communal decision, the most complex part of which is dealing with subliminal group pressure that distracts from the thoughtful evaluation that needs to be made.

Build anchors efficiently. This is the reason I've spent so much time discussing the reasoning behind building anchors. Most texts, and indeed most instructors, spend a lot of time describing strong anchors, rather than focusing on the more important issues of thoughtfully building anchors of adequate strength that are secure against all possible directions of pull. That's why I harp on the point that it's not the belayer's anchor that demands the most strength, but the first climbing anchor after the belay that will require strength in the event of a fall. Learn to use cordelettes; they make for efficient anchor building with static or dynamic equalization. Use your long length of 6 mm accessory cord to build anchors for rappelling and belaying the second; it's plenty strong and may allow use of reliable natural terrain features instead of slower-to-place hardware. Building secure anchors quickly is challenging when you carry only a light rack—one of the fast/light tradeoffs that requires judgment to make.

Place protection quickly. This requires practice, so that you'll be able to guess accurately which piece will fit a particular placement opportunity without requiring multiple tests. It means knowing the full potential of the hardware on your rack, and sometimes it means knowing how to make tricky opposing placements if no other options are available. On easy terrain you can move faster by placing protection, especially natural protection, when you spot good opportunities, rather than spending time fiddling with tricky pro placements. Get in the habit of spotting terrain features that will require only long runners to create strong and secure anchors, and get in the habit of carrying plenty of long runners.

Clip quickly. Sport climbers know the importance of this. Efficiently clipping the anchor and then clipping in the rope should become a habit. You shouldn't have to research the situation and then fumble around with both hands just to make a clip, even with gloves on.

Focus on the beginning and end of each pitch. The leader and second must work simultaneously. When the leader reaches a belay stance, the objective is to get the second climbing as soon as possible; for the belayer, the objective is to be ready to climb without further ado as soon as he hears "Belay on!" The leader will immediately make herself secure to a good anchor and signal "Off belay!" The second, as soon as he knows that the leader cannot fall directly on his belay system, can begin taking it down without waiting for the leader to construct a complete new belay anchor. As soon as the second hears "Off belay!" he can remove all the nearby anchors except any minimally necessary for his hanging support. The leader will have quickly set up a belay anchor, even if she knows she'll want to add placements before using it as Anchor #1 for the next lead. The second will pull the last placement and answer "Climbing!" without delay as soon as he hears "Belay on!"

Communicate before and during the climb. That means being sure that both climbers agree on the rules (such as, "If the rope runs up very fast and then goes tight, climb even if you can't hear a signal"). It

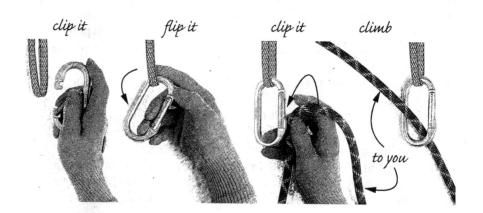

Clipping and flipping.

means agreeing on any rope tug signals or whistle blasts; tugs and even rope tension are often unreliable on mountaineering routes. I've often used the principle that an even number of widely spaced whistles means something good ("Belay on!" "Belay off!" "Climbing!"); the more blasts the better things are. An odd number of blasts means something bad ("Slack!" "Up rope!" "Watch me!"), the more the worse. The exact meaning is contextual. Another system bases the number of tugs or blasts on the number of syllables in the corresponding official shout. These systems are basically bogus.

The simplest but slowest protocol is for the leader to set up a complete belay anchor, bring up all the rope slack through her belay device, and then start pulling the belayer up the route as he attempts to take down the lower belay anchor. If the leader speeds things up by pulling up slack first and then putting the rope into her belay device, the second must know to allow a little time after the rope stops moving upward for the leader to take the rope out of her mouth and get it into her B-52. If the second begins climbing but the rope fails to keep moving up, he can assume his conclusion that he was on belay was premature; of course, that means the leader is not on belay either, and the climbers are actually simul-climbing on slack rope. That would be bad. If no communication scheme seems like it will work, the only alternative may be short pitches—another potential time sink common to mountaineering routes that makes anchor building skills even more important. Better than all these is to carry GMRS (or the weaker FRS) radios. Radio communication will speed belayed mountaineering immensely. I'd say that radios are essential for double-rope technique in the mountains, but I just know there'll be some Brit who will insist you can get the hang of it after only a year or so of climbing with the same partner.

Cheat. Pull on slings (use "French free" technique). Use simple aid. Tension the second. Do whatever's necessary to avoid delays while climbing in the mountains. Cheating is helped by using an autoblock to bring up the second; even a Münter hitch belay from an anchor is more efficient than a conventional tube brake at the waist. Use your time belaying to suck down gel and water. (I recommend cheating many times in this book, but let me be clear. When I'm rock climbing, trad or sport, I don't pull on pro, and I don't hang dog—it's just not fun. If I can't do the route without cheating and falling, I'll do something easier. But mountaineering is different. If I can't easily traverse around the difficulty, I'll do whatever it takes to avoid pointless delay.)

Optimize changeovers. Changeovers at the end of one pitch and the start of the next can consume a lot of time if deliberations must be held to make decisions. Best make them in advance. Who leads? Who carries the weight? Why are we not taking a break? The biggest time sink at changeover usually involves dealing with the rope: flaking it out for the second time, removing tangles, fetching it from below where it has become tangled in rocks; many such opportunities for delay will present themselves. Such delays are compounded if two ropes are used; two ropes require extra skill and dedication to avoid wasting time with tangles. It's the leader's duty to keep the belay stance organized and simplified, so that when the second arrives it will be obvious what needs to be done. During the changeover, each climber should verbalize every action and intention, especially if either involves a modification of the safety system and in no uncertain terms if an action involves even temporarily removing the other climber from it. Transferring gear to the new leader must be made efficiently; if swinging leads, using a shoulder sling makes swapping a light rack much faster than pro carried on gear loops on the harness or climbing pack (unless you swap the pack).

Learn good rope management technique. Bad rope management is what kills speed and efficiency. The belayer of the second must accept responsibility for keeping the rope neatly organized as it's taken in, so that changeover will be simple and efficient. If you lead in blocks on easy routes, avoid the problem of transferring a pile of rope and risking getting it tangled by tying in to lockers instead of directly to harnesses. That way you can simply swap the rope ends, unclip your tether, and be on your way.

Agree upon a speedy style. For example, the leader can end a mountaineering pitch quickly by rapidly going off belay. As soon as she places a solid piece or slings a good horn, she can clove hitch herself to a biner on that placement and yell "Off belay!" because she's now secure; there's no need to remain on belay while setting up the remainder of the anchor. Down below, the second has gotten ready to climb by having already taken down all or most of his anchor and Anchor #1; the other anchors placed on lead are plenty of protection. The leader knows the belay anchor needs only to hold the low forces of a second's fall, so she can immediately pull up rope until it goes tight, put on a Münter hitch, and yell "Belay on!" This takes little time, so the belayer had better have the belay already taken down and be ready to climb, because the leader's about to start winching him up. The leader can add more placements to the anchor system while she's belaying, if she thinks that the anchor will need extra placements to become Anchor #1 for the next pitch, and she's picked a spot to make that easy. Such a style might scare the bejesus out of a partner who expected something more conventional (and slow).

Climb faster if you're the second. You're on top rope, so go for it. Use success-oriented climbing style. Expect to be on tension (but agree first). If even heroic tension by the belayer above isn't getting you over a tricky section, let the belayer know to lock you off, put some prusiks on the rope, and haul yourself up; this is usually faster than trying to aid up the rock while on belay.

Climb easy terrain faster yet. Not all parts of a mountaineering route will be difficult; usually only a short part is hard, and the rest is much less challenging, so don't use the same techniques on the easy parts as you're required to use on the hard stuff. Mountaineers, more than any other breed of climber, must learn to move fast on relatively easy terrain—because there's so much of it. If you're using a rope, set anchors opportunistically, but don't skip them, even on easy terrain; quality anchors support the confidence to keep moving fast.

Learn to climb rock in crampons. Practice on a top rope at a climbing crag, but don't scratch up popular routes. Learn to use your ax or axes to hook rock and move up with confidence. Mountaineering routes often involve bands of rock on

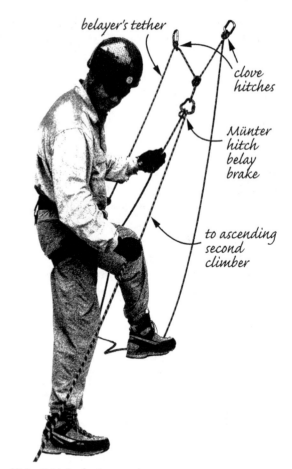

belayer's tether

clove hitches

Münter hitch belay brake

to ascending second climber

Minimalist belay for the second.

snow where removing your crampons soaks up too much time—so don't.

Simul-climb. This means that the leader, the second, and the rope will be moving at the same time, and no fixed belays will be established except at the start and finish. There must always be a minimum of two anchors between the climbers (or otherwise it could be safer if they just climbed unroped). There's more detail in Chapter 24 on group climbing, but the three basic rules should be clear: don't fall, don't fall, and don't fall. Well, actually, if the leader falls, the party might survive, but it would be a major time waster. If the second falls, the leader will probably be pulled off, too, so both might end up dangling and injured. A good day for hungry ravens, perhaps, but a bad day for the climbers.

Carry the rope up. If the pitch is short, as many

mountaineering pitches are, rather than have the leader drag up the rope through a belay brake and the friction of anchors and rock, the second should simply tie a butterfly knot and clip to the rope, throw the remainder of the rope into his pack, and immediately begin climbing.

Double up on seconds. A party of three or more on a rope can be cumbersome, especially if the seconds must be belayed up one after the other, and the rope must somehow be gotten back to waiting climbers. One way to avoid having a party of three drag on forever is for the seconds to simul-climb on belay, about 20 feet apart (so the rope must be that much longer than the pitch). Climbing in series like this is tricky, because if the last second falls, the middle second could be pulled off, too; that leaves the belayer holding two climbers, who may have different requirements—usually not a serious problem on easy terrain. This problem can be addressed by having the middle second connected through a Tibloc, which will prevent the middle second from being pulled backward if the other falls. One reason to climb with two ropes (double or twin) is so that two seconds can be brought up in parallel, typically using an autoblock belay brake; this can be almost as fast as a party of two. When that's your plan, the first follower should remove most anchors (except for those that protect traverses), skipping those that are difficult to remove rather than holding everything up; let the third climber clean them so that gear sorting and changeover can begin as soon as possible. If you have only one rope, but the pitch is rappel length, or you decide to make it so, the leader can tie in to the middle of the rope, lead on a doubled rope clipped as if it were twins but be belayed only on one strand. Belaying with both strands would result in doubled forces on climber and anchors in the event of a fall, so don't do it that way, but the leader should clip both stands to keep them organized. The leader can then set up an autoblock belay and bring up both seconds simultaneously, one on each strand several feet apart to avoid interfering with each other. Two pitches done this way may be faster than one long pitch with two sequential seconds.

Don't select routes that are over your limit. Thrashing and aiding are slow, particularly if you didn't

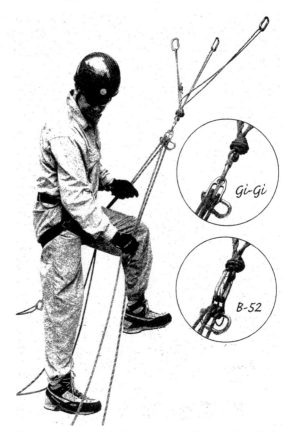

Bringing up two seconds simultaneously with an autoblock brake.

plan on them and particularly when wearing a pack. Placing additional protection out of fear is also slow. Equivocating is slowest of all, save for screwing your courage to the sticking point, which can take forever. Being ambitious is a part of growth and development, but getting in over your head unwisely is a recipe for an unintended moonlight stroll.

Don't fall. This might seem self-evident, but on top of being dangerous, taking a whipper consumes an inordinate amount of time. There are many things a leader can do to avoid falling, such as placing more pro, pulling on slings, resting on the rope, aiding, backing off, and downclimbing. Downclimbing is an important leading skill, different from being lowered, that you should practice from time to time; try it as an alternative to rappelling off a sport route. All of these take less time than taking a fall and dealing with the consequences, so do what you gotta do, but *don't fall*.

PART 4

Snow and Ice

All discussions of snow in the mountains tend to wax rhapsodic about its wonderfully changing character—but it's true. From the moment snow begins to fall to the time it runs down the mountains as a babbling brook destined to water golf courses in distant cities, snow is constantly undergoing change. Month by month, day by day, and even minute by minute. In Chapter 26 on glaciers and crevasses I'll mention snow changing over many years; in the section of Chapter 5 on avalanches I discussed changes in snow taking place month by month and in the days after storms. In Chapter 15, Equipment for Snow and Ice Climbing, and Chapter 16, Climbing Snow and Ice, I'll be most concerned with changes taking place during a single day or even in a period of minutes.

15

Equipment for Snow and Ice Climbing

Mountaineers climb snow, a lot of snow. So much that the term "snow slog" becomes all too familiar. We climb steep, hard snow that no one would call slogging, and we also climb alpine ice, which is frozen, metamorphosed snow. Rarely, we climb water ice in a short section of bergschrund or re-frozen meltwater. Of course, I'm thinking about the fun I've had climbing long runnels of late-season ice in alpine gullies, but that ice wasn't vertical and wasn't formed by water splashing down a waterfall—a rare habitat for mountaineers. Late-season glaciers can be solid ice, too, but though they may be steep, they're never continuously vertical. Let's have a look at the gear you'll need to get started on snow and moderate alpine ice.

MOUNTAINEERING AX

The ice ax isn't just a classic symbol of mountaineering; it's a fundamental tool. Unfortunately, there's often confusion as to its main purpose. First, let's be clear about which animal is under

discussion. The general mountaineering ax has a long, mostly straight shaft and head with adze and gently curved pick. It's not the same as the axes used for pure water ice climbing, now commonly called ice tools, having paired adze and hammer versions and often radically curved shafts and picks.

The model illustrated has an almost ideal design, making it easy to describe desirable features. Curiously, the manufacturer offers a marginally lighter *Pro* version with shorter pick, diminutive head, and sharper narrower adze; what were they thinking?

▲ **Head.** The head has smooth curves with no sharp edges anywhere to snag gloves or ropes. The cross section is T-shaped, with the upper surface about 14 mm wide; this makes it easier on your hands when shoving the ax into snow for hiking or self-belay and also makes it more effective for bashing in pickets, which is done by pounding with the top of an inverted ax rather than by swinging the shaft. Attach your leash or lanyard to

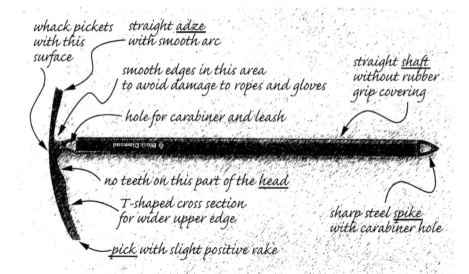

whack pickets with this surface

straight *adze* with smooth arc

smooth edges in this area to avoid damage to ropes and gloves

straight *shaft* without rubber grip covering

hole for carabiner and leash

no teeth on this part of the *head*

T-shaped cross section for wider upper edge

sharp steel spike with carabiner hole

pick with slight positive rake

The mountaineering ax.

avoid this area. Notice that there are no teeth under the middle of the head; if there were your gloved fingers would progressively become ungloved and ropes used for ax belays would get shredded. This model's head is made of cast stainless steel, which allows for the fancy shapes and eliminates corrosion worries.

▲ **Adze.** The adze is wide, slightly arced, and only moderately sharp. This is fine for chopping steps in most alpine ice and for cutting trenches in snow. If you want slightly better cutting of ice, you can sharpen the adze on its underside at the risk of inviting trouble from one more sharp edge in your gear.

▲ **Pick.** The pick is gently curved to match your arm's natural swing. Most axes have slightly positive pick angles, like the illustration, which I prefer. Don't agonize about whether the point angle is positive or negative; that has little effect one way or the other in most conditions. What matters most is how well the pick penetrates hard alpine ice, and how well it sticks and removes. In my experience, you can't tell how an ax will perform just by looking at the pick; you need to go out and test it on real ice. Maybe the frozen water off the roof of the climbing shop or the refrozen snow scraped out of the parking lot would be good for a test. If the pick penetrates well but is difficult to remove, try

relieving the top front edge with a file. The illustration suggests ways to transform a snow pick into an ice pick.

▲ **Spike.** The spike should have a sharp, effective point and a smooth curve joining it to the shaft, making the shaft easier to plunge into hard snow. The point must be steel; aluminum spikes do not stick well in hard ice—just when you most need them to. Lightweight axes with aluminum spikes may be fine for snow only, but stay away from them for your all-around ax. My ultralight ax has such a great pick that I machined a stainless steel spike to replace the aluminum one

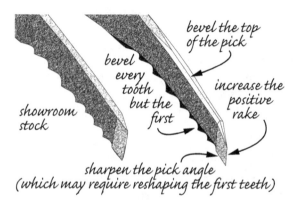

bevel the top of the pick

bevel every tooth but the first

increase the positive rake

showroom stock

sharpen the pick angle (which may require reshaping the first teeth)

Modifying the pick to make it easier to plant and remove in hard ice.

so I can use the ax on hard glacier ice. It's sometimes said that the spike should have a flat profile for use when glissading; I'm dubious that this is crucial. The spike, like the head, should have a hole that will allow you to clip a conventional carabiner; some carabiners won't fit.

▲ **Shaft.** The modern aluminum shaft has an oval cross section to make the swing easy to control and either a straight shaft or, rarely, one with a slight bend near the head. Avoid rubber coverings on the shaft; they don't add much to grip security, and if the bare shaft is sized for optimum holding, the covered version could be too fat, which is usually the case. Rubber shaft coverings do make the shaft a bit warmer in the hand, but that's seldom how you hold a general mountaineering ax. Shaft coverings inhibit penetration into hard snow and reduce the effectiveness of the ax as a crevasse probe, should you fail to follow my advice on a better way to do that.

Now comes the eternal debate over the optimum shaft length for a general mountaineering ax. As you may expect by now, my views are not in the mainstream, for reasons having to do with the actual main purpose of the ax.

The purpose of a mountaineering ax is not fashion accessory (so don't consider an aluminum-headed ax) nor to serve as a walking stick (trekking poles are infinitely better). The main purpose is to ensure the safety of the mountaineer, mainly against falling. Falls occur most often during descents, therefore *the main purpose of a general mountaineering ax is to avert falling while descending.* To serve this purpose, the ax must be long enough to reach down slope, and its spike must be pointy enough to bite into ice or hard snow, where falling is most likely. There has been a trend lately to recommend short axes—shorter than the customary measurement made by grasping the head, letting the ax hang at your side, and noting that the spike reaches your ankle. The claim that short axes are better when climbing steep slopes is debatable, but who cares? That is when falls are least likely. They are most likely when descending, usually in a traverse, when your boot slips and you fall on your butt. Or, if you're wearing crampons, when descending and you snag a

point on a pant leg or boot and pitch forward, face down.

I advise going slightly longer than the recommended length, perhaps as long as the pick touching boot sole level. Another way to establish the optimum length is to rest the ax on the floor, spike up; tradition says your fingers should just touch the spike, but I'd say the spike might want to reach as far as your palm. Test to see what planting the spike down ahead of your toes feels like when descending (make use of that sloped thing in the shoe department, crampons optional). Most illustrations, including those in The Classic, show axes that are far too short for general mountaineering. Just try reproducing their descending illustrations with a short ax, and imagine hiking in that crouched position for a thousand vertical feet wearing crampons. Test what chopping steps downhill might be like with that short ax the salesperson is trying to sell you. Plan on at least 70 cm length for most mountaineers, and 75 cm or longer for tall ones. If you're concerned about a longer ax being too heavy (the old-school complaint), not to worry: modern axes are incredibly light no matter what length. If you're worried that a longer shaft will make climbing steep, firm snow more difficult, fuggedaboudit. You'll be able to climb even steep water ice with an ax having a long, straight shaft; it's the ability of the pick to stick that matters most. With a long shaft you can move your hand up the shaft, using it like a handrail, and so plant the ax fewer times when climbing steep snow. Most of the time you'll likely use techniques other than *piolet traction*—planting the pick and hauling yourself up with the shaft. Self-arrest won't be affected by a slightly longer shaft and might even be augmented; self-belay will likely be improved as well. Functionality as a buried deadman will be better—the list goes on, as you'll see when I go over how you'll actually put your ax to use.

Leash

A leash is essential for preventing loss of your ax should it slip away for any reason—a disaster that could end your outing, or worse. There are basically two varieties of leashes: short leashes for

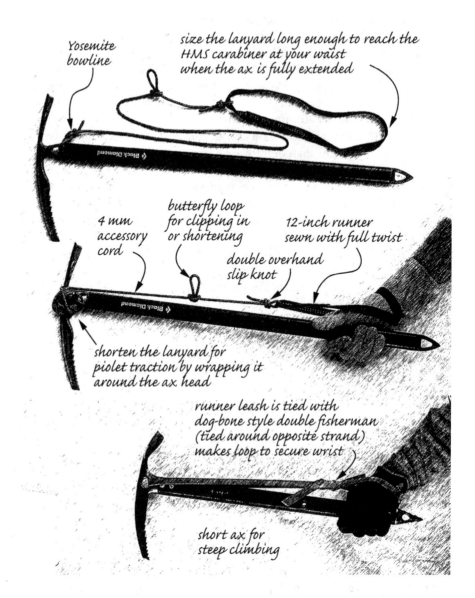

Yosemite bowline

size the lanyard long enough to reach the HMS carabiner at your waist when the ax is fully extended

4 mm accessory cord

butterfly loop for clipping in or shortening

double overhand slip knot

12-inch runner sewn with full twist

shorten the lanyard for piolet traction by wrapping it around the ax head

runner leash is tied with dog-bone style double fisherman (tied around opposite strand) makes loop to secure wrist

short ax for steep climbing

Leash and lanyard options.

short climbing axes, and longer lanyards for longer general mountaineering axes. Making your own of either type is easy using $9/16$ or $11/16$ webbing. Select a short ax only if you expect terrain to be so consistently steep that self-belay and self-arrest would be infeasible and climbing would be the exclusive use of your ax. In this case, you'd size the leash to support your grip on the ax shaft (which might be rubber covered). There are three options for securing the leash to your wrist: form-

ing the leash loop dog-bone style by tying a double fisherman's knot that includes the opposite strand, adding a pinch loop that you can slide with your teeth, or making the wrist loop long enough to wrap once around your wrist. The dog-bone leash will allow you to shrink one side of the loop to hold your wrist. The wrist wrap isn't as medieval as it sounds; even without a heavy glove, the pain inflicted is comparable to the other methods, and a mountaineer won't hang for long by an ax leash. It's my preference; you can combine it with a sliding closure. If you think you might want to hang at length, or if you're reluctant to tie your own knot, get a commercial leash with all the accoutrements, if you can find one long enough; I like the Yates Handcuffs for many reasons. All options will have the leash travel from the back of your wrist to the top of the ax; don't pass the leash between the palm of your hand and the ax shaft, or tether it to the shaft. Don't use a sliding ring leash attachment, either. You must be able to grasp the ax head easily without interference from the leash, and you might use the leash of a mountaineering ax, even a short one, as an attachment when setting up a belay that uses the ax as an anchor.

Most mountaineers will undoubtedly select a longer ax and a lanyard attachment. The lanyard will usually be clipped to your harness to prevent the ax going AWOL, even after you've lost it in your first attempt to self-arrest—reel it in promptly and try again. The lanyard might be superior to a wrist leash in such a circumstance, in that the flailing ax and its sharp points will be a bit more distant until you can bring it under control. You must *always* tether your ax when traveling on a glacier. Without a harness you can attach the lanyard by clipping it to a shoulder sling, or casual mountaineers can make the loop in the end of the lanyard big enough to *be* a shoulder sling on its own. Size the lanyard so that it's long enough to extend the head of the ax as far as you can reach when swinging the ax. This will make it plenty long enough to switch hands on the ax as you switchback when climbing or descending and to easily plant the ax for a boot-ax belay. Use a 48-inch runner as an emergency lanyard. Don't make the lanyard any longer than necessary, or you'll increase the risk of catching it with a crampon point during a steep ascent. When you encounter steep climbing and want a wrist leash, wrap the lanyard around the head of the ax a few times to shorten it. If you've chosen a wrist leash instead of lanyard, the tether can be extended while traveling by clipping it with your ever-useful daisy chain. If you worry about a lanyard

made of $\frac{9}{16}$ inch webbing becoming unwieldy when it gets soaked and frozen, consider making most of the lanyard out of 4 mm accessory cord (it's stronger than the ax); tie it to the ax head with a Yosemite bowline and to a 12-inch (30 cm) runner using a double overhand slip knot. Add a small butterfly loop in the cord to clip in shorter if you foresee the need. This is probably the most svelte solution for general mountaineering and glacier travel.

Ax Head Cozy

If you have cold-sensitive hands or use your ax in very cold conditions, consider adding insulation to the head—an aluminum ax shaft makes an effective heat sink, cooling your hands even through gloves. The usual method is to attach a scrap of sculpted sleeping pad foam with artfully applied duck tape. The pad becomes semi-permanent; it may interfere with your means of attaching the ax to your pack, it gets in the way of certain climbing techniques, and it will be destroyed the first time you use your ax to whack in a picket, but your hand will stay warmer when you're using your ax as a walking stick. Commercial versions are available that attach with Velcro or are made of rubber for more ready removal.

Second Tool

Ice climbers and extreme alpinists commonly carry two tools, maybe a third in case they drop one. One tool of the pair is typically fitted with an adze and the other as a hammer; both are at most 50 cm long. Mountaineers don't need this kind of fire power and seldom climb with axes in each hand. When we do, it isn't so critical that the axes be a matched pair. Even if you don't anticipate extensive steep climbing with a tool in each hand, you may want to carry a second tool to more efficiently bash in pickets or pitons, or spin in or out an obdurate ice screw. For this ax, select an old-fashioned ice tool with a straight shaft and hammer head; it will work much better as a hammer than the fancy modern ice tools with wildly curved shafts, but you may have to search yard sales to find one. Put a lanyard on this ax as well, as it's even more likely to escape as the result of finger trouble.

CRAMPONS

There are plenty of crampons on the market, and, fortunately, a few are good choices for mountaineers. The first requirement is that the crampon must fit your boots, much easier to achieve these days than in the past. All crampons are adjustable for boot size, so start your search by worrying about boot design, mainly sole stiffness. Crampons are available in flexible, semi-rigid, or rigid models. Don't give much thought to the rigid variety; they're for boots with nearly rigid soles. They're also heavy and tend to have vertical rails that are especially prone to "balling up"—the accumulation of big clumps of snow underneath your feet that makes hiking cumbersome and descending dangerous. There's no reason to choose crampons with vertical rails for general mountaineering even if they have anti-balling (antibot) plates.

Crampon designs have features making the crampons easier to put on. That's progress, compared to ancient models that required a macramé project for attachment (try it with frozen fingers or wearing gloves, and you'll see why this approach won't be missed). Many of the newer attachment schemes place requirements on boot design, however; some require a heel groove and perhaps a toe groove at the rand, and a stiffer sole to resist bending that might allow the binding tension to release. You can certainly choose a boot with the required features, but it's better to select crampons that don't require them and thus open up your boot options; there are plenty of good crampon models with perfectly adequate attachment systems that don't require rand grooves or a stiff sole. These models also allow you to don gaiters that insulate the boot welt, or move your crampons to other boots for different conditions. Unless you're sticking to vertical ice, pick crampons with an attachment system variously called *new classic* or *strap on*. This design uses a molded plastic toe trap that doesn't require a special groove for a front bail, and it uses a plastic cup in back instead of a heel lever, so no groove is required there either. You can fit them to lightweight hiking boots, should the need arise, and they'll fit your big plastic boots, too. Don't let the salesperson tell you they're more likely to fall off; seriously rad models use the same system. Front bail bindings may not fit every boot with a toe groove, and heel levers can easily appear correctly latched when they're not, especially when you're in an awkward position and things are covered with snow. Gaiters are accommodated better by the new strap-on crampons.

Next you encounter the common, but outmoded, distinction between 10-point and 12-point crampons. It used to be that 10-point meant no front points—very old-fashioned. Not so today; some of the most radical new designs have 10 points, or 9. A modern 10-point model is optimum for most mountaineering short of water ice climbing, and every manufacturer offers at least one. Any will work fine unless you have a special boot fit problem, such as telemark ski boots with wide toes. Stay away from aluminum crampons; sure, they save a few ounces compared to steel models, but they're limited to pure snow routes. Make up those ounces by careful boot selection; modern 10-point steel crampons are pretty light anyhow. I encourage you to learn to climb rock confidently in your crampons—a basic mountaineering skill that will trash aluminum.

Let me make my recommendation more specific: pick a 10-point, strap-on model with rounded, rather than sharp, points; such points tend to be a bit shorter, too, which is a good thing. These are perfect for mountaineering, even on moderate ice, and they're lighter than other models. If I were to tackle a route that I knew would be steep, rock-hard ice all the way, I'd opt for rigid boots and sharp 12-point crampons with agro front points or point, but for everything else, I prefer the rounded points. The reasons are simple: slightly shorter, rounded points are far less likely to snag on your clothing or on your other foot and are less likely to cause a trip by dragging unexpectedly. Such snagging and tripping is the most common cause of falls when wearing crampons. Plus, sharp points shred your pricey pant legs and they dull quickly when climbing rock. The slightly

10-point mountaineering crampons.

rounded points are more user-friendly and work just fine even on hard névé.

Consider adding antibot plates if you hike when balling up is a frequent problem (snow between new and old, when air temperatures are just above freezing). Mountaineering ax manufacturers invariably proscribe the classic habit of whacking the side of your crampons with the end of your ax to dislodge the ball of snow, and I agree. If balling up is rare for you, just sandwich the bottom parts of your crampons with duck tape to take care of the problem when it arises; duck tape antibots may last as long as the commercial versions. Some mountaineers make their own antibots by cutting up a plastic jug or truck tire inner tube and attaching the shape to their crampons with cable ties (zip ties)—lighter than the spendy commercial versions, too. Better yet, when your crampons start balling up, just take them off; balling up is nature's way of telling you that crampons are no longer needed. Antibots actually impair performance in some conditions, such as a hard surface covered with ice pebbles, and they slide more on slush.

While you're cruising the crampon department you may see models with heel spurs and wonder what that's about. The answer is gymnastics on frozen waterfalls and nearby rock. Not for mountaineers, and if you've ever absentmindedly knelt down while wearing them, you'll know why.

SNOWSHOES

There are two approaches to snowshoes: those designed for mountaineering and those intended for hiking on rolling terrain (the traditional design). The latter don't work well on steep terrain and are terrifying on icy traverses. For American mountaineers the options come down to three: the MSR Denali Ascents (in the newer Evo version), MSR Lightning Ascents, or the Grivel Promenade/Violino. The MSR models have built-in forefoot crampons and additional traction rails. The Promenade has an aggressive, full-boot, built-in crampon intended for "moderate" terrain; the Violino is the same frame intended for use with your regular crampons and is marketed for more technical climbing; the Grivels convert to each other with adapter kits. Both brands have heel lifts that can be flipped up to take pressure off your calves on steeper climbs, similar to the heel lifts of back-country ski bindings—essential. Neither MSR or Grivel models work well on slopes steeper than about 35° (that old angle of repose thing). Weights and pricing are comparable. The Violinos are cool, but I own the Denali Ascents because their serrated steel rails nicely back up their crampons on traverses and over the undulating hard ice of late season. I also like their bindings, which don't excessively compress boots to get a firm grip.

Another snowshoe option would be Verts. These are light, one-piece molded plastic plates that work well for climbing steep snow and clamber over rock reasonably well, but without any sharp metal components they're dicey if it's icy. They're less pleasant, if that's possible, than the others for trudging on flat snow. Frankly, instead of snowshoes, when the snow is too soft for hiking I'd rather ski.

New-School Snowshoes

One cool alternative to snowshoes is very short skis, sometimes called *firngliders*. The best I've stumbled across are Rossignol Free Ventures, but there are several brands. They're 99 cm skis with a three-position binding that will take mountaineering boots; they come with full-width climbing skins for monster traction. Firngliders climb well, better than snowshoes, and are much better in the flat, though they ain't no cross-country ski. Skis are great for safer glacier travel and are far more efficient than snowshoes for movement on snow of all degrees of steepness and consistency. Best of all, firngliders are a barrel of fun on the descent. You don't even have to be a good skier—being a fun hog is all it takes.

TREKKING POLES

Trekking poles are becoming a favored tool of new-school mountaineers. I've already mentioned them in Chapter 3 on hiking fast, and they're increasingly used instead of an ax whenever snow and moderate ice are involved. With good reason. First, an arbitrary definition: a ski pole is what you would expect, having either a fixed-length shaft or a two-section adjustable-length shaft. A trekking pole is a ski pole in three or four sections so that it can be collapsed down to around 25 inches (64 cm) to make for easy stowing when the rock or ice climbing starts. I anticipate that trekking poles will evolve to better suit alpinism, at which point they'll be called mountaineering poles; some day mountaineering poles and a hammer tool may become the new-school alternative to the ubiquitous mountaineering ax, even for demanding routes.

Trekking poles are superior to a mountaineering ax for preventing falls. Two relatively long trekking poles provide much more stability than a single ax by making it easier to keep your center of gravity balanced over your feet. As a ski mountaineer, for many years I've climbed (and descended) slopes using ski poles where other parties were roped and using axes, and I was having more fun. When I'm not skiing I still prefer poles unless I know an ax will be needed for *piolet traction* on hard ice—conditions where I'd carry a short ax and hammer tool. I've climbed steep snow with poles having self-arrest grips using technique equivalent to low and high dagger (*piolet panne*

and *piolet poignard*) ax climbing. Poles work just fine, and two such poles work much better for me than one ax. Poles are much easier and inspire more confidence than an ax when traveling on moderate slopes of hard snow, especially when descending steep snow or easy alpine ice. They're also better for resting on as you climb. A pair of trekking poles weighs about the same as one lightweight ax. I suggest you start pushing your use of poles onto more challenging terrain as you explore modern mountaineering—you'll be pleased. Trekking poles will continue to evolve and include more mountaineering features, such as self-arrest grips that make poles more like axes and ready conversion into avalanche probes. At the other end you see evolutionary axes from Stubai and Charlet that have extensions, making them more like poles. I wouldn't be surprised to see trekking poles replace mountaineering axes in almost every application, with or without crampons. For that to happen, self-arrest pole grips need to evolve, and arrest techniques need to evolve as well. Mountaineers can then work out the details of retention lanyards (a must on glaciers and anywhere else where losing a pole would be dire), whether or not to use wrist straps on dicey terrain, optimal pole tip and basket design, self-arrest features, and other issues of actually using poles to replace mountaineering axes.

The importance of not only the continuing refinement of trekking poles and techniques of self-arrest with them, but also of inculcating their skilled application among mountaineers, was brought home to me during the completion of this book when a fellow climber was killed in a fall. The slope was moderate, one I've skied on the way to more challenging terrain, but it was icy; my friend died with his ax on his pack and poles in his hands.

PULKKE

A pulkke, or pulk, is a sled intended to be dragged by the ultimate beast of burden: a mountaineer. Commercial versions are available in volumes from 12,000 to 18,000 cubic inches (195 to 295 liters), with weights starting around 10 pounds.

They're ideal for carrying loads on moderate terrain, up or down. Good sleds are far more manageable on irregular terrain than drag bags, which are large bags made of heavy vinyl-coated fabric intended to be hauled in straight lines on easy terrain by masochists. Drag bags have no directional stability; to the contrary, they seem to confirm the existence of perverse intelligence in inanimate objects. Kiddie sleds are comparably intransigent and have given pulkkes a bad name (not to mention adding colorful trash to the Kahiltna glacier). Commercially made sleds are a different animal; they have rigid towing poles to keep them off your heels or skis, a front rope drag brake for moderating downhills, a rear anti-reversal plate for uphills, and bottom rails to prevent the sled from passing its puller on traverses. A good pulkke is highly maneuverable, too; you'll find it easier to

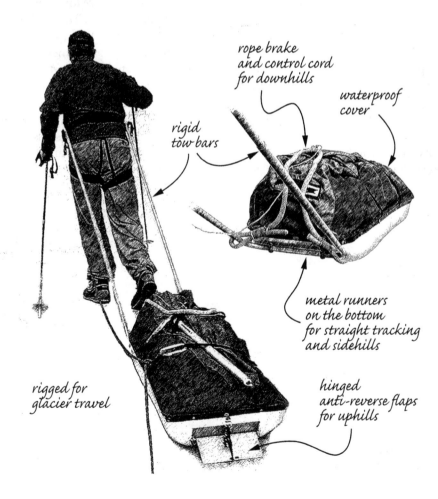

rope brake
and control cord
for downhills

waterproof
cover

rigid
tow bars

metal runners
on the bottom
for straight tracking
and sidehills

rigged for
glacier travel

hinged
anti-reverse flaps
for uphills

A mountaineering pulkke.

climb and descend—even ski descend—with 12,000 cubic inches of stuff in a sled compared to having it on your back. Especially if your routes involve long approaches on snow-covered roads, trails, or glaciers, the expense of a sled will be well worth it, particularly if you can convince your partner or dog to share the pulling.

GOGGLES

It's needless to say that protective eyewear is important for mountaineers. "Snow blindness" caused by wind and high altitude light can painfully terminate an outing. Glacier glasses with side shields are the old-school solution; closely wrapped sunglasses work as well and are much cooler looking; just be sure they have back-coated lenses and the 100 percent UV protection you need. New-school mountaineers will prefer ski goggles any time high winds blast them with snow, ice, or sand; they're not just for skiing any more. Plus, they keep a big part of your face frost free; just test their fogging propensity prior to committing to them on a serious route.

SHOVEL

If you're camping or traveling at length on snow, you'll want a shovel. Don't go for one of the plas-tic-bladed versions; they just bounce off ice, hard snow, and avalanche debris. Test by shoveling that hard snow around a parking lot, and you'll see. That worry also applies to the wonderfully light SnowClaw, though the new aluminum version may be better, but it's great for moving lots of soft snow if you have a strong back. The proper way to move hard, set-up snow is to chop at it furiously and then scoop away the debris; don't force the blade in and then try to lever out chunks, or you'll destroy your shovel, aluminum or plastic. Add holes near the corners of the blade to lash it to your pack and for attaching a cord to make your shovel into a hasty deadman anchor.

PROTECTION HARDWARE AND PERSONAL GEAR

I've covered protection hardware for snow and ice in Chapter 11, Climbing Forces. The list is short: pickets, flukes, and ice screws. For casual crossing of snow slopes on the way to summer summits, maybe one or two pickets is all a party needs to consider. Travelers on active, crevassed glaciers will likely be more circumspect if they spend much time there. If that's you, you still have a list of personal hardware to collect; I'll discuss the options in Chapter 26, Glacier Travel and Crevasse Rescue.

16
Climbing Snow and Ice

ASCENDING SNOW

Techniques for climbing snow are steeped in history, originating before the advent of modern mountaineering axes and crampons; the consequence is that the contemporary beginner is assailed by all manner of legacy inefficiencies. The truth is that the requirements are pretty obvious, even if you can't remember the French names. You want to step up or down using your ax or, better, your trekking poles, for balance. If you lose your balance, use your ax or poles to catch yourself (self-belay). If you don't immediately catch yourself, attempt to stop your slide (self-arrest—a last resort).

The techniques for moving your feet up depend on conditions; the main idea is to keep your weight balanced over your feet. Step up on natural features of the snow. When suitable features aren't handy, you'll have to make your own by kicking steps into the snow; make them with as few solid kicks as necessary to get the entire forefoot of your boot into the surface. Most climbers, with or without crampons, kick step their way up a slope with a rhythm of a tentative kick to assess firmness followed by a positive kick to plant their boot, then repeat with the other foot. When following someone else's steps, kick each one a little to strengthen it. If the snow is too hard to get adequate penetration of your boot, or sometimes even when you can, you'll soon find your legs tiring. Switch to a diagonal ascent rather than heading directly up the slope and make steps with the sides of your boots; this often works well when there is a soft surface over alpine ice. Don't think that your feet must be positioned symmetrically; one of the most effective ascents is with one foot into the slope and the other across it; this is called *pied troisième*, harkening to the third foot position of classical ballet. Make steps in firm snow with the edges of your boot soles using a scraping motion to saw out a purchase. If you can maintain your balance (trekking poles are a better aid than an ax), you can ascend on the edges of your boot soles with only a fraction of an inch of penetration into steep, firm snow—spooky, but it works. The tricky part of climbing difficult snow and alpine ice is switching leads to turn your traverse in the opposite direction. Change direction where you can take advantage of terrain features; if these are unavailable, spend extra time scraping out a few wider steps and sinking your ax or poles more deeply. You normally carry your ax in your uphill hand, so reversing directions involves a shift to the other hand; plant the ax spike with extra emphasis and keep both hands on the head until you have reoriented your feet and are stable in the new direction.

You may see mention of the self-belay grip and self-arrest grip; with a well-designed ax there's no reason for the self-belay grip. When you're climbing using the spike, grasp the ax head with the adze near your thumb and the pick extending from your little finger. Don't think you must swing the ax and bury the pick in order to climb or maintain security; in most cases the ax is used mainly to assist balance—another argument for trekking poles. Plant the spike (and the pick, when it's needed) assertively, but make each plant work for as many steps as possible, up or down, on moderate terrain. Always (always!) wear gloves when climbing on snow or ice; snow, especially granular snow, is extremely abrasive and will cause wrack and ruin to your bare hands if you take even a short slide.

If the snow is so soft that your boots sink in deeply as you climb, pause briefly after kicking each step and hope that the snow sets up enough before you transfer your weight onto it; this kick-and-wait process is faster and easier than attempting to wallow up steep, weak snow. This is similar to, but not the same as, the *rest step*. The rest step technique calls for a brief pause after advancing the uphill boot, while resting on the locked trailing leg; the idea is to relax the muscles in the trailing leg to spare them, and maybe to catch your breath. Mountaineering poles are a great supplement to the rest step. At lower altitudes, the rest step is too often overused by unfit climbers, resulting in very slow climbs.

Then there's the debate as to whether it's best to march directly up a steep slope or to zigzag in a series of traverses. Ski mountaineers who have ap-

Self-arrest grip.

plied a smattering of science to this question have concluded it's a toss-up in terms of energy efficiency. For me it's a matter of the hardness of the snow; if I can kick my boots in easily I prefer to go straight up, but if the snow is too firm for easy step kicking, I'll revert to traverses. Straight up seems easier with crampons, too; I guess my calves are stronger than my ankles are flexible.

When you're hiking with your ax, carry it by its shaft with the spike forward and pick down. This is supposed to make it less dangerous for other hikers, but it will mainly avert disapproving glances from more experienced mountaineers. Keep pick and adze covers on your ax until you're about to climb. If you temporarily stow your ax by slipping the shaft between your shoulder blades and your backpack, likely you'll forget about it when you take the pack off—another reason to tether your ax with a lanyard.

Self-Belay

Just about any self-belay technique is effective; it's usually described for hikers on softer snow, not for difficult climbing on steep, firm snow when you're more or less continuously belayed by your planted pick. The idea is that if your feet slip out from under you, you can plunge in the shaft of your ax and avert a slide. If conditions are that easy, you'll likely stop without much effort, and a hands-only self-arrest will work as well or better than anything you can accomplish with your ax. If your feet slip out and you can manage to stop yourself with your uphill hand holding the head of the ax, that's great; if you can grasp the ax shaft at the snow surface with the other hand, so much the better. Try not to end up as you often see illustrated: lying flat on the snow and thereby turning your body into a sled, which minimizes its stopping power. Don't waste any time if you lose your grip or the ax pulls out. Instead, get your body prone, facing uphill, as rapidly as possible and dig in your toes and hands; get your butt up so your stomach is off the snow. In other words: initiate a hands-only self-arrest. If your feet slide out when using trekking poles, it's the same story: do what you can to stop immediately using the poles as you might have used an ax (grab a pole just above the basket and jab the tip into the snow or even attempt to sink in the hand grip), but your best chance to stop is by immediate application of a hands-only self-arrest.

Hands-Only Self-Arrest

This, in my opinion, is the most generally effective self-arrest technique. Strangely, many texts don't emphasize it. The reason it's so effective is that you can apply it immediately, without gear, before speed develops and hopefully before you even move slightly down the slope. Here's how: As with all arrest techniques, be alert and maintain kinesthesia. If you have to run through a mental process to figure out your orientation on the snow and then decide the best way to twist or roll, you'll have already built up the speed that makes any kind of arrest much more difficult. If cats had to go through such a process, they'd never land on their feet; you must react like a cat, should you fall. That won't always be easy, but it's always necessary. Even as you're falling you want to be reorienting your body, curling up a bit if necessary, so that you end up prone, with your head upslope and both hands in front of your face. Immediately do a push-up. Not a girl push-up, either, even if you're a girl (you only have to do one). You must get your body off the snow (so it doesn't act as a sled) and get your butt in the air. Make a scoop with your hands and forearms that you hope will catch some snow, and push down with your cupped hands so your elbows are above the surface if possible. Dig in the front ends of your boots but keep the rest of your lower body off the snow. Aggressive application of these techniques will be successful; passive limpness won't.

The hands-only self-arrest technique is surprisingly effective, even on very firm snow where you might be skeptical that any arrest would work. It will work while holding poles in your hands and it will work while holding an ax in one hand (watch out for the adze). It's a method ski mountaineers use when they lose it in the steeps—and ski mountaineers tend to be moving briskly when they lose it. It's the best method by far if you've lost your ax as you pitch forward or backward—far better than gaining speed while you reel in your ax and attempt a traditional ax arrest.

If you're curious to evaluate the hands-only arrest, compare it to the more traditional ax arrest when you practice. You do practice self-arrests, don't you? Practice is your only hope of training your body to respond reflexively. If you and your mates are practicing, and you use the instant, hands-only technique, you'll stop before they even get into position (if you do it right). They'll accuse you of cheating and make you use an ax.

The hands-only technique is effective even if you're holding your ax and wearing crampons. If you can plant the spike as you are falling, so much the better; call it self-belay if you must. If you fall

-get your butt in the air
-plant your feet wide apart
-weight on your toes, stomach off the snow

-cup your gloved hands
-do a push-up on your hands
-look downslope

Hands-only self-arrest.

and begin sliding, you mustn't allow your crampon points to touch the surface, because they will catch suddenly and create new hinge points in your legs; maybe some new ventilation in your body, too. You may then tumble, but you won't stop. The hands-only technique is essentially the only one that makes use of the very effective stopping power of your crampons, because it's applied even as you fall. Call it *stick where you land.* Sticking where you land is about the only thing that will work on bare glacier ice or on steep névé, where you get only one shot at sticking before you take the long, bumpy ride into a hungry crevasse. A conventional arrest on such surfaces is virtually impossible.

Self-Arrest with Ax

The secondary purpose of a mountaineering ax is to help arrest a fall upon failure of its primary purpose of preventing falls in the first place. There are two terrain conditions on which you might attempt self-arrest: feasible and infeasible. When a self-arrest is feasible, almost any technique will be effective. Some techniques are more efficient than others, but prompt application favors success; inaction guarantees adverse consequences. The goal of all body gyrations is to end up as quickly as possible in the *self-arrest position.*

The most effective self-arrest position has a few key elements. Most importantly, you must perform a push-up on the head of the ax while locating it as close to your upper torso as possible, with the pick pointing into the slope. If you allow the ax to be pulled any distance away from your body, the effectiveness of the arrest plummets. Avoid having your body act as a sled; get it off the snow and put the most weight possible on your boot toes and the ax. To do that you want to keep your legs straight and push your butt up well off the snow surface. Keeping your feet apart increases stability. Less important elements include lifting the spike of the ax to put more weight on the pick and facing downslope, away from the adze. When you've come to a halt, you'll find yourself in an awkward position on the very slope on which you slipped moments before; vigorously kick in your boots and revel for a moment in your good fortune to have stopped.

The various techniques for ending up in the self-arrest positions involve rolling your body *toward the head of the ax* and planting the pick as soon as possible, even downhill below you, then contorting to swing your feet around and beneath you and getting your body into a prone orientation. Success requires practice.

If you're wearing crampons, unless you're able to stick where you land, you must prevent the crampon points from contacting the snow until you have brought your slide to a halt. To prevent contact, hold your feet in the air and brake with your knees—a much less effective technique than braking with your boot toes. It's a cruel irony that when the snow gets so firm and steep that crampons must be worn, a less effective arrest technique must be employed. There are many snow and alpine ice slopes on which self-arrest will be infeasible, but if you're on such a slope and have imprudently fallen, you have no choice but to at-

-butt in the air
-feet wide apart
-weight on the toes

-crampons off the snow
-weight on the knees

-stomach off the snow
-weight on the spike
-hold the spike close
to your shoulder
(but not too close)
-face downslope, away from the spike

The classic self-arrest position, with and without crampons.

tempt to arrest, and to continue attempting, with every last ounce of your strength. Even if you can't stop quickly, you may be able to slow yourself or contribute to your team's arrest if you're roped up.

It's absolutely essential that every mountaineer learn confidently to self-arrest no matter what the conditions or what your orientation as you fall. Even if you never actually fall, you may be called upon to hold your team when simul-climbing, catch a companion who has fallen into a crevasse, or bail out of a glissade that has gotten to be a little too much fun.

Self-Arrest with Trekking Poles

Trekking poles are becoming the tool of choice for new-school mountaineers (and guides) when climbing and descending snow, so properly self-arresting with them is a requisite skill. Fortunately, generations of skiers have explored the most efficient techniques; unfortunately, their favorites tend to involve skis and are often initiated from a failed hip check. I'll be the first to admit that a body of experience (and equipment) has yet to evolve that establishes the best arrest techniques for climbers using trekking poles, but a few are in favor.

Reasonably effective techniques for prompt self-belay with an ax would fail completely if used for self-arrest, after a little speed has developed. The same can be said for arresting with trekking poles. The key is starting the stopping process as

soon as possible; that's why one of the favored techniques with poles looks lamentably like the "don't do it this way" example of arrest with the spike of an ax.

For this technique to be effective, the climber must get a substantial fraction of his body weight uphill of the braking point where the poles contact snow; otherwise, the poles or pole can be ripped out of control, just like an ax with the spike planted. Unfortunately, in this position the climber's body lies on the snow, acting like a sled and making it difficult to press boot edges into the surface so they'll do their part to slow the fall. It's worse wearing crampons, where not even knees can be brought to bear. Either end of the trekking pole can be jammed into the snow; pick the most convenient at the moment of need.

Using another technique, the falling climber throws his arm over the poles or pole and rolls onto his back or side. He then levers the pole shafts upward, digging the tips into the snow by using his armpit as a fulcrum, and simultaneously adds more weight to his boot edges by arching his back. This is much easier if you have your hands out of the wrist straps, as many ski mountaineers prefer in steep terrain. The possibility of the poles being torn away is reduced by trapping them in your armpit. Control of the braking effect is easier, and recovery from the pole tips breaking off during the fall is conceivable. Getting your boot edges into the surface isn't easy, but it's well worth the effort. This

get as much weight
as possible
off your butt and
on to your
pole tips
and heels

brace your
holding
hand
against
your hip

feet braced
wide apart

Conventional self-arrest with poles.

capture your
poles in
your armpit

arch your back
as much
as possible
to get weight
off your butt

feet braced
wide apart

New-school self-arrest with poles.

technique has the additional feature of offering a view down the slope; possibly a benefit, depending on one's composure at the time.

At this stage of the evolution of mountaineering poles, there are two alternatives for more serious conditions: using poles with self-arrest grips and bringing an ax into the equation. Self-arrest pole grips either mimic an ice ax's pick or project plastic claws designed to bite into amenable snow; I have proposed a design that projects a pole tip from the top of the hand grip, to allow an arrest even when wrist straps are used. Self-arrest pole grips are no more effective at stopping a slide once it gets going than is a self-arrest with an ax, which is poor on a hard, undulating surface. Strapping a lightweight ax to a pole shaft with shock cord or even duck tape is an awkward solution, but not uncommon among adventuresome ski mountaineers. Some climbers use an ax in the uphill hand and a pole in the other, but steep skiers in the Alps don't

Ax-style self-arrest with poles.

bother—they learn to arrest with poles. These approaches are functional but are best thought of as means to stop immediately, rather than eventually. They all require practice. With poles or ax, the key is quickly getting your body oriented and off the surface in order to apply pressure with points—pick, pole, boots, or even just hands.

Trekking poles involve a trade-off: more security than an ax and less likelihood of a fall, but at this evolutionary stage, less capacity to arrest a fall on serious terrain. Arresting falls on truly difficult terrain is infeasible irrespective of tool choice, so your best bet is to assiduously avoid falling in dire conditions (by using trekking poles) or, better, to use a rope and anchors to prevent falls from becoming terminal on terrain where arrests are infeasible.

Don't Fall

Arresting a fall on steep, hard snow or alpine ice is in the realm of the infeasible. Quick and simple belays on snow are weak, but don't let that stop you from using them. Most falls occur when descending; the forces created by a falling descender on a snow slope are relatively low, so a weak belay is likely to be effective. The safest way to descend precarious terrain is to set up a quick belay from a jiffy anchor, such as a stomper. Get good at this, and you won't find yourself yelling to your partner as he disappears down the slope, "Arrest! Arrest!"

CRAMPON TECHNIQUES

When conditions become precarious due to increasing grade or firmness of slope, or both, an awareness creeps over you that you should have put on your crampons. If things are really dicey and you've procrastinated, hack out a stance with your ax, set an anchor, and clip yourself in before you begin the crampon attachment ballet—you don't want the petty distractions of self-preservation to result in an escaped crampon. It's not infrequently that mountaineers confront this "Will I die if I do, or will I die if I don't?" dilemma. In Europe it's more common for mountaineers to march out of the hut in predawn hours and spend

the entire day with crampons attached—on snow, ice, and rock.

French Technique

Before the development of crampons with front points, elaborate foot techniques and elegant terms describing them were developed for ascending moderate (by today's standards) alpine ice and firm snow. These techniques were predicated on ankle flexibility, flexible boots to exploit it, and, above all, keeping all 10 points of each crampon in contact with the surface. The ballet terms have been mostly forgotten, but the central principle remains: when climbing moderate slopes with crampons, keep all your bottom points in contact with the surface. There's no crampon equivalent of the rock climbing technique of "edging."

When the slope angle increases to the point where ankle flexibility can't keep up (about 35° even for skilled climbers), the mountaineer must turn at least one boot into the surface and utilize the front points of her modern crampons. Being smart, she'll revert to placing at least one of her boots across the slope, or even angled down it, whenever conditions permit such less-tiring technique.

The riskiest part of climbing with crampons is the transition from one foot position to the next when traversing. When moving up from a balanced "open" stance (when your upper leg is nearest the slope, and your hips are turned outward—the stance in which you'll want to move your ax up) to a stance with your hips turned inward toward the slope, your lower boot will cross the upper and then attempt a higher foothold—an invitation for a fatigued climber to snag a crampon.

Flex your ankles to keep the bottom points in contact with steep ice or hard snow.

Moving up in balance using poles and using *piolet canne* with ax.

You may want to avoid the crossover by taking more small steps, but that will be slower. To be honest, French technique, no matter what ax positions accompany it, requires unusual ankle flex, skill, and practice. It's becoming a lost art.

MOUNTAINEERING AX TECHNIQUES

Don't jump to the conclusion that the main use for a mountaineering ax is whacking the spike into the surface and hauling yourself upward. That technique, *piolet traction*, is slow and best reserved for steep, firm slopes where it's truly necessary. An ax is better used as an aid to balance, making it possible to ascend or descend using leg power; in the simplest case the ax is used like a walking stick, a technique called *piolet canne*. Trekking poles are a better aid for maintaining balance than an ax, which is why they are increasingly replacing axes except for steep technical climbing.

When using the ax or poles for cross-body support, pay special attention to keeping your body balanced above your feet and avoid leaning into the slope, which encourages your feet to slip outward.

The mountaineering ax is also used to create

don't lean into the slope

Moving with ax and poles in the cross-body position.

hand holds on terrain lacking them by chopping with the adze. This is seldom worth the time except for short sections; otherwise, it's better to be prepared with crampons or to find another route.

Plant the pick for *piolet traction* solidly, then work your feet up several steps using the ax shaft for hand holds. When you've moved up on the

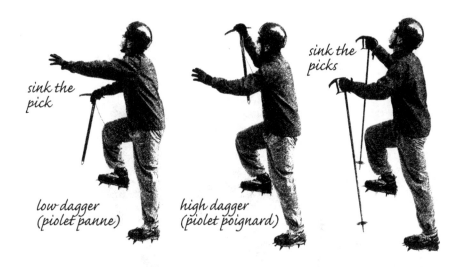

sink the
pick

low-dagger
(piolet panne)

high dagger
(piolet poignard)

sink the
picks

sink the
picks

Moving up on steep, firm
snow or soft ice.

shaft as far as possible, mantle up on the head of
the ax before you place it anew. Normally you'd
want to avoid overplacing the pick because that
makes it difficult to remove, but this technique
leaves you above the ax head where the pick can
easily be lifted up and out. If you must struggle to
remove an overplaced pick, in snow or ice, don't
wank the shaft side to side lest you break the pick.

DESCENDING

It's remarkable that a climber can turn around and
look down in terror at the prospect of descending
a slope that he's just climbed up with alacrity. That
sentiment is an accurate assessment of the peril,
as descending is more difficult than climbing. Far
more falls occur during descents. Competent descending is an essential mountaineering skill; it
requires confidence and maintaining a posture
with your weight balanced over your feet.

Glissade

The most enjoyable descent, save skiing, is glissading. After securing everything on or in your pack,
you turn your boots or butt into a sled, and gravity
becomes your friend. Augment the sliding and extend it to more gradual slopes by sitting on plastic
sheet sold as rolled-up kids' sleds; some mountaineers don slippery nylon overpants to spare
their spendy soft shells and enhance their glisse.

Regardless of whether boots can mimic skiing or
whether a frosty butt is in order, developing competence in glissading is an important component
of moving fast in the alpine world. You'll glissade
a slope in a few minutes that would require an
hour to boot down in total security. Competent
self-arrest is the backup technology, should the
spike of your ax or tips of your poles and progressively digging in of heels fail to sufficiently augment your personal coefficient of friction. On wet
snow you may be able to initiate a small surface
avalanche that you can ride down in greater comfort, but unless you're confident of a compassion-
ate runout, it's best to let the avalanche go its own
way; your self-arrest won't be effective applied
atop moving snow. Don't initiate a glissade if
you're uncertain of the terrain below. Glissading
over rocks, even small ones, or patches of ice is an
unwelcome experience. You have little directional
control when glissading so if you find yourself approaching an unpleasantry, stop and hike to the
side before continuing. Everyone knows that you
must never, ever glissade wearing crampons, yet
every annual accident list mentions glissaders
needing novel orthopedic procedures because they
kept their crampons attached.

Plunge Step

For more security at the cost of speed, plunge stepping may better suit the terrain, visibility limita-

finally, mantle up on the ax head before removing the ax and planting it higher

change your grip to low dagger (piolet panne) and keep moving

grasp the ax head and keep moving up

plant the pick and move up using piolet traction

Making the most of one solid plant of the pick.

Sitting glissade using poles for control.

tions, and your desire to maintain a warm, dry tush. The fastest plunge stepping aggressively plants your heels farther down the slope than you can reach with the pick of your ax or even poles, so balance and confidence when facing outward on a steep slope are what make for success. With trekking poles it's possible to reach farther and more easily maintain balance and a confident, upright posture; poles make for greater plunge stepping speed and security.

When conditions are too problematic for plunge stepping or glissading, it's still possible to descend faster than simply giving up, turning to face the slope, and downclimbing. Plant your ax as far down as you can and use the shaft as a hand rail as you descend in a crouch; competent French technique keeps this approach efficient. At some degree of difficulty you're likely to conclude that

Keeping your weight balanced over your feet when descending moderate ice or firm snow.

less daylight will be burned by constructing an anchor and rappelling. Hack out a bollard and back it up until the last person descends; in extremis, leaving hardware may be the least costly alternative overall.

One of the most terrifying descents is of hard, late-season glacier ice with a grade of 20 to 30°, where hiking down without anchors makes sense, but only barely. You'll be wearing crampons, the surface of the ice will be undulating with vestiges of sun cups, and you'll have the accurate apprehension that self-arrest is infeasible for any number of reasons. Even on lower-angled slopes, the contours and hardness of the surface guarantee a long, unpleasant ride—or worse—if you fall. In such conditions you must carefully ensure that all bottom points of your crampons contact the ice and that your weight is balanced over them; that could mean descending for many hundreds of feet in a tiring, crouched position. If you stumble, stick with desperation where you land, because arrest is infeasible; even sticking is dubious. Do everything possible to avoid falling, and aside from paying

close attention every time you relocate a crampon, the best way to prevent falls is to use trekking poles with tips stuck assertively into the surface. Next best would be planting a longish mountaineering ax having a sharp, steel spike. If neither are at hand to inspire confidence, the alternatives are to belay or rappel; both require establishing anchors in hard (too hard to drive pickets) but relatively low-angled ice. On such solid surfaces, ice screws or V-threads may be mandatory; placing protection is much faster than conducting a rescue of a fallen climber. Downclimbing takes forever.

ROPED TRAVEL ON SNOW

A solo climber: a man who falls alone. A roped team: climbers who fall together.

That was Tom Patey's sardonic view of roping up as a team. The decision of whether to rope up on perilous snow is the subject of innumerable and inconclusive debates. I happen to think that roping up when climbing snow is one of the most commonly misused mountaineering techniques. Let me cut to the chase: if the party doesn't set anchors, tying in to a rope offers psychological benefit only; roping up actually decreases the safety of the party.

That's certainly not the view you'll read elsewhere, so I'd better offer explanation and counsel for when you face that decision yourself. First, eliminate the irrelevant outliers: one member of the party is injured or freaked or dropped his ax; an improvident decision was made to include a member whose skills prove to be grossly inadequate (in other words, we'll assume that party members are more or less equally competent; we're not discussing guides and clients); the party is traveling on a snow-covered, crevassed glacier. In cases such as these it's better to rope up. If the terrain being crossed is suspect for avalanche hazards, the situation is also anomalous: *never* rope up when exposed to avalanche danger—cross terrain threatened by avalanche hazard one person at a time while others in the party watch attentively from positions of safety. Any time the terrain is suspect for avalanche, travel unroped at least 35 feet (10 meters) apart; if that doesn't seem sensible, go home. Those situations out of the way, let's consider three categories of terrain: conditions where individual self-arrest is feasible, conditions where individual self-arrest is infeasible, and conditions that are unclear or changing.

Feasible

Self-arrest is feasible on slopes where the grade and snow hardness are moderate, in other words, on slopes not too much steeper than the angle of repose on which a skilled climber would forgo crampons. Trekking poles provide more stability than a mountaineering ax on such snow, and arrest is easier without crampons. Where individual self-arrest is feasible, the rope is unnecessary and actually adds more danger, not solely because it encourages overconfidence. Even if you can arrest yourself, arresting yourself and others tangled in the rope at the same time has got to be more challenging. The party moves more nimbly without a rope but can still take advantage of the strongest climber by following in her boot track. Climbing in a roped team is always more awkward than climbing solo. Without some slack in the rope you'll be constantly jerked forward and back as you climb, which certainly impairs stability. To reduce some of the jerking, old-school advice is for each climber to allow additional slack in the rope or carry a few coils of rope in a free hand—*don't do it*. This is tantamount to asserting that individual arrest will be very easy. Here's why: There's no way you can slow another falling climber until all the slack is out of the rope between you. If party members are carrying coils or allow appreciable slack in the rope, other climbers won't be able to arrest a falling climber until after he's failed to arrest himself and has built up some speed; that makes his arrest even more difficult. Conditions must be highly favorable if a speeding climber is to be stopped—he would have been able to arrest much more easily on his own immediately as he fell, when his speed was nil. This is even more apropos of the ascending leader or final descender on the ends of the rope. It is not unheard of for a falling roped team to dislodge and entangle another team below, and for injuries and deaths to occur in both teams.

Carrying coils on easy snow is unwise, and carrying coils on a glacier is suicidal—never do it. Instead, learn to climb harmoniously when roped up, keep ropes as tight as possible (lightly dragging on the snow usually does it), and keep groups small. Even then, tying into a rope when climbing easy snow is imprudent; the team is better off without a rope. I was amazed to see a photo showing this poor technique, complete with carrying multiple coils of rope on easy terrain, used as the cover shot on a recently published book claiming to be from outdoor experts; no wonder bad technique is so hard to quash.

Being unroped on steep snow, even if the climbing is easy, may be disconcerting for some, but they should have practiced self-arrest until confident of their ability, and their team members should be confident that they've done so. Roping together a number of overextended, marginally skilled climbers is metastable at best and increases the difficulty and danger for all. Every person on the team can't be relying on others to stop them if they fall—can they? Because team arrest is more challenging than self-arrest, it's only possible where individual arrest poses no difficulty. It's important to drive home the point that a rope in such conditions increases, not reduces, danger. Reading the many accounts of teams that have fallen as a roped group will help convince you. It sounds cruel, but better that one should perish than all. Even better, one should self-arrest.

Infeasible

On terrain where individual self-arrest is infeasible because it's too steep or too icy, the team must rope up and place protection, even though that will slow them down. It makes no sense to hope that the balance of the team could execute an effective group arrest should one member fall and load the rope, applying unwelcome force to the other climbers, whether they've managed to get into self-arrest positions or not, and irrespective of whether the fallen climber is sufficiently composed to scream "Falling!" and his companions are able to hear him. There may be isolated examples of successful team arrest (invariably on snow where individual arrest would have been feasible), but common sense and evidence to the contrary are overwhelming in conditions where individual arrest is infeasible. This old-school form of communal brain dysfunction is so common that a couloir has been named for it: the Orient Express on Denali—frequently the scene of fallen-team rescues (or recoveries), even though it's also frequently skied. When self-arrest is infeasible and protection isn't going to be used, having no rope is far safer for the party than tying in. Only advanced mountaineers will consider such climbing, which is equivalent to unroped soloing on rock. I and many other mountaineers have fallen on such slopes and have arrested successfully, but I certainly wouldn't try it while holding another climber (wearing crampons makes things more difficult). Though it slows the party, prudently climbing perilous terrain demands placing protection. There are two styles of climbing with protection: pitch-by-pitch belayed climbing and simul-climbing. A skilled party will select the best approach based on conditions of terrain and team and may alternate or combine them to suit circumstances.

CLIMBING WITH PROTECTION

Leading fifth-class pitches on snow commonly involves long runouts, because placing protection is so time consuming. Nevertheless, falling on steep, hard snow or névé is comparable to falling on rock; there's little braking of the falling climber, who may frequently be airborne. Even if the potential for lithobraking isn't there, snagging a crampon or ax adds serious danger. When calculating where to place pro, snow climbers must be at least as attuned to minimizing fall factors as rock climbers, but that isn't the norm. Optimizing fall factors means that the distance between intermediate anchors should progressively increase, not decrease, and the tendency to run out the first placement after leaving the belay should definitely be avoided. That dictum is counseled by the fact that the farther snow climbers with crampons and axes fall, the more likely they will be impaled by their own equipment or increase the range of motion in their ankles or shoulders.

A modern leader may carry two tools, a mountaineering ax and a straight-shaft ice tool with hammerhead and wrist leash, to be used for driving pickets. If you're using both axes in *piolet traction*, wrap the long tether on your mountaineering ax around the head to shorten it into a leash. While you're placing pro, firmly sink your ax as a temporary belay; it'll be at least as strong as a self-arrest. Attach by clipping to a butterfly loop in the leash or to the hole in the spike, whichever gives you more freedom to work.

Belaying the Leader

There are situations where snow is steep, loads are heavy, and climbers are fatigued, when a simple belay could mean the difference between a long slide and a *very* long slide; such situations are rare and should not be the basis of general decisions about safe methods. Invariably, more common circumstances illustrate the psychological rather than the practical benefit of a rope. If a stomper belay is used to belay the leader, the direction of fall load will change from downslope, until the leader places the first intermediate anchor, to upward in the direction of the first anchor after it's placed; none of the weak snow belays, including the stomper and boot-ax belay, are adroit in dealing with that change of direction. After a good anchor is placed on lead, the belayer should take down the stomper, remain tethered to his planted ax by its

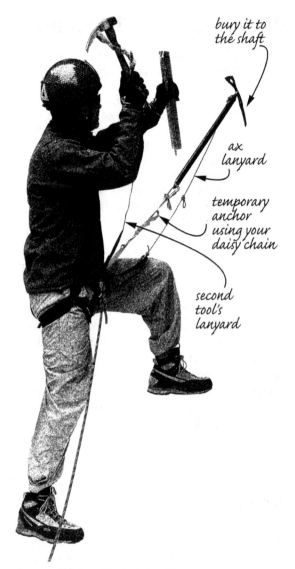

bury it to
the shaft

ax
lanyard

temporary
anchor
using your
daisy chain

second
tool's
lanyard

A hasty self-belay with a buried ax pick.

angled upward, away from the downward direction of force of the belayer's weight. Say also that the leader climbs above the belay and places an anchor, then climbs higher before falling. The force on the belay anchor is now upward toward the first anchor, in line with the angles of the picket and ax shaft, so the placements of the belay anchor have little holding power and may be pulled out easily if the belay anchor pulls out, the belayer enters a tugging match with the falling leader, both hanging on that anchor the leader just placed.

A new-school mountaineer knows to focus on Anchor #1. She'd hope for nearby rock placements, but absent those she'd build an anchor similar to that previously described, but she'd use it for Anchor #1 and not for herself. If there were any danger of her being pulled into Anchor #1 by a fall, she'd tether herself below it with her ax. If the leader, belayer, or both fall, Anchor #1 will hold them; remember, Anchor #1 limits the fall factor and prevents a fall directly on the belay, so the force on the belayer is always in the direction of Anchor #1, never downward, and any upward movement of the belayer's body will help reduce the peak force on anchors the leader has placed.

Leading on snow can and should be fast, so the belayer should be prepared to feed rope rapidly. The rope may be stiff or frozen, making it difficult to pass through a belay plate. A Münter hitch could be used, but it isn't a very dynamic brake. The desire to minimize forces on potentially weak anchors suggests using a hip belay, but the rope should be directed through carabiners at the belayer's waist to add holding power and prevent unwinding if the belayer is pulled off his feet and out of balance. If things are seriously insecure or the belayer foresees holding the leader for an extended time, a friction knot such as a Klemheist can be added to the rope as it feeds out; experiment to get the length right so the knot can be held to prevent it from locking accidentally. Some snow belayers may opt to forgo a belay device entirely and use only a friction knot or an ascender that they hold half open; this allows them to immediately dive into an ax arrest without losing control of the rope. Hardcore, but effective so long as Anchor #1 holds.

lanyard, and belay into the first intermediate anchor (the familiar Anchor #1).

Belaying the leader on challenging snow raises the same concerns of anchor building as on rock, except that anchors and fall forces will be weaker, and, of course, the medium will be constantly changing. In Chapter 14, Climbing on Rock, you learned to avoid the old-school miscalculation of building a serious anchor focused on supporting the weight of the belayer. Say the anchor is a driven picket equalized to an ax driven as a picket, both

sink the shaft to make the belayer's tether

Anchor #1

The belayer's anchor and Anchor #1 for belaying the leader on snow.

Belaying the Second

When bringing up the second on serious terrain, it's best to belay directly off a sound hardware anchor, not your body, and use a Münter hitch or autoblock device with tension. There's less likelihood on snow, compared to rock, that a fall by the second might require fancy techniques to release a locked autoblock B-52 or Gi-Gi, so take every opportunity to exploit this effective technique unless frozen ropes thwart it. Running the rope up from the belayer's harness through a redirecting carabiner places almost twice the fall force on the redirect's anchor so it's poor technique, but using a Münter hitch or autoblock at the same anchor increases the fall force on it by less than 10 percent; that difference can be important on snow. Digging a U-shaped pit for the belayer and using an unanchored sitting hip belay for the second is feasible only on easy snow, where a belay shouldn't even be necessary.

Poles or Ax?

Admittedly, the question of using trekking poles or an ax on terrain where arrest is infeasible yet where continuous *piolet traction* is not required is unresolved. Personally, I've done it both ways. Stability with poles is greater than with an ax—noticeably greater when descending. Yet arrest is probably, though not demonstrably, inferior using poles, particularly when crampons preclude using your feet to augment the tool of choice unless you can stick where you fall. Arrest is infeasible by definition, so sticking where you land is crucial and equally uncertain either way, but self-arrest ski poles may level the playing field, so to speak. I admit that my personal choice of ax or self-arrest poles has been influenced by irrelevant factors—whether I was mainly skiing or climbing, the seriousness of exposure rather than the difficulty of the slope, what my companions might think, and so on. Evolution in the use of poles is on the leading edges of modern mountaineering technique.

Between Feasible and Infeasible

It's sometimes said that climbing with the party roped is justified if the conditions are uncertain or likely to change. Being already tied in, so the argument goes, will speed up the transition to anchored simul-climbing or belayed technique. This may be true in rare cases, but I'm deeply suspicious that most such claims are made by climbers or theoreticians who have not undergone the fundamental paradigm shift from the old school's psychological rope to the new-school understanding that the rope creates additional danger in the absence of anchors. There's one other possible exception, comparable to glacier travel, and that's traversing on exposed snow where a cornice fall is possible. Herman Buhl died in a cornice fall on Chogolisa but might have been saved had he roped up—or Kurt Diemberger might then have also perished; we'll never know. Otherwise, the rules are simple: if you tie in, place anchors; if anchors aren't justified, don't tie in. The point of demarcation is whether a climber considers herself to be sensibly traveling on terrain where self-arrest is feasible, or to be free soloing where self-arrest is infeasible. In neither case does being tied to one's companions increase overall safety in the absence of anchors.

Descending the Infeasible

Descending is more perilous than climbing, so special attention is needed to avoid contributing to the many tales of groups of sliding climbers tangled in their ropes and falling into crevasses, impaling themselves, or lithobraking when runouts run out. These incidents happen every season, even on relatively easy climbs. Descent in a group on an unanchored rope is even more foolish and dangerous than climbing up on one, but somehow the psychological reassurance of the rope is seductive. It's actually better to untie, because jerks on the rope are especially unwelcome when descending tricky terrain, and team arrests are inevitably less effective than individual arrests. Things are particularly dangerous if the last climber falls; he'll have gained considerable speed by the time he comes on the rope—to the surprise of his team members, who didn't see him falling until he passed them on the way down. If the party is simul-descending (all tied in to the rope), the strongest climber and least likely to fall should go last, where she can keep an eye on the party and quickly apply the most competent arrest; this also minimizes the lengths of falls other team members take before coming on the rope, but better team organization is not enough to make it safe to descend difficult terrain with a rope unless anchors are placed. The good news is that forces of slips are low, so even a weak belay at the top—a single picket or a Münter hitch stomper—can do the job. If the party members are moving down a semi-fixed rope attached by prusiks (using Klemheist or autoblock knots, but not Tiblocs or even mechanical ascenders, which are a pain for descending because they must be held open), the last climber (who descends on belay) is the only one facing a serious fall, assuming climbers keep their prusiks tight enough to actually lock on the snow-covered rope. It's also possible to set up a single strand rappel for all but the last team member; only one climber at a time can be on the rope. There are enough relatively easy ways to avoid team falling that one could callously observe that team falls reveal Darwinism at work in the mountains.

MOVING FAST ON SNOW

I've already discussed techniques for moving fast on the trail (Chapter 3) and on rock (Chapter 14), and I've woven hints into this chapter, too; there's more on moving groups fast in Chapter 24. Plenty of opportunity exists to move fast on snow, alleviating the frequent description of mountaineering as a "snow slog." The first item of business is the same as previously: dial in your brain to the notion of moving fast and commit to making efficiency a priority. The next most important component of faster travel on snow is becoming competent and confident with self-arrest techniques. Get good at self-arrest when wearing a pack, using ice ax and mountaineering poles, falling face first and flat on your back, on soft slopes and firm; for extra credit and significant risk of injury, learn self-arrest while attached to a sled if you anticipate the utility of such skills. While you're at it, practice downclimbing steep snow and ice; the ax techniques, while obvious, are more challenging to execute than for ascending.

If there are three in a roped party, common practice is for the weakest climber to be in the middle. This climber can be clipped to the rope at a butterfly and belayed up, perhaps under tension, while the last climber follows at a fixed distance. It's faster and more efficient for the middle climber to ascend the rope somewhat independently, secured by a prusik (or, much better, a Tibloc or ascender); this gives the belayed last climber more flexibility in stopping to remove pro and allows the middle climber to continue moving up rather than wait while that goes on. Just remember that friction knots, especially those tied with webbing or fat cord, are not entirely reliable when called upon to lock on a snowy rope in the course of a gentle fall; they should never be expected to catch a hard fall. Four millimeter cord locks readily and is plenty strong for this application so long as slack in the rope is avoided.

The seconding climber faces lower length and danger of falls than the leader, so he can and must climb as fast as possible, using boot and ax techniques that might be too precarious on lead, even to the point of risking an occasional slip. Call this "success-oriented" style, but it's not unsafe because the second should be on tension, especially when removing pro, so falls will be very gentle. The second can also carry a heavier pack; the efficient party will embrace the concept of "leader's pack, second's pack." Speed on the part of the second is a key element of moving fast on steep snow or névé when you must belay.

Learn to place pro competently. Placing protection on snow and ice is inevitably more time consuming than on rock; strive to minimize the discrepancy. Since most placements are significantly improved by stomping the snow around and beneath the anchor site, stomp away while you contemplate the more subtle issues you intend to address. If you anticipate frequent picket placements, suffer the weight of an extra hammer tool; it will earn its keep by increasing speed and ease of placements.

Learn to descend with gusto. Confident descending on boots or butts is essential to moving fast. Consider firnglider skis rather than snowshoes; they're faster on climbs and much faster on flat ground or descents. Any snow you gotta slog up is an invitation to ski down—fast as well as a fun part of alpinism.

CLIMBING ICE

What is ice? The answer isn't simple. Technically, ice is frozen water with air either entrapped or excluded; that covers a wide variety of climbing media. Chouinard distinguished two types: *soft ice*, which allows ample penetration of axes and crampons, and *hard ice*, which makes you wish for soft ice. A mountaineer might say that soft ice takes pickets for pro while hard ice holds screws. I've already discussed the metamorphism of snow, which yields wet granules of ice at the end of the season. Surviving granules freeze to form névé, which is usually a pleasure to climb because it's "soft." Waterfall ice or ice that's refrozen from meltwater in gullies can certainly be "hard." Alpine ice might be either variety in the environment above tree line; mountaineers hope to find névé or something close but must learn to deal with hard ice when it's encountered.

Climbing alpine ice or névé isn't much different from climbing firm snow. Climbing waterfall ice, however, is a whole 'nuther thing, whether the ice forms as a true waterfall or as a flow in an alpine gully. Similar ice can form at the gap of a bergschrund. The details of climbing hard water ice are beyond the scope of this book, but some general comments will introduce that aspect of alpinism.

Falling while climbing ice must assiduously be avoided; there are just too many sharp points around that could do bad things, even if the rope catches your fall. Placements are weak in aerated ice, like that at the base of a frozen waterfall, so Screamers are often used there. A smart belayer would avoid the temptation to stand next to the lead climber as she starts up the waterfall or bergschrund, and instead stand well back, so that after an anchor is placed, the fall factor will be lower, and there will be more rope to absorb force and spare the anchor.

Water-ice gear has evolved to suit the technique, which is based almost exclusively on front pointing and hanging from axes (unless you count the outrageous new techniques of heel hooking, figure fours and nines, steinpullers, and figure fours on steinpullers). Crampons, like their boots, tend to be rigid, and models with single vertical front points are increasingly popular, though they more easily shear out of steep snow. You can climb water ice with mountaineering axes, but specialized axes make it far easier when the going becomes vertical and lumpy. Modern specialized axes for climbing waterfall ice are called *ice tools*; they have shorter shafts with significant curvature, and the picks have a reverse curve for better stick or hook in ice and rock features. Yes, rock. The leading edge of both bolted sport and alpine mixed climbing involves ascending routes using tools and crampons on both ice and rock, to the extent that a friend of mine asked, "If I poke the ice, is that off route?" Climbing on rock with tools and crampons is called *dry tooling*. Minimalist crampons with heel spikes are standard fare as are leashless ice tools with radical grips; wait till these climbers

Tools for hard alpine ice and mixed climbing.

Front pointing with heels low.

discover Gripec gloves and gReptile. Hammer and adze heads are shaped to work like chocks for climbing rock; many devotees use two such hammers and no adze. A few tool models, or their replaceable picks, have evolved even more to suit the stresses of leading-edge alpine mixed climbing and bullet-proof ice.

It's sometimes said that ice climbing is either the most mental form of climbing, or the least, but even though these specialized techniques and gear are uncommon in general mountaineering settings, lessons from water ice climbing serve mountaineers who venture onto steeper terrain. Keep your heels low when front pointing, and avoid rocking up and down, lest you lever yourself off or fracture the surface. Until the grade gets so close to vertical that it's impossible, climb as always, with your body balanced over your feet. Leading on ice demands, as does leading on rock, the ability to downclimb out of difficulty. The moves are pretty much the same as when climbing up, but shorter and with even less visible foot placements.

Avoid placing crampons or axes close to each other, so that fracturing of the ice by one tool doesn't affect the other; a shoulder width apart is about right. "Matching hands" doesn't work on ice, because the second tool placement will weaken the first, but both matching and stacking ice tools can be used on rock. Keep steps less than knee high when you move up on steep ice, and don't place your tools so high that you'll get spread out and flattened against the ice. Avoid the tendency to overplace your tools; hooking rather than hacking works better on waterfall ice. A delicate touch is especially important when confronting rock covered with verglas, even if you're lucky enough to find thicker flows in nooks and crannies. While you're at it, don't bash away the route with your crampons, either. It's amazing how little penetration of pick and point is necessary for ascending gossamer ice by a poised and balanced climber. On the other hand, don't hesitate to use your tools to bash verglas off rock when you need access, including when placing pro. Sport climbing on waterfall ice is great practice for techniques, and attitudes, that will improve your alpine ice climbing—and it's another great reason to head for the gear shop.

PART 5

Base Camp Basics

Establishing base camp means much more than throwing your heavy pack on the ground and putting your aching feet in the air. Arriving at base camp comfortably will require determined dedication to decreasing your load, and remaining there comfortably will mean selecting the best up-to-date equipment for alpine travel and camping. Arriving at base camp ready to tackle the upcoming climb requires mountaineering-specific nutrition and fitness training. Leaving base camp means leaving no trace of your presence.

Lightweight Mountaineering

From studying the outcomes of past expeditions, I believed that those that burdened themselves with equipment to meet every contingency had fared much worse than those that had sacrificed total preparedness for speed.

When Ernest Shackleton made those comments nearly a hundred years ago, he wasn't talking about a casual weekend of peak bagging. Yet he well understood the fundamental trade-off mountaineers must confront: trading skill for weight in order to move fast. Shaving the margin of safety on the gear side to increase the margin of success. In Shackleton's case, he certainly proved himself up to the task.

For mountaineers, going light is a philosophy, a comprehensive and systematic methodology, and a commitment to thoughtfully balancing total preparedness against increased speed, agility, and success. And fun. The lightweight approach is taking hold among backpackers, and it's just beginning to move above the horizon for recreational mountaineers. The problem is that mainstream equipment manufacturers have yet to sign on with conviction. When you browse your outdoor gear shop, the salesperson will extol a long list of features and will claim products to be "bombproof"; "lightweight" is either an afterthought, an empty promise, or an aspect to be avoided lest it connote "flimsy." Overbuilding equipment and adding tons of features is what sells products to weekenders, who are the majority of buyers, and reduces returns of products that fail when abused. This means that mountaineers looking for lightweight alternatives will have to search a bit more and in many cases will have to chart their own courses through the maze of gear selection. To find truly lightweight, well-designed equipment and clothing, modern mountaineers will have to turn to specialty manufacturers (in Canada, perhaps, eh?) who cater to the new-school, lightweight niche.

Lightweight mountaineers may even have to make or modify their own gear.

Going lightweight is a technique that must impact your entire equipment selection as well as your mountaineering style and objectives. If your tent and bag are lighter, you'll be able to use a lighter backpack; that will allow you to use lighter boots, which will make you faster and more nimble as you climb; climbing faster will reduce the time your objective requires so you can reduce the food and fuel you carry, making your pack lighter. Going lighter will reduce stress on your feet and knees, which will allow you to hike faster and longer each day and over your lifetime. Moving faster will reduce your exposure to objective dangers and will increase the route options you can consider. And so on. Hanging over this wonderful new approach are a thousand what-ifs: What if it rains? What if you sprain your ankle? What if you get lost? You may have to call off an outing if too many what-ifs arise, but I'd hazard a guess that this happens no more frequently to lightweight mountaineers than it does among those burdened with conventional kit. Dealing with all those contingencies requires skill—skill that doesn't come mainly from experience. It comes from being acquainted with the technology of lightweight gear and from following a process that reduces the equipment you require and the weight of every component of that equipment, a process that must maintain adequate safety and comfort margins as you learn these new skills.

STEP LIGHTLY

At this early stage of the art, most lightweight aficionados have independently taken very similar steps to going light. Let's look at those steps in prioritized order.

Analyze Every Piece of Your Equipment. You don't have to become obsessive about it (though many do), but a certain amount of technical effort is required. Start by compiling a list of everything you own that you might want to carry on a mountaineering outing. Use a spreadsheet to organize your list. Then weigh every item and enter the weight into your spreadsheet. Include boots, accessories, and clothing as well as items that will be in your pack. A spreadsheet makes it easy to express weights in both grams and ounces and to create what-if columns that will allow you to explore a virtual backpack and examine the effects of the items you plan to lug. Some mountaineers even include food and compute total weight and calories. Keep a steely eye on the base weight of your pack: the weight less food, water, and fuel. You'll need to acquire a reasonably accurate kitchen scale, postal scale, or triple-beam balance with a range up to 20 pounds (10 kg). Gram accuracy isn't essential at first. A scale is a fundamental piece of climbing hardware for the modern mountaineer, but you can get started by dragging stuff to the post office or REI on a slow afternoon.

Reduce the Number of Items. You'll have to give up on those "50 essentials." Look at your list as you plan your next outing and see what you can do without. Seems simple enough, but it can be painful the first time. As Antoine de Saint-Exupéry said, "In anything at all, perfection is attained not when there is no longer anything to add, but when there is no longer anything to take away." If you start with the bare minimum, your spreadsheet will clearly show the consequences of tossing in items "just in case" or that "might be nice to have." The only valid "just in case" items are a first-aid kit and a few well-chosen repair items; both must be optimized for function and weight. These elimination decisions require knowledge: of yourself, of the capabilities of your equipment, of the weather and environment, and of your companions. One way to reduce the number of items is to share things among your party; do you really need two cell phones? As the high priest of spartan lightweight backpacking, Ray Jardine (same guy who invented Friends), says, "Leave your home at home." Just don't be frugal to the point of guaranteeing yourself a miserable outing, which the Ray Way would be for most of us.

Reduce the Weight of Each Item. Invariably this means substituting another, lighter item, though it's not uncommon for lightweight fanatics to cut off unnecessary features and labels from backpacks, tents, and clothing. Make weight an important criterion any time you acquire new clothing or equipment. Look first at your heaviest items: sleeping bag, tent, backpack, and boots. That's where the biggest gains can be made. As you browse the isles of your outdoor gear shop, you may find yourself asking, "But how light is light?" You can find many opinions on that; I express plenty of mine throughout this book. A general rule for major items is three pounds is a good weight, but two could be better. The next group of sleeping pad, stove and cookware, and 10 essentials should weigh half that or less. Go down your entire list looking for opportunities to reduce weight; every ounce counts. Water is the heaviest item you'll carry, so thoughtfully minimize what's in your pack by resupplying frequently; winter makes this calculation more difficult.

Take Out Your Wallet. The dirty little secret behind going light is that lighter gear isn't less expensive—high-fill down and titanium ain't cheap. Figure it will set you back $10 to $15 for each ounce of weight saved. The way to minimize the pain is to thoughtfully factor in weight each time you make a purchase, so you don't end up with lots of clothing and gear that go unused.

Change Your Style. In order to effect significant weight reductions, you'll probably have to change the style of your backpacking and mountaineering. Take shelters, for example. There's no such think as a lightweight, four-season tent, however cozy you may find yours. A light one-person tent will weight less than 3 pounds, and a really light bivy sack will come in at half a pound. Sleeping under the stars can be a new experience that will significantly reduce the weight you carry. What if it rains? Adding a tarp tent can be done for the cost of another pound, and you'll still be ahead of the game; a poncho tarp tent will protect you as you hike and as you sleep. Augment your forecasting skills so that you don't carry a tent when precipitation is unlikely. Ultimately, you may decide that an 8-ounce silnylon poncho tarp is an adequate backup shelter. Just be aware that surviving a mountain thunderstorm, with its high winds and hail, requires more skill with a tarp than with a tent; it can be done, but you'll want to be very familiar with your poncho tarp before you take on Mother Nature at her most malevolent.

Don't Go Too Light. There's no question that shaving weight can also shave your safety margin, even as it increases your chances of successfully achieving your mountaineering objective. This harkens back to the old conflict between sieging the mountain and climbing it alpine style. The former offers better outcomes for old-school clients; the latter promises more satisfying success for fast-moving new-school alpinists. Be especially wary of *ultralight*. This realm of equipment and technique requires special skill and circumstances to avoid shaving the safety margin to nil; it may be inappropriate in the hostile alpine environment. Even with climbing equipment there are certainly some weight-saving options that should be avoided *ab initio*; one example (in my opinion) is aluminum ice axes and crampons. On rock they begin to disintegrate; on ice they don't penetrate. You may save half a pound per pair of crampons, but if you encounter ice or rock you'll regret the decision to go with aluminum; your success, and maybe your safety, will be threatened. That's the kind of decision you'll confront at every step along the lightweight trail.

Rethink Your Food. If you habitually bring a stove and prepare freeze dry, you're in the majority, but if you want to go light, here's food for thought. If you use freeze dry, at least repack it into Watchful Eye Designs's O.P.Sak zip-seal bags to shave weight. If you're resourceful enough to prepare your own dried meals or if you're in bear country, the odorproof bags are a great idea. On longer outings you don't want to carry unnecessary water, even in your food, but on short outings you may reason that you can tolerate tasty but cold ready-to-eat meals and can come out ahead by leaving the stove at home. If you just have to warm water for a couple of meals, an Esbit stove may be all it takes. When I cook, my system is light: a titanium kettle and a plastic two-cup cup are the only containers. You don't need pots and pans for most outings; if you must bring them, share among several people. "Extra" food should be minimal, so nothing remains at the end of your outing. In Chapter 19, Performance Nutrition for Mountaineers, you'll read that a balanced kilogram, dry weight, is about all the food you can metabolize

As an example of the kind of head scratching that lightweight mountaineers go through, let's take a look at your water container. Say you require a widemouthed bottle so you can easily dip into streams or add snow. Following our spreadsheet concept, here's a little table of options:

Container	Volume (ml)	Weight (gram)	ml/g	Note
Classic 32 oz. Lexan water bottle	1,050	170	6	
24 oz. widemouthed cycling bottle	700	88	8	1
100 oz. hydration bladder, no holder	3,000	200	15	1
48 oz. widemouthed fruit juice bottle	1,450	80	18	2
32 oz. widemouthed sports drink bottle	1,000	50	20	
20 oz. widemouthed sports drink bottle	650	42	29	
48 oz. Nalgene flexible Cantene	1,825	63	29	1

Notes
1. I wouldn't put this in my sleeping bag at night
2. Getting too large to pack easily

A pattern, as they say, emerges. The ubiquitous old-school Nalgene water bottle is the least weight efficient of all these options. The most weight-efficient container is the 20-ounce sports drink bottle, even for bulk storage. If you tote three liters of water, you'll save over 10 ounces by using lowly sports drink containers compared to using traditional water bottles. Saving that much weight of your sleeping bag would cost a hundred bucks. Sports drink bottles have other benefits, too: they're widely available and cost a dollar or less, plus they come filled with free sugar water. A 20-ounce sports drink bottle is the ideal size for an hour's worth of water, making it easy to keep up with your hydration plan. Breaking down your water into 20-ounce containers makes packing water a little easier; the bottle is ideal for use as a pee bottle; it fits bike bottle- and beer can-sized accessories, so many are available, including insulated backpack holders; it gives the mountaineer carrying it a jaunty, dirt-bag appearance; and it's made with PETE, so it doesn't retain flavors, rinses clean easily, and is readily recyclable. You can look at PET or PETE sports drink bottles as the larval form of pile jackets—they recycle into polyester, making them among the most valuable post-consumer waste. Recycling yours from time to time is a very good idea, because you're much more likely to encounter hostile microorganisms that have colonized your water bottle than from drinking untreated mountain runoff. Flexible containers like the Cantene and hydration bladders, though they do lose volume when empty, have lots of cracks and crannies that require vigorous cleaning and strong bleach or TSP treatments to fend off microcritters. The urban legend that reusing PET (or Lexan/polycarbonate, for that matter) water bottles releases a dangerous plasticizer is untrue; the only danger is failing to rinse and dry them between uses to avoid microorganism growth. For the thoughtful mountaineer with a scale and Excel, the best water container choice becomes obvious.

daily, even when you're working at full tilt; most days you'll need less, so plan carefully and don't carry more.

Bear canisters are painfully heavy, no doubt. The conventional model adds 3 pounds of single-purpose weight (the purpose being to avoid killing bears). Share them whenever possible. The Bear Vault is a bit lighter and bigger, while the Bearikade weighs "only" 2 pounds. Expect the $10/oz. rule to apply; at least the latter containers don't require remembering to turn them upside down in case of rain. In areas where the bear canister principle applies but the law doesn't, an Ursack seems to accomplish almost the same thing, but at 4 ounces, it weighs considerably less; it certainly foils varmints, but it isn't waterproof. Where bears are an issue, keep everything with a scent, including used feminine hygiene products, in a bear canister—using odorproof zip-seal bags helps keep scents separate. Bears, especially those who have graduated from the Yosemite Problem Bear Academy, are increasingly able to outwit food-

You may decide to hang your food to thwart bears or rodents; you may even decide to hang your backpack, hat, or anything else that contains animal-attracting salt. Forget the old-school "counterbalance" method—and you probably know that hanging stuff over a tree limb and tying the cord to the trunk is considered jocularity by bears and clever varmints. Instead, use this method: Tie a cord at least 10 yards or meters long to a light, keychain carabiner. Clip on a weight, such as a full-size carabiner or a stuff sack for a rock or dirt, and throw the weight over a branch about 15 feet off the ground and as far out as possible from the tree trunk. Remove the weight and clip the keychain carabiner to your food bag and to the free end of the cord. Pull the cord until the carabiner slides up into contact with the branch; then reach as high as you can and tie something to the cord that will serve as a stopper, such as a clove hitched twig or carabiner. When you release the cord the food bag carabiner will slide down until it hits the stopper twig, but the bag will be hanging far above the ground. Retrieve your food bag by pulling down the cord and untying the stopper. If wind threatens to make the free end of the cord inaccessible, leave a weight hanging on it. Above tree line, bears are less frequent, but varmints are more voracious, so hang things out of their reach on a cord suspended at each end; sometimes that works.

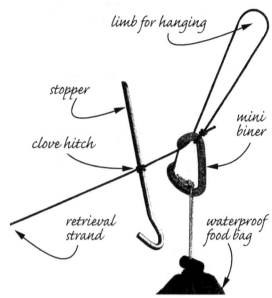

New-school food hanging technique.

hanging schemes; a bear's success at this will result in the end of your outing and, eventually, in the end of the bear.

Switch to New-School Clothing. This means "86" the traditional, heavy waterproof/breathable parka and go with a wind shirt and single layer of wool insulation. In cold conditions, whip on the belay jacket when your activity level drops, and you begin to chill. Phase out your heavy pile and fleece in favor of lighter down or synthetic insulation. Wear nylon pants instead of cotton. Carry a silnylon poncho tarp as a storm backup instead of a parka. On a serious outing you can plan on either moving, being in your sleeping bag, or belaying; don't carry clothes for other activities, and plan on efficiently using the insulation you must carry. This book's discussion of clothing systems (see Chapter 18) reflects the importance of a new-school approach to clothing and its place in lightweight mountaineering.

Weed Out Inappropriate Items. Amazingly, some people habitually carry items they have no use for. They carry filters on winter outings when their wa-ter will come entirely from melting snow. They carry winter sleeping bags on summer outings. Extra fuel bottles on one-night outings. King-sized bottles of sunscreen and insect repellent. A friend of mine started an above–tree line ski mountaineering trip with a hammock! The list goes on—snap out of it.

Favor Multiuse Items. This is actually a game played by lightweight mountaineers—trying to find items that can fulfill several requirements. Another way of saying this: avoid redundancies. One of my favorite items is a homemade stuff sack made of fleece; it has an open end shaped like a cap with earflaps. It's a clothing stuffsack, a base-camp food-hanging bag, a camp hat, and a comfy pillowcase.

Search the Internet. You'll find any number of resources, equipment, and suggestions from others on how to lighten your load. You'll even find free software to help analyze the weight of your kit. Many of these sources relate to hikers, not climbers or mountaineers, and pertain to outings on summer trails rather than snow-covered peaks, so you'll have to sort through endless suggestions for stoves made out of beer cans to find what might be useful for you. Mountaineers also tend to be more focused on specific objectives than backpackers and may be more willing to suffer in pursuit thereof. Beware: Internet content has no veracity check.

Deflate That Spare Tire. Painful for many, but I have to mention it. You may spend considerable effort and money removing 5 pounds from your pack weight, but you can lighten your load by the same amount at no cost by losing adipose tissue around your waist that does you no good. This is the only lightweight tactic that's not made easier by experience.

Go Light Slowly. But persistently. Sure, light-weight backpacking can make mountaineering much more successful and enjoyable, but keep reminding yourself that you're trading knowledge and skill for weight, and it will take some time to become accustomed to the new gear and the back-country protocols you'll need to acquire to exploit this gear. Some of your experience can be gained by weathering storms while camped in your back yard, some from watching others exploring the lightweight philosophy. If you increase your knowledge and skill at the same time you shave weight, you can avoid decreasing your margins of safety and comfort. In fact, many will assert that lightweight mountaineering is safer as well as more successful than old-school techniques. That's basically the argument that Shackleton made.

Equipment for Base Camp

BOOTS AND SHOES

Mountaineers are challenged by footwear demands few backpackers face. We typically hike rapidly on milder trails to reach climbs, thrash up talus, ascend snow or névé to reach rock, then climb rock or even mixed rock and ice to the summit. The ideal footwear on such a route would be comfortable hiking shoes, burly mountaineering boots capable of supporting crampons, and then rock climbing shoes. Unless you intend to be the Imelda Marcos of mountaineering (a title already held by one of my climbing partners), compromises are in order.

As you select footwear, function may require compromise, but never ever compromise fit. I've cramponed up snow couloirs and climbed fifth-class routes in lightweight hiking boots simply because most of the ground on the routes was hiking rather than climbing, and that pair of boots fit exceptionally well—well enough to motivate me to work around their functional limitations when I had to.

Fit to Be Tied

Fit trumps features every time, so let's start there. Purchase your boots from a shop having a skilled boot fitter, a wide selection of brands, plenty of size and width options, and the special tools needed to make any custom adjustments that prove necessary. That's the modern approach—gone are the days (or months) of agony trying to break in heavy leather boots. Modern boots have lots of synthetic components that don't respond to breaking in; neither do they require it. All this is a dream world, of course. The reality is that finding a boot that fits almost perfectly and making adjustments to achieve a great fit is going to fall largely on you, not on the kid in the shoe corner of the outdoor shop.

First and foremost, don't head to the cash register until you've done everything possible to evaluate the fit and comfort of the boots you've selected and you're satisfied that you've found the perfect fit for your feet. Plan on taking a lot of time, hopefully in the afternoon when your feet have swollen to their largest. Don't be influenced by seductive features, miracle liners, or cool colors, and don't expect annoying issues to go away after a few miles on the trail. Inevitably, the fit gets worse, not better, as you put on the miles with sweaty feet, rough trails, and the weight of your pack.

Start by measuring both your feet with a Brannock device; you may have to show the salesperson how to do it right. Put a heel in the labeled cup at one end of the device and press your toes down a bit to read off your foot length size based on your longest toe. Next, measure your arch length size by moving the weird little slider along your foot until the ball joint near your big toe is cupped by the slider; putting your thumb atop your ball joint may help position the slider. This measurement is important in shoes and boots with flexible soles because the flex of your footwear needs to align with the ball of your foot, which is where it flexes. Read out your arch length on the slider's scale in the same units (shoe size) as foot length. Measure both feet with your actual hiking socks on, both unloaded and with your full weight on one foot. Most people measure about a size larger when bearing weight; this is not an indication of fallen arches. Determine the width of your feet by sliding the side barrier against your foot while the arch length slider is correctly positioned; read the width that corresponds to the shoe size you've just determined. If you seem to be between widths, go for the larger width if your foot is fat or you have high arches; consider the narrower measurement if you have low volume feet. A boot fitter can be helpful with this and even at this early stage will have learned more about your feet than you'd ever imagine. Knowing the official, two-dimensional size of your feet doesn't mean you can find boots to fit; it's just a place to start. Start with a shoe size corresponding to the largest of the measurements of foot and arch length for both feet.

The salesperson should be able to walk you through models that are appropriate for your feet—with suitable volume and arch height, for example, among the factors that don't show up in length/width sizing. A few boot companies, Dunham, for example, make boots in several widths. Put on your first test pair wearing the same socks, footbeds, and orthotics you expect to use with them. Consider using a thinner pair of socks to fit insulated boots, to compensate for the eventual packing out of the liner and the compensating switch to thicker socks; modern synthetics don't pack out nearly as much as traditional loden and leather boots. Lace the boots from the toe, pull up on the tongue and carefully tighten the laces again, beginning at the toe. The aim isn't to clamp your feet but to eliminate loose material and create a uniformly close fit; you or the salesperson should squeeze your hand around the boot while you're standing to feel for localized looseness and to accentuate pressure points. Move your feet around vigorously. You sometimes hear the recommendation that you should be able to fit a finger behind your heel when you push your bare foot forward forcibly, but maybe that says as much about your finger and socks as your feet. Now stand up and close your eyes; think about the fit, being particularly attuned to pressure points over the instep (the top of the metatarsals and cuneiform bones) or other places where you've had problems in the past. Bend your knees and rock forward on the balls of your feet, spreading your legs a bit; concentrate on how much your feet move around and how much your heels rise as you perform this half squat, an unrealistically exaggerated test. If this test reveals pressure points or excessive movement, try another pair. If all seems well, hike up a slope of about 20°; nearly every outdoor shop shoe department has a ramp for this purpose. Stand on your toes and note where the boot sole flexes and how much your heel moves up and down. Hiking up and standing on your toes will allow your heels to move fully into the boots' heel cups. Then face downhill and repeat. Hope for a flex in both orientations that indicates your foot isn't moving around; that will indicate a good fit over the critical instep, boot flex that matches your arch length, and appropriate heel volume. As you turn to face down the slope, be especially aware of any movement of your foot toward the toe of the boot; the nap of your socks will allow some movement, but a quarter inch (6 mm) is excessive. If you're fitting boots in which you'll climb or hike rough trails, find an edge somewhere and try standing on it with your weight supported only by the inner edges of your forefeet. Some shops have a synthetic rock where you can test whether the sole is stiff enough to handle reasonable edging or whether the sole is too soft and will flex and let your foot roll off edges if you attempt to clamber or climb. You should be able to stand on a 1-inch wide ledge, even with hiking boots.

You're looking for adequate, but not excessive, toe room, absence of looseness that will let your foot slip around, and freedom from pressure points. Be especially wary of pressure, even slight contact, at the tips of your toes. That ends the test, because such boots will unmercifully attack your toes when you hike downhill and especially if you front point wearing crampons or kick steps up a snowfield. During the downhill test, it might be acceptable to feel your toes very slightly touching the end of the boot so long as you still have enough room to move your toes around; more pressure than that is a fatal test result. Length is a fit characteristic that cannot be altered. If things seem pretty OK but you still notice your feet sliding forward on the downhill test, carefully lace the boots more tightly and test again. Be especially attentive to fit across the instep. That's the part of the boot that holds your foot in place, keeping it from sliding forward and crushing your toes when you hike downhill, and keeping your heel in place to prevent heel blisters when hiking uphill. Many boots have special lacing features in the instep area, reflecting its critical importance to fit.

Many people, me included, have narrow heels. A boot that fails to provide adequate heel retention may not be evident in the shop; in fact, a loose heel may actually feel more comfortable. Beware. A loose fit in the heel or Achilles tendon area is a recipe for heel blisters when you hike uphill—hiking uphill is what forcefully pumps your heel up and down in the boot. Even boots that will assassinate your heels on steep uphills may not reveal their bad intent when tested by simply hiking on the flat, much less in the shop, so pay special attention to heel movement if you're prone to heel blisters. Having a foot with a narrow heel makes it especially critical to find boots with narrow heel counters, extra comfy instep fit, and flexible lac-

ing options. Similar comments can be made about other foot shapes that don't fit the norm. If you experience similar problems with all your footwear (calluses that indicate movement in a particular area, for example) you will pay special attention as you make these tests. The stiffer the sole of the boot, the more critical the heel fit will be, because the natural flex of your foot is fighting the stiffness of the sole. Really stiff-soled boots, such as you might choose for front pointing or kicking steps up steep snow, are starting to appear with lacing eyes all the way back at the Achilles tendon, making for much improved heel retention. Nevertheless, heel movement will occur when hiking uphill in any shoe or boot, stiffer soles just make it more pronounced. The real issue is how the boot deals with the combination of heel movement and your particular feet. Unfortunately, not even climbing stairs will reveal the truth; you'll have to put in some uphill distance hiking on your forefeet, and that may make your boots unreturnable.

Don't stop the fitting analysis when you leave the store. Take your new treasures home and wear them around the house. All the while, carefully go over the fit analysis I've just described. Return the boots if you aren't confident of their fit.

Do-It-Yourself Customization

If you have a low-volume foot or high arches, a footbed may help take up the excess volume in the boot. You can try a heel cup to make up for a too-loose heel counter; sometimes they help, sometimes not. Such devices are basically crude *volume* adjustments and they're directed at the average problems of average feet. To make *structural* adjustments you must employ a serious, semi-rigid footbed. Fixing structural fit problems may even require a custom footbed, which can cost as much as the boot. If you have unusual arches or excessive pronation (inward rolling of the ankle as you move your weight onto an extended foot—very common), custom footbeds may be your only option, but they'll work wonders that no off-the-shelf products can—and they'll be fitted by a professional. Overpronation is sometimes indicated if, when crouching barefoot just enough that your knees block your view of your toes, you are unable to lift your big toes off the ground; accurate diagnosis requires a podiatrist. If you ignore your pronation problem it could lead to plantar fasciitis, probably the most common foot complaint, when you start hiking with the weight of a pack. Don't expect a boot fitter to lengthen a well-made boot, certainly not by the third of an inch that separates men's shoe sizes, or to make much impact on the width, either.

Part way in between off-the-shelf footbeds and custom footbeds fall heat-it-yourself moldable EVA foam footbeds. These do a good job of reducing pressure points under your feet but can't go as far as custom footbeds in correcting structural problems where the design of your foot conflicts with the design of your boot, particularly arch length.

Lacing

Don't feel that you must follow a conventional lacing pattern. More and more, boots are being made with slippery laces and eyelets, so that a firm pull at the top puts equal tension throughout the laces; if that's not the effect that works best for you, you may have to skip eyelets or tie knots to put the lacing pressure where you want it. Some newer boots have lacing arrangements that, like rock shoe laces, allow tension to be highly customized. By skipping a lacing crossing and just passing the lace to the next eye, hook, or ring, you can relieve pressure under the region where the laces would have crossed. By putting a twist or two in laces where they cross you can isolate lacing tension on either side of the twist. Nothing in the rule book says you must lace your boots all the way up; if you want more ankle flex for hiking or for sidehilling with crampons, try skipping the top lacing points or lace the top hooks backward. Passing the laces through rings or loops from bottom to top or lacing hooks top to front as you work from the toe will "lock" the laces, making them tend to retain the tension you apply to each crossing; lacing in the conventional manner allows lacing tension to spread out. The goal is to have a uniformly snug fit across the instep while leaving your toes unbound.

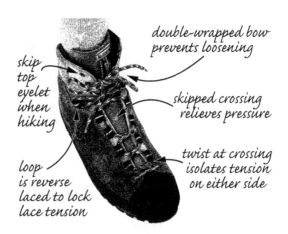

skip top eyelet when hiking

loop is reverse laced to lock lace tension

double-wrapped bow prevents loosening

skipped crossing relieves pressure

twist at crossing isolates tension on either side

Boot lacing options.

If you can't get a friendly fit under all circumstances, your only recourse may be to apply tape or padding to vulnerable points on your foot prior to donning your boots, most commonly at your heels. Moisture will inevitably cause tape to release even if you first apply tincture of benzoin, but here are a few approaches: tape with soft medical tape and then cover with duck tape, whose slippery top surface won't intensify the frictional interface between your fair skin and that malevolent boot. Try a modern blister dressing, perhaps covered by duck tape. Finally, a full ankle tape job could be necessary, but try for waterproof tape with a slippery outer surface. (Some people are allergic to substances in tape adhesive; you can test for this by wearing a bit of the tape on your inner forearm.) Break in your boots as gradually as possible, keeping in mind that synthetic materials stretch out very little. When you first wear your boots for real, take along extra first-aid supplies to deal with blisters, maybe a Spenco Blister Kit. Stop and treat a hot spot the instant you notice it or you'll soon regret it. Don't forget to trim your toenails.

Socks

Socks are part of the footwear system and deserve mention. The right socks will go a long way toward reducing blisters and keeping your feet happy. Old-school ragg wool socks are, well, old school. You might be tempted to mate them with liner socks that promise wicking comfort, but that's still old school. Socks that claim to manage moisture are available knit entirely from modern plastic fibers. I've found that what works best for me in terms of comfort and avoiding blisters are the new high-tech merino wool hiking socks worn without liner socks. They don't manage moisture quite as well as their plastic cousins, but somehow they're much kinder to my feet. And wool socks don't stink as plastic socks do. In cold conditions, wear vapor barrier liner socks over thin liner socks and under your insulating socks; just be sure to let your feet dry out each night. Vapor barrier socks not only keep your feet warmer, but they prevent moisture from your feet from condensing and freezing in the insulation layer of your boots—difficult to remove overnight, even if you sleep with your boot liners in the bag with you.

Waterproof/Breathable, Again

Speaking of moisture, I'm certainly not sold on waterproof/breathable liners built into boots. Boot marketers present a conundrum: some models are hawked with claims of fantastic ventilation with no pretense of water resistance; companion models charge more for waterproof liners that substantially block ventilation. Unless you regularly hike across very shallow streams or very wet grass, you may find that such liners keep water in at least as well as they keep it out—until they spring leaks, that is, which seldom takes very long. After that, they seem better at keeping it in. Waterproof/breathable liners certainly make my feet feel hotter and my wallet feel lighter than doing without. Modern leathers can be treated to be almost waterproof and still breathe well; that puts the water barrier on the *outside* of the boot, instead of at the very inner layer, inside the insulation. You can augment or renew the water resistance of synthetic boot materials by spraying them with one of the Nikwax waterproofing products, McNett's ReviveX Weatherproofing Spray, or Tectron Extreme Sport Shoe Guard. For a thorough job, first seal the stitching with SeamGrip. Your feet give off several ounces of water as vapor each day, more when you're working hard, so good moisture management is an issue of both comfort and safety; ignore marketing hype and select your boots thoughtfully.

Features

The first feature you'll have to settle on is the amount of sole support you need. The answer is probably less than you would imagine. My personal observation is that most mountaineers and backpackers wear boots that are more supportive, and therefore heavier, than they actually require; guides are invariably a glaring exception. Start by taking a short mental inventory of the demands you'll place on the boot you're about to acquire, and recognize that no boot will do it all. A lot of mountaineering is trudging. If you follow the lightweight philosophy, you'll be trudging with a relatively light pack; that means you can go with lighter boots that will help you trudge faster and more nimbly—and you won't feel like Frankenstein's monster when you tackle second- and third-class climbing. Don't wait to give up your big boot habit until the day a smiling party blasts past you wearing sandals.

If you plan to climb second- and third-class routes in the same boots you wear for hiking, as many summer mountaineers do, look for boots with more rigid soles (not necessarily more weight) than ordinary hiking boots and test them for edging ability before they leave the shop; stiffer soles usually mean more rocker for easier hiking but more awkward climbing. This will bring you into confrontation with a fundamental paradox: hiking boots are made with a roomy toe box to make them more comfortable on the trail; climbing boots are made with a low-volume toe box to give them more edging power and more precision when climbing, especially in cracks. Your personal choice may ultimately depend not only on your mountaineering objectives but also on your personal foot dimensions.

TREKKING?

You may find boots specifically designed for crossover use, between hiking and climbing. Some manufacturers refer to such models as trekking boots. Look for a wide rubber rand, which will help with durability and when climbing cracks, and a sole pattern that's less lugged under the big toe area, which will help with edging. Such boots won't have soles that are as sticky as shoes specifically made for rock climbing, but they'll be close, and their soles will wear longer. The soles will be flexible enough for reasonably comfortable hiking, and most models provide enough support for crampons and enough toe strength for kicking steps in moderate snow. A big appeal of these models is their light weight, about a kilogram (2.2 pounds) per pair; avoid the trendy sole patterns that squirm when climbing rock.

GENERAL MOUNTAINEERING BOOTS

If you're buying boots that you know will be used for snow climbing, maybe cramponing up moderate alpine ice, colder conditions, and plenty of hiking on talus slopes, you may have moved your options from backpacking boots into the category of general mountaineering boots—and added a pound or more to each foot. Whether or not it's entirely precise, the ancient maxim that a pound on your feet is worth five pounds in your pack is getting at a fundamental truth: strive for lightweight footwear. If you wear heavier boots, you may be allowed a bit less precision when stomping downhill, but you'll also sacrifice uphill speed as well as nimbleness when it comes to actual rock climbing. This is not the place for a new-school mountaineer to start the selection process, despite the pitch you may get from manufacturers and gear shops. If you're drawn, check out the modern synthetic boots designed specifically for alpinism.

MADE OF UNOBTANIUM

It seems that every manufacturer of technical boots has one or two models that lie between full-on mountaineering boots and climbing shoes. One model might look like a high-top rock shoe with a cushioned, lugged sole having "edging platforms" (unlugged areas under the forefoot), and the manufacturer may even offer a version with insulation to suit colder conditions. Sometimes these models are sold for big wall climbing, because their soles are rigid enough to stand somewhat comfortably in aiders for hours on end; sometimes they're marketed for *alpine plaisir*. Although these boots may resemble many ordinary styles, you wouldn't want to hike for miles in most of them because their foot cushioning features are minimal. Their virtues are realized in actual but moderate climbing. Another model might look like a lightweight mountaineering boot with a lighter sole, wide crack-climbing rands made of sticky rubber, and lacing reminiscent of climbing shoes. These models are often called alpine climbing boots, and the soles are beefy enough to support crampons. Boots of either of these styles are ideal for third-, fourth-, and even moderate fifth-class alpine climbing, depending on the season and the possibility of snow or ice on the route. Try them at your local crag to see what they can handle; my alpine climbing boots seem to top out at about 5.8, but I'm sure a better climber could push them harder. The problem with them is that North American distributors may not bring them in from foreign manufacturers, so you may have to search sources that serve the greater demand from European mountaineers. The first style would be ideal for summer rock routes, the latter for routes that include some snow or ice. Don't worry about crampon compatibility when selecting these or any other boots; there are plenty of good crampon choices to fit everything from sandals to snowboard boots.

You may be tempted by *approach shoes*, basically running shoes with slightly more rigid soles made of climbing shoe rubber. Be warned that many of these are intended to approach climbs at the local crag, not climbs in the mountains. Most have soles with only light lug patterns, so a pronounced heel is necessary for descending scree or snow without sliding. Some have soles stiff enough for mountaineering routes and crampons. And they sure are light.

ROCK CLIMBING SHOES

Many mountaineering routes can be climbed in hiking or climbing boots, but wearing rock shoes invariably speeds things up and makes climbing much more enjoyable; for me it's worth carrying the extra weight. If you plan to tackle fourth- and fifth-class mountaineering routes wearing actual rock climbing shoes, you'll want to fit them so you can stand with your toes flat on the soles rather than scrunched up as you would with normal climbing shoes; your sport climbing shoes would

Rock shoes for mountaineering.

have your feet screaming in agony after a few hours in the mountains. Pick a high-top model to provide ankle protection; focus on stiff, board-lasted shoes that get their rigidity from the insole instead of relying on clamping your toes; and size them for good fit when wearing a light sock—socks won't sacrifice significant performance for moderate fifth-class climbing.

L'IL ABNERS
At the other end of the spectrum are plastic mountaineering boots. Consider these for that part of your climb that involves kicking steps up hundreds or thousands of feet of hard snow (a chore I try to leave to my partners) or continuous front pointing on steep névé. Modern alpinists are switching from plastic back to high-tech leather except for expedition routes or very cold conditions—conditions where the ability to remove liners and keep them from freezing at night overcomes all objections—unless your boots use heat-formed foam liners, which are waterproof to begin with. Wear VBL (vapor barrier liner) socks to keep your liners or boots dry. None of these burly boot versions are much fun for hiking trails, even if only partly laced, or climbing rock either, so hope your approaches are on snow, or wear another shoe. Learn to climb rock in your crampons when doing mixed routes in these behemoths. And don't wait until your big climb to break them in; there's plenty of flexibility in what's acceptable for "business casual" around the modern office.

BIG ABNERS
Just so you'll know, there are boots designed specifically for expeditions in the high and cold. Certainly worth considering if you plan to trudge up a Himalayan peak, but of potential interest even to those considering Denali or other Alaskan objectives. Along with a bit more weight, you'll pay a big price, especially considering the number of outings these monsters will be used for. Cheap, perhaps, for those with an unseemly emphasis on returning with all their toes. If you read *Into Thin Air* you know that Beck Weathers spent a night high on Everest, face down in the snow after being left for dead. His fingers and most of his face froze off, but his toes and possibly his life were saved by a pair of Millet expedition boots (and of course, by his spirit and his determination to live). You most likely won't find such boots at a local shop in the United States.

IMELDA AGAIN
Don't feel like you have to do the entire climb in one pair of boots. You'll gain a reasonable amount of speed and an immense amount of comfort if you simply carry rock shoes for the difficult rock climbing or mountaineering boots for the alpine ice climbing, and do the approach in lighter, more comfortable hiking boots.

CASUAL
Don't forget to bring water shoes or sandals for stream crossings and hanging around base camp. I always regret it when I leave them at home. New sandals have rubber toe covers that not only reduce stubbing your toe, but they're deflected less by strong currents during water crossings. You can easily make your own pair of ultralight camp sandals from shoestrings and a pair of foam insoles or a patch of sleeping pad foam; mine weigh less than two ounces.

BACKPACKS
You'd think with all the versions and vendors out there, a mountaineer could walk into the local gear shop and find the perfect backpack model. You'd think. Unfortunately it isn't so easy. Most back-

packs are designed for the most numerous buy-ers—casual backpackers. Packs are adorned with all manner of features that make them undesirably heavy, and they omit other features that are important to serious mountaineers. The first thing out of the salesperson's mouth will be, "Yeah, this baby's bombproof! And look at all these zippered pockets." That's what people want who don't know better, and overbuilding minimizes complaints and returns for manufacturers and retail shops. Weight isn't a big factor in mainstream designs; the marketing department will refer to them as lightweight anyway, and who's to know? It's probably impossible to come up with a mountaineering backpack in the two-pound range, but aiming in the neighborhood of three pounds (1.5 kg) is a reasonable, if challenging, goal.

The first thing to consider is your intended application. This will determine the pack capacity you need, suggest some important features, and help you balance the light/durable equation. If you follow the lightweight philosophy I espouse, you'll start out ahead of the game, before you even start packing up. For outings of a few days, the most common, aim for a pack volume of 50 liters (3,100 cubic inches; one liter is about 61 cubic inches); that should be adequate, even in winter if the pack has a top sleeve that allows it to be expanded and you're willing to carry a few things strapped to the outside. Too small, you say? An ultralight devotee might say it's too large. For certain, if you start with a larger pack, it'll weigh more to start with and you'll fill it up with more weight. A smaller pack enforces a certain discipline that's easily learned; don't start out by coming up with all the stuff you might carry and use that to gauge the pack size you need. Selecting a smaller volume also makes it easier to find a pack on the lower end of the weight range. If you want to keep more of your base camp items on the inside, maybe because you don't want them to be rained or snowed on, indulge yourself with a heavier 60-liter model for longer outings (or use featherweight silnylon stuff sacks). Mountaineers tend to prefer packs with a single main compartment having an extension collar and top pocket design that allows the volume to be expanded on the way to base camp; a removable top pocket eliminates unnecessary volume and weight during the actual climb.

I've mentioned a pack's volume because it's a readily available specification. The real criterion however is a pack's weight carrying capability. This will depend on its suspension, on your tolerance for weight, and on how the pack fits your body. About 35 pounds is a good upper target for mountaineers who've successfully adopted the lightweight philosophy, extending to 40 pounds if you have extra climbing or skiing gear to haul. That said, look for a pack that weighs 10 percent or less of its load capacity.

Criterion #1

Once you weed out the choices that are just too heavy or the wrong size, your most important criterion will be the way the pack carries. Sacrifice weight, if you must, to get a pack that fits your body and manages your load. Packs always carry better in the retail shop (even better on the Net), but you can get an idea after some serious testing. If you follow the light-is-right approach, you'll carry about 20 percent of your body weight, at most. That should be easy for a hiking pack, whatever its design, but mountaineering, especially ski mountaineering and alpine climbing, places more demands on load-carrying élan. Go shopping with enough water bottles to load the pack to whatever weight you actually expect to heft. A 16-ounce bottle of water weighs just over a pound, so show up at the shop with 35 or more. They'll fit—50 liters or quarts of water weighs over 100 pounds. After the salesperson fits the pack to your body, see how it feels when you swing your weight from side to side. If you're a ski mountaineer, the first thought that will go through your mind is, "I can't ski with this gorilla on my back!" Crawl with the loaded pack; jump with it. If the shop has a climbing wall, give it a go. You'll find a surprising difference in the way pack models handle weight, even after the salesperson adjusts them perfectly to your body. Don't settle for one that acts like it wants to climb another route or slam you with a judo throw every time you turn around.

Also don't expect very lightweight packs, even those with attractive volumes, to carry weight nimbly. You may ultimately ignore its gossamer construction and select one of these because you want to save a pound or two (a serious amount of weight) on the approach, but your shoulders will pay the price. Ultralight designs that have no frame or rely on a sleeping pad to act as a frame won't transfer much load to the waist belt; that makes carrying more than 25 pounds very uncomfortable and makes your movements not very nimble compared to carrying a lightweight internal frame pack. Careful loading of a light pack can make a big difference in the way it carries, but mountaineers will doubtless want a pack with a functional frame for all but day-hike outings. A pack with a functional suspension can feel like it takes 10 pounds off the load, compared to a lightweight sack without a functional frame and waist belt. You may also question whether the ultralight's fabric will stand up to constant contact with rock; ultralight packs are mostly designed for hiking, not climbing. One exception is climbs that will be mostly on snow; snow doesn't attack fabric the way stone does. More potentially useful lightweight packs are becoming available for adventure racers and thru-hikers, so do your research; you'll reap the rewards on every outing. You may have to search out lesser-known manufacturers like Go-Lite, Osprey, and Granite Gear who are pushing the envelope with climber-specific designs and high-tech fabrics.

Features for Mountaineers

A benefit of a 50-liter pack, assuming it has the right construction, is that you can carry it on the climbing part of your outing and not suffer. It helps if the top pocket is removable and if the pack has features that allow it to be easily reduced in size, pulling the remaining volume close to your back. These features allow you to transform your freight hauler into a reasonable climbing sack after you leave your commissary, bivy sack, and sleeping bag behind. The frame of a smaller pack will also be more narrow; that's what you want for a climbing pack, even if it's tippy when you set it down. Backpackers like packs with bulbous bottoms that make them stable when set down, but moun-

taineers want a trim, tapered bottom that won't interfere with downclimbing or glissading and can be maneuvered in narrow confines; take a look at the Osprey Aether 60 to see what I mean.

One option is to carry a small, lightweight day pack for use only on the way to and from the summit. This would make the most sense if you establish a climbing base camp—a hike into the Circ of the Towers for several days of climbing, for example. Many climbers opt for this approach in every case, and some packs have a detachable summit pack as part of their design. I've never seen an off-the-shelf model that executes this successfully. Either the smaller pack doesn't climb well, or it's too small, or the combination is way too heavy. A top pocket that converts to a fanny pack is no solution, because it's too small to carry the necessary gear and water, and it will definitely get in the way of your climbing hardware and harness. I'll admit, though, that I've modified my two favorite main packs to piggyback a smaller pack. My small summit pack has been modified so it's large enough for a day of climbing or skiing and it has certain advantages: it carries well, has no waist belt to interfere with my harness, and it hangs below my shoulders so I can carry runners conventionally. Maybe you can find a combo pack that works well out of the box, or maybe you can find a hydration pack you can lash aboard your big bag to serve the same purpose. Just be sure that whatever pack you climb with has a sternum strap or waist belt so that it won't escape if you happen to take a tumble.

Let's assume you've found a 3-pound, 50-liter pack that carries well, has enough but not too many attachment points (for your sleeping pad, rope, crampons, ax, helmet, and whatever else ends up on the outside), and accommodates a hydration system, either internally or externally depending on your preference. Now try it on while wearing your climbing harness. Is it manageable, or does the pack belt get in the way of everything? Does the pack belt have gear loops that can substitute for those on the harness? Might carrying pro on shoulder slings be feasible, or does the pack design rule it out?

You may notice that the pack is made of fabric that's coated on the inside; don't expect it to be waterproof. Backpack rain covers don't work well for mountaineers who need access to equipment that's lashed on their packs. There's an easy solution to protecting the contents from rain or snow: silnylon stuff sacks. Some light hikers use turkey-baking or trash compactor bags, but silnylon is light and very slippery, so it's easier to stuff into the pack. A big stuff sack can effectively form the waterproof inner liner of the entire backpack; seal the stuff sack seams with SilNet or thinned silicone sealant if you're genuinely paranoid.

If your likely choice has made it this far, put on a climbing helmet and attempt to look up. If your helmet gets pushed forward over your eyes, your search is not yet over. Removing the top pocket may help provide helmet clearance; choosing a small pack in the first place helps, too. While you're in that neighborhood, look for a beefy haul loop, one that can support the pack's fully loaded weight as you drag it up the stone or out of a crevasse.

Now let's really fine-tune the selection. In many cases, the pack will go on late in the loading-up sequence so than it can come off early, particularly when traveling on glaciers, but you'll also have to put things on top of the pack, such as runners, cameras, and rope. Most packs attach ice axes using loops to secure the heads. To access your ax you must take off the pack and all the stuff on top (or impose on a partner). Packs designed for alpine ice climbing may secure axes so they can be removed by reaching back and unclipping a fastener—an ounce heavier, but potentially very handy if you unexpectedly discover you urgently need your ax. Might as well worry about getting the rope on and off, too, without using the top pocket as the sole means of securing it.

If you've managed to find a 50-liter pack that meets all these criteria, seems to be well made, is constructed of durable fabrics, and still comes in around 3 pounds—even better if it can carry skis and a shovel—please get in touch with me. I'm looking for one, too.

CLOTHING SYSTEMS

*Beware of all enterprises that require
new clothes.*

Easy for Thoreau to say, but George Mallory and Sandy Irvine perished on their Everest summit bid in 1924 wearing heavy boiled wool and waxed cotton clothing; if they had the benefit of modern fabrics and technology, might they still be alive today? Of course not, they'd be over 100 years old, but fabrics have come a long way since then. A big step was the invention of nylon in 1935, and the introduction of waterproof/breathable laminates by W. L. Gore in the early 1970s. Be cautioned that the outdoor industry thrives on selling garments to people who have no idea what they're buying or why, so expect to find the most outrageously unsubstantiated performance claims when you check a garment's hang tag. Also expect a bewildering and ever-changing plethora of catchy fabric names, often with different names applied to the same material by different clothing manufacturers.

Waterproof/Breathable Fabrics

Gore enthralled generations of consumers with the tale of pores too small to let water drops enter but big enough to allow water vapor molecules to escape. Amazing! What's even more amazing is that this isn't how Gore-Tex works. Gore found that their PTFE (think: Teflon) microporous membrane absorbed oils and soon lost its water resistance, so they protected it with a monolithic polyurethane membrane. Monolithic means no holes for water drops *or* molecules; polyurethane coatings and laminates transport water using hydrophilic polymer components to convey water molecules through the rubber membrane, from humid air on one side to the opposite surface where drier air evaporates the moisture. The benefit of the PTFE layer in Gore-Tex is that it allows a thinner polyurethane membrane than can be applied directly to nylon—about one-third as thick, so it's able to transport more moisture than ordinary urethane-coated nylon. Gore never mentions this, probably because they don't want to base marketing success on a claim that "our polyurethane membrane is thinner than their polyurethane membrane." But it is, and that's why Gore-Tex has a somewhat higher water vapor transmission rate (breathability) than other urethane-coated or laminated waterproof/breathable fabrics; Gore-Tex XCR is a bit better yet. Waterproof/breathable fabrics have essentially no air permeability whatsoever—a major limitation to their performance in outdoor garments.

Newer fabrics have been developed with higher moisture permeability than Gore-Tex XCR. One of the most interesting is eVENT, which uses a different kind of PTFE membrane that doesn't require a urethane coating or special laundry products, though it does need a protective layer of tricot. eVENT has about the same test permeability as Schoeller Dryskin Extreme (more than double that of Gore-Tex), but it's much more waterproof. Other fabrics with better moisture permeability than Gore-Tex include Entrant G2-XT, Nextec, and Low Alpine's TriplePoint Ceramic at low humidity. These fabrics are increasingly appearing in outdoor garments, and eVENT is starting to appear in single-walled tents. Nextec's EPIC is actually a process, not a fabric; it permanently coats individual fibers to achieve high water repellency without a membrane, and it, too, is starting to appear in bivy sacks and single-walled tents.

"Tent" may be what comes to mind when you exercise in waterproof/breathable garments, because though such fabrics are capable of transporting some moisture, the amount they can move is less than what you'll put out at moderate levels of exertion. Urethane membrane fabrics (including Gore-Tex XCR, Gore-Tex, Entrant Dermizax, Membrain, Hydroseal=XALT, Sympatex, Conduit, and Schoeller WB-formula, in order of permeability) double their breathability at high relative humidity (when you're perspiring) compared to low (when you're not yet warmed up). Nevertheless, except in very cold conditions, serious exercise by the wearer will overload their moisture-transport capacity. Waterproof/breathable fabrics can transport several ounces of water vapor per hour for each square yard of available fabric (the fabric area that's not blocked by your backpack, belts, straps, zippers, seam tape, pockets, etc.), but when your effort level pushes 75 percent of your maximum, and the air temperature is near or above freezing, you'll experience water vapor condensation inside your shell, and your base layers will become wetted with liquid water.

Making Tents with Sleeves Work Better

To get the most out of your waterproof/breathable shell (or any shell), choose and learn to use smart ventilation features; garment ventilation is more important than claims of fabric breathability. Avoid lined jackets—very old-school and virtually guaranteed to produce interior condensation. Newer parka designs feature mesh pocket materials and pocket openings located so that pack straps don't prevent pockets from being used for additional ventilation. Unfortunately, ventilation features conflict with completely excluding rain and rain excluding features reduce the available breathable fabric. Adjusting your level of effort also helps avoid overloading your garment's breathability—even a slight scaling back can make a substantial difference in the amount of perspiration and resultant condensation inside your shell. Slow down or open up vents early, before your base layers become soaked. Wear as little base-layer insulation as possible; you'll be cooler, but your shell will be warmer, and that makes it move moisture faster. Change base layers, if you must, to avoid overheating when you're in motion, then quickly throw on an insulating jacket to prevent chilling when you stop. No fabric can breathe properly if soaked with water, a condition called *wet out*. Wet out from rain is bad, but wet snow is even worse because it drops the temperature just inside the fabric, which will substantially reduce moisture vapor transport and increase condensation. To prevent wet out, durable water repellent (DWR) treatments have been developed (well, actually borrowed from the carpet industry) and most shell garments employ them; you can see the effect when water beads up on the surface rather than wetting the fabric. To maintain DWR effectiveness, wash your garment to remove the dust and dirt that accumulate during use (use Atsko Sport-Wash, never laundry detergent or Woolite); rinse it very thoroughly and dry it in a dryer—heat reactivates the treatment.

Most DWR treatments last no more than a dozen washings; when you notice that water no longer beads up on a clean garment, you can restore some of the original performance by treating your shell with a product like Nikwax TX-Direct, or McNett's ReviveX.

Polypropylene and polyester knit inner layers with claimed "wicking" properties were developed as part of the old-school layering system—an admission that liquid water inside the shell is a major problem. Layering means starting with a thin, next-to-skin garment for wicking liquid perspiration away from your body and encouraging it to evaporate to water vapor. The next layer consists of a synthetic fleece or pile garment for insulation. On top of everything is the waterproof/breathable shell layer—the tent. The reason for wearing that tent is to prevent getting wet if you are caught in a continuous downpour. No one deliberately climbs in the rain, of course, but in many mountain areas getting drenched by a shower or wet snow is a real possibility. If you're soaked, even in mild weather conditions, hypothermia can result, to say nothing of discomfort. But you can be soaked from the inside out as well as from the outside in. Even used skillfully, the old-school layering approach has serious limitations when applied to strenuous outdoor activities, because hiking, climbing, and skiing simply create too much water vapor for a waterproof/breathable shell to handle. When activity increases, the layering approach requires stopping to "shed a layer," a common term in the vernacular of old-school hikers and climbers. Removing or exchanging an inner layer is complicated if you're climbing with hardware on shoulder slings, wearing bibs, or are rigged for glacier travel. When you stop, you chill down because of your wet base layer. There's gotta be a better way than the narrow range of temperature and activity level that the waterproof/breathable layering approach accommodates—and there is.

Paradigm Shift

The focus of leading-edge active wear development has dramatically shifted from protection against liquid water on the exterior of the garment to managing water vapor on the interior. (Thomas Kuhn would be proud.) Only very infrequently must your clothing shield you from a downpour or prolonged wet snow—most of the time good water vapor transport and protection from wind are much more important, especially for mountaineers. There are two basic approaches that acknowledge this gestalt: breathable, wind-barrier garments on top of single-layer insulation, and soft shells.

Soft Shell

British climbers have been enjoying soft shells for over a decade; lately even W. L. Gore has gotten in on the action. Instead of a waterproof/breathable shell (these days called a *hard shell*) over wicking and insulating layers, soft shell jackets and pants are designed to achieve a high degree of moisture transport while providing insulation, wind resistance, and water repellency in a single-layer garment. (Beware: marketing departments are free to call anything soft shell, even urethane-coated nylon that yesterday would have been called hard shell.) These garments achieve better moisture transport, marketing hype aside, by allowing a certain amount of air permeability. You can get a rough idea of air permeability by attempting to suck and blow through the fabric. Higher air permeability allows significantly greater water vapor transport—much higher than still air test numbers—at the sacrifice of wind and water resistance.

The development of new fabrics, particularly stretch woven fabrics and stretch coatings, is critical to soft shell designs; that development is just getting started, but there are a bewildering array of fabrics claiming to be "better." Schoeller and Malden Mills make dozens. Most soft shell garments strategically combine stretchy fabrics, abrasion-resistant fabrics, more permeable but less wind-resistant fabrics, and water repellency treatments—along with design lessons learned from the struggle to make hard shells more versatile—to yield garments that keep wearers dry and comfortable over a wider range of activity levels and outside temperatures than is possible with hard shells. Soft shell fabrics mean garments can (indeed, must) be styled with a trim, athletic fit instead of the wrinkly tent-like styling of old-school hard shells. Garments typically have a soft, pile-like interior surface, but to me soft shells next to skin still feel a little creepy (a frequently washed, ultra-sheer poly T-shirt takes care of that). The performance difference of soft shell garments compared to hard shells with old-school layering is pretty amazing. Soft shells are more breathable, more comfortable, more friendly to climbing because of the stretchy fabrics; they are more versatile, they don't flap in the wind, and they look cool.

The problems with soft shell garments, apart from jaw-dropping prices, are that they are relatively heavy, they don't do a really good job of blocking wind, their Lycra content means they dry more slowly, and some have a bulky feel reminiscent of a wet suit, particularly those with fabrics that sandwich a membrane. Many of the fabrics are unsuitable for the rigors of climbing, brush bashing, or carrying ice screws. If serious precipitation or cold wind are possibilities, you'll still want a waterproof, windproof backup of some kind. Soft shell jackets may not have hoods and may minimize pockets to maximize breathabilty.

Wind Shell

A wind shell is a light, highly wind resistant shirt-jacket worn over a relatively thin insulation layer; sometimes both are parts of the same garment, but that wouldn't be my choice. Microfiber fabrics and EPIC treatments are commonly used, but high-tech options are appearing, like Pertex's denier gradient Equilibrium and stretch Equilibrium fabrics. This approach is warmer than you would expect for the thickness of the insulation layer because the wind shirt prevents convective heat loss. I've been comfortable in a wind jacket over a light wool layer at temperatures around 20° in moderate winds—as long as my activity level was high. Blocking wind is extremely important, because heat loss increases as the *square* of wind speed, not in direct proportion; that adds up quickly. Compared to a waterproof/breathable shell, a thin wind shirt offers much less impairment of water vapor transport from the warm, high-relative-humidity region next to your skin to the lower relative humidity of the cooler air outside the wind shirt—that effect is the pump that moves humidity out of your clothing. Because wind shell fabric is thin, higher moisture transport is possible with less air permeability than with soft shell fabrics and certainly in comparison to heavier coated fabrics. You stay more comfortable, and your insulation stays dry and functional over a wider range of activity levels. Wind jackets and pants also provide resistance to light rain, mist, or dry snow, depending on fabric and DWR treatment, and bugs can't bite through as they can with many soft shells. For best performance, wind shells, like soft shells, need to fit closer than waterproof/breathables to minimize the volume of damp air inside—for climbers, that's a plus.

A down side of wind shells is that most fabrics don't stretch, so garments must be cut more bulky than soft shells. Some soft shell fabrics are more durable, but all are heavier and less wind resistant than wind shells. By selecting the optimum next-to-skin insulation layer—which may be none if only sun or insect protection is needed—wind shells are more versatile than soft shells, and they are certainly more affordable.

New-School Insulation

One advantage of wind shells is that they allow you to select the next-to-skin insulation layer that best matches your activity and conditions, and let you choose new-school insulation technology as it develops. Suspend incredulity as you read this, but the fiber that is *really* new-school is wool. Wool—new-school?! That's right; wool is actually the best fiber for next-to-skin insulation. Not just any wool, of course; it needs to be (still suspending incredulity?) wool from a special breed of sheep raised in the high mountains of an island in the South Pacific. If you don't know the story, you probably think this is a joke. They're called merino sheep, and the island is New Zealand. Selection from these special sheep yields the "super fine" merino wool used in new-school outdoor garments. Turns out that if wool hairs can be grown long and fine enough, the fabric will feel soft, like cotton, and it won't itch.

THE MYTH OF WICKING

So merino wool passes the itch test; what about moisture management? Cotton is far and away the best fiber for wicking because its fibers are very hydrophilic and absorb lots of water, but mountaineers long ago learned to shun cotton because when cotton absorbs water it goes limp, losing insulation ability because no dead air is trapped. Wool, however, is resilient and kinky on a microscopic scale, so it maintains its insulating ability even when wet, comparable to plastic fibers; the fine fibers of merino wool enhance this property. But wool doesn't actually wick. You may have heard wicking claims for wool, but I've done the tests: nada; nichts. All fabrics dry at about the same rate, even cotton; a given garment will lose about the same amount of water in a given amount of time no matter what fibers it's made of, though some fibers absorb more water before becoming saturated and so appear to dry out more slowly. (If you're saturating your base layer, whatever its fabric composition, you need to be wearing a lighter base garment, or none, and more effectively ventilating your outer garment.) On the other hand, wool fibers can take up and transport water *vapor* more effectively than plastic due to hydrophilic interior fibrils, which have "pores too small to admit liquid water but plenty big enough to pass water vapor molecules" (sound familiar?). I call next-to-skin wool a comfort layer instead of a wicking layer, and comfortable it is. It also doesn't stink the way plastic (polyester or polypropylene) underwear does. That means no more soaking in Biz or Oxyclean to restore your clothes to habitability after a day's use. At first only Smartwool was in the U.S. market, but now even mainstream manufacturers are joining in, and with the availability of new, lightweight fabrics, you can find merino wool next-to-skin layers for a wide range of conditions. Even the briefs work great. However it works, fine merino wool has a wider comfort range than synthetics according to outdoor activists who give it a try.

There's a subtle down side to wool, apart from impressively high prices: you must protect your precious garments from moths—not something mountaineers have had to worry about for quite some time.

Topping It Off

Whether you take the wind shell or soft shell approach, you'll need a plan for what to do if it rains hard, and how to stay warm when temperatures dive, winds pick up, or your effort level drops. If you intend to travel in steady rain, you may not be a candidate for soft shells or wind shells at all; you may be relegated to sweating it out in a hard shell. Same story for mountaineering at high altitudes or in very cold, windy conditions, where hard shell is still king.

The simplest option for topping off a soft shell system is a lightweight, hooded shell—maybe a wind shell, maybe a rain shell, maybe even one of the new ultralight waterproof/semi-breathable shells. There are many to choose from; some weigh only a few ounces and disappear in your pack. A modern option, if a bit too new-school for mainstream manufacturers, is a silnylon shell. Silnylon is light and 100 percent waterproof; a jacket can weigh less than four ounces and stuff down to the size of a baseball. Zero breathability may not be an issue if you expect to slow down significantly—or bail out—in the event of rain. A silnylon poncho ventilates very well and drapes over your pack to protect it, too. A new-school ultralight option is a simple jacket made from 3M's Propore, a waterproof/breathable fabric with twice the breathability of Gore-Tex, but one-fourth the durability. They are so cheap and light that you can carry one guilt-free for emergency use. The absolute minimalist approach to emergency protection would be a 4-ounce hooded Tyvek jacket intended for runners, painters, golfers, or haz-mat workers. These are not very durable and only slightly breathable, but they'll set you back only about $5 at your neighborhood industrial supply store; they fold down to wallet size. I'll admit that I expect only a small number of mountaineers to opt for Tyvek rainwear, but I mention it to show just how far from the traditional waterproof/breathable parka you can go while maintaining an adequate margin of safety and comfort.

Insulating Jacket

Quickly adding serious additional insulation when you stop to take over the belay, have lunch, or set up camp in cold weather is a bit more complicated. The old-school solution is the trusty down jacket, but down will retain moisture, originating outside or in, and then lose warmth. The new-school solution is a hooded belay jacket having synthetic insulation and mountaineering features, like a zipper that opens at the bottom to make way for a rappel/belay brake on your harness and internal mesh pockets for drying your spare gloves and keeping gel and water from freezing. New-school mountaineers throw on their insulating belay jacket over just about everything, including climbing harness, shoulder slings and pro, and helmet—maybe even over their summit pack. Size accordingly and test before you buy. New–school fast and light mountaineers may even swap the same belay jacket when they swap leads, called "hot bagging." Jackets bring up two classic Coke/Pepsi battles: that of down versus synthetic and Polarguard versus Primaloft.

FIBERS AND FEATHERS GO DOWN FOR THE COUNT

The down/synthetic argument should be familiar but bears repeating. Down is more compressible, offers better insulation for the weight, and may last longer. But down loses loft quickly when damp, is useless if wet, and takes forever to dry. Synthetic insulation is bulkier and less compressible but retains insulation performance when wet. Wet can come from perspiration, rain on leaky backpacks, wet snow or ice, dripping snow caves, lamentable creek crossings, or leaking water bladders. A rip or burn in a synthetic jacket is far less catastrophic than in a down jacket. With modern garments there is less difference in actual product weights than you might think. Synthetic jacket construction can be more efficient than sewn-through down jackets (whose insulation value is based on the average thickness, and the thickness at the seams is nil), so equivalently warm down jackets may end up with little weight advantage, especially if you carry a waterproof shell to guarantee that your down jacket never gets wet. Down jackets with DWR-treated microfiber fabric can be amazingly water resistant, but making jackets truly waterproof is foiled by the high number of seams. Waterproof fabrics, including Gore-Tex, are not options, as they have no air permeability. Jackets with synthetic insulation have plenty of design options, including very water- and wind-resistant breathable fabrics such as EPIC, simple construction, and various insulation options. Synthetic insulation is hypo-allergenic and easier to put where you want it in the jacket design, but it seldom drapes as well as down. If there is any possibility that your scheme to keep your down jacket dry might fail, synthetic is the only way to go. A damp synthetic jacket will actually dry out while being worn or slept in over night—with down you'd be out.

Polarguard 3D or Delta and Primaloft PL1 are so similar that the jacket design and shell fabric are more important. Polarguard fibers are very long and are sprayed with glue to make batts, whereas Primaloft fibers are cut to about two inches and stuck together in a three-dimensional matrix. The Primaloft story is that it takes up less water than Polarguard (maybe because its fibers are silicone coated), so it dries faster when both are saturated, but it appears to lose more loft than soaked Polarguard. Primaloft claims to have better drape and to be warmer for a given thickness, comparable to down. Polarguard claims to be more tolerant of abuse, such as stuffing and washing, and is warmer for a given weight. In actual use in jackets (or sleeping bags) where neither would become totally saturated, their performance is very similar, with Polarguard Delta having a slight edge. Manufacturers probably base their choices more on marketing relationships than performance.

What about conventional fleece and pile? New-school alpinists have given up using thicker fleece for insulation. Fleece still needs a shell for wind resistance, and shelled synthetic insulation is much more efficient in terms of weight than thick fleece or pile. It's also more compressible. Skip right through the fleece and pile jacket section of your outdoor shop.

The Lower Half

Mountaineers don't wear cotton pants anymore; the current standard is Supplex nylon, but there are several comparable nylon and polyester fabrics. Supplex is durable, and it transfers moisture well and dries rapidly because it's so thin. It's not particularly water resistant, but that can be substantially improved by a DRW treatment, same as you'd use to restore your jacket. Supplex pants are available with the features mountaineers and climbers need: minimum bulk around the waist, closing pockets located to clear a climbing harness, cuff closures, lightweight Cordura knee and butt patches, maybe even a front zipper that opens upward (imagine the convenience when you're wearing a harness). Supplex is reasonably wind resistant; you can use Supplex pants in mild winter conditions over lightweight (wool) bottoms so long as you are active. Choose wind pants in colder, windier conditions. The biggest complaint is that Supplex and its kin don't stretch, so pants tend to be baggy in order not to restrict movement, and baggy isn't trendy. Your legs kick out a lot of heat and moisture, so be very sure that you actually need waterproof/breathable fabric before you spring for pants or bibs; they're still like wearing a tent, and a tent on your legs is even less comfortable than a tent on your torso.

Current soft shell pants are heavier than plain nylon pants and less wind resistant, and their DWR treatments need rejuvenating even more frequently than jackets. You may still need to carry a pair of lightweight rain pants if you anticipate continuous rain or cold winds—or if you intend to glissade without inducing the premature demise of your precious soft shell bottoms, which will be heavier and retain more wetness if they contain Lycra (a trade name for spandex polyurethane). Soft shell pants have a wide comfort temperature range due to their breathability and fuzzy inner surface; they have found enthusiastic favor with mountaineers who can afford their impressive prices. Look for something functional in a lighter fabric with a hard face, such as Schoeller Dryskin Extreme. If you still insist on beefy pants (a bushwhack approach or desert peak in winter, maybe)

forget the Carhartt and have a look at Skillers cotton/polyester work pants—highly functional.

Survey Sez . . .

Smart mountaineers pick their tools to suit the context. I love to wear my soft shells when they're appropriate (active, cool to cold, not too breezy), but at this stage of technology, soft shells don't offer the versatility and warmth-for-weight performance of other options; they strike me as too specialized and too expensive for all-around mountaineering. For general mountaineering in cool conditions I prefer a hooded wind shell jacket, lightweight and medium-weight wool zip-T tops next to skin, and Supplex climbing pants, over light wool bottoms if it's cold. In seriously cold weather I carry a belay jacket with synthetic insulation and, as always, a balaclava. It would take some serious winter conditions to get me to drag out my hard shell jacket and bibs. I'm saving my pennies for the next generation of soft shells.

Gloves

Gloves have the same moisture management problems as body wear, only more so. They have no ventilation features and invariably result in wet hands. Old-school mountaineers may hope that high-tech fabrics and waterproof/breathable liners will keep their hands dry, but this approach is doomed for all but very cold weather and modest activity, hype notwithstanding. Plus, such designs are difficult to dry, so users often find themselves putting on frozen gloves. New-school mountaineers recognize that moisture management is the key to comfort, so they prefer lightweight, breathable gloves for climbing in all conditions short of full-on storms, then slip a shell over the gloves as soon as things slow down or cool down.

My personal favorites are the new technical work gloves that have become popular among mechanics, cyclists, NASCAR drivers, and wide receivers. They are tough and dexterous and have good grip strength—attributes I have not found in other synthetic gloves. Plus they're nicely padded and dry quickly. They're stretchy, so liner gloves (wool) fit inside when the going gets cold, and cold weather versions are available. Take a look at Ironclad. Best of all, they're less than half the cost of lesser gloves from your outdoor shop. After that my preferences would be gloves made from soft shell fabrics, wind-resistant fleece gloves, or no gloves at all, depending on conditions and how long and intense will be the period of climbing or skiing. When the climbing stops or things get really cold, I put my gloves into lined finger mitts. Finger mitts (mitts with the first finger isolated, sometimes called trigger mitts) are warmer than gloves but allow more dexterity than mitts—enough to tie knots and belay. The finger mitts stay mostly dry, and the gloves dry out in my sleeping bag over night. Most gloves have some grippy material on their palms to make it easier to hang on to an ax or poles; my finger mitts have two layers of leather. I have yet to find a satisfactory synthetic substitute for leather; the options are either durable but too slippery, or grippy but disintegrate on the first rappel with a wet, dirty rope—an easy way to make a $100 rappel if you've bought into mainstream hand coverings. 3M Griptec material on tech work gloves combined with stick-on patches of gReptile for ski poles and ice tools make a potential contender. Some three-season climbers simply use leather work gloves; when they're eaten up by rappelling, $10 gets you a new pair. Cut off the fingertips to climb rock in them.

Never Say Never

I should mention the next revolution in textiles: possum fur. OK, this *is* a joke—except that brushtail opossum fur really is starting to enter the garment market. Turns out it's kinda like mink and blends well with merino wool (and there are plenty of unwelcome Australian brushtails in New Zealand), so you just never know what fashionable new-school mountaineers may be wearing next season.

As you're standing in awe of the vast clothing section of your outdoor shop, you might reflect that, given the highly geared and guided traffic on Everest these days, the only real challenge remaining may be to climb it using 1924 gear, with woolen clothing and hobnail boots, like Mallory

and Irvine. I'll bet there will be few takers with that kind of mettle.

SHELTER SYSTEMS

Well could I curse away a winter's night,
Though standing naked on a mountain top,
Where biting cold would never let grass grow,
And think it but a minute spent in sport.

It might seem like only a minute to Shakespeare, but without effective shelter you'll curse mountain top nights that seem to last forever. Many of the equipment items you must select have design requirements that, for mountaineers, boil the options down to only a few choices. Shelter systems, on the other hand, have many suitable alternatives, depending on the specific application, the season, and the skills, knowledge, and personal preferences of the climber. It's not unusual for a party to be using several different types of shelters on the same outing. Let's look at a few.

Naked

Your sleeping bag, that is. The most basic shelter option is no shelter at all—just throw your bag on top of your sleeping pad. This is a reasonable choice during an approach with hospitable temperatures and no inhospitable bugs. If you camp in a low location and expect only light breezes, be wary that dew or frost may form directly on your exposed bag, which will wet its insulation before your climb even begins.

Bivy Sack

Another option for mountaineers is the bivy sack: basically a sleeping bag cover with something fancy at the head end. Waiting out a rainstorm or snowstorm in a bivy sack is a facet of the suffering for which we mountaineers are famous. Bivy sacks are available made with bottom and upper fabrics of varying degrees of waterproofing and breathability. Gore-Tex doesn't breathe well enough for making sleeping bags, and you may find the condensation inside a Gore-Tex bivy sack equally objectionable, particularly if your bag also has a less breathable DryLoft or Quantum fabric shell. Interior condensation or frost will almost certainly be a problem if such a bivy sack has nonbreathable waterproof fabric on its bottom. Freezing rain or wet snow will result in condensation inside even the most breathable bivies. My favorite lightweight "tent" design is actually a bivy sack in its foot end and a two-hoop mini-tent in its head half; it provides just enough room to include critical gear, struggle with clothing, and keep bugs off your face; it's limited to a 20-inch wide sleeping pad, like most bivy sacks. It has a large enough opening that ventilation isn't a problem and, at 2 pounds, weighs the same as the going rate for a more claustrophobic Gore-Tex bivy sack. My conventional bivy sack, with a breathable EPIC fabric top and silnylon bottom, weighs 10 ounces; this option offers a considerable weight savings over any form of tent, so it gets the most use. Protection is adequate against light rain, blowing dry snow, and frost, and I've survived a mountain downpour by rolling upside down—but it wasn't fun. You generally climb into a bivy sack after the weather and bugs have already done their number on you, so they're not always the best option. If you search for versions with lighter upper fabric, such as 0.9 ounce/square yard Pertex Quantum or Shield, you can get the weight under 8 ounces (230 grams).

A bivy sack adds 5 or 10° to the comfort limit of your sleeping bag, even inside a tent or igloo, so a lightweight model is a sensible option even if you're sleeping indoors, and especially if you want some additional water protection for your down sleeping bag.

In the section on sleeping systems you'll read that there are two main options for mountaineers' sleeping pads: closed-cell polyethylene foam pads and self-inflating mattresses containing open-cell foam. If your bivy sack has a waterproof bottom, you could conceivably go without a ground cloth, which would be redundant. This raises an interesting conundrum: do you put the pad inside the bivy sack, or outside? Silnylon is slicker than deer guts on a pump handle, as my granddad might say, so before opting to protect your gossamer bivy sack, first test the coefficient of friction between the bivy and the pad; you may spend the night greasing off onto the ground and discover in the

morning that having the pad outside your bivy sack results in lots of condensation on the inside bottom of the bivy sack. Using a partial length pad inside your bivy sack, however, can result in a cat and mouse game of chasing it up and down the interior. I put my full-length inflatable pad inside the bivy and then stake out the foot end with tent stakes and the head end with trekking poles in an inverted V. I run a length of light shock cord from the loop over the opening of my bivy to the apex of the V and a light cord from there to a third stake; this keeps the bivy sack off my face as I thrash around. I usually have a minimalist Tyvek ground sheet under the bivy, to fend off moisture, punctures, and sap. (Don't make your ground sheet larger than your bivy sack or tent unless you punch some holes in it; otherwise, it'll become a water basin in the rain.)

Tarps and Tarp Tents

The simplest and lightest option for an actual shelter is a tarp. New-school tarps, made of silnylon or other silicone-impregnated fabrics, are strong, lightweight, and cut with three-dimensional catenary curves. This is not your old-school tarp. If you use your trekking poles to set it up, an entire solo shelter, including bivy sack, can weigh about a pound. Modern tarps can be pitched low, to resist storms, or high, for space and ventilation. They are quick to set up, cover all your gear, and are ideal for cooking under in rainy weather, but tarps pitched low are highly vulnerable to condensation because silnylon has zero breathability.

Tipi tarp tents have been around for years; the latest multimountaineer models offer a lot of shelter for 2 pounds. A serious concern for tarp tents

A modern solo tarp.

and tarps is lack of protection from biting insects. This can be addressed with individual head covers or net interiors, but these subtract from the weight advantage and reduce flexibility. Tarp tents have evolved to the point that some models are actually minimalist single-wall, floorless tents. Some save weight with bug netting around all sides, but still have an open floor and no vestibule. Tarps and tarp tents don't offer as much protection from serious storms as a tent, so your gear is more vulnerable to blown rain or snow, or rivulets that you failed to anticipate. If you fear foul weather during your outing and are concerned about keeping your sleeping bag dry, carry a bivy sack, too. Still, their very light weight makes modern tarp tents an ideal shelter solution when conditions permit, which is more frequently than most mountaineers believe; tarp tents are another example of trading skill for weight.

To make a tarp or tarp tent function in alpine conditions, you've got to grapple with wind, weather, and extemporaneous tent sites. You're way ahead in these efforts if you start with a smaller, catenary-cut design; square-cut tarps and tarp tents can't be pitched tightly enough to avoid horrendous flapping in even moderate winds. You'll also want to use something for guy lines other than nylon cord, which stretches when wet; use braided polyester (Dacron) line, super-strong Spectra/Dyneema cord such as Triptease, or the more affordable high-tenacity line used for flying big kites. And carry plenty of line—not a bad idea for any tent, but especially important for a highly guyed tarp. A tarp tent set up inches above the ground is ideal, because there will be ventilation to fend off interior condensation; staking it out closer to the ground will be necessary in high winds. These factors require thought and ingenuity in order to use tarps and tarp tents effectively, particularly in the cramped spaces or rock rings that mountaineers often encounter. Why bother? Because a tarp tent can offer plenty of interior room for you and all your gear, and even one with the added weight of perimeter bug netting, plus the weight of a state-of-the-art bivy sack, will come in ounces under 2 pounds. Together the tarp and bivy sack pack down to sizes that could be mistaken for a couple of hoagies.

Silnylon is one of the newer fabrics that's been immediately incorporated into outdoor products such as shelters and clothing. The original version was a very light (1.1 ounce/square yard) 30-denier ripstop nylon fabric impregnated with silicone plastic, bringing the fabric weight to 1.35 ounces/square yard and making it essentially waterproof. It's only $5/1{,}000$ of an inch thick, translucent, and much more durable than you'd expect. It feels like thin wax paper, and it's incredibly slippery, so don't even think about using it as a ground cloth. Use Tyvek House Wrap instead; it weighs about 1.8 ounces/square yard, is way cheap, and can be run through a clothes washer to make it feel more like fabric; don't melt it in a drier, which won't be needed it because Tyvek (like silnylon) dries rapidly. Silnylon can't be seam-taped (seam-seal it with McNett's Silnet or 100 percent silicone sealant thinned with mineral spirits and applied with a brush), and it's flammable. You can now find high denier silnylon, sil-Cordura, sil-spinnaker cloth, and zero-permeability fabrics from parachute manufacturing that offer a range of options for durability and weight.

Money between You and the Elements

Next in complexity would be single-wall tents. There are an increasing number of silnylon models for backpackers, but let's consider full-on single-wall mountaineering tents made of fancy fabrics. Even with "mostly waterproof/not-very-breathable" PTFE fabric these tents are susceptible to interior condensation. Single-wall tents are not really suitable for warm weather or humid conditions, despite manufacturers' claims of fantastic ventilation, but indeed ventilation is key, as it is with waterproof/breathable clothing. EPIC and eVENT fabrics offer substantial improvement. One advantage some of these tents have is being very compact—so compact many won't fit a 6-footer like me. That and a low ceiling height help make them strong and storm resistant; some claim to resist 70 mph winds, but only from an optimal direction. Above all, these tents are extraordinarily expensive. Here's how I look at it. If you bring a ground sheet, or "footprint," to protect your pricey single-wall mountaineering tent, the total weight is more than that of a comparable conventional tent without a groundsheet. Conventional two-person, double-wall tents are now available weighing less than 4 pounds, and for what they cost you can omit a groundsheet and have more space than a single-wall mountaineering tent. Replace the conventional tent every few years—you'll always have a new tent, and you'll still be saving money. You're way behind the spending curve if you ever let a wayward snow shovel add ventilation features to your single-wall treasure (a double-wall tent might survive). Single wall tents also do not offer the warmth of a double-wall tent, often by 10 F° or more. Any time you size a tent of any kind, be sure it will fit a sleeping pad or pads of the type and size you prefer; many designs, especially two-person tents, limit your pad options because of the size or shape of their floors. Vestibules may be options.

Solo

My second personal preference, if a bivy sack or bivy tent is ruled out because of inclement weather or bugs, is a one-person tent, even when I'm among a larger party. You can find conventional models weighing under 3 pounds—heavier per occupant than a light two-person tent, but with many advantages. You can find light, double-wall, one-person tents with enough room to sit up in and wide enough for 25-inch-wide sleeping pads, my preference for lazy camping on snow when an igloo is somehow impractical, such as when going solo or with only canine accompaniment; you can cook in the vestibule. A mountaineer is more likely to find a suitable spot to pitch a one-person tent (or bivy sack) than something larger, and by sleeping solo you avoid awakening your partner, and he or she waking you, when sleep is hard to come by.

If Only . . .

There are some subtleties to consider when selecting a tent. I've always wondered why most tents are designed for the inner tent to be set up first, before pitching the fly. Maybe that's an easier design to execute, but it seems to me that if you're being rained on, you'd want to pitch the fly first and keep the inner tent dry. The ability to pitch the fly first is an unadvertised feature of some single-wall tents that set up from the inside and of some tents that assemble with clips and allow pitching the fly and

footprint only. Pitching only the rain fly is another way to achieve lighter weight if conditions permit—another way to get at the tarp concept, but with penalties of weight, cost, flexibility, and probably ventilation. Reduce weight by carrying only the inner tent if all you need is bug protection. Most tents are shaped so that condensation drips from the fly back into the tent door—potentially worrisome. Tents with door openings that slant outward at the top avoid this. If you anticipate snow, especially wet snow, avoid tents with flat or saddle-shaped tops; tents having pole crossings at the top are much better at shedding snow and avoiding sag if snow does accumulate. Snow is heavy; if you're buying a three-season tent for winter, lay some serious weight on it to satisfy yourself that it'll hold up, because not all do. If you intend to use a hanging stove contraption for cooking inside your tent, be sure the tent structure will accommodate it. Finally, polyester flies are generally more resistant to degradation by ultraviolet light than those made of nylon, and they don't stretch when wet. A colorful fly is easier to find when returning to camp in a whiteout; happening upon your tent is always a pleasure in such circumstances.

Whatever tent you select, it makes sense to treat it well. Keep your tent or tarp clean; set it up and hose it off at the end of the season and let it dry very thoroughly before you pack it away. Spray the fly with 303 Protectant or McNett's Thundershield for UV resistance, better water and snow shedding, and easy cleaning. Patch any pinholes in the floor before water enters them and soaks an outing.

The Fourth Season

As you're wandering through the tent department fondling your credit card, you may be wondering what the differences are between three-season tents and those that claim to be suitable for all four (often called "mountaineering" tents to underscore the point and justify the substantially heavier weight and hang tag shock factor). The four-season varieties generally have more poles to reduce areas of unsupported fabric and so make them tougher, stouter poles to make the tent more wind resistant, and often slightly heavier or higher thread count fabric to resist everything. Four-season tents are often designed with lower height, to better shed wind, and they have more tie-down features; some claim to resist 70-mph winds, but only from one direction. Their vestibules allow for indoor cooking. Three-season tents have more mesh panels on the inner tent, especially at the top, to improve ventilation, while four-season flies pitch closer to the ground to reduce ventilation and heat loss. This makes four-season tents actually work for only three, as they are uncomfortable in warm weather—reminiscent of solar ovens during the day. Four-season tents are also more prone to condensation in any season. Mountaineering tents typically weigh twice as much as comparably sized 3-season tents, though some single-wall versions approach 5 pounds. To make four-season tents stand up to really serious winds, high-altitude climbers point them away from the wind and hold them down with additional covers made from fishing net that's separately staked out with snow anchors; this is in addition to whatever walls of snow blocks can be built around the tent. You can apply the same principles to help your three-season tent work for four (assuming you're climbing when and where storms aren't too severe. If you're really serious, you can gain some strength and lose some weight by replacing your three-season aluminum poles with beefier DAC aluminum or Fibraplex graphite poles. I've seen my last four-season tent years ago; ever since then I've used these methods with three-season tents in the fourth season with no regrets—but there is a better solution . . .

Lyin' in Winter

It seems a cruel irony that in winter, when nights are long and daylight precious, getting a tent ready for use takes so much more time and effort than it does in the summer. Pitch your tent in the most protected spot you can find, face the door away from the prevailing wind, use all those tie-down and tie-out features you've probably been ignoring, be sure you have solid anchors all around (not always easy in soft snow), and build a snow wall or use existing rock walls for additional protection. Snow walls need to be well away from the tent, so you can trip over your tie-outs while you shovel snow that drifts in on your tent; this means the protective walls must also be tall if they're to be effective—about the same height as their distance from the tent. Removing snow that a storm has piled up around your tent isn't merely a cosmetic option; coated tent flies don't breathe, and the snow will cover the openings at the bottom of the fly, effectively sealing the tent. Even if you don't cook inside during said storm, you still run the risk of using up every last oxygen molecule inside without some means of ventilation.

The best shelter for winter mountaineering, or whenever there's movable snow, is a snow cave or, better, an igloo. They are warm, quiet, and storm proof. Let's start with the snow cave. New-school mountaineers no longer build them by digging out a small hole low on a snow bank and shoveling out the interior by passing snow between their legs or dragging it out on a ground cloth—very old-school and sure to get you wet. It's much better to dig out a T-shaped or inverted L-shaped opening that provides reasonable access for interior excavation and a space next to where you're working to heave out the snow. Fill in the opening with snow blocks made with set up shoveled snow after you've finished the interior architecture. Don't build your snow cave in an avalanche path, mark your excavation with wands to warn inadvertent interlopers, and keep a shovel inside, just in case you need it to exit the remains of your efforts. A snow cave requires a deep snow bank; hopefully you'll be able to locate one if you commit to this type of shelter. Probe with your poles or avy probe to confirm adequate snow depth before you invest time digging. You may see a recommendation to pile up snow to make your own spot to dig a snow cave—very laborious, and with most snow you'll need dynamite to make any progress inside once the snow sets up. However you dig a snow cave, plan on dealing with the wet clothing that will surely result.

Eskimos Know Better

Better than a snow cave is an igloo. Yes, I know, they take a long time to build, require perfect snow, and have unpredictable results—no longer.

New-school mountaineers now have a better solution because of a contraption called the ICE-BOX, made by Grand Shelters of Colorado. Basically, it's a packable slip form that rotates around a spike on an adjustable aluminum pole, laying down a spiral of formed-in-place snow blocks to easily construct several sizes of near-perfect igloos with just about any kind of snow, including sugar snow, spring slush, a few inches of powder on a frozen lake, and even snow on a parking lot it is claimed. You don't get wet, and you don't have to be concerned about high winds that frustrate tent setup. With another partner I've built a comfy igloo in just 2 hours. That's about the same amount of time it would take to stomp out a flat spot in the snow for a tent and the necessary space around it, wait for the snow to harden, set up a tent, set snow anchors for the tent guy lines, build a snow block wall around the tent, then trench out a kitchen area and protect it with snow block walls. If snow under the floor of your tent acquires an unfortunate contour, you will have to sleep in discomfort or move the tent while you make repairs; in the igloo you can just shovel a bit of snow from one spot to another.

If you think the igloo still takes relatively too long, remember that the next morning the people who spent the night in their tent will have the pleasure of digging out the frozen anchors, attempting to dry the frost and condensation in the tent, and packing the frosty tent away with a little extra weight to carry. In your igloo you can get another half hour of shut-eye and enjoy an indoor breakfast. If you dig a trench from the door opening partway across the igloo floor, you will be able to sit inside with your feet dangling and you can stand upright to move around, dress, and eat—luxuries impossible with a tent. No concern about tracking in snow either. The temperature inside an igloo will be about freezing even when it's very cold outside, and often it seems warmer because there's little moving air; you can use a lighter sleeping bag to save additional weight. Cooking inside may have you taking off your jacket and gloves, and one candle lantern or LED headlamp lights the whole interior. Use the construction pole as a clothesline.

No matter how hard the wind rages outside, inside an igloo it's calm and quiet. Smile to yourself as you think of your companions in flapping

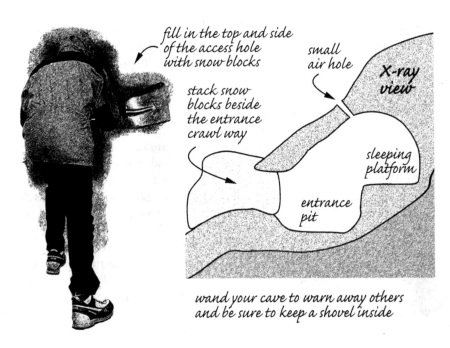

fill in the top and side of the access hole with snow blocks

stack snow blocks beside the entrance crawl way

small air hole

X-ray view

sleeping platform

entrance pit

wand your cave to warn away others and be sure to keep a shovel inside

Shoveling out a snow cave.

tents who must get out in the storm to shovel off snow by headlamp; you can discreetly empty your pee bottle in a corner of the igloo and go back to sleep. An igloo is much sturdier than a tent because worked snow sets up solidly; you can usually stand atop your igloo soon after it's finished, and it may last an entire season. The ICEBOX weighs pounds less than a four-season tent that is much more cramped than the igloos it will build (the larger sizes will hold four or more people), and it's far less expensive. One other significant advantage is that you can plan with confidence on taking advantage of the benefits of an igloo—no longer dependent on a roll of Mother Nature's dice for suitable snow. I could go on, but suffice it to say that the next time you see a photo of tents on snow you should say to yourself, "Those old-school dolts should get hip to the ICEBOX and build igloos."

SLEEPING SYSTEMS

There's no need to get deeply into sleeping bag technology; I'll just offer a few comments to help you sort out the myriad options. Basically, you're aiming for the lightest weight and most comfortable model that will keep you adequately warm. Lightweight can be measured, but what is comfortable and what is adequately warm are very subjective. There are plenty of well-made bags, but you may want to push the envelope, so to speak,

An igloo in the making.

and consider unconventional choices. Here's how the design elements play out.

Loft

The most important factor in retaining body heat is loft; loft is simply dead air. It's kept dead by filling it with fluffy stuff: down, Primaloft, Polarguard, or fancy blends of hollow and microfiber synthetics, about which plenty has been said in the section on clothing. Bag manufacturers put most of it in the areas they expect to be on top, because compression by body weight renders the fluffy stuff underneath you ineffective. Some manufacturers are willing to challenge buyer skepticism and completely do away with loft in the lower third of the bag; they design their bags to accept and require a sleeping pad—they may also require a rigid sleeper. Another scheme is to allow down to be shaken from the bottom side around to the top to make the bag warmer, or from top to bottom for more comfort in warmer conditions; this works well for bags intended for modest temperatures. All insulation, down or synthetic, loses some of its loft simply because of ordinary use. Definitely don't use a compression stuff sack with your synthetic bag; in fact, using an oversized sack will let the bag last longer.

Sealing

If outside air enters the bag or inside air escapes, you'll lose body heat. To prevent this, bags are designed with draft tubes around the neck and insides of zippers. A bag can be made lighter and better sealed by substantially shortening the zipper or eliminating it altogether, but this limits the comfort range. A drawstring closure at the neck (hope for elastic) and around the face opening of the hood also makes for better sealing. You can get by in a bag without a hood at temperatures down to freezing, though you may want to scrunch down inside a long-length bag or wear your camp hat (call it a *toque* to impress your friends), balaclava, or the removable hood from your insulating jacket. At temperatures below freezing the effectiveness of a hood is critical because of the substantial amount of heat lost from your head and neck.

Internal Volume

Volume is a principal point of trade-off between comfort and weight. A bag can be made lighter and warmer for the same amount of loft if the internal volume is reduced. Doing so reduces the amount of air around you that isn't dead air, and that reduces cooling of you, the heat source. The colder the conditions for which the bag is designed, the more important this will be, with the result that lightweight bags for subzero temperatures may fit tightly—you'll be convinced the descriptor "mummy style" was chosen because of the feeling as much as the shape. Check the shoulder girth dimension to get a sense of the internal volume. Roomy semi-rectangular bags are more comfortable, but they're usually limited to temperatures not much below freezing because of their substantial excess internal volume; they're heavier for a given temperature rating, but because of their high volume, you can sleep in your insulating jacket to extend the comfort range, which can then be quite wide.

Outer Shell Fabric

Surprisingly, there are trade-offs here, too. You'd think you'd want the lightest downproof fabric—material that doesn't let the little down thingies weasel through it—that allows the least amount of air exchange. Indeed, shell fabrics have gotten really light, lighter than 1 ounce per square yard—that's probably OK if there are no environmental hazards threatening the bag. You no longer see Gore-Tex sleeping bag shells, even though they were warmer, because of complaints about condensation; Gore switched to DryLoft. It isn't as waterproof as Gore-Tex (it's hard to make a bag truly waterproof anyhow, because of the many seams), nor does it make the bag quite as warm, but it allows more moisture (and warm air) to escape. Your body gives off water vapor continuously throughout the day and night, even if you're not sweating. At night that water vapor enters the insulation of your sleeping bag and heads toward the outer surface, driven by your body's warmth; when it reaches air that's cold enough to cause it to condense (the dew point), it becomes liquid water.

Unless the moisture can easily escape, it'll be there in the morning. If the temperature drops further, that water can even turn to ice in the insulation of your bag. This is a real problem on multiday trips when you must pack your bag without letting it dry; many mountaineers, myself among them, have seen their down bags go flaccid and, at temps below 0 °F (20 °C), see stiff, icy sections appear—brrr! This is a significant concern in cold weather with bags that use less breathable DryLoft or even Pertex Quantum outer shell fabrics. To avoid this problem, the aim is to use a downproof shell fabric that's highly permeable to water vapor but not too open to air exchange and then to protect the bag from drafts.

Target

The typical mountaineer's three-season bag will be rated, conventionally, for around 20 °F (5 °C). That's a starting point for temperate alpine conditions during the main climbing season when nighttime temperatures drop to freezing or just below. The target loft for the upper layer would be at least 2 inches on average, more at the foot, and the target weight for this bag is 2 pounds, a little more for synthetic bags. To be comfortable at temperatures several degrees below freezing in a bag this thin, most people will have to wear additional clothing. Several manufacturers offer such lightweight bags, but the general rule of $10 to $15 for every ounce saved applies. For temperatures only as low as 35 °F (2 °C) a well-sealed inch of loft and a layer of light thermal underwear may get you by. Don't forget to consider the weight of whatever sleeping pad you choose, or the bag requires. Mainstream sub-2-pound bags, even synthetic fill bags, are appearing with comfort ratings around 20° F and abbreviated features; that might be just the ticket if on cold nights you sleep in your insulating jacket (providing the bag's internal dimensions accommodate you and your jacket). If you're willing to diverge from a mainstream mummy-style bag, you can find a 1-pound 20° bag for a reasonable price; it just won't have zippers, a hood, or down on its lower side—it may not even have a lower side—and you won't find it at your neighborhood outdoor shop.

Sleeping bags have been temperature rated for decades, generally using a combination of controlled instruments and subjective human reports. Methods and ratings vary widely between countries and manufacturers, with ratings in the United States tending to be the most optimistic. Now the CEN (see Chapter 9) has produced European Norm (Standard) EN 13537:2002 to end all that. Likely all manufacturers who sell in Europe will adopt it after 2005, however painfully, if only out of liability fears if they don't.

EN 13537 includes four areas of standardized specifications: sleeping bag requirements, inner dimensions, thickness, and compressed volume. The requirements are the most interesting because they amount to temperature ratings. The *Upper Limit* reports the highest temperature at which a "standard man" can sleep comfortably without sweating. A standard man is a fit 20-something; you'll prefer more warmth if you're older, younger, or less fit. The *Comfort* rating is based on the lowest temperature at which a "standard woman" will sleep comfortably (read that again). Women kick out less heat per surface area than men. The *Lower Limit* is the lowest temperature at which a standard man can sleep comfortably. The *Extreme* rating is the lowest temperature at which a standard woman can survive, irrespective of comfort. Bags rated lower than about -24 °C (about -12 °F) may fall outside the standard, because the clothing and sleeping pad a person might use at such temperatures are different from that of the tests.

These new standards will mean that European manufacturers will have to use comfort temperature ratings that are about 5 C° (about 10 F°) higher than they have been reporting and American manufacturers will have to raise comfort ratings by about 10 C° (about 20 F°). The down side for manufacturers is that the tests (performed at independent certified labs) not only drop the veil but are expensive and must be done on every model and size of sleeping bag that will be sold in Europe. Ultimately EN 13537 should make it possible to select a sleeping bag based on realistic comparative ratings, which would be good for the consumer, but if it reduces options that would be bad.

Padding Your Options

Unless you're snoozing in a hut, the pad between your bag and the ground or snow is a crucial component of your sleeping system. It prevents heat loss where your bag below you is compressed to nothingness. Like the loft in your bag, the aim of the pad is to provide a thickness of dead air adequate to keep you warm; it may secondarily provide a modicum of comfort. Lightweight backpackers delight in sleeping on thin foam pads cut as short as the lowest bones in their butt; that's maybe OK if you can bed down on comfy forest duff, but it doesn't work for everyone. For fair-weather camping, there are many sleeping pad options (most from Cascade Designs, but also look for Pacific Outdoor Equipment and others). Mountaineers who face less hospitable conditions will have to be more selective. For them the option of waffle-patterned pads is out—these pads collect snow, and when the snow melts under you, they collect ice. Such pads are too thin for adverse conditions even apart from their ability to make ice cubes, and the foldable versions are notably cold. Avoid any pad designs that employ exposed open-cell foam, which will absorb water. These considerations bring the choices down to two: self-inflating mattresses or slices of closed-cell foam.

VALUE YOUR R

Setting comfort aside (you're a mountaineer, right?), the ability of a sleeping pad to insulate you from cold beneath can be expressed, like the insulation of your house, as an R-value. It's generally accepted that for sleeping on snow a minimum R value of 3 is required, if only to prevent you from melting your way downward. Self-inflating mattress pads are generally of two kinds: those with open-cell, solid foam innards, and those using perforated or hollowed-out open-cell foam (the "lite" versions). Truly diminutive ultralight inflatable pads are available that claim a high R-value despite their 1-inch thickness, but Cascade Designs is candid enough to admit that their lightest 1-inch models have an R value of 2.3 and don't recommend them for winter use. You'll need 1.5 inches (38 mm) of perforated foam to get an R-value of 3.8, or 3.2 in the lightest models. Keep in mind that manufacturers report these values for "fully inflated" pads, whatever that means; you'll be more mechanically comfortable with the least amount of inflation that keeps your bones off the ground. If the pad's internal foam isn't perforated (and it therefore traps more truly dead air), a 1.25-inch (32 mm) pad will buy you an R-value of 4.2, along with more weight. Unfortunately, the newer light models don't feel as warm and comfortable to me as the older, heavier equivalents.

Compare that to a yellow closed-cell foam pad of 0.6-inch (15 mm) thickness, which will have an R-value of about 2.2. Somehow, these pads feel warmer to me than self-inflating models having a slightly higher R-value; maybe that's because they're made with closed-cell foam instead of open cell, or maybe it's because my self-inflating model wasn't "fully" inflated. Warmer, maybe, but not as comfy on rocky ground; possibly OK for snow (no lumps) or for a hard-core summit push, but I usually prefer to lug self-inflating foam pads for comfort. A partial-length self-inflating pad that weighs 13 ounces (370 g) in combination with a full-length closed-cell foam pad beneath promises the best of both worlds.

It's hard to compare weights of the various pad options, or directly compare closed-cell foam pads to self-inflating pads, because the choices come in length/width combinations that don't match up; actual pad thicknesses vary considerably from what the manufacturers quote. For similar R values, yellow foam pads and "lite" self-inflating pads will have similar weights; the self-inflating pad will cost much more and is more vulnerable, but it packs smaller. You could save even more weight by trimming your closed cell pad to eliminate surface area that you never sleep on. There seem to be two varieties of the foam in closed-cell pads: the blue foam, once called Ensolite, with about 9 percent EVA, and the yellow version with about 18 percent EVA, called "Evazote" though Zote Foams makes both versions. The yellow foam is tougher and is supposed to remain flexible at lower temperatures; both colors aren't available in the same thicknesses.

Hardcore mountaineers may opt for a foam pad instead of a self-inflating model, because if the later encounters environmental adversity, its R value quickly becomes zip to nil. If they so opt, mountaineers face two problems: in the cold, a rolled up foam pad attempts to stay rolled up, and, curled or flat, these pads like to take off on the slightest breeze and zoom down any old snow slope. To fix the former, cut the pad (in the warmth of your living room) into panels of a width that will easily fit your pack, preferably inside it; this will carry better on a climb than rolling it up and tying it on the outside, colorfully photogenic though it may be. Tape the panels together with duck tape, making sure you do so in a way that will allow the panels to unfold flat (tricky, unless you're sober). Duck tape sticks well to this foam. Then, to prevent your pad from heading for home before you do, run a cord through one corner (reinforced with duck tape) and use it to keep your pad on belay.

How to Snooze Warmer

The warmth of a sleeping bag depends on many things beside the bag itself, including drafts, moisture inside the insulation, but principally on the sleeping pad and the warmth of thermal underwear worn by the sleeper. If you've followed my advice, you've selected a wind-protected campsite that's not at the very bottom of a narrow alpine valley or below a big snowfield. Protect your bag from breezes that will cause convective cooling of its outer surface. If you sleep in a bivy sack instead of a tent, give thought to the condensation issue previously mentioned, and if you awake to find such dampness, get rid of it as soon as possible. No matter how dedicated you are to condensation eradication, such moisture will become a problem on trips of several days or more unless you get rid of it. Better to use a bivy sack (and bag, for that matter) having a more vapor-permeable fabric, such as EPIC ripstop or Pertex Microlight. A lightweight bivy sack adds considerable warmth, so it's a weight-efficient means of adding cold-weather comfort to your bag, even inside a tent. Using a thicker pad in colder conditions and keeping pads fully inflated can also make your bagged hours warmer; bag ratings are usually based on a fatter pad than most mountaineers use.

A sleeping bag with lower internal volume will be warmer, but if you can't deal with that boa constrictor feeling, use a roomier bag and fill up excess internal volume with spare clothes, socks, and sacks; you may still have room to toss and turn. Wearing at least light underwear bottoms and top while sleeping provides twice the insulation comfort as the same weight of bag filler because it provides a layer of dead air right at the skin surface, where it is most noticeable; it's certainly more effective and weight-efficient than using a single-purpose sleeping bag liner. This layer also prevents skin oils and salts, perspiration, sunscreen, and bug repellent from soiling your bag and leading to that lived-in nylon ambiance. Every backcountry traveler should bring an extra pair of socks and wear the dry pair at night; many bring extra thick socks to wear only while sleeping. Having warm feet substantially reduces the sensation of freezing to death at night. In cold conditions wear light gloves or liners and a balaclava. In fact, why not wear your insulating jacket, too, or at least lay it across your bag, rather than take it off at night when you most need insulation.

Another way to add warmth without any weight penalty is to zip two sleeping bags together. This can be done even with bags from different manufacturers, as most mainstream bags and zippers are designed to mate—providing one has a left-hand zip design and the other is right handed. Since right-hand zip is more common, purchasing a left-hand model may improve your chances of zipper compatibility. It may be considerably more difficult to find another climber with personal-habit compatibility, so this measure is probably best for emergency use only, but it's very effective.

The standard tip to bring a bottle of warm water into the bag with you won't work for hydration bladder users, who are justifiably paranoid about leaks, but any strategy for starting out warm may at least let you fall asleep. What will help you stay asleep is fat in your evening meal and jumping into the bag soon after it has been eaten. Add fat to a low fat dehydrated meal by pouring on olive oil. The fat keeps your internal flame on simmer during the night. Staying thoroughly hydrated helps, too. Sit around in the cold after dinner as your blood moves to your gut and your insulin rises, and you'll start the night out chilled.

Using a pee bottle also helps keep you warm at night, and it addresses the consequence of copious hydration. I don't know whether a distended bladder *makes* you cold or just reminds you that you *are* cold, but there certainly seems to be a syn-

ergy. The 20-ounce, widemouth sports drink bottles I like so much work very well in this application; the need for a positive means of tactile identification goes without saying. Another benefit of using a pee bottle is that you'll provide yourself with a cozy new bottle of liquid warmed to 98.6 °F (37 °C in Canada).

Sweating the Details

Use a vapor barrier bag liner when temperatures are around or below 0 °F (20 °C); consider one any time the nighttime temps are appreciably below freezing, especially if you're in a down bag. A VBL is a big stuff sack of impermeable fabric that you cinch up around your neck. You gotta wear thin long underwear to make this tolerable, but a VBL will add 15 F° to your bag's bottom temp. A modern VBL made of silnylon can be cut amply and still weigh only a few ounces—less than the weight of condensate your bag will retain on the first cold night. VBLs keep you warmer in two ways: they prevent your losing water by insensible perspiration and heat by evaporation, because when the relative humidity next to your body reaches about 80 percent, insensible perspiration slows to a stop. You don't actually sweat inside the VBL, and there's no liquid water, but you do feel damp. VBLs also keep the stuffing of your bag dry, so it doesn't gain water and lose loft. This is vitally important on a multiday outing in very cold weather, or any time in colder conditions when you won't be able to dry out your down sleeping bag, which takes time. Some people can't tolerate the claustrophobia and the damp feeling, but they'll have to carry bigger synthetic bags and waste an occasional fair-weather rest day to dry them. You can't dry your thicker insulation clothing layers as effectively inside your bag when using a VBL; you certainly can't have them inside it with you, but you probably can't dry them in your down bag anyhow on a multiday outing because that would just transfer the water into your sleeping bag. Air leaked into your VBL when you scratch your nose or tug on your hood closure will feel like you've been doused with ice water; that's one reason you want to wear *light* long underwear: to hasten the drying time when the time comes. When you exit your bag, work the VBL down around your ankles before unzipping the bag and letting the cold outside air slam your precious body. And finally, you can carry your silnylon VBL as an ultralight emergency bivy shelter on a summit push; they're much more durable than space blanket bags, whose claimed benefit of significant warmth from reflecting body heat is science fiction.

Drying It Out, or In

You'll have to decide whether you want to bring damp clothing inside the bag with you in hopes of drying it out. That's usually the strategy on long outings, but depending on conditions, your things might dry better lying atop the bag, and you might prefer to keep your down drier. Wet gloves hold an amazing amount of water, but putting on frozen gloves is no fun at all. If you bring your damp clothes in, especially if you bring in your boots or liners, put them in a stuff sack made of uncoated fabric (sleeping pads used to come with these); they'll be able to dry, but won't soil your bag. If your bag and insulating jacket have synthetic insulation, under many conditions wearing the damp jacket will dry it out overnight without catastrophically impairing the insulation of your bag. This won't work with down, where your bag will end up carrying the water that was in your clothes until you can devote a sunny day to drying it out. These considerations may impact your decision on bag size; even if your height doesn't require a "long" sleeping bag and even though the additional air space may be otherwise undesirable, you may decide that the additional space is needed for boot liners, water and other liquid bottles, and clothing.

What Works for Me

For short-term three- or three-and-a-half-season mountaineering, I use a semi-rectangular down bag that works reasonably well as low as 20 °F (-5 °C) with the down shifted to the top. This costs me a pound of extra weight compared to the lightest alternatives, but it's much roomier than a mummy-style bag and more easily adapted to a wide range of temperatures. I sleep better, given all the other stressors of altitude and anxiety, and

when push comes to shove my dog can even fit inside. When it's above freezing, I use the bag as a quilt. When it's cold, around 10 °F (-15 °C), I also wear my insulating jacket, which has a hood, and most every other item of clothing I've brought— and keep it all on until almost ready to leave camp in the early morning. Any fabric I don't wear I put into the bag around my knees. Because the bag is so roomy, this isn't uncomfortable, and I can thrash around as I tend to do. I sleep in a 10-ounce, vapor permeable bivy sack or, in very cold weather or if rain or snow is a possibility, a bivy tent; this increases the warmth of the air around the bag, compared to being in a larger tent. I'll use the same setup inside an igloo in midwinter. The ultralight bivy sack keeps my down dry and is lighter overall than going with synthetic insulation; I get it off the bag immediately after I rise, so that I can shake out any frost that rarely forms on the bag or inside the bivy. On short outings the bulk of a synthetic bag isn't justified, because my relatively thin down bag can be laid out flat to dry well enough to retain most of its loft; on short trips a damp bag isn't terminal. My eyes are peeled for a 20° semi-rectangular synthetic bag with a light EPIC shell and the high-tech features my down bags have. I have a reasonably light, roomy 0 °F (-20 °C) synthetic bag that I use for multiday winter trips when I know that making use of every available hour of daylight to cover ground means I won't be able to dry my bag, except by my own body heat while sleeping in it, when I'll also be drying clothing, socks, and gloves. This works with a synthetic bag, but isn't feasible with down. On especially serious, cold-weather climbs I carry a beefier but more constrictive down bag and use a VBL as well as the lightweight bivy sack— even in a tent. You get used to being damp and mummified in a VBL, or maybe you're just too tired to notice how uncomfortable you really are.

Keep It Clean

Now that most shell fabrics are treated with DWR finishes or have water-resistant coatings or laminates, sleeping bags are tricky to wash. Gently wash even synthetic bags by hand in the bathtub to avoid loss of loft. This is especially important if your ultralight down bag is made with more delicate netting baffles or stretch fabric instead of ordinary tricot baffles. Use barely enough soap or detergent to have a few suds left over and rinse very thoroughly multiple times; if your shell is Gore-Tex or a variant that requires special cleaner, or even if it isn't, use Atsko Sport-Wash, never laundry detergent or Woolite. I'll repeat the ancient admonitions to be cautious about using commercial laundry dryers with erratic heat settings, use tennis balls instead of tennis shoes when tumble drying your bag, and stop the dryer periodically to gently hand massage the clumps of down. Before your bag is completely dry you may want to spray a new DRW treatment on the shell and complete the drying process with the temperature boosted from cool to warm.

Get the Cat Out of the Bag

The ambient temperature drops lowest in the hour just before dawn; that's when many mountaineers are awakened by chilly feet and a full bladder. Just look at it as nature's way of telling a mountaineer that it's time to put on the headlamp and get going on that alpine start. None of this plays well with the bourbon-before-breakfast crowd; they should stick to backpacking.

FUEL AND STOVES

There are a huge number of stoves on the market that could be appropriate for mountaineering; it seems every manufacturer offers a dozen models or more. Stoves can be classified according to the type of fuel they burn.

Types of Fuel

WHITE GAS

Also called naptha and "Coleman fuel," white gas is just a blend of hydrocarbons (approximately 60 percent hexane and 40 percent heptane, if you care) that distill together at your local refinery. Don't use actual automotive gasoline, leaded or unleaded, or mineral spirits (paint thinner) unless your stove's manual agrees (as many do); lighter fluid might be OK, too. All these are similar, but fuels made specifically for stoves contain rust inhibitors and preservatives, are cleaned up for stove use, and are probably safer than gasoline because of a slightly lower boiling point. White gas may be hard to find outside North America and the UK, but it's becoming more available in parts of South America. If you're studying for extra credit, properly burned white gas produces heat energy to the tune of about 10.2 kcal/gram.

KEROSENE

Also called paraffin, kerosene is a petroleum distillate mixture of hydrocarbons (mostly decane) that is less volatile than white gas. That makes it a bit safer than white gas, but it also makes it necessary to use another fuel to preheat the stove's generator coil. Use alcohol, acetone, white gas, or priming paste (napalm, basically). These also work for white gas stoves but aren't essential. If you use alcohol, go for pure ethanol (grain alcohol) or denatured alcohol, not isopropanol, and be careful: alcohol flames can be almost invisible. Your kerosene stove will burn with a smoky yellow flame if it isn't adequately preheated; if that happens, shut it down, let it cool, and start over. Kerosene may be the most reliably available option for international travel, but it needs to be clean, or it will gunk up your stove even faster that it normally does; it always burns a bit sooty. Kerosene (not Ultrasene) stinks and taints food flavors, but Jet-A Fuel, available at airports, is water clear with little smell. Kerosene yields 10.1 kcal/gram.

LIQUEFIED PETROLEUM GAS

Liquefied petroleum is more commonly called butane in the United States, even though the canisters no longer contain pure butane, and is commonly called LP elsewhere. There are actually three chemicals that may be used or blended; they are turned into a liquid by compression, with the resulting liquid kept under pressure in canisters. There's butane, of course—technically n-butane. It boils at 30 °F (-1 °C) at sea level. Isobutane is also a hydrocarbon with four carbon atoms, but it has a branched, rather than linear, chemical structure and a boiling point of 10 °F (-12 °C). Propane, a lighter hydrocarbon, has a boiling point of -44 °F (-42 °C). Butane yields 11.8 kcal/gram and propane 12.0 kcal/gram. There were once multiple standards for the canister connection, but stoves nowadays fit most all resealable, Lindahl valve canisters (except the proprietary Camping Gaz, common in France and Australia, and Coleman X types). Modern canisters may be hard to find outside North America and Europe, and you can't take them (or probably any other fuels) on a commercial airliner.

ALCOHOL

Methyl alcohol, also called methylated spirits or meths, is popular among lightweight backpacking enthusiasts, who fancy making their own featherweight stoves from pop cans. Ethyl alcohol can also be used, so you might consider Everclear a multiuse item. Alcohol, a carbohydrate, produces much less heat (6.3 kcal/gram) than hydrocarbon fuels, and alcohol stoves function poorly above 10,000 feet (3,000 meters). This makes alcohol stoves impractical for mountaineers except as pot warmers on a sunny approach; they are quiet and light, though. Alcohol fuel is widely available, but you need as much as three or four times the amount to produce the same heat as white gas or butane, depending on your stove and elevation. Alcohol burns with a nearly invisible flame. Avoid isopropyl alcohol, even the 91 percent version (rubbing alcohol is 70 percent isopropyl alcohol in water), because it burns sooty.

OTHER FUELS

There are stoves, such as the MSR XGK, Brunton Optimus Nova (strange name in Spanish), and Primus Himalayans, that, sometimes by swapping parts, burn white gas, kerosene, auto gasoline, aviation gas, diesel fuel, rape seed extract, and others; some even convert to burn butane mixes. You may have to rebuild them every day and do a lot of fiddling, but such stoves offer the assurance that you can burn any hydrocarbon, however inefficiently, that you stumble across anywhere in the world.

You may also come across micro stoves, holders really, that burn hexamine pellets (Esbit fuel). Hexamine (hexamethylenetetramine) is a solid with no storage issues other than keeping it dry,

you can burn it in your tent, altitude is no problem, and it's non-explosive despite being the starting material for plastic explosives. These stoves are a great lightweight option if the amount of hot water you need on your outing is modest. The illustration shows the author's homemade hexamine "stove." The windscreen is a section of aluminum "handyman coil" from a hardware store and the stove part is just a 2 × 2 piece with ventilation holes made with a paper punch and the corners folded down. The windscreen rolls up and fits in the titanium cup for transport, with a plastic cup inside it. An Esbit tablet weighs half an ounce, costs 50 cents, and half of one will boil two cups of water in 5 minutes (in my setup); one tablet is plenty to prepare a 2-course home-dried meal. The stove and windscreen weigh 0.8 ounce.

Fuel and Stove Equivalency

All hydrocarbon fuels, liquid or compressed gas, produce roughly the same amount of heat for a given weight of fuel. There's nothing particularly outstanding about any fuel option, although you will often hear persons who should have paid more attention in chemistry class making baseless claims that one type of fuel produces significantly more heat than another. Stoves aren't magic either. No matter what fuel they burn—liquid hydrocarbons or compressed hydrocarbon gases—the heat output for a given weight of fuel will be similar among all well-designed stoves. If a particular

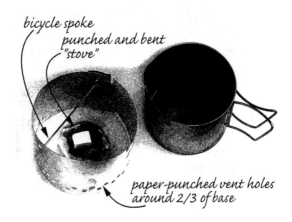

bicycle spoke
punched and bent
"stove"

paper-punched vent holes
around 2/3 of base

Homemade hexamine stove/windscreen.

stove produces more heat, it's because it burns more fuel in a given period of time. Liquid fuel stoves have heat outputs that top out around 10,000 BTU/hr (2,900 watts). Higher heat output is limited by the difficulty of vaporizing enough liquid fuel in a simple generator coil. Butane stoves have no such limitation, and some models produce over twice that heat output—by burning more than twice the weight of fuel in the same amount of time. Manufacturers like to separate the "burning time" specification from that for "boiling time," but these are connected; a stove that boils water faster will also burn up its fuel supply faster—simple laws of chemistry. Don't expect to reproduce quoted times in actual field use, and don't run out and invest in a Jetboil until you confirm the speed claim—it didn't jet for me, the piezo lighter is as lame as most others, it uses expensive little fuel canisters, the integral pot limits it to solo cooking, and you can't invert it to improve cold weather performance. MSR has a similar model that runs on white gas but requires no pumping; they claim it's super efficient.

Improving on Physics

Fuels and stoves may be nearly equivalent, but there are things you can do to make any choice perform better. As a starting point, figure on being able to boil about 8 liters or quarts of water with 100 grams of fuel or you could figure that a quart of white gas will last one person about a week or 10 days, but there are many environmental factors that will adversely impact fuel consumption; don't miscalculate and end up touching the void. The most important measure is to protect the burner from wind. Wind can increase boiling time and fuel consumption by a factor of three. If your stove doesn't have a windscreen, you can adapt an MSR model or make your own from the bottom of a recyclable baking pan, an oven liner, or aluminum flashing from the hardware store. That is, unless your stove is a canister-top butane stove; except for models intended to be hung inside your tent, canister-top stoves should not be used with a windscreen lest the canister overheat. A ground-level heat reflector as part of the windscreen increases efficiency, too, and using black

pots also helps reduce fuel consumption by up to 25 percent. MSR, Backpackers Pantry, and GSI make black pots, or you can paint your titanium favorites with header paint (from your auto parts store) or barbeque paint. Keeping lids on pots helps conserve fuel, too. Speaking of pots, although stainless and titanium have pretty much replaced aluminum for mountaineering, heat transfer differences have nothing to do with it—all three alloys cook pretty much the same. Stainless is easy to clean, and titanium is light, but a thick aluminum pot that weighs the same as a stainless pot may actually cook more uniformly and may clean better if it has a non-stick coating. The association of aluminum with Alzheimer's has been disproved for more than 30 years. Take care not to overheat coated pots, which can happen easily when melting snow; that may produce toxic fumes. At high altitude your stove will burn rich, so open up the windscreen and back off on the pump pressure of liquid fuel stoves. Keep your stove tuned up and its jet clean—unless you use a butane stove, which eliminates maintenance chores. Keep the fuel bottle of your liquid fuel stove insulated in very cold weather; you can use a sock or your stove's stuff sack, or both—years ago I used a beer can cozy because it made me nostalgic. Set the stove on your shovel blade. Stoves burn more efficiently at less than full throttle, so if you're not in a hurry, back off. Finally, minimize your fuel consumption by planning meals that require as little heating as possible—certainly no baking or protracted simmers of rice and beans—and avoid any actual boiling that isn't necessary.

White Gas Stoves

Kerosene offers no particular advantage over white gas, except maybe for less likelihood of inadvertent detonation, so North American mountaineers will see white gas stoves as the main option for liquid fuel stoves. Liquid fuel stoves work by pressurizing a fuel container with a pump that's part of the stove assembly; 40 or more pump strokes are needed. After pressurization, the control valve is opened enough to allow a small amount of white gas to enter the burner. This fuel is lighted and allowed to burn (inefficiently) in order to heat up the generator coil. If the preheating process is successful, the control valve can be opened just before the priming flame goes out, and the stove will fire up and produce a hot, blue flame. If unsuccessful, the stove may release unvaporized fuel, with the result being a flare-up. Every mountaineer has experienced singed hair, perhaps a singed tent, as a result. The priming process results in messy soot on the stove, especially if a flare-up needs to be burned off, and unnecessarily consumes fuel. The Nova stove minimizes this ritual by lighting quickly, plus it works well in cold weather, simmers nicely, shuts off cleanly, and its jet can be cleaned while the stove is operating. Even if you are compelled by storm to cook in the vestibule of your tent, or even inside your tent, light the stove outside and be sure to have an effective means of jettisoning the stove should it flare up when being started. If you must bring the stove inside once it is burning properly, have plenty of ventilation to provide adequate oxygen to the stove and yourself. In cold conditions or at altitude, liquid fuel stoves need persistent assistance from the pump and a hungry mountaineer.

Butane Stoves

The other principle option for mountaineers is stoves burning liquefied petroleum gas: "butane" stoves. These stoves are models of simplicity compared to liquid fuel stoves. They require no maintenance, plus they light, start, and extinguish instantly, and they don't make soot. At one time they were considered to be inefficient, perhaps because windscreens are inappropriate for canister-top models for fear of overheating the canister(!), seals, piezo igniter, or the control valve. Don't be tempted to use a windscreen; just cook in a protected spot and forget about using backcountry oven contraptions. However, modern remote-canister models allow use of a windscreen and heat reflector at the expense of a few more ounces (and dollars), which may be recovered by better fuel efficiency. Butane fuel is 30 times more expensive than white gas, but stove fuel is a small fraction of your outing budget. If you elect a light, canister-top stove for summer outings, use the Primus folding legs to add stability to the canister. For serious mountaineering you'll want a remote-canister model that can accommodate a windscreen and heat reflector—and inverted canister. Read on.

If the liquefied gas fuel for "butane" stoves were actually butane, you can see from the initial discussion of fuels that at around freezing temps the butane would fail to vaporize and would instead behave like a liquid fuel; canister-top stoves are designed for fuels that spontaneously turn into gas, so in freezing temps, burning drops way off or even ceases. As the fuel is used up, pressure in the canister drops, and stove output falls further; there's no way to pump up the pressure as there is with a liquid fuel stove, other than by warming the canister. When a liquid vaporizes and expands it also cools (that's how your refrigerator works); you can see this effect on gas canisters in use when, especially in humid air, frost forms on the outside up to the level of the cold liquid fuel on the inside. For all these reasons, if air temperatures are close to freezing, vaporizing butane will cool itself down and the stove will begin to die for lack of fuel. At higher altitudes (lower atmospheric pressure), the boiling point of butane drops, which is good. At 10,000 feet (3,000 meters) the boiling point is 12 °F (11 °C), so the stove will work better in the cold. At 20,000 feet (7,000 meters) the boiling point of butane will drop to 2 °F (19 °C), so the stove will work better yet—except for the fact that the vaporizing fuel is cooling itself as it's being burned. Altitude is the butane stove's friend, but cold is a mortal enemy.

There are any number of ways to address this problem. One is to keep your winter butane canister warm by keeping it in your sleeping bag or inside your jacket, stand it in water, swap canisters as they cool, or use a chemical heat pack. Admittedly, these solutions are lame. Do not insulate the canister, as this will make the cooling effect worse. If you're always cooking in an enclosed space like a tent vestibule, cooling may not be a huge problem because the ambient temperature soon rises, and all you need to do is insulate the canister from the ground. To tackle the problem of pressure loss in cold weather, mountaineers have for years made their own heat exchangers to keep canisters warm. Usually these are made from heavy copper wire, hammered flat and bent to contact the flame and make a couple of wraps around the canister. I made mine out of heavy copper foil used for roof flashing. They get surprisingly hot, but the goal is only to warm the canister above freezing; you should be able to grip the stove and feel only warmth, not heat. Stove manufacturers avert their eyes, because the amount of heat transfer can get out of hand, with the potential result of exploding canisters or stoves becoming uncontrollable flame throwers—it happens.

Another solution to the self-cooling problem is to blend the gases that make up the fuel. Why not just use 100 percent propane and be done with it? With today's technology that would require heavy steel canisters to retain the propane's higher pressure; OK for car camping stoves but not for stoves you'd want to carry in a backpack. Instead, canister manufacturers blend n-butane and/or isobutane with a percentage of more volatile propane to improve cold-weather performance. You'll see 80/20, 70/30, and a combination of 70 percent n-butane, 10 percent isobutane, and 20 percent propane. This isn't a perfect solution either, because the propane will mostly burn off first. Shaking the canister has no effect. You'll soon be left with straight butane—and a fading flame.

DOING SOMETHING ABOUT THE WEATHER

Here's what I recommend for dealing with cold weather: use a remote-canister butane stove that features a preheat coil (every manufacturer offers one nowadays). It will have all the benefits of a liquefied gas stove (instant lighting, no fuel wasted in priming, simmering ability, no flare-ups, no smoky flame, no smelly fuel spills, no maintenance issues), plus it will allow the use of a windscreen around the burner and a heat reflector below it, an efficiency boost that isn't sensible with canister-top stoves. These two items substantially improve efficiency, just as they do with liquid fuel stoves, and that could offset the increase in weight over canister-top models. Remote-canister models might even be more stable (if you're going to melt snow for water you'll want a big pot and a stable stove). In cold conditions, invert the canister; that may send liquid butane (or blend) to the stove, but

it will vaporize in the preheat pipe. This should work with any remote-canister model, since they should all be resistant to failure (or detonation) in the event of an accidentally tipped canister; some manufacturers tacitly recommend this tactic. A few stove designs even perform the same way without actually inverting the canister. Be prepared for a *substantial* increase in firepower when the liquid butane hits the preheat coil if you invert the canister of an operating stove, and definitely test this system with your stove before you switch from less aggressive winter techniques. If things are so cold that the pressure in the canister isn't pushing the liquid fuel out, just raise the inverted canister enough so fuel drains into the burner.

WHAT ARCHIMEDES SAID

That completely takes care of one of the major objections to butane stoves: flagging cold-weather performance. Another common objection is that you can't tell how much fuel is left in a partially used canister. People who make this objection didn't pay attention in high-school physics class, because the solution is simple. Just take a full canister (whichever model you prefer) and float it in water. Mark the level of the water line on the canister. Then float a completely spent canister and note its water line; this canister will ride higher in the water. A partially used canister will float somewhere in between, and the difference in waterlines precisely shows the fraction of fuel remaining, from 0 to 100 percent. You can perform this simple test using any pot barely big enough to float the

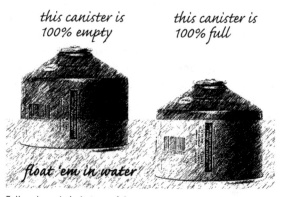

Full and empty butane canisters.

canister, even in a lake or stream. This is not a whole lot less convenient than opening a liquid fuel bottle and peering into the interior. An operating canister stove may also show the level of the fuel remaining by frost on its outside, especially if you dampen the canister.

Power and Altitude; Advantage: Butane

Now we have leveled the playing field for stove selection, save for two final observations. Because of stove physics, above 21,000 feet (6,500 meters) compressed gas is the only fuel that vaporizes well enough to work effectively; in fact, butane stoves generally work better than liquid fuel stoves at any high altitude. Butane stoves are also the only option if you really need double the heat output of liquid fuel stoves; it doesn't require a super-special stove either—high-output models look like ordinary backpacking stoves, and several manufacturers make them. If high output and altitude are issues, your only choice is a butane stove.

Weight; Advantage: Butane

Historically, butane stoves have been considered to be convenient, but not a serious alternative to white gas or kerosene stoves for extended, cold-weather outings. I've dealt with the cold-weather issue, and I've mentioned that you can find butane stoves with twice the heat output of, say, the venerable XGK rocket. Let's take a look at weight, because you'll hear that butane stoves' canisters make them heavy compared to white gas stoves. If you add the weight of a common remote-canister butane stove to the weight of its empty 8-ounce (227-gram) canister, you have 12 ounces (335 grams); a canister-top model for mild conditions would cut nearly 4 ounces (105 grams) off that. Taking a common white gas stove with the same heat output (a bit less actually) from the same manufacturer and including its empty 11-ounce fuel bottle (which holds 8 ounces of fuel since you must leave air space) you get 14.5 ounces (410 grams). The white gas stove's pump makes it heavier than the remote-canister butane stove. The fuels weigh the same, but the butane or butane blend will produce almost 20 percent more heat energy, and no fuel will be used up for priming.

The butane stove setup is actually 2.5 ounces *lighter* than the white gas model and will boil significantly more water for the same amount of fuel weight. Both stove types benefit from exactly the same heat reflector and windscreen. The advantage begins to shift to white gas only if you have to carry more than about 32 ounces of fuel per stove (about a week's worth). You have to pack out empty fuel containers for either choice; liquid fuel containers don't get weight competitive unless you carry gallon cans. It could be argued that the spare parts kit you'll need for the white gas stove on such longer outings needs to be factored in as well.

So here's my bottom line (cue the trumpets): at all altitudes and in all seasons, new-school mountaineers will prefer remote-canister butane stoves for their heavy-duty heating.

TEN ESSENTIALS RETHOUGHT FOR MOUNTAINEERING

Once when I was a Boy Scout I came home and, with great excitement, told my grandfather about all the cool things on this list, called "the ten essentials," that I was about to collect. My grandfather, who makes cameo appearances elsewhere in this book, was unimpressed. "You need all that stuff?!" was his more than typically incredulous response. My granddad's idea of ten essentials were a Barlow knife, eight kitchen matches, and a pack of Lucky Strikes.

Well, he was a Native American and I was a Boy Scout, so inevitably and inescapably we communicated across a vast chasm of antithetic agendas when it came to the acquisition of paraphernalia. When you look at the many lists of ten essentials, you can see that most are indeed aimed at Boy Scouts and backpackers, even though the concept originated with The Mountaineers in the 1930s. Today's mountaineers will have honed their lists much more selectively, aiming to increase safety and decrease weight, using the number 10 as a suggestion more than a rule. This is a personal process, so I'll offer you my list and suggest that you come up with your own.

I define "ten essentials" as those specific items that I bring on every single outing. A map, for example, wouldn't be on the list, because I'd bring a different map for different areas. Most of these things get put into a 6 × 9 × 2 travel pouch that has lots of little pockets inside, like a first-aid kit bag; my particular model has a removable internal pouch, which is where I keep the items that can remain in base camp. A reflective zipper tab helps locate the pouch in darkness. This setup adds ounces of extra weight, but it helps me keep the whole business organized and replenished. On short hikes: why not carry my ten essentials? They don't weigh much, so they always come along. And on longer outings I most definitely carry them—they are essential, after all. I just throw the pouch into my pack, and I know I'm covered. Here's what's included:

Medical ID card. Just a 2 × 3 laminated card with pertinent ID, contact info, and medical data.

Reading glasses. Half-framers. Hey, I'm over forty, and I might want to read the fine print.

Soft iron wire. One meter of 20-gauge (0.5 mm) galvanized steel wire. With this stuff you can repair anything, including human flesh (though perhaps not your own).

Whistle. One of those big, unbearably loud guys. Used more often than I would have imagined; far better than shouting.

Compass. A small model with mirrored cover and 2° protractor, but without declination adjustment, which is suggested by red tape on the underside of the capsule.

LED lamp. A 1-LED model with switch, hung on the internal zipper of my pouch; the brightest model available, with fresh batteries. It's for finding stuff in my "ten essentials" pouch or nearby, but it's bright enough to hike with in an emergency—one reason for a model with a switch instead of requiring constant finger pressure.

Paper. Two 3 × 4 sheets of waterproof note paper. Whack up a FedEx envelope, they're free.

Pencil. A 3-inch stub, like a golf pencil—if you have any idea what that is.

Ear plugs. Stuff in these foam puppies, and you can hear the volume dropping on flapping tents, snoring partners, or a brook that won't stop babbling.

Poop tickets (aka toilet paper). Some people count the sheets and ration themselves; not needed when snow is available (by guys anyhow). In a heavy zip-seal bag from McMaster-Carr, with lighter zip-seal bags for packing out the used tickets.

Multi-tool. Of the micro size, with pliers and other tools that might come in handy. Heavy, I suppose, but very useful, even as tweezers. As a ski mountaineer, I have used this gadget a lot to make repairs; don't skimp on quality.

Swiss Army knife. All I need is the smallest size; I move it and a 1-LED micro-light to an OSHA-approved neck lanyard while I'm climbing. I like the Wenger brand for functionality, but Victorinox for style. It's also a component of my first-aid kit.

Dental floss. One meter, at least. Better for oral care than a toothbrush and multipurpose, including minor repairs, tick removal (lasso those little suckers in an overhand knot), etc. Don't neglect dental hygiene just because you're climbing.

Toothbrush. Yeah, I cut the handle down, but only to make it more compact. If I think of it, I moosh some toothpaste into the bristles before leaving home, just for the taste, but I don't pack toothpaste. Some people use Dr. Bronner's, but I'd rather do without.

Saline solution. Half ounce. For my contact lenses, should my pocket bottle run dry.

Surveyors' tape. Two meters of Day-Glo route marker. Used and removed every so often, especially in winter.

Butane lighter. Backup for the one in the stove's stuff sack when I carry a stove; thoroughly tested for functionality. I used to carry a cool refillable butane lighter that I bought at a flea market in China; it had a big picture of Mao, went off like a blowtorch, and played *The East Is Red* as it did. Retired it when I got the lightweight religion.

Accessory cord. Two meters of 2 mm accessory cord, enough to replace shoelaces or tent lines, make minor repairs, or snare tasty ground squirrel bush meat. I also carry 10 meters of 3 mm accessory cord. Ten meters because I teach avalanche classes, and that's a handy length for establishing a visual reference (of 20 meters). Normally used to hang backpacks out of the reach of voracious but gymnastically challenged varmints.

Sun block. Half ounce of SPA 45, as backup in

case I screw up and take off without any—easy to do in the wee hours.

Chamois. Small piece for cleaning sunglasses and goggle lenses, which can't be done with synthetic fabric.

Balaclava. Mid- to lightweight. The most warmth you can get for the least weight. Used every so often, year round.

Cotton fabric. A 24 × 28-inch piece of white cotton gauze sold as a diaper for newborns, despite its inadequacy in this application. It may be the only absorbent fabric I carry. It can be used to clean lenses, make a helmet sunshield, serve as washcloth or towel, wipe condensation off tent interiors or sleeping bag exteriors, and become an emergency medical dressing. Some people carry bandanas for these purposes, just be sure yours is 100 percent cotton; women prefer patterned fabrics for use as their pee rag. Get big bandanas in camouflage or blaze orange from Generation Gap.

Trash bag. Grocery bag size. I search out versions with extra-strong plastic and solid welds that will carry a gallon of water and won't burst or leak. Essentially weightless.

Insect repellent (seasonal). With the increase of Lyme, West Nile, and other exotic mosquito and tick vector illnesses, this issue is becoming more than just a matter of annoyance. I favor 3M Ultrathon lotion repackaged from 2-ounce tubes (32 percent DEET, time-released for "12 hour" protection) or repellent sprayed on at the trailhead. DEET is surprisingly nontoxic, but it may eat your compass and some plastic watch and camera parts. The only benefit of the more noxious concentrations above 35 percent is more enduring effect, and that has been addressed by time-release products from Sawyer and 3M. You can still use the stronger stuff on your clothing. Keep an eye out for Skeeter Shield, based on a less toxic and more effective chemical called IBI-246. If mosquitoes, ticks, and chiggers are rampant, treat your clothing and tent opening with a 0.5 percent permethrin (synthetic pyrethrum) fabric spray; it will last two weeks or several washings, longer if you keep your stuff in black plastic bags. You can even buy clothing that's been impregnated with it, but its effect is modest. Permethrin doesn't work directly on your skin, because chemicals there deactivate it. If black flies are anticipated, use a repellent containing R-326 or Rutgers 612, which work better than DEET against these insects; you can find products with these in combination with DEET and MGK-264. I wouldn't apply any of these things to sunburned or abraded skin. (I'm sparing you the technical names for these chemicals; see the Resources appendix—if you dare.)

Women on longer outings—when menstrual cycles can become unpredictable—may want to include a Keeper Menstrual Cup or DivaCup in their ten essentials. These lightweight, reusable products are a rather convenient and eco-friendly alternative to the weight and bulk of paper-and-cotton feminine hygiene products.

FIRST-AID KIT

The contents of the first-aid kits you can buy in your outdoor shop are pretty much confined to conventional minor wound dressing. They're usually weak on wound cleaning, which is often more important, the contents themselves are very old-school, the packaging is poor, and the analgesics they contain are of the weak-to-useless variety. The thinking is probably that such items, even in the hands of a moron, could do no harm. I strongly encourage anyone who spends time in the backcountry to take a wilderness first-aid course; that will greatly expand your knowledge and influence the choice of first-aid items you carry, the array of which will be influenced by the character of your outing and the number of participants for whom you are responsible. The course will teach you to improvise all manner of first-aid supplies, replacing weight with skill. My first-aid stuff goes into an airtight Aloksak zip-seal baggie and weighs a little over 3 ounces (90 grams). This first-aid kit is actually slightly overkill for an outing of a few days, but I have erred that way because of the greater likelihood of a more serious injury when climbing compared to backpacking, because I have had training that makes me feel more responsible for providing care, and because my companions cannot be counted upon to be well accoutered. I carry additional supplies if I'm responsible for a larger party; for a really large party, the first-aid kit should be split up among participants, not carried in one big bag by the leader. Go through your first-aid kit at the start of every season and ensure that tired and expired items are replaced and recheck it against a written list before each outing. Here are the annotated contents of my personal "ten essentials" first-aid kit, which I offer not as a recipe, but to get you thinking.

Exam gloves. One pair of nitrile gloves.

SOAP note. One sheet. The standard format for recording medical information; Subjective (what the patient communicates to you), Objective (data you collect about the patient), Assessment (your short-term diagnosis), and your treatment Plan— all of which you'll learn about in that wilderness first-aid course you've signed up for. (I have a pencil in my "ten essentials").

Very sharp knife, tweezers, scissors. All are parts of a small high-quality knife, such as a Victorinox Swiss Army Classic or Wenger Esquire. Save a little weight by jettisoning most of the knife itself. Don't include these if you have another such knife elsewhere in your ten essentials.

Sterile gauze sponges. Two 3 × 3, two 4 × 4. If things get more serious than that, I have nonsterile gauze fabric elsewhere. Multipurpose.

Tape. One 1-inch × 2-yard roll of waterproof medical tape. Multipurpose.

Steri-Strips. Packet of three, $\frac{1}{4}$ × 3. Or use Spenco Self-Healing Cut Closures. Butterflys are old-school.

Moist wound-care pads. Two medium, four large; or generic equivalent. Some brands contain silver oxide as a bacteriostat. Band-Aids, and dry dressings in general, are old-school.

Blister Pads. Two Spenco hydrocolloid pads; new-school. I wish they were larger.

Bioclusive Transparent Dressing. One 2 × 3. I no longer carry the larger size.

Adaptic. One 3 × 3 non-adhering dressing.

Waterproof bandage strips. Two large (2 × 3) strips, two medium (1.5 × 1.5) squares. If you can find waterproof alginate dressing strips, go for it.

Potato starch. Two tablespoons. The civilian version of TraumaDEX, an effective hemostat to control serious bleeding; maybe not as effective as QuickClot, but my whole kit weighs less than a QuickClot packet.

Bactroban Cream. Weapons-grade topical antibiotic, priced accordingly. You'll need a script from your MD.

Imodium (loperamide HCl, 2 mg). Four tablets. Anti-diarrheal that slows down your gut when bugs have speeded it up. This is mainly for my companions, and they've needed it.

Hydrocodone (Vicodin ES; also contains 500 mg acetominophen). Two tablets. A moderately strong analgesic that works for some. I stopped carrying OxyContin out of concern that someone might react adversely, and there I'd be, handing out Schedule II drugs. Not to be used for someone with head injuries or altitude illness.

Naproxen sodium. Six 220 mg tablets of conventional NSAID (Non-Steroidal Anti-Inflammatory Drug).

Celebrex. Four 200 mg tablets of industrial-strength NSAID.

Benadryl (diphenhydramine HCl, 25 mg). Two tablets. Antihistamine. Might work for bee sting sensitivity or to reduce itching from bug bites.

Povidone iodine solution (Betadine). Two 0.5 ml ampoules.

Povidone iodine prep pads. Four. Tiny, but very useful.

Safety pins. Two, large size.

First-aid cream. One micropacket, with benzethonium chloride and 20 percent benzocaine. Works for bug bites, because of the benzocaine. Cheaper than the Bactroban when you don't need power.

Women may want to bring along 150 mg of Fluconazole or a topical cream with butoconazole, clotrimazole, miconazole, or triconazole for the treatment of a yeast infection.

I expect to improvise splints, collars, slings, large bandages, sutures, irrigation syringe (from zip-seal bag), and litters. I don't carry a PPV barrier, despite the likelihood that anyone who recovers while receiving Positive Pressure Ventilation will vomit, because of the unlikelihood that anyone will need CPR in the backcountry.

NON-ESSENTIALS

Traditional "ten essential" items that I don't carry include, but are not limited to, the following:

Map. I usually print one specifically for the area I'll be in, which is why this item isn't in my ten essentials bag.

Extra clothes. I don't carry "extra" anything, except maybe water; I just carry what might be required by the temperature extremes I foresee, or a little less.

Duck tape. Duck tape was originally named for the cotton duck fabric on which it is based. Somehow I've never carried this stuff, and I've never missed it. Perhaps that will change, but so far my wire and medical tape has gotten me through. Whoever recommended wrapping duck tape around ski or trekking poles must have spread the word before trying to use their stash—it doesn't hold up well to water or wear, even the preferred contractors' grade; if you carry it, keep yours inside your pack. Better choices would be boaters' repair tape, military surplus 100 MPH tape, or radiator hose repair tape—we're talking burly tape here.

Extra food. You can do without food for many days in an emergency; besides, what is "extra" food?

Water treatment. Chemicals or filters. Unnecessary in alpine regions.

Pepto-Bismol (bismuth subsalicylate). How come this stuff keeps showing up on lists?

Fire starter materials. There's enough stuff in my first-aid kit to get a fire going; I could even whittle kindling out of my pencil, so I don't carry anything specific for starting fires. Above tree line or on snow, there may not be enough material to burn anyhow. If you insist, my granddad would have you carry char cloth, juniper bark shavings, flint, steel, and a leather patch, all in a Bag Balm tin.

Most mountaineers bring a small camera and carry it where it can be quickly accessed. As an audio professional, I'd like to suggest an alternative, or at least an adjunct. For me, listening to recorded sounds of my activities, from grunts and clanks while climbing to street sounds in Asia to the voices of my companions, transports me back to those experiences much more vividly than do photographs. I'm sure you'll share that feeling, if you give it a try; as an example of the importance of sound, note that it's easier to follow a movie with your eyes closed than with the sound off. Recording the sounds of your adventures is easy nowadays, with miniaturized digital recorders and tiny stereo mics.

Elimination of all non-essential and just-in-case equipment can be referred to as a lightweight mountaineer's "success oriented" strategy. It makes sense only if your skills have developed enough to be able to respond effectively to unforeseen adversity and if you're prepared to abandon your objectives should your safety margin become too thin. Those whose skills are up to the challenge can expect more success and more fun in the mountains.

TEN ESSENTIALS FOR COOKING

These are the items I carry any time I'm on a multiday outing that will involve food preparation. Like my personal ten essentials, I keep them together so I don't have to think about the basics I bring. Everything fits in the Ti mug. A stove, lighter, and windscreen aren't listed, because I often try to live without them. If I plan meals thoughtfully, this is all I need for solo culinary art on a short excursion.

Soap. Half ounce of liquid antibacterial dish/hand soap, with a 1 × 2 inch piece of scrub sponge. Personal hygiene is the most important means of avoiding intestinal illness. "Friction" is not an effective cleansing method. In winter I add alcohol gel hand cleaner, which is even more effective against pathogens than soap.

Mug/pot. Titanium. Realistically holds up to 28 ounces (850 ml), with handmade aluminum cover (to replace the fitted lid that took a screamer).

Cup. Two-cup HDPE measuring cup that holds 22 ounces (650 ml); fits inside the Ti mug. A luxury maybe, but two-container meals are much easier to manage.

Spoon. Titanium, with stove tools punched into the handle. I broke my Lexan spork.

Olive oil. One ounce. Somehow I always end up

using it, so I always bring some along.

Headlamp. Light, 4-LED model. With the new high-output, variable intensity units, no longer do mountaineers have to carry a bulky headlamp (*head torch*, as the Brits would say), extra batteries, and extra bulb. One to 3-watt, HyperBrite LEDs are even replacing halogen lamps, and the truly weight-abhorrent climber can cut headlamp heft even further by using lithium batteries. Now you can read *War and Peace* without guilt on long winter nights; change batteries, and maybe you can polish off those last volumes of *Remembrance of Things Past* you've been meaning to get to. I bring an LED headlamp on any excursion where returning in darkness is a possibility that two ounces of precaution might alleviate, which is most of them.

Trash bag. More trash potential, so another high-tech trash bag.

I might as well pass along my advice to carry alcohol, especially on longer winter outings. Rubbing alcohol, I mean, but I suppose you could consider this another application for Everclear. You can give yourself a sponge bath (well, cotton rag bath) with this stuff, which will be much easier than trying to get clean and dry with soap and water, and you'll save fuel and water at the same time. Just mop yourself with a small cotton cloth dampened with rubbing alcohol. On a longer outing you can wash out your manky cotton cloth with soapy water every few days, and you're back in business. The more genteel may prefer to employ single-use cotton balls and pack them out.

WATER PURIFICATION

There are several reasonable means of water purification for new-school mountaineers. Let's start with chemical treatment and begin that discussion by eliminating any old-school treatment methods that use forms of iodine, chlorine, or hypochlorite (aka bleach, which is sold in camping stores for 50 times what you pay in grocery stores). Bacteria, protozoa, and viruses in the natural environment aren't generally floating freely in the water; a few may be, but most live in slime coatings, called *biofilm*, on the surfaces of waterborne material.

That's what makes them difficult to kill with chemicals, but easier to filter. Iodine and chlorine aren't completely effective in killing bacteria living on invisible "filterable material" in natural water sources, their purveyors don't claim effectiveness against cryptosporidium, and they certainly don't improve the water's flavor, even if you reduce residual iodine to iodide with vitamin C.

Treat

The chemical treatment that *is* effective is *chlorine dioxide*. In fact, ClO_2 is almost completely effective in killing bacteria, protozoa, and viruses, and even in getting rid of funky tastes. Any lingering scent of chlorine soon disappears. At this time there are only a few means of using chlorine dioxide in the backcountry, though it's commonly used in municipal water treatment plants. The Aquamira kit sold by McNett consists of two small dropper bottles of stuff that's mixed together, allowed to react for a few minutes, added to suspect water, and then allowed to do its thing for 15 minutes to an hour. The kit for treating a couple dozen gallons weighs a little over 3 ounces and costs around $14; you can break it down into smaller bottles to save an ounce. The Katadyn Micropur MP1 chlorine dioxide system consists of 30 one-liter tablets for about $14. Katadyn are candid enough to admit that killing crypto may take up to four hours.

A high-tech source of chlorine dioxide (or as the manufacturer says, "mixed oxidants") is a company called Miox. They've condensed their commercial treatment system, under military contract, into a cigar-sized, battery-powered device that uses only table salt. Mix up a salt solution, zap it, and add the result to suspect water. And, of course, wait; and, of course, killing crypto means a longer wait: four hours. This gadget, sold by MSR (owned by REI), also weighs a little over 3 ounces, but it costs a stiff $130; presumably it will last forever and will eventually pay itself off.

And for the truly high-tech, there are special, battery-powered ultraviolet lamps that will nuke every kind of critter, including crypto, in a pint of water in about 40 seconds. The catch is that the lamp dies after processing about 600 gallons, and the thing is heavy—about half a pound, a bit less with lithium batteries. The Steri-Pen goes for $200. Taste is not affected, for better or worse, but if there is light scattering gunk in the water you need to prefilter.

Filter

Ah, yes—filtration. When it comes to filtration, you'll find the claims are somewhat murky. Filtering out viruses doesn't work because they're so small, so some kind of iodine post-treatment is usually combined with filtration to claim effectiveness against viruses, but filters do work against crypto. The main sales pitch for filters is their effectiveness against giardia, but that's probably a baseless fear for mountaineers. To be effective, filters need an "absolute" pore size of 1 micron or less, referring to the guaranteed largest opening. What filters can do that other common treatments can't is remove suspended material, including glacial flour from glacier-fed streams and lakes; of course, the filter element quickly loads up when used this way. While there may be some fumbling, there's not much waiting with a filter, except in cold weather when your filter freezes solid.

Boil

The brute force method of boiling kills everything. In fact, boiling isn't even necessary; no pathogens or viruses can survive 140 °F (60 °C), the temperature of a very hot cup of coffee. Milk, a notably complex mixture, is pasteurized at about 170 °F (77 °C) for 15 seconds, mainly to kill TB; the USDA recommends consumers cook hamburger to 160 °F to kill the hardy E. coli, though most state laws require only 140 °F for restaurants. Water appears to start boiling at about 175 °F (80 °C); it boils at 185 °F (85 °C) at 15,000 feet. If you barely get the water to "boil" when stirred with a (then sterilized) spoon, the bugs are all dead, and you're done, no protracted boiling is required. Boiling consumes stove fuel and doesn't improve flavors or reduce particulate matter. Boiled water, like melted snow, tastes flat; you really want to put it into a bottle and shake some air into it. If you're going to heat the water close to boiling as you cook, you don't need additional means of sterilization.

Food poisoning is a brief illness having symptoms similar to waterborne illness: stomach pain or cramps, diarrhea, and perhaps vomiting and fever. It is caused by toxins produced by bacteria growing in food before it's eaten (in which case the effects can come on within an hour) or growing in the intestine after the food is eaten (when symptoms will appear in 7 to 15 hours). In most people, symptoms abate after a day or so without treatment. If you're curious, Staphylococcus aureus is an example of the first kind of bacterium, and Clostridium perfringens is an example of a bacterium that grows in food then produces toxins in the small intestine after it's eaten. Avoiding food poisoning means washing hands and utensils with soap before and after preparing food, keeping food that requires cooking separate from food that won't be cooked, and cooking food thoroughly and eating it hot. Warm, moist food is an invitation to bacterial growth. Travelers' diarrhea is a range of similar symptoms usually caused by a toxic strain of E. coli in food, not water. It comes on after about a week and lasts several days, usually clearing up without treatment. Intestinal illness caused by amoeba produces the same range of symptoms but may also result in blood or pus in stools. If you have diarrhea, increase your water intake to compensate for the dehydration; consider taking a 12-ounce course of bismuth subsalicylate (Pepto-Bismol) (the resultant black stools do not indicate bleeding) or loperamide (Imodium)—which slow down your gut in hopes of reducing water loss. Or, you could do nothing and just hope for the best. Note that although antibiotics (such as Cipro or Doxycilin) are effective in killing bacteria associated with intestinal illness, they don't kill parasites such as giardia and cryptosporidium.

Ignore

That leaves the best method: do nothing. Drinking water without any form of treatment is probably the most reasonable approach for mountaineers in North America because there aren't enough pathogens in alpine water sources to bother with. While you're recovering from the apoplexy this statement has caused, let me run down a few facts. There are tens, maybe hundreds of thousands of cases of intestinal illness each year in the United States. Nobody knows for sure how many, because most go unreported. Nobody knows exactly what organisms cause the problems, because diagnosis requires rare and sophisticated lab tests. The U.S. Center for Disease Control estimates over two million annual cases of giardiasis exposure in the United States. Nearly every victim recovers without treatment, save those with weak or compromised immune systems. Often such illnesses, including giardiasis, confer subsequent immunity to the specific pathogen. Of reported cases, only a tiny fraction are associated with backcountry travel, and of those essentially none can be pinned down to drinking the water. Rainwater runoff from municipalities is usually highly contaminated, but the dry alpine environment apparently significantly reduces the viability of pathogen cysts in mountain runoff, if any are present to begin with. What's the best way to contract an intestinal illness? Probably having a toddler in day care; next would be eating undercooked chicken or hamburger. Traveling to developed countries other than Scandinavia is also dicey; I've gotten sick drinking water in a pricey Parisian hotel—unthinkable in the United States, but de rigueur in most other places. Russia? Fuggedaboudit. But in the North American backcountry? Doesn't happen. There, intestinal illness including giardiasis is invariably caused by "oral-fecal contamination." That means poor personal hygiene—failure to wash your hands.

Surprisingly, people who are absolutely paranoid about water filtration and drinking giardia often fail to wash their own hands, and ensure their mess mates do, too, when eating and preparing food. They're content with cleaning their hands, cookware, and utensils by a process best described as "friction." Everyone's gut is full of alien organisms—some beneficial, some not. About a third of human fecal bulk is bacteria. It is estimated that 70 percent of folks have one kind of intestinal parasite or another. About 20 percent of the world's population harbors giardia, as does at least 5 percent of the U.S. population, including mountaineers. Back in the 1940s before water treatment became universal, almost every American was drinking giardia. Intestinal pathogens are found everywhere, yet somehow the whole world isn't perpetually on the can.

Found everywhere, that is, except in backcountry water sources. The actual science directly contradicts the advice of purifier manufacturers and hysterical land agencies, who may be practicing CYA or may simply be unaware. Where there are good data, reasonable wilderness lakes and streams of North America invariably prove to have lower concentrations of pathogens than municipal water (so you should filter your home water before you filter alpine water). Taking the California Sierra as an example where good data exist, the concentration of giardia cysts in the untreated Los Angeles aqueduct that drains much of the Eastern Sierra is so low, according to the LA Department of Water and Power, that you'd have to drink over 300 liters a day to have a 50 percent chance of contracting giardiasis. This makes sense, because giardia cysts die after a few weeks in water, and they're killed by drying or freezing—facts the Park Service and Forest Service probably forgot to mention. (Cryptosporidium, however, is much hardier.) It has been reported that the highest concentrations of giardia cysts found at test sites in the Sierra were a tenth of that in San Francisco municipal water. Similar rates have been reported outside the Sierra in other Western states and Canada. Even at the very highest concentrations reported you'd have to drink over 10 liters of untreated water a day to have a significant chance of contracting giardiasis.

I could go on, but there are a couple of points to highlight: You need to have a certain minimum number of pathogens or pathogen cysts in your gut at a given time to get sick. Your immune system can dispense with fewer, and backcountry water isn't a good place to find enough. With most pathogens, and certainly with giardia, even if you become infected, you'll most likely not develop significant symptoms. Even if you become infected, and even if you develop symptoms in a week or so, you'll likely recover without treatment.

And if you're thinking, "Eeuuww! I'd be drinking fish whiz," remember that your filter removes particles, not chemicals. You're already drinking fish whiz.

But Wait, There's More

Let's run down the rogue's gallery of waterborne intestinal pathogens. I've already introduced a common one, giradia lamblia, but it may not be the most worrisome. One thing that, for connoisseurs, somewhat distinguishes diarrhea caused by giardia is that giardiasis screws up one's fat metabolism, so the poop floats (not recommended for in-field diagnosis). You may also experience sulfurous burps, depending on the amino acid profile of your dietary protein. Otherwise the symptoms of all the nonviral critters are variations on a common theme: copious and persistent diarrhea, horrific flatulence, and stomach pain. The incubation period for giardia is a week or so but is, as for all such bugs, highly variable. Again, the wisdom among scientists is that coming down with giardiasis from drinking untreated water in the North American alpine backcountry is extremely unlikely. The drug most commonly used to treat giardiasis in Europe and developing countries, tinidazole (Pfizer's Fasigyn), isn't approved in the United States because there isn't enough demand to justify the expense of getting it through the FDA; get it from Mexico or wait for new drugs just over the horizon. The drug commonly used in the US, metronidazole (Falgyl), is a carcinogen and causes changes in genetic material; its side effects include diarrhea and stomach pain.

Next, let's dispense with *viruses*. They'd be hepatitis A or maybe poliomyelitis; neither are found in backcountry water. Rotaviruses, the most common cause of severe diarrhea among children, resulting in the hospitalization of approximately 55,000 children each year in the United States and the death of over 600,000 children annually worldwide, are transmitted by the oral-fecal route and not through surface water, and certainly not in North America. Echoviruses, another common type of enterovirus attacking mainly children, can be transmitted through water, though oral-fecal transmission is far more common; it's not a concern in alpine surface water. In short, there's essentially no danger of viral infection from ordinary surface water in North America, although the danger in developing countries is significant, and travel to them warrants precautions with all water and food. At any given moment about half the population of the developing world suffers from a water-related illness. Filtering is ineffective against viruses, due to the small size of the organisms, but boiling and chemical treatments readily nail 'em.

Campylobacter. "Campy" is one of the most common bacterial causes of diarrheal illness in the United States; the CDC thinks it affects about a million persons every year. It is particularly prevalent in poultry, with infection rates of about 100 percent; about half of purveyed poultry flesh is thought to become contaminated during preparation. Most people who get campylobacteriosis recover completely within two to five days without treatment; that's also the incubation period.

Cryptosporidium. "Crypto" is a protozoa found throughout the United States and is a common cause of intestinal illness. The infection rate in American cattle is near 100 percent; these animals alone excrete over four and a half tons of crypto spores annually. Those oocysts have a tough shell that enables them to resist many disinfectants and harsh environmental conditions, comparable to nasty forms of E. coli; giardia is a comparative wuss. Symptoms appear after about five days and last several days more. Some infected persons never develop symptoms; some people continue to shed spores months after symptoms disappear. Persons with healthy immune systems recover without treatment, which is a good thing because there is no treatment.

Other suspects. Additional waterborne pathogens that can and do cause illness in humans include Salmonella (food poisoning, enteric fever, or typhoid, depending), Shigella (dysentery), Yersinia, Aeromonas, Clostridium, Cyclospora, Pseudomonas, Entamoeba histolytica (amoebic dysentery), and E. coli. If that list doesn't convince you to pack Perrier, visit parts of the world where you can add Vibrio cholerae (cholera), another of the ways to get diarrhea and, as with its pals, one where most people who become infected don't get sick, and 90 percent of healthy adults who do become sick have only mild symptoms; however, severe symptoms can be fatal. Then, there's typhoid, leptospirosis . . .

Bottom line: if you come down with the symptoms (more than customary flatulence, big-time diarrhea, and stomach cramps) you've got one of these bugs, and you probably picked it up a week ago, although if you're infected you're more likely to be asymptomatic. It's hard to tell exactly which bug you've contracted, but more than likely you'll recover without treatment. Treat for dehydration due to diarrhea, but using anti-diarrheal drugs, such as Imodium (loperamide hydrochloride), may be contradicted for some pathogens—don't overdo it. If symptoms don't resolve spontaneously after a week or so, or if a high fever develops, see a doctor, who will probably be clueless.

The good news about all these pathogens is that, among the many cases of waterborne illness that the CDC reports each year, none come from any kind of water above several thousand feet elevation except for swimming pools, hot tubs, water parks (chlorine, as I've said, doesn't work well against giardia cysts), and, rarely, municipal water. The reason appears to be that there just aren't enough of these bugs, including giardia, in backcountry water to cause reportable problems.

Recommendations

▲ Practice good personal hygiene by washing your hands with soap after pooping and before preparing food; insist your companions do, too. Use the more effective waterless hand gel if washing with water is impractical.

▲ Most people who have giardia and other pathogens have no symptoms, so habitually prevent human feces and any other waste from entering watercourses.

▲ In the alpine environment of North America, particularly above about 8,000 feet (2,500 meters), nonstagnant water is safe to drink without treatment, especially if it obviously comes from snowmelt or a spring. Collecting water from the center of a flow reduces the concentration of potential pathogens by a factor of hundreds or thousands compared to the bottom or surface. I and just about everyone I know, including my toddler daughter, never treat such water and never become ill.

▲ Backpackers who collect water elsewhere, especially immediately downstream of persistent human habitation or livestock corrals, should treat suspect water used for drinking or preparing food with chlorine dioxide. If crypto is suspected (due to proximal livestock pens, for example), the treatment should be doubled and treatment time extended.

▲ Water that isn't clear or has an organic scent should be pre-filtered with a paper towel or paper coffee filter. Chlorine dioxide usually removes such scents.

▲ If you have known immune impairment or anticipate unavoidable exposure to serious pathogens, consider taking prophylactic antibiotics, under doctor's direction, during travel in developing countries. I have taken Cipro daily during travel in India and China when I knew I would be sharing food (eaten with hands), water (bottles passed around), and utensils (washed?) with ordinary folk, and I avoided illness. This strategy nukes your friendly personal bacteria, so it's not a general-purpose solution, and you must take your vitamins and consume active cultures to restore the benign flora in your gut when it's over.

▲ When collecting snow to melt, avoid snow at the surface and discolored snow. That pink or magenta tint ("watermelon snow") comes from algae that could make you queasy. And just what is that filmy stuff in melted snow that we call elk snot?

19
Performance Nutrition for Mountaineers

I gave [the cook] leave to kill our little dog, (Tlamath,) which he prepared in Indian fashion; scorching off the hair, and washing the skin with soap and snow. . . . Shortly afterwards . . . we had to-night an extraordinary dinner— pea-soup, mule, and dog.

That was John C. Fremont as he celebrated nearing the end of the first winter crossing of the Sierra Nevada in 1844. You can't really get to like the guy. Not only did he eat the pet dog that had accompanied him through months of adversity, but he and especially his guide, Kit Carson, were notably fond of slaughtering Native Americans, using sabers on the women and children to save gunpowder. Not much of a gastronome, either. Times change, thankfully, as have ideas about nutrition for mountaineers.

New research on the performance of athletes at altitude shows conclusively that what a mountaineer eats and drinks profoundly affects health, body weight and composition, ability to recruit en-

ergy stores, recovery time after climbing, performance on the mountain, and even cognitive acuity. Gone are the days when a mountaineer simply tossed a salami and a block of cheese into his pack, threw a rope over his shoulder, and suffered to the summit. New-school mountaineers take advantage of the progressing understanding of optimal endurance nutrition and new science on performance at altitude. Top-level mountaineers are among the most fit athletes in the world, but even weekend climbers on roadside attractions should think of themselves as endurance athletes—that will bring nutritional requirements into focus. You don't have to be a super alpinist to take advantage of the best science; even weekend peak baggers can perform better, enjoy themselves more, and climb more safely when their bodies are optimally nourished.

The body deals with nutrition differently during exercise and when recovering, so I'll separate my discussion into nutrition on the go and nutrition for recovery. I'll mix science and practical recommendations.

CALORIE CONSUMPTION

Energy consumption is measured in calories; for consistency with food labels I'll use dietary calories; they're each equal to 1,000 science lab calories (kcal), which are themselves equal to 4.2 joules, to be insufferably scientific. Calorie consumption measures how much energy your body is putting out to move, stay warm, digest food, and think about things. Maximum calorie consumption for a given weight is indicative of an individual's fitness. The calories burned by a couch potato are called *basal metabolism*; this daily figure is added to calories burned by activity. You can approximate your basal metabolism (assuming you are the reasonably fit climber I refer to throughout this chapter) by multiplying your weight in kilograms (pounds divided by 2.2) by 13.7, adding 66, adding 5 times your height in cm (inches times 2.54) and subtracting 6.8 times your age. Females use 9.6 × (wt. in kg) + 65.6 + 1.7 × (height in cm)–4.7 × (age in years). Simple enough? Above basal, most calories are burned in muscle. Even couch potatoes burn about 50 percent more than basal, just changing channels.

Mountaineering activities result in calorie consumption of from 300 to 800 calories per hour. Trained athletes can go as high as 1,000 cal/hr; world-class endurance athletes can kick out 1,500 cal/hr or more for limited periods. You can get at this number knowing that it requires about 5 calories to burn a liter of oxygen; if your VO_2max (detailed in the next chapter) is 50 ml/min/kg and you weigh 165 pounds (73.6 kg), that means your absolute maximum burn rate will be around 1,100 calories per hour (but you probably couldn't go that hard for a whole hour). Calorie consumption for an entire day can range to 6,000 or more at altitude and in the cold. Cyclists in the Race Across America may burn 10,000 calories for days on end, but the RAAM is basically a battle of metabolic capacity; mountaineering presents challenges that preclude anywhere near this level of exertion. My climbing buddies refer to 4,500 calories as an "El Cap day." That's a good number to figure for a hard, but not debilitating, day; a fit mountaineer could string together many of these days, given proper rest and nutrition. Many reasonably fit mountaineers will find a 4,000-calorie day challenging, and in a moderately sized group, attempting 4,500 will probably exhaust at least one member. Your vigorous hike up the trail to base camp may require only a 3,000-calorie day.

PARTIAL REPLETION IS BEST

During athletic activity your body will consume water, calories, and micronutrients (minerals, electrolytes). During high-output exercise it isn't possible or desirable to replace 100 percent of the water, calories, or electrolytes you expend. About 35 to 45 percent (call it a third to a half) repletion of water, calories, and electrolytes is optimum to avoid gastrointestinal violence and performance degradation (the gut bomb). Another way to say this is that humans can resupply energy from ingested food only up to a maximum of about 280 calories per hour (depending on lean body mass), irrespective of output. This means that the remainder burned during the day must be replaced at sit-down meals. Let's see how this partial repletion principle plays out, starting with water.

HYDRATION

With all those calories being burned, your body's core temperature will rise—exercise literally warms you up. A temperature of about 102 °F (39 °C) is to be expected, but your body must cool itself

---

VO₂MAX

By *high output* is meant exercise at or above about 75 percent of your VO_2max; that's vigorous, sustainable for several hours if you're a conditioned athlete, but still less than your maximum effort. Effort at 85 percent of VO_2max is the level of effort where lactate builds up in the blood of most athletes, indicating the onset of anaerobic exercise. Effort at 65 to 75 percent VO_2max, while still considerable, can be sustained much longer; athletes refer to this level or a bit less as an active recovery day. The high end of this range is the high end of the calorie consumption range, near or a little over 800 calories per hour. Moderate effort pulls the greatest fraction of energy from fat; higher effort requires more carbohydrate.

---

to prevent its core temperature from rising much higher. It does this mostly (at least 75 percent) by evaporative cooling of sweat. The efficiency of sweating varies with environmental factors (in high humidity you'll sweat, but the sweat won't evaporate and therefore won't cool you as much), and it may be supplemented by convective cooling (a cool breeze), but you can figure on sweating about a liter (34 oz) of water during each hour of exercise. Heat, humidity, and exertion can raise that by a factor of three, and it will also be higher in cold dry air and at altitude. Some of this water comes from glucose metabolism (as much as a pint per hour), but most comes from your store of bodily fluids, which become increasingly concentrated as you sweat unless you deliberately replenish your water loss.

Unreplaced water loss (dehydration) is a bad thing. Take a look at the table to see what happens.

Loss (as percentage of body weight)	Consequence
1–2%	You become thirsty, performance suffers, and your heat regulation mechanisms become less effective. This amount of loss is safe and to be expected.
3–4%	You feel parched, performance declines by 20–40%, and heat regulation becomes increasingly maladaptive.
5%	Heat exhaustion, headache, dry chills, decreased mental abilities.
7%	Heat stroke, collapse, hallucinations. You must cease activity and hydrate.
10%	Loss of consciousness. Preventing death requires medical intervention.

The importance of replacing water loss is reflected in the many admonitions to do so, from "drink before you are thirsty" to "hydrate or die." Drinking at rest stops falls short of optimum; it's much better to drink frequently from a handy bottle or a bladder inside your pack. To attempt to rehydrate at the end of the day is not only old-school; frankly it's stoopid in light of modern science—and it's ineffective because of the limit your maximum gastric emptying rate places on water absorption, to say nothing about the performance degradation you will inflict on yourself as you become increasingly dehydrated during the day.

How much *can* you drink? Your stomach can absorb up to a liter per hour if you keep it full (600 ml is about full) and if the weather is really hot and humid; otherwise figure on maximum gastric emptying of about 750 ml (25 oz) per hour with a filled stomach. It's actually possible to drink too much water; it will sit in your stomach and impair performance, and in extreme cases of exertion and sweating, it could lead to hyponatremia (debilitating sodium depletion) unless you also thoughtfully consume electrolytes. Twenty ounces per hour is a good number to use as a repletion target for just about any athlete on the go; in extreme circumstances, that would go only slightly higher, and you'd want to superhydrate with a glycerol supplement—beyond our scope. Don't kid yourself and think you can get away with less—your performance will suffer, and your body will, too. Even if you're drinking the right amount of water, it may not be doing you enough good because it's poorly absorbed in your stomach. For proper, maximal absorption (gastric emptying), your fluid intake needs to be isotonic.

Here's a summary of recommendations for adequate hydration:

▲ Drink 16 to 24 ounces (475 to 710 milliliters) of water, in several aliquots, during each hour of strenuous exercise. This is likely less than you are losing through sweating and breathing, but it's the most your stomach can absorb; be sure to make up the difference later.

▲ Drink an isotonic carbohydrate solution containing electrolytes.

▲ Drink another 80 to 100 ounces (2 to 3 liters) of water each day when you are vigorously active, in addition to your sweat replacement scheme.

▲ In cold weather, sweating will decrease, but dry air and high altitude cause more respiratory water loss for the same activity—up to twice as much as at sea level.

▲ Water is more readily absorbed when it's cold; freeze a bottle (or even smarter: half a bottle) or stuff yours with wet snow to keep your hydration source cool.

Osmotic pressure is the effect of water pushing through a membrane when there's a difference in osmolality on either side. *Isotonic* means that solutions on both sides of the membrane (such as a cell wall or stomach wall) have equal osmolality; that's what makes for fastest transfer of both water and chemicals. *Hypotonic* solutions have lower osmolality, and *hypertonic* solutions have higher osmolality than the reference solution (which in this case is bodily fluids). Blood plasma has an osmolality of about 300 mOsm/kg —that's the target, so we refer to physiologically isotonic as an osmolality of 270 to 330 mOsm/kg. Simplistically, osmolality is a measure of the concentration of *molecules* (not material) in a solution; don't worry about the units. Water comes in around 10, sweat about 200, cola about 600 (which is why some athletes drink it diluted by half), and some fruit juice close to 700. "Sports drinks" made by dissolving about 6 percent sugars in water are isotonic. A sports drink made with about 24 grams of glucose or fructose in 16 ounces of water will result in an isotonic solution, but 48 grams of sucrose (table sugar) would be needed to make the solution isotonic because each sucrose molecule weighs twice as much as a molecule of glucose or fructose (sucrose is actually a molecule of glucose bonded to a molecule of fructose).

▲ Use caffeine advisedly; in high doses it helps endurance athletes on the go, but it's a diuretic when consumed at rest. Some energy gels provide 20 to 40 milligrams (equivalent to about a fifth to a half of a cup of coffee) per serving. Read the labels carefully.

▲ When you calculate anticipated water requirements, work out what you'll carry, what you can obtain from streams or drips, and what you must obtain by carrying a stove and melting snow. If you have only the option of melting snow, it's not efficient to carry more than about three liters, or quarts, of water.

ELECTROLYTE REPLETION

In sweat you lose sodium, potassium, a little calcium, and smaller amounts of lots of other things. The sodium loss can be 1 or 2 grams for each hour of copious sweating. Potassium loss amounts to a few hundred milligrams per hour; other constituents are much less. Actual numbers are all over the map, because individuals have huge variations and heat acclimation reduces electrolyte loss. You'd suffer greatly if you tried to replace all the electrolytes you sweat out during the time you're active; you'd probably vomit or cramp up. A better strategy is to replace about 200 milligrams of sodium per hour of exercise along with about 100 milligrams of potassium. Be sure your hydration fluid provides that, or do it yourself. Morton Lite, available in grocery stores, is about 21 percent sodium and 24 percent potassium, the rest is chlorine. If you mix two parts, by volume, of ordinary table salt (39 percent sodium) with three parts Morton Lite, you'll have a mix that's 29 percent sodium and 14 percent potassium. A heaping quarter teaspoon of this mix weighs about 2 grams and an eighth of a teaspoon provides an hour's worth of the sodium and potassium you're looking for; precision is not required. Your body has stores to hold you for at least three or four hours, and just about anything you eat, including most sports drinks, contain sodium and potassium, so replacing electrolytes isn't normally an issue unless you're drinking a lot of pure water and sweating like a beaver. If you're obsessive/compulsive you could ensure, by your choice of maltodextrin gel or by another supplement, that you're not only getting the right amount of sodium and potassium but also calcium, magnesium, and manganese chelates. Be sure you're not overlooking the requirement to replenish electrolytes and that you restore daily net losses in the course of your sit-down recovery meals.

CALORIES ON THE GO

Remaining in your on-the-go nutrition planning is replacing the calories you burn. Here again, it's not possible to achieve complete repletion. You may be burning 600 to 800 calories per hour (more at altitude and in the cold), but the maximum your body can ingest and process while you're exercising is only 200 to 350 calories per hour, no matter how high your energy output. Any more will just hamper performance until it gets converted to fat. To get a slightly more accurate number for maximum repletion calories per hour, multiply your weight in pounds by 1.75 or figure 1 gram of carbohydrate per hour for each kilogram of body weight; a gram of carbohydrate yields four calories. Your most accurate personal number depends on your lean body mass, tolerance for food during exercise, and other individual factors. The best way to obtain those calories is from carbohydrates in liquid (solution) form. The solution should be isotonic for best absorption, but does this take care of the problem? Not quite.

Isotonic sports drinks contain 6 to 8 percent carbohydrates in the form of simple sugars. Simple describes pretty much all of them, and simple carbohydrates are pretty much all the same, too: "sugar" (table sugar: sucrose) is glucose + fructose, high fructose corn syrup is about equal amounts of glucose and fructose, and fructose and glucose are, well, glucose and fructose. A 6 percent sugar solution provides only about 120 calories in 20 ounces (carefully read the labels on those sports drinks). We're shooting for closer to 300 calories in 20 ounces for optimum repletion. If more sugar were dissolved in the water to deliver the needed calories, the solution will be hypertonic (not to mention obnoxiously sweet) and will mostly sit in your gut until you secrete enough water to dilute it—just the opposite of your hydration objectives.

Glucose Polymers = Maltodextrin

The answer is hydration fluid made with 18 to 24 percent maltodextrin. Maltodextrin is a carbohydrate, just like sugar, and it provides the same amount of energy—4 calories per gram or 113 calories per dry ounce—but it's molecules are mostly much bigger. Maltodextrin is basically partially digested corn starch; it contains about 2 percent glucose, maybe 6 percent maltose (glucose + glucose), and about 85 to 90 percent polysaccharides (complex, but not too complex, carbohydrates). Data suggest that glucose polymers such as maltodextrin are absorbed and used more quickly than plain old glucose, especially after an hour or so of exercise. You may see maltodextrin rated with a dextrose equivalent (DE) number (dextrose is another name for glucose); lower numbers mean faster absorption in the stomach. A DE lower than 20 is good. That 18 to 24 percent solution of mal-

todextrin will be isotonic and will quickly provide about 300 calories in 20 ounces of solution, with only small amounts of simple sugars and no fructose. And it's way cheap. Miraculous!

All Gooey about Gel

Another approach to drinking isotonic carbohydrate solution is to consume maltodextrin in the form of a concentrated gel (gel is the marketing term, but syrup would be more accurate), immediately followed by a drink of plain water. GU was the first such gel readily available in the United States, and it became famous among mountaineers; now there are many others, or you can make your own from bulk maltodextrin. Fortunately some of the others are formulated without fructose, most add electrolytes, but many make specious claims of benefits from trace ingredients. New-school mountaineers (and adventure racers) prefer to purchase maltodextrin gel in larger, 23-ounce (650 ml) bottles and transfer it to fist-sized, graduated 5-ounce flasks for on-the-go consumption. A 1-ounce gulp of gel (about 110 calories) washed down by two or three big mouthfuls of water (about 7 ounces or a third of your 20-ounce bottle) every 20 minutes is just the ticket to provide optimum repletion of both water and energy. The necessary electrolytes are formulated there, too. Set your watch to beep a reminder until you get into the 20-minute habit. If you find swallowing gel troublesome, you can dump the necessary amount into your water container to make your own energy drink (some flavors work better than others), or find new products that let you mix up maltodextrin-based sports drinks yourself. If you're not working at high output, cut back on the gel and water, but don't extend the 20-minute intervals.

Consuming maltodextrin this way has other benefits, the first being lower cost compared to the single-serving packets. There's no temptation to discard those empty packets or their opening tabs along the trail, and no need to fiddle around with the gooey empties or store them in your pack. Your water containers will hold only plain water, so they'll neither encourage the development of alien life nor preclude use of the water for other purposes. And there's no complexity if you add more water or snow to your water container. Finally, maltodextrin doesn't keep my teeth full of sugar or create the scum and aftertaste in my throat the way sports drinks do, but maybe that's just me. There are a couple of practical cautions: some of those little flasks leak, so test them out first in zip-seal baggies, and the gel gets very thick in cold weather, so keep your working flasks close to your body for warmth.

But What about GORP?

Good old raisins and peanuts is definitely old-school. Trail mix is mainly low-grade fat and low-grade protein, and it's difficult to digest, however yummy you may think it tastes—check the nutritional contents on the label. Don't eat GORP or its variants for on-the-go nutrition. In general, for optimum performance, don't eat fat and don't eat solid foods of any kind, including energy bars, during high-output exercise. Those bars claim to be balanced for daily nutrition, not for consumption during vigorous exercise, and even that claim is questionable. Always aim for mountaineering food that's high in carbohydrate and low in fat.

Don't put your calculator away just yet. Let's look a little closer at mountaineering nutrition, starting with a digression that will lead to sit-down nutrition planning.

Riding the Krebs Cycle

Carbohydrate metabolism can be viewed simplistically as the conversion of glucose to work in your muscles. Muscles can't simply pull the required glucose out of your blood stream because the limited amount there would be depleted in a few minutes of hard work. Since your brain runs on glucose and doesn't store any, depleting glucose from your blood would be, well, brainless. Running out of glucose (the "bonk") does indeed lead to cognitive dysfunction, though in males the principal cause of that may be testosterone oversufficiency. Instead of relying solely on blood storage, your body stores glucose in the liver and muscles in the form of glycogen, a polymer than can readily be converted back to glucose. Male athletes store about 90 grams of glycogen in their liver and 400 grams in muscle (about 2,000 calories total); female athletes store about three-fourths of that. Attempting to increase these stores is called carbo-loading—a shift to a higher fraction of dietary carbohydrate calories in the day or so before an event lasting more than an hour. Even this energy store will be exhausted after a few hours of hard exercise, so replenishing as much as possible—as much as the body can accommodate—during exercise is crucial for maintaining high output effort for an extended time. Replenishing the remainder of your glycogen debt with sit-down recovery meals is crucial if you expect to continue high-output effort on successive days.

THROWING FAT ON THE FIRE

The relative contributions of fat and carbohydrate to energy vary with exercise intensity. At low exercise effort your carbohydrate needs can be obtained from blood glucose and the conversion of glycogen. As your body continues hard exercise and faces depleting glycogen stores, the balance shifts to other energy sources: fat and protein. At effort near 40 percent of VO_2max the availability of fat for energy reaches a peak, but the actual utilization of fat peaks at about 60 percent of VO_2max. A single pound of body fat provides about 3,500 calories, so don't worry about running out. The balance of fat versus carbohydrate used for energy shifts when an athlete is exposed to altitude and then re-adapts during acclimation. Burning fat is less efficient than the conversion of carbohydrates to energy, and fat can't be converted directly to glucose or glycogen. Nevertheless, body fat becomes the fuel of choice during moderately hard exercise lasting more than a few hours. Then it should provide around two-thirds of your caloric requirements. Ingested fat inhibits gastric emptying and lowers blood glucose levels, so avoid consuming it during exercise. Conversion of fat to energy requires glucose, so when glycogen and blood glucose are thoroughly depleted, fat conversion nearly stops, and your body consumes muscle for energy—that's bad. Promoting the conversion of fat to energy is the challenge. There are plenty of supplements that claim to promote fat utilization, caffeine among them, but the biggest factor in building your body's propensity to make fats available for conversion to energy is protracted, regular endurance training—unwelcome news for couch potatoes, who were hoping for a pill.

Fat deserves a place in your recovery meal, but not because you're ever likely to run out of this important energy supply during a typical extended outing. Fats containing omega-3 fatty acids help replete the intramuscular triglycerides that are a significant energy source during extended exercise, and fats in your diet support fat-soluble vitamins and supply essential fatty acids for things like hormone (testosterone) synthesis. Fat in your dinner also seems to keep you warmer at night. Don't over do it by eating lots of fatty foods on longer, higher climbs; that old-school approach is nutritionally unsound. Getting an unnecessarily high fraction (more than 30 percent) of your sit-down energy from fat instead of carbohydrate tends to exacerbate the symptoms of altitude illness. On the other hand, mountaineering shouldn't be thought of as a weight-loss or fat-reduction program, even though that often happens. There is anecdotal evidence that your body, when nutritionally stressed, attempts to spare its fat stores but that this mechanism can be fooled by eating a dollop of fat. I think I've seen this myself, based on the olive oil that's in my "ten essentials for cooking," but it's for sure that your body won't efficiently convert fat to energy if glycogen has been depleted and you're in a state of bonk. I'll spare you more complex details on fats, triglycerides, and essential fatty acids except to offer my personal admonitions to favor liquid vegetable and fish fats (oils) and to avoid solid animal fats, processed and hydrogenated fats, and tropical oils.

PROTEIN—YOU EAT WHAT YOU ARE

Protein, too, is thrown into the cooker to produce glucose during endurance efforts. About 10 to 15 percent (call it $^1/_8$) of expended energy comes from the conversion of protein to glucose, a very inefficient process called gluconeogenesis. When I say protein, I mean your muscles. The amount you burn going full tilt is about an ounce (28 g) per

hour—a few pills won't replace it. Ideally, you'd replace protein in liquid form during any vigorous exercise lasting more than a few hours, but this proves to be problematic in practice, and protein can be difficult to digest when on the go. Once again, the best you could do is partial repletion. Because it's difficult to maintain protein balance during exercise, it's absolutely essential to replace it conscientiously in your sit-down recovery meals.

Protein is a class of complex molecules composed of amino acids; the ones that humans can't synthesize are called essential amino acids. The amino acids most important to building or rebuilding muscle are leucine, valine, and isoleucine, in the ratio of 1:1:2. These are called the *branched chain amino acids* (BCAAs). Ideally you'd just add these to your hydration plan in order to avoid burning muscle for energy (catabolism—a bad thing). Throw in some alanine, too. There are numerous studies that show that supplementing these amino acids during recovery spares muscle mass, prolongs the ability for high-output exercise, and even improves mental function, even though it doesn't boost raw performance. And they don't taste too bad. The problem is that the amount of BCAAs you'd have to consume on the go (about 25 percent of 10 percent of the El Cap day calorie expenditure, or 5 to 10 grams per hour during exercise) is economically infeasible. You're going to have to consume protein and break it down into amino acids yourself in order to get the BCAAs you need. There are several options.

You might think that a whole protein such as meat or eggs would be your first choice. You'd be wrong. There are several ways to rank protein sources according to how efficiently they provide the amino acids humans need and whether certain components are available undenatured, not just whether the protein has a desirable amino acid composition; one such index is the Protein Digestibility Corrected Amino Acid Score. At the top of the quality list is *whey protein*. Cow milk is about 6.5 percent protein; of that, 20 percent is whey protein, and the balance is casein (or "curds" as Miss Muffet sat down to eat). Roughly 25 percent of whey protein is BCAAs in approximately the correct ratios. There are several ways of refining whey protein, a byproduct of cheese manufacturing, and the results find their ways into supplement powders and protein bars along with other often unidentified bulk protein sources. Cross-flow microfiltration whey isolate is apparently the best form, made by a process patented by Glanbia Nutritionals. It is available with 99 percent undenatured protein. Whey "concentrates" are less concentrated and cost half as much.

Next on the list is soy protein in its various qualities. Then conventional whole protein from egg whites followed by meat protein (light skinless chicken and fish). Casein is down the list, too. Soy doesn't build muscle quite as well as whey and doesn't have as favorable a balance among the BCAAs, but it causes less ammonia waste, so soy might be the choice for consumption during or immediately before exercise. It also contains phytochemicals that are proving to have numerous health benefits. In principle, partially digested (hydrolyzed) protein would be the best form to consume for easy assimilation during exercise; in practice, the taste of hydrolyzed protein is a gastronomic disaster. Last on the quality list is whatever protein you eat in the course of casual consumption—catch-of-the-day protein.

Various formulas have been offered for daily protein requirements, but it's clear that athletes need more than couch potatoes. Plan on 1.2 to 1.7 grams daily per kilogram of body weight (about 0.5 to 0.8 grams per pound), depending on exercise intensity and the quality of the protein; teenage athletes need more. This, as always, refers to dry weight. It's a surprisingly large amount of protein by the time it's eaten (a McDonald's Quarter Pounder contains less than 30 grams of dry protein). Drink the suggested amount of water to ensure removal of uric acid waste from protein metabolism.

Among the protein and amino acid supplements you may come across, you'll see glutamine. It's the most plentiful amino acid in the body and in wheat protein; claims have been made that supplementing 5 grams before and after workouts, along with BCAAs, helps increase muscle growth. The actual science is inconclusive, and I'm unconvinced that quality whey protein wouldn't do the same thing better.

REALITY NUTRITION AND ALTITUDE

I recognize that not all mountaineers will burn 4,500 calories every day of their outing, and that the optimal nutrition I'm describing here may be difficult for many to achieve. I've presented it as the best recommendation current science has to offer for protracted, high-performance, high-output exercise. Then there's reality.

One aspect of reality is that everyone's appetite suffers at altitude. Many climbers lose 1 to 2 pounds per week, often several times that in the first week of an expedition at altitude. Caloric needs increase by 10 percent or more above 10,000 feet, but appetite goes down by at least that amount. There are many reasons for this, principally "hyperbaric hypoxia," but it's common for mountaineers to consume 60 percent or less of the calories they expend—that's a worry. Cramming enough food down your throat when you sit down to eat is difficult, but essential. This problem is not to be taken lightly; addressing it requires deliberate and concerted dietary management and forced eating, especially on extended outings at high altitude. You may hear statements along the lines of "any calories are good calories at altitude," but the more you succumb to junk calories, the more your performance will suffer. Strive to maintain a high-carbohydrate diet, even though you must force down powders and gel in addition to tolerable real food. On short trips you can ignore dietary recommendations and just eat whatever tastes good enough so that you'll eat enough, irrespective of any nutritional profile—live off the fat of your waist. On longer outings, and especially at altitude, you need to plan much more thoughtfully for total calories, caloric balance, and palatability.

A DOG'S BREAKFAST

Well, let's hope not. Backpackers may have the luxury of preparing elaborate cooked breakfasts, but climbers usually need to get going as soon as possible, often before daylight. Our breakfasts tend to be, as Duncan Hines said, "the bolt it and beat idea of dining." A big breakfast, concocted without regard to glycemic index, needs to be given several hours to make it out of the stomach before exercise commences. If that amount of time isn't in the cards, perhaps because you wisely conclude that sleep is more important, take more care to eat breakfast thoughtfully. If you're on a short casual climb, cold pizza makes just as tasty a breakfast in the mountains as it does at home; it beats Oak Meal or Cream of Weeds. I avoid cooking breakfast to save time and fuel; I've learned to tolerate body builder powder in cold water—sort of a high-tech powdered instant breakfast mix without fructose. If you haven't put away that calculator and want to follow the best science, start your day with a light carbohydrate and protein breakfast about a half hour before you hit the trail; that snack would contain about 50 grams of carbohydrate and 5 to 10 grams of soy protein. If you start your day with a big slug (two ounces) of energy gel, wait until you've started warming up. Whatever you eat for breakfast, don't eat too much; that would bog you down, and you'll be throwing more fuel on the fire as soon as you get moving. If you expect a hard, hot day, ensure that you are fully hydrated by slugging down a 20-ounce bottle of isotonic water about two hours before the intensity begins.

NUTRITION ON THE GO

Once you're moving and warmed up, begin your on-the-go nutrition and hydration plan; go easy on the gel in the first hour. After the first hour, maintain the 250 to 300 calories from maltodextrin gel and 16 to 24 ounces of water, spread out over each hour. If you're clever, you could add 20 to 40 calories from soy protein per hour (about a half ounce of protein stirred into a 5-ounce flask of gel), but the science is not entirely conclusive on the real value of doing so. I find that the gel regimen keeps me going, but doesn't keep my ribs from banging together once breakfast fades from memory. That's the purpose of lunch. Lunch should not be a big calorie hit; just something quick and easy to get down that hopefully emphasizes protein—another bolt-it-and-beat-it snack. My current favorite is tuna repacked into a 150 ml specimen jar (ask your doctor), dumped into a French roll and slathered with mayo from those little food service packets. One of my partners likes cream cheese and jelly on a bagel. Pick your personal favorite snack, but make it easy to digest and, unlike my examples, deemphasize fat. Some folks like Intermountain's Bear Valley Meal Packs—basically oversized energy bars that pack over 400 calories into not quite 4 ounces; they have about the same amount of protein as that can of tuna, but its quality is unknown and probably not as good. Cooking is definitely out unless you also need to melt snow for water. Don't be surprised that you become chilled as your blood shifts from muscle to gut, or that you feel like it's nap time right after lunch; minimize these effects by eating light and fast. After your lunch snack, it's back to the carbo and water routine.

GET STARTED AS SOON AS YOU STOP

When things wind down, whether it's back in base camp or setting up a new camp, you may be tempted to ignore your empty stomach and begin some important project. That would be a mistake. Immediately after vigorous activity stops is by far the best time to refuel for recovery; the longer you wait, the less efficiently you'll replace expended glycogen and conserve muscle protein. The best plan would be to consume a concoction of 200 grams of complex, high-glycemic-index carbohydrates, or about 1.25 grams per pound of body weight (an amount equivalent to about eight servings of energy gel), along with 50 grams of whey protein, washed down by plenty of cold water. In other words, a carb to protein ratio of four to one. These amounts are higher than were once thought effective, but ingestion immediately after exercise is well accepted. The idea is that the protein both promotes repair of metabolized muscle and causes a heightened insulin release that enhances glycogen repletion; this protocol also reduces illness, reduces muscle and joint problems, and reduces susceptibility to heat illness. Details are being actively researched. Mix gel plus whey protein powder in advance, so that you can scarf it down as soon as possible; it will have the consistency of runny peanut butter—the sweetest-tasting peanut butter ever to cross your tongue. If getting that down is challenging no matter how hungry you are, it's nearly as effective to consume half the amounts immediately after you stop and finish off the remainder over an hour or so as you are setting up camp, building an igloo, or preparing that seven-course sit-down meal. Promptly getting glucose into your blood is what's most important to glycogen repletion, so eating a complete meal soon after you stop exercising, especially one containing fat and fiber, is much less beneficial than eating only carbohydrate and protein solution. If you opt for something other than maltodextrin gel to supply carbo calories, look to high-glycemic-index carbs that go quickly into your blood stream, such as quick-cooking rice or instant potatoes; avoid fat until later and always avoid fructose altogether. Be wary of one down side: you may get an insulin spike and crash that can lead to a party of fatigued mountaineers who are very, very crabby.

REPLETION STARTS WITH WATER

If you've successfully replaced 35 to 45 percent of your fluids, energy, and electrolytes consumed during exercise, your first concern at the end of the day will be to drink enough water to rehydrate and support optimal renal function. This isn't the same thing as allowing yourself to become dehydrated during the day and then attempting to rehydrate afterward—that won't work. Don't depend on your sense of thirst; it may be depressed by exertion at altitude. Aim for 0.5 to 0.6 ounces of water

for each pound of body weight (35 ml/kg), in addition to your on-the-go intake. You'll have to consume about 150 percent of what you intend to replace, due to losses from normal urination, high-altitude-induced diuresis (maybe an extra half to a full liter per day), and increased respiration losses (up to 1.5 liters or quarts of water per day; twice what you'd see at sea level, and at very high altitude, twice that again). Some water is also lost in feces, and some is gained as a byproduct of glucose metabolism. Alcoholic beverages don't count, and coffee counts only half, because they are diuretics. Plan on 2 to 4 liters or quarts per day, made isotonic with dissolved carbohydrates unless consumed during meals, in addition to your on-the-go hydration intake. Failure to achieve adequate hydration will depress your appetite even more than it will already be depressed by high altitude, and can augment symptoms of altitude illness. The only down side is that you'll pee like a racehorse, but that's a good thing if you're careful to replace minerals and soluble vitamins that are washed out. In Chapter 20, Training for Mountaineering, you read that a principal gain of cardiovascular training is an increase in circulatory capacity; when you lose water, the bulk of the loss comes from blood plasma, so maintaining hydration is absolutely essential to maintaining cardiovascular fitness on an extended outing.

THEN TOTAL CALORIES

Next, consider total energy replacement. We've been looking at 4,500 calories as the burn on a solid day of mountaineering, but it can easily be more. Some of that you've already replaced during your on-the-go nutrition/hydration scheme. The optimum ratio of macronutrient calories is about 65 to 70 percent (two-thirds) from carbohydrates (at 4 calories per gram), 20 to 30 percent (one-fourth) from fat calories (at 9 calories per gram), and 10 to 15 percent (one-eighth) from protein (at 4 calories per gram). These ratios work out to around 2.1 pounds (960 grams) of total dry weight per day to hit 4,500 calories. Even "dried" food contains 5 to 10 percent water, so you end up looking at 2.25 pounds or about one kilogram per day of total "dry" weight, on-the-go plus sit-down recovery food. Interestingly, this is the same weight worked out through trial and error by thoughtful mountaineers, long-distance backpackers, and others who go hard for days on end. If you ignore the science and eat an old-school diet, you'll have to accept suboptimal performance as your reward.

Typical appetite loss at altitude, especially in the first few days, means that getting this amount of nourishment into your gut will be a challenge. Of more scientific concern is that 650 grams (23 ounces), or about 2,600 calories, is about all the carbohydrate that a human can convert to glycogen stores daily. Any carbohydrates eaten in excess of that get converted to fat; fructose in particular is more likely to be converted to fat rather than glycogen. The precise amount you can convert depends on your lean body mass and level of exercise, so if you're a really big guy and go very hard all day, that figure could go up by 50 percent, but you get the picture. This limit, in combination with an optimum balance of fats, protein, and carbohydrates, places a total limit on daily useful caloric consumption of around 4,400 calories, irrespective of the amount you actually burn. This figure matches nicely with our model El Cap day, but the 2,600 calorie maximum places a limit on attempts to carbo-load—you can end up just fat loading, and for most of us, carbo *un*loading is a greater concern.

Those 6,000-calorie burns hauling heavy loads on long Denali days will cost you. Hopefully the cost will be in body fat that you can do without, but don't compromise on protein, or you'll lose muscle, too. On a day like that aim for 0.8 grams of protein per pound of body weight. That's around 140 grams (5 oz) dry weight; consuming that amount from native sources can be daunting.

REALITY DINING—AGAIN

On typical outings of a day or so, the guide for a mountaineer's dinner is comparable to that for breakfast: forget nutritional science and eat what tastes good and is easy for you to digest. For dinner, eat foods that are easy to prepare, and eat all your appetite will tolerate. I've been discussing

If about 2.25 pounds per day is all the food you can reasonably metabolize, why carry more? Some authorities, such as the National Outdoor Leadership School (NOLS), advocate carrying a lot more, presumably to increase comfort and safety, but there's a good argument that mountaineers would be better off carrying extra insulation instead of extra food. This is a nontrivial judgment, because the ability to carry light and move fast is unquestionably critical to safety in the mountains (as well as success and fun). Carrying extra food, especially food that requires extra time and fuel to prepare, works against the new-school fast and light style and could very well result in decreased safety (and success), compared to a party that carries only the fuel and food weight they require and that speeds their climb by doing so.

---

powder as if it were food, and indeed powders and gels make good and easily computed adjuncts to real food, but their sparse profile of micronutrients, absence of components like soluble fiber, and marginal palatability make them unsuitable for steady main courses or as substitutes for that rarity of modern life, a healthy diet. Unless you're an astronaut or nutritional scientist, eat well-balanced real food when you can, even though you consume powder when it's more convenient during critical stages of a climb.

On short outings you'll be eating to accommodate your attitude more than attempting to maintain a perfect energy balance. Stop by a bun-and-run on the way to the trailhead, if that's your pleasure. On excursions of only a day or two, it may be more efficient to carry ready-to-eat sandwiches and forgo cooked meals and the means of cooking them. If cooking is going to happen, I like to bring semi-prepared food, like fresh tortellini, a prepared sauce in a zip-seal bag, and freshly grated Asiago cheese. On the outing this is easier to prepare than freeze dry, and it actually cooks faster and so uses less fuel (I often get by with a home-made hexamine stove, and you can pour boiling water right into a reusable O.P. Sak zip seal baggie just like into a freeze dry packet); I'm willing to carry an extra ounce or two to get the flavor that my appetite needs for encouragement. On longer outings I bring home-dried delicacies. Most back-

Committed mountaineers, like ultra-endurance athletes and adventure racers, need to optimize their performance nutrition, even at the expense of satisfying dining. For them, powders represent the best nutrition at minimum weight—but this only applies to exceptionally well-formulated powders accompanied by supplements that provide the missing micronutrients. For high-output effort over a few critical days of a serious climb, the mainstay powder would contain mostly maltodextrin, about 15 percent of calories from soy protein isolate, a small amount of well-chosen fat (flax or olive oil, maybe lecithin), 200 mg/hour total sodium and about 100 mg/hour potassium, perhaps 250 mg/hour calcium, and 300 to 400 mg/hour of phosphate in the form of tribasic sodium phosphate. To this you'd expect to add carnosine, carnitine, choline, and antioxidants such as lipoic acid, vitamin E, vitamin C, and the other questionable suspects that supplement companies might be hawking. Including soluble fiber would be a good idea, too; it will help keep you regular as well as give you a leg up in flatulence competitions with your climbing partners. I know this sounds like the formula for Elmer's Glue, but trust me. Products like these are being formulated for ultra-endurance athletes who demand optimal nutrition during multiday, high-output events—just don't expect to find them in your local health food store.

---

country cooks follow a similar principle: if you carry spicy condiments, you can make a tasty meal even out of grass and pinecones (well, I think I've seen it done). I like fresh garlic for its flavor (and its claimed benefits for altitude performance) and fresh Italian parsley for its durability in the backpack and ability to impart a fresh taste to any entrée, even freeze dry. Speaking of freeze dry, survivalists may swear by it but it's very old-school for mountaineers. Because freeze-dry packaging is so wasteful, it has no weight advantage over carefully selected dry food, and its cost is certainly out of proportion to its nutritional value. As an example, Bear Creek powdered soups average ¾ of the weight for the same number of calories from freeze dry. If you shop carefully, you can find plenty of tasty dried foods at your supermarket; start with flavored basics: instant potatoes, instant rice, and ramen noodles; then work your way into exotica. Look for foods that require minimal cooking time and no boiling. The boiling temperature of water

drops by about 1 F° for every 540 feet of altitude increase (1 C° for every 275 meters), so boiling times increase (about double at 5,000 feet), but not cooking times at lower temperatures. The lesson is to avoid foods that require actual boiling. Anytime you select prepared foods, check the Nutrition Facts label to see just how many fat versus nonfat calories you're getting; be prepared for disappointment.

If you're truly interested in optimum nutrition for athletic accomplishment, you'll have to forgo the cavalier advice I've given about eating whatever tastes good. What you eat has a tremendous effect on your physical and mental performance. An athlete cannot hope to approach her full performance potential unless she eats a carefully planned diet. Such a diet would be one that all agree is "healthy," but few people actually follow. Start by dumping any fashion diet you may be on or considering and aim for the caloric balance among protein, carbohydrate, and fat that I've already given. You'll have to get your protein from very lean meats (not beef) and isolates, get your sedentary carbohydrates from low-glycemic-index, complex sources, and minimize fats, especially processed and animal fats. Ditch fructose, even in honey but especially the omnipresent high-fructose corn syrup. Plan on eating lots of cruciferous vegetables (brassica), tomatoes, and highly pigmented vegetables—which will also help you get a healthy 35 grams of fiber each day. The benefits from such a diet begin to kick in after a couple of months. The challenge for mountaineers is that such foods have high water content and cook slowly, making them impractical for extended outings if prepared fresh—hence my recommendation to prepare your own meals and dry them in a food dehydrator. Americans who actually adhere to such foods are dietary deities.

CATCHING UP ON ELECTROLYTES

I haven't yet mentioned replacing electrolytes lost in sweat that were only partially replaced during your on-the-go scheme. If you eat a reasonably balanced sit-down meal, you'll replace basic electrolytes without supplementation, along with cal-

There are plenty of recipe books for backcountry cooking, and I've listed a few in the Resources appendix. The key is creativity and individual expression, and probably nothing expresses individualism more than the varied diets among mountaineers. Most mountaineers don't like to cook, but they all like to eat. One of the best ways to have tasty meals on the mountain is to make a variety of flavorful meals at home and dry them in a food dryer, so you can just add water and prepare one-pot meals quickly, even on a winter outing when cooking by headlamp is the least fun of all. It takes no more fuel than freeze-dry, maybe less as no boiling is required. Package your results in a reusable O.P. SAK (odorproof zip-seal bag) from Watchful Eye Designs; you'll not only eat better, but you'll save money. There are special techniques for this type of home cooking, such as cutting things up more finely than normal, avoiding oils (which can be added when rehydrating), and selecting special ingredients. You can even take the bachelor approach and dry ready-to-eat grocery store casseroles, though you may have to dice up large chunks of vegetables, pasta, and animal flesh to keep the cooking time down. You may want to raise the carb calories to 65 percent with cooked rice or instant mashed potatoes. The results are worth the effort when you are dining sumptuously as your companions are force-feeding themselves with crispy bits of cold freeze dry.

---

cium, magnesium, and most of the other minerals. It doesn't hurt to supplement electrolytes, because any excess washes out quickly, but don't overdo it in hopes of eliminating cramps or out of sweat-loss paranoia. One serving of just about anything contains around 300 mg of potassium; bananas are not nearly as good as preserved dried fruit. An easy source of known amounts of potassium is Morton Lite salt, which is about 21 percent sodium and 24 percent potassium (table salt is about 40 percent sodium; the remainder is chlorine); you might add extra Morton Lite to your mountaineering meals, but drink plenty of water. Eating a teaspoon of salt doesn't work.

NUTRITIONAL SUPPLEMENTS

There is a wide range of substances subsumed under the moniker of vitamins or nutritional supplements. Since athletes require more food for energy and recovery, you might expect that they'd benefit from consuming more than the Dietary Reference Intakes (formerly the Recommended Daily Allowances) of vitamins. In fact, it appears that athletes benefit from having several times the RDAs (or DRIs) of vitamins in their diets, although there's no commercial incentive to work out the exact amounts and benefits for individual micronutrients. There's a wide spectrum of opinion on the general subject of supplementation. Medical professionals have been schooled to preach that if you eat eight to ten servings of fresh vegetables daily, you'll get the recommended allowances, and that's all you need. That view is definitely old-school and is falling out of favor except among drug-dispensing professionals and within the government, their advocate. The problem with recommending a healthy normal diet is that a normal diet isn't healthy. Anti-vitamin folks and drug companies constantly produce unresearched scare stories about vitamin toxicity; these inevitably prove to have nothing to do with vitamins and the stories fail to compare the danger to, say, aspirin, which kills thousands of people every year. My favorite scare stories are about how you might die from taking vitamin A supplements. If those stories were ethically honest, they'd have to say that the only instances of vitamin A toxicity have been caused by eating the livers of animals who store high concentrations of retinal ester (sharks, dogs, and, principally, polar bears), so the ethically honest conclusion isn't "so don't take supplements"; it's "so don't eat too much polar bear liver." The conservative American Medical Association is now recommending a one-a-day multivitamin in order to promote general health and even recommends omega-3 fatty acids in supplemental form. Nor do I care much for the concern about "expensive urine"; if you want truly expensive urine, drink beer. At the other extreme are supplement fanatics, who can lose sight of sound science. I'm closer to the latter view—a confessed recovering supplement guinea pig—but I wouldn't recommend it as a place to start. Micronutrient supplementation is a lifelong daily commitment to long-term benefits, combined with skeptical evaluation of mostly bogus commercial claims.

One "supplement" that's now in favor is aspirin; the conventional wisdom is to take one baby aspirin (81 mg) daily to prevent heart attacks and some forms of cancer and maybe to counter some consequences of chronic NSAID use. Some mountaineers increase that to a full 325 mg every 8–12 hours when over 10,000 feet, in order to relieve headache due to high-altitude illness; don't take that much aspirin for many days unless you really need it.

The B-complex vitamins are required for production of energy and for rebuilding muscle after exercise. There is evidence that, for athletes, the requirements are several times more than the usually quoted recommended daily allowances (or dietary reference intakes). One B vitamin, riboflavin, or B2, turns your urine bright amber, almost fluorescent in high mountain sunlight. In my opinion that's a good indication that you're getting enough water-soluble B vitamins; consider a multivitamin supplement if your urine is merely "straw colored" or "clear." On the other hand, downplay niacin (vitamin B3), if possible, prior to and during exercise, because it appears to reduce the metabolism of fat for energy.

Antioxidants protect cell membranes from oxidative damage; these include selenium, lipoic acid, vitamin C, and the fat-soluble vitamins E, D, and A, or beta-carotene, which the body converts to vitamin A. Since endurance athletes have 10 to 20 times higher oxygen consumption than typical sedentary television watchers, you might think that supplementation of antioxidants would be a good idea for us. The science isn't conclusive; some research finds appreciable but not dramatic benefits, and other research finds none. The studies that find no benefits are invariably conducted using laughably small doses compared to what supplementation enthusiasts consume. Studies at high altitude have shown that vitamin E improves exercise performance, and that vitamins C and E improve recovery after strenuous exercise. The amounts consumed were many multiples of the DRIs or RDAs—comparable to typical supplementation quantities. As far as I know, all the studies on antioxidants and mountaineers at altitude have shown beneficial results in terms of maintaining appetite and VO_2max, indicating that antioxidant supplementation is a good idea under these stressful conditions. Other than cost, there are no down sides.

Calcium supplementation is no longer controversial, especially for female athletes who eliminate dairy, restrict calories, or suffer menstrual dysfunction; the amount of calcium should be balanced with about half as much supplemental magnesium. Calcium supplementation has been shown to promote fat metabolism and help manage body composition, though the effects are modest. I suspect that vitamin D supplementation will soon be widely recommended, especially for dark-skinned people or those who bundle up all year. Supplementing trace minerals, such as selenium, germanium, manganese, chromium, vanadium, and boron, is becoming less controversial as they are depleted from tilled soil and therefore disappear from our food supply, but there's little evidence that supplementing them has ergogenic benefits for athletes. It's generally recognized that zinc consumption is below the 1989 RDAs for most of the American population. Zinc preserves immune function that's likely to be depressed in athletes. Zinc's also involved in growth, muscle building and repair, and energy production. Its best natural sources are animal protein and fats, which may be in short supply for mountaineers, and zinc is especially likely to be deficient in athletes who wisely adopt high-carbohydrate diets. Conservative supplementation of minerals is cheap and safe; if you're not sure of getting at least 20 mg of zinc daily, give serious thought to supplementation. Iron supplementation, on the other hand, is not beneficial except for the tiny fraction of the population known to be anemic, most of whom are female. If that's you, you need serious medical intervention starting with a blood test. In industrialized countries there are about twice as many men suffering iron oversufficiency compared to deficiency, and 2 percent of people of northern European descent have a condition known as hemochromatosis, in which damaging amounts of iron are retained in the body's organs. Iron promotes free radical production, a bad thing, and a high intake of iron, especially in combination with manganese supplementation, may be related to increased risk for Parkinson's disease—in addition to making you constipated. I recommend choosing multivitamin supplements that specifically exclude iron—an indication they're thoughtfully formulated according to modern science.

SPORTS SUPPLEMENTS

Beyond these basics there are a bazillion sports supplements vying for the wallets of endurance athletes, all claiming astounding benefits despite the small amounts of unproven active ingredients they contain—it's a multibillion dollar industry, after all. I consider myself well informed on these matters, and sympathetic, too, so I'll make a recommendation to get you started: save your money. Focus on training and the basic nutritional guidelines I've just offered—that's complex enough. Be happy that success in mountaineering depends on so many different factors that you can ignore any purported marginal gains from sports supplements. The other option would be to give it serious study in peer-reviewed journals; after a year or so you'll have done a lot of reading, will have incurred a hefty bill for broadband services, and may have shelves full of expensive supplements, but you'll end up making the same recommendation that I have. In arriving at the following comments on specific supplements, I looked at nearly 500 scientific articles, including review articles, in journals as recent as the winter of 2004; all the many other supplements that I don't mention that you may find being hawked by supplement manufacturers either have inconclusive or contradictory evidence supporting their effectiveness in human athletes, or when properly tested have been shown to have no significant benefit, or are dangerous. There are very few published studies on the effects of combining more than one supplement.

Sodium Phosphate

Phosphate loading has been studied for decades; it's been found to increase maximal oxygen uptake, raise anaerobic (lactate) threshold, increase power at anaerobic threshold, and improve endurance exercise capacity by 8 to 10 percent, without increasing heart rate or lactate production. That's an amazing benefit, comparable to blood doping with the banned drug EPO (erythropoietin), yet sodium phosphate is cheap and nontoxic. Sodium phosphate could be especially interesting to mountaineers, because it's been shown that EPO improves respiratory acclimation to hypoxia. Phosphate supplementation is effective for endurance efforts; it does not augment high-intensity intermittent exercise. The complete story of why phosphate loading is effective is still being worked out, but it seems to be more than its buffering effect on lactate. The loading that's been studied most consists of consuming one gram of trisodium phosphate (about a quarter to a half teaspoon, depending on the grind) four times a day for five days prior to your most important day; dissolve it in sports drink or orange juice because it's too caustic for many to keep down in pill form. Mix up an entire day's supply in advance, or even the complete loading amount. The benefits seem to last for about ten days.

There are several forms of sodium phosphate; the one shown to have considerable benefit for endurance athletes is the tribasic hydrate: trisodium phosphate dodecahydrate, $Na_3PO_4 \cdot 12H_2O$. That's right: plain old TSP, the caustic agent that was taken off the market as an industrial cleaner when it launched concerns about nonbiodegradable products. The main impurity is sodium hydroxide: drain cleaner. Of course, the studies on athletes have been done with food-grade TSP; it is Generally Recognized As Safe by the FDA and has been safely used for many years, particularly in processed cheese. Apparently potassium and calcium phosphate aren't effective, and it seems the dibasic sodium form used in the now discontinued PHosFuel probably isn't either, for reasons beyond my ken. Chronic excess phosphorous intake may cause calcium loss from bones, so phosphate loading should be restricted to only several times per year, and the loading period should not be increased lest your body overadapt and begin peeing out more phosphate than it's taking in. Phosphate is cheap, safe, effective, and legal.

Caffeine

Caffeine affects almost every organ system, the most obvious being the central nervous system. This stimulant increases alertness, reduces perceived effort during exercise, and decreases reaction time. At high doses (more than 15 mg/kg body weight), caffeine can also produce bradycardia, hypertension, nervousness, irritability, insomnia, and gastrointestinal distress. Many studies indicate that ingestion of caffeine can improve endurance capacity by as much as 20 to 50 percent in trained athletes engaged in moderate exercise. There are several mechanisms proposed for caffeine's effects; it appears that increased fat utilization and glucose sparing occur only in the first half hour of high-output exercise, but that's the most critical time. The overall caffeine benefit continues for a few hours at least. The effective amount is 3 to 9 mg/kg of body weight consumed 1 or 2 hours before exercise; this amounts to about 3 or 4 cups of strong coffee, although pills are used in tests because of interference from other compounds in coffee (drugstore caffeine pills contain 100 or 200 mg). People who regularly consume caffeinated drinks appear to experience much smaller ergogenic benefits from caffeine; the recommendation for them is to desist in caffeine consumption for a few weeks prior to the outing where they hope to enjoy its benefits. I've never observed this recommendation actually being practiced by coffee lovers. Although concern has been raised that consuming caffeine, a diuretic, may contribute to dehydration, the most recent studies show this doesn't occur during exercise. Side effects, particularly at doses above 6 mg/kg, include headache and insomnia (not to mention abdominal cramps and diarrhea), so use of caffeine by acclimating mountaineers may augment the symptoms of altitude illness.

Creatine

There's a great deal of excitement about creatine among strength athletes and body builders because of studies that show it increases muscle growth in the course of strength training. Recent studies have questioned whether all the benefits seen are really muscle growth or are mainly increases in extracellular water that looks like muscle because of the indirect means of measurement. Numerous performance tests have shown that creatine supplementation is safe, expensive, and beneficial for sprinters and athletes whose sports involve cycles of sprinting and jogging, such as soccer and perhaps climbing. Studies evaluating creatine for benefits in endurance exercise are mixed, with pure endurance performance apparently unaffected or even slightly diminished due to the weight gain creatine causes. Endurance athletes may nevertheless benefit in that creatine appears to aid carbo loading, and taking creatine and carbohydrates simultaneously has been shown to optimize both creatine loading and carbohydrate loading. Most endurance athletes also perform interval training, which creatine might help, and mountaineers frequently practice rock climbing where creatine would aid in specific muscle development and improved strength training adaptation.

The typical creatine-loading protocol is to consume 20 grams of creatine monohydrate (the phosphate form is poorly absorbed) each day in four doses of 5 grams spread throughout the day during the first 5 to 7 days—the "loading phase." Thereafter, during the "maintenance phase," only one dose of 2 to 5 grams is needed each day, as any additional creatine is excreted in the urine. Other protocols of 3 grams daily for a month have been found to be comparably effective.

ß-hydroxy ß-methyl Butyrate (HMB)

Hydroxy methyl butyrate is a natural metabolite of leucine; about 5 percent of the leucine in your body is converted to HMB each day (about 0.2 to 0.4 g of HMB). Supplementing with 1.5 to 3 grams per day of calcium hydroxymethylbutyrate has typically been reported to increase muscle mass and strength in untrained or elderly subjects initiating training; it doesn't appear to offer benefits to endurance athletes except perhaps to slightly delay onset of the lactate threshold or mitigate the catabolic effects of prolonged exercise. Gains in muscle mass are typically 1 to 2 pounds greater than controls during 3 to 6 weeks of training. HMB has a half-life of 2 to 3 hours after ingestion, so vendors recommend it be taken in several divided doses throughout the day (for example, 1 gram of HMB 3 times daily). Current research suggests that HMB may also enhance the benefits of creatine supplementation. Creatine worked about three times as well as HMB in increasing lean body mass during progressive resistance training, but the combo was almost twice as effective as that. In these studies the doses were 20 grams of creatine per day for a week, followed by two weeks at 10 grams per day, with 3 grams of HMB taken every day. Use of HMB as a supplement is heavily patented by Iowa State University, and all genuine forms must bear the U.S. Patent number 5,348,979.

That's it. If your favorite supplement didn't make the cut, sorry. At this time only these four have incontrovertible scientific backing for ergogenic benefits, though there are many other promising possibilities that may or may not eventually prove worthy of the claims that suppliers are making based on anecdotal evidence or studies of rats. Or maybe you'd prefer to spend your money and rely on the placebo effect.

VEGETARIAN MOUNTAINEERS

Just what kind of vegetarian you are has a big impact on how difficult it will be for you to maintain good nutrition under the demands of strenuous activity at altitude. Little of what I've covered precludes ovo-lactarians; they'll just have to be more deliberate than omnivores. Vegans, however, will have special difficulties getting the calories they need without becoming overloaded with fiber. Getting the necessary amino acids, particularly branched chain amino acids, will be especially challenging. The best strategy is to eat unprocessed grains and legumes with complementary protein compositions, the best-known combination being rice and beans. Tofu provides high-quality protein and other valuable nutrients, but it's comparatively heavy. Vegans may have to raise their total protein intake to compensate for incomplete digestion— not easy given the problem of appetite loss at altitude. If you're eating a vegetarian diet that consists primarily of grains, fruits, and vegetables, you're probably eating an unbalanced diet that will adversely impact performance at altitude. Cooking times for vegetarian foods are apt to be long, so emphasize precooked, dried meals and carefully calculate fuel consumption. Vegetarians are often at risk of low vitamin B-12, riboflavin, zinc, and calcium, stores of which are stressed by mountaineering. Iron is less available from vegetable sources, and some common vegetables actually lower its bioavailability. If you've chosen vegetarianism partly as an aid to weight control, you'll need to be especially attentive to nutrition. Take on the demands of serious mountaineering in small steps and monitor your body composition as you do. That's good advice for everyone.

20
Training for Mountaineering

That which does not kill us makes us stronger.

Nietzsche died of syphilis, not overtraining, but he was hitting on training's fundamental truth. The human body is an amazingly adaptable system. When stressed, it changes to better deal with that stress; in essence, it becomes a slightly different organism. Adaptation to stress means your body's hormonal systems change their chemical balances, and physical components of your body grow and change. Generally, adaptation doesn't mainly occur during the stress, but during recovery periods afterward. This means that planning your recovery is as important as planning your exercise. Failing to plan is the most common error made by athletes who are exercising to improve performance. The stress level and focus must be enough to stimulate adaptation but not too great to break down the system and prevent adaptation. Recovery requires adequate rest and nutrition and must be long enough to permit adaptation to occur yet not so long as to allow reversion to pre-

stress physiological balances. Not all your body's systems adapt at the same rates; for example, blood circulation volume increases dramatically in the first week of hard training, enzyme systems take longer to adapt, and capillary growth and adaptation of fat metabolism require many months or even years.

FOLLOW THE TRAINING ADVICE OF GERMAN EXISTENTIAL PHILOSOPHERS

Mountaineers need to have good physical fitness, but just what does it mean to be in shape? How should one get in shape and stay that way? How long will it take? Sports physiologists know the answers to these questions, but most of what you read in the popular press are merely anecdotal accounts of exercises that seemed to work for one person or another in one sport or another. Seldom do you read solid science. What's more, you almost never read about conditioning that's specific to mountaineering, which combines the aerobic requirements of endurance sports with occasional high demands on anaerobic strength and speed much like those of games athletes. Rather than recommend a specific exercise regimen, let me introduce the science behind conditioning for mountaineers, so that you can design a program that effectively fits your specific background, ambitions, and available time.

Physical conditioning for mountaineering involves improving endurance capacity and strengthening muscles specific to hiking and climbing. The desirable characteristics of muscles involved in endurance efforts and those best suited for fastest contraction turn out to be, at the cellular and enzymatic level, exactly opposite. The optimal muscle fiber type for endurance can't be maximally quick, and the muscle type that produces the most force in a relatively short burst can't be developed for optimal endurance; your personal ratio of the two types of fibers in specific muscles is genetically determined. When designing your training program, you must work on each muscle type separately. Attempting to develop both types simultaneously fails to optimally stimulate either strength or endurance adaptations; an example of such an attempt is circuit training. Endurance training is more important to mountaineers, so let's start there.

Endurance training focuses on three areas: circulatory system capacity, commonly measured by VO_2max, which reflects the body's ability to deliver raw materials (primarily oxygen) to exercising muscles; the ability of specific muscles to burn fuels and oxygen and to produce energy for extended periods of time without overload, commonly referred to as one's lactate threshold; and biomechanical efficiency, a catchall category. Circulatory system performance applies to your entire body and not to specific muscles. Lactate threshold applies to muscles, and increasing it reflects adaptation, primarily by mitochondria, in the specific muscles being trained. Efficiency applies to muscular, skeletal, and neural systems associated with the specific activities training is intended to benefit. These three aspects of performance are somewhat independent, as are the optimal means of augmenting them.

Delivering more oxygen means delivering more red blood cells, and since you can't increase the maximum rate at which your heart can pump, that means developing a bigger pump (increasing your heart's stroke volume). Increasing the rate at which your body can burn fuel and oxygen for a longer period of time (your lactate threshold) means increasing the metabolic capacity of specific muscles by physical and biochemical adaptations. In order to stimulate successful adaptation in these systems, you must stress them with exercise of sufficient, but not too great, intensity. The biggest problem with a scientific approach to endurance conditioning is the difficulty of objectively measuring the intensity of your effort and scoring your results. Without such measurement you could be wasting your time, or even making things worse.

Most recreational athletes tend to overestimate the amount of effort they are putting out; they can become discouraged when they fail to achieve their desired goals even though they devote substantial time to training. Elite athletes, on the other hand, tend to spend too much time at high-intensity effort and too little time recovering—this overtraining leads to injury that sidelines athletes, drops their training levels, and leads to depression. That's why understanding how adaptation works is much more important than having a recipe of training routines—which need to be individualized in any case. The cure for both conditions, over- and undertraining, requires a measure of your body's actual effort during exercise—and that's the problem. Exercise physiologists rely on tests that involve hooking athletes up to sophisticated machines and analyzing blood samples. For most of us, measuring our heart rates is the only practical option, although it isn't a very good one.

VO_2MAX—THE MEASURE OF AEROBIC FITNESS

VO_2max means, unsurprisingly, the maximum volume of oxygen (O_2) that your body can convert to energy each minute at sea level, expressed in milliliters of O_2 per minute per kilogram of body weight. VO_2max is mostly genetically determined but can be increased with regular endurance training and, temporarily, with certain supplements. A typical 25-year-old untrained man will have a maximal oxygen consumption of 40 ml/min/kg; some may hit 65, if they selected their mother carefully. By undertaking an effective endurance exercise program, that typical man might increase his VO_2max to 50 or 55, which is the range for regularly training male recreational athletes; females will be about 20 percent lower. A champion Olympic 10k runner will probably have a value around 80 or more, but he was probably that guy with an untrained value of 65. Training is important, but good genetics is critical. Species is even more critical; a well-conditioned canine can have a VO_2max of 150 ml/min/kg, a fact my dog brings to my attention at every opportunity.

In mountaineering, it turns out that VO_2max has little impact on absolute success. It does, however, have a strong influence on the speed at which a mountaineer can climb at a given altitude. Mountaineers with higher VO_2max scores climb faster, so they're potentially able to minimize objective dangers and give themselves more options than climbers of high determination but low VO_2max.

PERCENTAGE OF VO_2MAX—THE MEASURE OF YOUR PERSONAL AEROBIC EXERCISE INTENSITY

If you're a complete couch potato, almost any form of exercise will produce immediate improvements in your fitness level, but if your VO_2max is over 40 ml/min/kg, you'll need to exceed a threshold of training effort to see benefits in cardiovascular fitness. That threshold seems to be around 50 percent of VO_2max (about 70 percent of your maximum heart rate). In elite young and older athletes, the threshold for a positive training response may exceed 80 percent of VO_2max, but sustaining such a level of effort for long periods without adequate recovery will likely result in diminished returns overall. Some people tolerate and even thrive on a high volume of training to reach peak fitness; others need more rest days but are able to reach similar performance levels. All athletes produce most of their training gains during recovery, not during the actual exercise.

HEART RATE—THE MEASURE FOR MOST OF US

You've probably seen the old-school formula for calculating your maximal heart rate: subtract your age from 220 beats per minute. That formula is equivalent to saying that every newborn's heart maxes out at 220 bpm and inexorably declines by 1 bpm each year; basically, the formula is ridiculous, and there's no science behind it. Determining your actual maximum heart rate requires sophisticated testing, but it's possible to get an approximation by comparing yourself to measurements of many athletes. Start by subtracting 85 percent of your age from 217; this will better correspond to actual test results from treadmill running or using a Versaclimber. Women should subtract 70 percent of their age from 209. Subtract 5 beats per minute from the result to compare with cycling tests. Subtract 3 beats if you are an elite athlete under 30 years of age; very well trained mountaineers should add 2 beats if they're 50 years old and 4 beats if they're over 55. Fit mountaineers can estimate their maximum heart rates by pushing themselves on a track or exercycle so they hit their maximum effort after about 4 minutes and then reading out the result on a heart rate monitor. The inescapable truth is that your maximum heart rate declines with age, and training won't change that.

The Karvonen formula for determining your training heart rate uses the percentage of the range between your resting heart rate and your maximum heart rate (called your heart rate reserve) and then adds that to your resting rate. For example, if your heart rate range from resting to maximum is 140 bpm and your resting rate is 50, and you want to train at 85 to 90 percent of your anaerobic threshold, you would take those percentages of your range and add the result to your resting rate to get a target training range of 169 to 176 bpm. The older you get, the more the simple maximum heart rate formula works better than the heart rate reserve calculation.

Since heart rate is the only measure available to most athletes, many formulae have been developed to suggest training zones based on a percentage of one's maximal heart rate. Comparable zones have been based on VO_2max and blood lactate concentration, too. Usually four or five ranges are suggested. At about 50 percent of maximal heart rate (HRmax, not to be confused with VO_2max), you won't be training anything; this is usually referred to as a recovery zone. I exceed this zone when talking to attorneys and editors. The next zone is usually described as fat burning or basic aerobic endurance building and centers on 65 percent of HRmax; this is noticeable to the athlete as real training but not as significant effort; spending time in this zone is a waste of time. Aerobic endurance is built by training at 75 to 85 percent of HRmax, where real effort is felt, but where training can be maintained for hours (by determined athletes). The anaerobic threshold zone from 85 to 100 percent of HRmax is when lactate accumulates, and effort cannot be sustained beyond short periods. If you're thinking in terms of percent VO_2max levels, you can approximate the percentage of your maximum heart rate by adding 37 to 64 percent of the percent VO_2max number—a handy, if approximate, connection between VO_2max and HRmax. (Example: if you want to train at 75 percent of your VO_2max, that would be 37 + .64 x 75 percent = 85 percent of your HRmax.) This approximation applies to trained middle-aged athletes, keeping in mind that VO_2max can be increased by training but HRmax cannot.

There's endless debate as to how to perform these kinds of calculations and what effort ranges accomplish what forms of benefits; without an actual determination of your personal maximal heart rate (or better, personal VO_2max) all such calculations remain interesting but hypothetical. Most recreational athletes learn to train according to perceived effort; some are successful, but for most this subjective form of feedback is what leads to poor results and frustration.

Up the Mountain, Over the Hill

Absent training, VO_2max declines about 1 percent each year after age 25. If you avoid gaining fat and

keep physical activity levels high (serious problems for the aging athlete), the decline in VO_2max due to aging can be limited to 0.5 percent per year. Prior to age 50, this decline may even be as low as 1 to 2 percent per decade in hard-training athletes, but cardiovascular capacity is ultimately reduced by the relentless decline in maximal heart rate. There are other effects of aging that impact training: your body fat inevitably increases, though this may be slightly beneficial to those without Olympic aspirations, and your sweat production decreases, suggesting a greater need for caution when climbing in hot, humid conditions. Interestingly, if you take a look at climbers who have reached the summits of all fourteen of the world's 8,000-meter peaks (an incredibly difficult challenge), you notice Reinhold Messner completed the list at age 42, Jerzy Kukuczka at 41, Krzysztof Wielicki at 46, Juan Oiarzabal at 43, and Sergio Martini at age 49. There are probably many other examples of highly successful mountaineers whose accomplishments have continued at ages far beyond what you might expect. Among American mountaineers, Fred Becky comes immediately to mind; he's in his 80s and is still putting up first ascents. I hear he's damn hard to keep up with.

HOW LONG DOES TRAINING TAKE?

It depends on what systems you're training. If it's VO_2max, the good news is that if you're now a complete couch potato, your VO_2max will improve in only the first week of training, and it will do so no matter how you train! This results from a nicely increased blood circulation capacity—your heart will pump more blood and transport more oxygen to your muscles. It's oxygen transport by your heart, not oxygen consumption by your muscles, that limits VO_2max. If you're untrained but able to exercise for 30 minutes without becoming sore, you're ready to start serious training. After three months of regular endurance exercise of appropriate intensity and duration you may increase your VO_2max by 15 to 20 percent, given typical starting values. Results can vary considerably among individuals undertaking identical training. The greatest gains in VO_2max occur in the first 6 weeks of serious training, and training benefits seem to hit a plateau after about a year, irrespective of training regimen.

The bad news is that after 3 or 4 months, improvement will begin to level off, no matter how you train. You may start out with a VO_2max of 35 ml/min/kg and end up with 45; this is a substantial improvement, especially if you've lost weight during your training—decreasing the denominator as you increase the numerator. An increase of 25 percent would indicate a dedicated athlete and very successful regimen. You'd really have to crank up the intensity in the next 6 months in order to eke out a few more percentage points. Unfortunately, in the following years you won't even be able to maintain your increases, as you begin confronting the inevitable decline in VO_2max with age. Although it would be best to accomplish your VO_2max training and your conditioning maintenance using the muscles most closely related to mountaineering, working any large muscles will be effective because it's your body's entire circulatory system that's being trained.

Lactate Threshold Training

VO_2max training refers to what's often called building your cardiovascular base. You also want to be increasing the endurance capacity of your skeletal muscles that are specific to mountaineering. When you first start training, an effort of about 50 percent of your VO_2max will cause your muscles to reach a threshold, called your lactate or lactic acid (same thing) threshold, where your muscles will start accumulating lactic acid, and you won't want to push harder. You'll feel fatigued at this relatively low effort.

Over time your muscles will adapt. Mitochondrial synthesis will increase, more enzymes necessary for fatty acid metabolism within your muscle cells will be produced, and more capillaries will appear around your muscle fibers. At the end of 6 months of training, your lactate threshold may have increased to 70 percent of VO_2max in the muscles you've been training—a very good result. This means your sustainable level of exercise-specific effort will have increased by more than the increase in your VO_2max. That's a benefit you can continue to increase to a lesser degree over several years of mountaineering training. If you switch to a sport that uses different muscles, such as kayaking, most of your lactate threshold increase won't apply, and you'll start over from the cardio base you've built. Another way of making this point is to say that cross-training is inefficient for raising your lactate threshold.

Efficiency

There are additional gains to be made through training, apart from the wisdom of experience. As you practice the various movements involved in mountaineering, your biomechanical efficiency improves, and this improvement can continue to grow over many years, although the contribution to your overall performance is much less than that due to increasing your VO_2max and raising your lactate threshold. I'm unaware of efficiency studies on mountaineers, but in other sports the more complex the activity, the greater will be the gain from improved efficiency as your accumulated sport-specific training and experience increase.

AT WHAT INTENSITY SHOULD I TRAIN?

The fundamental principle is to stress systems slightly beyond their current capacity, and then allow adequate recovery time for the systems to adapt. To increase your VO_2max, you need to spend training time working near or slightly above your current VO_2max, and to raise your lactate threshold you must spend training time at or just above your current lactate threshold (which will be below the heart rate of your VO_2max). There are two fundamental types of training: continuous and intermittent or interval.

Cardiovascular Training

If you're just beginning to train, your first efforts should go to increasing your VO_2max. The best way is unquestionably with interval training. By that is meant short (about 5 minute) high-intensity effort followed by periods of low-intensity effort that allow your body to recover (clear lactate) almost completely. The principal gain of cardiovascular training comes from the intensity of workouts, not the number or duration. By high intensity I mean at 85 to 100 percent of VO_2max (it's possible to exceed 100 percent of your VO_2max heart rate by 10 percent or more; sprinters do it in every event). The problem with such high-intensity training is that it really knocks your body for a loop. Even if you think you're OK, your biochemical systems will be out of balance for days, and your muscles and connective tissue can't keep up with the stress. Things only get worse if you do another intense interval session before you're fully recovered.

What's optimum for interval training is a series of high-intensity efforts lasting 4 to 8 minutes, with rest periods of at least 2 minutes, accumulating to about 30 or 40 minutes. Another strategy is to perform longer intervals of 10- to 20-minute duration at 75 to 85 percent of VO_2max, with rests of 5 minutes, and accumulating up to 40 to 60 minutes total, depending on your level of conditioning. The longer interval strategy is probably more effective than shorter, more intense intervals for simultaneously developing muscle endurance (pushing up your lactate threshold), and

recovery is quicker and easier because you won't be pushing your peak lactate accumulation as severely. As you progress, increase the level of intensity during the intervals; don't decrease the recovery periods. Don't think of rest between intervals as a weakness and try to eliminate it. Clearing lactate is essential to enable you to reach the level of effort that stimulates the adaptation you're looking for. You're hitting the proper level of intensity if you can sustain the final intervals in each session, keeping up the same performance but only by increasing your perceived effort. If you're forced to reduce the intensity of your final intervals, you're working too hard and need to back off. Unfortunately, heart rate monitors don't effectively report interval intensity; they may provide some help in evaluating longer intervals, but they are ineffective for shorter, higher-intensity training. You can do two or three of either the short or longer interval series in a session, but limit yourself to only one such session per week or fortnight to avoid doing more damage than good.

Lactate Threshold Training

Continuous training is what will raise your lactate threshold and improve your biomechanics. Aim for steady state effort at 65 to 75 percent of VO_2max lasting 45 to 120 minutes—the hour of power. These sessions should be done three or maybe four times each week. This takes dedication. They're a bit more intense than maintenance training, which needs only two or three 20- to 30-minute sessions weekly at a comparable level of effort, but their purpose is to increase, not merely maintain, your performance capacity. The adaptive gains you're looking to stimulate occur primarily during periods between exercise sessions. Don't overtrain; monitor your resting heart rate daily to forestall doing so. Take a look at this book's chapter on performance nutrition (Chapter 19) for suggestions on optimal nutrition for recovery; it should begin in the minutes immediately after a workout. Both the longer, low-intensity workouts described in this paragraph and the high-intensity intervals described just previously are necessary to build endurance fitness. Either form alone won't produce the results you're looking for.

WHAT AEROBIC EXERCISES WORK FOR MOUNTAINEERS?

The facile answer is: those exercises that stress the main muscles involved in mountaineering. Some sports, such as rowing and cycling, have machines that can give a workout very similar to competing—not identical though, as significant additional gains will come from actually working out on the road or on the water. Mountaineering doesn't have even these—the Versaclimber is a long way from being a simulation of mountaineering, and FitTrek seems aimed mainly at selling hiking poles. That means you'll have to design your own routines, ones that best utilize your personal resources. For mountaineers this may mean (short) uphill training hikes that deliberately carry extra weight and push speeds; some carry a pack containing jugs of water, whereas I carry my daughter and bottles of formula. Do intervals on the uphill, and take it easy on your knees going down. Snowshoeing rapidly requires an untoward amount of effort, should you find it attractive. You might even run up long stairways at a local stadium, à la Walter Payton, but a stair machine will allow you to make higher steps that work your muscles over a wider range of motion if you use it properly, without hands for balance. (Come to think of it, didn't Payton run two or three steps at a time? I'm sure he had the sense to walk back down.) Recognize that a stair machine and gadgets like them tend to repeat a single motion, which can be hard on your knees; anyone who recommends working out on a stair machine while wearing a pack is ill informed. Stairs are superior to stair machines, and hiking is better yet if you can get the intensity up.

Be sure you appreciate the difference between intervals and continuous training. Attempting continuous training at interval intensity will only burn you out. Doing intervals at continuous-training effort levels won't produce results. The trick will be to design hard intervals with adequate rest periods, for your VO$_2$max workouts, and longer, steady routines at a sufficiently high level of effort to stimulate lactate threshold gains. The longest exercise period will be about an hour. Longer hikes at lower effort won't produce gains; runners call this "junk miles." Slogging along for hours with a heavy pack is worse than worthless. Trail running may not work either, unless you can get the intensity up, and that will expose beginners to injuries. Start out on dirt roads and bridal paths until you build ankle and knee conditioning; develop an efficient running posture by looking well ahead and committing on the downhills.

Peaking for Mountaineers

Exercise physiologists understand nowadays that striving for maximum workout effort all the time isn't as effective as a targeted level of efforts with plenty of recovery time in between. Purely aerobic athletes spend only a small percent of their training time at all-out intensity. But what about peaking (increasing your training effort immediately prior to a big climb)? Unfortunately, this hasn't been scientifically studied for mountaineers as it has for athletes preparing for shorter events. The best advice is to increase your interval intensity, slightly increase the intensity of your continuous workouts, don't decrease the periods of recovery, and then back way off in the several days immediately prior to your most important day. Pay attention to proper rest and nutrition in those days of backing off, to allow your body to completely clear lactate. Increase the amount of carbohydrate in your diet by about 250 grams daily to ensure that your body recharges its stores of glycogen, which is what you've been training it to do all along. It's better to be undertrained and well-recovered than to begin a major climb in an overtrained condition—advice not always easy to follow given the addictive appeal of aerobic training.

Female mountaineers may be concerned that menstruation will interfere with their strength or endurance; that appears not to be the case, and the opposite could be true, but many feel that they can perform at a higher level when they're not menstruating and so manipulate their cycles. A typical protocol is to take birth control pills for several cycles until 10 days prior to the major effort; menstruation will start in 3 days and will stop before the critical day. Female mountaineers could be affected by higher body temperature after an egg is released during the last half of the cycle, which could cause a moderate increase in cardiac load. It's hard to find conclusive science behind any of these possibilities, perhaps because athletic women have a higher incidence of menstrual dysfunction, particularly if they have low body fat, making responses highly individualistic. I suspect that the real reason for lack of science is that mountaineering remains a male-dominated sport.

STRENGTH TRAINING

Strength training is intended to increase the bulk of targeted muscles, generally those that will augment particular aspects of a sport or those that will alleviate imbalances that impair performance. It consists of *progressive resistance exercise*. For most mountaineers, the goal of such exercise is likely to be strengthening connective tissue, developing motor control, and reversing the catabolic effects of climbing at altitude more than simply bulking up, but the basics are the same. Progressive resistance exercise means repeatedly performing a motion that challenges the targeted muscle to contract and relax for a minute or so total for all the repetitions—the effort is mainly anaerobic. The load must be sufficient to exhaust or nearly exhaust the muscle. Each repetition of the motion is called a "rep," and a series of reps is called a "set." Typically there are ten reps in a set, but smaller muscles with shorter movement duration benefit more from more reps of lower intensity. Usually several well-separated sets are performed during a session that targets the particular muscle or muscle group. As the muscle adapts (mostly by growing), the resistance is progressively increased to maintain the challenge.

The most effective regimen for building muscle requires surprisingly high intensity. Before starting serious training, lift easy weights for a month or so while you formulate your plan. When targeting a muscle or muscle group, pick a load that demands a struggle to smoothly complete the last few reps in the first set of ten. Then increase the load by several percent and have your partner quickly do most of the lifting so you can *lower* the load about six times (i.e., perform six negative reps). Then add a few percentage points more

weight and perform three negative reps; your partner should be standing by to take over if you can't control the load. This protocol will cause significant pain during the last set and soreness the following day. The pain is caused by tearing of muscle fibers, which is necessary to stimulate muscle growth. Wait a few days for the soreness to abate, then do three sets of light reps; repeat light sets after another few days. Connective tissue, with its reduced vascularization, grows and heals much more slowly than muscle, so give it time. If the soreness has gone, perform another hard workout on that muscle no sooner than a week after the first. If you target unrelated muscle groups and stagger hard workouts, you can work your major muscle groups every week or so—and be rewarded with soreness somewhere every single day. A program of this intensity is hard on your body, but it produces results.

For mountaineers, the first issue will be determining which muscles should be targeted and deciding what exercises stress them most effectively—there's an endless variety of exercises from which to choose. The big issue, however, is finding the time to perform the exercises without abandoning any component of your more important aerobic conditioning program. Unless you're a professional climber, you'll find it difficult to allot an hour on three days during the week for aerobic exercise to maintain, much less increase, your endurance conditioning. Adding more days for strength training is difficult for most of us, so we'd certainly want to optimize the benefits of any such program. The key is to plan a program that's manageable for you and then assiduously carry it out.

First, Do No Harm

The first challenge in designing your personal strengthening program is to identify your own weak points. Certainly, if you're truly a couch potato, you may need a program of general strengthening exercises—all the usual exercises that you see illustrated on posters at the health club. And you'll need the facilities of a health club to cram enough such exercises into a reasonable period of time. Avoid exercises that involve an excessive range of motion or awkward angulation against resistance. If you're already reasonably conditioned, you're ready to take a closer look at any specific weaknesses that may be troubling you.

As an example, consider the common patellofemoral syndrome—knee pain exacerbated by hiking downhill that old-schoolers call chondromalacia. It takes a clinician to make a definitive diagnosis and rule out causes from other musculoskeletal alignment problems, but the common therapy is to build the strength of the muscles that stabilize the patella, such as the vastus medialis if it's not adequately balancing the vastus lateralis. Ace bandages or neoprene foam around your knee won't do the job; neither will rest and ice, or NSAIDs. A common strengthening exercise is leg extensions, and it isn't unusual to find some mountaineers spending time in the evening doing leg extensions with their loaded backpacks as weights. Unless you're a clinician yourself, it will be impossible for you to accurately assess your weaknesses and prescribe safe, specific exercises to address them, but addressing any worrisome weaknesses is certainly the first order of business. Progressing with a training program, strength or aerobic, prior to addressing weaknesses will exacerbate the weaknesses and preclude success in the remainder of your training efforts, and it'll cause you to postpone progress while you recover.

But Don't Do Too Much Good

Although mountaineering involves many different muscle groups that strengthening will benefit, having larger muscles is not always beneficial. Muscles developed for size alone may actually become more easily fatigued as they get bigger. This is called mitochondrial dilution; it happens when mitochondrial density is not increasing at the same rate as muscle volume. Mitochondria are the components of muscle cells where fuel and oxygen are burned for energy. In order to gain muscle size and yet maintain mitochondrial density and therefore endurance capacity, you must maintain your endurance training intensity at the same time you perform your strength training.

Training by Exaggeration of Normal Loads?

Normal loads (normal mountaineering activities) won't make you a stronger climber; using them as exercises may only prevent you from becoming less fit unless you manage to focus and heighten the intensity. Activities like carrying a heavy pack on long hikes will only overload smaller muscles before larger muscles are adequately stimulated. Analyze which muscles to target and then apply the principles of overstressing followed by recovery so that you don't simply put in junk miles. Pushing your grade at sport climbing will increase your climbing-related strength, increasing flexibility and building power for subtle movements, but more importantly it'll teach you the gymnastics of rock. Careful it doesn't teach you indifference to falling. Don't expect hard climbing to make you massive, an awareness that will hit you when you watch a teenage waif sending a 5.13. Rock climbing will make you nimble, and it'll build hand and shoulder strength if your tendons can keep up. Sport climbing requires leading even if it doesn't require placing protection and running things out (I suppose you could skip alternate clips, but you'd get some stares). Gym climbing and bouldering, on the other hand, are overly focused on face climbing, whereas alpine rock routes, certainly the

---

STRETCHING: THE TRUTH

Most athletes include some form of stretching, flexibility, or range of motion routine in their exercise regimens. Many enthuse about stretching as an adjunct to other training, mostly because they believe it reduces injury or simply because it feels good. The basic purpose of stretching is to increase range of motion and the principles are the same as for other training: stress systems slightly beyond their current limits and then allow adequate recovery time. The problem with stretching is that the systems involved are slow to adapt and the balance between effective stress and overstress and injury is narrow. The consequence is that unless you confine your stretching to the conventional, feel-good variety you should be guided by a skilled instructor who will ensure that your motions are appropriate to your personal physiology and objectives and that you don't injure lesser structures while trying to train major ones. Skilled instructors for athletes, despite self-certification claims, are hard to come by. A general book or class is no substitute.

longer, harder ones, tend to involve cracks. Getting competent with crack climbing won't come from pulling on plastic; neither do mountaineers seem to have personalities that fit the rock gym scene. Test yourself: do you start climbs sitting down and use "dude," "like," and "awesome" multiple times in each sentence? If so, like your diction is as bad as, like, whatever, but you'll make an awesomely rad climber, dude.

Training in the Cold

Mountaineers exposed to cold air initially find their immune systems depressed, but athletes who regularly train in the cold seem to adapt and become more resistant to acquiring infections than those who train in cold air only occasionally. Training in cold air also results in a lower heart rate (by as much as 20 bpm) for a given workload; this is good news but should be taken into account if you use heart rate to guide your exercise intensity. Training in the cold means you should warm up thoroughly, maintain your hydration regimen, avoid dressing in clothes that will accumulate moisture, and recognize that you'll be burning additional calories to maintain body heat and to move heavier clothing and footwear.

Training at Altitude

Training at altitude is different from acclimatization—or is it? There's ongoing and unresolved debate on the merits of "training high, living low" versus "training low, living high." The goal is to train in enough oxygen to support the level of intensity that will stimulate the sought-after adaptive responses yet take advantage of the stimulative effect of altitude to increase your number of red blood cells and other components of aerobic capacity. It appears that the answer lies at moderate altitudes, and the best answers are different for different sports and events of different lengths. For mountaineers, the science suggests that effort above 8,000 feet (2,440 meters) cannot be made intense enough for ultimate aerobic conditioning, so mountaineers who live that high should conduct their interval training at a lower altitude. Mountaineers who live at sea level will benefit from bouts of steady effort at 5,000 feet (1,500 meters) to begin their altitude adaptation. When climbers first go high, their heart rate increases substantially for a given level of effort; then as they acclimate, their maximal heart rate declines, and their resting heart rate increases. The amount of HRmax decline is about 10 percent at 12,000 feet (3,600 meters).

PERSISTENCE

I've discussed two of the three main causes of lack of training success: lack of results from too low intensity and overtraining with too little recovery. The third cause is perhaps the most difficult to deal with: lack of persistence. It's often said that everyone wants to be a winner, but only champions want to train. Yet train you must. Build variety into all your workouts, to keep your interest up. Compete with your training partners in ways that support persistent effort. If deceased martial arts heroes inspire you, drag out that Bruce Lee poster and tape it to the back of your bathroom door. Put a Rainier screen saver on your computer so that your objective is there to inspire you at every opportunity and remind you to keep your training promises. Set personal short-term and long-term goals. Achieving short-term training goals is essential to maintaining commitment, but long-term goals are the real objective of your training. Goals must be specific, measurable, and attainable—but not too attainable. Train your will by forcing yourself to spend a fraction of your training time budget doing something you know you should do, but just loath doing.

MENTAL TRAINING

Just as your physical ability adapts to stress by becoming stronger, so also does your mental ability. The beneficial exercise principles are remarkably parallel. To improve your mental conditioning you must slightly exceed your comfort zone and then recover. Too much mental stress will be debilitating; too little won't produce results. Insufficient recovery will result in burnout without growth. From time to time you should permit yourself to go beyond the degree of mental challenge you're confident of surmounting—perform mental intervals. This doesn't mean behaving recklessly—you want to face genuine punishment if you fail, but not flirt with disaster for yourself or your companions. Mental comfort zones are different for every person, so everyone must explore his or her own limits and respect those of others. The challenges could be overcoming fear, dealing with loneliness, improving leadership skills, enhancing team dynamics, exploring new decision-making paradigms, and many other areas of mental growth important to mountaineers. Your confidence will grow if you succeed; your wisdom should grow even if you don't. If you're fortunate enough to encounter a mountaineer with significant physical impairments who's accomplishing things you'd never have thought could be achieved, you may realize that your own development of mental toughness has only scratched the surface of what is possible.

21
Wilderness First Aid

First aid is one of those things you can't expect to learn from a book, much less a chapter. I've suggested a great text in the Resources section as well as a list of accredited wilderness first-aid trainers. First aid requires competent instruction and hands-on learning; this is even more important for wilderness first aid.

What distinguishes *wilderness* first aid?

▲ More than 2 hours from definitive medical care (advanced life support, a hospital).

▲ Materials will have to be improvised.

▲ Performed in an adverse environment.

The consequences of these distinctions are profound. Wilderness first aid is a far cry from Red Cross first aid or the treatment delivered by EMTs. It's much more hands-on and based on actual treatment rather than stabilizing the patient prior to transport to a medical facility. Wilderness first aid deals primarily with trauma sustained in the backcountry and spends little time on more common urban afflictions, such as heart attacks and poisoning. There are several protocols taught that

directly contradict the usual training for urban settings.

WILDERNESS FIRST-AID INSTRUCTION

What should you expect to learn in a wilderness first-aid course? More than just a collection of Red Cross protocols. You'll learn a systematic approach to diagnosis and treatment based on the principal body systems: circulatory, respiratory, nervous, and musculoskeletal. You'll be taught diagnostic and reporting tools along with a lexicon of terms to support organized thinking. You'll learn protocols for systematic assessment, monitoring, and documentation. And you'll learn the importance of the progression of symptoms and the range of responses to trauma and treatment. Expect much more than learning how to clean a wound and apply a bandage—that's old-school. One of the pivotal protocols you'll learn is cervical spine assessment; if you can rule out spine injury after an incident that involved a mechanism of injury for spine, your options open up; if not, things can get pretty grim in a wilderness setting.

In addition to requiring a practicum for learning, first aid is also like self-rescue in that it is a seldom-used skill set. This means that it must be practiced regularly if skills are to be kept sharp. Outdoor programs require their instructors or guides to maintain current wilderness first-aid certificates, requiring retraining every few years. Not a bad idea for conscientious mountaineers. With the proper knowledge, training, and experience, you'll avoid the dead ends of panic, despair, myopic judgment, and irrational behavior that yield the many "what not to do" examples you'll study—humorous in the retelling, but doubtless not in the actual experience.

FIRST-AID KIT

In Chapter 18, Equipment for Base Camp, I list, by way of example, the items in the first-aid kit I carry as part of my "ten essentials." If you've ever thought about commercial first-aid kits, you've noticed that they're pretty much limited to topical antiseptics and materials for dressing wounds and treating headaches. These simple items are about all an untrained climber could use without the risk of doing more harm than good. It makes no sense to carry a SAM Splint or nasal airway if you're not trained to use them. If you have the training, you'll be able to assemble your own new-school first-aid kit that glues together the items you know you can improvise from other things you carry into a response package that can handle an amazingly wide range of problems. The real first-aid kit is your personal knowledge and training.

SHOCKING

I'm now going to indulge in a rant about one of my pet peeves: misuse of the word "shock." You often hear of people being treated for shock because they've received bad news. This is baloney; there's no such thing as psychogenic shock. *Shock* is a physiological condition that requires specific, aggressive medical intervention—treatment that's probably impossible in a wilderness setting. What

the cub reporter or uninformed friend was talking about is properly termed ASR: acute stress reaction. Knowing the difference is significant.

Shock is the consequence of abnormally low blood pressure and volume and the resultant inadequate perfusion. Its classic symptoms are cold, pale skin and an increase in pulse and respiratory rates caused by shell/core effects as the body attempts to compensate. If volume shock progresses to the point of impairing mental status, the patient will soon die without advanced life support (hospital treatment).

ASR, on the other hand, is a temporary condition, controlled by the autonomic nervous system. It's a common response to emotional or physical stress, but *it ain't shock.* ASR caused by adrenalin release yields an increase in pulse rate and circulation, and it shunts blood to the muscles; this results in the "fight or flight" condition that enables extraordinary effort, but it may also mask pain and complicate diagnosis. ASR can also manifest itself by feelings of lightheadedness or nausea, caused by a temporary loss of perfusion pressure due to a drop in heart rate. These symptoms are harmless except that they mimic the shell/core effects of true volume shock.

The key to distinguishing ASR from shock is the method of injury (MOI) and progression of symptoms. ASR will remit without treatment, though reducing pain and anxiety will help. The patient should be seated and calmed. ASR can appear along with minor or serious injuries, even true shock. The MOI suggests the patient's treatment.

TAKEAWAY EXAMPLE

As an example of the difference in new- and old-school approaches, one of the principles you'll learn in a new-school wilderness first-aid course is the treatment of stable or unstable musculoskeletal injuries. In old-school first aid, an injured ankle (the most common mountaineering injury) would be classified as broken or sprained; if sprained, it would be subclassified into three grades, depending on the extent of damage to ligaments. Fractures would be subclassified as avulsioned, comminuted, angulated, displaced, and so on and so forth for a dozen other descriptors. The new-school approach recognizes that these descriptors, along with sprain, strain, fracture, dislocation, contusion, and many more like them, are irrelevant to treatment in a wilderness setting. In fact, all these categories require imaging equipment to make a proper diagnosis. The new-school approach is to forgo portable X-ray equipment in favor of practicality.

Instead of complex diagnostics, in a new-school class you'll learn to classify injuries of this sort into only two categories: *stable* or *unstable*. This distinction has great utility in planning treatment; it allows training to be focused on effective wilderness treatment rather than diagnosis. Unstable injuries need to be stabilized; some may require reduction, and sometimes the injury may require the entire body to be immobilized. To determine instability, you look at symptoms and mechanism of injury. A mechanism of injury with sufficient force to cause ankle fractures or severe sprains is not always easy to determine. The symptoms of instability include the inability to move the ankle or to bear weight, obvious deformity or unnatural angulation, feeling or hearing a pop during the injury or bones grating against each other afterward, and the sense of instability. In my own case, a broken ankle wasn't particularly painful, but after the pop it felt like I was standing on a greasy ball bearing inside my boot and it made a click with every step on the several-mile hike to a road.

Treatment for an unstable ankle is the same irrespective of the degree or cause of the injury. A sprained or broken ankle isn't life threatening, but it's important to prevent additional injury to the soft tissue nearby. It's also important that efforts to stabilize the ankle don't cause additional decrease in blood supply to the area than might already have been caused during the injury. To ensure that neither the injury nor your stabilization methods aren't cutting off blood supply, you'll want to monitor blood circulation in and distal to the injury area. You know that nerve tissue is most vulnerable to insufficient circulation, so you check CSM (circulation, sensation, and movement) in the foot and toes. Circulation can be checked by looking for a pulse or noting skin tone and prompt restoration of color under a mashed toenail. Sensation is the best test; loss of sensation is the first sign of insufficient circulation. Early signs of loss of blood supply are tingling, then numbness. Inability to move the foot or wiggle the toes sets in more slowly. Restricted blood supply can be tolerated in soft tissue for an hour or so, but if you can't restore CSM by moving the ankle or using traction-into-place, you're facing a life-threatening emergency, and you must consider immediate evacuation. If CSM isn't being impaired by the injury itself, your next chores will be to get the ankle into a natural position and make it hand stable, and then to improvise an appropriate splint and make the ankle splint stable. You'll continue to monitor CSM until the patient receives definitive medical care.

This little section isn't meant to be instruction, and it's certainly not a substitute for a good text. It's meant to illustrate the complexity of dealing with even a common, non-emergency injury in backcountry conditions and the utility of new-school approaches. Hopefully it will prompt you to seek out a recognized wilderness medical training program and learn not only the science of treatment but also the art of improvised splinting, wound cleaning, evacuation, and the many other skills you'll want to master.

PSYCHOLOGICAL FIRST AID

Anyone who's witnessed a serious injury or death or who's been involved in a rescue or recovery effort may be severely stressed, even if uninjured. Although only a small fraction of such persons go on to develop post-traumatic stress disorder, administering psychological first aid is a good idea. Make the person safe and reassure them that they actually are safe. Make them comfortable without making a big deal about it. Let them know what the plan is and that you're available and accessible, but don't intrude on their thoughts and coping mechanisms, which are likely different from your own.

22
Protecting the
Natural Environment

*We do not inherit the earth from our ancestors,
we borrow it from our children.*

Supposedly this is Native American wisdom; that would make sense. Mountaineers should embrace it, too. The high mountains have special problems when it comes to maintaining the pristine environment that we find so compelling. The alpine ecosystem has relative little soil, sparse vegetation, few bacteria, and a short growing season; for much of the time it's a giant refrigerator that will preserve for many years the waste we leave as well as any trace we make by our presence. Thoughtful mountaineers enjoy a special, custodial responsibility to minimize their own impact and to model behavior that encourages others to minimize theirs.

LEAVE NO TRACE

Protecting recreational lands, particularly wilderness areas, against the ever-increasing onslaught of visitors has become so crucial that the U.S. Forest Service, Bureau of Land Management, and National Park Service have joined with the National Outdoor Leadership School (NOLS) to develop a nationwide educational program called Leave No Trace; a nonprofit with dozens of member firms and organizations has been created to spread the word. The program now has international outreach. The Leave No Trace Ethics principles have been condensed to seven points that apply to all recreational users; I'll offer comments that pertain particularly to mountaineers.

Plan Ahead and Prepare. When getting ready for your outing, give consideration to creating the minimum amount of waste and causing minimal impact. Freeze-dry food-unit packaging materials, for example, are notably wasteful. Come prepared to pack out all your trash, especially toilet paper and personal hygiene materials. Food scraps and peels are trash. Old slings are trash if you wouldn't rap on them; they go in your pack. Increase your karma by packing out others' trash you come across. As Carlos Buhler points out, it never hurts to make deposits in your karma bank; some day you may need to make a withdrawal.

Travel and Camp on Durable Surfaces. Or even better, on completely recyclable surfaces—snow and natural forest duff. Sand is the ideal camping surface for mountaineers. I have mixed feelings about rock rings for mountain tent sites. I don't build them, but I've improved a few; I've also disbursed some that were particularly sloppy and unnecessary. In general, "improving" alpine campsites is more a habit of backpackers than mountaineers and should be avoided. A key principle in pristine areas is to avoid compacting soil or trampling vegetation to the point that it cannot recover, which doesn't take much in the alpine environment. Where vegetation is growing it's better to move to a new site than to prolong impact on a single location.

Dispose of Waste Properly. In the mountains and desert, foil is forever. There's no "disposal" option for alpinists—pack out your waste. That increasingly applies to human waste. In remote, subalpine areas, feces should be buried in soil well away from camping areas and water; soap, for those mountaineers who use it, should not be rinsed into watercourses. In alpine areas there are no soil bacteria to decompose fecal matter; there, feces should be spread on exposed, sunlit rock surfaces. Scientific research (I'm not making this up) has shown that human feces spread out on rocks in alpine or arid forest regions do not contribute fecal microorganisms to the environment; all microorganisms are killed within a few weeks and the fecal matter desiccates and vanishes or is disbursed by critters. On alpine snow, feces spread out on the surface do not contribute fecal microorganisms to the surrounding snow, because the bugs are killed off faster than they spread. On glaciers, don't dump garbage in crevasses; fecal matter alone is probably OK, but not trash, bags, or tampons. If you use toilet paper (and if snow is available, you may not), pack out your used poop tickets. On many highly used mountains, particularly the popular volcanoes and Mt. Whitney, packing out your own feces and waste paper

is becoming a requirement. Land management agencies are exploring the requirement to pack out all waste, rather than rely on conspicuous latrines, which require helicopter cleaning. Packing out all waste makes special sense for larger parties, and it's a great way to build your karma account. Specialized products, such as the WAG Bags from Phillips Environmental, are widely available; use them. If cleaning up after yourself makes you squeamish, get over it; the experiences of parenthood should help.

Leave What You Find. And take care as to what you leave. Don't place or remove bolts on established routes or summits. Don't leave brightly colored rappel slings; drab webbing is readily available. Don't build cairns, or if you must build them on the way up, disburse them on your return. It's better to use surveyor's tape from your ten essentials; there's no doubt about its removal. Don't disburse cairns you stumble across, as someone else may be relying on them. It goes without saying that you must never disturb archeological artifacts (anything over 50 years old) or climb near ancient rock art; that will get you some very bad karma.

Minimize Campfire Impacts. I don't know about all mountaineers, but my companions tend never to build campfires, except maybe at trailheads where there are picnic tables and iron pits. Campfires are no good for cooking, and they make your clothes smell like weekend campers. In the alpine environment there's usually not enough fuel or time to bother, and in many locales fires above 10,000 feet are prohibited—as they should be. Don't be tempted to build a fire to burn your trash; campfires, even if the fire site is subsequently disbursed, leave enduring scars on Mother Nature and will bring you more bad karma.

Respect Wildlife. This means don't feed them, deliberately or accidentally. Many climbing areas are home to raptors, bighorn sheep, and other wildlife that deserve special protection. Be honored to share the alpine world with each of the critters you meet; it may be your play area, but you're in their home.

Be Considerate of Other Visitors. I'm happy to say that the mountaineers I've encountered are uniformly the most considerate of all users of backcountry and wilderness areas. Keep up the good work.

ACCESS

Users of wilderness areas, climbers and mountaineers in particular, face relentless efforts by land management agencies and concessionaires to eliminate, restrict, or levy access to the backcountry. There's constant pressure to convert lands from public resources into profit centers, to shift funding to mainstream recreation, and to close areas to less conventional use. To ensure that such restrictions are minimal, reasonable, and fairly applied, climbers must behave responsibly when they use these resources, but they need to go beyond that by also becoming aware of and involved in the issues of wilderness preservation and access. There are many opportunities to do so, and one of the best places to start is the Access Fund, "a national, non-profit organization dedicated to keeping climbing areas open and to conserving the climbing environment"; you'll be in good company.

BE LIKE ED

No one talks much about it, but one allure of mountaineering is "knocking the bastard off" and thinking of ourselves as being as heroic as Ed Hillary in that famous photo by Karsh, appearing most recently on the May 2003 cover of *National Geographic.* That's the ideal, and it's certainly heroic, yet we know what climbing big mountains is really like. That photo was a studio shot, and by the time it was taken, then-Sir Edmund had had several years to wash off the grime, gain back some weight, get rid of the reverse-raccoon tan, have his hair fashionably coiffed (properly mussed, of course), and practice looking heroic. As I'm writing, tomorrow is the 50th anniversary of Hillary and Tenzing Norgay Sherpa's impressive climb. There are some of us who cling to the romantic notion that Mallory and Irvine managed to make the summit 29 years earlier, but it doesn't matter. Hillary went on to many more mountaineering adventures, but in reflecting on his life he said his most worthwhile accomplishments were building schools, hospitals, and reforestation projects with the Sherpa people. Appreciation of indigenous cultures and protecting the natural environment—as well as bold mountaineering—are values shared by every alpinist. Hillary's life is full of impressive accomplishments in all three areas. Not bad for a beekeeper. Heroic indeed.

PART 6

Advanced Techniques

I n this section I've collected a number of seldom-used techniques. Although I've labeled them advanced, they build on the simple methods and principles discussed earlier. I put them here because not every mountaineer will want to commit them to memory at first. When your experience grows, when you want to increase your ability to deal with unusual circumstances, or when you want to consider using more leading-edge equipment, bring these techniques into play.

23
Lightweight Ropes

Mountaineers have a special affinity for lighter ropes because they carry their ropes so much. Strength has never been an issue, and durability is being addressed by modern designs. The remaining problem is that most available hardware wasn't designed for thin ropes. That means special techniques are necessary to use thin ropes safely, particularly when they're extra slippery due to snow or gloved hands, or when the load is unusually high because of backpacks—issues unique to mountaineers.

RAPPELLING

Assiduously test the systems on which you bet your life *before* you head into the mountains. If you use a skinny rope, make sure that your rappel brake will produce enough force multiplication so you can easily control your descent with a single hand, even if that gloved hand is fatigued and even if you're wearing a bigger pack than you planned on. But what if you find yourself confronting a sit-

uation that you haven't tested beforehand? Suppose you're caught on a ridge by a lightning storm and decide to fix your skinny rope in order to flee on a long single-rope rappel; would you know how to handle this situation? There are several ways to add additional friction during a rappel, but in every case use an autoblock self-belay in the event the rope gets away from you. Test your autoblock at home, with two strands of your new rope and with one, and with a Klemheist instead of the autoblock knot if you're concerned about the autoblock knot having adequate grip on a snow-covered rope. If you start to lose your grip during a rappel and the autoblock saves your bacon, add a wrap of the rappel rope around your back or leg to increase the friction before releasing the autoblock and continuing. If you anticipate problems before you start down, consider adding a Münter hitch on a carabiner before the rope heads into your usual brake; that will almost certainly result in too much friction, which may be just what you want.

If you find yourself short on gear and facing

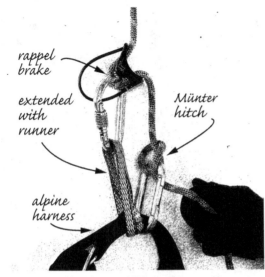

rappel
brake

extended
with
runner

Münter
hitch

alpine
harness

Adding a Münter hitch for extra holding power on a skinny rope.

right hand
grips
four strands

Klemheist on
24-inch
runner
to waist

one wrap
around your
boot
should do it

Reversing a rappel using one prusik and the rope wrapped around a foot.

an unusually dicey rappel or the need to lower two climbers simultaneously, use a Super Münter as described in Chapter 13. It will produce a lot more friction than a Münter hitch. For example, with it you can make a no-thrills rappel on a single strand of 6 mm cord; that means you could consider carrying such a cord to use as part of an emergency bailout system or for descending unanticipated difficulties.

Reversing a Rappel

When your luck runs out you may need to reverse a rappel, skinny rope or otherwise—hopefully for only a short distance. The causes include getting clothing or hair jammed into your rappel brake (this happens surprisingly often, and it's one more good reason to extend your rappel brake with a short runner), inadvertently descending below a hung rope strand, or finding no place to stop when you reach the end of your rope. To reverse a rappel you must create a connection from your harness to the ropes that will grip the ropes and hold your weight and another connection to a foot that will allow you to step up and move your harness connection upward. The most primitive harness connection is simply your autoblocked belay device (when the rappel rope is held by your autoblock self-belay). Don't overlook this ready option; it

may be all you need if you can attach a foot loop to the ropes above the brake in order to take off tension and move your autoblocked brake up the rope. A 48-inch runner with a Klemheist might do, or a prusik loop extended by another runner. Another hasty approach would be to attach a shorter prusik from your harness to the rope above the brake and then wrap the ropes around a foot, grab the ropes from below the wraps, and grip them against the rope. Stand up on the wrapped foot, and you can move up enough that your weight will shift from the rappel brake to the prusik when you back off on foot effort; at that point you could

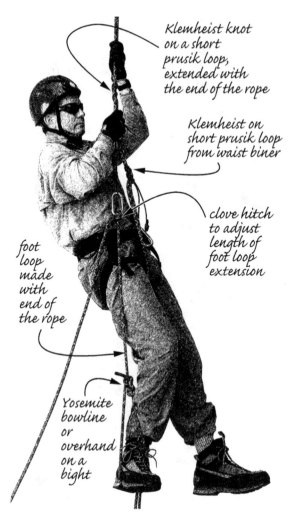

Klemheist knot
on a short
prusik loop,
extended with
the end of the rope

Klemheist on
short prusik loop
from waist biner

clove hitch
to adjust
length of
foot loop
extension

foot
loop
made
with
end of
the rope

Yosemite
bowline
or
overhand
on a
bight

Double-rope ascent using the end of the rope to extend a short
prusik loop.

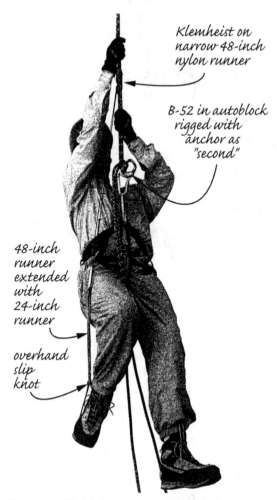

Klemheist on
narrow 48-inch
nylon runner

B-52 in autoblock
rigged with
anchor as
"second"

48-inch
runner
extended
with
24-inch
runner

overhand
slip
knot

Using an autoblock belay brake as a rope grab.

remove the clothing or hair from your brake, or re-move the brake entirely and thrash your way up. You wouldn't want to ascend far with these meth-ods if other options were feasible.

A prusik foot loop attached to the rope works better than wraps around your foot, if you have the materials to make one. This setup amounts to a traditional prusik ascent, except that it's on a pair of ropes (which precludes using mechanical ascenders, the optimum means of ascending a single rope). The illustration shows two short prusik loops, the holding prusik from the waist (attached to the ropes with a Klemheist) and the

pulling prusik extended using the end of the rope.

You can re-rig your autoblock belay device to use it as a rope grab, using a single prusik foot loop on the rope above your brake, extending your prusik with a runner if necessary. Run your upper prusik connection through a carabiner at your waist to help keep your balance under control.

These examples are offered to illustrate meth-ods that could be used in extremis to improvise means to reverse a rappel descent gone awry. It's unlikely that you'll have practiced these techniques when you find yourself forced to invoke them; tie backup knots (mule knots or overhand-on-a-bight) on the ropes below you, and anytime you face a long rope ascent, even using mechanical ascenders, clip in short to limit your fall if everything goes awry.

Retrieval Cords

Some climbers are tormented by angst because, with only one rope, descending a route by rappels potentially requires setting twice as many rappel anchors as belay anchors. Climbing on half ropes or twins solves this problem, but at the cost of weight and, in the case of halfs, complexity while climbing. A common solution for adventuresome climbers is to carry a long, very small cord used as a retrieval line or pull-down cord, so that full-length rappels can be made. That cord is strong enough for other purposes, too, including hauling, and some aspects of rescue. The typical diameter is 7 or 8 mm, but 6 mm works as well and is lighter yet; some rope manufacturers make 7 mm ropes just for this purpose, and even an 8 mm static line could be used if you happened to have it along for other purposes. A 35-meter half rope plus a 35-

meter length of 6 mm cord has many advantages for mountaineers. There are two concerns when rappelling: First, light retrieval ropes provide little support to the rappel; they're just along for the ride as far as friction goes, so the descent is basically a single-rope rappel. Second, very skinny cords have a remarkable affinity for stone and shrubbery; they get hung up and tangled at every opportunity, especially if it's windy.

The setup is always rigged for pulling the skinny rope first. The joining knot will bind against the rappel sling, so the thin rope is not supporting significant weight during the rappel—and it can't, due to stretch. If the rappel anchor were set up with the joining knot some distance from the anchor point, the differences in rope stretch between your climbing rope and retrieval cord could be a concern; this is something that must be worked out in advance for your particular ropes, to allow more terrain options for establishing rappel anchors when you use this technique. Compare stretch by

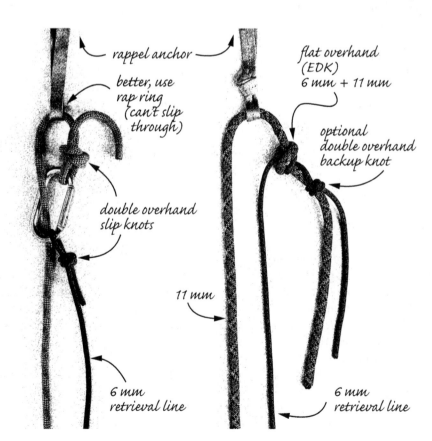

rappel anchor

better, use rap ring (can't slip through)

double overhand slip knots

11 mm

6 mm retrieval line

flat overhand (EDK) 6 mm + 11 mm

optional double overhand backup knot

6 mm retrieval line

The rappel anchor with retrieval cord setups.

substituting a large pulley for the rope anchor and note movement of the joining knot as you make a test rappel. Pulling the skinny rope first reduces the likelihood it will become stuck when coming down, but this also reduces the amount of pull that can be applied if something does get stuck, again depending on stretch of the retrieval cord. Either way, climbing up to free a stuck retrieval cord rappel system is more thought provoking, if that's possible, than when conventional ropes get stuck.

BELAYING THE LEADER ON A THIN ROPE

Using a conventional belay brake with a rope that's around 9 mm in diameter may not result in the holding power you expect, and "thin" is coming to mean closer to 8 mm. You read earlier that the rope has little effect on forces throughout the safety system when fall factors are around 0.3 or higher, even static ropes used for lead climbing. The rope's energy absorption does affect the amount of slip at the belay; however, ropes with higher impact force ratings result in more slip. Lighter ropes used as singles cause less slip at the brake because they stretch more. The amount of additional stretch compared to the reduced slip through the belay is more complex than you'd want to worry about, especially while climbing, but the bottom line is that falls on thin ropes will be longer than falls on less stretchy ropes, but not by as much as you'd expect.

Since thinner ropes have more energy absorption, you can use a less dynamic belay (less rope slip through the brake) and still have lower forces throughout the safety system than you'd produce with a fatter rope. The least dynamic brake for skinny ropes is a Münter hitch. The increasing popularity (and availability) of thinner ropes has resulted in the introduction of belay/rappel brakes specifically designed to accommodate smaller-diameter ropes; get one if you use a thin rope, including a half rope used as a single. Some thin rope brakes even have an autoblock feature; the Mammut Matrix is designed specifically for auoblocking with thinner ropes, and Mammut ships one with its new skinny single ropes, but the B-52 and XTC-XP handle thin ropes well, too, as does the venerable Gi-Gi when rigged appropriately.

Belaying the Leader for a Very Short Distance on a Very Skinny Rope

Some mountaineers carry very short, thin ropes for safety on short sections of precarious climbing or lowering themselves or others down a tricky move or two. If you're willing to depend on a 7 mm cordelette, you should be comfortable making a few moves while belayed by 7 mm accessory cord. It's strong enough to catch a slip or even a short, low-factor fall; I can think of a few airy step-across moves that fit this description—what mountaineers call 3.12. To my knowledge, no hardware brakes are intended for use with 7 mm cord. Without investing a lot of science, the belayer (or rappeller) can revert to a Münter hitch off her anchored waist or directly off an anchor such as a sling around a permanent terrain feature. That will limit force at the belay to around 2 kN, but the belayer should be prepared for rope slippage by wearing gloves. If there's any chance that the cord could slip entirely through the belay, secure the end or use a stopper knot—that's good advice no matter what rope you're using.

There will come a time when your rope is too frozen to cram into a belay brake. The autoblock brakes perform better with this challenge, due to their longer rope slots, but you want to have a backup. Your options would be a Münter hitch or a hip belay. If you use a hip belay, definitely increase its low holding power and security by passing both the incoming and outgoing strands through carabiners at your waist—and be prepared to deal with substantial rope slip when catching a leader fall, made worse by an icy rope.

BELAYING THE SECOND

Belaying the second involves much lower forces than those possible during leader falls. You know that I favor belaying the second directly off an anchor using a Münter hitch or autoblock brake and applying tension when possible. Take care that your choices of thin rope and belay brake are compatible. The Reverso probably has the best information available. I interpret Petzl's cartoons as saying that when belaying a leader on a single rope, 10 mm is the minimum suitable diameter; when belaying a single second on two strands, 8 mm is the minimum; and when belaying one or two seconds in autoblock, 8.5 mm is the minimum. If you're using modern, skinny ropes, consider the newer Reversino. The Reverso has two orientations for different holding power. Adding a second carabiner in the conventional orientation results in more friction; I've measured a 40 percent increase with most brakes. Trango says the B-52 is suitable for leader belay on two 7.8 mm twins, but some new twins are slightly thinner, so do your own tests. You'd expect the B-52 to be functional for belaying two seconds on such ropes; I have used it successfully with 8 mm ropes in autoblock mode.

RELEASING AN AUTOBLOCK

Autoblock means that tension on the second's rope automatically locks it in the belay brake; it's not a hands-off device until it locks (it's not "auto-lock" like the GriGri). Autoblock belay brakes are efficient for bringing up a second and are especially effective for bringing up two seconds simultaneously, but independently, on two strands. The essential feature of an autoblock brake is two long slots parallel to the rope. The second's rope enters at the top of a slot, passes around a second carabiner's spine (not the carabiner that's anchoring the brake), and exits at the bottom of the slot into the belayer's hand. Tension on a second's entering strand pinches the belayer's exiting strand into the slot, locking the rope against the relatively modest force of a short fall. Bringing up a second with an autoblock brake requires two hands to simultaneously pull up rope and pull it through the brake, so the brake should be anchored a couple of feet above the belayer for efficiency; using an autoblock brake off your waist would be stoopid. The trick is releasing the lock if the second falls and is weighting the rope. Depending on the particular belay brake (Gi-Gi's work well, B-52's not so well, try yours), if the autoblock carabiner has an oval cross section you may be able to let out rope simply by hinging it up and down; beyond that it gets tricky.

When you find yourself with a blocked brake and a second who can't climb up, you have two approaches. While you contemplate them, fiddle with

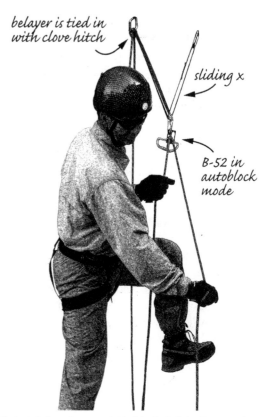

belayer is tied in with clove hitch

sliding x

B-52 in autoblock mode

Typical rig for using an autoblock brake to belay the second.

gear, or chat with the second, put a backup knot (such as an overhand-on-a-bight) in the rope and clip it to the anchor; the autoblock isn't guaranteed to be a positive lock forever. You'll then proceed based on whether or not the hanging second can be lowered or must be raised. Lowering, as always, is far more attractive in terms of time and effort.

If lowering is feasible for the second's situation, all that's necessary is to release the autoblock. The traditional solution is simpleminded but not easy: raise the autoblock carabiner until the autoblock effect goes away, whereupon the rope will run conventionally. Caution: as soon as the rope runs conventionally, the second will be free to drop rapidly; another belay brake, such as a Münter hitch, must already have been put in the system for control. Raising the carabiner (by attaching to either the autoblock carabiner or the brake itself, depending on the brand of brake) means, in effect, raising the second who's hanging on it. Most brakes help out with only a small amount of leverage; the Gi-Gi is more helpful. You'll probably have to rig some kind of pulley system attached to a higher anchor to create adequate mechanical advantage, even if the second can provide a little assistance. If you're getting the sense that this could turn into a science fair project, you're on the right track.

Here's a better approach. The illustration shows the use of a carabiner acting as a force-doubling pulley cleverly attached to the rope and to the belayer's harness. It shows using a section of the climbing rope for pulley cord, but you could also use our ubiquitous 48-inch skinny webbing runner. The force of the belayer's leg power, pulling off the harness, will be multiplied by two (minus pulley inefficiency). As soon as the fallen climber's weight is off the belay brake, the rope in it will be slack enough to remove the autoblock carabiner; at that point the brake will be out of the system, and rope control will revert to the Münter hitch belay already added. If you need both hands or just want to be cautious, put a mule knot on the rope ahead

of the Münter and snug it up. After letting out on the pulley and allowing the rope tension to come onto the mule knot, it can be released to let the Münter hitch take over to control the lowering of the second. (The mule knot, simple as it is, is very handy; it is described in detail in Chapter 25.)

Many texts, even manufacturers, teach releasing an autoblock using a setup in which the autoblock carabiner is pulled upward by a cord or runner through a higher redirect carabiner, so that the belayer can use body weight to pull. They haven't read *The Mountaineering Handbook,* or they'd know that such a setup will apply only about 85 percent of the belayer's weight to pulling, while the method I've described applies 130 percent of the belayer's leg strength—at least twice as much force as his weight, for over three times more total pulling power. Additionally, the method I've described only requires taking tension off the autoblock briefly before reverting to the Münter hitch, whereas the traditional method requires the autoblock to be pulled farther and for tension to be continuously maintained; it effectively hangs the weight of the belayer plus the climber off the single placement where the redirect is clipped (which may be high above and difficult to reach anyhow). Use my method; it'll work better unless you're in a hanging belay with no footholds, which is rare for mountaineers. It's easier to set up and much more efficient, plus it utilizes the strength of the entire anchor system. It's also easier to revert back to normal belaying once the second can resume climbing. If there's too much friction on the rope down below for even my approach to be effective, you'll have to set up a Z-pulley or something more complicated.

If the fallen climber must be raised or assisted in ascending, rather than lowered, you can readily set up a Z-pulley using the autoblocked brake as the holding device—just add a friction knot or rope grab to the climbing strand and connect the belaying strand to your harness with a clove hitch or, better, another friction knot. This isn't as energy efficient as using pulleys and prusiks, but it's quick and may do the job. Z-pulleys and other pulley and rescue systems are described in detail in Chapter 25. Hopefully you won't have to raise the second far before he can resume climbing, because

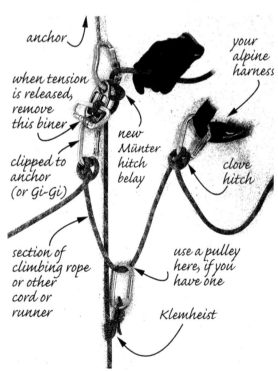

anchor

your alpine harness

when tension is released, remove this biner

new Münter hitch belay

clove hitch

clipped to anchor (or Gi-Gi)

section of climbing rope or other cord or runner

use a pulley here, if you have one

Klemheist

Releasing an autoblock brake using a section of the climbing rope.

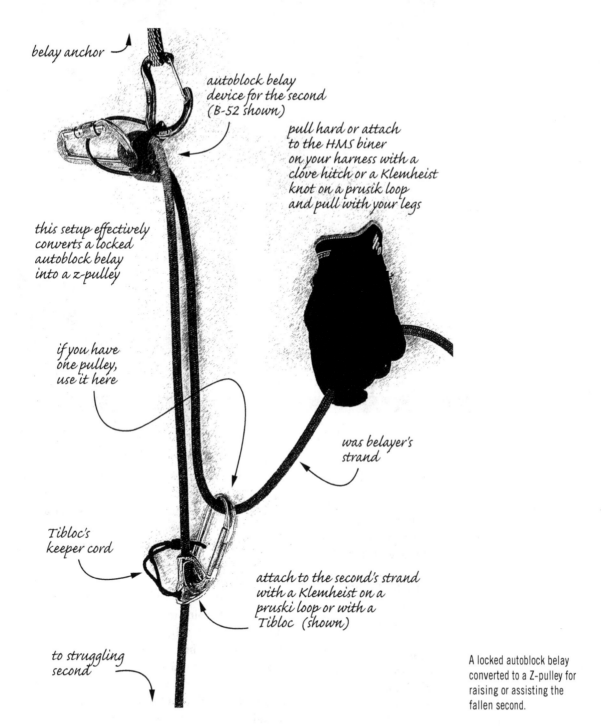

belay anchor

autoblock belay
device for the second
(B-52 shown)

pull hard or attach
to the HMS biner
on your harness with a
clove hitch or a Klemheist
knot on a prusik loop
and pull with your legs

this setup effectively
converts a locked
autoblock belay
into a z-pulley

if you have
one pulley,
use it here

was belayer's
strand

Tibloc's
keeper cord

attach to the second's strand
with a Klemheist on a
pruski loop or with a
Tibloc (shown)

to struggling
second

A locked autoblock belay
converted to a Z-pulley for
raising or assisting the
fallen second.

it's going to be a grunt. Once the second is back to climbing, it's easy to remove the "pulley" and revert back to the autoblock brake.

When the fallen second can't be lowered, perhaps because she's swung over featureless terrain, for example, don't ignore the possibility that the fastest solution might be for the second to attach prusiks to the rope and climb up on her own. Hauling a climber up, Z-pulley or not, is always the last option.

24
Roped Parties

Roped climbing is significantly slower than climbing unroped, and climbing in a group of more than two can be notably slower than climbing in pairs. Climbing in a large roped group compounds the slowness, so be prepared with specialized techniques to minimize the delays whenever a group of climbers must move over fourth- or easy fifth-class terrain.

The section at the end of Chapter 14 with suggestions for moving fast on rock describes using a single rope folded in half as if it were a pair of halfs or twins to enable bringing up two seconding climbers simultaneously using an autoblock belay brake. Basically, the leader ties in to the middle of the rope and leads on one strand; then the leader belays up the other two climbers simultaneously, one on each strand. This works well but limits the length of the pitch to half a rope length. That may still be faster than other ways for a party of three to climb. Releasing the autoblock if one climber falls isn't noteworthy, but if both fall and can't climb, Herculean efforts will be required.

SIMUL-CLIMBING

Simul-climbing means that the party members and the rope move as a unit, using only intermediate anchors and no fixed belays except at the start and finish of the pitch. This technique is applicable to climbing on rock as well as snow, but on snow more flexible options may avail. Simul-climbing with a large party is asking for trouble; try to limit the rope to three climbers. Here's why. For simul-climbing to be sensible, you must allow at least one anchor between each climber, at least two between the first and last. More climbers mean more anchors and more time stopping while anchors are placed and removed. More climbers also mean more jerking on the rope and more stopping to wait for others, particularly if they're rest stepping; excess slack or having climbers carry coils of rope is definitely not the way to resolve these delays. If a large party must be moved over roped terrain, simul-climbing may be impractical, and some form of fixed rope may work better.

No climber on a simul-climbing rope can fall—that's the overriding rule. The leader has the best chance to recover after falling, but if a second falls, likely the leader will be pulled down from behind. The whole party could end up hanging on the top anchor. That means that all climbers must climb as if leading, and that means the rope moves safely only at the leading pace of the slowest climber—the apparent benefit of a top rope for following climbers is purely psychological. The seconds bear more responsibility for not falling than does the leader, so it's sensible for the strongest climber to give up the lead when simul-climbing, both ascending and descending, unless routefinding or anchor-setting skills are at issue.

As the leader heads off, the second will be belaying normally until out of rope. As soon as the leader places the first anchors, the second should remove any belay anchor and prepare to climb. When the rope is entirely out, the belayer should let any belay device just hang on the rope where it is, signal the leader, and get moving. The goal of simul-climbing is speed.

Old-school advice for the rope to lie on climbers' downhill side is just lame compensation for sloppy rope management. New-school moun-taineers know that having the rope across the uphill hip when simul-climbing on snow favors a successful arrest should the rope come tight; if it runs on your downhill side, you'll be more strongly pulled away from the slope. Climbers in the middle of the rope attach to butterfly loops with their locking HMS carabiner and easily pull the rope past anchor carabiners without unclipping.

Advanced Topic

A technique that makes simul-climbing on snow or rock significantly safer uses the Tibloc. A Tibloc is a tiny, one-piece rope grab—basically a minimalist mechanical ascender. If the leader runs the simul rope through a Tibloc at an anchor carabiner (preferably one with a short runner), a fall by someone lower will be caught there and won't be felt by the leader, yet the rope can move upward freely. The force that the Tibloc will have to hold from a falling second is less than a kilonewton; they're rated over 4 kN. A fall by the leader is held by the anchor carabiner, not by the Tibloc. Dozens of Tiblocs aren't needed; only one is required between the leader and other climbers to get the job done, so a few will suffice even for a long simul-climb pitch, where anchors are typically widely

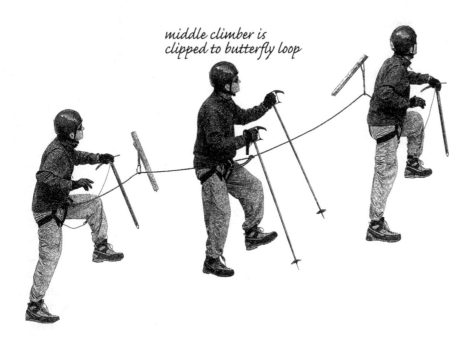

middle climber is clipped to butterfly loop

Triplets simul-climbing on snow.

anchor

you are here

butterfly knot

pull through

Clipping past an anchor.

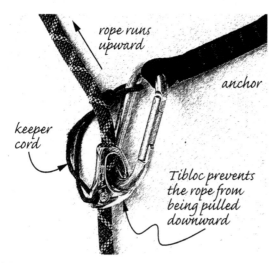

rope runs upward

anchor

keeper cord

Tibloc prevents the rope from being pulled downward

A Tibloc on a simul-climb anchor.

spaced. The second who removes a Tibloc needs to let the leader know to place another.

Encountering a Tibloc at an anchor requires a following simul-climber to temporarily clip in with his daisy and unclip the rope, so Tiblocs on anchors work best for teams of two climbers when they will be removed rather than passed. Don't forget to tie a security loop of 3 mm cord through the retaining feature of your Tiblocs; they're able to jump out of gloved hands with practiced agility.

Tiblocs can be further exploited if middle climbers attach to the rope with Tiblocs instead of attaching to a butterfly loop. They'll then be able to continue moving upward even while the last climber stops to remove anchors. With the anchor removed, the last climber may be able to move up faster and make up time, yet the Tibloc will lock to the rope in the event the middle climber falls; this isn't an excuse to allow slack in the rope. A Tibloc attachment can be pulled right through an anchor carabiner without being detached, just like

a friction knot. If the leader falls, the second climber's Tibloc will lock and hold the upward pull on the rope, as you would hope, while if the last climber falls, a middle climber on a Tibloc may not be pulled off, though the leader may.

Decision Time

Give thought to whether simul-climbing will actually be faster than pitching it out. A belayed pitch can extend at the leading speed of the best climber, and seconds can follow using more success-oriented techniques, even on rock (climbing on tension, using a single ax, using the ax more for balance and less for traction, climbing steeper slopes without sinking the pick, using rope tension while removing pro, etc.; in other words: hanging it out more). This is significantly faster than climbing on lead. Simul-climbing is fast only if the weakest climber isn't significantly slower than the leader climbs while also placing pro; using Tiblocs can help even things out, but only to a point, so simul-climbing is mainly a technique for uniformly competent parties. Such teams switch nimbly between simul-climbing and belaying (of the leader or seconds) depending on terrain. The first and last pitches of a simul-climbed section will be belayed in any case, which is good because belayed climbing is unquestionably safer than simul-climbing.

FIXED ROPES

If you fail to follow my advice to avoid larger groups, as we all sometimes do, you'll inevitably confront a situation in which that group needs to go up, down, or across a roped pitch using one rope. Approached conventionally, that could consume an incredible amount of time; it could even be impossible, if wind or traversing terrain precludes sending the second's end of the rope back to the group of waiting climbers. Simul-climbing becomes unwieldy with more than four climbers moving on the same rope. Using an autoblock belay to bring up two seconds simultaneously is a means of moving fast for a party of three, but only three. One alternative for larger parties on fourth-class terrain is to fix the rope—anchor the rope at top and bottom.

Describing all the various scenarios in which a party could climb or descend a fixed rope would be lengthy, so I'll describe the components, and you can put them together to match the terrain, available equipment, and skills of your party. Many decisions revolve around whether the rope will be mainly vertical or mainly horizontal. Vertical is easier to deal with, because anyone who falls will do so in a downward direction and end up beside the rope. Falling on a fixed line protecting a traverse can result in the fallen climber sliding forward or backward along the rope, with or without affecting other climbers on the rope, and the fallen climber may have difficulty getting back on the route. Establish fixed lines so they'll actually protect climbers who fall on them at any point; never set them mainly to provide psychological benefit.

Setting a Fixed Line

Mountaineers can fix a climbing rope for a larger party by clipping it through carabiners on intermediate anchors so it runs freely—basically leaving the lead rope in place and tying off its upper end. The alternative is to use clove hitches or butterfly loops to attach the rope at each anchor—called a rebelay. The benefits of a rebelay at each intermediate anchor are that the force of falling and pulling climbers will be more isolated between two anchors; the length of falls will be minimized, and other climbers on the rope will be jerked less. These might seem like good things, but there are negatives. The rebelay approach presents problems for the climber who sets the line. Unless the leader accepts a fair amount of misery and what amounts to a tied-off belay or no belay, the connections will be tied by the subsequent climber who travels the rope, and even that isn't trivial. The anchors must be able to resist forward and backward pulls; this might not be difficult to set

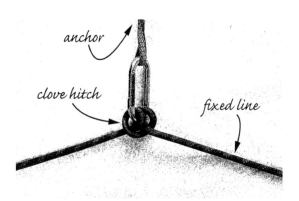

A fixed line with a clove hitch rebelay.

up for easy falls on snow but could be a problem on rock that lacks natural anchor opportunities. Rebelays also present problems for subsequent climbers, who must work around each anchor as they ascend. That's time consuming if climbers attach with prusik loops. If the fixed line is simply laced through carabiners at each anchor, a climber who falls or who pulls on the rope for aid will pull the entire line tight. Other climbers on the rope may or may not be jerked, depending on their means of attachment.

Connecting to a Fixed Rope

There are four ways for climbers to attach to a fixed line. In addition to their primary attachment, a backup attachment to the rope using their daisy and small locker should be added if there's any significant possibility of a fall or fumble; in general, keep the backup connection clipped above you and the anchors you pass, ascending or descending. Climbers on expeditionary fixed lines typically use mechanical ascenders to connect. When passing rebelays, climbers clip their backup carabiner higher, remove their ascender, and then reattach it on the higher side of the anchor. Removing and reattaching a conventional mechanical ascender while wearing mittens is a practiced art of expeditionary climbers. If you're tempted, test your potential ascender acquisitions for ease of deliberate release from the rope and for ease of holding the cam open without releasing it, which will be necessary when climbing down a fixed line. A simpler Tibloc connection is effective, lighter, and, with a wrist loop, even easier to yard on through strenuous sections. It doesn't require being pushed along like an ascender; plus it will fit through oval carabiners at anchors without being removed from the rope, making for faster progress if you've set your fixed rope without rebelays. Downclimbing a fixed line with a Tibloc is impractically fiddly. Conventional mechanical ascenders and Tiblocs are one-directional—they prevent the user from sliding backward only. If a climber were to fall on a traverse soon after passing an anchor, he'd fall forward and would slide along the rope to a low point between the anchors ahead and behind. If a climber ahead of you falls when you're attached with an ascender, you'll be jerked, but maybe not if a trailing climber were to fall, because of the one-directional lock of the ascender. A climber attached to the fixed line with a friction knot on a prusik loop would be jerked by a falling climber ahead or behind, but would travel the minimum distance in his own fall—assuming the friction knot locked and held. A friction knot attachment can easily be slipped through carabiners at anchors of the fixed line but must be retied to pass rebelays.

The fourth method to attach (after mechanical ascenders, Tibloc rope grabs, and friction knots on prusik loops) would be simply for a climber to clip to the fixed line with a carabiner that's cinched to her harness with a runner or her daisy chain. A carabiner attachment results in the longest fall, whether the fixed line is vertical or horizontal, but the climber would be unaffected by other climbers falling or pulling on the line, other than by the rope straightening. A carabiner can pass through an oval carabiner holding the rope, so it's unnecessary to unclip to pass a non-rebelay anchor. This kind of arrangement is equivalent to attaching to the fixed line by your backup connection; it might be appropriate for a line that gives climbers a simple hand hold or for backup security, to speed up a party scurrying over easy ground.

When setting the anchors for a mostly horizontal fixed line, think about the potential for force multiplication. The included angle of the rope at the fallen climber will be high, and so the load at anchors will be more than the climber's fall force—more than you might expect. A rebelayed fixed line has that concern at every anchor, a free-running fixed line mainly at the ends.

Downclimbing

Downclimbing a fixed rope on rock or snow can be faster than setting up a rappel or lowering climbers one by one, and sometimes it's the only option, even if rappelling equipment is available (which, if you have at least one carabiner, it will be). Expeditionary climbers descend by holding the cam of their ascender half open. Climbers can attach with a friction knot and push it along the rope as they descend; do not let the friction knot

Passing an anchor carabiner with a prusik connection.

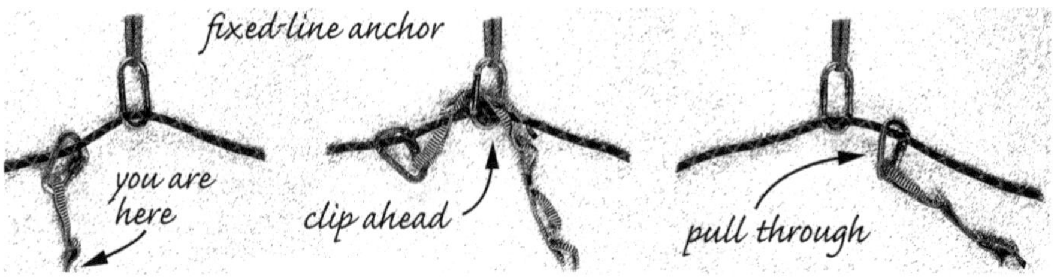

prusik shown, works with Tibloc

you are here

clip ahead

push through

Passing a fixed-line anchor with a carabiner connection.

fixed-line anchor

you are here

clip ahead

pull through

become loose enough to follow along on its own or it won't lock in the event of a fall. An occasional butterfly loop can be put in the rope below tricky sections, as safety catches against slips, even in the absence of intermediate anchors; if you're lucky, your safety connection may stop at the knot. Clip to such loops with your daisy as you move your friction knot around them. You know my view that it's foolhardy for a party to rope up without placing anchors, but simply setting a top and bottom anchor can be a very fast way to move a large group over easy terrain if they've practiced the basic techniques of moving up and down fixed lines.

RAPPELLING BY A GROUP

Rappelling safely requires following a protocol such as the one I detailed in Chapter 13, but a group of climbers gathered at a rappel station virtually guarantees distractions. It's a good idea to designate an experienced climber to manage the process and ensure that each descender starts out safely. This is particularly important if the group is stressed or if the rappel is somehow unusual—on a single rope, for example, or in darkness. Having supervision also minimizes wasted time, but time will be consumed in large quantities even in the best case.

The order of descenders shouldn't be based on weight; that rule is baseless and silly. The first descender has a number of responsibilities, including finding a good spot to stop and applying a fireman's belay if necessary. She must be able to reverse her rappel if something goes wrong. If an inexperienced or exhausted climber must be left behind, he can be made ready to go with his brake connected to the rope; the weight of the previous descender will keep him in place until the rope is unweighted. Then he needs only unclip his safety connection and descend with a fireman's belay from below.

You may conclude that it will be faster to set up a rappel on a single strand of the rope so that the group can make a longer rappel. The last descender will have to stop halfway down and set up an anchor for an ordinary two-strand rappel before continuing down to the remainder of the party, but that's probably faster than having the entire party make two rappels.

25
Self-Rescue

THINK AHEAD

The common admonition to think ahead for several steps through each decision and its consequences is nowhere more important than in the event of self-rescue. Self-rescue refers to the actions a party must take to deal with an emergency incident, typically a fall or rockfall, without relying on outside assistance. Making a cell phone call is not self-rescue. The same thinking and similar techniques apply to self-rescue on rock climbs and to self-rescue in the event of a crevasse fall. Many descriptions of self-rescue techniques imply a large, well-supplied party and, curiously, plenty of fortuitously placed trees; the reality is more likely to be a small party—one of whom is injured—who have only a small amount of climbing hardware with which to work, most of which may be with the victim. The techniques of self-rescue are among the most complex and least practiced climbing skills, and self-rescue circumstances, unlike search and rescue (SAR) operations, invari-

ably sacrifice safety margins. I won't pretend to cover the subject thoroughly, but I do want to present basic techniques and show how they can be applied. These techniques aren't rocket surgery, but you can't expect to learn technical self-rescue simply from a book. You can't memorize setups; you must strive to learn principles that you can combine to deal with each specific incident. A group of climbers might be able to teach themselves self-rescue, but they'll need a considerable amount of time and effort to work out and practice the skills safely. You might be able to get training from a school or guide, but unfortunately many guides are ill informed. Shop around. More important than skills, however, is judgment. I'll discuss self-rescue just enough to augment your judgment, so that you can make the most of your existing skills and resources, should you find yourself in a self-rescue situation some day.

There are specific steps in dealing with a self-rescue situation; you'll see slightly different versions, but the important thing is to have a structure and follow it.

▲ Don't get yourself into a self-rescue situation in the first place. Self-rescue isn't limited to roped rock climbing. It can occur anytime someone is injured in a precarious environment. It can arise from a rappelling mishap, or taking a fall on third-class terrain. You could even consider the possibility of becoming benighted as a self-rescue event, because it could require technical rope skills to deal with. After you read this section you'll understand the grave consequences that arise when self-rescue skills become necessary; you'll want to avoid such circumstances. When you're in the mountains, turn up the volume on that little birdie who's constantly complaining, "Hey, you know, this might turn out bad." Don't become paralyzed; just think ahead and carefully consider where your actions and decisions might lead and how you might have to respond if things do, indeed, go badly.

▲ If worse does come to worst and you realize that the game has abruptly changed from climbing to self-rescue, the first thing to do is *do nothing*. Clear thinking rather than prompt action is what will be required. You want to stand back from the shock and awe of what has just happened and get your mind in balance. This is particularly difficult among a group and when physical trauma is obvious. You'll soon begin a series of linked actions, and it's imperative that your mind be clear as you plan how you'll deal with the situation confronting you.

▲ Survey the scene. This is primary to every emergency response protocol. You want to think about how many victims and rescuers there are, what resources might be available, how remote you are, what's the most likely ultimate goal, and so on. Most importantly you want to be acutely aware of any factors, such as objective hazards, that threaten, because the first rule of rescue is not to jeopardize the rescuers.

▲ Quickly assess the victim. You may have to do this from a distance, perhaps out of sight. In a self-rescue situation the most critical bits of information are the approximate extent of the injuries to the victim and the degree to which the victim can assist in his own rescue. The victim may be uninjured but hanging where climbing is impossible, or the victim may merely have stumbled on talus but be unresponsive. It would be rare that a victim has a life-threatening injury that requires immediate intervention of a sort that could be provided in a wilderness context. It's likely more important to formulate an effective and comprehensive rescue plan than it is to give prompt first aid—no matter how loudly the victim may be protesting (protesting is good, because it means the victim is conscious and breathing; being unable to protest is bad). Of course, if you can easily and safely reach the victim and perform a thorough assessment (as you will learn in that wilderness first-aid course you've signed up for), then do so. Protect the victim from further injury.

▲ Inventory your resources. The best way to do this is for everyone to dump their gear on the ground so every item can be seen, including climbing hardware, first-aid supplies, tools, items with improvisational potential, and even food, water, and clothing. If you're holding the victim on belay, you may have to do a mental inventory of your resources and verbally query the victim as to hers. It would be great if, before the climb, your party discussed what gear is being carried and what first-aid skills are along, but that seldom happens on casual outings.

▲ Formulate a plan and communicate it to the other rescuers, if any, and to the victim. The plan may be designed using input from others, including the victim, but there comes a time early in a rescue scenario when a single person must assume leadership and direct the other rescuers. That person could even be the victim, but once a plan is established, there's no room for participatory democracy. The person best qualified to lead is the one with the best management skills, not necessarily the best climbing or medical skills—those persons may contribute more effectively by focusing their skills where needed. It's imperative that the rescue plan be well designed, because very often it will be difficult to alter a plan once it's under way; indecision and equivocation consume valuable time and send the wrong message to all involved.

▲ If your plan involves technical rope work,

Harness hang syndrome is a real puzzler, about which little is certain other than the seriousness of the problem. When a healthy person hangs motionless in a harness (any harness that supports the legs, including a full body industrial safety harness), perhaps because he's exhausted or has fainted, he inevitably falls unconscious in about 10 minutes; traumatized persons succumb faster. The cause is uncertain, and the condition only recently identified (among cavers and industrial workers); in the past the syndrome may have been confused with exposure or hypothermia. A person hanging immobile constitutes a serious medical emergency and must be attended to promptly, or he'll die within 30 minutes, often less. Industrial safety protocols are being developed suggesting rescue of an immobile person hanging in a harness should take place within 4 minutes. Any movement of the victim's legs or torso orientation will stave off the problem (so keep moving if you're hanging), but once the syndrome sets in, victims soon become less cogent and unable to help themselves. The problem is also called suspension syndrome, harness-induced pathology, and Compression Avascularization/RePerfusion syndrome. Very scary.

---

check and double-check every step you take. Likely these skills are seldom practiced, so you must be absolutely confident that your procedures are sound. Don't get fancy; you'll be under a lot of stress. And remember that the most reliable plan may be to give the victim your jacket and go for help.

A climber fall with you as the belayer could require technical rope work. As you recover your composure, you see that only a small number of possible alternatives is available to you: stay where you are to lower or raise a climber who can participate, or join the climber to administer first aid or assist moving up or down. The following discussions focus on actions a belayer might take to respond to a leader fall, but they could also apply to a second's fall or a crevasse fall, depending on circumstances; keep in mind the differences as you read. The scenario needn't involve a leader fall to be serious: a second won't take a serious fall unless it involves a pendulum or the belayer fails to keep the rope tight, but a second could find himself in a steep section of a fourth-class pitch, unable to climb up, with insufficient rope to be lowered to a safe location, and without any prusiking gear or skills—now what? Even if the leader doesn't fall, what do you do if the rope somehow gets too stuck for the leader to advance and downclimbing isn't an option?

Lower Is Better

Whatever the cause of the incident, if you can lower the victim to a position of security, you're in luck. This could require cooperation of an able victim or even lassoing a nearby victim. Do whatever you can to exploit a lowering tactic; it's well worth the effort, given that other options are odious or impossible. Taking in rope at the belay requires pulling harder than the victim's weight. After you've lowered the victim, you'll want to assist her, and you may want to keep her on belay as you do. That means you'll have to *escape the belay* that you're using to hold her, while keeping yourself secured for safety. This is also the first step in other rescue procedures.

PLAN YOUR ESCAPE

The basic goal of escaping the belay is to gain control of the tension that's being applied by your belay device to the main rope and smoothly transfer the tension to a separate, secure anchor point. We're talking body weight or less here, so the emphasis on this separate anchor is security more than strength; you probably don't have to worry about equalizing several placements, but the anchor should be backed up unless you have no option, because it's life supporting, and because the person who builds it is under stress.

Tie Off the Anchored Belay

If you're belaying off an anchor, as I recommend for belaying the second, you've already escaped the belay. Now you must lock off the rope at the belay device. Think ahead several steps and evaluate the consequences of your plan. You'll certainly want to remain tied in, if you already are, but you may need some extra slack in your connection. Will your tie-off result in any forces on the climber's anchor from unintended directions? Don't be paranoid about putting minor jerks on the belay anchor as you work; after all, it's just been tested by a fall.

If you're using a tube brake, pass a bight of the rope through the HMS carabiner and tie a mule knot on the spine of the carabiner. A mule knot (strange how knots get named for animals and animal parts) is simply an overhand slip knot tied on a bight—an overhand bow knot; its value is that it locks the rope at the belay device but can be released while the rope is under tension. You'll use a mule knot, even on paired cords, anytime you need a knot that can be released while the cords are under tension. The illustration on the following page shows how you put the mule knot to work holding the rope through the brake.

You could also tie the mule knot on the main rope, but it isn't necessary; it's easier to tie it on the carabiner. Tighten the mule knot before you ease off on the hand that's holding the brake. This same method can be used to tie yourself off when rappelling or anytime you want to keep tension on the belay rope but have both hands free. The mule knot is only holding the force on the rope divided by the force magnification of the brake— less than 10 percent of body weight. Increase security by clipping the mule's bight to some part of your harness.

Securing a Münter hitch is very similar, but it's easier to tie the mule knot on the main rope. This combination is so common and handy, for both ropes and prusik loops, that it's called the Münter-mule. See the illustration.

That was easy; now you can sort things out and continue with your plan of either lowering the victim, raising the victim, or climbing to the victim to give assistance. In any rescue situation, it's always wise to tie backup stopper knots in ropes and use to friction HMS knot loops to prevent belay ropes from slipping away unintentionally.

Anchored Belayer

If you and the belay brake are attached to the same anchor, you must establish an independent point to which you can transfer the rope tension. Hopefully you can use the anchor to which you're attached; it was set to keep you from being pulled into the leader's Anchor #1 (or downward toward

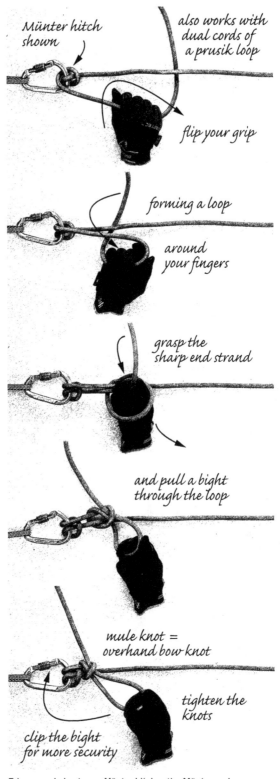

Münter hitch shown

also works with dual cords of a prusik loop

flip your grip

forming a loop

around your fingers

grasp the sharp end strand

and pull a bight through the loop

mule knot = overhand bow knot

tighten the knots

clip the bight for more security

Tying a mule knot on a Münter hitch—the Münter-mule.

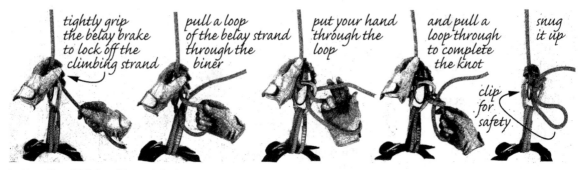

tightly grip the belay brake to lock off the climbing strand — _pull a loop of the belay strand through the biner_ — _put your hand through the loop_ — _and pull a loop through to complete the knot_ — _snug it up_ — _clip for safety_

Locking off an ATC belay with a mule knot.

your ascending second if you've unwisely elected to belay off your harness or through a redirect), so its optimum direction should still be secure. Whether the anchor point is new or part of your existing anchor, it'll have to be within reach—you may be dangling in the air at this point if the fallen climber has pulled you upward.

Start by putting a friction knot on the rope with a prusik loop and connecting that loop to a carabiner, preferably a locker, on the new anchor point with a Münter-mule, treating both strands of the prusik as one. The Klemheist is a good choice for the friction knot. Clip the free end of the Münter-mule prusik loop into its carabiner as a backup. You'll need a longish prusik loop; 32 inches (82 cm) is about the minimum, and a 6 mm cordelette would be ideal if you use at least four wraps in your Klemheist—maybe more on a skinny rope. Avoid hassles with the damn knot on a long prusik loop (which is how you'll refer to the loop's double fisherman's knot when you practice this technique) by using separate loops for the Klemheist and the Münter-mule, then clip them together with a carabiner after you get everything in place. If you need both hands while setting up the Münter-mule, wrap the belay strand of the rope around a leg a few times, or even wrap your leg with a long bight in the rope and clip it in your HMS biner; it won't take much tension to hold the belay rope.

Let out rope from your belay brake until tension is transferred to the new anchor. Managing this rope work takes practice as well as having those prusik loops somewhere other than in the bottom of your pack. Re-anchor yourself using

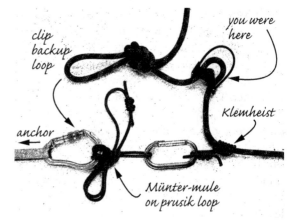

clip backup loop — _you were here_ — _Klemheist_ — _anchor_ — _Münter-mule on prusik loop_

Holding the rope with a Münter-mule on prusik loops in order to escape the belay.

your small locker and daisy chain. Tie a butterfly or overhand to create a loop in the rope and clip it in to the biner that's holding the Münter-mule, as a backup, but locate it far enough from the Münter-mule that it won't become tensioned accidentally, which will make it impossible to release. Remove your belay brake from the rope. You've escaped the belay.

LOWERING THE VICTIM

If you intend to lower the victim with the rope, you'll set up an HMS biner on the anchor that holds the Münter-mule, remove the rope's backup connection, and tie a new Münter-mule using the climbing rope. Take as much slack as possible out of this new Münter-mule and tie a new temporary backup in case it slips. Then transfer the rope tension to the new Münter-mule on the rope by releasing the one on the prusik loop. Remove the prusik loop and Klemheist. You will be able to let out rope under control of the new Münter hitch on the main rope after releasing the new mule knots on the rope and the backup knot.

If these instructions strike you as excessively complex, you've seen the light. Work out the details step by step with your own gear and a realistic load; you'll see it's pretty straightforward, once the processes come together for you.

ASCENDING

Now that you've extricated yourself from the belay you can set about lowering the victim from a better vantage point or preparing to climb up. An injured victim may need first aid or assistance while being lowered, but climb up only if you absolutely must; you'll likely be joining the victim in a precarious location—you don't want to also end up joining the victim in a predicament. If the victim needs first aid or is hanging and immobile, you'll need to work quickly because you have 15 minutes or less before harness hang syndrome sets in. However you do it, climbing up will consume vast amounts of time. The easiest way to climb up is simply to climb the rock as the leader did. In order to have some semblance of a belay, attach a friction knot to the rope and slide it along with you; slack in this connection encourages its failure. Passing intermediate anchors will require moving

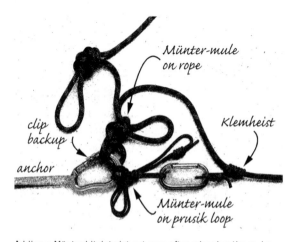

Münter-mule
on rope

clip
backup

anchor

Klemheist

Münter-mule
on prusik loop

Adding a Münter hitch to let out rope after releasing the mules.

PRUSIK WITH YOUR PRUSIK PRUSIK

The prusik knot is so pervasive that *prusik* is not only an adjective but also a verb and a noun. As a verb it means to ascend a rope using friction knots (to *jug* or *jumar* means climbing a rope using mechanical ascenders, such as a Jumar). As a noun, prusik refers to a loop of small-diameter accessory cord, typically 5 mm, but sometimes 4 mm for more reliable locking on skinny or frozen ropes, or 6 mm, for better tending by some pulleys, at the expense of more troublesome locking. The prusik knot isn't usually the best choice for the actual friction knot; others lock and release more easily, such as the 4-wrap Klemheist, which can also be made with webbing runners, particularly skinny nylon webbing. The Bachmann holds less strongly but can be more easily moved along the rope; you'll find it and the prusik described in Appendix A. Most friction knots (even the Bachmann, sorta) are bi-directional, whereas mechanical ascenders lock in one direction only—with implications for special climbing techniques and climber safety in some scenarios.

the friction knot through each clip, same as you would pass anchors on a fixed line except that the line may be held tightly by anchor carabiners or against terrain features along the way; that could force you to attach a second prusik above the impasse or to clip in with your daisy while you relocate the prusik you're using. Be wary of loading anchors from insecure directions.

If simply climbing up rock (or ice) isn't feasible, you must consider ascending the rope itself. This is complicated and time consuming. What you do when you reach the fallen climber is likely to be more complicated yet, so it better be absolutely necessary to go there, and you better have a clear plan for what you're going to accomplish if you manage to pull it off. Actually, prusiking up a rope isn't all that difficult; it's a necessary trad climbing and glacier travel skill. But it's awkward and slow—and miserable if you're on a slope where you aren't fully hanging but can't stand on your feet. You can enjoy the full measure of fun practicing ascending a rope using friction knots by climbing up toward a pulley while the other end of the rope is being slowly belayed out by a "friend."

The trick to efficient prusiking is working out

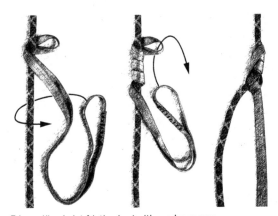

Klemheist knot on
waist prusik loop
made with
5 mm cord

Klemheist knot on
foot prusik loop
made with narrow
nylon webbing

backup
mule knot

overhand
slip
knot

Prusiking up a rope.

Tying a Klemheist friction knot with a nylon runner.

One exception to the difficulty of climbing to reach the fallen climber is rappelling to reach a second who needs assistance—if you have enough rope. Following my advice, you'll be belaying your second with a Münter hitch. To start the rescue, tie off the Münter hitch with a mule knot. Then anchor the second's strand using a prusik loop, with a Klemheist on the rope and a Münter-mule at the anchor carabiner, as I've recently described. Release the mule knot on the main rope so the prusik loop takes the load of your partner, and then take apart the Münter hitch on the main rope and run the rope through the anchor carabiner without a knot. Connect yourself to the belay side of the rope with your rappel brake; now your second is on one strand of the rope and you're on the other, with the rope through the anchor carabiner. Disconnect your personal safety clip from the anchors, put your weight on your rappel brake, release the Münter-mule on the prusik loop, and rappel to your second; you may want to clip yourself to the second's strand if it angles. Friction of the rope in the anchor carabiner will prevent the rope from slipping there. When you reach your second, you can attach with a short runner or prusik loop and continue down together in a counterweighted rappel, for half a rope length anyhow.

a prusik loop setup and lengths that work for you and getting them on the rope the way you intend; remember the mnemonic "put your foot down and waist away" to remind yourself that the connection from your waist to the rope usually attaches higher on the rope than the one from your foot. Size one loop to connect from the rope at forehead level to your HMS biner and another from just below the first to your foot when it's raised high. You might want to extend a short prusik loop with a slip-knotted runner on your foot, or maybe a 48-inch runner is all you need for the foot loop. If you'll use your system for glacier travel, figure in the effect of a chest harness and practice with it clipped to the rope so you can be sure it doesn't get in the way. A simple ascending setup works for me; I don't prusik far enough or often enough to rig a special-purpose Texas or Frog setup like those cavers use.

Tying in Short

Rope-ascending technique is also used in crevasse rescue, but that doesn't mean it's any easier when the rope is covered with snow. Normally the rope climber will tie an overhand knot in the rope behind himself every 10 feet and possibly clip it to his harness (not to a gear loop!) for safety should his friction knot slip (in which case it may melt and fail). This is called *tying in short* or *clipping in short*, and it should be done even if you're using mechanical ascenders, which can become unclipped inexplicably. Release and untie the previous safety knot when you connect the next if there's any chance of hang up when the rope is retrieved; if that's a big worry, you'll want to retain *all* of the rope and safety loops, but you'll have to thread them onto a runner loop in order to prevent a gigantic snarl at your waist. Use your daisy. If this sounds complex and time consuming, you're correct. Moreover, in our rescue scenario of ascending a tightly anchored rope that's holding the leader, it'll be impossible to tie safety knots—instead, clip the rope with a locker on your daisy that you hope will stop you at lower anchors should you fall, but mainly hope that your friction knots never slip.

A Turn for the Worse

It only gets worse. Prusiking up a tight, angled rope is much more difficult than climbing a slack rope that drapes vertically. If the rope being climbed takes a turn at a carabiner or over a rock edge (or over the icy lip of a crevasse in another scenario), it may be impossible to slip the upper friction knot (the one attached to your waist) up and over the biner or edge. To pass this impasse you may have to step up as high as possible on the foot loop and connect a new friction knot to the rope on the other side of the biner or edge on which the rope is pressing. Attach a new waist prusik, or if you haven't a spare, remove your waist loop and reattach it, all the while thinking pure thoughts. Don't try to remove the anchors (they're under tension), but reattach that safety locker on the rope above each anchor as you pass it. This whole business is a nerve-racking exercise—and, meanwhile, time marches on.

PULLEY SYSTEMS

The least attractive of your alternatives is raising the victim. This might be impossible for a two-person party, even one fairly knowledgeable and well equipped. The pulling force on the rope at the belay stance will need to be about twice the weight of the fallen climber in order to lift her, more if there's friction on the rope. This immediately calls either for a party of hearty climbers with prusik loops connected to the rope for better grip or, more likely, a force-multiplying pulley system.

Does Z Pulley Work, Monsieur?

Unfortunately, *je crois que non*—a little secret seldom brought out in climbing texts. The classic Z-pulley is supposed to have a 3:1 force multiplication. Practically, however, using ordinary climbers' pulleys and rope, the actual advantage will be only a little north of 2:1 due to inefficiencies and friction; using carabiners instead of pulleys will reduce the realizable force multiplication even more. If you attach both your hands to the rope with prusik loops to get a good grip and have a solid stance, you can pull steadily on a rope with about a quarter of a kilonewton (60 lbf), briefly maybe twice that. If you have a really good stance with lots of room, you can apply more force by attaching the prusik loop to your harness and using leg power to pull, but that's not something you'd want to plan on. On a small stance or one where you can't make your boots stick, you'll be lucky to get 25 lbf with one hand.

This means that a real-world, hand-pulled Z-pulley will deliver about twice 60 lbf to the load, maybe a bit more on a good day; that's about 125 lbf or half a kilonewton. If you were positioned to pull directly on a climber below you might, with gonzo effort, be able to lift someone of average weight for a short distance until you became fatigued, but a short distance is seldom the requirement.

Things are less favorable in the scenario where the rope from the belay stance to the fallen climber runs through at least one additional carabiner

Adding pulling power.

above, which acts as a redirect. Friction through that carabiner reduces the pull on the climber from the belay location by about a third. That 125 lbf (0.5 kN) of pulling force only amounts to 80 lbf of lifting effect on the hanging victim—not enough to pull her up if she's hanging free. In order to lift her, you'd need to apply at least 250 lbf (1.1 kN) at the belay—not possible, even using your body weight. Numbers like these will have wide variations in practice, depending on the particular hardware used, the rope, and your good or bad fortune.

Pulley systems are kinda like a blind date: they come highly recommended but often missing critical details. You even see examples that don't always work on the Web sites of national guide associations, and the illustrations in texts are replete with inefficiencies. I'll dig into what is admittedly somewhat complex and advanced for the average mountaineer, because when a hauling system becomes crucial in a rescue operation, on rock or on a glacier, you'll avoid a serious waste of time if you have a handle on how pulley systems work in the real world. I'll cover use on both rock and glaciers—and anywhere else you may need extra pull, even hauling your ox out of a ditch.

Pulley Operation

There are two modes of basic pulley operation: one that reverses the direction of force without changing its magnitude, and another that doubles the force without changing its direction. The turnaround pulley (first mode) is always anchored by its axle and has one strand of its rope connected to the load while the other is pulled. The force-doubling pulley always connects the load at its axle and usually has one side of its rope anchored and the other pulled.

Pulleys are not 100 percent efficient. Not only because of sheave-bearing friction but from the bending of the rope as it goes around the pulley. The larger the pulley diameter and the smaller the cord, the more efficient the combination will be. That's why a carabiner with a 10 mm diameter of rope-bearing surface soaks up so much pulling force on an 11 mm rope. The amount of the inefficiency depends on relative diameters of rope and

pulley, rope characteristics, rate of pull, short- and long-term rope history, and lots of other things, but some simple numbers help to illustrate the concept.

A conventional rescue pulley with a 54 mm (2⅛ inch) diameter sheave will have an efficiency of between 91 and 96 percent when passing climbing ropes. A small climber's pulley will have an efficiency of about 83 to 85 percent, while a carabiner used as a pulley may have an efficiency of only 50 to 70 percent. Two carabiners back to back or carabiners with narrow profiles are worse. Let's say we pick 65 percent for the efficiency of the carabiners we happen to have along; a system built with two of them used as pulleys will have a pulley efficiency of 65 percent of 65 percent, or only 42 percent of what you'd expect. Using such carabiners to build a 3:1 pulley system will reduce the advantage to 1.3:1. If you foresee any possibility that you'll be involved in self-rescue, carry two pulleys; those neat little Petzl Ultralegere wheels eliminate excuses based on weight or cost (and you already use oval carabiners because of their versa-

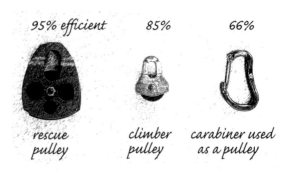

| 95% efficient | 85% | 66% |
| rescue pulley | climber pulley | carabiner used as a pulley |

Efficiencies of pulleys.

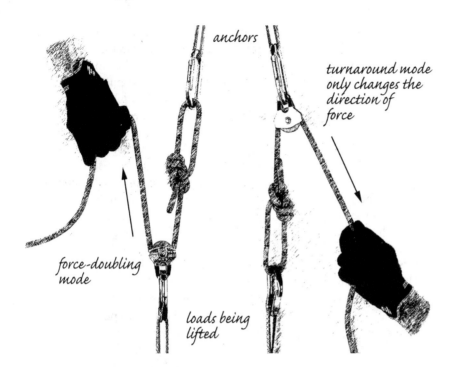

anchors

turnaround mode
only changes the
direction of
force

force-doubling
mode

loads being
lifted

Pulley modes.

tility, right?). Efficiency figures are based on the rope wrapping halfway around the pulley; inefficiency is less when the wrap is less, but the full force multiplying benefit of the 2:1 pulley requires the entire half wrap.

Now let's build a system. The simplest way to increase your pulling force is to attach a pulley to the load by its axle, anchor one end of the rope that runs through the pulley, and pull on the other end. This creates a force-doubling pulley (minus inefficiency); you'll have to pull twice the length of rope as the distance the load is moved. This approach is frequently recommended for pulling a victim out of a crevasse, but don't think you must set it up as normally illustrated, where a pulley is lowered to the victim. It's easier to attach a pulley's axle to the victim's rope with a friction knot and work with the pulley on the surface of the glacier; the only benefit of dropping the pulley is slightly less friction at the crevasse lip because the moving strand supports half the load. In the self-rescue scenario where you're pulling down on the rope, you could attach a pulley to the rope holding the victim and use your weight to pull. If you can get everything to line up and pull down with the force of your weight, which the pulley will in-

crease by about 200 percent × 83 percent = 166 percent; that might be enough to raise the climber unless there's more friction elsewhere.

If you can pull only with your hands, the pulley will increase your 60 lbf of pulling power by 166 percent to about 100 lbf. Any friction of the rope on rock or snow, or on something you put in the snow or on the rock to keep the friction from being even worse, will reduce your effective pulling force. For example, bending over an ice ax shaft will reduce force on a rope by about 25 percent, and a backpack will knock off about 30 percent. A backpack would be much better than a coarse rock edge. You can see where this is going: even with two people pulling with their hands, if you run the rope over an ice ax shaft (the best case edge), you'll be able to generate only about 150 lbf of pulling power with a C-pulley, and that won't lift most climbers. Either motivate the pullers, get some help from the victim, or go to plan Z.

Practical Z's

Here's where the Z-pulley comes in. After considering pulley inefficiencies, a Z-pulley will about double your pulling force, hopefully a little more depending on pulleys and rope. If the rope runs over an ice ax shaft you'll reduce the effect and end up with about 100 lbf effective pulling force from one puller using his hands. If that puller is going to raise a typical climber, he's going to have to be highly motivated or be able to pull with his harness and sound footing, or both. Two pullers, on the other hand, could produce 190 lbf of pull with their hands, and that will raise someone you'd find in a crevasse, even a person whose pack didn't evidence the lightweight philosophy. This is one reason for the common recommendation for parties of three on active glaciers. If pullers can use body weight or pull with their harnesses, things could get even better, especially for the victim. Physics is unjust: your pulling power is reduced by inefficiencies and friction, but you still have to pull three times as much rope length as the distance you want the load to move.

Most texts show Z-pulley rigs that are far from optimum. Here are some pointers to make yours better. The *holding prusik* wants to be *very* short, because the difference between where it holds and where it slips is lost length of lift every time you start a new pull on the rope; you might want to consider using a dedicated short prusik made with 6 mm cord if that's what it takes to cause your pulley's flanges to ensure that the prusik knot slips and doesn't get sucked into the pulley absent climber intervention. Feed the rope through a belay device at the turnaround to guarantee self-tending; it's better to have all hands on the rope than dedicate someone to tending the prusik—or use a prusik-tending pulley. If the climbing rope is 9 mm or thinner, use three prusik wraps instead

of the common two (never a bad idea). A Bachmann friction knot won't hold well on skinny ropes; a Klemheist is more reliable but may not be released automatically by your pulley as well as a traditional prusik knot. The *pulling prusik* loop needn't be long; just push it as far toward the load as possible each time you begin a take-in cycle to maximize the length of rope that can be pulled in before another reset is required; use a Klemheist for the friction knot. The main benefit comes from the force-doubling pulley; if you have only one pulley, use it there and use a carabiner as the turnaround pulley. If you have no pulleys and must use carabiners, figure your force multiplication will degrade to only about 1.3:1. After running the rope over an ice ax shaft you'll end up with no net gain, but that's better than a 25 percent loss if you simply haul without a pulley rig. All this will make more sense when you actually set up a Z-pulley. Don't blindly imitate illustrations in The Classic, Field Manual FM 3-97.61, or just about anywhere else.

A self-tending Z-pulley can be made without prusik loops using an autoblock brake as the "holding prusik." This configuration will produce a real force multiplication of about 1.8:1, which drops more if made without any pulleys. This setup was described in Chapter 23, Lightweight Ropes, as a means of assisting a climber below.

Stressed Out? Not Hardly

I've already mentioned misguided claims that pulley systems put extra stress on their anchors. Pulley systems reduce the load on the puller—their rai-

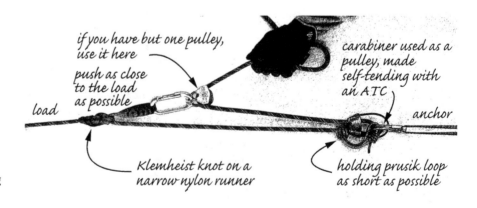

if you have but one pulley, use it here

push as close to the load as possible

load

carabiner used as a pulley, made self-tending with an ATC

anchor

Klemheist knot on a narrow nylon runner

holding prusik loop as short as possible

Classic Z-pulley rig using one pulley.

son d'être. The anchors will hold the remaining fraction of the load—considerably less than body weight while the victim is being raised. While the victim is hanging between pulls, the anchor will hold only the victim's weight, reduced by rope friction over the ax shaft or whatever. In other words, the anchor sees no more than body weight. The anchor in our rock rescue scenario that actually *does* take more force is that much abused uppermost anchor—the one that has just held the leader's fall. It will have to support the weight of the hanging victim plus almost twice that force coming from the pull at the belay stance; figure 300 percent of body weight (about 2 to 2.5 kN) while the victim is being raised—probably less than from the leader fall it just held.

What if you're the only puller available? First try getting help from the victim. If the crevasse or rock rescue victim could climb up even a little, that might be enough to turn the tide. Toss down an anchored rope and suggest that the victim attach her own prusiks. If nothing looks like it's going to work and you must haul the victim without assistance, the alternatives are substantially more complex.

4:1, 5:1, and 6:1 Pulley Systems

A sick, inventive mind can cook up any number of complex combinations of pulleys. Practically, only three should be needed to meet every contingency that could be managed by a small team (SAR teams will have more techniques and specialized gear). The 6:1 system (sometimes called a CZ or ZC rig) is conceptually simple: just rig a Z-pulley system on the pulling rope of your C-pulley, or use a C-pulley to increase pulling power of a Z-pulley. You'll have to pull six times as much rope as distance the victim is raised; this requires a lot of rope and implies a lot of prusik resets, which takes a lot of time. In tests I've done, the actual benefit is not much more than a 5:1 system, which has slightly lesser limitations. A 4:1 system can be constructed in the same way: add a C-pulley on the pulling rope of another C-pulley. This setup involves the same two pulleys and associated inefficiency losses as a Z-pulley but provides a little more mechanical advantage; however, by adding only one more carabiner you get the 6:1 system, so the CC rig hardly seems worth its additional complexity (the empty butterfly in the illustration is where the arresting climber was clipped).

A turnaround pulley added to a Z-pulley system on its pulling rope doesn't increase leverage; if you use a turnaround carabiner instead of a pulley, its inefficiency can decrease the actual advantage almost to the point that you might as well simply haul on the rope without any rig at all. The only

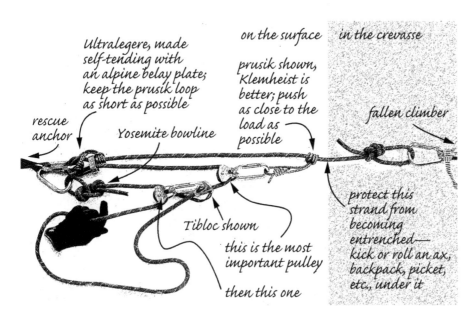

Ultralegere, made self-tending with an alpine belay plate; keep the prusik loop as short as possible

on the surface

in the crevasse

prusik shown, Klemheist is better; push as close to the load as possible

fallen climber

rescue anchor

Yosemite bowline

Tibloc shown

this is the most important pulley

then this one

protect this strand from becoming entrenched— kick or roll an ax, backpack, picket, etc., under it

C-pulley added to a Z-pulley for a theoretical 6:1 advantage.

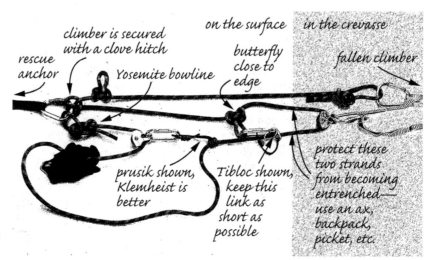

rescue anchor

climber is secured with a clove hitch

Yosemite bowline

on the surface

in the crevasse

butterfly close to edge

fallen climber

prusik shown, Klemheist is better

Tibloc shown, keep this link as short as possible

protect these two strands from becoming entrenched— use an ax, backpack, picket, etc.

C-pulley added to another C-pulley for a theoretical 4:1 advantage.

benefit of adding a turnaround pulley might be to allow use of body weight to pull or pulling from a direction that was otherwise physically impossible.

A downside of the 5:1 system is its complexity, including the need for an extra length of cord or a long runner. A cordelette works well; attach it with clove hitches and split the length between cord that will always be tensioned and cord that will always be slack. You could also use the end of the rope. You must pull five times the length of rope as distance you hope to lift the victim, and the system will require a reset when the load has moved half the length of the extra cord. If only two pulleys are available and a carabiner must be used, make it the turnaround at the anchor. Using an autoblock belay brake doesn't detract much from the benefit of an all-carabiner version, which is less than 3:1. To put things in perspective, a mariner haul made with carabiners will have about the same force multiplication as a Z-pulley made with climbers' pulleys, but a mariner haul using two pulleys will have twice the benefit of a Z-pulley made with carabiners—those two pulleys are like adding another rescuer to your party. Other than those caveats and, of course, the difficulty in remembering how to set it up, the 5:1 system, called the *mariner haul*, is very effective, yielding a practical force multiplication around 3.6:1.

Complex pulley systems can create an irresistible force on the load. Be sure not to injure the victim by pulling when he's stuck on rock or at the crevasse lip. An unresponsive victim should be monitored constantly during rescue operations (and his legs moved by rescuers to fend off harness hang syndrome).

ASSISTED DESCENDING

If the fallen climber is injured, it may be necessary for her to be accompanied by another climber as she's lowered. That could mean an actual lower by another member of the party or, if you're the only rescuer, a tandem rappel. A tandem rappel, with both climbers hanging on the same rappel brake, could be done like an ordinary rappel, after tethering both climbers together, but that would mean the load of two climbers on the rappel brake. You probably wouldn't be prepared, or practiced, for that. A better way would be for the rescuer to rappel, after tethering himself to the victim, on one strand of the rope while the victim is simultaneously lowered on the other strand as a counterweight; there would be so much friction through the anchor carabiner that the rescuer might have to push rope into his brake. Too much friction is better than too little.

Tandem Rappel

To set up a tandem rappel to rescue a fallen leader, the rescuer would tie off the belay with a Münter-

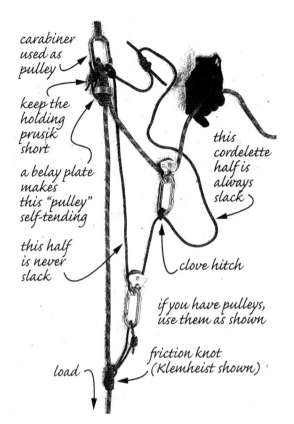

carabiner used as pulley

keep the holding prusik short

a belay plate makes this "pulley" self-tending

this half is never slack

this cordelette half is always slack

clove hitch

if you have pulleys, use them as shown

friction knot (Klemheist shown)

load

The 5:1 mariner haul.

mule as I've been describing and then ascend to the top anchor and clip in. In the best of all possible worlds, the rescuer would add components to the top anchor to increase its reliability. In real life, the fallen climber down below probably has the entire rack. Having two climbers hang on a single placement might be scary, but the anchor has already held a leader fall, so it's been tested. Of course, it would be preferable to reach the fallen climber, recover the rack, and build a nearby multi-placement anchor to which the victim could be secured and on which a new rappel anchor would be based. Attach the victim to such an anchor with a Münter-mule on a prusik loop and back that up with an unloaded runner or the victim's own daisy clipped to the master point of the new anchor. If you can't reach and anchor the victim, secure the victim's rope strand at the top anchor with a Münter-mule on a prusik loop; if you have a spare prusik, put a Münter-mule on both strands, the

one to the victim and the one back to the tied-off belay. Then downclimb back to the belay, using prusiks if necessary. I'll bet you've never practiced prusiking *down* a tight, angled rope; clipping your harness to it helps until you encounter an anchor or a sharp bend.

When you're back at the belay where this whole thing started, you'll remove the backup knot and release the Münter-mule on the main rope, letting the victim's weight come onto her Münter-mule up at the top anchor. Then you'll take down the belay anchor and re-ascend the rope; it won't be any easier this time because you'll want to remove the anchors, and that won't be easy if your climbing rope is putting outward tension on them; at least you'll be able to tie in short this time up.

When you reach the victim's Münter-mule at the rappel anchor (was top anchor), you have three options: clip in and lower the victim and then rappel yourself (since you now have enough rope), orchestrate a tandem rappel (which we don't like), or conduct a counterweight rappel (which was our original plan). Needless to say, the rappel rope must go through a carabiner, not simply a runner, or it'll melt through the runner surprisingly quickly; a locker is best, or a fat leaver biner with the gate taped shut. Don't use two nonlockers back to back, because that causes extra rope friction. Tie a stopper knot in your strand of rope and get yourself on rappel, remove any safety knots or runners, release the Münter-mule on the victim's anchoring prusik loop, and rappel to the victim, whose counterweight will prevent rope slipping through the top anchor carabiner. When you reach the victim, connect yourself closely with a runner or prusik loop; you may also want to put a chest harness on the victim, to help keep her upright. The victim's strand probably won't run until you put downward tension on the victim, who will be pulled above you unless you've engineered a runner between the two of you to prevent it. You may want the victim at your shoulder height or knee height, but there will be excessive interference if the victim is at the same height.

Tandem Lower

If you have enough climbers in your party and the

terrain permits, lowering the victim and attendant from above is easier than rappelling. After you've constructed a secure anchor and protected any abrupt edges with a backpack, you face the problem of lowering the weight of two climbers on one strand of rope. Conceptually, that requires four times as much holding power as a conventional rappel. You could use two brakes in series—a Münter hitch feeding into an ATC, for example. You could also use a Super Münter hitch without needing any other hardware. Either way, use an autoblock knot on the braking strand, just in case. If possible, the person doing the lowering should connect the autoblock to an anchor instead of his harness so he can be mobile and able to address any issues that arise during the lowering.

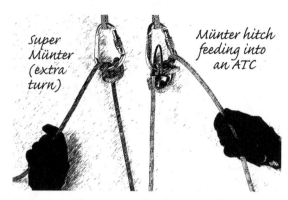

Adding additional control when lowering heavy loads.

EVACUATION

Once the victim is safely on terra firma, conduct a complete assessment and administer treatment called for. If you've made it this far without running out of daylight, you've done an excellent job. The next step is your evacuation plan. If you've ever rehearsed it, you know how incredibly difficult it can be to move a disabled patient along an easy trail; it's even more difficult over rough ground without a trail. Special training and equipment is usually required to conduct a lengthy evacuation over steep terrain. If you can't rule out spine damage, but the accident involved a mechanism of injury for cervical spine (such as violent whipping or impact to the head), you face the decision of continuing or hoping to get SAR assistance with backboard evacuation. Tough decisions for mountaineers, and another good reason to avoid falling and experiencing a self-rescue scenario.

There are many variations of these techniques that skilled rescuers adapt to suit circumstances. Think through your plan and its possible consequences before you begin. Be certain you have the hardware, cordage, belay brakes, and rope length your plan requires. Use the simplest techniques that will get the job done. Avoid scenarios that involve tandem rappels. Avoid scenarios that involve raising the victim. Use an autoblock anytime you're feeding rope through a rappel brake.

Hopefully reading this section has made you feel naked without good self-rescue skills, and you'll be motivated to get some hands-on training. If you're serious about learning self-rescue methods, do so with a group of experienced climbers. You're way ahead if you can find qualified instruction. These techniques are so complex that errors are likely, so practice with every participant on a separate belay. Always keep in mind that a self-rescue situation may arise in the worst of conditions; you may be called upon to put your skills to work in a storm by headlamp, and your partner may depend entirely on your skills and judgment.

26
Glacier Travel and Crevasse Rescue

Glacier travel and crevasse rescue is perhaps the most technically complex area of general mountaineering. In effect, a party traveling on a crevassed glacier must be in a perpetual state of self-rescue preparedness. Many mountaineers will never encounter deep crevasses or even active glaciers, but for those who do, it's often said that sooner or later you'll fall into a crevasse. Nor will skill or fame protect you: Mugs Stump, one of America's leading alpinists, and Babu Chhiri Sherpa, Everest climber who held the record for speed, are among those who perished in crevasse falls. Who can forget the chilling photograph of Louis Lachenal's final ski tracks disappearing into a crevasse on the Vallée Blanche. The bold Renato Casarotto fell into a crevasse in a seemingly safe area on K2 and died within sight of base camp and his wife; his body appeared in the ice 17 years later. Reinhold Messner and Joe Simpson fell into crevasses, though they somehow survived. Aircraft have fallen into crevasses and snowmobile crevasse accidents are not uncommon.

HOW THEY GET THAT WAY

Even as snow is falling it's undergoing metamorphism, a process mentioned in Chapter 5 in the section on avalanche hazard. If transformed snow lasts long enough through the warm season, it'll become ice when the weather cools as winter approaches. This ice, with lots of air entrapped, is called névé or alpine ice. Permanent snowfields haven't the depth to creep downhill the way glaciers do, but they may still have small crevasses. If the névé builds up and becomes increasingly dense over many years, a giant field of ice may form that can become hundreds of feet thick and miles long. When the ice is 80 or 100 feet thick, its weight causes ice at the bottom to become plastic, and the whole block will begin oozing slowly down its mountain valley as a *glacier*. Big glaciers can move several meters (yards) each day; some in Alaska move over 40 meters daily. Steep sections above the glacier don't build the depth for plastic flow, so the thick ice of the glacier pulls away, leaving a gap called a *bergschrund*. The bergschrund usually goes all the way to bedrock, but it can be filled with avalanche debris, blocks of snow and ice, and spindrift off the slope above. The bergschrund increases in size as snow melts in the spring and into late season, when it can turn into an overhanging water ice climb. Many times getting over or around the bergschrund as you approach from the glacier below is a climb's most challenging element; icicle fangs make it appear even more formidable as you peer into the dark and chilly depths. In late season, permanent snowfields develop gaps between them and surrounding rock walls as the snow melts away. This gap is called a *moat*, and large ones may be as challenging to cross as the bergschrund.

Every year's accumulation of snow adds to the glacier and presses it down the mountain, with solid ice being carried atop the plastic ice below. If the path of the glacier changes direction, the solid ice fractures. On the insides of curves and concave regions, compression ridges are formed, and on the outsides and areas where the glacier moves over convex terrain, cracks open far down to the plastic ice. If the drop of terrain below the glacier is steep enough, an *icefall* forms where large blocks of ice called *seracs* can tumble down without warning at any time of the day or night and during any season.

As the glacier travels to lower and warmer parts of its valley, the annual accumulation of snow becomes insufficient to make up for the ice that disappears in warmer weather. This lower region of the glacier is called the *ablation zone*; the region between it and the *accumulation zone* above is called the *firn line*. Ultimately, melting wins entirely, and the ice ends at the *glacier terminus*, where rocks and grit that have been picked up and carried along by the glacier are deposited. On large glaciers, the terminus area may be covered by stones, completely concealing the ice surface and making for miserable travel. The pile of rubble that gets dumped along the sides of a glacier is called a *lateral moraine,* and at the end it's called a *terminal moraine*; these are often piled as steeply as the angle of repose, leaving large boulders frighteningly unstable. The finely ground rock dust in icy glacier meltwater is called *glacial flour* and accounts for the milky tint of gray rivers and blue lakes that are fed from the glacier.

There are many other details of glaciers as well as polyglot terms to label them, but this generally describes active glaciers—those whose ice is thick enough to create the movement that results in the formation of crevasses. Glaciers change seasonally. In winter, snowfall and blowing snow form bridges that cover the openings of crevasses just as snow bridges form over mountain streams. Bridges build from the edges and are thinner in the middle. On glaciers of maritime mountain ranges, snow bridges are dense and remarkably strong, but in continental ranges the snow can metamorphose into weak crystals and hoar may form on the underside of bridges, within the crevasse, without any surface indication of weakness. In spring, travel over glaciers is relatively easy, but not carefree. Crevasses of unknown extent may be hidden by snow bridges of unknown strength, with only the slightest indication on the snow surface that danger lies beneath. A snowy surface on the glacier may require snowshoes or skis for travel, but it makes for good arrests. As the season progresses, the snow melts, and snow bridges sag and begin opening up, revealing crevasses. Where one is visible, others are often hidden nearby. Melting can be surprisingly rapid, dropping the snow by inches in a single day and calling for careful probing with something longer than an ax when selecting a camp site on the glacier—often a creepy proposition due to the creaking sounds of the moving ice as well as the omnipresent danger. Melting can also increase the size of the bergschrund considerably, even from the time you ascend it until the time you return. Finally, in late season, snow and snow bridges may have melted away entirely, below the firn line at least, exposing the ice of the glacier and making crevasses readily apparent; moats gape and the bergschrund may become virtually impassable.

Wide crevasses must be circumnavigated, and mountaineers wear crampons on the bare ice of even low-angle glaciers. As winter storms return, the glacial ice again becomes covered by snow, crevasses begin to fill in, and bridges begin to form across them. Metamorphism is beginning, so bridges on maritime glaciers will begin to strengthen, and snow bridges over crevasses of continental glaciers will begin to weaken, even before they're completely formed.

Wet or Dry

For a frame of reference, glaciers can be described as wet or dry, having nothing to do with their content of water or vermouth. A wet glacier is one that's covered by snow and where crevasses are hidden by snow bridges, but where the tractable surface offers the possibility of successful self-arrest. A glacier that's dry in late season has all, or nearly all, of its crevasses made visible, but the bare ice surface thwarts attempts to self arrest. These two conditions, wet and dry, bear significantly on a climbing team's decision to rope up, set anchors, or travel unroped. The most worrisome condition is a glacier that's primarily, but not exclusively, either wet or dry. Extensive glaciers may be wet above their firn line and dry below.

Crevasse Falls

Before we get to tactics, let's take a closer look at a crevasse. When first formed, the walls of a crevasse are smooth and parallel, and it is deep—80 or more feet—down to the ice made plastic by the weight above it. After a time the crevasse may become partly filled in with avalanche debris, old snow, collapsed snow bridges, and blocks of ice. Crevasses in more benign climates, such as in a good percentage of the Lower 48, tend to be much less deep and wide, but that may mean only that falling into one offers more opportunity to collide with something. In late season, the surface of a glacier may be bare ice with little snow cover, but during most of the season—and certainly the best time for easy glacier travel—there will be snow covering the glacier ice and snow bridging at least part of most crevasses. Despite the illustrations you may have seen, few people fall off the edge of a precipice when they take a crevasse fall; more likely they disappear down a small hole of their own making. Snow bridges are thicker at the sides, so when a climber falls through (and not all crevasse falls go completely through; many go only waist deep) she'll likely be free falling until caught by the rope, and then she'll hang, substantially in space. That's good, especially if the climber is wearing crampons, because injuries are less likely. The worst fall would result in the climber being wedged head down into a narrow crevasse after striking ice or snagging a crampon on the way down.

In the event of a serious crevasse fall, from the fallen climber's perspective, the ground drops away without warning, and the climber instantly finds himself hanging, hopefully upright, in a cold, quiet, and dimly lit vault, much different from the warmer, sunny surface of the glacier. After the snow and ice stop raining down, the climber looks up to see a patch of sky and the rope cut deeply into the snow at the edge of the hole above that he's just made. From the perspective of others in the party, a climber, typically the first on the rope, has suddenly vanished, sometimes without a sound and sometimes into a hole that isn't visible even from a short distance. If the party has been attentive, they immediately dive for the snow away from the hole and assume self-arrest positions as the rope comes tight first on the second climber and then on the third, the force being cushioned as the rope cuts into the snow of the crevasse lip. A party taken by surprise will be jerked and dragged toward the hole, but hopefully the snow that concealed the crevasse will slow them down and allow boots, axes, and adrenaline-inspired determination to bring things to a halt. The second climber on the rope may have no choice but to be a human haul bag anchor, but hopefully the third climber will have enough time to turn away from the fall and execute a face down arrest. In most cases, that's what happens. Parties of two must take special precautions, not the least of which is to attentively minimize slack in the rope between them.

Before we take a look at how the party deals with this situation, let's turn back the clock and see how they prepared their equipment and techniques beforehand.

ORGANIZING THE ROPED TEAM

Plan

The first order of business is sizing up your opponent. Will the glacier be wet or dry, or have parts of both? How steep is it? Are there extensive crevasse fields or icefalls? Will you be crossing the bergschrund? If so, how? What about moats? What about avalanche danger?

Next, choose your weapons. Will the party travel on boots only, boots with crampons, snowshoes, or skis? Everyone on the same rope should make the same choice. Will wands be needed? If so, make them out of 3- or 4-foot bamboo gardening stakes with flags made of surveyor's tape or folded-over duck tape in some color other than silver. How many wands will you need? What protection hardware will be appropriate? How much? When the potential for crevasse fall exists, the minimum gear for each mountaineer is at least one piece of snow or ice pro (a minimum of two pieces each for a team of two), a 4-foot webbing runner, 2 personally sized prusik loops, and a shoulder sling carrying a cordelette and 4 carabiners. Adding a prusik-tending pulley or a pair of Ultralegeres would be good, too. Beyond that, be guided by your experience in practicing rescue methods and by your assessment of the crevasse danger you anticipate.

Organize the rope based on the crevasse character (small, or deep and wide) and the number in the party. The optimum on a rope is 3 climbers; 4 is manageable; 2 requires special techniques and more skills in organization and rescue. You'll want 8 to 15 meters (yards) of rope between each climber, enough to span the likely width between crevasses; a party of 4 might use all of a standard length rope, requiring hasty reorganization when rope is needed for a rescue, especially if a prompt rappel to the fallen climber is required. Consider bringing a second rope, such as a shorter, skinny, low-stretch (static) rope, to use in rescues, hauling, and around glacier camp as a cordon and potty belay. In general, you'll travel roped if on

Experienced climbers may explore lightweight options to the traditional climbing rope carried for glacier travel. The applications for a glacier travel rope are substantially different from those for which rock climbing ropes are designed; for example, fall forces are much lower because the snow on a glacier absorbs fall energy and because the leader on a glacier doesn't climb much above the belayer. The main use for a glacier travel rope is safety and rescue, and rescuers invariably use static ropes. Strength isn't an issue, so a lightweight static rope would be ideal for many glacier travel scenarios, as might a low-stretch canyoneering rope. Not all glaciers are deeply crevassed, so travelers on those that aren't might opt for an 8 mm, 35 m long rope that will weigh substantially less than a conventional 10.5 mm, 50 m rope. If you intend to go light, don't simply choose half of a double or twin rope pair; it'll be very stretchy if used for rescue. Do, however, put more wraps on your friction knots and consider making them from 4 mm accessory cord for more reliable locking on thin, icy ropes.

foot, on snow-covered glaciers in the summer, when crevasse patterns are unknown or difficult to assess, when the snow cover is weak or variable, as it might be on continental glaciers, and whenever visibility is poor. You may deem it safer to forgo roping up on dry glaciers and may demur in winter when snow cover is consistent, deep, and of high density, as it may be on maritime glaciers. Many forgo a rope when skiing downhill in winter on well-covered glaciers; roped skiing is miserable.

After you've come up with a plan and a list, ensure compliant participation by every member of the group. You don't want to start out climbing in the wee small hours hearing the question, "So, what'd ya bring?"

Roping Up

Let's say your optimum party of three elects to leave a short 10 meters (33 feet) of rope between climbers, because you foresee only smaller crevasses. That leaves 30 m remaining from a standard rope, along with the question of where it should be carried. The choices would be 15 m with the first and last climbers, or all 30 m with the last. The tradeoff probably favors splitting the excess, but that could change if a longer gap were used between climbers. You could also divide the rope into fourths, about 13 m, with one fourth in the last climber's pack. A party of four would probably want to divide the rope into thirds (about 18 m), and leave no excess.

A party of two will want at least 20 meters (65 feet) of separation, to give the second plenty of opportunity to arrest. Because one climber must arrest the other without assistance, the party may elect to tie bulky knots in the rope between them, hoping the knots will add friction in the snow and contribute to the arrest. This works well in reasonable snow and would even give comfort to a party of three if tied between the leader and second. The knots will complicate rescue operations, but better that than the alternative. Use butterfly knots to create small loops every two meters, which will consume less than a meter each or 5 to 8 meters for all. When you practice prusiking up a rope having these safety knots, use the loops as part of your technique. This again raises the question of how best to distribute the excess length and whether to carry an additional short, light rescue rope.

Having allocated the rope, the party members will tie Yosemite bowline loops into the ends and butterfly knot loops between and will connect themselves. Each climber, even those on the ends, will attach from their harness loops to the rope loops with an HMS biner, carried with the two large webbing loops of the harness on the wide end of the carabiner and the rope on the small end (which is how the biner is designed).

Gearing Up

Now comes donning everything else. The focus of gear organization for glacier travel is to facilitate rescue in the event of a crevasse fall. This strongly influences the sequence of attaching things to your body. Specifically, you'll want to put things on in the reverse of the order that you'd follow in taking them off—whether it's you who falls or whether you're a rescuer. If you fall far, you'll want to take off as much as possible and be able to do so while hanging from the rope. You also don't want to lose anything, so that means that *everything* must be tethered. Positively everything: not just your ax,

but your skis or snowshoes, hiking poles, backpack, probe pole, protection and ascending hardware, camera, hat or helmet, sunglasses—the whole nine yards. If you're a rescuer, you'll want to be sure that you can reach whatever you'll need to set an anchor while you're simultaneously holding a face-down arrest.

The first items to adorn your body would be things like the chest harness sling and its nonlocking carabiner if it needs one (use my method and it won't), then the sling with pro and runners along with your rope ascending gear, next your walkie-talkie and camera on their sturdy shoulder lanyards (*never* loop *anything* around your neck that could turn into a garrote). Finally, throw on your backpack with any extra rope coiled up and secured under the top pocket, near the insulated jacket you may want to don when you stop for lunch or find yourself in a crevasse. The rope could also be carried in a bag or even wrapped around the pack's top pocket. Tether the pack's haul loop to your harness in any conveniently removable way, such as with an extra prusik loop clipped to your harness belay loop with a small nonlocker. The length of the tether should allow you to reach the pack if you've removed it and it's hanging on its tether. If the pack's haul loop isn't impressively burly, supplement it with a runner between the pack's shoulder straps. Sometimes you'll see the recommendation to tether your pack with a short end of the climbing rope, but I don't agree; if you fall into a crevasse, you'll probably want to remove the pack and either haul the pack out or clip it to the rope you'll ascend, so having its own tether is easier to deal with, plus you'll be spared a cold carabiner on your neck. If you're an arresting climber, you may want to utilize the rope while preventing your pack from departing on its own initiative, so it should be tethered independently.

Finally, you'll probably want to pre-attach your prusik loops to the rope using Klemheist knots, to save time in the event they're needed. The end of one of them will connect to a locker on your harness's belay loop or tie-in points, the other (the one for your foot) will just get stuffed into a pocket. Climbers in the middle of the rope won't know in advance which direction is up, so they'll pre-attach a prusik on each side of their clip-in loop. There are more elaborate systems for ascending ropes using friction knots or mechanical ascenders, including the Texas and Frog systems, but

crevasse rescue is used only infrequently and then only for short distances, so simplicity wins over the complexity and efficiency of single-use systems that cavers might prefer. When sizing and positioning your prusiks, give thought to potential interference by the chest harness's carabiner; when prusiking, you don't want to find that the chest harness frustrates your efforts to ascend the rope. As always with complicated systems, try before you fly.

Although each climber may start out with a chest harness in place, only the first climber should actually clip the rope to her harness (with a nonlocker). There are several reasons. If the second climber were to clip his chest harness and the leader fell, the second would be yanked forward from above his center of gravity, just like with a Kiwi coil; he'd be sprawled face first rather than have a fighting chance to lean back and quickly dig in his boots. Experiments have shown that falls caught by a full-body harness (waist plus chest) are actually more injurious, however counterintuitive that might be. If the leader might have to apply an arrest, on a team of two, for example, she also might want not to clip her chest harness until after falling, even though it may be a struggle to get upright (Mr. Backpack will not be your friend)— a struggle potentially made more difficult by injury from the fall.

All the careful organization and planning that has gone into getting ready to move can be nuked when you stop for a clothing change. As usual, you'll want to start the day off chilled, knowing that you'll soon warm up, but each time you take off some or all of the incredible amount of gear that's lashed to your body, you'll want to put it

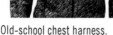
Old-school chest harness.

double wrap of 48-inch runner   *pick either strand and put it over a shoulder*   *put the same strand over the other shoulder*   *no biner needed! (same back view)*

New-school harness needs no carabiner.

The beast of burden ready for glacier travel.

back on with the same care as when you started the outing. And whenever possible, you'll want to check your companions and have them check you, just as you always do whenever you alter the safety system of a roped climb.

OFF WE GO

All this preparation and mutual checking has consumed a lot of time, which is a good thing, as the sun is now up so it's possible to scan the glacial terrain and plan the route. Many glacier ascents begin in the dark, but usually only on familiar trade routes, where you can follow the boot tracks of guided climbers. In many cases, the flow of the glacier won't be obvious or influential; you'll just have to rely on your visual evaluation, and perhaps

CAT IN THE HAT

The question invariably arises as to the proper chapeau for glacier travel. The weather will certainly influence your decision, as will the amount of sunlight (which is always much more than seems possible, even on cloudy days). The hard question is, what about a helmet? In principle, anytime you use a rope you should wear a helmet; both protect your most important asset in the event of a fall. In practice, wearing a helmet on a warm, sunny glacier slog can be miserable; a wide-brimmed sombrero would be much more pleasant; if you wear a helmet, augment it with a sun shade made from a bandana or gauze cloth, or use a slip-on neoprene brim. A helmet complicates removal of shoulder slings, camera straps, and coils of rope. The choice is up to you: if a fall is conceivable, if the glacier has major crevasses, if the glacier is dry, if actual climbing is anticipated, wear a helmet. If glacier travel is just an easy approach route and the rope is mainly precautionary, if the day is blazing hot, and if falls of any kind are unlikely, you may decide on modest comfort over maximum safety.

---

reports from previous climbers, to select a route that offers the best snow bridges, most predictable crevasses, and fewest cul-de-sacs—and, of course, avoids ice falls and seracs and subjects the team to minimum avalanche danger on the route itself or from nearby runs.

The leader has decided that she prefers not to crawl for the entire outing, so instead of using her ax as a crevasse probe, she has brought a long, basketless ski pole. On a serious continental glacier she might have elected a longer pole yet, and she knows that perfectly vertical probing isn't required until a weakness has been discovered. In most cases, she'll be probing the remains of a single season's snowfall, down to the ice surface. Other climbers follow, carrying their axes with the arrest grip and vigilantly keeping slack out of the rope, letting it barely drag on the snow. After a while, the group learns to match pace, and they actually do manage to keep slack out of the rope and avoid jerking each other, and they *never carry coils*.

This group is competent, so they *always* keep slack out of the rope, even when they stop for a clothing break or for lunch. They keep slack out

If the party has decided to tow sleds or a sled, hopefully they have a commercial model and not a kid's saucer; there's a detailed description and illustration in Chapter 14. The sled is the least likely object to fall into a crevasse on its own (it has the lowest ratio of weight to contact area), but it will cause endless problems if it gets dragged in by its tow person, especially if it falls on top of a climber. If there is but one sled, the second or last climber should do the towing, not the first, and the tower might want to be closely watched or even belayed when crossing a suspect bridge that might collapse or pull the sled in because of its sloping surface. The sled must be tethered to the climbing rope, but in a manner that allows it to be independently dragged out of a crevasse by rescuers after the fallen climber frees himself from the towing harness and poles. When a climber is towing a sled, the rear of the sled must be attached to the rope with a prusik or clipped to a butterfly loop to prevent it from taking out its puller in the event of a crevasse fall; climbers have been killed that way. Even if the sled is safely tethered, the tower may end up on the rope below the sled, and the climber will have to contrive a way to prusik around it if the sled cannot somehow be dragged out first by rescuers. Despite all this, dragging a sled is, in my opinion, far preferable to carrying a heavy pack whenever terrain permits, especially when skiing. Keep the load under 80 pounds, even if using a capable commercial sled. Similar precautions apply to use of drag bags, but with stronger epithets.

of the rope—even if they have to revert to belaying—when they change leads or maneuver around complex terrain features. They keep the rope tight when they probe out a campsite, and when they wand out the perimeter. They place crossed wands to mark danger or uncertainty. They're ever vigilant and follow the maxim *don't go where you don't probe.* Above all, they communicate, even if that means using radios.

Climbing

Not all glacier travel is trudging. Some glaciers are steep and require the same climbing techniques as steep snow or ice, made all the more interesting by the possibility of crevasses. Crossing open crevasses, like crossing an open bergschrund, can involve ice climbing and even aiding on hard ice. If the route is steep, the most competent climber may

lead on the ascent but will be the final climber on the rope coming down.

SAFE CAMPING

Camping on a glacier is pretty much the same as camping on snow, unless you are faced with no option other than camping on a rubble-covered glacier, when it's like camping on rubble. Camping on a dry glacier would be so miserable that I doubt if any climbers force themselves to do it. When you select a campsite, refer back to the section on avalanche hazard in Chapter 5 to inform your choice and avoid runout zones. Glaciers generally don't afford opportunities for protection from winds, so you'll have to construct your own. Even if things seem calm, glaciers can produce their own upslope or downslope winds during the day and night. I recommend constructing igloos rather than using tents (see the section on shelter systems in Chapter 18), but if you chose a tent, you'll want to construct substantial snowblock shelter walls if there's any possibility of storms or anabatic/katabatic winds, which is almost always. There'll be a lot of hiking around, setting up tents and quarrying snow blocks for tent and eating area shelters. That means you must keep reminding yourself: where crevasses are possible, *don't go where you don't probe.* The first order of business, while still roped up and belaying, is to probe out all the area you think you might need and then wand the perimeter. Place the wands close enough that they won't be missed during a nighttime biobreak or in a whiteout. Probe deeply enough, using that basketless ski pole or, better, avy probe to account for melting during the days you'll be using the site; probe again in a couple of days. It isn't unheard of for an unlucky glacier camper to step out of a tent and into a crevasse.

Some logistic concerns should be mentioned. You'll learn soon enough to separate your pee area from where you quarry snow for water; make it obvious and be sure everyone gets the word before a light snowfall causes lamentable confusion. Poop can be tossed into a crevasse; it can even be safely spread on the surface and allowed to become naturally neutralized (takes a few weeks). If the area is popular enough that it would be unseemly to leave visible fecal matter, pack it out if no safe and deep crevasse is available. A shallow burial pit or piling snow on top isn't a solution. Don't throw waste paper, plastic bags, empty fuel cans, or any non-organic material into crevasses—pack it out, however icky. Be cautious about leaving out anything that will attract ravens (think of them as smart marmots with wings). Even piles of snow or wands on a buried cache will attract trash-habituated ravens, so be sure your cache containers are raven proof; don't make the mistake of putting fuel in with food in those raven-proof pails, unless you think of petroleum as a spice.

WHEN LUCK RUNS OUT

Usually, a crevasse fall involves only modest forces, because the snow absorbs fall energy in various ways. The biggest worry is hitting something during the fall or snagging ice or self with ax or crampon, another reason to forgo crampons unless they're unquestionably necessary, to be added to the difficulty of executing a graceful arrest without snagging a crampon and getting flipped over. In the event of a surprise crevasse fall, there's a sequence of steps that the party must take, methodically and thoughtfully (and skillfully, too, one would hope).

Assess the Fallen Climber

Let's assume that in an instant the leader has vanished below the surface, the second climber is sprawled on the snow, and the last climber is holding an arrest. Whew! The first thing to do is attempt communication. Can the third climber hold her arrest? Does the second climber think he can get off the rope, or is he pinned or tangled? Most importantly, is the fallen climber injured? If communication is imperfect, but things seem stable, one climber can start getting free of the rope but remain on belay. If things aren't obviously stable, catching a downslope fall on thin snow, for example, one or both climbers will have to attempt to set a temporary anchor while simultaneously

holding their arrests; same story for the second on a rope of two.

If the third climber is solid for now, the second climber should move toward the fallen climber, probing ahead with his ax, and attempt to establish communication to determine if the fallen climber is in immediate need of assistance. Any response from the fallen climber is welcome, because it means she's conscious and breathing; there's probably no need, then, for the second to immediately approach the hole through which the leader fell and knock down a lot of snow and ice. In the best case, communication can be established (even using radios), and the fallen climber is stable. If reassuring communication can't be established, a furious effort must be made to build an anchor strong enough for a climber to approach the hole and possibly descend into the crevasse to assist the injured leader—a decision not lightly taken. This could be incredibly difficult, but it could be crucial to reach within minutes a person who's unable to breathe or who's hanging immobile in a harness and subject to harness hang syndrome.

Favor a Straightforward Approach

In most cases, the very snow that hides danger minimizes it upon a fall, making for effective arrests and gentle forces. Don't immediately go into Z-pulley mode. If the fall is short, and if the leader is prepared, she can immediately begin ascending the rope while the remainder of the team, knowing this to be the plan and having already held the force of the fall, simply use their arrests to hold the rope. If it's feasible, this is much faster than diving into engineering mode and setting anchors. The team has read *The Mountaineering Handbook*, so they know that, aided by friction, they'll only have to hold around 100 lbf (0.4 kN), probably less, between them to hold the fallen climber's ascent, and they can easily do that if the load is shared on their harnesses. In fact, under optimal conditions, two climbers may be able to pull the leader out using only cooperative hauling off their harnesses. The main problem will be negotiating the lip of the hole; that may require a lot of thrashing and grunting from the fallen leader and the belayers.

Keep your mind open to easy possibilities. As with any other self-rescue situation, the easiest option is always to lower the victim, even if only to a temporary rest that's more comfortable than hanging in a harness. If the fallen climber could prusik up the rope, could climb out under tension, or could even hike along in the crevasse under belay and reach the surface or a spot where climbing up is easier, such options would be more efficient than constructing a science fair project on the surface. If the fallen climber is able to prusik up to the surface, that makes things easy for the rescuers—they'll only have to help the leader haul herself over the lip. To make the lip-crossing process easier, the rescuers might first haul up most of the leader's gear; hauling her pack through the crevasse lip helps blast a nice path for the ascending leader.

Meanwhile, down in the crevasse, the leader has gotten herself oriented, taken off her pack and snowshoes, and removed her insulating jacket from her pack; since she was carrying an ax we know she's already wearing gloves. She's put her jacket on, pulled her toque out of the jacket and put it on, and stowed her sunglasses and camera. The pack and maybe snowshoes are clipped to the climbing rope at her waist; she has clipped her chest harness to the rope, attached her foot prusik to her strong foot using a slip knot, and is ready to prusik up. *Or*—she's done as much of this as possible but is unable to climb up; she keeps her legs moving periodically and dodges chunks of snow falling from above.

The second climber may now have to expand the opening in the snow in order to communicate effectively with the fallen leader and assess the crevasse—all the while probing ahead and remaining connected to the anchored rope with a prusik. After the assessment, all the facts are on the table, resources have been inventoried, and a plan must be formulated that fits the circumstances.

If a brute force haul or the leader simply extricating herself aren't feasible, the climbers on the surface must assess their predicament in terms of conducting a technical rescue. Do they have the gear that conditions require? How much rope is available? How much operating space is available on the crevasse field? Are there any other persons nearby who could assist? Let's assume that space is available to set up anchors, the crevasse is apparently vertical, and no easy exit is obvious, and no one else is available to assist (if there were, the simplest solution might be for several climbers to attach prusiks and simply haul on the rope).

To get a technical rescue started, the rescuer with the best arrest will hold it while the other removes his pack, clips its tether to the rope, and sets an anchor back from the crevasse opening, all the while probing before he steps ahead and probing the area where he'll set the anchor. This anchor could be temporary, or it could become part or all of the eventual rescue anchor. The climber has read the sections in this book on forces (Chapter 11) and anchors (Chapter 12), so he knows that the anchor won't have to hold more than body weight, but it really, really can't come out; he covers it with snow to prevent melt out during the upcoming processes. If the best location for an anchor is on the far side of the arresting climber, the rope can be connected to the anchor's carabiner with a clove hitch (which is what the pulley systems illustrated in Chapter 25 show) or a Münter-

arresting climber in the middle of the rope

prusik loop with Münter-mule on biner, Klemheist on the rope

clove hitch or Münter-mule

arresting climber on the end of the rope

Starting the anchor-building process for a crevasse rescue.

mule on the rope. If the best location for an anchor is between the arresting climber and the victim; the rope there will be taught, and the third climber will have to connect to the anchor with a friction knot. The arresting climber will take his longest prusik loop (or add a runner to a short one) and connect the taut rope to the biner on the anchor with a Klemheist and Münter-mule. He's even calmed down enough to remember to clip an over-hand-on-a-bight loop in the rope to the biner, for safety.

Build the Rescue Anchor

After a solid anchor is established, the arresting climber can ease the rope tension onto the anchor and stand up, finally. She probes her way over to the anchor scene (if things are really marginal, she may want to be belayed), drops her pack and clips it in, and begins building another anchor. If the first anchor can become a component of the rescue anchor, so much the better, and she sets another anchor several feet from the first (so one anchor doesn't weaken the other), approximately in line with the force on the rope (to limit force multiplication). If the rescuers first built a hasty anchor, using a ski or snowshoe as a deadman, for example, they'll now build a favorably located rescue anchor with at least two equalized placements, creating the master point of the rescue anchor. If an extra picket is available, they'll use it to anchor packs and extra hard-

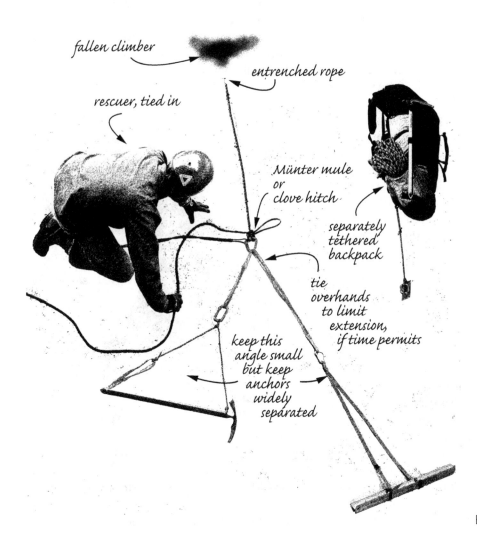

fallen climber

entrenched rope

rescuer, tied in

Münter mule
or
clove hitch

separately tethered backpack

tie overhands to limit extension, if time permits

keep this angle small but keep anchors widely separated

Building the rescue anchor.

ware independently of the rope anchor system; if the anchor should fail, you don't want to find yourself on the glacier surface without any resources. The second climber has been busy probing a wider path to the crevasse and has informed the fallen climber of progress on the surface.

Prevent Entrenchment

If hauling is the plan, whether you intend to haul on the climbing rope or conclude that a new haul rope must be set up (and you have enough rope to do so), you'd want to place something at the crevasse lip to prevent the haul rope from cutting into the snow and producing excessive resistance. A backpack works, but results in considerable friction itself; an ax shaft works better if you can work it into place; even a spare picket or fluke will suffice and won't have as many sharp points as an ax. It may be possible to kick and shove such an object under the leader's rope after excavating the crevasse lip; that would allow that rope strand to be used as part of the rescue pulley system and open up options. Rolling a picket into place may be easiest; you could try walking an ax by moving one end at a time and rolling it. Easier yet is starting over with a new rope strand over a supportive object placed near the climbing rope (the one that was entrenched in the crevasse lip during the fall). Prepare the crevasse lip while you're at it, which means clearing away most of the overhanging snow and digging a ramp down through the soft snow until encountering ice or hard snow that the fallen climber can climb or be pulled over. Whatever you use to prevent entrenchment, be sure to tether it somehow, or it's a goner.

Especially if there's only one rescuer and the fall is short, one possible rescue plan is simply to drop a loop in the end of the rope (connected to an anchor by a clove hitch and draped over an ax shaft or backpack at the crevasse lip) and have the fallen climber step up on the loop; clipping the rope to a chest harness helps with balance. Then the main rope to the fallen climber can be shifted atop the ax shaft and tightly re-attached to the anchor with a Münter-mule on a prusik loop or with another clove hitch before the victim transfers her weight back to it. The looped rope strand is then short-

ened and re-anchored, the fallen climber steps upward again, and the process is repeated. The climber on the surface tends the prusiks or clove hitches holding the two rope strands but doesn't do any hauling; the fallen climber doesn't use personal prusik loops but climbs out using the rope. An abbreviated version of this dropped loop technique can be used to assist the crevassed climber in getting over the lip. If twice as much free rope is available as necessary to reach the fallen climber, the easiest way to haul gear out (or the climber, if there were enough pullers available) is to lower a force-doubling pulley and have the fallen climber attach it to the load.

The climbing rope is anchored to the master point of the rescue anchor using clove hitch or, better, a prusik loop with a Klemheist on the rope and a Münter-mule at the master point locker, then the hasty anchor's Münter-mule is released to transfer the climbing rope tension to the rescue anchor.

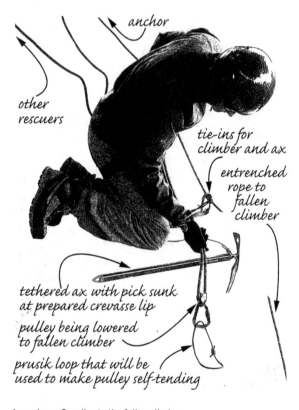

anchor

other rescuers

tie-ins for climber and ax

entrenched rope to fallen climber

tethered ax with pick sunk at prepared crevasse lip

pulley being lowered to fallen climber

prusik loop that will be used to make pulley self-tending

Lowering a C-pulley to the fallen climber.

I'll not repeat the painful details of the section on rescue pulley contraptions, except to remind you that a climber can pull steadily on a rope to which he's attached (with a prusik on the rope, for example) to the tune of about 60 lbf. If the rope runs over an ax shaft, that pull will be reduced to around 45 lbf and running it over a backpack will drop it more. The force-doubling pulley isn't perfect, so you end up with a deliverable pull of about 75 lbf. Two pullers would increase that to 150 lbf, and three to 225 lbf. In other words, one puller could haul up a backpack, two pullers could manage a sled or maybe a climber in favorable conditions, and three could pull out an unconscious leader. Getting these objects over the crevasse lip will still be a grunt. Watch out for the pointy parts of the ax that protects the crevasse lip.

The healthy fallen climber will ascend her rope with her prusiks while the rescuers drag pack, skis, and other gear (but not ax) out of the crevasse. Skis will be awkward to get over the crevasse lip unless they have mountaineering-type holes in the ends; a sled will be heavy as well as awkward and might be left in the crevasse until after the fallen climber has made it out, if the crevassed climber can maneuver around it. A composed climber may elect to delay egress in order to help wrangle equipment. After the gear has been hauled, you might as well use the hauling system to assist the fallen climber's efforts to ascend the climbing rope. At some point, the hauling rope could be passed to the crevassed climber, who'll transfer her prusiks to the anchored strand before continuing up to the surface, avoiding a struggle with the entrenched climbing rope at the crevasse lip.

Many scenarios are possible, using some combination of engineering by the rescuers and climbing by the person in the crevasse. If everything goes smoothly, the climber and rescuers can work simultaneously, and everything and everybody will be removed from the crevasse in short order.

Practical Hauling

If the fallen climber is unable to prusik up the rope, a serious hauling system must be con-structed. Pulley systems are described in excruciating detail in the previous chapter on self-rescue; just remember that an injured climber should be monitored anytime a hauling system is used. If two pullers are available, a Z-pulley system will deliver around 190 lbf (0.85 kN) through a rope that isn't entrenched, even figuring on friction over an ax shaft; maybe more with adrenaline-charged rescuers pulling from their harnesses with good stances. If only one rescuer is available for pulling, a more complex mariner haul may be necessary, or a CZ or ZC combination. The Z-pulley requires pulling up three times as much rope as distance the load is moved, and the mariner haul five times; that potentially requires a lot of carefully probed space on the glacier or a lot of resets of the pulley systems. Because the pullers must remain tethered for safety, the lengths of those tethers limit how far they can hike to pull before they must reset prusiks and start a new haul. The hauling rope is secured by a Münter-mule, which will allow slack to be released if necessary. The sticking point will be getting the climber and her equipment over the crevasse lip; that could require considerable excavation of the crevasse lip to avoid high forces and a painful thrash if the fallen climber is injured.

These descriptions of crevasse rescue procedures are only pedagogical examples. There's no fixed recipe for a crevasse rescue, and there's no point attempting to commit specific scenarios to memory, because it's likely they won't suit the actual situation that confronts your party. The specific techniques and anchors employed will depend on the terrain, available equipment and rescuers, ability of the crevassed mountaineer to participate, even the weather. It's much more important to understand the various techniques well enough to string together the specific rescue solution your circumstances demand. Here are some salient points:

▲ When moving on glacier, be attentive, always keep slack out of the rope, arrest promptly.
▲ In the event of a fall, calm down and sort things out before you leap into action.
▲ Don't go where you don't probe.

- ▲ Constantly communicate with your companions.
- ▲ Stay anchored and tied in throughout the rescue.
- ▲ As quickly as possible, determine if the fallen climber needs immediate assistance.
- ▲ Determine if the fallen climber can participate in the rescue.
- ▲ Consider brute force options before you attempt complex hauling systems.
- ▲ As soon as the climber is out of the crevasse, perform a first-aid evaluation and consider treatment for hypothermia.

The most important principle of all is to avoid crevasse falls in the first place. The lesson is not, "Hey, so what if someone falls into a crevasse? I read how to set up a Z-pulley," but rather that rescue operations, while feasible, are complex, tiring, and time consuming—and potentially dangerous to everyone involved.

PART 7

The Human Dimensions of Mountaineering

Having struggled through the often highly technical content of *The Mountaineering Handbook* you may be dismayed to near the end and read that just about every thoughtful mountaineer eventually concludes that the enjoyment, safety, and success of mountaineering hinge more on the human dimensions of the adventures than on complex technical skills. To paraphrase my granddad, that's a lesson that's essential to learn, but difficult to teach.

27

Human Factors and Not Technical Factors?

The personnel of an expedition of the character I proposed is a factor on which success depends to a very large extent. The men selected must be qualified for the work, and they must also have the special qualifications required to meet polar conditions. They must be able to live together in harmony for a long period without outside communication, and it must be remembered that the men whose desires lead them to the untrodden paths of the world have generally marked individuality.

To say nothing of the adventuresome women. What Shackleton knew as he planned his expeditions we all come to understand—it's human factors, rather than technical skills, that are most important to the success, safety, and enjoyment of mountaineering, whether the endeavor is a roadside outing or a Himalayan expedition. You can make the summit but return from the outing discouraged about mountaineering, or you can fail but be elated and eager for more, all depending on

the dynamics of the group you were with. It's easy to focus on more tangible things, like tying knots and purchasing gear, and lose sight of the critical importance of what are called "soft skills," such as risk management, judgment, cooperative problem solving, decision making, coping with fear, and leadership. Nevertheless, when mountaineers refer to personal growth, we're talking about character, courage, and cooperation, not technical expertise.

RISK MANAGEMENT AND DECISION MAKING

The old-school term was "safety," and the old-school approach was focused on maximizing safety. That didn't work, because the concept is out of sync with reality. The reality is that risk can't be completely eliminated—overcoming risk is an essential component of adventure—but risk *can* be managed. Risk management is first proactive and then, in an emergency, reactive. Experience and equipment may set your upper bounds, but it's the quality of your decision making that allows you to operate safely within those bounds. The first step is recognizing hazards, which is why there's an extensive section in this book on mountain objective or environmental hazards with enough detail to help in the next step: hazard analysis. People new to mountaineering tend to be naive about the presence and magnitude of objective hazards, particularly those that appear and disappear quickly, such as rockfall and avalanche. Such hazards manifest themselves so infrequently that climbers become overconfident of their ability to appraise and avoid hazards; then when a hazard does appear it's assumed to be an unavoidable random act of nature. Not a good approach to decision making.

Decision making the way most of us learned it (the rational, analytical method: identify objectives, gather data, evaluate hypotheses, decide) doesn't work well for mountaineers, even though popular books recommend it for that and just about every other context. In a wilderness setting the data are seldom certain or complete, and alternatives are not always apparent. Unacknowledged emotional motivations and desire for group approval can be more important than reaching a rational conclusion. Few people, no matter how well trained in the technique, actually use analytic decision making, especially when mountaineering and especially when decisions and plans of actions must be formulated by a group.

Instead, the most common means of decision making is simply to fixate on a principal aspect of the circumstances and apply a simple rule of thumb (a heuristic) derived from experience. This is a good method for making quick, simple decisions. You would hope that the smarter folks are, the more aspects they would consider, and the more complex would be the rules they apply. That's the way it usually works, except in groups. A problem with applying rules of thumb is that, when applied to objective hazards, there isn't the luxury of building up a history of progressive feedback that confirms successful decisions—feedback can be catastrophically fatal. This means you'll want to learn from others who've analyzed the particular hazard and thoughtfully evaluated their personal close calls to produce a few teachable

heuristics. This is why many climbers pore over *Accidents in North American Mountaineering*. Even so, it's possible to use inappropriate rules of thumb for years without mishap. Absent thoughtful evaluation of whether your rules of thumb actually fit the circumstances, you can come to mistake your luck for wisdom.

The use of heuristics is common and has been studied extensively, with the identification of what are called heuristic traps—common causes of poor decision making. *Familiarity* is one such heuristic trap; it turns out that when circumstances are familiar, even though threatening, experienced and inexperienced mountaineers have about the same degree of successful decision making. It's only when unfamiliar circumstances predominate that experience seems to be advantageous. *Social proof* is another trap and explains the notable failure of groups to make good decisions. After all, if others are continuing up as cumulous clouds build, it must be safe. Avoiding the social proof trap entails all the skills of group dynamics, cooperative problem solving, hazard assessment, decision making, and conflict resolution (so that decisions are based on objective criteria, not group hierarchies, interpersonal conflicts, wishful thinking, or denial). Another seductive trap that confounds good application of heuristics is *scarcity*. This causes mountaineers to compete for routes or summits while ignoring hazards, insufficient resources, or the deterioration of themselves or their group.

In the real world, neither analysis nor application of rules of thumb is effective in dealing with uncertain, ambiguous, or missing data, poorly defined and inconstant goals, and the stress of limited time and dire consequences, yet somehow good decisions are made under these conditions. Success is usually attributed to experience, but it actually comes from *expertise*, which is different. Experience doesn't require thoughtfulness or training; expertise does. Experts often make decisions without realizing how they do it, but there are characteristics of their methodology. They size up the context and successively compare it to contexts they have experienced before; they are assessing the situation, not looking for response triggers.

This means they must have personal or learned experience, but more importantly they must also understand the salient characteristics of that experience. Rather than attempt to shoehorn the situation to fit heuristics, they are critically attuned to characteristics that don't fit their rules of thumb. Expert decision makers are focused on action, not analysis, so after running through their mental library of familiar, prototypical contexts, they pick one and make it work, rather than spending time analyzing and developing a perfect plan. Experts exhibit the wisdom of Hick's Law, which says that the time to make a decision is proportional to the *log* of the number of alternatives; they know that examining more alternatives doesn't impair the speed of decision making, but it certainly improves decision quality over fixating on a small number of familiar rules of thumb.

How can you improve your decision making? Hopefully, understanding how decision making works will help. Here are some specific suggestions for assembling your own rules of thumb. Rules of thumb should be formulated according to easily recognized trigger characteristics, and these triggers should be connected to specific actions. Your heuristics will become increasingly sophisticated if you proactively analyze the experience you accumulate. Construct your heuristics so that they're specific and expressed in terms of positive action (not "when rappelling, don't be unsafe," instead: "always back up rappel anchors"). Focus your heuristics on the specific danger you intend to minimize, not on the entire activity. Look for characteristics of situations that appear to be exceptions to your rules of thumb. Broaden your expertise by thoughtfully reading or discussing actual scenarios where decision-making skills are highlighted—by their adroitness or by their lamentable absence. Be especially wary of the difficulty of making good decisions among a group of other mountaineers.

Group decisions can easily be inferior to decision making by individuals, particularly in the face of uncertainty and ambiguity. Decisions taken often have more to do with relationships within the group than with objective facts or accurate appraisal of consequences. The term "groupthink" was coined to describe the deterioration of mental efficiency, reality testing, and moral judgment that results from in-group pressures. Actively combat groupthink by encouraging dissenting opinions, having leaders express their views last, and playing devil's advocate.

CONTROLLING FEAR

They say miracles are past; and we have our philosophical persons, to make modern and familiar, things supernatural and causeless. Hence is it that we make trifles of terrors, ensconcing ourselves into seeming knowledge, when we should submit ourselves to an unknown fear.

Easy for the Bard to say, but his butt wasn't hanging over hundreds of feet of air with rockfall crashing all around. Fear is an important component of mountaineering; it tells us to marshal our resources, deal with the task at hand, and shut off that mind riot that's clamoring for our attention. When you're struck by fear, embrace it, because trying to deny fear or block it out will only consume energy you need for taking effective action. Think of adrenaline as a performance-enhancing drug, but be aware of the effects that fear has, physical and emotional, and deliberately compensate. You want to focus on the important issues before you, but you don't want to let tunnel vision make you blind to easy solutions that may lie just outside your physical or mental field of vision. If fear is creating a sense of urgency, know that it's probably inappropriate; the worst thing you can do is cut corners, fumble, or stumble trying to hurry when being deliberate and careful will save time in the long run.

I find that it helps me to categorize fear as rational, disproportionate, or nonspecific, each form demanding different coping strategies. Nonspecific fear can come at any time—in the parking lot or on the climb. When it strikes, you're overcome by dread for no reason, at least not a reason you can identify. If the feeling doesn't resolve itself by stopping and trying to relax, there's no point in continuing—you'll only find ways to equivocate, procrastinate, and otherwise guarantee failure.

Everyone experiences inertia or hesitation from time to time, but if you find yourself overwhelmed by genuine stark terror without tangible cause, bailing is your only option. You won't be the first.

Disproportionate fear describes being irrationally fearful of something that should elicit only caution or concern. Sometimes you can talk yourself through it by reminding yourself that you've done this before or that you're following a sensible course of action. Don't try to talk yourself out of your fear by trivializing the circumstances or minimizing the consequences (or by false bravado). Don't force yourself to go ahead until you've resolved whatever is making you afraid, unless there's no other option and no one else around who can help you out, physically or mentally. I prefer, when confronting disproportionate fear, to do something tangible, such as place additional protection even if it isn't necessary, or to go through a safety check to reassure myself that I'm not overlooking something crucial. After all, irrational fear can be your wise self pointing out that your smart self has overlooked something, or is about to—listen to what your fear is trying to tell you. In other words, *broaden your awareness*. Disproportionate fear can be minimized by adhering to a personal set of safety principles and protocols; in Chapter 14, Climbing on Rock, I mentioned the mutual safety check climbers perform on each other at the start of every roped climb, and in Chapter 13, Rappelling, a protocol for conducting safe rappels. Every person who deals with complex, dangerous systems relies on protocols rather than inventiveness to minimize hazard. If you're sure your protocols are sound and you haven't cut corners, you can be more confident that your fear is indeed out of proportion.

Rational fear is the accurate perception that bad things could happen and will, unless you act competently. This is when you must ignore extraneous factors and *focus on the task at hand*. If that task is making a difficult, exposed move, don't dwell on the anchor below or the wind or your belayer's attentiveness—make the move. You should already have dealt with the other factors, and you should have skills in reserve you can call upon—in this example that could be your ability to down-climb or your willingness to hang on your anchors. Even in situations where you have little apparent control, you must avoid panic and use every bit of your skill and strength to bring the danger and fear down to manageable levels. You'll be successful, and you'll become stronger and more confident as a result.

LEADERSHIP

Leadership doesn't mean going on an outing and inviting others to keep up if they can. Competent leadership is essential to effective risk management, though on many outings there isn't a requirement for a formal leader. Participants are nominally equals and have comparable levels of skills; they mutually agree on objectives and style (aggressive or casual) and the degree of commitment expected of everyone. Participants must communicate clearly to head off conflicts and disappointment, because the nominal objective (a summit, for example) is only one of potentially many personal objectives among the group. Participants need to be aware of informal rules, such as what will be done if someone chooses not to continue or becomes lost. Responsibility for safety of the party is shared, if unspoken, and no structured leadership is required so long as things go well.

As an informal party of companions reaches mileposts in the outing, leaders may emerge by consensus, based on appropriate expertise, with the leadership function assumed by the most technically competent group member, changing as circumstances change. The person who proposed the objective and secured the permits may defer to someone who has been in the area before to lead the approach, another who is skilled on snow may be the first up the glacier, and a third may become the rope gun on technical rock. There are other contextual styles of leadership: teacher, mentor, motivator, expert, all the way to guide—the position of absolute authority and responsibility.

When all is going well, seemingly little leadership is needed. Reality is more complex. That things are going well indicates effective leadership has already taken place. When problems arise, it's most often due to previous lapses in leadership, particularly procrastination in addressing a deterioration of group dynamics.

Being a part of a successful group is one of the joys of mountaineering; it also makes for more effectiveness. The military has long known that soldiers will perform far beyond their personal norms if they feel their performance is important to and recognized by their group; performance falls far below norm with impaired group cohesion. How do you create a sense of group identity? Most important is a constant, consistent, and obvious policy of inclusion. It helps to celebrate success in terms of accomplishment by the group; I have a friend who's always shouting, "¡Lo hicimos!" (We did it!), and, ya know, it's kind of infectious. As important as the nominal objectives of the group are, participants always have unspoken personal objectives that they associate with the objectives of the outing; this provides individual motivation and a sense of personal accomplishment. Everyone, leaders and participants alike, has emotional needs that are uniquely associated with tangible accomplishments that may or may not be among the identified objectives of the outing. Each person is striving to reach personal milestones; these should be recognized and celebrated by other members of the group.

Maintaining an appropriate pace is probably the single most important action for promoting group cohesion. Also on the list would be setting out a few understandings ahead of time, such as what will be done with a party member who drops out before the summit, whether the group will remain together until back at the trailhead and all cars are started, and what will be done if someone becomes lost. A group is a collection of people with common objectives, and a team is a group with common values. Alpinists share many values; a good place to start expressing them and building your team is by modeling environmentally conscientious behavior, such as Leave No Trace practices.

This section discusses leadership, but in a sense each person is his or her own leader. Every leader hopes that each member of the party will exhibit effective personal leadership by setting high but achievable personal goals, taking responsibility for personal and group objectives, showing willingness to go beyond personal comfort zones and be exposed to growth, interacting constructively with others in the group, and accepting assignments and carrying them out cooperatively and effectively should an emergency arise.

EMERGENCY RESPONSE

There's one context in which the style of leadership ceases to be optional: an emergency incident. Emergencies arise when the force of human factors (planning, skill, leadership, judgment, communication, physical conditioning) is overwhelmed by environmental hazards (weather, terrain, rockfall, avalanche, equipment faults). Dealing effectively with emergencies demands that a single person step forward and assume a directive style of leadership to orchestrate all the party's resources. That means clearly stating messages using "I" language ("Dave, I need you to . . ."), by making messages complete and specific with congruent verbal and nonverbal delivery, and by emphasizing importance with redundancy. To ensure the directions are understood, a leader uses body language that communicates attentiveness to the person being addressed and asks for feedback about how her messages are being received. The leader must be able to remain calm and manage others under stressful conditions but may not be the party member with the most advanced technical skills, such as first aid or navigation. The emergency response leader must see to the safety and security of the rescuers as well as other party members who may be emotionally affected by the emergency, even if they weren't physically involved, or even physically present.

It's out of the scope of this book to present an adequate treatment of every emergency response, although Chapter 25 goes into some detail discussing self-rescue—an emergency response to a climbing accident—and Chapter 26 discusses responses to crevasse falls. In the wilderness first-aid course you're signed up for you'll learn a protocol for emergency medical response. Every emergency response relies on specific, step-by-step protocols that are similar across a variety of emergency incidents. In terms of leadership, all response protocols include the following steps:

▲ Designate an overall leader/manager who takes charge.
▲ Ensure that others, rescuers or bystanders, are not endangered.
▲ Size up the scene in terms of the response required (search for lost person, administer first aid, etc.), victims involved, hazards present, and available resources. The leader will make sure everyone is accounted for.
▲ Formulate a response plan based on the nature of the emergency and communicate it to everyone involved, including any victims.
▲ Assign responsibilities to members of the party and require them to report their progress to the leader, who will balance resources to ensure objectives are met.

After an emergency incident, when your party gets its feet back on the ground, it will be faced with a triage: continue, delay, or retreat. If you're dealing with a medical emergency, you'll be faced with the decision to request outside assistance, either from other mountaineers, from a SAR team on the ground, or in the form of a helicopter rescue.

There's a lamentable increase in backcountry travelers relying on calls to outside agencies for rescue, along with a lessened perceived importance of parties' ability to conduct their own self-rescue and administer first aid, sometimes even to apply common sense. Calling for rescue works in the Alps, but in many mountain areas of North America rescue can be far away or unavailable. Even where it's available, rescue can be significantly delayed by environmental factors or by resources that are preoccupied with another incident. It's always expensive and frequently exposes rescuers to danger, so requesting outside assistance should be considered carefully. Calling for outside assistance may be your only option if a companion has been injured with a mechanism for spinal injury, and no one in your party knows how to rule it out; without a backboard carry, you're taking a chance that transporting the patient could cause serious and permanent additional injury. If you've ever prac-

ticed evacuation using a Stokes litter, you know how difficult and time consuming it is, and you'll have certainly come away with a valuable lesson: don't volunteer to be the "victim." A litter evac is not to be taken lightly, and a necessarily improvised litter makes it many times worse.

If you do carry communications equipment as backup for your group's self-rescue competence, or even with the thought of using it to confirm your safety and avoid an unneeded SAR response, you'll want to determine in advance that you can connect. The availability and response time of rescuers should be factored into your decisions, so you should research this information in advance, too, particularly if you're in a position of leadership. Rescues or flights at night are usually forbidden by SAR rules. Cell phone coverage in mountainous areas is spotty. I once accompanied a ski mountaineer in a long line rescue by a helicopter that was summoned with an FRS radio call that was received over 100 miles away—but I wouldn't count on FRS or GMRS for rescue.

Personal Locator Beacon

The PLB is a pocket-sized, 1-pound transmitter, a scaled-down version of those used by boaters and pilots for years. Thirty-six nations, including European countries, Russia, Canada, and Australia have adopted the system. Each PLB is equipped with a unique identifying code tied to the registrant's personal information. The position of an activated PLB is communicated to a base station by a complex satellite system within a 2-mile radius on the first satellite pass and to within a half-mile radius within three satellite passes, which occur about every 40 minutes. The time to notify a local SAR authority is about 45 minutes. At the same time, SAR will be monitoring with a tracking device to home in on a second signal put out by the PLB. Some PLB models have provisions to attach a GPS (global positioning system) receiver, and some even have built-in GPS receivers; these will broadcast the user's GPS location within a 100-meter radius on the first satellite pass (so, no, they won't work as avalanche beacons).

There's no question that PLBs will be used in non-emergency situations by persons who are overextended and who have the resources for self-rescue but fail to utilize them. PLBs will be activated by stranded motorists, confused Boy Scouts, and hunters low on bourbon. Such situations already cause the bulk of calls for SAR rescue; PLBs may increase such calls but will also make victim location easier for SAR squads.

You might think that PLBs could be ignored by mountaineers or at least treated like cell phones for emergency calls (except that PLBs appear to avoid reception problems), making their use a personal decision. But think again. PLBs are beginning to be required on Oregon mountains to escape rescue fees.

Helicopter Rescue

Helicopters are the most expensive and dangerous rescue technology available. Medical rescue helicopters are especially accident-prone, and wilderness search and rescue is the most dangerous job a civilian helicopter pilot faces. When you meet rescue helicopter pilots in the line of work, you'll be blown away by their competence and bravery—so don't expose them to risk by summoning them unnecessarily. In the event you may be involved in a helicopter rescue, you should have a basic understanding of how things work.

From a distance it may appear that helicopters can just fly anywhere they choose, but it's much more complicated, particularly at altitude and close to the surface. When the rescue helicopter spots you, the pilot will look for a landing spot. Pilots prefer to land into the wind with some forward speed; dropping straight down from a hovering position is a difficult maneuver. Pilots also prefer to take off into the wind. It's surprisingly difficult to spot poles and wires from the air, so avoid suggesting any areas that have such obstacles. Avoid brushy areas or places where there are stumps more than a foot high. It's also difficult to determine ground winds from the air in mountainous areas; you can help by hanging the strip of surveyor's tape in your ten essentials from your trekking pole so that the pilot can see it during the approach.

Flying in mountainous areas is problematic for several reasons. The less dense air at altitude reduces lift; warm air also lowers air density and reduces lift, plus it increases turbulence. Pilots may prefer to fly in mountains only in the cool of the morning, depending on the capabilities of their aircraft and its load. Mountain air is notably turbulent, particularly over ridges and in the lee of crests, so pilots may reject such areas for close flying. When a helicopter is close (about a rotor diameter) to flat ground, it gets an important extra boost of lift from ground effect; sharp ridges provide no ground effect. Landing on slopes is difficult and requires the pilot to constantly modulate the controls to maintain stability; avoid even gentle slopes as pickup sites. Pilots are increasingly unwilling to attempt toe-in or one-skid landings (hovers, really) on slopes because it's exceptionally difficult to keep the helicopter stable as cargo weight changes. Instead, rescuers will be lowered, and able victims will be raised using a horse collar on a wire cable. I can assure you that being long-lined off a steep mountain face is a thrilling experience, because you immediately swing out over hundreds of feet of air, suspended by only your armpits; then you swing back toward the slope and the rescuers. Injured victims are winched up in litters. Particularly in Canada, a fixed-length line is used to drop a rescuer and equipment near victims on precarious terrain, even fifth-class terrain; it's pretty amazing watching a guy in an orange jumpsuit swinging thousands of feet in the air under a small helicopter. The rescuer alights, unhooks, and prepares the victim by putting him in a sack; then the helicopter returns, and both the rescuer and victim are hooked up and carried to a location from which they can be further evacuated. Sling rescue procedures expose the rescuer, pilot, and victim to considerable danger, so it's a method of last resort.

Another hazard for helicopter pilots is the difficulty of estimating distance above snow-covered ground. If your pickup spot is snow covered, especially if the snow is loose, try to leave loaded packs, skis, or logs to help the pilot's depth perception; even boot prints will help. Stand where the pilot can see you, but well clear of the LZ (landing zone), and be prepared for the hurricane of detritus or snow driven by the 100 mph winds created by the helicopter as it approaches (Chinooks, the big ones with two rotors, are even worse). In general, climbers involved in a helicopter rescue should all be crouching together near the victim, well away from where the helicopter will be landing, preferably in view of the pilot. Protect the victim from the wind blast and secure all small items that will otherwise be blown away. Remove hats with brims or bills, and put on your sunglasses or goggles.

Anytime a rescue team appears, in a helicopter or otherwise, the incident commander will take over all leadership responsibilities. Only approach the helicopter when you are specifically directed to do so and from a direction forward of amidships where the pilot can see you; the pilot may decide to reorient the aircraft before anyone gets on or off. Never approach from the rear of the helicopter, even if you think that's what you've been told to do (unless it's a Chinook, which has its entrance door in the rear). Keep your head down, carry your pack and any other items low and in front of you, and be especially wary of skis and poles, which should be lashed into a single unit and carried low. Even though your head is down, keep your eyes on the pilot. If a horse collar or litter is lowered from a hovering helicopter, allow it hit the ground and discharge any static electricity before touching it or the person in it.

Rescue teams may use hand signals to communicate with helicopter pilots because radios can be ineffective in the roar of the engine and rotor (don't plan on verbal communication when a helicopter is near, including a chat with the rescuers). Unless you're familiar with these hand signals, keep your hands by your side. For example, the "wave off" signal to tell a pilot that she should move away rather than land is crossing your hands above your head, à la Village People; that's also how many people would attempt to attract the pilot's attention. Another useful hand signal is to stand just outside the landing zone with your back to the wind and your arms extended straight in front in the direction of the LZ; the pilot will interpret this as an indication of the wind direction and your awareness of her presence. Beyond this, the pilot will probably ignore any signals from someone with whom she isn't familiar.

28
Why Do We Do It?

I went to the woods because I wished to live deliberately. To front only the essential facts of life, and see if I could not learn what it had to teach, and not, when I came to die, discover that I had not lived.

Thoreau wasn't a mountaineer but his sentiments ring true for many of us. Mountaineering captivates and compels an amazing variety of people, and has done so for hundreds, maybe thousands, of years. The meanings and rewards for each person are highly individualistic. Trying to describe the philosophical aspects of mountaineering, undoubtedly a principal component, is fraught with peril, though many have tried. Words that are glowing inspiration for some come off as banal platitudes for others. Shop around. I'm not going to go on about the nature and significance of mountaineering; plenty of others have done it well, and it took more than a few paragraphs. Let me instead point out some notable examples.

If you're interested in the self-discovery aspect of mountaineering, a fine place to start is *The Snow Leopard*, by Peter Matthiessen. Great writing has kept it in print for 25 years. You get comparable romanticism from an accomplished mountaineer in Gaston Rébuffat's *Starlight and Storm*. For a taste of being there, *Annapurna* is Maurice Herzog's tale of the first ascent of an 8,000-meter peak; it's probably the most popular mountaineering book of all time, having sold 15 million copies in dozens of languages. If you want to read what really happened, check *True Summit* by Dave Roberts; it puts Herzog's three climbing partners, Louis Lachenal, Lionel Terray, and Gaston Rébuffat, into better perspective. Terray wrote *The Borders of the Impossible*, which in its original French was titled *Conquistadors of the Useless (Les conquérants de l'inutile)*. That book shows what can be accomplished by a great climber, certainly one of the best of the 20th century, with a great partner, Lachenal, plus it's a great read. One of the best British mountaineering books is *The Shining Mountain* by Pete Boardman, available in an omnibus with *Savage*

Arena, Sacred Summits, and *Everest the Cruel Way*, edited by his great climbing partner Joe Tasker. Another is *One Man's Mountains*, an entertaining and humorous collection by Tom Patey. Don't skip *The White Spider* by Heinrich Harrar, which covers his climb of many men's one mountain, the Eiger. Harrar also wrote *Seven Years in Tibet*, so you know he's a Nazi who looks like Brat Pitt; anyway, *Spider* is better mountaineering. Among other classics well worth reading is Herman Buhl's *The Lonely Challenge*, or in its British title, *Nanga Parbat Pilgrimage*. Mentioning Terray and Buhl among the greats leaves Reinhold Messner. Just about anything by Messner is worth reading, and there's plenty of it; start with *All Fourteen Eight Thousanders*, but don't stop there (unless you're turned off by his 'tude). Another prolific and highly readable mountaineer is Chris Bonington; here you might start with the gripping if not wholly accurate *Everest: The Unclimbed Ridge*. If you're looking for a tale of suffering and triumph of epic proportions, try the accident-prone Joe Simpson's *Touching the Void*; it has sold hundreds of thousands of copies and is now a movie, the best since *The Eiger Sanction*. I could mention *Thin Air* by Greg Child, not only because it's worth reading, but because its name is so close to *Into Thin Air* by Jon Krakauer; somehow that book creeps me out, popular as it is; maybe because so many of the characters are still a part of the climbing scene or have died recently. My favorite air book is Kurt Diemberger's *Spirits of the Air*. And finally I must mention another how-to book, *Mountaineering* by C. T. Dent, from 1890; now that's *really* old-school, but it sets a high standard for entertaining instruction.

I've enjoyed sharing this list of wonderful, life-changing titles with you; I hope you'll read a few if you haven't already. Yet, as I finished I was struck by how many of the authors and characters have perished in the mountains doing things that are difficult, dangerous, and pointless. It made me reflect on my own friends who've been killed climbing or skiing, several during the writing of this book, and even as I write this paragraph the search is on for the body of a fellow mountaineer who died in nearby mountains. You're not around adventure in high mountains for long before you begin to realize how many of your partners and acquaintances have lost their lives doing what they love most. I guess that's an inevitable component of mountaineering. It's not one I've yet explained to my daughter.

TRAVEL SOLO

Most of the content of this book is focused on climbing in the companionship of others. That's certainly one of mountaineering's greatest joys, but don't overlook the commensurate joy of climbing solo. Norman Clyde climbed alone extensively in the Sierra, as did Finis Mitchell in the Winds. When you climb alone you accept total responsibility for your own success and safety. You're free to choose your own pace and your own tolerance of risk, uninfluenced by the groupthink that can be so distracting. Alone, you can achieve your own focus and avoid the autopilot mode prevalent in groups. You compete only with yourself, and by climbing alone you come to know yourself much more clearly. Try it; it's good for the soul.

TRAVEL WITH CHARLIE

Nor should you overlook the soulful pleasure of mountaineering in the company of man's best friend. My own dog is a bold climber and an accomplished mountaineer, summer and winter. She roars up low fifth-class rock and has a number of 14,000-foot summits under her collar; she climbs alpine ice better than I and loves glissading down it, which terrifies me. The value of canine climbing companionship is well known. John Muir wrote of his pick-up partner Stickeen, "I have known many dogs, and many a story I could tell of their wisdom and devotion; but to none do I owe so much as to Stickeen. Our storm-battle for life brought him to light, and through him as through a window I have ever since been looking with deeper sympathy into all my fellow mortals." My own dog's hero is Tschingel, the celebrated climbing partner of the prolific climber, guidebook author, and mountaineering historian W. A. B. Coolidge. Coolidge's Victorian contemporaries considered him "eccentric," but that didn't stop Tschingel from accompanying Coolidge up a ferocious number of difficult climbs during the golden age of alpine exploration. She had at least 11 canine first ascents, including Mont Blanc in 1875 at the age of ten. Tschingel was proposed for honorary, nonvoting membership in the Canadian Alpine Club, but apparently she was rejected on the grounds of gender. If you've ever split your last bite of food and remained hungry, if you've shivered together in an inadequate sleeping bag, if you've hiked the long trail back to the car when both of you are limping but neither complains, knowing the other suffers as much, you know that bonds are built that transcend mere friendship. It's been my great pleasure to have shared such camaraderie with a few good men and one damn fine dog.

Then there's that other thing. It was my grandfather's firm conviction that dogs are able, when they're so inclined, to communicate directly with the Great Spirit. He believed that dogs' tolerance of human shortcomings is the Great Spirit's gift to mortals, and that kindness to dogs will inevitably be rewarded. In an unguarded moment I queried my dog as to whether there might be any truth to such ideas. She looked at me and cocked her head. Then she wagged her tail, which I took to be a response in the affirmative. So we went climbing.

Appendix A
Additional Skills

EXTRA-CREDIT KNOTS

Climbers should develop the habit of tying knots the same way every time, with the motions becoming a sort of physical mantra. This results in consistent-looking knots, so blunders are more apparent. Whatever method you use, avoid those that require lots of fiddling with both hands; unfortunately that's what most instructions call for. None of the knots that follow are essential.

Figure Eight on a Bight

Here's how I'd tie the figure eight follow-through, rethreaded figure eight, or figure eight on a bight: Grasp the rope palm down about 3 feet from the sharp end, with your thumb pointing toward the end. The exact distance from the end depends on

your specific technique, the diameter of the rope, whether you are wearing gloves, and other factors; figure out what's best for you and stick with it. Rotate your hand to palm up, forming a loop in the rope. Snag the short end of the rope and pull it back through the loop. You now have a figure eight. Either drop the sharp end down through your harness attachment points or feed it upward through them, and then carefully retrace the figure eight with the end. The precise way the knot is tied, and even the neatness of tying it, make no significant difference in the strength of the knot, but you should tie it neatly anyhow, as a part of achieving consistent appearance so that knots that are tied incorrectly will be readily apparent. You want to end up with a remaining tail that's 5 or 6 inches long.

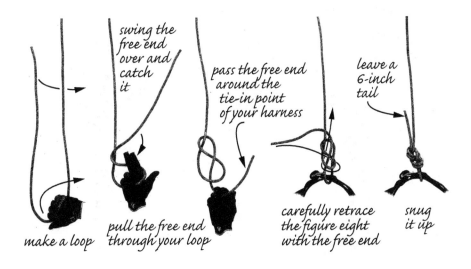

The figure eight tie-in mantra.

make a loop

swing the free end over and catch it

pull the free end through your loop

pass the free end around the tie-in point of your harness

carefully retrace the figure eight with the free end

leave a 6-inch tail

snug it up

The figure eight on a bight, like the overhand on a bight, is very useful and adequately secure and strong; it just gets overused. As a tie-in knot, it falls short of the Yosemite bowline.

Figure Nine

A figure nine on a bight is stronger and more secure than the figure-eight version. Cavers and SAR teams use it regularly.

You'll have to work out for yourself how to tie this knot in a follow-through version if you want

A figure eight on a bight and figure nine on a bight, loose and tight.

to use it to tie your rope to your harness. It's for the truly paranoid.

A Three-Loop Knot

In the modern, cordelette era there's seldom a need to make a multiloop knot in the end of the rope, but here's how. Start by tying a figure eight on a bight, a knot you already know. Leave the length of the bight beyond the knot about three times as long as the average distance you require from the knot to your three placements; be sure to make the lengths long enough to avoid force multiplication. You'll be able to adjust the relative lengths of the three loops before you tighten up the knot. Then wrap the end bight through the distal loops of the figure-eight knot (this is the only tricky part). You're done.

If you pass the bight through the distal loops from the wrong side, you'll still get a functional knot, but it won't be as good as if you do it right. Study the illustration; you'll see that you want to pass the bight through the same way it went through when you tied the figure eight. Now fiddle around to adjust the relative lengths of the loops so as to equalize your placements and then tighten up the knot. Trust me, this knot is the best one around to make three anchor loops in your climbing rope. But wait, there's more.

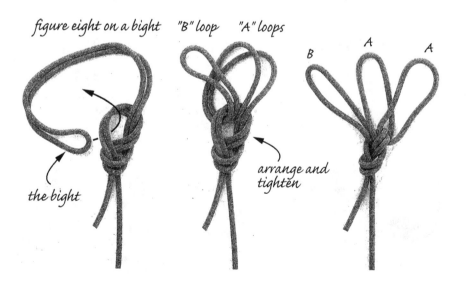

Putting three loops in the end of your rope as part of a complex anchor.

let one of the
A loops
shrink to nil

A two-loop knot, for free.

Now: Two Loops

If you want to make a knot that will equalize *two* placements, the joke, as they say, is over. All you have to do is tie exactly the same knot (this time leaving a length of bight beyond the figure-eight knot amounting to *two* times the average distance you want from the knot to the placements), and then allow one of the A bights to shrink to nothing.

So, for the price of a knot you almost already know, you solve the two-loop and three-loop problems; that ought to free up a hill or two. If you hang those loops over rock features, use overhand slip knots in them for a little additional security. If you intend to sling features that are 10 feet away, you'll end up using half your 50 m rope to set up the anchor. I'll just end this bit with a warning that I've tried to examine every published multiloop knot, and all but this one flunk for one reason or another; caveat emptor.

Another Way to Tie the Alpine Butterfly Loop Knot

Some may find this method easier to commit to memory.

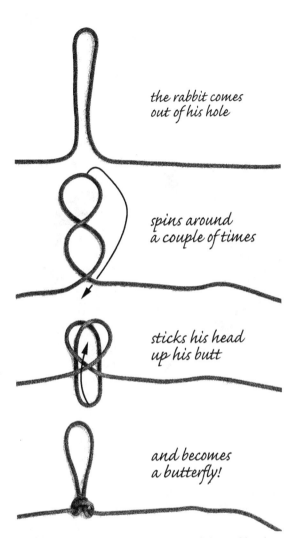

the rabbit comes
out of his hole

spins around
a couple of times

sticks his head
up his butt

and becomes
a butterfly!

Alternative method of tying the alpine butterfly loop, with rude mnemonic.

Bowline on a Coil Alternative

The bowline on a coil is another legacy knot that you should never have to consider, for two reasons. First, you should always carry a 48-inch runner and locking carabiner if you carry a rope; don't rely on coils to tie in. Second, one step in the tying requires twisting a loop; if you twist it the wrong way, the result is a defective knot that isn't readily apparent. The idea is to put three wraps of the climbing rope snugly around your waist and tie a sort of bowline to hold the coils. You can accomplish the same thing by simply using a con-

Yosemite
bowline

you are here

Three wraps around your waist, held by a Yosemite bowline.

The Bachmann friction knot.

ventional bowline or Yosemite bowline, knots that you already know and that are easy to inspect. Theoretically, this results in a potentially constricting loop, but practically the difference is indistinguishable, especially if you make the last loop spiral around the previous two. Little force will be put on this knot, and it certainly isn't meant for supporting body weight no matter how you tie it—painful, and you'd find breathing seriously hindered.

Additional Friction Knots

The knot I use most frequently to tie a loop of nylon webbing or small cord to a rope is the Klemheist knot; it works by friction and constriction. You've also learned the weak autoblock knot (aka French prusik) as a backup during a rappel. It only has to be as strong as your grip, and it can be released while under tension. There are two other common friction knots: the classic prusik knot and the Bachmann. The prusik is quite se-

cure, but if slipping is a concern because the rope is frosty or skinny, use four wraps or a 4 mm diameter cord. The Bachmann is handy because you can use the carabiner as a handle to move it along; it doesn't hold as well as the prusik or Kleimheist on frosty or skinny ropes. All these knots, even the Bachmann to some degree, hold when pulled from either direction, whereas mechanical ascenders or rope grabs hold in one direction and slip when pulled from the other.

Tautline Hitch

Adjust tension on your tent lines the smart way, especially if the lines are nylon and will stretch when they encounter rain or dew. Once the knot is tightened, you can push it along, but it will self-lock.

Primitive Loop Knot

You may think I'm ape for the overhand knot—that you could get by just using variations of the overhand knot for all your mountaineering. Here's a

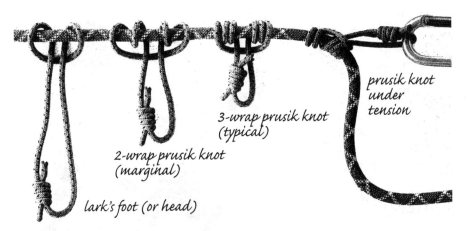

prusik knot
under
tension

3-wrap prusik knot
(typical)

2-wrap prusik knot
(marginal)

lark's foot (or head)

Prusik knots on a prusik loop.

Double fisherman on a bight.

for adjusting tent lines
not for climbing

Tautline hitch.

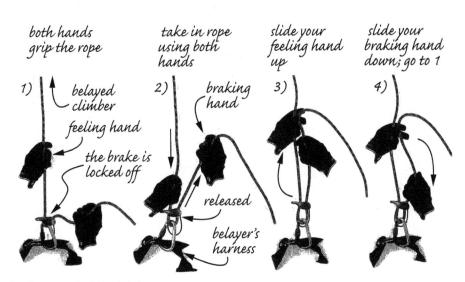

both hands
grip the rope

take in rope
using both
hands

slide your
feeling hand
up

slide your
braking hand
down; go to 1

1) belayed
climber

feeling hand

the brake is
locked off

2) braking
hand

released

belayer's
harness

3)

4)

Hand sequence for taking in belay rope.

way to tie a loop using two double overhands. It's as strong as a figure eight on a bight, easier to remember for some, but harder to untie. You could call it a double fisherman on a bight.

Hand Sequence for Belaying

Bringing up a second by belaying off your harness is a technique I discourage, but the hand sequences you'd use are a routine every climber learns. It's the same method you'd use when belaying a top-roped climber. There are two important points. First, minimize the amount of time when rope is being taken in and the belay isn't locked off, positions 2, 3, and 4; there'd be trouble if the belayed climber were to fall when rope is being taken, because the belay is very weak when the rope strands are nearly parallel. And second, *never take your braking hand off the rope*.

DÜLFERSITZ RAPPEL

I can't recommend using this rappel method for any reason unless you're on easy ground; no one in your group was clueful enough to bring a harness, sling, or carabiner; and you're wearing your partner's jacket. It's more challenging when wearing a pack, and it's easy to flip out of because it attaches below your center of mass, but if you have a taste for shoulder pain, you may want to learn it. Maybe its retro aspect will appeal; it was developed by Hans Dülfer before WWI, when mountaineers were men, carabiners were steel, and ropes were hemp. Hold the rope in your right hand, step over it, then, using your left hand, pull a bight from your right hand and pass it over your head to your

The Dülfersitz rappel, straight out of history.

left shoulder so that the rope drapes down your back to your right hand (you've never released the rope from your right hand). Keep your feet wide apart with the foot on the holding hand side below the other, don't let your feet slip, and don't let go of either hand.

Appendix B

Resources

Some references include Internet links, which typically have only a fleeting existence. Conduct your own searches using a few keywords.

PART 1

Cox, Steven M., and Kris Fulsaas, eds. *Mountaineering: The Freedom of the Hills*, 7th ed. Seattle: Mountaineers Books, 2003. The classic bible of old-school gear and methodology.

Field Manual FM 3-97.61: Military Mountaineering. Washington, D.C.: Department of the Army, 2002. All the same stuff as Freedom of the Hills, including weather, first aid, climbing, hazards, snow and ice—all solidly old-school. Even the illustrations are remarkably similar, except for the uniforms. Free on the Net at: http://155.217.58.58/cgi-bin/atdl.dll/fm/3-97.61/toc.htm or www.adtdl.army.mil/cgi-bin/atdl.dll/fm/3-97.61/toc.htm

PART 2

Start exploring avalanche forecasts at the Colorado Avalanche Information Center's page of links to many areas: http://www.geosurvey.state.co.us/avalanche/Link.html
Canadian avalanche forecasts may be found at: http://www.avalanche.ca/weather/bulletins/index.html

To learn more about high-altitude illness check The International Society of Mountain Medicine's site at www.issmmed.org/np_altitude_tutorial.htm. Or read the standard refer-

ence for medical professionals: Hackett, Peter H., and Robert C. Roach, "Current Concepts: High-Altitude Illness" *New England Journal of Medicine*, 345 (2001):107–114.

Long, John. *Close Calls: Climbing Mishaps and Near-Death Experiences*. Helena, MT: Falcon Publishing, 1999. Learn from others' mistakes and John Long's advice.

Williamson, Jed, ed. *Accidents in North American Mountaineering*. Golden, CO: American Alpine Club and Alpine Club of Canada, annual editions.

To get started with more sophisticated weather forecasts, check out the National Weather Service's Storm Prediction Center, Mesoscale Discussions, at www.spc.noaa.gov/products/md/. Much of this data is updated hourly. For all manner of weather information covering the United States (with links to Canada), start out at the NWS home page: www.nws.noaa.gov or for Western states, www.wrh.noaa.gov.

PART 3

Petzl, innovative French climbing and caving equipment manufacturer's product instruction sheets, catalogs, and Web site (www.petzl.com) are filled with sensible, up-to-date information and guidance. Plus, Petzl's product names are très clever.

Klassen, Karl. *Technical Handbook for Professional Mountain Guides: Alpine, Rock, and Ski Guiding*

Techniques. Kamloops, BC: Association of Canadian Mountain Guides, American Mountain Guide Association, 1999. Get it with your membership.

Long, John, and Bob Gaines. *More Climbing Anchors*. Guilford, CT: Falcon Press/Chockstone Press Books, 1996. Clear photos and old-school discussions of lots of complex anchors.

PART 4

Chouinard, Yvon. *Climbing Ice*. San Francisco: Sierra Club Books, 1977. Classic, but not old-school, this is the real deal from the guy who engendered hard ice climbing while espousing fast and light.

PART 5

For up-to-date information on fabrics and breathability, search the Net for "Elizabeth A. McCullough" and "Phil Gibson" + Natick.

Townsend, Chris. *The Advanced Backpacker: A Handbook for Year-Round, Long-Distance Hiking*. Camden, ME: Ragged Mountain Press, 2001. Excellent, clear, and practical advice for backpacking, especially over long distances.

Townsend, Chris. *The Backpacker's Handbook*, 3rd ed. Camden, ME: Ragged Mountain Press, 2005.

O'Bannon, Allen, and Mike Clelland (illustrator). *Allen and Mike's Really Cool Backpackin' Book: Traveling and Camping Skills for a Wilderness Experience*. Helena, MT: Falcon Publishing, 2001. A great place to start, if a tad old-school in approach. You gotta love Clelland's illustrations.

The following is a list of the chemicals used in various insect repellents. I offer them should you care to read the fine print on the containers you're considering: The best repellents contain the chemicals DEET (N,N-diethyl-m-toluamide same as N,N-diethyl-3-methylbenzamide), Indalone (butyl 3,4-dihydro-2,2-dimethyl-4-oxo-2H-pyran-6-carboxylate), Rutgers 612 (2-ethyl-1,3-hexanediol), and DMP (dimethyl phthalate); DEET is probably the best choice. Di-n-propyl isocinchomeronate (R-326) has been promoted as useful against biting flies. MGK-264 is N-octyl bicycloheptene dicarboximide; it's a synergistic agent for DEET. IBI-246 is 2-undecanone, a Category IV chemical used in cosmetics.

Connors, Christine. *The Lip Smackin' Backpackin' Cookbook*. Helena, MT: Falcon Publishing, 2000. This, and the following cookbooks, while highly recommended, are aimed at backpackers not mountaineers. Even though they feature the use of dehydrators, mountaineers may have to adapt the recipes for efficient preparation in alpine conditions. Still way better than freeze dry.

McHugh, Gretchen. *Hungry Hikers Book of Good Cooking*. New York: Alfred A. Knopf, 1982.

Fleming, June. *The Well-Fed Backpacker*, 3rd ed. New York: Vintage Books, 1986.

Marrone, Teresa. *The Backcountry Kitchen*. Sedona AZ: North Trail Press, 1996.

For more information on the science of vitamin supplementation and life extension, search the Net for Dr. "Bruce Ames."

Hammer Nutrition, Ltd. Makers of Hammer Gel and other nutritionals for ultra endurance athletes, with an emphasis on cyclists. Check their J.O.E. for random scientific research. See www.e-caps.com.

Life Extension Foundation, a source of every possible health (not necessarily sports) supplement, reasonable prices, and tons of peer-reviewed research. See www.lef.org.

Various interactive ways to determine VO_2max and fitness without medical tests: "Assessing Physical Fitness of Participants and Staff using Non-Exercise Screening Techniques," Rich Curtis: www.outdoorsafety.org/articles/article.asp?ArticleID=144, based on Jackson, A. S., S. N. Blair, M. T. Mahar, L. T. Wier, R. M. Ross, and J. E. Stuteville, "Prediction of Functional Aerobic Capacity without Exercise Testing" *Medicine and Science in Sport and Exercise* 22(6) 1990: 863–870.

Isaac, Jeffrey. *The Outward Bound Wilderness First-Aid Handbook*. New York: Lyons Press, 1998. New-school wilderness first aid, up to the level of Wilderness Advanced First Aid.

Morrissey, Jim. *Wilderness Medical Associates Field Guide.* Colorado Springs: Wilderness Medical Associates, 2000. A tiny guide to the content of Wilderness Medical Associates's excellent wilderness first-aid instruction; useless without the course. See www.wildmed.com

Check out the National Outdoor Leadership School (NOLS) Wilderness Medical Institute at www.nols.edu/wmi/.

PART 6

Fasulo, David J. *Self-Rescue.* Guilford, CT: Falcon Press/Chockstone Press Books, 1999.

Tyson, Andy, and Mike Clelland (illustrator). *The Illustrated Guide to Glacier Travel and Crevasse Rescue.* Carbondale, CO: Climbing Magazine Publications, 2000. A great example of a book that pretty much nails its subject dead-on.

Instructions:

~ Copy this page onto clear plastic film such as used for overhead projections.

~ Check the 7-inch line to be sure your copy machine isn't overly helpful.

~ Make as many copies as you need to best utilize the lamination step, based on whichever version works best for you—the ruler or the UTM grid.

~ Cut up the rulers or grids and place them carefully in a heavy lamination sleeve, then laminate.

~ Cut out each ruler or grid, leaving a border of laminated film around each.

7 inches exactly

five 20m contour lines

0 10 15 20 25 30 35 40 45 50

1 MILE

Telemarkers Rule!

© Craig Connally 2004

7.5' 1:24,000

five 40' contour lines

2000' 1000' 0

50 45 40 35 30 25 20 15 10

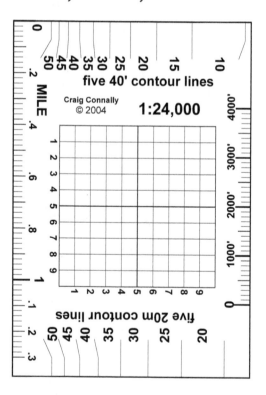

0 .2 MILE .4 .6 .8 1 .1 .2 .3

five 40' contour lines

10 15 20 25 30 35 40 45 50

1:24,000

Craig Connally
© 2004

.4000' .3000' .2000' .1000' 0

five 20m contour lines

20 25 30 35 40 45 50

To read a slope angle directly off a 1:24,000 topo map, match the gaps on these tools with five contour lines.

Map tools for skiers and mountaineers.

Appendix C

Glossary

ablation zone The region of a glacier below the firn line that experiences annual net loss of snow and ice by melting, sublimation, and calving.

abseil Same as rappel: descending by sliding down a rope under control of friction.

accumulation zone The area of a glacier above the firn line, that retains more annual snow than it loses to melting and sublimation.

aid climbing Ascending using fixed or removable anchors to support the climber's weight.

alpha angle The angle, measured from horizontal, from where you are to the likely start zone of naturally triggered avalanches on slopes above.

alpine The terrain above tree line.

alpine climbing Rock and ice climbing that requires mountaineering skills.

alpine start Beginning a day of mountaineering at a very early hour.

AMS Acute Mountain Sickness. Headache, nausea, insomnia, and other symptoms caused by hyperbaric hypoxia (low pressure, low oxygen).

anabatic A wind that moves up a slope; compare katabatic.

angle of repose The steepest slope angle (measured from horizontal) at which irregular materials can be piled. For sand, scree, and small talus it is about 35°.

arête A narrow, often very narrow, ridge.

ascender A mechanical device used to hold or climb a rope; a rope grab.

autoblock A friction knot that tightens automatically but can be made to slip while under tension, commonly used to back up a rappeler's grip on the rope; aka French prusik. A property of a belay brake that causes the rope to a climber below to jam and hold the climber's fall; not intended to hold hard or leader falls or to be used hands-free.

autolock A property of a belay brake that causes the rope to another climber to become locked and hold the climber's fall; intended to hold leader falls and to be used hands-free by some.

avalanche A mass of snow, mud, rocks, scree, or talus sliding down a mountain, with snow being the most common.

B-52 Trade name for a belay/rappel brake with autoblock functions.

bail To give up on a climb.

bearing The angle between the direction to an object and a reference direction that is typically geographic north.

belay To make secure by use of a rope.

bergschrund (Or simply 'schrund.) A crevasse formed where the moving ice of a glacier pulls away from a permanent snowfield higher up.

beta Information, usually regarding a climb or route.

big wall A long, steep rock climb that may require several days.

bight A section of rope that curves back on itself.

biner Short for carabiner, or karabiner.

bivy Short for bivouac: an impromptu, primitive encampment during a climb.

black ice Old, dense ice containing rock and grit, often found deep in north-facing gullies.

bollard A rounded object used for securing a rope, dug out of snow or ice for use as an anchor, or part of a strength-testing machine.

bolt A permanent anchor made by drilling a hole in the stone and placing an expansion screw and hanger.

bomber Same as bomb proof: a hold or anchor (or just about anything else) that inspires great confidence in its strength and security.

bootie Found hardware, lost or left by a previous party.

bouldering A style of climbing that forgoes belays, usually involving exceptionally difficult moves on routes close to the deck.

bounce test Putting one's weight, and as much extra force as possible by jumping around, on an anchor in order to test its security.

cairn A form of mountain graffiti made by piling rocks, used to mark a route; aka duck.

cam Generic term for active (spring-loaded) mechanical camming devices, such as Friends, Camalots, Aliens, etc., used for anchors in rock.

carabiner A snap link of various kinds, with many uses; also "karabiner."

chock A category of passive devices used as anchors when wedged into openings in rock; also called rocks, nuts, stoppers, and wires or wireds.

chockstone A stone firmly wedged in an opening in the rock.

choss Loose, broken, or exceptionally weak rock; aka kitty litter. To a Brit, choss means dirt and vegetation in cracks.

chute A steep, narrow gully, used by mountains to dump their garbage.

cirque A steep-sided basin forming the high end of a mountain valley.

clean To remove a climbing route's anchors. Climbing without falling or pulling on anchors. Climbing using removable anchors only.

clinometer An instrument for measuring the angle of a slope, often built into compasses and sometimes incorrectly referred to as an "inclinometer."

continental A location far from the effects of the sea; describes weather, climate, and snowpack.

contour line A line of constant elevation on a topographic map.

cordelette A long, versatile runner loop made of about 20 feet of 6 or 7 mm accessory cord or of 5 mm high-tenacity cord.

cornice Wind-sculpted snow projecting beyond the crest of a ridge on its lee side.

couloir A steep chute or gulley on a mountain, typically containing ice or snow.

crab Or krab, short for carabiner—which should be "karabiner."

crag A small, easily accessible rock-climbing area.

crampon One of a pair of metal attachments for boots that feature spikes for traction on snow and ice.

crater The ground terminus of a serious fall; aka splat.

crevasse A chasm in the ice of a glacier.

crimper A small hold that barely admits fingertips.

cross loading Applying loads to a carabiner other than along its long axis, the strongest direction and the one for which it was designed.

crux The most challenging section of a climb.

daisy chain A runner sewn or tied to create a number of pockets along its length, allowing length adjustment.

deadman An object buried in snow to serve as an anchor.

deck The ground or a substantial ledge. Falling to the ground or onto a ledge.

denier The weight in grams of a single fiber that is about 5.6 miles (exactly 9 km) long; pronounced dun-yay' (sort of) and abbreviated d, used to express fabric weight.

diaper harness An improvised harness made with a long runner, suitable only for short periods on easy terrain.

directional An anchor or runner whose primary purpose is to control the direction of applied force.

downclimb Descending a route without weighting a rope and often without protection.

drag bag A large, robust sack intended for hauling equipment and provisions over snow-covered terrain by masochists.

dry tooling Using ice tools (axes) and possibly crampons on rock when climbing.

dynamic belay A belay of the leader that allows some rope to slip in the event of a fall, absorbing energy and reducing peak forces.

dynamic rope A climbing rope having energy-absorbing and force-limiting properties such that it's suitable for lead climbing.

Elvis When a climber's legs are so tired or stressed that they shake uncontrollably; aka sewing machine legs.

epic A climbing adventure that goes badly, requiring extraordinary effort to complete or survive.

equalization The property of a complex anchor that balances the applied force among its component placements.

escape the belay Actions by which the belayer disengages from the belay setup while keeping the climber safely belayed, usually as the start of a self-rescue process.

European Death Knot EDK; a name given by sardonic American climbers to the simple "flat overhand" knot used to join rappel ropes.

exposure The character of terrain that makes climbers especially fearful of a lengthy fall.

extension Movement of the master point of a complex anchor in the event of failure of a component placement.

FA A guidebook term indicating the first ascent of a route. FFA means first free (without using aid) ascent.

fall factor A coarse index of the severity of a fall equal to the length of the fall divided by the length of rope available to absorb fall energy; fall force is proportional to the square root of the fall factor.

fall line The most direct, not necessarily straightest, line down a slope; it is the line down which a ball would roll and it crosses contour lines perpendicularly.

fifi hook A small metal hook shaped like a question mark and intended to hold body weight but not fall force.

firn Well-consolidated granular snow and ice remaining from previous seasons; intermediate in density between snow and ice; aka névé.

fixed line A rope, usually static, left attached to anchors for an extended period.

fixed pro Protection anchors that are not readily removable, due to accident or intention.

flake A relatively thin, flat feature detached from the main rock face. The act of untangling a rope while arranging it in a pile.

fluke A snow anchor, usually with attached cable, made from slightly bent aluminum sheet metal.

follow To climb after the leader, typically while being belayed from above; same as "second."

free climb Moving up a climbing route without putting weight on anchors, using only hands, feet, and natural holds for progression.

free solo Climbing without a safety rope when one would typically be used.

French free Climbing by pulling on anchors, irrespective of who placed them.

French technique A style of climbing moderate snow or ice emphasizing adroit ankle flexibility and eschewing the use of crampon front points.

Friend The trade name of the first common spring-loaded camming device (active cam), used as a generic term for them and successors.

funkness A cable runner intended to be clipped to a piton and hammer to help jerk the piton out of its placement, i.e., to funk it.

gardening Removing organic material and loose rock to improve a climbing route; cleaning up a climbing route in general.

gendarme A sharp pinnacle of rock on a ridge that typically impedes climbing along the ridge.

Gi-Gi A simple plate belay/rappel brake with auto-block functions.

glacial flour Rock dust ground by moving glaciers that makes streams cloudy and alpine lakes appear opaque pale blue.

glacial ice Ice formed from the continuing transformation of névé to the point it is impermeable to water, condensed further by the weight of snow and ice atop it so that its density approaches that of solid ice.

glissade Descending snow by controlled sliding on feet or derrière.

GPS Global Positioning System; a satellite-based navigation system accessed by consumers using portable receivers.

GriGri A mechanical, auto-locking belay brake, unsuited for mountaineering because of its weight and lack of rope slippage.

gripped Incapacitated by fear.

HACE High Altitude Cerebral Edema; swelling of the brain due to edema caused by hyperbaric hypoxia (low pressure, low oxygen).

hang dogging Hanging on the rope while resting and trying to figure out the climbing moves that have defeated you thus far.

hanging belay A belay that requires the belayer to hang in a climbing harness without significant support from the feet.

HAPE High Altitude Pulmonary Edema; fluid accumulation in the lungs due to hyperbaric hypoxia.

haul bag A robust sack intended for dragging

equipment and provisions up big wall climbs; aka the pig.

headwall Terrain where the grade steepens dramatically.

hex Generic term for a type of pro having an irregular, hexagonal cross section, used as a chock and in passive camming modes.

HMS Halbmastwurf sicherung—German meaning half clove hitch; another name for the Münter hitch, or a large pear-shaped carabiner with which it goes well.

horn A large, sturdy protrusion of rock.

hueco A substantial hole or pocket in a rock face that may surround solid rock, around which a runner can be placed by passing it through the hole.

hypoxia Unusually low or deficient oxygen reaching tissues of the body.

icefall A section of a glacier where a steep slope cracks the ice into large blocks, called seracs.

intermountain A location between maritime and continental, sometimes having maritime characteristics west of mountain crests and continental characteristics to the east; describes weather, climate, and snowpack.

jug A substantial and easily grasped climbing hold. Ascending a rope using mechanical ascenders, such as a Jumar and so also "jumaring."

katabatic A mountain wind that flows downslope due to cooling, usually at night.

kernmantle Rope or cord construction with a woven exterior and braided interior.

kilonewton A unit of force equal to about 225 lbf (pound force), abbreviated kN, meaning 1,000 newtons; gravity causes a kilogram (2.2 pound) mass to press down with a force of about 10 newtons.

Kiwi coil An obsolete and suboptimal means for a glacier-travel team member to tie in to the rope and coil the excess.

lead To be the first climber, typically the one charged with routefinding and placing protection anchors if a rope is used; leading takes place on the sharp end of the rope.

lithobrake Impacting rock as a means of reducing the velocity of a fall.

locker A carabiner having a means to lock its gate closed.

mantle A rock climbing technique for moving up onto a ledge mainly using downward pressure of one's hands on the ledge.

maritime A location close to the sea and subject to its effects; describes weather, climate, and snowpack.

master point The point at which the component placements of a complex anchor come together and to which the load is connected, usually at a large locking carabiner.

mitochondria Structures in cells that are responsible for energy production.

mixed climbing Climbing that involves ice, maybe snow, and rock.

moat A gap between a snowfield and adjacent rock.

moraine Rock, gravel, sand, and mud deposited by a glacier.

Münter hitch A simple, slipping hitch used to create friction on a rope for belaying, rappelling, or lowering.

névé Well-consolidated granular snow and ice remaining from previous seasons, intermediate in density between snow and solid ice; aka firn.

new-school An approach to learning and practice based on objective evaluations rather than historic precedent and tending to be eager for advancement.

off width A crack having a width that's inconvenient for typical climbing methods and that's therefore unusually awkward and strenuous; it can be off hands, off feet, off body, etc.

old-school An approach to learning and practice for which tradition outweighs objective evaluation.

orienteering A sport in which competitors race from one checkpoint to the next using a map, compass, and navigation skills.

picket An aluminum stake, typically with a T-shaped cross section, driven or buried in snow as an anchor.

piolet canne Climbing snow or ice using the mountaineering ax (piolet) as an aid to balance, like a cane.

piolet panne Climbing snow or ice using the mountaineering ax (piolet) by holding it with one's hand atop the head and plunging in the pick at about waist height; aka low dagger.

piolet poignard Climbing snow or ice using the

mountaineering ax (piolet) by holding it with one's hand wrapped around the head and plunging in the pick at about head height; aka high dagger.

piolet traction Climbing snow or ice with a mountaineering ax (piolet) by sinking the pick of the ax and holding or pulling on the ax shaft.

pitch A portion of a climb between two successive belay anchors, or the conceptual equivalent.

placement An anchor in rock, snow, or ice or a component anchor of a complex anchor.

posthole Hiking in snow so soft that one's legs sink deeply with each step.

pro Protection hardware; a variety of permanent or temporary means to achieve climbing anchors in rock, snow, or ice.

prusik The original friction knot: a knot used to connect a smaller diameter cord to a rope, allowing the knot to hold or slip along the rope. A runner (loop) of small diameter cord used to create a prusik knot or any other friction knot. To ascend a rope using friction knots on prusik loops.

quickdraw Or simply "draw"; two carabiners joined by a relatively short runner, so called because they were originally intended to be pre-attached to the rope to make them quick to clip to anchors.

rack The compliment of equipment, including pro, once carried on a shoulder gear sling, now also carried on harness gear loops. To attach hardware and sort the rack prior to climbing.

randonée A form of skiing using a binding that allows the boot heel to rise when ascending or to be locked down for conventional alpine skiing; French for "can't telemark."

rappel Or just "rap"; to descend with one's weight supported mainly by the rope under control of a brake device; most of the world refers to this as abseil or to "ab off."

redirect A carabiner or pulley whose purpose is to change the direction of the dress of a rope or runner and thereby the direction of force.

redpoint Leading a route from bottom to top without falling or hang dogging while placing one's own protection.

resection A technique for determining one's location by taking compass bearings and plotting them on a map; aka triangulation.

rime A thin crust of icy snow deposited by storms on the windward side of objects.

runner A circle of webbing or cord used, for example, to create or extend an anchor; same as "sling."

running belay Either an anchor through which the rope runs freely or a style of climbing in which only the beginning and end of a pitch are protected with belay anchors, and the climbing party moves simultaneously using intermediate anchors (simul-climbing). Not used in this book because of this confusion.

runout A portion of a pitch characterized by an uncomfortably long distance from the last anchor or secure stance.

sandbag A climb rating inappropriately low for the actual difficulty.

SAR Search and rescue; a specific or generic organization with the training and resources to conduct search and rescue operations.

scum To use body parts other than hands and feet while making a difficult climbing move; considered aesthetically poor form.

screamer A long fall, accumulating impressive air time.

Screamer The original load-limiting runner, which allows stitching to rip and limit the applied force while absorbing some fall energy.

scree Rock fragments forming a slope, sometimes defined as being composed of stones too small to be individually stepped on by a climber.

screwgate A carabiner whose gate can be locked shut; same as "locker."

second A person who climbs behind the leader and is belayed from above as on a top rope; same as follower.

self-arrest Stopping a slide on snow by a climber's individual efforts.

send To climb a route with ease.

serac A block of ice in a glacial icefall.

sew up To place a copious amount of pro on a trad route.

simul-climbing Roped climbing in which the party and rope move simultaneously; the party sets and removes intermediate anchors while moving several rope lengths and only sets belay anchors at the beginning and end of the extra-long pitch.

solo Climbing a route alone.

spindrift Loose powdery snow often blown by the wind or sluffing off steep terrain during storms.

sport climb A route, usually of one pitch, protected by bolts and on which the holds are often indicated by gymnastic chalk residue.

static belay A belay of the leader allowing no rope slip and consequent energy absorption in the event of a fall.

static equalization The attribute of a complex anchor making for minimal extension, but also resulting in imbalance if the direction of applied force is other than that intended.

static rope A rope with less energy-absorbing stretch than a "dynamic" rope and which therefore cannot safely be used for lead climbing where the fall factor could exceed 1.

steinpuller A hold created by a climber on mixed terrain by inserting the pick of an ice tool into what would be an undercling for a rock climber, then pulling outward on the tool's shaft.

sun cup One of many depressions covering a snowfield, from an inch to several feet deep and wide, that form in fair sunny weather and which may be destroyed by windy, warm, wet, and cloudy weather only to reform when the weather again becomes sunny and dry.

talus Rock fragments forming a slope, sometimes defined as being composed of stones large enough to be individually stepped on by a climber.

team arrest An attempt to stop the fall of a member or members who cannot self-arrest by a party that is roped together on snow.

telemark A form of skiing based on a binding that allows the boot sole to flex and its heel to rise and so requiring a kneeling turn with the outside ski ahead of the other; French for "face plant."

terrain trap A terrain feature (such as a narrowing gully) that concentrates avalanching material, encourages avalanching material to pile up, or forms barriers (such as a stand of trees) to persons being carried along by avalanching material.

Tibloc Trade name for a rope grab with no moving parts but using a carabiner to achieve the slide/lock functions of a minimalist ascender.

top rope Climbing in which climbers are protected by a rope from above that is usually passed through a single anchor point and back to a belayer at the ground (a "slingshot belay").

topo A topographic map, such as those of the USGS, showing elevation by contour lines. A sketch of a climbing route indicating identifying features and the locations of fixed anchors and belay stances, as well as the style and rating of each pitch.

trad Traditional lead climbing, where the leader places removable intermediate anchors while being belayed from below and the second removes them while being belayed from above.

traverse A portion of a climb that's relatively horizontal.

tri-axial loading Loads connected to a carabiner from three directions, reducing the strength of the carabiner.

Ultralegere Trade name for a minimalist pulley, in fact, just a pulley wheel intended to be used with a symmetrical carabiner.

UTM Universal Transverse Mercator; a map projection that overlays small regions of the earth's surface with rectangular metric grids that nearly, but not exactly, align with lines of latitude and longitude and used to simplify navigation within such small regions.

verglas A thin, transparent layer of ice over rock, formed by frozen rain or melt water.

via ferrata A climbing route consisting of iron rungs permanently attached to mountain faces; protection is by an adjacent, periodically anchored steel cable to which climbers clip short leashes; originally constructed in Europe to move troops, now climbed as sport.

V-thread An anchor in ice made by drilling connected holes and lacing them with cord or webbing, which is then tied into a loop; invented by Vitaly Abalakov.

windslab A layer of unusually firm and dense snow deposited by wind.

wired A chock or hex with a short, factory-applied runner made of wire cable. Being in complete command of the difficulties of a climb.

yard To move upward by pulling on the rope with your hands. To take in large amounts of rope.

zipper When falling on a climb, to pull out several, or all, of the intermediate anchors.

Z-pulley A common 3:1 pulley system.

Index

self-belay techniques, 196–197; auto-block self-belay, **96**; while rappelling, 162–**163**

self-rescue: anchors, building, **336**–338; assisted descending, 324–**326**; crevasse falls, 335–337; escaping the belay, 314–**317**; lowering the victim, 314, 316–317, 325–**326**; rappelling to the victim, 318; tandem rappelling, 324–325; climbing to the victim, 317–319, **318**; steps to deal with, 312–314; techniques, 326

Seventh Grade (Messner), 76

Seven Years in Tibet (Harrar), 351

shell layer, 321

shelter systems, 236; bivy sacks, 236–237, 239; igloos, 240–**242**; lightweight mountaineering, 216; naked, 236; selecting, 239; sleeping pads, 237, 244–245; snow caves, 240, **241**; tarps and tarp tents, **237**–238; tents, double-wall, 238–239; tents, four-season, 239–240; tents, single-wall, 238; tents, three-season, 239–240; for winter mountaineering, 240–241. *See also* sleeping bags

Sherpa, Babu Chhiri, 327

Sherpa, Tenzing Norgay, 139, 296

Shining Mountain (Boardman), 350

shock, 292

shock loading, 148–149

shoes. *See* boots and shoes

shovels, **132**, 194

Sierra Club, 73

silnylon, 233, 238

Simpson, Joe, 112, 327, 351

simul-climbing, 8, 182, 306–**308**, *367*

single rope, 81, **82**, 85–86

sixth-class climbing, 73

ski mountaineering, 192

skis, 191–192

slab climbing, 173

SLCDs (spring loaded camming devices, active cams), 110, 123, 145

sled, mountaineering, **193**–194, 334

sleeping aids, 69–70

sleeping bags, 236, 242; cleaning, 247–248; drying damp clothing, 247; fabrics, 243; internal volume, 243; loft, 242; ratings, 243–244; recommendations, 247; sealing features, 242; vapor barrier liners (VBL), 246–247; EN13537, 244; warmth of, 245–246

sleeping pads, 237; R-value of, 244–245

slings. *See* runners

slip knot: overhand, **141**, 315, 318; double overhand, **103**

slopes: bearing of, 25; fall line, 25; slope and grade chart, 17, 20; steepness of, 21–22, **362**. *See also* angle of repose

small rack, 110, 111

snow, 184; anchors in, **124**, 126–127, 129–133, **130**, **131**, **132**; pits for checking, 47; types of, 45–46, 47

snow blindness, 58, 194

snow bollards, **124**, 126–127

snow bridges, 41, 64, 328–329

snow caves, 240, **241**

snow climbing: descending, 203–**205**; fabric choices for clothing, 201; falls, 201; glissade, 203, **204**; hands-only self-arrest techniques, **197**–198; moving fast, 210–211; plunge step, 203–205, **204**; with protection, 207–210, **208**, **209**; with rope, **205**–207, 307, 331; self-arrest grip, **196**; self-arrest techniques with ax, 198–**199**; self-arrest techniques with trekking poles, 199–201, **200**; self-belay techniques, 196–197; techniques, 195–196

snow flukes, 131–**132**

Snow Leopard (Matthiessen), 350

snowshoes, 191–192

snow stakes (pickets), 8, 129–**131**

snow walls, 240

socks, 223–224

sodium phosphate, 277

software for mapping, 30

solo climbing, 351, *368*

sound recording, 257

spandex, 235

Spectra/Dyneema runners, 81, 102, 106

speed. *See* fast movement

Spirits of the Air (Diemberger), 351

sport climbing, 75

sports supplements, 277–279

SRENE concept, 145–146

Starlight and Storm (Rébuffat), 350

State Plane Coordinate Systems, 34

static belay, 117–118, *368*

static forces, 114–**116**

static rope, 81, 84, *368*

Stickeen (John Muir's dog), 351

stomper belay, 127–**128**, 201, 207, 210

stopper knots, 102–**103**

stoves: altitude and stove performance, 253; butane, 251–253; fuel consumption, 250; heat output

and, 249–250; hexamine stoves, **249**; multiple fuels, 249; recommendations, 253; weight of, 253; white gas, 250–251; windscreens, **249**, 250. *See also* fuel types

strength training, 6, 287–289

stretching, 288

Stump, Mugs, 164, 327

sugar snow, 46

sun-related illness, 58

sunglasses, 59, 194

sunrise and sunset data, 36

Super Münter, 154, **157**

swami, **96**, **97**

swinging leads, 177

taking a bearing, 22, 24, **25**

Taquitz, 74

tautline hitch, 356, *357*

Tech Cord runners, 108–109

technical climbing, 3

Technora, 106

Telemarkers Rule, 47, *362*

temperature: air temperature and training, 289; altimeter accuracy and, 28–29; time of day and, 248; weather predicting and, 64; inversion, 64

Ten Essentials, 253–255. *See also* essentials

tents: selecting, 239; tarps and tarp tents, **237**–238; double-wall, 238–239; four-season, 239–240; single-wall, 238; three-season, 239–240; for winter mountaineering, 240–241. *See also* shelter systems

Terray, Lionel, 350

The Mountaineers: rating system, 76; Ten Essentials, 253

Thin Air (Child), 351

third-class climbing, 9, 72, 73, 78, 79

three-loop knot, *354*; how to avoid, 149, 150

thunderstorms, 62–63, 65–66. *See also* lightning; rain

Tibloc, 210, **305**, 307–**308**, 309, 310, *368*

time, estimating travel, 35–36

topographic maps, 16–19, 28

topo, 78, *368*

top roping, **115**–**116**, *368*

Touching the Void (Simpson), 112, 351

trad (traditional) climbing, 2–3, 75, *368*

training for mountaineering, 280–281; aerobic exercise, 286–287; age and, 283–284; air temperature

CPSIA information can be obtained
at www.ICGtesting.com
Printed in the USA
JSHW032019250222
23377JS00005B/59